BEHAVIORAL INTEGRATIVE CARE

BEHAVIORAL INTEGRATIVE CARE

Treatments that work in the primary care setting

Edited by
William T. O'Donohue
Michelle R. Byrd
Nicholas A. Cummings
Deborah A. Henderson

Brunner-Routledge
Taylor & Francis Group

NEW YORK AND HOVE

MT

Published in 2005 by
Brunner-Routledge
270 Madison Avenue
New York, NY 10016
www.brunner-routledge.co.uk

Published in Great Britain by
Brunner-Routledge
27 Church Road
Hove, East Sussex
BN3 2FA
www.brunner-routledge.co.uk

Brunner-Routledge is an imprint of the Taylor & Francis Group.
Printed in the United States of America on acid-free paper.
Cover design: Elise Weinger.

10 9 8 7 6 5 4 3 2 1

Library of Congress Cataloging-in-Publication Data
    Behavioral integrative care : treatments that work in the primary care setting / editors, William T. O'Donohue ... [et al.].
        p. ; cm.
    Includes bibliographical references and index.
    ISBN 0-415-94946-7 (hardback : alk. paper)
    1. Mental health services—United States. 2. Integrated delivery of health care—United States. 3. Primary care (Medicine)—United States.
    [DNLM: 1. Mental Disorders—therapy. 2. Delivery of Health Care, Integrated. 3. Mental Health Services—organization & administration. 4. Primary Health Care—methods. WM 400 B419 2004] I. O'Donohue, William T. II. Title.
    RA790.5.B366 2004
    362.1'068—dc22
                                                        2004011580

10/22/09

Contents

About the Editors

William T. O'Donohue, Ph.D., earned his doctorate in clinical psychology at SUNY–Stony Brook and a master's degree in philosophy from Indiana University. He is the Nicholas Cummings Professor of Organized Behavioral Healthcare Delivery in the Department of Psychology at the University of Nevada–Reno, where he also holds adjunct appointments in the Departments of Philosophy and Psychiatry. He is also currently the president and CEO of the University Alliance for Behavioral Care, Inc., a company providing integrated-care services. In addition to this book, he is editor and coeditor of a number of other volumes including *Management and Administration Skills for the Mental Health Professional, Behavioral Health as Primary Care, The Impact of Medical Cost Offset on Practice and Research,* and *Early Detection and Treatment of Substance Abuse Within Integrated Primary Care.*

Michelle R. Byrd, M.A., is an assistant professor in the Department of Psychology at Eastern Michigan University. Her research interests include pediatric primary care integration and the incorporation of acceptance strategies in the treatment of medically ill populations.

Nicholas A. Cummings, Ph.D., Sc.D., is a distinguished professor in the Department of Psychology at the University of Nevada–Reno and president of the Cummings Foundation for Behavioral Health. He is chairman of the board of the University Alliance for Behavioral Care and the Nicholas and Dorothy Cummings Foundation. He is the founder of over two dozen organizations including the California School of Professional Psychology, American Biodyne, and the National Academies of Practice. He is a past president of the American Psychological Association and a recipient of the gold medal for a Lifetime of Achievement in Practice. He is the author of over 400 journal articles and book chapters and has authored or coedited 30 books.

Deborah A. Henderson, M.S., is a doctoral candidate in clinical psychology at the University of Nevada–Reno. She is the author of several journal articles and book chapters and is currently completing her predoctoral internship at the Reno Veterans Administration Medical Center.

Contributors

John G. Arena, Ph.D., is lead psychologist at the Augusta Department of Veterans Affairs Medical Center and professor of psychiatry and health behavior at the Medical College of Georgia–Augusta. He is widely published in the area of psychological assessment and treatment of chronic pain disorders, with his major emphasis being headache and lower back pain.

Kristoffer S. Berlin, M.S., received his B.A. from the University of California–Santa Cruz and is currently completing his doctoral degree in clinical psychology from the University of Wisconsin–Milwaukee. His research interests include behavioral pediatrics, pediatric/health psychology, and utilizing functional analytic psychotherapy, and acceptance and commitment therapy approaches with parents and individuals with medical conditions.

Edward B. Blanchard, Ph.D., is distinguished professor of psychology at SUNY–Albany and is an internationally recognized expert in the area of headache and behavioral medicine. He has published widely and held numerous federally funded grants in the areas of headache, posttraumatic stress disorder, and hypertension. He is director of the Center for Stress and Anxiety Disorders at the University at Albany, and he has received numerous accolades in his long career, including the distinguished scientist award from the Association for Applied Psychophysiology and Biofeedback.

Timothy A. Brown, Psy.D., is a research professor of psychology at Boston University and director of research of the Center for Anxiety and Related Disorders. He currently serves as associate editor of the *Journal of Abnormal Psychology* and *Behavior Therapy*. He was a member of the *DSM-IV* and *DSM-IV-TR* Anxiety Disorders Workgroups, and he is currently an executive member of the *DSM-V* Research Planning Committee. His NIH-supported research is focused on the classification, nature, and course of anxiety and mood disorders.

Glenn M. Callaghan, Ph.D., received his doctoral degree in clinical psychology from the University of Nevada. Currently, he is associate professor and director of clinical training for the Master of Science in Clinical Psychology Program at San Jose State University. His research interests are in the areas of psychosocial interventions in primary care, alternative approaches to psychological assessment and classification, and research on interpersonal psychotherapies, including Functional Analytic Psychotherapy.

Laura Campbell-Sills, Ph.D., received her doctorate in clinical psychology from Boston University. Her research is focused on factors that may affect the development, course, and manifestation of anxiety and mood disorders. She is currently a postdoctoral fellow at the University of California–San Diego.

Mark W. Conard, M.A., is a doctoral student in the clinical health psychology program at the University of Missouri–Kansas City and supervising research assistant at the Mid-America Heart Institute. He is also a licensed professional counselor. His research interests include cardiovascular health outcomes and psychosocial issues in organ transplantation.

Janet L. Cummings, Psy.D., received her doctorate in clinical psychology from Wright State University School of Professional Psychology and is a licensed psychologist in the state of Arizona. In addition, she is currently an adjunct professor in the Department of Psychology at the University of Nevada–Reno, and she frequently provides workshops for mental health professionals throughout the United States and Europe. With over 15 years of clinical experience and particular expertise in the area of substance abuse, she has authored six books as well as numerous journal articles and book chapters.

Andrea Diloreto, M.A., is an advanced graduate student in the clinical psychology training program at the University of Nebraska–Lincoln. Her research interests are primarily in the area of child maltreatment, with particular emphasis on the long-term psychosocial, behavioral, and physical correlates of various types of abuse.

Gregory A. Fabiano, M.A., is a clinical psychology graduate student at SUNY–Buffalo. Current research interests include studying effective behavioral and combined behavioral and pharmacological treatments for children with ADHD.

Kyle E. Ferguson is a doctoral student in clinical psychology at the University of Nevada–Reno. He earned a master's degree in behavior analysis from Southern Illinois University. His research interests include managed behavioral health care and, in particular, medical cost offset. In addition to other publications, he has coauthored two books and coedited three recent volumes.

John P. Foreyt, Ph.D., is a professor in the Department of Medicine, Baylor College of Medicine, Houston, Texas, and director of the Baylor DeBakey Heart Center's Behavioral Medicine Research Clinic. His research interests include the development of behavioral strategies for the reduction of cardiovascular risk factors, including obesity, hypertension, diabetes, and dyslipidemia. He has published more than 260 articles and 17 books in these and related areas.

Alan E. Fruzzetti, Ph.D., is associate professor of psychology and director of the Dialectical Behavior Therapy (DBT) and Research Program at the University of Nevada–Reno. He received his Ph.D. from the University of Washington. His research focuses on the interplay between psychopathology and couple and family interactions, and the development of effective treatments for these problems. He is research advisor and member of the board of directors of the National Education Alliance for Borderline Personality Disorder; he maintains a clinical practice with individuals and families; and he has provided extensive training in the United States, Europe, and Australia in DBT with individuals, couples, and families.

Margaret Gardea, Ph.D., conducted her dissertation research at the University of Texas Southwestern Medical Center–Dallas, and is currently in private practice in El Paso, Texas.

Robert J. Gatchel, Ph.D., ABPP, is a professor in and chair of the Department of Psychology at the University of Texas–Arlington.

Elizabeth V. Gifford, Ph.D., is a research scientist at the Center for Health Care Evaluation, Department of Veterans Affairs and Stanford University Medical Centers. Her interests include smoking cessation and tobacco control, social context and coping, and health-care practices, policy, and evaluation.

Jennifer A. Gregg received her Ph.D. in clinical psychology at the University of Nevada. She currently works as an education coordinator at the Palo Alto VA Health Care System. Her research interests are diverse, and they include application of Acceptance and Commitment Therapy to medical populations and the role of avoidance in PTSD, chronic illness, and other co-morbid conditions. She also conducts research and writes in the areas of the dissemination and implementation of effective interventions and the detection and treatment of mental health problems in primary care settings.

Jessica R. Grisham is a doctoral candidate in clinical psychology at Boston University. She received her B.A. in English and psychology from University of Pennsylvania and her M.A. from Boston University. Her current research interests include personality and neuropsychological characteristics contributing to the co-morbidity of various mood and anxiety disorders, diagnostic issues related to obsessive-compulsive disorder, and the etiology and treatment of compulsive hoarding.

Arthur C. Houts, Ph.D., is professor emeritus and former director of clinical training at the University of Memphis. He currently sees patients and conducts research at West Clinic, a leading community oncology center in Memphis, Tennessee. He is interested in assessing and improving quality of life in cancer patients by using knowledge from empirically supported psychological interventions.

Negar Nicole Jacobs, Ph.D., earned her doctorate in clinical psychology at the University of Nevada–Reno. She is currently a staff psychologist at the Veterans Administration Sierra Nevada Health Care System in Reno. Her primary research area is in the area of integrated care with an emphasis on the psychological factors in infertility treatment.

Terence M. Keane, Ph.D., is professor and vice chairman of research in psychiatry at the Boston University School of Medicine. He is also the chief of psychology and the director of the National Center for PTSD at the VA Boston Healthcare System. The past president of the International Society for Traumatic Stress Studies, he has published six books and over 160 articles on the assessment and treatment of PTSD.

Rodger S. Kessler, Ph.D., is a clinical health psychologist practicing in family medicine at Berlin Family Health in Montpelier, Vermont. He is on the staff at Central Vermont Medical Center where he is chair of the quality management committee and a member of the credentials and contracts committees. His current research focuses on patient compliance with psychological referral in integrated practice and the impact of integrated medical psychological care on medical and cost outcomes. He is a fellow of the American Psychological Association and is also past president of the Vermont Psychological Association.

Adrienne H. Kovacs, Ph.D., is currently a postdoctoral fellow at the University Health Network in Toronto, Canada. Her focus is the enhanced quality of life of cardiac patients and the promotion of healthy lifestyle behaviors. She provides clinical services to cardiac patients and is currently conducting several research projects with this population.

Gregory A. Leskin, Ph.D., is a health research scientist at the National Center for PTSD, VA Palo Alto Health Care System. He chairs the National Center for PTSD initiative to increase integrative behavioral health models of care into VA primary care settings.

Eric R. Levensky, M.A., is a doctoral candidate in clinical psychology at the University of Nevada–Reno. The author of several journal articles and book chapters, he is currently conducting a randomized, controlled trial evaluating a behavioral intervention to promote treatment adherence in HIV patients.

Elizabeth A. Lillis, M.A., is currently a doctoral student at the University of Nevada–Reno. She received her B.A. from the University of California–San Diego. Her research interests include couple and family interactions, dialectical behavior therapy (DBT), psychotherapy outcome, brief interventions, and crisis management.

Ann Matt Maddrey, Ph.D., is the director of consult liaison psychiatry and behavioral medicine at the University of Texas Southwestern Medical Center–Dallas.

David Meichenbaum, M.A., is a doctoral candidate at SUNY–Buffalo. His current research interests include studying effective treatments for children and adolescents with ADHD and exploring the impact of prolonged stimulant medication use on later life functioning.

Leslie A. Morland, Psy.D., is a health research scientist at the National Center for PTSD–Pacific Island Division in Honolulu, Hawaii, and an assistant clinical professor in the Department of Psychiatry in the John Burns School of Medicine at the University of Hawaii.

Erin M. Oksol, Ph.D., earned her doctoral degree in clinical psychology at the University of Nevada. She is currently an outpatient therapist at Children's Behavioral Services in Reno. Her research interests include behavioral pediatrics and improving compliance with pediatric diabetic treatment regimens.

Enrique Ortega is a doctoral student at the University of Southern California in health behavior research. Enrique received his B.A. in psychology from San Jose State University. Currently he is studying the effects of subcultures on smoking (for the Transdisciplinary Tobacco Use Research Center) and the effects of ethnic categorization on tobacco use statistics. His primary interest is in chronic disease management in cancer.

Kathleen M. Palm, Ph.D., completed her doctorate in clinical psychology at the University of Nevada–Reno. She is currently a postdoctoral fellow at Brown Medical School. Her current research interests include smoking cessation and treatment development for substance use disorders.

William E. Pelham, Jr., Ph.D., is professor of psychology, pediatrics, and psychiatry and director of the Center for Children and Families at SUNY–Buffalo. His summer treatment program for ADHD children has been recognized by the American Psychological Association as a model program and is widely recognized as the state-of-the-art in treatment for ADHD. He has authored or coauthored more than 200 professional papers dealing with ADHD and its treatment.

Walker S. Carlos Poston II, Ph.D., M.P.H., FAHA, received his Ph.D. from the University of California–Santa Barbara. He is currently an associate professor at the University of Missouri–Kansas City Clinical Health Psychology Program and School of Medicine, associate chair of the Department of Psychology, and codirector of behavioral cardiology research at the Mid-America Heart Institute at Saint Luke's Hospital. He is a fellow of the North American Association for the Study of Obesity, the American Heart Association Council on Epidemiology and Prevention, and the Council on Nutrition, Physical Activity, and Metabolism, and a cardiovascular health fellow alumnus of the American Hospital Association's Health Forum. He has published over 120 peer reviewed journal articles and book chapters on the etiology, assessment, and management of obesity and eating disorders.

Patricia Robinson, Ph.D., provides consultation and training services in primary care behavioral health integration for Mountainview Consulting Group, Inc. She is also a clinical supervisor and clinical provider for Yakima Valley Farm Workers Clinic system in Washington state and Oregon. She worked as a clinical and research psychologist at Group Health Cooperative of Puget Sound for 15 years. She is the author of two books and many book chapters and articles.

Richard C. Robinson, Ph.D., is an assistant professor at the University of Texas Southwestern Medical Center–Dallas.

Kirk D. Strosahl obtained his Ph.D. in clinical psychology from Purdue University. In more than a decade of clinical practice in primary care, he has worked as a practicing clinician for 11 primary care teams and over 150 primary care providers, including adult medicine providers, OB-GYN physicians, and pediatricians. He has written numerous articles on the subject of primary care behavioral health integration and has presented workshops on the subject both regionally and nationally. He currently is research and training director for Mountainview Consulting Group, Inc., a firm specializing in providing consultation and training for health-care systems that are attempting to integrate primary care and behavioral health service lines.

Preface

We decided to compile this book because we thought it would be useful for clinicians and researchers who are a part of, or want to become a part of, an important emerging trend in health-care delivery: integrated care. There are several reasons to believe that in many cases health care delivered by a multidisciplinary team of medical and behavioral health providers is better than health-care delivery that is disjointed or delivered by providers who are not functioning as a collaborative unit. By "better" we mean treatment that is both more effective and efficient. Specifically, integrated care envisions treatment that better fits with what the patient actually needs and thus leads to more adequate service delivery, healthier patients, and increased patient and provider satisfaction. In addition, particularly in an era of a major health-care crisis, integrated care has the potential, in the long term, to be more cost efficient.

However, many providers do not have the skill sets to deliver integrated care. To address the gap between training and the demands of practice, there are two obvious strategies. First, new providers in the field must be trained to function competently in an integrated-care environment. For the past 5 years at the University of Nevada–Reno, we have attempted to prepare new clinicians for the particular demands of functioning in an increasingly managed and integrated-care environment through innovative courses and practicum experiences. However, by providing a new model for training scientist-practitioners in the field of psychology, we are succeeding only in changing the skills of new professionals, leaving existing psychologists in the field still unprepared for the integrated-care environment. Therefore, a second strategy to bridge training- and practice-demands must serve to supplement the training of existing providers. This book is aimed at reaching both trainees and seasoned professionals with the overarching goal of improving care for our clients, present and future.

Here we will introduce behavioral clinicians to the overall ecology of primary care (e.g., fast-paced, oriented more toward action, acute problem solving, population management, stepped care, and, obviously, physical complaint resolution). In addition, this book will attempt to teach specific skill sets related to the assessment and treatment of particular types of problem presentations as they occur in primary care settings, so that behavioral health providers will be aware of and better prepared for their potential role in this environment. Thus, the book addresses assessment and treatment strategies that are effective in the primary care setting, as presented by known experts in each subfield.

In summary, based on current trends in the research literature and the practice marketplace, we believe the inclusion of behavioral health care in medical settings is an important development that makes both clinical and financial sense. We are concerned that one impediment to its growth may be that training-program leaders do not have sufficient access to relevant training materials and are not retooling fast enough to provide the health-care economy with well-trained clinicians and researchers. There are some key exceptions to this; we hope there will be a trend in training to keep pace with the inclusion of multidisciplinary teams in practice settings. We hope this book will become a seminal text in training future scientist-practitioners.

We have many people to thank for this book. First, we would like to thank our publisher, Brunner-Routledge. In particular, we are grateful for the patience and support of our editors, Dr. George Zimmar and Mr. Dana Bliss. We would also like to thank Nanci Fowler and Sara Ashby for their administrative assistance. Finally, we would like to thank each chapter author for his or her ability to think in novel ways while applying high standards and outstanding scholarship.

Introduction
The Case for Integrated Care: Coordinating Behavioral Health Care With Primary Care Medicine

MICHELLE R. BYRD, WILLIAM T. O'DONOHUE, AND
NICHOLAS A. CUMMINGS

Behavioral health care in 2004 bears little resemblance to the not-so-distant days of burgeoning private practices, limitless sessions of psychotherapy, and the work of the psychologist occurring more or less independently. In the past two decades, health-care funding has undergone a veritable systemic revolution resulting in significant and seemingly permanent changes in the field of clinical psychology, with traditional models of practice and financial viability rapidly changing. Although psychologists and other mental health-care providers cannot bend at the will of economic contingencies alone, they also cannot deny the realities of current reimbursement practices and related limited access to mental health services. These changes in the marketplace call upon behavioral health providers to cultivate innovative models of care.

The purpose of this book is to provide an overview of what may become the new standard of mental health-care provision—the integration of behavioral and medical care. In this introductory chapter, we provide some context in which to best understand models of integration, to explore the rationale for integrated models, to operationally define forms and functions of integrated care, as well as describe how we have conceptualized this book.

The Context of Integrated Care

As a consequence of what has been called a "health-care crisis" in America, mental health care appears to be especially hard hit by reimbursement cuts and limits on services, perhaps because mental health care has long been viewed by legislators and third-party payers as secondary to medical/surgical care. Although health-care expenditures continue to rise exponentially, with $1.4 trillion spent in 2002 (14% of the GDP) and expected growth of 7.3% each year in the next decade, only a small proportion of these funds is earmarked for mental health care. For example, in 1996, of the $943 billion spent on health care in the United States, only 7% was devoted to mental health care, with another 1% devoted to addictive disorders and 2% to dementia/Alzheimer's disease. Clearly, the apportioning of dollars, at least in part, represents the value placed on mental health care by decision-making bodies.

As this book goes to press, the largest "carved-out" managed behavioral health-care organization, Magellan Health Services, is in bankruptcy. Its stock has dropped from a high of $30 per share to nearly zero. More changes are on the horizon as the health-care carve-out industry attempts to deal with its serious financial problems. However, rather than spelling the end of clinical psychology, in many ways economic uncertainty has actually pushed the science and practice of our discipline beyond historical parameters. With the trends toward increasingly managed and empirically driven care, new models of practice have begun to emerge for clinical scientist-practitioners.

Today at least a part of clinical decision making has been externalized to third-party gatekeepers (through means such as preauthorization of sessions and utilization review), who may not have sufficient training to make clinical decisions and who must form opinions based on limited understanding of specific cases. For many data-oriented clinicians, the current contingencies governing practice may not be too different from their traditional emphasis on providing efficient and effective treatment for their clients. For practitioners who were not basing their clinical decisions on the empirical literature, the mandated changes in service delivery may be cause for, at minimum, a reorientation of their practice, retraining, or even a career change or early retirement. Integrated care provides a means of restructuring clinical practice so as to maximize existing human and financial resources.

Defining Integrated Care

Integrated care is a term with many meanings, which can vary according to what is integrated (dental, nutrition, alternative medicine, etc.) as well as the extent to which a particular system is integrated (ranging from more screening and referral to collocation to integrated medical management groups). Though integrated care can be defined in many ways, we conceptualize it as the process and product of medical and mental health professionals working collaboratively and coherently toward optimizing patient health through biopsychosocial modes of prevention and intervention.

Integrated care, then, cannot be defined by one type of service or one type of setting. The primary function of integration remains constant, but the system may actually take many forms. One way to understand the topography of integrated care is to classify systems based on their level of integration between medical and mental health care. The level of integration is a way of describing the degree to which services are provided collaboratively by a multidisciplinary team of clinicians. O'Donohue, Cummings, & Ferguson (2003) provide the graphic in Figure I.1 to illustrate the continuum of integrated care.

As described above, although integrated care may differ in terms of level of integration, the function and related goals of integrated systems remain constant. Some of these treatment targets are the same as or consistent with goals articulated in traditional models of care; however, integrated models also have the potential to broaden the scope of practice. Specifically, integrated care has the following aims:

1. Improved recognition of behavioral health needs in medical settings.
2. Improved collaborative care and management of patients with psychosocial issues in primary care.
3. Increased availability of an internal resource for primary care providers to help address patients' psychosocial concerns or behavioral health issues and provide rapid feedback to the provider, without referring to a specialty mental health clinic.
4. Improved fit between the care patients seek in primary care and the services delivered.

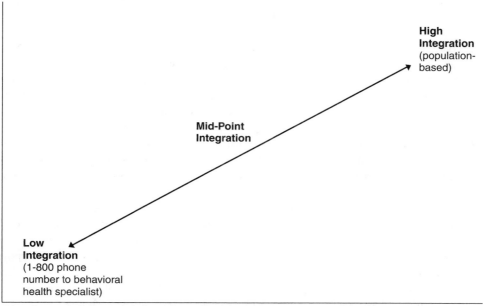

Integration can occur at any point in the continuum of intensity, depending on customer readiness and market receptivity

Fig. I.1 Continuum of integrated care (from O'Donohue, Cummings, & Ferguson, 2003, p. 38).

5. Prevention of more serious behavioral and physical health problems through early recognition and intervention.
6. Triage when appropriate, into more intensive specialty health care by the behavioral health consultant.

As described above, integrating a system of care is no small task—a team effort is required. Integrated care is inherently collaborative and multidisciplinary, as a close working relationship between all care providers is essential for the model to be successful. In the integrated care model, medical health professionals, such as physicians, nurses, and nurse practitioners, serve as the primary referral sources for behavioral care providers (BCPs), ideally located onsite. Behavioral care providers may be clinical psychologists, psychiatrists, or master's level clinicians with specialized training in primary care.

In most models of integrated care, behavioral services are delivered in the primary care setting. *Primary care* is defined as the medical setting in which patients receive most of their medical care, most frequently staffed by a general practitioner or family practice physician. By definition, then, primary care is the first source patients look to for treatment. Primary care is distinguished from specialty care, wherein patients receive care by more highly trained providers such as cardiac or mental health specialists.

In the integrated care model, when, in the course of a routine medical visit, a medical professional notices that the patient may be presenting with psychological symptoms, he or she may invite the BCP into the visit to provide immediate assessment and possible brief treatment for the psychological sequalae. In doing so, the patient has the opportunity to receive seamless care more coherently addressing all of the presenting problems, rather than artificially compartmentalizing his or her physical and psychological complaints. Furthermore, patients do not suffer any additional delay in receiving treatment necessitated by the referral process, nor do they incur the stigma of being referred to the mental health sector for treatment.

There are four main types of problems targeted in an integrated care model. First, integrated care directly targets psychological problems, such as anxiety and depression, which may be presented in the primary care setting. Patients may complain of symptoms such as sleep or appetite disturbance, irritability, or marital/family problems. The diagnosis of psychological disorders in primary care is given by BCPs based on the referral of medical professionals who are primarily responsible for the patient's care.

Second, problems that include both physical and psychological components are explicitly targeted in integrated models of care. These problems include substance abuse (drugs, alcohol, nicotine) and are often identified in routine primary care assessment. However, in traditional models of care, treatment of co-morbid problems is unlikely to occur in the primary care setting, thereby creating a chasm between identification and treatment of the problem behavior into which the patient is likely to fall.

Not only is there an apparent need for the recognition and treatment of behavioral health problems as independent entities in primary care as described above, but behavioral issues also play a key role in the development, detection, and successful treatment and management of primary medical disorders. Therefore, integrated care aggressively targets psychological components of physical illnesses, both acute and chronic. Many relationships between both acute and chronic physical disorders and secondary behavioral processes have been empirically established (cardiac disease and hostility; panic and asthma, etc.). Chronic illnesses with identifiable psychological components that may contribute to the development or exacerbation of physical symptoms include coronary artery disease, arthritis, and asthma. Depending on the specific variables in question, psychological processes may be conceptualized as either components of the cause or effects of physical processes. Indeed, a transactional model may also be appropriate in many cases.

Finally, integrated care models also address nonspecific factors related to both acute and chronic illness states that account for a substantial proportion of treatment failure and increased medical costs. These factors include stress, noncompliance with regimens, subclinical mood or anxiety disorders, coping styles, personality characteristics, sociodemographic factors, social support factors, sleep, and dietary considerations.

How Is Integrated Care Different from Psychological Practice Already Occurring in Medical Settings?

Although the relevance of psychological issues in the assessment and treatment of medical patients has long been recognized, the participation of psychologists in this process is relatively novel. For the informed reader, however, integrated care will obviously appear to be an extension of two already existing areas of practice—behavioral medicine and consultation-liaison psychiatry. *Behavioral medicine* is commonly defined as "the interdisciplinary field concerned with the development and integration of behavioral and biomedical science, knowledge and technique relevant to health and illness and the application of this knowledge and these techniques to prevention, diagnosis, treatment, and rehabilitation" (Schwartz & Weiss, 1978, p. 250, as cited in Belar & Deardorff, 1995, p. 2).

Although we acknowledge that a fundamental competency in behavioral medicine is a prerequisite for practicing in an integrated care environment, it is not sufficient. Behavioral medicine, while collaborative in nature, is typically practiced in specialty mental health settings following the referral of the treating physician. Behavioral medicine specialists, then, serve more the function of a consulting provider than a treatment team member, as in integrated models. Furthermore, many behavioral medicine providers have built their practices around particular groups of patients or diagnoses (e.g., pulmonary patients), whereas integrated care requires a greater breadth of knowledge and skills to treat more medically diverse primary care populations. Integrated care differs from traditionally practiced behavioral medicine in that it requires collaboration at the logistic and theoretical levels, which exceeds that required for the practice of behavioral medicine alone.

More closely resembling integrated care is the discipline of consultation-liaison (C-L) psychiatry. The field of C-L psychiatry has long been in the business of providing mental health service within medical settings, albeit with historically different targets and strategies than are being discussed in this text. Thus, the C-L literature provides a strong foundation on which to base new models of integrated care. C-L has traditionally been the link between psychiatry and the rest of medical practice, providing two primary services. First, C-L services provide direct patient care for psychiatric problems in medical settings (consultation), a form of behavioral medicine. Second, C-L services also provide indirect care by educating and consulting with primary care teams on the appropriate care of patients with co-morbid psychiatric conditions (liaison). Although the development of integrated models of care in psychological practice is relatively new, C-L psychiatry has been in practice and been actively studied since the 1970s.

Although C-L literature is a useful springboard for building understanding of integrated models of care (see Stern, Fricchione, Cassem, Jellinek, & Rosenbaum, 2004 for an excellent reference.), there are several ways in which C-L psychiatry differs from the models we suggest in this book. First, C-L psychiatry is by definition the domain of medical doctors whose training and expertise differ drastically from the classic training of other (non-MD) mental health professionals. As such, the C-L literature assumes a level of understanding of disease processes and an overall orientation toward the medicalization and pharmacological treatment of psychological disorders. In addition, C-L psychiatry has been developed in hospital settings. Although we support the integration of care for medical inpatients, we also assert that behavioral care is imperative in outpatient care, including both primary and specialty care clinics. Finally, C-L psychiatry is more focused on the task of assessment within the medical setting and referral for follow-up in specialty psychiatric clinics when warranted, with limited emphasis on treatment. So, even though the practices of traditional behavioral medicine and C-L psychiatry undoubtedly provide the foundation for integrated care, integrated care is a unique model with unique advantages and challenges.

Rationale for Integrated Care Model

Integrated care appears to offer a number of advantages over traditional models of providing medical and mental health care independently and has, therefore, been proposed as a primary area of expansion in psychological research and practice (Cummings, O'Donohue, Hayes, & Follette, 2001).

Integrated Care Treats Psychological Disorders Where Treatment Is Sought

First, primary care is already the de facto arena in which mental health services are provided. Statistically, the majority of patients who meet DSM-IV diagnostic criteria see their primary care physicians at minimum once per year and receive psychological services more often during their primary care visits than from specialty mental health-care providers (Reiger et al., 1993). Furthermore, subclinical psychological problems that do not meet diagnostic criteria for a DSM-IV disorder are most likely to be "caught" in the medical setting, with an increased chance of prevention or early intervention. By integrating mental health care into primary care visits, we would be providing mental health services in the same venue in which they are already being sought. However, services would be provided in a more responsive, appropriate, and organized manner to improve both the effectiveness and the efficiency of treatment provided. In addition, providing integrated care in medical settings also has the potential to reduce the stigma typically associated with specialty mental health services.

Integrated Care Provides More Service to More People

In addition to the argument that integrated care offers a better match between where clients seek and receive care, a second rationale for integrated care is the ability to broaden potential client base. The large epidemiological studies of the past 20 years have taught us that while psychological disorders are highly prevalent, a great proportion of individuals who endure psychological suffering do not seek or receive behavioral health care in any forum (e.g., Epidemiologic Catchment Area Study; Reiger, Myers, & Kramer, 1985). Integrating care would provide a means of accessing populations who could benefit from behavioral health care but would not otherwise seek treatment. Thus, by integrating care, we may remove some of the barriers to access for those most in need of behavioral health services.

The primary care setting has been viewed as the preferred setting for the delivery of behavioral health-care services because (a) this setting does not carry the stigma that a mental health-care setting often does; (b) the patient does not have to experience the inconvenience of making another appointment, resulting in more completed referrals (for example, when a physician refers a patient to a specialty mental health-care provider in another setting, patients follow through approximately 15% of the time, whereas when referrals are made to an onsite behavioral health provider, they are followed through approximately 90% of the time [Strosahl, 1998a]); (c) the behavioral health provider is more skilled at handling disease management issues that stem from treatment adherence and education problems than the primary care physician; (d) the physician's time is considered more costly than that of the behavioral health provider; therefore, assigning behavioral health issues to the onsite behavioral health provider means more patients can be seen by the physician; and (e) patients initially receive more services.

Although the argument can be made that initially costs for providing care for those not currently receiving care would be prohibitive, ultimately, delivering more mental health services may well lead to a reduction in other forms of expenditure related to un- or undertreated mental illness (unemployment, judicial costs, medical costs, etc.). Ultimately, then, providing more care to more people may actually result in reduced costs.

Integrated Care May Improve Treatment of Physical Problems

Not only are people with identified psychological problems more likely to seek treatment in primary care settings, but the primary care setting is also where physical problems with psychological correlates or causes are most likely to be treated. By treating psychological problems we may also improve a patient's (actual or perceived) physical health.

Of the presenting problems in primary care settings, pain/somatization accounts for 18%, depression 14%, and anxiety/panic 14% (Fries, Koop, & Beadle, 1993). Furthermore, research indicates that approximately 90% of the 10 most common presenting problems in primary care settings do not have an identifiable medical etiology (e.g., Kroenke & Mangelsdorff, 1989). Even for presenting symptoms that appear to have an organic etiology, such as chest pain, fatigue, dyspnea, and dizziness, in a high percentage of cases no organic cause is ever identified, suggesting psychological causes or correlates (Kroenke & Manglesdorff, 1989). Although the insufficiencies of modern medical technology and diagnostic procedures may account for the lack of positive medical findings in some cases, the data suggest that a substantial number of medical visits may actually have a "hidden" psychological driver (Fries et al., 1993). Furthermore, even when diseases have a known physical etiology, the management of many chronic diseases requires concurrent behavioral care.

Chronic diseases such as diabetes, chronic airway and respiratory diseases, ischemic heart disease, pain, and arthritis are highly prevalent, progressive, costly, and, we argue, best treated by an integrated care approach. The medical care costs alone for people with chronic disease total more than $400 billion annually. This accounts for better than 60% of all health-care expenditure in the United States. When indirect costs such as work absenteeism and disability are considered, it is impossible to calculate the costs of chronic disease.

There is a substantial body of literature showing a high prevalence of psychological co-morbidity with chronic disease. Specifically, depression, anxiety disorders, and/or substance abuse often accompany chronic diseases but are all too often undetected and untreated. Chronic disease patients have been reported to experience high levels of psychological distress (Erdal & Zautra, 1995) compared to controls. The psychological impact of having a chronic medical condition, however, is not well addressed by conventional treatments (Fore, 1996; Friedman, Sobel, Myers, Caudill, & Benson, 1995).

Furthermore, chronic diseases frequently require patient self-management and lifestyle modification. Behavioral and psychological factors have repeatedly been shown to have a profound impact on the onset, progression, and management of chronic diseases. For example, patients experiencing mild depressive symptoms may be less likely to adhere to dietary and exercise recommendations. These factors in turn are related to treatment costs. In one study, the introduction of an arthritis self-management group at the Stanford Arthritis Center resulted in not only a 20% reduction in pain, but also an average 4-year savings of $648 per person in reduced physician visits (Lorig & Holman, 1993).

The importance of treating behavioral problems in the context of chronic medical illness is also reflected in studies evaluating impact of care on patient satisfaction and outcome. Recent studies report that patients with chronic illnesses have poor disease control and are generally unhappy with the care they receive (e.g., Wagner, 1997). In order to improve care for chronic disease patients, systems of care must be reconfigured. The primary care system was designed to treat individuals experiencing acute problems in the form of a short appointment. This functional triage system relies on two treatment modalities: prescription medications and brief patient education with an expectation of patient follow-up. In managing chronic medical illnesses, integrated care emphasizes extensive patient education about his or her disease, assistance in patient decision making regarding his or her treatment, managing treatment adherence, treating co-morbid psychological problems such as depression, and providing change strategies for lifestyle problems such as diet and exercise (see Figures I.2 and I.3).

Finally, there are sound financial rationales for integrating care. As Cummings, O'Donohue, Hayes, & Follette (2001, p. 804) remind us, the current writing in integrated care has a certain "Willie Suttonism" in that the literature strongly suggests that we "go where the money is." Much excess spending or "fat" has been carved out of the traditional mental health system. However, it appears as though more carving will be done in the traditional medical/surgical system owing to this system's lack of recognition of behavioral health pathways to medical utilization. One outcome of integrating care, therefore, is the potential to increase the economic base for the behavioral health professions through medical cost offset.

Medical Cost Offset

The vision for integrated care is that not only would more people receive more appropriate services, but that, in doing so, some other, potentially more expensive, services could be avoided or reduced, resulting in an overall cost savings. This principle is known as *medical cost offset* (see Cummings, O'Donohue, Ferguson, 2002, for a review). More precisely, medical cost offset refers to reduced medical and surgical expenditures attributed to decreased utilization of services when behavioral health care is provided within that system (Cummings, Johnson, & Cummings, 1997).

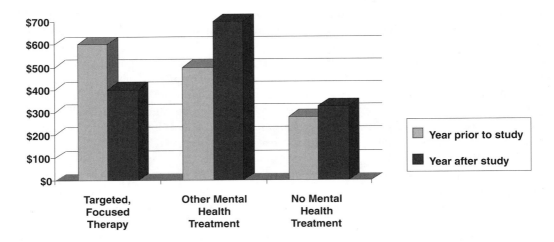

Fig. I.2 Chronically ill group. Average medical utilization in constant dollars for the year before (lightly shaded) and year after (darkly shaded) intervention (from Follette & Cummings, 1967).

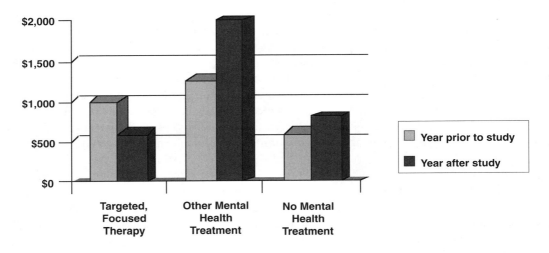

Fig. I.3 Nonchronic group. Average medical utilization in constant dollars for the year before (lightly shaded) and year after (darkly shaded) intervention (from Follette & Cummings, 1967).

The primary route to achieving medical cost offset is adequately treating psychological problems that may be presented as purely medical problems. It has been shown that patients who have known psychological disorders use approximately 50% more physical health-care services each year than patients who are not experiencing psychological distress (Simon, VonKorff, & Barlow, 1995). Research has demonstrated (e.g., Cummings, Dorken, Pallak, & Henke, 1990) that medical cost offset can be achieved through efficient and effective treatment of behavioral problems by reducing direct medical costs (such as office and emergency department visits). By providing these patients with more comprehensive and appropriate psychological treatment, the literature suggests that not only will their psychological symptoms be ameliorated, but they will require and subsequently utilize fewer physical health resources as well. Cost savings have been estimated to range from 20–40% (Figure I.4; Cummings & Pallak, 1990; Strosahl & Sobel, 1996).

Medical cost offset was initially witnessed in the mid-1960s by Cummings and his colleagues at Kaiser Permanente in California (e.g., Cummings, Kahn, & Sparkman, 1962; Follette & Cummings, 1967). These researchers found that medical utilization was reduced up to 62% over the 5 years following the application of behavioral interventions, and that the reduction in costs substantially exceeded the cost of providing the behavioral health service. Additionally, they found that without any additional behavioral care services, utilization of medicine and surgery, both outpatient and inpatient, steadily declined to an ultimate level and stayed down, as compared with a comparison group that did not receive any behavioral health services (see Figure I.4).

Following the release of this finding, researchers began studying the medical cost offset effect, with varying results. Discussions regarding factors that may influence a study's ability to detect medical cost offset (Jones & Vischi, 1980) led Cummings and colleagues to conduct a large-scale,

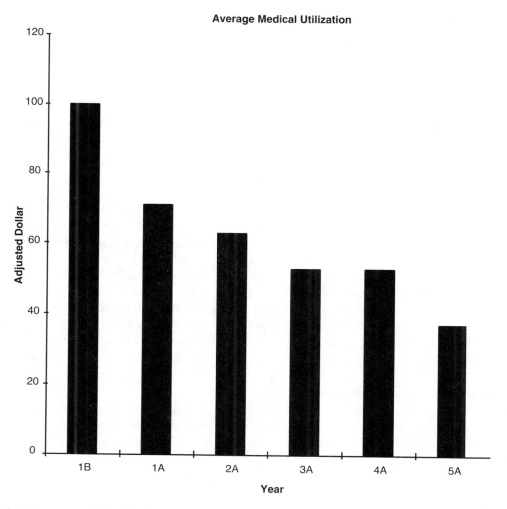

Fig. I.4 Average medical utilization for the year before (1B) and the five years after (1A, 2A, 3A, 4A, and 5A) behavioral intervention was instituted (from Follette & Cummings, 1967).

well-controlled medical cost offset study in the state of Hawaii (Cummings, Doerken, Pallak, & Henke, 1993; Pallak, Cummings, Doerken, & Henke, 1995). The Hawaii Medicaid Study, as it was known, was conducted over a period of 7 years with the entire Medicaid population of the Island of Oahu and in a managed behavioral care setting specifically organized for that purpose under the auspices of the federal Health Care Financing Administration (HCFA). The study was designed to address the several scientific criticisms leveled at the medical cost offset research endeavor.

The Hawaii Medicaid Study was prospective in design with all Medicaid eligible persons ($N = 36,000$) randomly assigned to experimental and control groups, keeping families intact. The study was conducted in an organized setting with a staff model. An aggressive outreach program was combined with programs designed to encourage physician, social work, agency, and community participation. This controlled prospective study confirmed the results obtained in previous retrospective studies. The cost of creating the behavioral health-care system was recovered by the medical-surgical savings within 18 months, and the significant reduction in medical utilization observed initially continued thereafter with no additional behavioral health care required to maintain the cost savings.

The highest savings were seen in a group consisting of individuals with diabetes, hypertension, chronic airway and respiratory diseases, ischemic heart disease, and rheumatoid arthritis, who account for 40% of all Medicaid costs in Hawaii (Cummings, Cummings, & Johnson, 1997). The control group, which was seen in the fee-for-service private sector for psychotherapy, exhibited a 17% increase in medical-surgical utilization, a finding not statistically different from the 27% increase in control group patients who did not receive mental health services.

The Hawaii Medicaid Study exemplifies the possibility of observing medical cost offset as a result of integrated care. Although economic reasons alone may not be considered sufficient rationale for restructuring routine clinical care, in the context of improved patient satisfaction and functioning, little additional justification for examining a new model is needed.

Summary of Rationale for Integrated Care

In summary, there are several reasons why serious consideration of integrated systems of care is warranted. The presence of patients in primary care with clearly stated psychological concerns and the apparent importance of assessing for psychological contributors to physiological symptoms suggest a profound mismatch between the primary care environment as it exists and the demand characteristics of primary care patients. In addition, the traditional model of service delivery does not appear to be maximizing the available economic resources to provide the highest level of service to patients for the least cost to payers. Thus, there is currently much interest in integrated care because it is hypothesized that this type of service delivery will improve patient access, increase the rate of evidence-based practice, and improve patient health and satisfaction, in addition to reducing long-term costs.

Implementation of Integrated Models of Care

Although strong rationale can be provided for integrating care, actually conceptualizing how implementation of such systems could occur requires another level of analysis. There are a number of factors that must be carefully considered when planning to develop a new integrated system or shift an existing system to becoming more integrated.

First, adopting an integrated model requires changes in roles for clinicians. For each member of a multidisciplinary team, being integrated necessitates understanding enough about the disciplines and training of one's colleagues to communicate effectively to design collaborative interventions that will best meet patients' needs. For most providers, functioning as a team member rather than an independent operator is a significant shift. Most often, multidisciplinary teams are led by physicians, not behavioral health providers. For some behavioral providers, this apparent loss in solitary decision-making power may prove difficult to accept. However, if the longer term goals of integration (such as providing increased and improved levels of care) meet the values of the clinician, they may function well as a team member. According to a seasoned integrated care clinician, behavioral service providers need to conceptualize their role in integrated care as being the medicine, not the doctor (Friman, 2001).

Strosahl (1998b) has outlined several key points relevant to the role of behavioral health providers in primary/integrated care settings and identified core assumptions of the model:

1. The behavioral health clinician's role is to identify, triage, treat, and manage primary care patients with behavioral health problems.
2. The behavioral health program is grounded in a population-based care philosophy that is consistent with the mission and goals of the primary care model of health care.
3. All services are based on a primary behavioral health model.
4. The primary care medical team members are key customers (of the behavioral health clinician).
5. The behavioral health clinician promotes a smooth interface between medicine, psychiatry, and specialty mental health as well as other behavioral and social services.

There are several specific steps that have been suggested for establishing a new integrated system of care (or retooling an existing system). First, in order to provide behavioral health services in this new setting, we must emphasize adequate assessment of probable symptom domains. Given our training in assessment, this step in the process can often be led by behavioral health providers. Health screening instruments such as the HEAR or the PRIME-MD (Spitzer, Williams, Kroenke, & Linzer, 1994) can be utilized for screening for behavioral problems in primary care. Using standardized screening instruments in an integrated setting will be a critical component of conducting a needs assessment, the goal of which would be to determine which kinds of interventions would be most useful for the specific clinic population.

Second, based on needs assessment, priority areas should be targeted. Priority areas can be defined either by high frequency or severity in a given sample. Although targeting particular clinical presentations based on frequency or severity clearly meets patient demand, this rubric will likely also target areas that are the most costly. For example, chronic illnesses such as depression, diabetes, and hypertension are typically managed in primary care and have a high incidence, which would likely result in these diseases being targeted. In addition, these illnesses often present with and may be exacerbated by co-morbid behavioral health problems, resulting in lower adherence rates and more significant (and costly) disability. Ultimately, if poorly managed, chronic illnesses could require invasive interventions, and result in permanent disability or death.

Although priority areas will certainly differ based on population served, Friedman et al. (1995) have described specific pathways that might be utilized to produce healthier patients in primary care. These pathways could be considered a starting point for examining probable priority areas, a roundup of the "usual suspects," clinically speaking. These pathways are:

Information and Decision-Support Pathway. Teaching patients the nature and treatment of their disease, appropriate self-care, and optimal professional utilization increases patient satisfaction and reduces future medical usage. Psychoeducational groups, bibliotherapy, individual consultation, and Internet services are means for capturing this pathway.

Stress Management Pathway. Stress is both a key cause of illness and an effect of illness. Progressive muscle relaxation, meditation, exercise, and other stress management techniques have been shown to provide positive health benefits in a number of psychological and medical problems. Stress management, bibliotherapy, and group and individual consultation are means for capturing this pathway.

Behavior Change Pathway. Changing how a patient, eats, drinks, smokes, uses substances, and exercises has been shown to have profound implications for health. Lifestyle change groups, bibliotherapy, smoking cessation psychotherapy, and substance abuse treatment are ways of capturing this pathway.

Social Support Pathway. Some patients enter the health-care system to obtain social support. Even patients who have high levels of social support under ordinary circumstances may develop feelings of isolation when experiencing chronic illness. Increasing social support through peer-led groups and activation of natural support networks have been shown to improve health and reduce future medical utilization.

Undiagnosed Psychological Problem Pathway. In many cases patients present with medical complaints but actually have an undiagnosed psychological problem such as depression and anxiety. Training in the accurate diagnosis of these as well as the use of less expensive but highly effective psychological treatments result in significantly less medial utilization. Managing successful referrals to specialty care is also part of the service.

Somatization Pathway. Some patients who very frequently present with multiple somatic complains may have increased emotional reactivity to bodily changes. These individuals tend to be high utilizers of medical services. Psychological consultation involving relaxation training, cognitive restructuring, and psychoeducation have reduced medical costs significantly in patients with somatizing patients.

Once particular problem areas have been chosen and targeted, the next task in establishing an integrated model is to apply evidence-based interventions. It is critical to the functioning of an integrated system that protocols are in place to guide the practice of the multidisciplinary team. As described above, protocols should be in place for (at minimum) high base-rate psychological problems, co-morbid psychological/medical problems, and patterns of behavior that could exacerbate the disease process (e.g., not following medical directions). Disease management protocols have been developed for a variety of medical and behavioral conditions and some have been shown to be effective. Strosahl (1998b) and Cummings (1996a) propose that the lack of effectiveness of some (medically focused) disease management programs has been due to their relative insensitivity to common behavioral health co-morbidities such as depression, anxiety, and substance abuse. Likewise, few psychological treatment protocols have been empirically tested in primary care environments. These limitations of the current literatures may prove to be a significant barrier in choosing protocols to implement. Mindful of this fact, if available, system administrators should plan to implement practice guidelines that have been derived from the empirical literature and, when such guidelines are not available, be prepared to follow current best practices and collect data with an eye toward developing empirically supported practice guidelines.

Finally, once protocols have been implemented, ongoing quality management is essential for the maintenance and further development of an integrated practice. To do so first requires systems administrators to define the outcome variables of interest. Of course, outcomes related to disease processes (e.g., improved physical or behavioral functioning) should be measured, but integration also invites the examination of a novel set of outcome variables. For example, variables such as medical utilization, direct and indirect costs of providing care, adherence to prescribed treatment regimens, and patient and provider satisfaction may be additional variables of interest. Ultimately, ongoing data collection will provide a means of evaluating existing programs and making necessary changes to improve effectiveness and efficiency of products.

What Is the Evidence for Integrated Care?

Integrated care appears to be very much "at the edge" of science and practice. As a result, there has not yet been a proliferation of published research in the area. However, the available data are promising. Studies have shown that integrating behavioral health services into primary care can (a) improve patient satisfaction (e.g., Katon, 1995); (b) improve provider satisfaction (Katon, 1995); (c) improve patient outcome (Cummings, 1997; O'Donohue et al., 2002); and (d) decrease health-care costs (Chiles, Lambert, & Hatch, 1999). Strosahl (1998b), Cummings (1997), and other experts in integrated health-care delivery suggest that the common elements of successful integrated programs are: (a) full integration of mental health providers and services within the primary care clinic; this typically involves colocating the behavioral health provider in the primary care setting; (b) structured treatment programs; (c) emphasis on follow-up care; and (d) sensitivity to the ecology of primary care.

Putting Theory Into Practice: The Purpose of This Book

The theoretical underpinnings of integrating behavioral and primary care practice have been thoroughly discussed in previous books (Cummings, O'Donohue, & Ferguson, 2002; Cummings, Johnson, & Cummings, 1997). However, to our knowledge, no texts to date have provided guidelines on *how* to practice integrated care. That is the intention of this book. We have structured this book to provide specific examples of behavioral problems targeted in integrated care and guidelines for behavioral health providers in treating these problems, including conducting assessments and performing triage functions. This book is intended to extend and bridge the existing literatures of integrated care, behavioral medicine, consultation-liaison psychiatry, medical cost offset, and health-care economics.

To this end, the contributing authors were required to provide a detailed definition of the problem area their chapter addresses, recommendations for assessment, a proposed protocol for the treatment of said problem within a medical context based on relevant research findings (when available), a discussion of medical cost offset (either observed or hypothesized), and suggestions for future research directions. Chapter topics were chosen based on two factors: prevalence of the problem and the extent to which integrated models of care have been established for the problem.

We have chosen three main content areas for this text. First, the treatment of psychological problems in the context of primary medical care will be addressed in several chapters (3–9). In these chapters, the psychological problem is considered to be the primary treatment target, and, indeed, the probable raison d'etre of the primary care visit. In addition, several chapters (10–17, 19) address co-morbid psychological factors that play key roles in the effective management of physical diseases, either acute or chronic. Finally, several chapters (1–3, 18) address issues relevant to the overall practice of integrated care.

In summary, the aim of this book is to provide a comprehensive and current handbook of clinical protocols that may be applied in integrated care. We hope that this book will facilitate both expanded and enriched practice. In addition, we hope that these chapters will educate readers to the existing empirical literature on integrated care, which has previously existed primarily within specialty medical journals. In doing so, we hope to inspire clinicians and researchers to engage in and contribute to the burgeoning practice and study of integrated care with the ultimate goal of improving patient health and well-being.

References

Belar, C. D., & Deardorff, W. W. (1995). *Clinical health psychology in medical settings: A practitioner's guidebook* (revised edition). Washington, DC: American Psychological Association.

Chiles, J. A., Lambert, M. J., & Hatch, A. L. (1999). The impact of psychological interventions on medical cost offset: A meta-analytic review. *Clinical Psychology: Science and Practice, 6,* 204–220.

Cummings, N. A. (1996a). Does managed mental health care offset costs related to medical treatment? In A. Lazarus (Ed.), *Controversies in managed mental health care* (pp. 213–227). Washington, DC: American Psychiatric Association.

Cummings, N. A. (1996b). The new structure of health care and a role for psychology. In R. Resnik & R. Rozensky (Eds.), *Health psychology through the lifespan: Practice and research opportunities* (pp. 27–38). Washington, DC: American Psychiatric Association.

Cummings, N. A. (1997). Behavioral health in primary care: Dollars and sense. In N. A. Cummings, J. N. Johnson, & J. Cummings (Eds.), *Behavioral health in primary care: A guide for clinical integration* (pp. 3–21). Madison, CT: Psychosocial Press.

Cummings, N. A., Dorken, H., Pallak, M. S., & Henke, C. J. (1990). The impact of psychological intervention on health care costs and utilization. The Hawaii Medicaid Project. *HCFA Contract Report #11-C-983344/9.*

Cummings, N. A., Dorken, H., Pallak, M.S., & Henke, C. J. (1993). The impact of psychological intervention on health care costs and utilization: The Hawaii Medicaid Project. In N. A. Cummings & M. S. Pallak (Eds.), *Medicaid, managed behavioral health, and implications for public policy, Vol. 2: Healthcare and utilization cost series* (pp. 2–23). South San Francisco, CA: Foundation for Behavioral Health.

Cummings, N. A, Johnson, J. N., & Cummings, J. (1997). *Behavioral health in primary care: A guide for clinical integration.* Madison, CT: Psychosocial Press.

Cummings, N. A., Kahn, B. I., & Sparkman, B. (1962). *Psychotherapy and medical utilization: A pilot study.* Oakland, CA: Annual Reports of Kaiser Permanente Research Projects.

Cummings, N. A., O'Donohue, W.T., & Ferguson, K. E. (Eds.). (2002). *The impact of medical cost offset on practice and research: Making it work for you.* Reno, NV: Context.

Cummings, N. A., O'Donohue, W. T., Hayes, S. C., & Follette, V. (2001). *Integrated behavioral healthcare: Positioning mental health practice with medical/surgical practice.* San Diego, CA: Academic Press.

Erdal, K. J., & Zautra, A. J. (1995). Psychological impacts of illness downturns: A comparison of new and chronic conditions. *Psychology and Aging, 10,* 570–577.

Follette, W. T., & Cummings, N. A. (1967). Psychiatric services and medical utilization in a prepaid health plan setting, *Medical Care, 5,* 25–35.

Friedman, R., Sobel, D., Myers, P., Caudill, M., & Benson, H. (1995). Behavioral medicine, clinical health psychology, and cost offset. *Health Psychology, 14,* 509–518.

Fries, B. E., Mehr, D. R., Schneider, D., et al. (1993). Mental dysfunction and resource use in nursing homes. *Medical Care, 31,* 898–920.

Fries, J., Koop, C., & Beadle, C. (1993). Reducing health care costs by reducing the need and demand for medical services. *The New England Journal of Medicine, 329,* 321–325.

Friman, P. C. (2001). Personal communication to authors.

Jones, K. R., & Vischi, T. R. (1979). Impact of alcohol, drug abuse, and mental health treatment on medical care utilization. A review of the research literature. *Medical Care, 17,* 1–82.

Katon, W. (1995). Collaborative care: Patient satisfaction, outcomes, and medical cost-offset. *Family Systems Medicine, 13*(3–4), 351–365.

Kroenke, K., & Mangelsdorff, A. D. (1989). Common symptoms in ambulatory care: Incidence, evaluation, therapy, and outcome. *American Journal of Medicine, 86,* 262–266.

Lorig, K., & Holman, H. (1993). Arthritis self-management studies: A twelve year review. *Health Education Quarterly Special Issue: Arthritis Health Education, 20,* 17–28.

O'Donohue, W. T., Cummings, N. A., & Ferguson, K. E. (2003). Clinical integration: The promise and the path. In N. A. Cummings, W. T. O'Donohue, & K. E. Ferguson (Eds.), *Behavioral health as primary care: Beyond efficacy to effectiveness* (pp. 15–30). Reno, NV: Context.

Pallak, M.S., Cummings, N. A., Dorken, H., & Henke, C. J. (1995). Effects of mental health treatment on medical costs. *Mind/Body Medicine, 1,* 7–12.

Reiger, D. A., Myers, J. K., & Kramer, M. (1985). The NIMH Epidemiological Catchment Area Program: Historical context, major objectives, and study population characteristics. *Archives of General Psychiatry, 41,* 934–941.

Reiger, D. A., Narrow, W. E., Rae, D. S., Manderscheid, R. W., Locke, B. Z., & Goodwin, F. K. (1993). The de facto US mental and addictive disorders service system. *Archives of General Psychiatry, 50,* 85–94.

Schwartz, G. E., & Weiss, S. M. (1978). Behavioral medicine revisited: An amended definition. *Journal of Behavioral Medicine, 1,* 249–251.

Simon, G. E., VonKorff, M., & Barlow, W. (1995). Health care costs of primary care patients with recognized depression. *Archives of General Psychiatry, 52,* 850–856.

Spitzer, R. L., Williams, J. B. W., Kroenke, K., & Linzer, M. (1994). Utility of a new procedure for diagnosing mental disorders in primary care: The PRIME-MD 1000 study. *Journal of the American Medical Association, 272,* 1749–1756.

Stern, T. A., Fricchione, G., Cassem, N. H., Jellinek, M. S., & Rosenbaum, J. F. (2004). *Massachusetts General Hospital handbook of general hospital psychiatry, 5th edition.* New York: Mosby.

Strosahl, K. (1998a). The dissemination of manual-based psychotherapies in managed care: Promises, problems, and prospects. *Clinical Psychology: Science and Practice, 5,* 382–386.

Strosahl, K. (1998b). Integrating behavioral health and primary care services: The primary mental health care model. In A. Blount (Ed.), *Integrated primary care: The future of medical and mental health collaboration* (pp. 139–166). New York: W. W. Norton.

Strosahl, K. D., & Sobel, D. (1996). Behavioral health and medical cost offset effect: Current status, key concepts, and future applications. *HMO Practice/HMO Group, 10,* 156–162.

Wagner, E. H. (1997). Managed care and chronic illness: Health services research needs. *Health Services Research, 32,* 702–714.

Chapter 1
Training Behavioral Health and Primary Care Providers for Integrated Care: A Core Competencies Approach

KIRK D. STROSAHL

Managed behavioral health care has had a profound effect upon the delivery of behavioral health services in the United States. What was once a "cottage industry" has been transformed into a mature industry that is subject to increasing scrutiny by accrediting bodies, purchasers, and consumers. The ferocity of the managed behavioral health-care movement itself is based on recognition that the behavioral health industry is a "player" in the American health-care scene. Although proponents and opponents of managed care can argue the merits and drawbacks of this socioeconomic movement, one truth is clear: behavioral health care in the United States has been and will continue to be transformed by the same influences that have transformed general health care.

Despite the success associated with this rise to prominence, it is useful to remember that behavioral health care is embedded within a larger system of general health care. Of the approximately $1.6 trillion spent annually on health care, less than 10% is allocated to behavioral care (Coffey et al., 2000; Strosahl, 1994). Although the United States spends more of its gross national product on health care than any other country in the civilized world, the health "report card" for America does not look good when compared with countries that spend far less on their systems of health care. A recent Institute of Medicine (Richardson, 2001) report concluded that the American health-care system (including behavioral health care) is broken, characterized by a profound mismanagement of available resources, which frequently results in decreased quality of care. Although inordinate financial resources are being poured into the American health care every day, the final product leaves much to be desired. In the past 2 years, health-care premiums have once again begun an upward trend. This is disconcerting because most health-care financing experts agree that the floor of cost-cutting strategies has been reached. Many health plans are refusing to participate in insurance programs that cannot generate reasonable operating profits (i.e., state Medicaid programs), indicating a growing willing-ness to sacrifice economy of scale for greater profitability. One must conclude that the Draconian cost-cutting strategies of Generation One of managed care have failed to cure very basic flaws in the way health care is delivered in this country

(Strosahl, 1995). What will be required to correct this sad state of affairs is a reengineering of the basic process of health care, not simply the modification of long-standing practices.

Integration of Services: A Major Driver of Health-Care Redesign

The integration of primary care and behavioral health services is an integral part of health-care redesign (Dobmeyer, Rowan, Etherage, & Wilson, 2003; Pruitt, Klapow, Epping-Jordan, & Dresselhaus, 1998; Strosahl, 1995, 1996, 1997, 2001). The explosion of interest in primary care behavioral health integration is demonstrated by the appearance of authoritative texts on the subject, pre- and postdoctoral fellowships devoted to working in primary care, and Websites, as well as the appearance of crossover training programs for family physicians and psychologists. Large systems of care in both the public (e.g., Bureau of Primary Health Care, U.S. Air Force, U.S. Navy, Veterans Administration) and private sectors (e.g., Kaiser Permanente Northern California) have launched full-scale, primary care behavioral health integration initiatives. Although it is tempting to create a simplistic picture of the factors driving service integration, there are three major drivers of the integration movement: health-care utilization patterns, consumer preferences, and the economics of health-care reform.

We Built It and They Didn't Come: Failure of the Segregated Model of Mental Health Care

For more than two decades, it has been widely accepted among health-care researchers that primary care is the "defacto behavioral health system" in the United States. There is compelling health services and epidemiological evidence indicating that the vast majority of behavioral health services are delivered solely by general medical providers (Narrow, Reiger, Rae, Manderscheid, & Locke, 1993; Regier et al., 1993; VonKorff & Simon, 1996). There is incontrovertible evidence pointing to a strong relationship between psychological distress, increased medical service utilization, and poor health outcomes (VonKorff & Simon, 1996; Wells et al., 1989). Indeed, many studies have demonstrated that the majority of primary care visits are driven by psychosocial factors (Kroenke & Mangelsdorff, 1989). At the same time, primary care providers point out that the work pace of primary care medicine, as well as physicians' lack of behavioral health intervention skills, makes it difficult if not impossible to address the behavioral health needs of their patients. Sobel (1995) has suggested that the tremendous demand for psychosocial services, combined with the improper configuration of the health-care system, results in a chronic mismatch between what most primary care patients are seeking (i.e., psychosocial interventions) and what most are receiving (general medical services, tests, and procedures). This mismatch generates a "revolving door" problem in primary care that leaves providers demoralized and patients dissatisfied.

With this information in hand for so long, why have health-care systems not been interested in integration earlier? Frankly, the economic incentives in the premanaged care era favored waste and fragmentation. The more wasteful health systems were, the richer they became! Managed care reversed the rules of the game by shifting financial risk to the provider of service through such strategies as case rates, capitation, and various types of utilization management. Now, health-care systems are discovering that it is difficult to manage both the service burden and financial risk when a chronic and pervasive need such as behavioral health is simply ignored.

Ironically, behavioral health carve-outs, with their much-heralded success at cutting behavioral health costs and improving access to services for selected segments of the population, have created a significant impetus for integration. In essence, carve-outs have not only formalized the segregation of health and behavioral health services, but have effectively shifted the service and financial burden for behavioral care to the health-care system (see Strosahl & Quirk, 1994). The inadequacy of most health-care insurance databases has allowed this population shift to go largely undetected. Further, carving out behavioral health care has resulted in poor communication, lack of care coordination, and a basic confusion of roles between health-care and behavioral health-care providers. Whether knowingly or unknowingly, the progenitors of carve-outs have steadfastly ignored the overwhelming population data that point to the need to deliver behavioral health services in primary medical settings. Instead, most carve-outs refuse to pay for such services or, if payment is made, it is at a steeply discounted rate. This means that, contrary to the claims of carve-out executives, behavioral health care is inaccessible to the vast majority of Americans who will not agree to receive their behavioral health in the settings and from the providers dictated by the carve-out companies. In essence, the first generation of managed behavioral health care has resulted in an expensive system of care that most consumers will never use.

Consumer-Centered Care

A second major factor in the drive toward integration is the increased role of consumer preference in determining not only how services will be delivered, but where they will be delivered. For decades, a "provider-centered" model of service has characterized American health care. Generally, this means that the provider community determines when, where, and how services are to be delivered. The consumer's role has been to comply with these systemic rules. Managed care has inadvertently contributed to the rise of "consumer-centered" care. In their marketing efforts to enroll and retain new consumers, health-care systems began the dangerous process of asking consumers what they wanted in their health care. One clear theme that has emerged is that consumers want a less fragmented system of care that emphasizes "one-stop shopping." Most consumers would prefer to receive behavioral health services in the same location and in the same time frame as they receive health-care services. It is extremely inconvenient to have to attend several appointments on several different days in several different facilities, when the same services could just as easily be delivered during a single health-care visit. Consumers generally would like access not to just behavioral health services, but oral health, physical therapy, and other adjunctive health services. It is fair to say that the voice of the consumer will be a major determinant of how the American health-care system of the future is designed.

Economic Drivers of Integration

The economic forces pushing the integration of behavioral health are closely tied to service population characteristics. A service need that exists in 70% of the medical population is a serious economic issue. Systems analysts and health-care administrators are well aware that recycling patients because their behavioral health needs are not adequately addressed converts directly into uncontrollable medical costs. Essentially, patients never leave the health-care system; so when service needs are not addressed, the patient's general health status deteriorates, leading to a greater medical services burden in the future. Further, the burden of managed care is "to do more with less." Up until recently, health-care premiums were rising at about the rate of general inflation, while insurance coverage increased to include more services. Expanding services without adding significant revenue means that the productivity of health-care providers is a central concern to system administrators. Inefficient delivery systems that drain away the capacity of medical providers will simply not be able to compete in the health-care marketplace of the next decade. At the same time, as productivity standards have increased (i.e., some general physicians now are responsible for as many as 3,500 patients), the feedback from medical providers is that their productivity is severely hampered by the ongoing problem of having to address behavioral health needs during medical exams. Furthermore, the ongoing mismatch between what the patient seeks and what the provider is prepared to deliver demoralizes medical providers, increases the risk of provider burnout, and creates difficulties in recruiting and retaining medical providers. Finally, the financial burden of maintaining highly segregated systems with many core administrative redundancies results in an unacceptably high percentage of the U.S. medical dollar's failing to reach the field. The segregation of health and behavioral health is so complete that separate administrative and governmental infrastructures exist from the level of federal government all the way down to the community. It is impossible to calculate how much of the health-care dollar is drained away by the bureaucratic maze of health care. It suffices to say that no other country devotes so much money to such an unproductive and unnecessary administrative infrastructure.

This rather long background on the integration movement is necessary because it creates a context for understanding the basic nature of health-care redesign. Integrating behavioral health services into primary care systems is not simply a matter of taking the traditional mental health specialty model and dropping it in a primary care center. The volume of behavioral health needs in the primary care population will far outstrip the capacity of the traditional specialty model of behavioral health care. Primary care centers and practice groups are searching for far more basic answers to the problems that confront their medical providers on an hourly basis. This will require building behavioral health service delivery models that are modeled after primary care medicine in mission, goals, and strategies (Dobmeyer et al., 2003; Strosahl, 1996, 1997, 1998, 2001). There is no precedent for this in the United States and most training programs for behavioral health- and primary care providers remain steadfastly rooted in mind-body dualism and a segregated system of care. However, we can capitalize on the experience of other countries such as the United Kingdom, where there is a long history of both service integration and clinical research (Goldberg, 1990). Analysis of these systems of care suggest that, in order to successfully integrate behavioral health- and primary care services, medical and behavioral health providers will have to learn new strategies for working together. This book addresses one very basic issue in this quest: how to build clinically effective and cost-efficient intervention protocols for high-volume, high-impact conditions seen in primary medicine. This chapter examines one of the most basic and perplexing aspects of the transformation to integrative primary care: how to "retrain" behavioral health- and primary care providers to work together effectively to respond to the overwhelming behavioral health needs of primary care patients. To provide some answers to this multifaceted question, it will first be of value to examine the characteristics of the primary care milieu, to understand characteristics of the most effective models of integration, and to appreciate the demands these new models of care will make of primary care and behavioral health providers. This will allow for a better appreciation of the substantial training issues involved in this type of system redesign. The final sections of this chapter will introduce a skill-based, core-competency training model that has been successfully implemented in both small- and large-scale primary care behavioral health integration initiatives. I will identify and discuss the core competencies required of primary care and behavioral health providers when working in a primary care team model. Finally, I will describe the sequence of training strategies that have produced the most successful training outcomes.

The Gestalt of Primary Care: Implications for Training

The primary care milieu is vastly different from the mental health clinic/office practice setting. These differences have profound implications, not only for the types of services that will be provided, but also for the goals and methods of training programs for primary care and behavioral health providers. The most basic difference lies in the contrasting missions of primary care and mental health systems of care. Grounded in the basic concepts of public health and epidemiology, primary care systems seek to raise the health of the entire population, not just a portion of it. The guiding mission of primary care is "population based care" (Eddy, 1996). The goals of population-based care are to (a) prevent the onset of illness through the management of health risk factors, (b) engage in early detection and management of illnesses, (c) provide stepped care for health-care problems in an attempt to manage most conditions within primary care, (d) provide palliative and chronic medical management for patients with chronic or progressive diseases, and (e) manage the total health-care needs of patients through referral to and coordination with medical subspecialists and adjunctive services such as behavioral health. In general, a primary care system must be prepared to address the full spectrum of health-care concerns that are likely to exist in the community being served.

In contrast, the concepts of population care are largely absent in the design of behavioral health systems of care, and few behavioral health providers understand even the most basic principles of this model. Most mental health training programs do not provide any education in such basic content as health-care economics, evidence-based care, and population health. Few postgraduate programs in any discipline other than psychiatry provide practicums in primary care centers, so that graduate students can get a "feel" for the primary care milieu. Consequently, entering the primary care setting can be daunting to the behavioral health provider. First, the work pace in primary care is much faster than that in a behavioral health setting. Primary care providers will average 24–34 patients per day, seen in 10–15 minute medical appointments. Often, three or four patients will be processed simultaneously, in a highly choreographed service-delivery model involving nurses, midlevel providers, and the general physician. The goals of population-based care can be achieved only by constructing a delivery system that has the capacity to provide basic medical services to a very large portion of a community population. Typically, a primary care system will provide at least one ambulatory medical service to 80% of the members of a community on an annual basis. In contrast, the typical behavioral health system will provide services to only 3–7% of the population, depending upon the service setting (Strosahl, 1996, 1997). This relatively low penetration rate allows behavioral health providers to be trained to provide longer episodes of care in the fabled 50-minute hour model.

Second, primary care patients tend to be more ethnically diverse and older, and have a much higher proportion of males than is true for the mental health populations. In addition, primary care patients present with a bewildering diversity of psychosocial issues. As has been highlighted in other writings (Strosahl, 2001), most of the major psychosocial drivers of health-care seeking are not related to mental health or chemical dependency factors, as classically defined. For example, a patient with a new diagnosis of diabetes might fail to follow behavior-change guidelines for diabetic self-management. Another patient might present for care repeatedly owing to migraine headaches that can be triggered by stress, smells, physical exercise, and so forth. These types of problems are commonplace in primary care, but they are not traditional mental health or substance abuse problems. They are, however, deeply rooted in patients' ability to change habits and behaviors.

As might be expected, the interaction of these health and psychosocial factors is a basic feature of working in primary care. Primary care patients are much more likely to have health issues that both impact and are impacted by behavioral health factors. Such patients frequently require a combination of interventions that are rarely used in mental health settings. At the same time, the volume of patients streaming through primary care generally requires less intense episodes of care and a much greater reliance on management of the patient by the health-care team over time.

Finally, one of the major transformations occurring in health care is the growing influence of the health-care team (HCT) model. This approach molds the traditional solo physician practice into a team-based enterprise, so that the doctor-patient relationship is changed into a team-patient relationship (Taplin, Galvin, Payne, Coole, & Wagner, 1998). Members of the typical health-care team include the medical assistant, nurse, physician assistant, advanced nurse practitioner, and general physician. The behavioral health provider in primary care will operate within a team milieu that is constructed very differently from that encountered in traditional behavioral health settings.

Training Implications. Adapting the mission, goals, and strategies of mental health to fit the primary care environment will require both a modification of the mental health service delivery model and the acquisition of new skills by behavioral health providers and their primary care colleagues (Robinson, Wischman, & Del Vento, 1996; Strosahl, 1996, 1997, 1998, 2001). At the level of post-graduate training, mental health providers need much greater exposure to concepts of population care, health-care economics, and evidence-based care. All of these are central and defining features of contemporary general medicine. In addition, students need to learn about aspects of the primary care population that will require a different "lens" to be used in both conceptualizing cases and delivering appropriate interventions. Providers will need to be trained to identify medical conditions that produce symptoms that mimic mental disorders and become conversant in psychopharmacology, behavioral medicine, and health psychology. If these skills are not acquired in graduate training, they will need to be learned as part of the "on the job" retraining process.

Models of Primary Care Integration: Implications for Training

The first principle in developing effective integration training programs is that the model of integration drives the content that must be mastered and the skills that will have to be acquired. It is important to understand that a range of primary care behavioral health integration models have been used with varying degrees of success (see Dobmeyer et al., 2003, and Gatchel and Oordt, 2003, for reviews of these approaches). Most health-care administrators have limited knowledge of behavioral health services in general and might not appreciate the training needs associated with different approaches to service integration. Therefore, it is important that behavioral health providers understand the central characteristics of the most common integration models. These models vary considerably in their underlying philosophies and associated clinical goals, strategies, and practice structure.

The Primary Behavioral Health Model

The primary behavioral health model is a framework for developing and delivering behavioral health services in a manner that is consistent with the mission, goals, and strategies of primary care (Strosahl, 1996, 1997, 1998, 2001). Briefly, this consultation-based approach emphasizes providing basic behavioral health services to a wide variety of patients seen by members of the primary care team. The behavioral health consultant functions as an integral part of the health-care team and attempts to improve the quality of psychosocial interventions delivered by any team member. To achieve this objective, the behavioral health provider consults with health-care providers and may engage in temporary comanagement of certain patients.

There are two distinct but complementary dimensions within the primary behavioral health model: general consultation services and chronic condition programs. It will be useful to describe the two components in more detail.

General Consultation Services. General consultation services are the behavioral health equivalent of a general primary care practice. The goal is to see any referred patient regardless of the type of problem or level of need. Drawing from the classic *Peanuts* cartoon series, this approach is often called the "Lucy is in" model. In the cartoon, Lucy is seen sitting in a Kool-Aid stand with a sign saying, "See the Psychiatrist for 5 Cents." Similar to Lucy, the behavioral health consultant offers such easy access to general consultation services by "setting up shop" in the exam room area.

The approach is to "see all comers" regardless of the type of behavioral health issue that is involved. When working in a general consultation service, it is not at all unusual for the behavioral health consultant to see 14–18 patients in a practice day. Consultation sessions tend to be very brief and focused on helping the doctor and patient successfully address a specific problem.

Chronic Condition Programs. These programs are also referred to as critical pathways, clinical roadmaps, disease management, or chronic-condition management programs. There is a growing emphasis in general health care on developing evidence-based clinical practice protocols for common disease conditions such as diabetes, asthma, and cardiovascular disease (Geyman, 1998). Similarly, chronic condition programs focus on a specific condition that is commonly seen in general medical practice. The goal of such programs is to create standard treatment guidelines, care protocols, and processes that produce the best clinical outcomes for the most patients. In chapter 2, Robinson describes various parameters for selecting behavioral health conditions that are good candidates for such programs. Generally, the condition needs to be well represented in the primary care population (i.e., depression, panic disorder) and/or have significant impact on service utilization and cost (i.e., chronic low-back pain). Second, there is one or more behavioral or psychopharmacological treatment that is known to be effective. Finally, an analysis of the cost savings and/or improvements in clinical outcomes justifies the institutional costs involved in developing the pathway (Geyman, 1998).

In chapter 2, Robinson also describes various principles for adapting evidence-based behavioral health treatments to the primary care setting. She concludes that we cannot just transfer evidence-based behavioral health treatments into primary care, any more than we can simply transfer the specialty mental health model into primary care. Evidence-based treatments must be adapted to fit the primary care milieu and address the unique preferences of primary care patients. This will require the developers of such protocols to be highly attentive to the factors that will make these models of care acceptable to both patients and providers (Robinson, 1998; Robinson & Strosahl, 2000). However these protocols are developed, they must still be delivered by a team comprising medical and behavioral health providers in the context of daily practice.

Training Implications. Behavioral health providers working in the primary behavioral health model need to be comfortable with very fast-paced sessions and need to possess a variety of assessment and intervention skills in the areas of mental health, chemical dependency, behavioral medicine, and health psychology. They need to be very effective communicators and have the ability to consult with medical team members. The skills needed to deliver chronic condition protocols overlap with, but are distinct from, the skills required of the general consultant. The provider must still adopt a brisk work pace, conduct brief and structured sessions, and continue to see many patients in a practice day. In addition, the behavioral health consultant must understand the clinical evidence for treatment of a certain condition and be able to convert this knowledge into a psychoeducational format that emphasizes skill building and home-based practice. The consltant must also understand how to assess, monitor, and quantify clinical response during each visit.

Colocated Specialty Model

An alternative integration model is the *colocated specialty approach*. This involves locating a behavioral health provider within the primary care clinic with the goal of providing traditional mental health and chemical dependency services to patients referred by general medical providers. The behavioral health provider is responsible for providing specialty treatment while attempting to coordinate care with referring medical providers. A full range of traditional mental health services is available, including individual, couples, or family therapy. A traditional service delivery model is employed that includes 1-hour therapy sessions and/or longer group therapy sessions. The services may even be delivered in an evidence-based care framework using treatment manuals or other protocols.

The "family systems health-care" model is a variant of the colocated specialty care approach (Doherty, McDaniel, & Baird, 1996; McDaniel, Campbell, & Seaburn, 1990). In this approach, the behavioral health and primary care providers conduct regular staff reviews of shared patients and may even conduct conjoint therapy sessions. This model is designed to increase collaboration between medical and behavioral health providers and support the delivery of specialty behavioral health care. Although the behavioral provider is physically colocated, he or she does not function as a core member of the primary care treatment team, but rather is viewed as an in-house specialist that is available to take same-day referrals. In this model of care, the patient flow is significantly smaller than in the consultation approach and the work pace of the behavioral provider more closely resembles that seen in a mental health clinic.

The chief drawbacks of this approach are indigenous to the specialty model of care. First, specialty care by design is labor intensive and lacks the capacity to serve a meaningful percentage of the primary care population. There is a tendency for colocated specialists to be bombarded with the most difficult patients early on (many require the most intensive forms of clinical management), and it can develop the same access problems that have plagued mental health specialty settings. For all intents and purposes, this is not a "population health" model because it does not seek to provide services to a large segment of the primary care population.

A second, subtle drawback is that the specialist approach, even in the collaborative health-care model, reinforces the idea that health care and behavioral health care are separate processes. When primary care providers send patients with behavioral health problems out of the medical exam room area, they are communicating that behavioral health is not a core aspect of quality health care. Finally, the colocated specialty approach is unlikely to have a great impact on the way primary care providers intervene with commonly seen behavioral health problems. If a specialist is needed to handle behavioral health problems, then primary care providers will continue to believe that they cannot be expected to deal with them during medical exams.

Although proponents of the collaborative family health-care approach contend that physicians learn basic mental health skills by conducting conjoint therapy sessions and attending weekly case conferences, years of experience in applied primary care settings suggest that most physicians do not have the time or interest to participate in conjoint sessions or behavioral health case conferences. Nevertheless, my experience is that primary care providers generally have positive evaluations of colocated specialty services. After years of finding such specialty services virtually unavailable for their patients, primary care providers will see the addition of an onsite specialist as a definite step forward. At the same time, medical providers will readily admit that this model does not really promote the behavioral health of the population served to any meaningful extent, nor have they learned much about how to intervene with behavioral health issues in the exam room. When health-care systems are given the choice between adopting a colocated specialist approach or the primary behavioral health model, they choose the latter almost without exception. This is because the primary behavioral health model is really a basic form of primary care.

Training Implications. The chief benefit of the colocated specialist approach is that it requires the least adaptation of existing skills by behavioral health- and primary care providers. The model is familiar to both medical and mental health providers and does not strain any existing paradigms. Most reasonably trained behavioral health providers can deliver an array of specialty services and can adapt to the primary care milieu. Further, primary care providers can easily be taught to detect and refer patients who could benefit from specialty behavioral health services. I believe that the vigor with which the colocated specialist model is being supported by the mental health industry is largely due to the fact that it requires little change in training programs or the practice patterns of providers in the field.

An Integrated Training Approach for Behavioral Health and Primary Care Providers

Practice in integrated care settings can range from slightly modified versions of the specialist approach to models of care that are much more like primary care services. The general rule is the more traditional and "mental health–like" the integration program is, the less retraining is needed. As noted, however, the more traditional colocated specialist models lack the population health focus and capacity to have a significant impact on the primary care population. Consequently, I generally recommend that primary care clinics and systems adopt the primary behavioral health approach and, in the overwhelming majority of situations, system leaders agree with this assessment. When this bridge is crossed, implementing an effective in-the-field training program for both behavioral health and primary care providers emerges as a central issue. The rest of this chapter will be devoted to describing an integrated training model designed to help primary care and behavioral health providers succeed in this primary care team-based approach. The training program is "integrated" in two senses: (1) It nearly always involves providing didactic training to both medical and behavioral health providers; and (2) the model incorporates multiple training methods ranging from didactic workshops to "shadowing" medical and behavioral health providers in practice. All of the training methods have the same central goal: to improve the providers' intellectual understanding of this model and its underlying philosophies, as well as to build concrete practice skills that will make the provider as effective as possible. Table 1.1 presents some of the training methods that are employed, as well as some of the hoped-for training outcomes.

Generally, the training sequence starts with didactic workshops that introduce participants to the primary behavior health model in general. When behavioral health and medical providers are introduced to this model of integration, their reactions are somewhat different. Medical providers have trouble believing they can deliver effective behavioral health interventions in the 2- to 3-minute time frame of a routine exam, and they are unclear about how the team-based behaviorist can assist them in the exam process. Mental health providers are generally skeptical about the feasibility of 15- and 30-minute sessions, and they find it hard to imagine how they could "handle" 12–16 patients in a practice session. In my experience, most of these reactions originate from an "attachment" to a specific mental model of human psychopathology, how behavior change occurs, and the role the intervener plays in producing change. As the didactic training proceeds, I begin to examine these issues in more detail, primarily to reveal the widespread controversies that exist in each of these fundamental paradigmatic arenas. My goal is to reveal beginning assumptions for what they are: just assumptions. The most dangerous thing about beginning assumptions is that, although they seldom can be scientifically proven, they take on the aura of being eternal "truths."

Understanding Basic Issues in Behavior Change

To a very significant extent, the way we conceptualize human suffering and psychopathology, how behavior change occurs, and the role of the intervener in producing behavior change defines the magnitude and feasibility of the job at hand. Whereas medical providers get trapped in their assumptions without knowing it, because of the general inadequacy of their mental health training, behavioral health providers are wedded to their assumptions from graduate school onward. These assumptions are near and dear to behavior health providers, and letting go of them in the face of conflicting evidence is very difficult. Most graduate training programs have a specific theoretical

TABLE 1.1 Educational Methods and Learning Goals for an Integrated Primary Behavioral Health-Care Training Program

Training Method	Learning Goals
Didactic training	Understand prevalence and impact of behavioral factors
	Understand major psychosocial drivers of health-care seeking
	Appreciate basic concepts of population health care
	Understand model of care and continuum of integration
	Appreciate concepts supporting effective assessment, brief and strategic interventions
	Understand how to adapt and apply evidence-based treatments in primary care practice
Clinical case vignettes and best-practices video training sessions	Learn to apply basic concepts of functional and diagnostic assessment
	Apply brief and strategic intervention concepts in practice
	Understand how to monitor progress and track at-risk patients
	Appreciate how to structure ultrabrief clinical encounters
Clinical and administrative services manual	Appreciate philosophy and service parameters of integrated care program
	Understand administrative requirements, policies, and procedures underpinning program
In vivo job shadowing, academic detailing, supervised clinical practice using core competencies framework	Promote increased awareness of primary care practice styles
	Develop core practice competencies
	Improve effectiveness in adapting evidence-based treatments to primary care milieu
	Adapt to the gestalt of primary care and the team-based treatment setting
Mentoring and extended practice consultation	Create framework for developing core competencies over time
	Provide forum for identifying and solving practice issues over time

doctrine (i.e., cognitive behavioral, humanistic, psychodynamic) that explains how human suffering originates, what is required to "fix" it, and what the role of the therapist is in that process. Moreover, there are other hidden conventions that nearly all programs adhere to, regardless of the theoretical model (i.e., the 50-minute hour). These beginning assumptions carry an air of sanctity that drives the a priori rejection of innovative ideas about behavior change. For example, many behavioral health clinicians will chafe at the idea of brief 15-to-30-minute encounters. They will emphatically claim that such brief encounters lead to clinical errors and only superficial treatment effects.

Observing this rigidity in their behavioral health colleagues, primary care providers claim that anything short of a specialty approach to assessment and intervention is ineffective. Since primary care exams do not allow for such comprehensive assessments and interventions, a primary care provider cannot deliver effective interventions. Thus, patients requiring mental health care should be referred out of primary care. This is one of the chief benefits of conducting didactic training with an intermixed group of medical and behavioral health providers. It allows providers on each side of the fence to witness the conceptual struggle of their colleagues while at the same time noticing that the struggle takes on different forms based on one's training background. Therefore, the struggle has to be related to what has already been learned and how new perspectives and information can be integrated into the previously existing "mental map."

Medical Illness Versus Stress-Coping Models of Human Psychopathology

The first and most salient issue involves the assumptions implicit in various models of psychopathology and human suffering. For a variety of political and economic reasons, the medical model of psychiatric illness has been and will continue to be the mainstay of the medical community, including primary care. The medical model holds that behavioral health conditions are disease entities that can be described in terms of *DSM-IV* (*Diagnostic and Statistical Manual of Mental Disorders*, 4th edition) categories. Once the correct diagnosis is made, a specific treatment is indicated. A major informal assumption of this approach is that psychological well-being is the natural resting state of human beings, much as health is the natural physical state. Similar to diseases on the medical side, behavior disorders are a deviation from that state of healthy equilibrium. This leads to terms such as *illness* or *disease* being used to describe various psychiatric syndromes. In other writings (Hayes, Strosahl, & Wilson, 1999; Hayes, Wilson, Gifford, Follette, & Strosahl, 1996), this assumption has been shown to be not only logically flawed, but to a great extent inconsistent with the empirical literature on the causes of psychopathology and behavioral dysfunction. The strongest predictors of human behavioral dysfunction are not biological or genetic factors, but rather basic coping styles (i.e., problem-focused versus emotion-focused coping, experiential escape, and avoidance). Even in contemporary medicine, health is conceptualized not only as the relationship between pathogenic and disease-buffering processes, but also as a state of mind and a sense of well-being. This means that a patient with a chronic disease such as diabetes can be "healthy" if he or she is managing his or her blood sugar; pursuing work, intimacy, family, or spiritual goals; and experiencing a sense of psychological well-being. Unfortunately, this more advanced conception of health has not been transferred to the psychiatric taxonomy, and it is still common to hear medical and behavioral health providers describe mental health and substance use syndromes as biologically driven disease states that require specialized treatment. By default, most primary care clinicians are exposed only to the medical model of human psychopathology in their graduate training. One physician commented to me that his formal mental health training in residency was to memorize the *DSM-IV!* The concepts of syndrome and illness are familiar to most medical providers, and it drives much of their overreliance on medicines as the first-line treatment response for almost any psychological complaint.

The vast majority of behavioral health clinicians in the United States are not medically trained and, in general, do not share the same allegiance to the medical model as their medically trained colleagues. Most forms of brief and strategic therapy have originated in the nonmedical wing of the behavioral health industry, and most assume that psychopathology is the by-product of increased life stress or ineffective coping responses. Indeed, a strong case can be made that most empirically-validated cognitive behavioral treatments are rooted in a stress-coping framework. Many of the core interventions in these treatment packages build coping and stress-reduction skills.

In general, stress-coping models hold that humans exist in a dynamic environment that involves responding to internal and external stresses with stress-buffering or coping responses. Generally, human psychopathology involves the interplay of three major social and psychological components: recently occurring stresses that can vary in magnitude from daily hassles to major life events, personal dispositions that determine the "reactivity" of the person to stresses (traits, genetic vulnerabilities, resources, and liabilities derived from remote learning histories), and the patient's repertoire of coping responses (stress reduction skills, self-care skills, ability to mobilize social supports, problem-solving skills, etc). Problems in functioning develop when (a) stress in the form of life events is introduced, (b) personal dispositions lead to heightened reactivity, and (c) the level of coping skills is insufficient to address the level of reactivity (Brown, 1981; Skodol, Dohrenwend, Link, & Shrout, 1990; Zubin & Spring, 1977). Often, the clinical presentation of a patient may be suggestive of severe psychopathology from a medical model perspective, but may actually be the result of a small shift in that patient's stress-coping equilibrium, as exemplified by the following clinical vignette.

A 34-year-old single mother of two children screened positive for depression in a medical exam and was referred to the behavioral health consultant. Her depression score and clinical presentation both indicated she was severely depressed. When asked if there had been a shift in her life over the past 2 or 3 months, she gave the following report. Three months prior, she had been working both a daytime and a nighttime job. Money was so tight that she couldn't afford the gas to drive to work. So, she had to walk approximately 30 minutes each way. After the daytime shift ended, she would walk home, feed her children, and then walk to her other job at a fast-food establishment nearby. About 2 months prior, she received a much-hoped-for promotion to manager at her daytime job, along with a hefty pay raise. The increased pay allowed her to quit her nighttime job and also provided the gas money for her commute to work. When asked how she had coped before with the pressure of being a single mom working two jobs, she recalled that the process of walking to and from work had helped her get organized, reduce her stress level, and increase her general energy level. When asked if she was still exercising each day for 30–45 minutes, she reported she had not done any exercise since the promotion.

A medical model analysis of this patient would result in the diagnosis of "major depressive disorder, single episode, severe." A stress-coping analysis would conclude that a very basic stress-buffering response (her daily walks) had disappeared from her repertoire, while to some extent her stress level (being at home with her two young children) might have increased. After 2 months of this "out of balance" lifestyle, she was unable to maintain an adaptive relationship between the stresses of her life and how she took care of herself in the face of stress.

Theories of Change: Cure Versus Strategic Change

As should be obvious from the previous vignette, how one conceptualizes a mental health problem leads directly to an assumption about what the intervention goal must be. If depression is an "illness" that is characterized by a specific set of "symptoms," then the goal of treatment is to eliminate those symptoms and, inferentially, remove the underlying illness. This is the predominant model of change for most primary care providers at the outset of training. I point out during training that there are many potential problems with the "cure" theory of change. One problem is that it flies in the face of evidence about the natural resting state of human existence. Rather than being divine beings free of "issues," mood swings, and dark moments, human experience seems to involve highly variable mood states, frequent negative self-referent thinking, and an ongoing struggle to acquire and maintain a sense of well-being. Is the woman in the vignette experiencing an "illness" or is she experiencing the natural effects of a positive life shift in which she has not made a necessary adjustment in her self-care strategies? A second major problem is that patients with long-term psychological problems seldom get "cured." They struggle with psychological symptoms of one type or another for decades. Assessing whether treatment is "working" with such patients based upon the presence or absence of symptoms is going on a fool's errand.

In contrast, the key feature of the stress-and-coping approach is that even small changes in any domain can produce symptoms of distress that can take on the appearance of a full-blown mental disorder. Thus, the goal of treatment can be to reduce the impinging stressor, work on reducing reactivity, or heighten any number of coping responses. Not only is there a vast literature linking stress, coping, and social support to the development of psychopathology, but many evidence-based behavioral interventions and brief therapies implicitly adopt this approach. The goal is not necessarily to fix what is broken, but to equip the patient with the skills needed to reduce stress, cope with the impact of stress, and/or increase social integration and support. The result is a model of change that does not require heroic actions on the part of the patient or the provider. Rather, helping patients make small, positive changes can have a tremendous impact. I train primary care providers to understand that working with stress and coping repertoires may be more important than eliminating the symptoms of mental illness. This type of change can actually be achieved without the need for intensive, specialized services. Not surprisingly, behavioral health providers who have substantial exposure to the brief therapies and time-limited, cognitive behavioral interventions resonate to this message during training and will also tend to prosper in the primary care environment.

Primary care providers typically receive very little formal training in basic principles of behavior change. During didactic workshops, they will candidly point out this lack of specialized training as a chief reason they are not prepared to work on behavior-change issues with patients. The one intervention they are trained in, and the one they feel most comfortable with, is the use of medications. As mentioned earlier, using medication is both quick and consistent with the biomedical paradigm of mental disorders.

To be fair, primary care providers are faced with a daunting task: to deliver behavioral health interventions in a 1-to-3-minute time frame within a comprehensive medical exam. Given the enormous volume of patients seen in any given practice day, a poorly conceived behavioral health intervention may cause the provider to be late for appointments the rest of the day. From this perspective, it is understandable that primary care providers are leery of behavioral interventions and are much more likely to reach for the prescription pad when time is tight. Giving a patient medicine is a major practice management strategy in primary care. The act of prescribing a medicine (even if it is not warranted) is a culturally accepted sign that the provider has listened and responded to the patient's complaints.

Fortunately, primary care providers know from experience that concrete, bite-sized functional interventions can dramatically affect functioning, health, and the patient's sense of well-being. Indeed, the impact of such 2-to-3-minute interventions in medical practice is supported by clinical research (Robinson et al., 1995). Establishing a better understanding of the conditions that promote behavior change is a basic requirement of training for primary care providers. For example, most primary care providers are receptive to the idea that selecting small, positive behavior change goals has an incremental, positive effect on functioning. During didactic training, I might use vignettes like the one above and then ask primary care providers to tell me what is wrong from a stress-coping perspective and then what the behavior change target would be. The use of clinical vignettes teaches both behavioral health and medical providers to apply the stress-coping model to conceptualize a problem and then develop a "bite-sized" intervention that will work.

In the previous vignette, the behavioral health consultant worked with the patient to develop a stepped exercise plan (i.e., start at two exercise periods weekly and then add one additional period each two weeks, up to five). No antidepressant medication was prescribed pending the results of her coping plan. She returned 2 weeks later reporting more than a 50% reduction in her depression level and that she had spontaneously gone from two exercise periods in week 1 to four in week 2 because she felt so good after working out. The consultant recommended that she continue the exercise plan, after consulting with the referring medical provider, and return in another 2 weeks for a brief checkup. At that visit, her depression inventory score was in the nondepressed range, and she did not meet diagnostic criteria for any depressive disorder. When primary care providers see that something as simple as building an exercise plan is a legitimate intervention for major depression, the goal of delivering effective behavioral health interventions in a medical exam seems much more achievable.

In most settings, primary care providers should look to the behavioral health provider for education and guidance on behavior change issues. The behavioral health provider needs to know both the evidence-based literature on treatments for various types of problems and to be conversant in such topics as strengths-based intervention models, stages of change interventions, or motivational interviewing, to name a few. In a basic sense, primary care providers are the world's ultimate pragmatists. If a behavior-change intervention works and its rationale is well understood, the primary care provider will integrate it into routine practice. If a behavioral health consultant is going to help reshape assumptions about behavior change, it is important to "walk in the shoes" of the primary care provider and see patients for only 15–25 minutes. This experience will help the behavioral health provider appreciate the challenges inherent in developing effective, tangible interventions in a fast-paced session. The interventions that originate in very short visits will be far more relevant to primary care practice than those developed in an hour. Without this type of role modeling, most primary care providers will quickly return to an overreliance on medication treatments.

Therapist-Guided Versus Patient-Guided Change

The traditional mental health service model is an office-based, specialty model. A cardinal feature of the specialist model (even in medicine) is that the specialist's expertise is the active ingredient in promoting a positive outcome. The patient is not expected to acquire or use the specialist's knowledge independent of the guidance of the specialist. For example, a thoracic surgeon does not expect the patient to learn how to conduct heart-lung surgery. The patient's job is to participate as the recipient of the procedure, to follow the specialist's recommendations, to follow up for required medical examinations, and so forth. If the patient does all of these things, then the chances of success are increased.

The analogy of the behavioral health provider as specialist breaks down on closer scrutiny. From a stress-coping perspective, one can hardly claim that most behavioral health interventions are highly specialized. Most of the strategies incorporated in mental health and chemical dependency treatments have been available to and used by the community for decades. One only need examine the self-help section of the local bookstore to support this notion. For example, Was the exercise intervention with the depressed patient in the previous vignette really that different from having a friend tell her that she needed do get out and do something to take care of herself? In most situations, the behavioral health provider possesses a degree that allows culturally sanctioned interventions to be endorsed. This is powerful medicine, but it is not unique and specialized compared with the skills required for open-heart surgery. If there is a distinctive benefit of "therapy," it may be that the process itself provides a structure for approaching and resolving problems, rather than avoiding and exacerbating them. However, this benefit may be costly in other respects. Essentially, the patient is required to participate in sequentially organized treatment sessions over time and the therapist "releases" information in stages according to his or her perception of the patient's readiness to learn new strategies. This places the patient in a subordinate role where the therapist is responsible for the transmission of key knowledge.

This service delivery model may work for providers, but it does not coincide with the preferences of patients. Primary care patients want advice, support, and the responsibility for managing their own conditions. In this sense, the patient education model dominant in health care is not philosophically organized to be consistent with the intervention models of various psychotherapies. During didactic training with primary care providers, I try to draw an analogy between the exercise plan created for the depressed patient and the formation of a self-management plan for a newly diagnosed diabetic patient. Both involve educating the patient about the nature of the condition, discussing the various types of self-management activities that will help the condition, and then assisting the patient in developing a specific self-management plan that the patient will be responsible for implementing. The goal of such plans is to get the patient to practice new strategies outside of the primary clinic in their native environment. In discussing clinical vignettes like the one above, it is important to highlight that the active ingredient of the exercise intervention is not the 15 minutes spent with the behavioral health consultant or the medical provider. Rather, the active ingredient in behavior change is the extent to which the patient engaged in coping responses (i.e., exercise) known to be effective in reducing depression. The goal of strategic interventions is to get the patient to do something different in response to challenges that are being faced on a daily basis.

In primary care contexts, it is unusual for a behavioral health consultant to be in a long-term consulting relationship with a patient. The goal of the consultant is to fully inform the patient about self-management strategies available to address a particular life circumstance and develop a "patient-centric" action plan. Pamphlets, classes, and brief consultative support visits replace the therapeutic process. Most behavioral health providers struggle with these ultra-brief regimes, where they cannot exercise immediate control over the flow of treatment. They are uneasy about shifting so much responsibility for behavior change to the patient. However, evidence for the clinical effectiveness and consumer acceptability of this approach is indisputable (Katon et al., 1996; Robinson et al., 1996).

Attacking Myths and Misconceptions That Fuel Resistance

Although philosophical assumptions define whether the job of behavioral health in primary care is "doable," the mental health field has fallen prey to many myths about clinical assessment, how effective working relationships are formed in therapy, and how therapy itself works. When providing didactic training to behavioral health and medical providers, it is important that we directly discuss these myths and misconceptions. Left unaddressed, these beliefs can impact the provider's level of confidence in the selected interventions.

Traditional Versus Functional Assessment Models

Most behavioral health providers spend 60–90 minutes in their initial meeting with a patient, collecting a voluminous amount of information and developing a comprehensive treatment plan. They are trained to believe that this level of detail is required to make accurate assessments and deliver clinically competent care. When confronted with the idea that a new patient will be seen for 15–30 minutes, behavioral health providers will contend that it is impossible to accurately assess a patient in this amount of time. What they do not understand is that there are no studies linking much of the information obtained in the traditional mental health intake with improved clinical outcomes. The most important and often least attended to component of an intake interview is to figure out what the patient's current problem is and to design a strategy to solve that problem. Many studies have found that agreement on a definition of the problem to be targeted is a powerful nonspecific predictor of positive outcome (cf. Garfield, 1994). It is highly related to the development of an intervention that is viewed as credible by both the therapist and patient, another powerful nonspecific predictor of change. Unfortunately, a good deal of the traditional behavioral health intake (i.e., relationship histories, family, work and educational histories, genograms) seems peripheral to this goal. It appears that the work requirements have expanded to fit the work pace of a specialty model of service. In obligatory fashion, the peripheral aspects of assessment become reified as a standard of practice. As the old saying goes, the work will expand to fill the time!

Within the behavioral health industry, there are competing schools of thought about how much information is needed about a patient in order to deliver effective treatment. Many popular strategic intervention models emphasize that patients will readily provide information about the most important components of their current and immediate past circumstances, if the therapist provides the necessary session structure and avoids reinforcing certain types of time-consuming therapeutic transactions (Budman & Gurman, 1988; De Shazer et al. 1986; Hoyt, 1991). A hallmark of many brief therapies is the philosophy that it is not the patient's problem that is causing dysfunction, but rather the solutions that are being used to solve the problem. Within the brief therapy framework, the information required for an effective intervention can usually be obtained in 20–30 minutes. Although there may be cases that require more information gathering than is possible in a 20–30 minute visit, this is the exception rather than the rule. It is also important to remember that the behavioral health consultant is practicing in a medical team context in which other medical providers have additional information and perspectives about a patient's behavioral health history. This information normally is not available in a mental health or chemical dependency clinic unless there is an established history with the patient. It is striking how much corroborating information is available from other primary care team members; often they may have a multiyear history a referred patient.

The Therapeutic Versus Team Relationship

The therapeutic alliance has been shown in many studies to be a strong predictor of both adherence to treatment and positive clinical outcome. Far less well understood are the conditions that are both necessary and sufficient for a therapeutic alliance to develop. Many behavioral health providers believe that the strength of the therapeutic alliance is linearly related to the amount of time spent with a patient. Therefore, spending less than the traditional amount of time with a patient damages the therapeutic relationship and decreases clinical efficacy. Although there is a host of literature supporting the importance of the therapeutic relationship as a predictor of clinical response, there are no studies establishing this as a function of time spent with the patient. In other words, rapport can be established within 5 minutes of the first encounter or never established in 20 one-hour sessions. In fact, it appears that the quality of the therapeutic relationship is to some extent independent of the amount of time the therapist and client spend in session (cf. Beutler, Machado, & Allstetter-Nuefeldt, 1994). Finally, it is important to remember that almost all studies of the therapeutic relationship have been conducted in the mental health specialty setting and the rules for forming effective therapeutic relationships may not generalize to the primary care patients.

As noted previously, there are drastic differences in the gestalts of primary care and a mental health clinic. One profound difference is that in primary care, the patient's relationship is with the health-care team, not necessarily with just one individual on the team. In primary care, there is a conscious effort to substitute the single provider–single patient relationship with the team-patient relationship. Clinical outcome studies with primary care patients clearly indicate that this model produces lower dropout rates, better adherence to treatment regimens, and better clinical outcomes (Katon et al., 1996; Mynors-Wallis, Gath, Day, & Baker, 2000; Mynors-Wallis, Gath, Lloyd-Thomas, & Tomlinson, 1995; Robinson, Wischman, & Del Vento, 1996). Because of this feature, primary care providers typically are more comfortable with the idea that the team relationship is just as powerful as the 1:1 therapy relationship. They often are perplexed by the emphasis behavioral health providers place on the 1:1 relationship because it is inconsistent with their direct experience working in the team model.

More Therapy Is Better

Many behavioral health clinicians assert that patients with significant behavioral health issues cannot possibly overcome these problems by participating in such brief team-oriented intervention regimens. This is really a throwback to the controversy regarding the acceptability and efficacy of brief therapy in general (Hoyt, 1991). The argument is that it takes time to build a therapeutic relationship, to work through client resistance, manage transference, and eventually engage the client in meaningful attempts at behavior change. The "dose-effect" literature (Howard, Kopta, Krause, & Orlinsky, 1986) provides only modest support for this idea. Although nearly all the dose-effect data are derived from studies of specialty mental health patients (making inferences to behavior change in primary care settings an issue), it is clear that a great deal of behavior change happens very quickly in psychotherapy. Specifically, approximately 50% of the total benefits of therapy are realized before the completion of the eighth session (Howard et al., 1986). Indeed, many new generation behavioral therapies emphasize important concepts such as acceptance rather than change, as well as the notion that change may be a qualitative rather than quantitative process (see Hayes et al., 1999; Hayes and Strosahl, 2004).

A second commonly held misconception is that consumers prefer longer-term treatment for their behavioral health problems. This is the basic assumption of the fee-for-service model of mental health private practice, but it is well documented in health services research that the average psychotherapy patient will participate in four to six sessions of treatment. The psychotherapy dropout rates in most mental health settings (i.e., patients who stop on their own without discussing it with their behavioral health provider) approaches 50% (cf. Garfield, 1994). Empirically validated treatments in behavioral health routinely involve 12–24 hours of treatment, vastly greater than most consumers are willing to tolerate. Evidence-based behavioral programs in primary care, using far less session contact time, have produced clinical outcomes that are comparable or superior to those in specialty treatment (Katon et al., 1996; Mynors-Wallis, 1996; Mynors-Wallis et al., 1995, 2000, Robinson, Wischman, Del Vento, 1996).

I have found it very important to talk about the active ingredients of therapy when training primary care providers as well. Primary care providers have many stereotypic beliefs about what goes on in the process of therapy and what the science says are the active ingredients of successful therapy. In prior, often limited contacts with behavioral health providers, medical providers have learned that the process of behavior change is very complicated and that it takes a specialist to do the work. On the other hand, primary care providers know from experience that concrete, bite-sized functional interventions can dramatically affect functioning, health, and sense of well-being. In most settings, primary care providers will look to the behavioral health consultant for guidance on these matters. If the behavioral health provider is resistant or negative about the power of strategic or behavioral interventions, this will influence the medical providers on the team. On the other hand, medical providers will aggressively pursue a brief behavior change model, if it is well understood and advocated by the behavioral health specialist.

Practice-Based Core Competencies Training

When the didactic phase of training is completed, the goal shifts from equipping behavioral health and medical providers with knowledge to providing them with the practice skills needed to apply their knowledge. In this section, I will present a practice-based, core competencies training model that has been used with significant success in several large-scale, primary care behavioral health system initiatives.

During the past two decades, employee training programs in business and industry have shifted from content-based to skill-based models. Essentially, content-based training attempts to convey the intellectual knowledge about a specific task or role to the employee, usually in the form of training workshops, tutorials, and guided instructional curricula. These methods are didactic in nature; they assume that the employee will incorporate intellectual knowledge and convert it to practical application, once in the job context. The main problem with content-based training is that research into its effectiveness is very equivocal. Attending a workshop has only a temporary effect on the subsequent work behavior of the participant.

As a remedy for these disappointing findings, training experts have developed skill-based training programs. In contrast to the emphasis on intellectual knowledge of content-based programs, skill-based training emphasizes developing task fluency through structured and supervised practice. Job shadowing, guided modeling, and in vivo skills training are typical skill-based training methods. In medical training programs, these strategies are often collectively referred to as academic detailing. Skill-based training divides job-related skills into core groups, known as core competencies. The goal of training is to help the trainee acquire core competencies through guided practice, with real-time modeling and performance feedback available from the teacher. In contrast to didactic training methods, which have proven to be relatively ineffective in promoting lasting changes in medical practice, skill-based training (academic detailing) has been shown to promote stable changes in various medical practices (see Lin et al., 1995, for a discussion of these issues).

The dilemma facing behavioral health and primary care providers in an integrated model of service delivery is similar to the problems businesses face when they retrain workers to function in computerized work environments. New skills have to be acquired to function successfully, and it is not feasible to re-educate the entire workforce; approaches must be developed that allow education and skill development to occur quickly and cheaply. The core competencies training model described in this section is an attempt to address this significant challenge. Table 1.2 highlights many of the core competencies required of behavioral health and primary care providers practicing in an integrated service delivery model.

Note that the "front end" of this training program involves exposure to the content of the primary behavioral health model. If the provider does not understand the model at the conceptual level, it is very difficult to conduct the hands-on training. On the other hand, all the concepts in the world do not prepare the provider for the reality of sitting in front of a patient, gathering data in an efficient way, and then picking an effective behavior change intervention. This requires in vivo supervision from an expert trainer, often spaced over weeks or months, to promote fluency with the primary behavioral health approach (see Dobmeyer et al., 2003, for a similar argument).

The core competencies to be targeted in training have some important features. First, there is significant overlap in the practice skills required of behavioral health and medical providers because they are working in a shared philosophical framework. At the same time, there are some distinct differences resulting from different roles and responsibilities for each provider on the primary care team. For example, clinical practice skills for primary care providers anticipate that roughly 1–3 minutes of a medical visit will be devoted to behavioral health issues. The behavioral health provider may have 15–20 minutes of uninterrupted time with the same patient, leading to different expectations of what can and should be accomplished during the longer visit. For example, the behavioral health provider can conduct a more in-depth assessment and generate a more detailed behavior change plan in a 20–25 minute session.

A second feature to note is that the primary behavioral health model requires both medical and behavioral providers to change their practice styles. No miraculous changes are going to happen through the simple act of placing a behavioral health provider on a medical team. Primary care providers need to change how they conduct exams in a setting where the behavioral health consultant is available in real time to assist with patient care. For example, behavioral chronic condition programs may create a specific set of responsibilities for both the behavioral health and medical provider. New core competencies might include knowing how to employ structured diagnostic and symptom severity checklists, practice guidelines, behavior change plans, conjoint visits with patients, and new charting practices. Space does not permit a detailed examination of each core competency in the program, but it will be of value to briefly discuss each core competency domain and how this training approach targets the skills of primary care and behavioral health providers.

Clinical Practice Skills

Clinical practice skills are required for effective, brief interventions that are medically appropriate and can be supported and reinforced by other primary care team members. In general, this requires primary care and behavioral health providers to quickly align with the patient, conduct rapid,

TABLE 1.2 Core Clinical Domains and Practice Competencies Required for Integrated Primary Behavioral Health Care

Clinical Practice Skills

Identifies problem quickly and accepts patient's point of view

Efficiently describes and employs biopsychosocial model of behavior change

Limits number of target problems consistent with strategic theories of change

Applies patient strengths and resources to identified problems

Uses patient education and home-based practice model

Focuses on functional outcomes

Interventions emphasize acceptance as well as first-order change

Evaluates client's readiness to change and emphasizes client-driven change

Interventions are simple, racially and culturally sensitive, and supportable by other primary care team members

Uses brief, culturally appropriate assessments and interventions

Shows understanding of relationship of medical and psychological processes

Shows knowledge of psychotropic medicines and adherence strategies

Understands evidence-based treatments and can develop primary care protocols

Shows understanding of behavioral medicine principles and interventions

Can apply health psychology concepts and interventions in prevention protocols

Ready to provide primary care lifestyle class or group care clinic alone or with a primary care team member

Practice Management Skills

Measures outcomes of behavior change plan at every visit

Uses 30-minute sessions efficiently*

Stays on time when conducting consecutive appointments

Uses community resource and social support strategies

Evaluates outcomes of interventions and develops alternative treatment when indicated

Uses intermittent visit strategy to support home-based practice model

Choreographs patient visits within existing medical services process

Uses flexible patient contact strategies (i.e., phone, letter)

Uses patient-care modalities designed to manage caseload (classes, group care clinics)

Coordinates triage of patients to and from external specialty services*

Consultation Skills

Understands distinction between consultation model and psychotherapy model*

Can explain role of consultant accurately to patient*

Focus is on referral question*

Provides feedback to referring providers on a same-day basis*

Tailors recommendations to work pace of medical units*

Conducts effective curbside consultations

Recommendations are concrete and easily understood by all primary care team members*

Consultations incorporate health and behavioral health factors*

Willing to aggressively follow up with health-care team members, when indicated

TABLE 1.2 (continued)

Leads efforts to develop clinical pathways for behavioral health conditions*

Focuses on recommendations that reduce primary care physician's workload*

Uses prescribing psychiatric consultant appropriately

Documentation Skills

Documents BHC response to primary care physician referral question

Writes clear, concise chart notes indicating BH treatment plan, treatment response, and patient adherence to homework

Gets chart notes and feedback to physicians on same-day basis

Chart notes are consistent with curbside conversation results

Protects sensitive and confidential information

Knowledgeable of reporting requirements for physical abuse, sexual abuse, and neglect

Team Performance Skills

Shows awareness of medical provider roles within the primary care team

Understands and operates comfortably within primary care culture

Frequently circulates through medical practice area to create top-of-mind awareness among primary care team members*

Develops various strategies to build a consulting practice by dovetailing on common teamwork processes

Readily provides unscheduled services when required

Is available for on-demand consultations by pager or cell phone

Willing to provide brief educational talks during lunch hour meetings

Administrative Skills

Understands relevant policies and procedures from services manual

Understands and applies risk-management protocols

*Indicates core competency specific to the behavioral health provider; all others are shared competencies.

appropriate diagnostic and functional assessments, limit the scope of the target problem, and select "bite-sized," behaviorally oriented interventions that can be supported by any team member. As should be obvious, the foundation for these skills is the ability to conceptualize behavior change in stress and coping terms, to understand the interaction of medical and psychological processes, and to shift to an intervention model that uses patient education and home-based practice in lieu of frequent provider-patient contacts. Because of the formidable demand for behavioral health services within the primary care population, behavioral health clinicians simply cannot afford to engage in more traditional and time-consuming forms of assessment and treatment. Instead of conducting extensive family, work, or psychiatric histories, the goal is to get into the "here and now" with the patient. How is the patient functioning at work, with family, at church, or with friends? How has the patient addressed problems like this before in life? What types of coping strategies is the patient using now and with what success? The definition of what is an appropriate assessment shifts from patient to patient, depending on the needs of the referring medical provider but, in general, the focus of the assessment and subsequent behavior change plan is on improving the patient's current functioning.

For different reasons, primary care providers must learn efficient ways of generating an agreed-upon definition of the patient's problem and then selecting interventions that are limited in scope. There is simply not enough time in a typical medical exam to get anything resembling a comprehensive social or psychiatric history. The goal is to minimize the service burden associated with managing the general health-care needs of a panel of 2,000–3,000 patients. The concept of "working diagnosis" is applicable here. A working diagnosis allows the provider to treat the presenting problem based on an incomplete set of data, then observe the results of treatment and refine the diagnosis. Only if the patient fails to respond does the search for more comprehensive assessment data begin (i.e., referral to specialists, specialty tests).

In general, behavioral health providers working in primary care need to understand empirically supported interventions and deliver them in a highly condensed fashion. Not only will the number of contacts with the patient be smaller, but session times will be shorter as well. The first requirement is to keep current on empirically validated treatments. This can be accomplished by purchasing one of several excellent volumes devoted to this subject (i.e., Nathan & Gorman, 2002). In addition, the behavioral health provider needs to be an accomplished Web surfer, accessing evidence-based-care Websites on a frequent basis. When delivering care in an evidence-based chronic condition program, the same basic intervention principles apply as in a general consultation. The main exception is that the number of interventions and frequency of sessions may change. Instead of seeing the patient one to three times, as would be the case in the general consultation approach, behavioral chronic condition protocol might call for four to six short visits. For example, asking a patient with heightened stress levels to exercise on a regular schedule is a commonly used intervention that can be implemented in a very short time frame. Regular exercise is good for almost any person who is not medically constrained from doing so, and the provider can plan on seeing the patient back in 2–4 weeks to review the success of the plan. However, if the patient is clinically depressed, the exercise goal might be only one component of the evidence-based intervention program to be recorded on a standard depression management form in the medical chart. This form in turn could be included in an interactive patient education pamphlet on depression (see Robinson, Wischman, & Del Vento, 1996, for an excellent example of this strategy). Subsequent 20-minute visits might expose the patient to other evidence-based self-management strategies, such as personal problem solving, behavioral activation, cognitive disputation, and so forth. Each session would result in the development of a new self-management goal. Thus, the depressed patient might end the program with three or four specific self-management goals, because the severity of the patient's presenting problem warrants a higher intensity of stepped care.

Given the frequency with which medicines are used in primary care, both medical and behavioral health providers need to have an excellent grasp of functional psychopharmacology. It is important to understand the pharmacokinetic bases of these compounds, important drug-drug interactions, common side effects, and basic medical contraindications. There are several excellent textbooks on psychopharmacology for nonmedically trained providers, and I usually encourage the provider-in-training to purchase one. Another excellent way to stay current is to attend workshops on psychopharmacology as well as lunches sponsored by the various pharmaceutical companies.

I train medical providers in particular to understand that their use of medications needs to be consistent with clinical practice guidelines designed for primary care populations. Medicines are both over- and underprescribed in primary care. They are often given to patients who do not have the problem the medicine is designed to treat and often not given to patients who could benefit from them. To correct this problem, I will often advise medical providers to use screening tools designed to help define the nature of a presenting complaint more accurately. In some clinical settings, brief screens for depression, alcohol and drug abuse, domestic violence, pain, and anxiety states have been implemented as "vital signs." The screens are administered before every medical exam and the results are passed on to the medical provider by the support staff.

Given the pervasive problem of nonadherence to medicines, both primary care and behavioral health providers need to be skillful in describing the complementary role of medicine and psychological interventions. Generally, it is useful to describe medicines as a short- and intermediate-term treatment for improving functioning, so that the long-term solution of learning specific coping and self-management skills can be accomplished. Both primary care and behavioral health providers need to be acutely aware of and respond to patient beliefs and expectancies about medications that influence both adherence and response to psychopharmacological treatment. When medication occupies a major role in the management of a condition (i.e., antidepressants for major depression), behavioral chronic condition programs must contain strategies for systematic patient education and risk assessment and management (Robinson, Wischman, & Del Vento, 1996). For example, the typical primary care patient still believes that antidepressant medication is addictive and that a lifetime regimen of medication treatment is required to manage depression. This type of misinformation is easy to correct if the behavioral health and medical provider is sensitive to the role that beliefs and expectancies play in determining adherence to medical care.

Practice Management Skills

Practice management skills are required to see 10–12 (and often more) primary care patients in a practice day, to stay on time, to monitor clinical response in time-efficient ways, and to effectively respond to the behavioral health needs of the entire population using population care strategies. Effective practice management is absolutely essential for both primary care and behavioral health providers, although the skills required for success may vary. For behavioral health providers, perhaps the greatest challenge is the ability to organize and conduct 15-to-30-minute patient contacts. This is a major focus of training in the core competencies approach. Most behavioral health providers are trained to work in the traditional 50-minute hour that supports the specialty model of behavioral health. By primary care standards, this is a luxuriously slow work pace. Most primary care providers will have seen four to five patients in the same 1-hour time frame! To a large extent, the behavioral health provider's credibility is determined by the ability to work at the pace of primary care and develop interventions that will work in the 1-to-3-minute time frame that is the bread and butter of the medical exam structure. To routinely accomplish 15-to-30-minute sessions, the behavioral health provider must reduce the emphasis on rapport building, eliminate unneeded, time-consuming assessments, limit the problem focus, and stick with functional interventions. As is the case within a brief therapy approach, the emphasis is on helping the patient develop practical goal-oriented interventions.

Behavioral health providers that can master the 15-to-30-minute visit space typically do well with the other core competencies. The interventions that fall out of such accelerated visits tend to end up being small and concrete, precisely the type of strategies that are called for if one is using the stress-coping philosophy. Consequently, I train the behavioral health provider to organize and manage the 30-minute visit using the following time frames:

> *2–5 minutes*: Introduce the service and the provider, link the general process to quality health care, develop patient understanding/buy-in, and review previous home-based practice results (in follow-up sessions).
>
> *10–15 minutes*: Discuss current issues, identify problems, make differential diagnoses, conduct functional analyses, assess what is working and not working, hunt for solutions already in place, and create a shared problem definition.
>
> *5–10 minutes*: Develop, justify, and troubleshoot a patient-centered intervention, set up monitoring strategies, and agree to a follow-up plan.

5 minutes: Consult with primary care provider, implement any medical treatments, and chart for the medical record.

The most common problem that behavioral health providers have is running late with one or more patients, so that patients who have arrived on time for their appointments are required to wait for unreasonable lengths of time. This requires both an awareness of the passage of time while intervening with sometimes complicated clinical situations and acquiring skills that both prevent falling behind and allow the provider to recapture time when running late. Any provider who cannot effectively organize and conduct a 20-to-30-minute session will habitually struggle with staying on schedule. This has a snowball effect throughout a day of practice. For example, if the behavioral health provider runs 5 minutes late for each of the first six appointments, the provider will be 30 minutes late for the seventh appointment. Most behavioral health providers have no experience with very high volume practice models like those common in primary care, so it should come as no surprise that this is an area that frequently requires significant emphasis in training.

There are both effective and ineffective strategies for maintaining control of a busy practice schedule. Effective strategies include anticipating a certain number of no-shows, scattering brief charting and consultation slots throughout the daily schedule, or shortening a scheduled 30-minute, follow-up visit to 10–15 minutes if the patient is doing well. Less-effective strategies include ending the visit by requiring the patient to return for a second appointment to complete the assessment and intervention planning process, implementing an intervention without gaining patient buy-in, or simply referring the patient to some other community resource to get him or her out of the room.

For prescribing primary care providers, the least effective practice management tool is to precipitously reach for the prescription pad. In the busy world of primary care practice, the pill has become a central practice-management strategy. This is compounded by the fact that very few medical providers have any access to real-time behavioral health support in the context of their daily practice. In essence, they are trapped in the room with a patient who may or may not comply with nonverbal and verbal cues to end the medical visit. When this occurs, and it does on a daily basis for most medical providers, prescribing a pill is the way to end the visit. It signifies to the patient that the medical provider has listened and is doing something to help. The medical provider learns that offering medicine can very rapidly conclude a visit that is spiraling out of control. The problem is that this is a hit-or-miss solution. Some patients may actually benefit from the pill that has been prescribed; others have little chance of a positive response. For example, research suggests that only about 50% of depressed primary care patients who are prescribed an antidepressant actually meet diagnostic criteria for major depression (Katon et al., 1996). Patients with subthreshold depressive symptoms are less likely to respond to medications. A second problem is that adherence to medication is alarmingly low. As many as half of all primary care patients receiving a psychoactive medication will discontinue on their own within 30 days (see Robinson, Wischman, & Del Vento, 1996, for a more thorough discussion of this issue). In the world of primary care, it is very difficult to track who is and is not taking medication as prescribed. Consequently, prescribing is a double-edged sword. It works to manage the individual contact, but it is difficult to monitor adherence and even more difficult to discontinue medicines in an appropriate clinical time frame.

Primary care providers are typically familiar with the practice implications of population-based care. Patients are seen in brief medical visits that are organized around various practice algorithms. The theory behind algorithmically stepped care is that, in most cases, the least intensive intervention that is clinically indicated will work. It is only when a patient fails to respond to this first level of care that a second level of care is initiated. This is a primary strategy for managing a scarce resource, in this case the primary care provider's time. At a certain point in the process of stepped care, the complexity of the patient's complaints exceeds the training level or time management requirements of the primary care provider. This typically results in referral to a medical subspecialist, who then takes on a significant role in managing the patient's subsequent health care.

In contrast, behavioral health providers have little experience with the practice management requirements of population-based behavioral health care. Typically, the strategies that work for medical providers need to be translated into similar tactics and strategies for the primary behavioral health provider. For example, a behavioral health provider will need to adopt a brief intervention and team-based management approach that allows the needs of most primary care patients to be addressed in one to three visits. Obviously, there may be patients who require more visits, and the percentage of such patients varies dramatically according to the population being served. However, even in an at-risk population, the behavioral health provider is responsible for managing resources so that all members of the population have access to behavioral services. The conceptual shift and skills required to adapt behavioral health practice to the demands of population care is a core focus of the competency-based training program. This really involves a subtle combination of clinical practice skills and a change in practice philosophy. In addition, this approach requires the use of alternative, flexible, service-delivery strategies such as telephone follow-ups, psychoeducational classes, nursing-based interventions, and group medical care clinics (Kent & Gordon, 1997; Robinson, Del Vinto, & Wischman, 1998). One central theme in my training is to have the behavioral health provider understand that his or her "panel" is the entire population of the primary care clinic. This means the behavioral health provider is a "scarce resource," so the goal is to distribute services to patients and consultations with medical providers in a way that maximizes the benefit for the most patients. Each decision about when a patient is to return for follow-up and with what intended effect must be weighed carefully. For example, having patients return in 1–2 weeks for follow-up visits is the tradition in mental health specialty settings, but it can be disastrous in a high-volume, primary behavioral health practice. When a provider is seeing 20–25 new patient referrals per week, it only takes a month of practice management errors like this to create significant problems in the daily practice schedule.

For some behavioral health providers, population management philosophies can create standard-of-care concerns, founded on the belief that delivering abbreviated services is tantamount to inappropriate treatment. It is important to understand that the traditional specialty practice model defines the existing standard of care, and primary behavioral health is based in an entirely different set of philosophies. Hence, the standard of care for primary behavioral health providers is not, and should not be, defined by the practice of specialty mental health. This is analogous to holding primary care physicians to the same standard of care as cardiologists with respect to the assessment and treatment of heart disease. Practice standards for primary behavioral health-care need to be derived in the same way that standards of care for primary medical providers are derived.

As is true for the primary care provider, the primary behavioral health provider needs to effectively manage the needs of the entire population to be served and to appropriately refer patients who cannot be helped in this approach to the behavioral health specialty system. In other words, just as the primary care physician needs the cardiologist's special skills and expertise, so too will the primary behavioral health provider need the specialty mental health specialist to intervene in more difficult cases. Unfortunately, many chronically distressed, multiproblem patients who could benefit from specialty mental health or chemical dependency care are simply not willing to receive these services in the specialty setting. These patients are often among the first referred when a new, integrated, behavioral health service is made available to the primary care team. Because of their level of clinical need and provocative style of help-seeking, these patients can have a very disruptive influence on a primary care center. The multiproblem medical patient must also be managed within a population-care framework, otherwise, 5 or 10 such patients could consume all a behavioral health provider's time and schedule. In a population management model, the central focus is not on providing long-term therapy to such patients, but rather is on managing unnecessary medical utilization and forestalling further deterioration in the patient's general functioning. This requires the primary behavioral health provider to use a behaviorally oriented, case and crisis–management oriented approach that may span months or years. This approach emphasizes forming a strong team-based management plan that restricts the patient from using both excessive and unplanned medical services. It may include any or all of the following strategies:

Create a yearly visit bank that the patient can manage but not increase.
Create specific crisis management protocols for unplanned medical visits.
Create a planned monthly medical visit schedule, do not permit unplanned visits.
Alternate planned monthly visits between the nurse, physician, and behavioral health provider when the capacity of primary care team members permits it.
Develop a limited set of functionally oriented treatment goals that are consistently monitored and reinforced during all medical contacts.
Engage in regular updating of the crisis management plan and functional treatment goals, based upon the patient's response.

The major philosophy in managing such patients is that no member of the primary care team should have to absorb a disproportionate share of the service burden when addressing the plethora of problems presented by the patient.

When providing interventions to patients using behavioral chronic condition care programs, population-management strategies are even more essential. As Robinson states in chapter 2, the goal of such programs is to coordinate the efforts of all medical team members with the aim of providing a consistent, structured process of care to all patients presenting with a specific behavioral health issue. The primary behavioral health provider never adopts a specialty behavioral health relationship with the patient. Rather, the visits with the behavioral health provider are interspersed with medical visits, and the goal is for all providers to understand, monitor, and reinforce the behavioral aspects of the patient's health-care plan. In essence, any medical team member can function in the role of behavioral health provider with the patient. It is only through such collective management that the medical team has any chance of addressing the vast demand for behavioral health interventions in the primary care population.

Consultation Skills

Consultation skills are required for a behavioral health provider to provide clinically useful advice about the nature of and interventions for behavioral health problems that are encountered during routine medical exams. Primary care providers also need to develop specific skills that allow them to maximize the impact of the behavioral health provider. This includes understanding what types of patients might benefit from a behavioral health consultation, how to sell the patient on the value of the service, how to frame an appropriate referral question for the behavioral health consultant, and how to integrate behavioral health recommendations into the patient's health plan.

The most important core competency for the behavioral health provider is a clear understanding of a consultation practice and how it differs from a traditional psychotherapy practice. First, the goal of the consultant is to answer a specific referral question generated by a referring medical provider. This means that the consultant must be adept at "coaching" medical providers on how to develop a specific referral question. Second, because the consultant's job is to answer a specific question and provide a set of recommendations, consultation episodes are typically brief and focused. The consultant does not take over responsibility for treating the patient, but operates in a temporary comanagement role with the referring medical provider. Another defining feature of a consultation practice is that it is completely dependent on referrals from medical providers. This means the consultant has to build the practice, a topic I will address in more detail in the next section. A more basic premise is that the rate of referral is directly related to whether referring medical providers believe involving the consultant adds value to the medical visit. If the consultant's assessments and recommended interventions are helping patients, the consultant will be used more and more. Another important element of a consultation practice is that the referred patient *must* understand the role of the consultant in relation to the referring medical provider. Because it is relatively rare for patients to see a behavioral health provider in a primary clinic, the temptation is to assume that the provider is there to deliver psychotherapy. This can lead to a different mind-set for the patient and sometimes the referring medical provider. Thus, a major point of emphasis in my training is to make sure the behavioral health consultant clearly articulates the role of the consultant in relation to the referring medical provider and the primary care team.

Generally, quality consultation both helps generate a set of strategies for the index patient and teaches the medical provider how to address patients with similar presenting problems. The goal of the behavioral health provider ultimately is to increase the ability of all medical providers to deliver effective behavioral interventions. This is best accomplished through a consultation and brief comanagement relationship between the behavioral health and primary care provider. Many behavioral health providers have no graduate training in or practical experience with consultation with medically trained providers. A major goal of the core competencies program is to help the behavioral health provider acquire these skills.

When a patient is referred to the behavioral health consultant, there are two primary customers to be served. One is the client, who will be the recipient of a set of brief consultative services. However, the primary customer is the referring medical provider, who is asking for assistance in such important areas as differential diagnosis, the relative merits of a drug, or behavior change intervention. The primary behavioral health provider must focus on responding to the questions raised by the referring provider. When the referring medical provider asks for an opinion about a patient's level of depression, the consultant must provide feedback that answers the referral question. This does not prohibit the behavioral health provider from providing additional information that may be of use in better understanding or treating the referred patient. At the same time, the cardinal rule in consulting is that the referral question needs to be answered. On occasion, novice behavioral health consultants are tempted to pursue clinical issues that may not be the central focus of the medical provider. Although the medical provider is concerned about a patient's depression level and whether a specific treatment is indicated, the novice consultant might identify a history of trauma related to sexual abuse as a child. The consultant might conclude that some type of in-depth psychotherapy is needed to address the trauma and overemphasize this point while placing less emphasis on the patient's current mood functioning. In many such cases, the medical provider will leave the consultative interaction less than satisfied. The medical provider may rightfully feel that the referral question had to do with depression and related treatment recommendations, while the consultant's answer was focused on historical events that might be important in their own right, but did not address the immediate treatment needs of the patient. In core competency training, I always emphasize that the first job of the consultant is to answer the referral question. After that, the behavioral health consultant can provide additional information and perspectives that enrich the medical provider's understanding of the patient.

Commensurate with the highly compressed time frame of a medical exam, the behavioral health provider must generate a limited set of practical, workable strategies that fit the skills and competencies of the referring provider. For example, recommending that the physician discuss "introjected libidinal rage" with the patient is not likely to be helpful, whereas a recommendation to ask the patient to participate in at least three social activities weekly to decrease social isolation can easily be accomplished in a 2-to-3-minute discussion. Creating this level of simplicity, while remaining consistent with the evidence-based care framework, is a major focus of core competency development. Many behavioral health providers use psychological jargon in their professional discussions with colleagues. They assume that mental health professionals speak a common language, but the same assumption cannot be made about primary care providers. The behavioral health provider needs to remember that most medical providers have limited mental health training and do not understand jargon or many of the nuances discussed in mental health staffings. In general, even modestly specialized recommendations will tend to overshoot the sophistication, interest, and skill level of most primary care providers. The primary behavioral health provider must be able to extract the core principles associated with an evidence-based intervention, eliminate jargon, and simplify the operational definition of an intervention. Further, any recommendations must be tailored to fit the skills, abilities, and interests of the referring provider and be understood and supported by other members of the primary care team. One philosophy used in core competency training is that a consultant actually has as many clients as there are primary care providers in a medical clinic. Each provider has a different level of interest in and skill in dealing with behavioral health. The consultant must understand and address each primary care provider within these parameters.

Most consultations in primary care practice occur in what are commonly known as "curbside consultations." These are informal 30-to-60-second interactions during breaks in medical practice, in which the behavioral health and primary provider discuss what to do with a patient that has been evaluated by the consultant. Because of the busy work pace, such communications are brief and to the point, and they convey a substantial amount of "core" information. Often, these curbside encounters trigger important treatment decisions, such as whether the physician will start a patient on a psychoactive medication. On other occasions, the primary behavioral health provider will need to interrupt the physician during a medical visit to address an immediate medical service issue. All of these encounters require brevity, an ability to discern relevant from irrelevant information, and the ability to communicate directly and make clear and concise recommendations. Just as the work pace of primary care emphasizes speed and efficiency, discussions about patient care need to happen quickly and lead to positive results.

Often, integrated behavioral chronic condition protocols will provide additional aids to facilitate the communication process, including such documents as goal-setting forms, intervention checklists, written relapse prevention plans, and patient progress-tracking systems. The goal is to standardize the way information is delivered to and shared among members of the primary care team (see Robinson, Wischman, & Del Vento, 1996, for excellent examples of such communication devices).

The pragmatic value of integrated behavioral health services is in large part determined by the amount of work that is either saved or created by involving the behavioral health provider in the routine process of health care. Behavioral health providers who find ways to reduce medical visits, eliminate unneeded or ineffective treatments, or develop more effective ways to manage patients will quickly be integrated into the medical team. Those who create additional work for referring primary care providers will not be used over time. The goal of effective consultation and comanagement is not only to create new intervention strategies, but also to eliminate interventions that are less likely to be effective. As simple as this principle sounds, it requires the behavioral health consultant to engage the medical provider in discussions about which treatments are likely to work and which can be stopped. For example, many patients started on antidepressants are not likely to benefit from that treatment, but they get medicine as a sort of "default" response. The intervention picture with such patients can be greatly simplified by focusing on practical problem-solving goals and stopping medicines for the time being. Many behavioral health providers, particularly those with master's level training, do not regard themselves as peers with medical providers, particularly physicians. This can result in a reluctance to discuss assessment or treatment issues that might place the consultant in the role of critic. The primary behavioral health provider must develop the mind-set that primary care providers are overwhelmed with work, and they need help selecting small, manageable intervention strategies. One way to achieve this goal is to be relentless about reducing the number of interventions and taking on some of the burden of follow-up care. This allows precious medical resources to be preserved, so they can be made available to more patients in need.

Primary care providers, as "customers" of integrated behavioral health services, have to develop the core competencies that will allow them to capitalize on these services. Most medical providers have adapted their medical practice to a world in which there is no practical access to behavioral health services in general, not to mention a behavioral health provider on the medical team. Consequently, most medical providers develop a set of practice habits that may interfere with the upside potential of integrated behavioral health services. As part of their core competency development, medical providers need to open up their practices to discussions about behavioral health issues, rather than take a "don't ask, don't tell" approach with patients. For many medical providers, taking this step requires an almost complete revamping of their practice philosophy and style.

For example, most primary care providers have stereotypic notions of the behavioral health issues that would be addressed by integrated behavioral health services. Most commonly, this stereotype includes heavy utilization of medical services for depression, anxiety, and substanceabuse. Very few medical providers think of behavioral health in a broad way that places it in a central role in quality health care. When I provide core competency training to medical providers, this is the "net" I want them to cast as they integrate behavioral health considerations in the exam room:

> Behavioral health includes any behavioral factor that might affect a patient's current or future health status, broadly conceived as real or perceived physical health, emotional health, quality of life and health habits, and behaviors that determine health risk.

Along with the traditional referrals (i.e., depression, anxiety, alcohol/drug problems), medical providers are encouraged to refer such problems as sleep hygiene, weight management, smoking cessation, headache management, disease management, job stress, marital conflict, parenting issues, and high-risk sexual behavior, to name a few. In general, primary care providers need to open up their routine medical practices to include the primary behavioral health provider in a much wider array of human problems. Using the broadest definition of behavioral health, one could make the argument that, just as every primary care patient has a health-care plan, every patient should also have a behavioral health-care plan. For primary care providers, appreciating the broad scope of behavioral health factors in general medicine is a key factor in providing effective, population-based behavioral health services.

When a primary care provider refers a patient for behavioral health consultation, it is important to sell the patient on the service and the provider. It is important not to use stigmatizing words and concepts (i.e., mental health, chemical dependency, therapist, counselor, psychologist) when discussing the potential value of seeing the behavioral health provider. Generally, terms associated with traditional mental health will increase the "stigma level" of the transaction and lead to resistance. For example, instead of using the word "therapist," the medical provider should use terms such as "team member" or "practice partner." Instead of implying that the absence of a known medical cause means that stress is responsible for chronic headaches, the medical provider must learn to portray stress as an integrated physiological and psychological process. Developing this biopsychosocial lexicon in medical providers not only requires hallway and lunch-time discussions about mind-body medicine, but also written scripts, case vignettes, and role-playing exercises. I generally place great training emphasis on how to introduce and describe the behavioral health consultation service in a way that keeps the stigma level low and the patient acceptance rate high.

When the behavioral health consultant sees a referred patient, the existing health-care plan for that patient should be modified to incorporate the recommendations made to the referring medical provider. This allows every member of the medical team to understand, support, and monitor the behavioral health plan. An important core competency for medical providers is to "close the loop" on the consultation-feedback process by integrating the results into the medical treatment plan. In a team-based management model, failing to do this can have dramatic negative consequences. A nurse might be unaware of a plan developed by the behavioral health provider and physician because it is not in the patient's medical chart. The nurse inadvertently recommends that the patient engage in a type of self-management strategy that has been tried without success, so that the patient now perceives that different recommendations are coming from different members of the same team. Therefore, the patient may leave with the perception that members of the medical team disagree about what the patient should do or that team members are not sharing information and coordinating care. Both of these perceptions can be detrimental to the patient's confidence and participation in the behavioral management plan.

Team Performance Skills

Team performance skills allow the behavioral health clinician to integrate with and function effectively as a primary care team member and to build a high-volume primary care practice. On the flip side, primary care providers need to understand and integrate the special, complementary skills that the behavioral health clinician brings to the medical team. In most cases, behavioral health providers are nonmedically trained professionals (psychologists, social workers, counselors) entering a practice environment dominated by medically trained providers (physicians, physician assistants, nurse practitioners, registered nurses). In many venues, the general stress of contemporary primary care, the multitude of new initiatives that seem to emerge weekly, and the unrelenting work pace make it difficult to maintain a focus on blending in the new member of the team. In most cases, it will be incumbent upon the behavioral health provider to blend into the primary care culture and build a vibrant practice.

Behavioral health providers must understand that the primary care medical setting is an altogether different gestalt from traditional mental health settings. There is a different formal and informal power structure; there are different medical disciplines represented on the team, and there are different cultural norms. Most behavioral health providers have little if any experience with the inner workings of a primary care team. One of the first tasks is to determine how the process of team-based care is organized and who makes what types of decisions. Although physicians are almost universally acknowledged as the formal leaders of a medical team, a nurse may be the de facto decision maker, and the support staff may in actuality manage and control the daily work processes. It is also important to understand how the rules of a primary care team differ from a typical mental health team. A good example is the issue of privacy during visits. It is common in primary care practice to be interrupted during an exam. A behavioral health provider who insists on not being interrupted while in session is working contrary to the culture of the primary care team. In general, behavioral health providers need to be flexible and open minded in their interactions with medical team colleagues. During core competency training, I emphasize the importance of taking additional steps to develop good relationships with both medical providers and support staff. These are the individuals who can solve problems in real time, find the chart that has disappeared, or locate an unused space in the exam room area when an emergency arises. To work effectively in a primary care team requires a certain comfort level with the fast work pace, continuous multitasking, frequent interruptions, and the ability to adjust to rapid changes in the daily schedule.

The next major goal in team-related performance is to develop a variety of strategies for "injecting" the behavioral health provider into the daily practice routines of medical providers. To build a referral-based practice, it is necessary to build "top-of-mind awareness" among all members of the medical team. The eventual goal is to have medical providers conditioned to look for and assess behavioral factors in their routine medical exams. I typically encourage behavioral health providers to develop a "laundry list" of marketing strategies to create this top-of-mind awareness.

- Develop and distribute a monthly behavioral health newsletter highlighting the impact of behavioral health factors in certain populations (diabetes, pain, headache).
- Develop a consultation service flyer that informs medical providers of how the service can be accessed and what types of patients to refer.
- Shadow medical providers in practice to better understand their practice style and, when solicited, provide feedback about interview style, assessment strategies, and intervention options.
- Identify high-utilizing medical patients and develop behavioral health management plans in consort with the medical providers.
- Schedule brief monthly meetings with each medical provider to review the status of jointly managed patients.
- Secure "privileged time" in each provider staff meeting to review progress of the consultation program and highlight recent referrals that demonstrate a new type of problem to refer.
- Review schedules of medical providers each morning and use highlighter to indicate patients that may be presenting because of behavioral health factors (e.g., headache, limb and joint pain, gastrointestinal distress, insomnia).
- Build practice protocols that incorporate the behavioral health consultant in routine processes of care (e.g., screening for medical adherence risk and depression in all newly diagnosed diabetics).
- Adapt screening tools for common behavioral health conditions that are applied at each medical exam or on a regular schedule.
- Develop exam room posters that screen for behavioral health issues that should be mentioned to the medical provider.

When an emergency situation arises in the context of daily practice, the behavioral health provider needs to be part of the solution. If it is a psychiatric emergency, the behavioral health provider will see the patient at lunch or after scheduled work hours, if no other times are available. It is contrary to team culture to refuse to provide an unplanned or unscheduled service, even if it means disrupting an existing practice schedule. This type of team-oriented response, even though it may be an inconvenience, will increase the likelihood that the behavioral health provider will be viewed as a member of the medical team.

In many settings, the behavioral health provider will not be in the primary care practice setting every day of the week. This may include situations where the provider is splitting time between a specialty mental health clinic and the primary care clinic. It is important to ensure that all primary care team members have immediate access to behavioral health support. Normally, a good strategy is to carry a pager, a cellular phone, or a two-way radio. The process for making emergency contact should be explained in both verbal and written form to all medical team members. The philosophy is to encourage medical providers to call whenever the situation demands it. When a call for help comes, the behavioral health consultant should immediately respond with at least a brief 2-to-3-minute assessment on the phone to see whether the clinical situation can be addressed immediately or whether a longer, follow-up call is needed. In practice, requests for emergency consultation are rare, but a swift and effective response will be remembered for months.

Documentation and Feedback Skills

Documentation and feedback skills are required for the primary behavioral health provider to write brief, to-the-point, evaluation summaries and progress notes in the medical chart and to protect sensitive patient information from unneeded circulation. Although the majority of consultative discussions with medical providers occur in the hallways, effective note-writing may be the only communication vehicle to other members of the primary care team who are more distant in the care-giving process.

The accelerated pace of primary care practice demands that consultation reports and other notes in the medical chart quickly convey key assessment and intervention information. This is similar to the process of curbside consultations, in which assessment information is pared to only the essential data needed to formulate a plan of attack. For example, the typical two-to-four-page intake report generated by a behavioral health specialist would not be useful to most medical providers. They have neither the time nor the interest to sort through a large body of information. In the typical case, chart notes should be no longer than one page, and often may be shorter. These notes generally should incorporate the following components:

A description of which provider referred the patient and what the referral question is.
A very brief summary of core symptom complaints and other stresses.
A very brief summary of the patient's general functioning.
A summary diagnostic impression or problem statement.
A limited number of recommendations designed for all members of the team.
A description of the follow-up plan, if any, and what medical team members are to do during
   subsequent patient contacts.

It is not unusual to address any one of these content areas in one or two sentences. The majority of the note should focus on core symptoms, precipitating stresses, functional status, and the behavioral interventions that are being recommended. All this should be written in concrete language that does not contain jargon. In the majority of cases, writing the note will be preceded by either a face-to-face consultation with the provider or a voice-mail message if the provider is not available. Therefore, it is important that the note is consistent with the consultative feedback already given.

On occasion, a patient may disclose personal and sensitive information to the behavioral health provider that may not be appropriate for placement in the general medical chart. In general, medical charts are less-secure documents than the mental health or chemical dependency treatment records maintained in specialty settings. The behavioral health provider must weigh the risks and benefits of placing such information in permanent written form. In most cases, it is preferable to communicate such information verbally to the referring medical provider and to write more circumspect notes that present the core factors that led to recommended treatment strategies.

Dissemination of the Primary Behavioral Health Care Model: A Train the Trainers Approach

One of the major challenges facing larger primary care systems is how to disseminate the primary behavioral health model across multiple sites, with differing local cultures and several different medical teams. My experience as a trainer has taught me that it is important to maintain a core consistency in the model of care, while allowing specific sites to respond to local population requirements. Once the primary behavioral health model is spelled out in sufficient clinical and administrative detail, it becomes immediately obvious that both behavioral health and primary care providers need to receive skill-based training and support over time. The safe assumption is that very few, if any, medical or behavioral health providers will be as effective as they need to be without some form of standardized training. The goal of training is to help shape provider skills and behavior to be consistent with the model of care. It is one thing to put behavioral health and primary care providers in practice together. It is quite another to get them to practice together.

Faced with a similar challenge to ensure a consistent consumer experience with the delivery of new products across multiple sites, national and multinational businesses have developed and refined the "train-the-trainer" dissemination model. Essentially, the train-the-trainer model is a positive example of the pyramid scheme. It involves creating a group of expert trainers and distributing them strategically so they can train other lead employees, who in turn can train their subordinates. In this model, dissemination of new products and service processes can happen within months, often involving thousands of workers. The same principles have been used to implement systemic changes in large, multisite health-care systems. By identifying and training a group of local champions, health-care systems have successfully implemented medical practice guidelines and desktop medicine initiatives, as well as visit process redesigns (Stuart et al., 1991). Similarly, this basic technology transfer model has been used to implement the Primary Behavioral Health Care Model in large primary care systems (see Dobmeyer et al., 2003, for one such example).

For this dissemination model to work, both the clinical and administrative components of the integrated program must be clearly defined. Normally the first step is to develop a detailed program manual that documents both the clinical and operational characteristics of the primary behavioral health program. Development of the services manual often reveals flaws in the model of care design, legal or risk management issues, and gaps in administrative infrastructure. In the case of integrated behavioral care programs, the process of program definition might involve conducting pilot tests of patient education pamphlets with consumer focus groups and determining if assessment tools and standard treatment forms are "primary care provider–friendly." If these issues are not addressed in the initial design process, then they will surface in unpredictable ways once the program has gone "live." Typically, problems that arise once a program is up and running do not lend themselves as readily to rapid resolution, so the goal is to use appropriate planning to avoid these problems. Further, the services manual is used as a living, breathing document designed to help medical and behavioral health providers to quickly access important clinical and administrative information (e.g., practice guidelines for chronic pain patients, billing codes, staffing ratios).

Once the integrated care program has been thoroughly articulated, it is possible to define the core competencies required for providers to implement the new model of care. As was previously noted, the core features of the model of integrated care will help highlight the core competencies required of medical and behavioral health providers. This, in turn, allows administrators to take the appropriate steps to supply needed training through a variety of methods.

Central Role of the Mentor–Trainer

The key player in this dissemination model is the mentor, or champion, who is responsible for shaping, monitoring, and maintaining the core competencies required for behavioral health and medical providers. Thus far, this chapter has focused exclusively on the skills and abilities that primary care and behavioral health providers must acquire in order to implement a primary behavioral health program. When dissemination across a system of primary care sites is the goal, the focus of training turns to ensuring that trainers demonstrate the following abilities:

- Significant clinical proficiency in the core competencies required in the primary behavioral health-care model.
- The ability to help trainees understand the model and learn core competencies using both didactic and hands-on methods.
- Positive interpersonal attributes that allow the trainer to form a mentoring relationship with the trainee over time.

A mentoring relationship is not simply established by designation. The mentor must earn the trust of the trainee, deliver both negative and positive feedback in a way that generates behavior change, and act as a "cheerleader" to enhance the trainee's motivation to excel. On a trainee-by-trainee basis, the mentor is responsible for identifying the best methods for disseminating skills over the short, intermediate, and long term. Effective mentors are willing to create clear performance expectations, model the behaviors desired, and create a sense of "can do" confidence in the trainee. During clinical proctoring and supervision, an effective mentor individualizes feedback and looks for "trainable moments." These are times when the trainee is open to receiving new knowledge or is looking to acquire or modify practice skills in a positive direction. Most providers come into primary care practice with a set of strengths and weaknesses. It is important in mentoring to help the trainee become aware of existing strengths and modify them to fit the demands of primary care practice. It is also important to examine how weaknesses are going to be corrected through a targeted learning process. Successful mentoring is a long-term undertaking, and trainees must accept that they will have periodic contact with the mentor over months, if not years.

Cotraining Medical and Behavioral Health Providers

In this chapter, I have discussed the many ways that primary care and behavioral health providers will have to alter practice habits to make integrated care a success. Although the modifications may be different, the one binding similarity is that this constitutes a major paradigm shift for both disciplines. Often, team camaraderie is built by going through a difficult change together and, for this reason, it is important to avoid segregating behavioral health and primary care providers in the process of training. Just as it is bad practice to design an integrated-care system without the participation of all provider groups, it is equally misguided to focus training on one provider group alone. Generally, the best results occur when primary care and behavioral health providers go through the experience of service integration together. This might involve such exercises as having medical and behavioral health staff members craft a patient brochure that explains the integrated care philosophy of the medical team. Another activity might be to develop and role-play referral "scripts" so that medical providers become more efficient at handing the patient off to the behavioral health consultant. Many of the teaching methods in the core competencies approach are ideally suited for this type of conjoint training. For example, case vignettes can be more interesting when both primary care providers and behavioral health specialists are responding to the same stimulus piece. Best practice videotapes might include interactions between medical providers and patients demonstrating the best ways to frame a behavioral health issue in a nonstigmatizing way.

In the real world of primary care practice, time is a scarce commodity, and time-intensive training experiences are hard to arrange. The focus of any in vivo training program should be to take advantage of existing work processes as opportunities to deliver competency training. This means that exercises such as script development, guided case discussion, and best-practices training need to occur in the context of weekly staff meetings or medical team meetings. On the other hand, the overwhelming temptation in the busy world of medicine is to short change the training process resulting in an inadequate grasp of the primary behavioral health philosophy within the medical team. In any integrated care initiative, senior leaders need to remind themselves, as well as their managers, team leaders, and staff, that adding behavioral health services is an investment; it is not simply a luxury. Part of this investment is to carve out the time necessary to optimize the chances for success.

Graduate Training and the Future of Integrated Care

Obviously, the root cause of the need for field-based retraining is the failure of graduate programs in behavioral health and general medicine to properly prepare their students for what awaits them in the real world. Academic training programs are bastions of both regressive and progressive forces. Although many of the most innovative medical and psychosocial treatments have been discovered in these contexts, the same programs routinely produce professionals that are ill equipped for the contemporary health-care environment. We still have graduate training programs in clinical psychology that are preparing students to work in the office-based, fee-for-service, private-practice model in a world that is largely dominated by managed care! Many training programs fail to properly train their students in how to negotiate managed-care contracts or to use procedure codes that are required for insurance reimbursement. With a few notable exceptions, most medical training programs do not adequately prepare residents to address behavioral health factors in general health care. Most mental health training programs appear to be oblivious to the primary care system in toto!

There are many ways graduate training programs can prepare behavioral health professionals for the primary care environment. Coursework should include basic anatomy and pathology, detection and treatment of acute and chronic disease, and the behavioral manifestations of medical illness. Graduates should be exposed to functional psychopharmacology, behavioral medicine, and health psychology. Some rudimentary exposure to public health and epidemiology would better help behavioral health providers understand the central precepts of population-based care. Clinically, students need to learn functional assessment skills, brief intervention strategies, and how to provide consultation to other professionals. Requiring internship and postdoctoral experience in primary behavioral health care should be a core element of all behavioral health training programs.

Within general medical and residency training programs, there are two basic deficits in the behavioral health training medical students receive. First, the behavioral health training rotations are too short, often involving 3 months or less of in vivo training. If integrated primary care is to succeed, medical schools must stop the abysmal practice of undervaluing the behavioral health component of general medicine. It is ironic that many of the same physicians who teach evidence-based care so brilliantly when it comes to the medical assessment and treatment of disease, then proceed to systematically ignore the evidence base on the necessity of treating the behavioral sequalae of those same diseases. Medical schools must allocate more didactic coursework and residency training time to the assessment and treatment of behavioral factors in general health care. Instead of implicitly or explicitly communicating that the behavioral health rotation is the least important part of medical training, the message should be that medical care and behavioral care are integral parts of general health care. One cannot be an effective health-care provider without being competent in both realms.

A second shortcoming is that the behavioral health scientist model that has been adopted in most family practice residencies is basically ineffective. The behavioral health providers functioning in these roles are not teaching the behavioral health skills required for success in the field. Few behavioral health specialists have prior experience working in the primary care milieu and tend to teach and role-model traditional mental health strategies that simply do not fit the real world of primary care. Medical and nursing students are then graduated into the professional sector, only to discover that their mental health "tool kit" is woefully inadequate. Rather than teaching arcane interviewing strategies designed to build rapport with the patient, behavioral health specialists should teach the skills required to assess and intervene with behavioral problems in 2 to 3 minutes. Didactically, medical students need less exposure to the medical model of mental illness and much more education in behavioral medicine, health psychology, brief strategic therapy concepts, cognitive behavioral therapy, evidence-based interventions, and full-spectrum psychopharmacology. In general, medical providers need to develop an individually tailored, flexible tool kit for understanding the role of behavior factors in all aspects of general medicine.

Until the training institutions take responsibility for developing professionals who can understand and work in integrated service models, we will be forced to retrain these professionals in the field. There are some encouraging developments in this regard. Brantley and Jefferies (2000) describe a combined clinical psychology internship and family practice training program housed at Louisiana State University. This program is designed to prepare psychologists and physicians for integrated primary care. The program involves a fully integrated curriculum that provides extensive cross training in common areas of care, in addition to exposing students to more advanced aspects of each discipline's professional tool kit.

The U.S. Air Force psychology residency program now requires all predoctoral psychology interns to undergo at least one 3-month rotation in primary care (Dobmeyer et al., 2003). Interns are systematically trained using the core competencies training approach described in this chapter. Achievement of a minimum standard of proficiency in the core competencies is a basic expectation of the training rotation. These trained professionals are subsequently deployed to Air Force primary care sites around the globe, supported over time by their residency-based mentor–trainers.

A highly innovative clinical psychology training program at the University of Nevada, Reno, offers graduate students the option of enrolling in a training track in organized systems of care. The courses offered in this track teach psychology students the basic principles of health economics, epidemiology, population medicine, and performance benchmarking/program evaluation. Field-based training experiences allow students to deliver clinical and research services in primary care and hospital-based settings. The goal of the training curricula is to prepare psychologists to operate effectively in the integrated health-care environment of the future.

Role Differentiation Among Behavioral Health Disciplines

A final issue that needs to be addressed in the era of integrated care is how to differentiate the roles of various mental health disciplines. An all-too-common notion within general medicine is that all behavioral health providers are essentially interchangeable, regardless of their training background or degree. Which behavioral health discipline (if any) is best suited to work in the primary care setting? With the growing popularity of integration, this issue is likely to be more on the front burner than the back burner, and most medical administrators will candidly admit that they have limited experience with these types of personnel questions. In general, administrators obtain fragments of information from the behavioral health industry where, for cost containment reasons, managed care companies have created the impression that all nonmedically trained behavioral health providers are essentially interchangeable. The perception that "one size fits all" is also reinforced by turf and guild issues within the behavioral health industry that have more to do with market positioning than a rational analysis of the issues.

One might approach this question in the following way. If no link exists between the type and intensity of training and the resulting skills of the provider, why do separate schools of social work, psychology, psychiatric nursing, and psychiatry exist in nearly every university or college that is large enough to support such training programs? If there is no difference between a social worker and a doctoral-level psychologist, then why bother train psychologists? This ongoing debate is quite mystifying to primary care providers, who work in a team model and readily accept role differentiation as a basic requirement for effective teamwork. It would be a rare event indeed for an advanced-practice nurse to claim to have the same professional skills as a general physician. Yet, this type of reasoning is used every day to equalize a social worker and a doctor of psychology. Ultimately, it is the responsibility of both behavioral health professionals and medical administrators, not only to reject this homogenization, but also to work diligently to identify the unique contributions of each discipline in the primary care milieu. This will allow behavioral health providers to comfortably work within their scope of practice while allowing the primary care team to benefit from the diverse skill sets represented in all the behavioral health professions.

Summary

In this chapter an attempt has been made to articulate the training issues associated with the integration of primary care and behavioral health services. As should be obvious, the integration of primary care and behavioral health services is better conceptualized as a system redesign. It is not merely adding a new service to the primary care milieu; it more accurately reflects a rethinking of the goals and process of general health care. This means primary care and behavioral health providers have a very basic role to play in determining the structure and function of the integrated systems of the future. In the world of everyday health care, it will be impossible to escape the practical implications of rejoining the mind and the body. Although behavioral health providers are often the initial targets of core competency development, there are equally fundamental changes in the skill sets required of health-care providers. Perhaps the most important implication is that good intentions alone will not make integrated primary care successful. It is only by taking a systematic approach to identifying the skills required for success and developing cost-effective training strategies that the potential benefits of integrated care can be realized.

References

Beutler, L., Machado, P., & Allstetter-Neufeldt, S. (1994). Therapist variables. In A. Bergin & S. Garfield (Eds.), *Handbook of psychotherapy and behavior change* (pp. 229–269). New York: Wiley.

Brantley, P., & Jefferies, S. (2000). Daily Stress Inventory (DSI) and Weekly Stress Inventory (WSI). In M. Maruish (Ed.), *Handbook of psychological assessment in primary care settings* (pp. 373–390). Mahweh, NJ: Erlbaum.

Brown, G. (1981). Life events, psychiatric disorder and physical illness. *Psychosomatic Research, 25*, 461–473.

Budman, S., & Gurman, A. (1988). *Theory and practice of brief therapy.* New York: Guilford.

Coffey, R., Mark, T., King, E., Harwood, H., McKusick, D., Genuardi, J. et al. (2000). *National estimates of expenditures for mental health and substance abuse treatment, 1997.* SAMHSHA Publication No. SMA-00-3499. Rockville, MD: Substance Abuse and Mental Health Services Administration.

DeShazer, S., Berg, I., Lipchik, E., Nanally, E., Molnar, A., Gingerich, W. et al. (1986). Brief therapy: Solution focused development. *Family Process,* 207–221.

Dobmeyer, A., Rowan, A., Etherage, J., & Wilson, R. (2003). Training psychology interns in primary behavioral health care. *Professional Psychology: Research and Practice, 34*, 586–594.

Doherty, W., McDaniel, S., & Baird, M. (1996). Five levels of primary care/behavioral health collaboration. *Behavioral Healthcare Tomorrow, 5*, 25–27.

Eddy, D. M. (1996). *Clinical decision making from theory to practice: A collection of essays from the journal of the American Medical Association.* Sudbury, MA: Jones and Bartlett.

Garfield, S. (1994). Research on client variables in psychotherapy. In A. Bergin & S. Garfield (Eds.), *Handbook of psychotherapy and behavior change* (pp. 190–228). New York: Wiley.

Gatchell, R., & Oordt, M. (2003). *Primary care psychology: A practical guide for clinical health psychologists in primary care.* Washington, DC: American Psychological Association.

Geyman, J. (1998). Evidence based medicine in primary care: An overview. *Journal of the American Board of Family Practice, 11*, 46–56.

Goldberg, D. (1990). Reasons for misdiagnosis. In N. Sartorius, D. Goldberg, G. Girolamo, J. Costa e Silva, Y. Lecrubier, & U. Wittchen (Eds.), *Psychological disorders in general medical settings* (pp. 139–145). Toronto: Hogrefe and Huber.

Hayes, S., & Strosahl, K. (Eds.). (2004). A clincian's guide to acceptance and commitment therapy. New York: Springer.

Hayes, S., Strosahl, K., & Wilson, K. (1999). *Acceptance and commitment therapy: An experiential approach to behavior change.* New York: Guilford.

Hayes, S., Wilson, K., Gifford, E., Follette, V., & Strosahl, K. (1996). Emotional avoidance and behavioral disorders: A functional dimensional approach to diagnosis and treatment. *Journal of Consulting and Clinical Psychology, 64,* 1152–1168.

Howard, K., Kopta, S., Krause, M., & Orlinsky, D. (1986). The dose-effect relationship in psychotherapy. *American Psychologist, 41,* 159–164.

Hoyt, M. (1991). Teaching and learning short-term psychotherapy. In C. Austad & W. Berman (Eds.), *Psychotherapy in managed health care: The optimal use of time and resources* (pp. 98-107). Washington, DC: American Psychological Association.

Katon, W., Robinson, P., Von Korff, M., Lin, E., Bush, T., Ludman, E. et al. (1996). A multifaceted intervention to improve treatment of depression in primary care. *Archives of General Psychiatry, 53,* 924–932.

Kent, J., & Gordon, M. (1997). Integration: A case for putting humpty-dumpty together again. In. N. Cummings, J. Cummings, & J. Johnson (Eds.), *Behavioral health in primary care: A guide for clinical integration.* Madison, CT: Psychosocial Press.

Kroenke, K., & Mangelsdorff, A. (1989). Common symptoms in ambulatory care: Incidence, evaluation, therapy and outcome. *American Journal of Medicine, 86,* 262–266.

Lin, E., VonKorff, M., Katon, W., Bush, T., Simon, G., Walker, E. et al. (1995). The role of the primary care physician in patient's adherence to anti-depressant therapy. *Medical Care, 33,* 67–74.

McDaniel, S., Campbell, T., & Seaburn, D. (1990). *Family-oriented primary care: A manual for medical providers.* New York: Springer-Verlag.

Mynors-Wallis, L. (1996). Problem solving treatment: Evidence for effectiveness and feasibility in primary care. *International Journal of Psychiatric Medicine, 26,* 249–262.

Mynors-Wallis, L., Gath, D., Day, A., & Baker, F. (2000). Randomized controlled trial of problem solving treatment, antidepressant medication, and combined treatment for major depression in primary care. *British Medical Journal, 320,* 26–30.

Mynors-Wallis, L., Gath, D., Lloyd-Thomas, A., & Tomlinson, D. (1995). Randomized controlled trial comparing problem solving treatment with amitryptyline and placebo for major depression in primary care. *British Medical Journal, 310,* 441–445.

Narrow, W., Reiger, D., Rae, D., Manderscheid, R., & Locke, B. (1993). Use of services by persons with mental and addictive disorders: Findings from the National Institute of Mental Health Epidemiologic Catchment Area Program. *Archives of General Psychiatry, 50,* 95–107.

Nathan, P., & Gorman, J. (Eds.). (2002). *Treatments that work* (2nd ed.). Washington, DC: American Psychological Association.

Pruitt, S., Kaplow, J., Epping-Jordan, J., & Dresselhaus, T. (1998). Moving behavioral medicine to the front line: A model for the integration of behavioral and medical services in primary care. *Professional Psychology: Research and Practice, 29,* 230–236.

Reiger, D., Narrow, W., Rae, D., Manderschied, R., Locke, B., & Goodwin, F. (1993). The de facto U.S. mental and addictive disorders service system: Epidemiologic Catchment Area prospective 1 year prevalence rates of disorders and services. *Archives of General Psychiatry, 50,* 85–94.

Richardson, W. (chair) (2001). *Institute of Medicine report: Crossing the quality chasm: A new health system for the 21st century.* Washington, DC: Institute of Medicine.

Robinson, P. (1998). Behavioral health services in primary care: A new perspective for treating depression. *Clinical Psychology: Science and Practice, 5*(1), 77–93.

Robinson, P., Bush, T., VonKorff, M., Katon, W., Lin, E., Simon, G. et al. (1995). Primary care physician use of cognitive behavioral techniques with depressed patients. *Journal of Family Practice, 40,* 352–357.

Robinson, P., Del Vento, A., & Wischman, C. (1998). Integrated care for the frail elderly: The group care clinic. In A. Blount (Ed.), *Integrated primary care: The future of medical and mental health collaboration* (pp. 123–141). New York: Norton.

Robinson, P., & Strosahl, K. (2000). Improving outcomes for a primary care population: Depression as an example. In M. Maruis (Ed.), *Handbook of psychological assessment in primary care settings* (pp. 687–711). New York: Erlbaum.

Robinson, P., Wischman, C., & Del Vento, A. (1996). *Treating depression in primary care: A manual for primary care and mental health providers.* Reno, NV: Context Press.

Skodol, A., Dohrenwend, B., Link, B., & Shrout, P. (1990). The nature of stress: Problems of measurement. In J. Noshpitz & R. Coddington (Eds.), *Stressors and the adjustment disorders* (pp. 3–20). New York: Wiley.

Sobel, D. (1995). Rethinking medicine: Improving health outcomes with cost-effective psychosocial interventions. *Psychosomatic Medicine, 57,* 234–244.

Strosahl, K. (1994). Entering the new frontier of managed mental health care: Gold mines and land mines. *Cognitive and Behavioral Practice, 1,* 5–23.

Strosahl, K. (1995). Behavior therapy 2000: A perilous journey. *Behavior Therapist, 18,* 130–133.

Strosahl, K. (1996). Confessions of a behavior therapist in primary care: The odyssey and the ecstasy. *Cognitive and Behavioral Practice, 3,* 1–28.

Strosahl, K. (1997). Building primary care behavioral health systems that work: A compass and a horizon. In N. Cummings, J., Cummings, & J. Johnson (Eds.), *Behavioral health in primary care: A guide for clinical integration* (pp. 37–68). Madison, CT: Psychosocial Press.

Strosahl, K. (1998). Integration of primary care and behavioral health services: The primary mental health care model. In A. Blount (Ed.), *Integrative primary care: The future of medical and mental health collaboration* (pp. 43–66). New York: Norton.

Strosahl, K. (2001). The integration of primary care and behavioral health: Type II change in the era of managed care. In N. Cummings, W. O'Donohoe, S. Hayes, & V. Follette (Eds.), *Integrated behavioral healthcare: Positioning mental health practice with medical/surgical practice* (pp. 45–70). New York: Academic Press.

Strosahl, K., & Quirk, M. (1994, July). The trouble with carve-outs. *Business and Health*, 52.

Stuart, M., Handley, M., Chamberlain, M., Wallach, R., Penna, A., & Stergachis, A. (1991). Successful implementation of a guideline program for the rational use of lipid lowering drugs. *HMO Practice, 5*, 198–204.

Taplin, S., Galvin, M., Payne, T., Coole, D., & Wagner, E. (1998). Putting population-based care into practice: Real option or rhetoric. *Journal of the American Board of Family Practice, 11*(2), 116–126.

VonKorff, M., & Simon, G. (1996). The prevalence and impact of psychological disorders in primary care: HMO research needed to improve care. *HMO Practice, 10*, 150–155.

Wells, K., Steward, A., Hays, R., Burnam, M., Rogers, W., Daniels, M., et al. (1989). The functioning and well being of depressed patients: Results from the Medical Outcomes Study. *Journal of the American Medical Association, 262*, 914–919.

Zubin, J., & Spring, B. (1977). Vulnerability: A new view of schizophrenia. *Abnormal Psychology, 86*, 103–126.

Chapter 2
Adapting Empirically Supported Treatments to the Primary Care Setting: A Template for Success

PATRICIA ROBINSON

Primary care physicians and other primary care providers, including physician assistants, nurses, and clinical pharmacists, provide a great deal of care to patients suffering with mental disorders (Shapiro, Skinner, & Kessler, 1984). On average, primary care physicians spend 12.1 hours per week (23.1% of a 52.8-hour workweek) providing direct treatment for psychiatric conditions (Howard, 1992). More than half of the mental health services in America are delivered in the primary care setting (Knesper & Pagnucco, 1987; Magil & Garrrett, 1988), and at least half the depressed people who receive mental health care do so through their primary care provider (Narrow, Reiger, Rae, Manderscheid, & Locke, 1993). Regier et al. (1978, 1993) described the situation well when they referred to the primary care system as the "de facto mental health system" in America. Collectively, the number of patients seeking care for behavioral health problems in the primary care setting is dramatically larger than the number seeking care in mental health settings (Strosahl, 1996a), and this number is likely to increase as we move further into the new century. Current managed health-care trends favor gatekeeper models that direct patients toward primary care providers who can then assess the appropriateness of various specialty referral options (Hoy, Curtis, & Rice, 1991). Perhaps more importantly, the initial outcome studies of primary care–based behavioral health interventions suggest that patients report higher levels of satisfaction when their treatment is delivered in primary care (Katon et al., 1995, 1996). Further, cost effectiveness analyses have indicated that the expenditure of behavioral health resources results in greater value (i.e., degree of clinical improvement relative to the cost of delivering treatment) in the primary care as compared with the mental health setting (Von Korff et al., 1998).

Patients are comfortable in the primary care setting for several reasons. Many patients have ongoing relationships with primary care providers. These relationships often precede the development of significant psychosocial stresses and behavioral disorders. Patients see providers as capable of providing a big-picture perspective during difficult periods of development. Further, primary care providers often provide services to multiple members of a family and may function as important advisors on family matters. Some patients, particularly older adults, prefer the primary care setting because they feel less stigmatized in seeking care from a physician as opposed to a mental health provider (Robinson, Wischman, & Del Vento, 1996).

Although epidemiological and health services research suggests that there are many patients in need of psychological interventions in primary care, little has been written to guide behavioral scientist practitioners in the development and dissemination of primary care–based protocols that incorporate efficacious interventions. Unlike the traditional mental health treatment setting, the primary care setting employs a population care model. Consequently, treatments in primary care are brief, focused, and rely on patient education and self-management strategies. In a typical year, 80% of all persons in a primary care catchment will have at least one ambulatory outpatient medical visit. In contrast, behavioral health services are accessed by only 3–7% of a catchment in any given year. This results in radical differences in the service delivery culture. Primary care providers may often see 30 or more patients a day in 10-to-15-minute appointments. The typical behavioral health provider sees six to eight patients a day in 50-minute appointments.

There is a host of primary care service delivery structures that supports a high-volume public health model. These include the use of wellness and prevention visits, algorithmically based stepped care, team-based patient management, patient education, and an emphasis on home-based self-management. Most of these strategies are foreign to traditionally trained mental health providers. If behavioral scientists and practitioners are to bring the most efficacious psychological interventions to primary care patients, they must tailor protocols so that they are supportive of primary care provider skill strengths, the expectations of primary care patients, and the basic philosophy of primary care.

In 1995 a task force of the American Psychological Association (APA) Clinic Division issued three reports on dissemination of psychological procedures. These reports identified a number of psychological interventions as empirically supported treatments (ESTs). The efforts of the APA occurred in response to a broader movement known as evidence-based medicine (Sackett, Richardson, Rosenberg, & Haynes, 1997), which began in the United Kingdom. Psychologists in the United Kingdom have been leaders in identifying ESTs, and they promoted the work leading to publication of *What Works for Whom?* (Roth & Fonagy, 1996). The Clinical Psychology Division of APA approved creation of a standing committee charged with ongoing evaluation of efficacy and effectiveness of psychological interventions in 1999. Their most recent report is of great value to behavioral health providers who plan to implement efficacious psychological interventions in the primary care setting (see Chambless & Ollendick, 2001).

The Chambless and Ollendick (2001) report specifies levels of empirical support for specific conditions. For adults, well-established treatments for various anxiety disorders include cognitive-behavioral therapy (CBT), exposure, applied relaxation, exposure response prevention (for obsessive-compulsive disorder (OCD)), and stress inoculation. Community reinforcement, motivational interviewing, behavioral marital therapy plus dissulfinam, and social skills training with inpatient treatment are well-established treatments for alcohol abuse and dependence. For depressed adults, behavior therapy, brief psychodynamic therapy, CBT, psychoeducation, reminiscence therapy (for mild-to-moderate levels), behavioral marital therapy (for those with marital discord), and interpersonal therapy are well-established methods. Behavioral family therapy, social-learning programs, and social-skills training are highly efficacious interventions for schizophrenia that can be adapted for implementation in the primary care setting.

There are numerous efficacious psychological interventions for health-related problems. For example, behavior therapy and cognitive therapy have well-established efficacy for anorexia, and CBT is a well-established intervention for binge eating disorder and bulimia. For chronic pain, CBT is highly efficacious, and, for headache, behavior therapy meets the criteria for the well-established level of evidence. Multicomponent CBT is highly efficacious for rheumatic disease pain and smoking cessation. Behavioral interventions applied at the environmental level for behavioral problems are efficacious treatments for dementia.

Chambless and Ollendick (2001) report a variety of efficacious treatments for relationship-related problems for which patients frequently seek primary care. For example, behavioral marital therapy has strong efficacy support for patients with marital discord. CBT and behavior therapy are effective for several types of sexual dysfunction. Social-skills training is well established as a treatment for avoidant personality disorder. For geriatric caregiver distress, psychosocial interventions are highly efficacious.

The most effective empirically supported psychological treatments for children have great importance in primary care because of the prevention potential inherent in the primary care setting. These include behavioral parent training for attention deficit hyperactivity disorder and CBT for distress due to medical procedures. For conduct disorder, cognitive behavioral therapy, cognitive problem-solving skills, functional family therapy, multisystemic therapy, videotape-modeling parent training, and parent training based on living with children (for both children and adolescents) are interventions meeting standards for being well-established treatments. Behavior modification is highly efficacious for encopresis and enuresis. For phobias in children, participant modeling, rapid exposure (school phobia), and reinforced practice are highly effective. Contingency management is effective for undesirable behavior associated with pervasive developmental disorder. For the high-impact condition of psychophysiological disorder, family therapy is an efficacious treatment. Finally, relaxation with self-hypnosis is a highly efficacious treatment for recurrent headaches, which is common among young primary care patients.

Although the APA task force reports are helpful to clinical providers and generally well received, some writers (e.g., Elliot, 1998) have criticized them for their focus on the efficacy of treatment in randomized clinical trials (RCTs) and their relative lack of emphasis on effectiveness (i.e., whether the ESTs work in real clinical practice). There are numerous effectiveness trials in progress that will help clinical providers further select the most viable treatments, and some of these effectiveness trials are being conducted in primary care settings. Related to the efficacy and effectiveness debate is the controversy about clinician adherence to manualized protocols versus development of individualized treatment protocols. Available studies do not provide strong support for one approach being better than the other (see Emmelkamp, Bouman, & Blaauw, 1994; Jacobson, Schmaling, Holtzworth-Munroe, Katt, & Wood, 1989; Schulte, Kunzel, Pepping, & Schulte-Bahrenberg, 1992), and in primary care adaptations, clinicians need to be prepared to work from manuals and to provide individually tailored interventions.

This chapter introduces readers to key concepts that underpin the adaptation of ESTs to the primary care context. These include understanding the unique characteristics of the primary care system, the principles of population-based care, and the use of evidence-based medicine in the primary care setting. The Primary Behavioral Health Model (Robinson et al., 1996; Strosahl, 1996a, 1996b, 1997, 1998) will be examined. This model holds promise as a service delivery platform for ESTs. The Primary Behavioral Health Model has already demonstrated clinical utility in defining and guiding adaptation of ESTs for treatment of depressed primary care patients (Katon et al., 1995, 1996; Robinson et al., 1997). Finally, a functional and structural template will be presented for building EST-based, population-specific protocols and pathways for primary care.

The Primary Care Setting

Primary care physicians are generalists committed to improving the health of all members of a community. In the United States, primary care physicians include family practice physicians, pediatricians, general internists, obstetricians-gynecologists, and general practitioners. The generalist nature of the primary care setting requires providers to play multiple roles in the health-care system. These roles include being direct providers of treatment for the majority of health problems, case managers regarding chronic medical health conditions, and gatekeepers who determine patient referral for specialty services.

The primary care setting and patients seen in this setting differ significantly from the mental health clinic and clients seen in this traditional health-care setting. Further, primary care patients may differ significantly from the research subjects who participate in studies that define EST. Behavioral health providers new to the primary care setting are more likely to be successful when their initial and ongoing efforts reflect an appreciation of the following five features of the primary care setting: primary care is diverse, it is medically oriented, it is driven by psychosocial factors, it is fast-paced and immediate, and it is "primary."

Primary Care Is Diverse

Primary care is the melting pot of the health-care delivery system. Primary care providers see members from every socioeconomic, racial, and ethnic group. They see patients in all stages of development—from the first moment of life to the last. Their patients suffer from a wide variety of acute and chronic diseases, as well as behavioral health problems. In a day's work, they may see patients who are mildly distressed and patients who are psychotic. The range of behavioral health issues seen in primary care is truly remarkable. For example, it has been well established that the higher utilizers of primary care often have substantial mental health and chemical dependency problems. A substantial subgroup of high utilizers is clinically depressed (Katon et al., 1992), while another sizable group suffers from co-occurring mental, substance-abuse, or dependency disorders. Common mental disorders in primary care include depressive disorders, anxiety disorders, alcohol and other substance-abuse and dependence disorders, somatization disorders, and eating disorders (Spitzer et al., 1995). Other disorders of concern in primary care include high acuity disorders, which are less common, but require intensive service. These include schizophrenia and other axis-one and -two disorders with psychotic features, as well as pain disorders associated with psychological and medical factors. Among children, high-prevalence disorders include attention deficit disorder, sleep disorders, conduct disorders, and depressive disorders. Along with patients who meet the criteria for a mental disorder, there are at least as many and probably more that are affected by the stress of medical illness, social disenfranchisement, job loss, economic hardship, or relationship problems (Robinson et al., 1995). The daily life of a primary care provider involves not just addressing the diverse health-care needs of primary care patients, but also an incredible range of psychosocial issues as well.

Like their patients, primary care providers are also diverse. Primary care providers vary in practice styles and interest and specialization areas. Older primary care physicians tend to have older patients, while younger doctors tend to attract younger patients (Robinson et al., 1995). Provider panels vary in composition and size, and this is reflective of the practice setting and provider interest and skill areas. Some providers deliver babies and provide care for numerous young families, while others serve a large group of diabetics. Some providers enjoy treating patients with mental disorders, while others have little interest in this area. Primary care clinics also vary significantly in accordance with their organizational structure, with some emphasizing team-based management (Taplin, Galvin, Payne, Coole, & Wagner, 1998), while others employ a solo practitioner model (Rivo, 2000).

Primary Care Is Medically Oriented

Given a highly diverse group of patients, primary care physicians are challenged to diagnose and treat myriad medical problems on any given day. In the medical setting, interview strategies and level-of-care assignments are made quickly, and the tendency is toward ruling out medical conditions and attempting to describe presenting complaints in biomedical terms. This reflects preparation and training for primary care providers who can readily explain the medical basis of psychological symptoms (e.g., depression related to hypothyroidism) and assess the physical symptoms related to depression more thoroughly than the psychological ones. Primary care providers are trained to evaluate the whole person. Predictably, they are more likely than psychiatrists to give physical exams, neurology exams, and to obtain multiple lab tests (Epstein, 1995) and prescribe psychotropic medications differently from their psychiatrist colleagues (Beeardsley, Gardocki, Larson, & Hidalgo, 1988).

Primary Care Services Are Driven by Psychosocial Factors

In contrast to the biomedical orientation of most primary care providers, patients frequently seek health care because of psychosocial stresses. In fact, most primary care patients present with symptoms that do not meet the criteria for an organic disease, but are of a medical concern. Kroenke and Mangelsdorff (1989) found that only 1 out of 10 of the most commonly seen complaints made in primary care was determined to have a medical etiology 1 year after the initial complaint. In this very large group of patients with vague symptoms, there is a huge opportunity for preventive behavioral health intervention programs. Although user-friendly screening instruments can help providers tease out behavioral health-care issues, the development of generic behavioral health patient education materials designed to improve coping and stress management skills can be tremendously helpful. Primary care is the ideal setting for teaching patients problem-solving skills, as these skills have wide applicability to the many psychosocial factors that drive care (Mynors-Wallace, Gath, Lloyd-Thomas, & Tomlinson, 1995). For all of the potential promise, there still appears to be a significant mismatch between what primary care patients are seeking and what primary care clinicians are prepared to provide (Sobel, 1995). This mismatch results in lower levels of patient and provider satisfaction as well as poorer health and behavioral health outcomes.

Primary Care Is Fast-Paced and Immediate

Diagnostic and treatment interventions, by necessity, are brief in primary care. Providers work in 10- and 15-minute units of time. Although visits with depressed patients are slightly longer than visits with nondepressed patients, they are far shorter than patient visits with psychiatrists (Olfson & Klerman, 1993). Consultations with colleagues and other medical team members are brief and occur at the time of need. They may be initiated by a knock on the door of a treatment room where a colleague is working with a patient or spontaneously in a "curbside consultation" between providers as they move between patients. The knock-on-the-door rule is a significant cultural difference between primary and many mental health-care settings. Primary care providers often marvel at how long behavioral health providers take to accomplish a treatment session. They view the 50-minute visit as a luxury they can ill afford in their busy daily practices. Generally, behavioral health interventions requiring more than 2–3 minutes cannot be accomplished during typical medical encounters. In mental health terms, primary care providers operate using a "15-minute hour."

Primary Care Is "Primary"

Regardless of the presenting problem or the levels of care involved, patients begin and end episodes of care with their primary care teams. Often the longest health-care relationship a patient will have is with his or her family doctor. In many managed health-care systems, primary care physicians act as care managers or "gatekeepers." They are responsible for coordinating referrals to various subspecialties, including mental health and chemical dependency services. In most instances, it is the primary care provider who is the first and the last professional involved with a patient during a period of compromised psychological functioning. Therefore, primary care providers are in a key position to detect escalating symptoms of psychological distress as well as to support long-term treatment gains associated with effective, ancillary psychological and psychiatric treatments.

This feature of the primary care setting is critical to achieving improved clinical and cost outcomes with behavioral health conditions. For example, nearly 70% of depressed primary care patients report at least one previous episode of depression (Robinson et al., 1995). It is in primary care, not specialty care, where recurrent psychological conditions, like depression, can be managed proactively on a long-term basis. Primary care is an ideal setting for applying risk-based protocols and other population-management strategies to recurrent or chronic medical and psychological health conditions. This "hub of the wheel" nature of primary medicine also has a dark side. When treatment protocols fail in mental health or chemical dependency treatment settings, the patient ends up returning to the primary care provider, often in a state of greater disrepair than before the initial referral was generated. Primary care providers tend to view mental health and chemical dependency services with great skepticism. They experience these services as a "black box" in which communication with the primary care provider is nonexistent and treatment practices are both mysterious and ineffective. The negative images of mental health and chemical dependency providers that are commonly held by primary care providers are in large part due to the apparent failure of these specialists to appreciate the central role of the primary care provider as a care coordinator.

Population-Based Care

Population-based care is grounded in public health concepts that may be unfamiliar to many behavioral health providers. The population-based care approach is designed to help the healthcare system achieve satisfactory levels of basic preventive care, accessibility to acute care, and effective chronic disease management. This approach uses public health and epidemiological principles to describe a population, analyze care for problems of highest priority, and design and modify services to deliver that care and monitor the results. This approach has been applied to community-oriented primary care, as well as to age-group and chronic-disease-group populations. There are two basic principles of population-based care that are relevant to the migration of ESTs into primary care. First, population care is effective only to the extent that basic clinical services can be accessed by a large percentage of the medical population. This generally involves the philosophy of providing limited services to many members of the population, instead of providing intensive services to few members. Second, population-based care interventions work best when they are designed to address the preferences of consumers. When consumer acceptance of interventions is high, consumers are more likely to seek the service and to follow the required steps of an acute or preventive intervention.

Table 2.1 lists five steps involved in the development of population-based care programs. These steps can be applied to behavioral health problems as well as medical problems. In the last section of this chapter, these steps are woven into a functional template for developing population-specific,

TABLE 2.1 Five Steps to Development of Population-Based Primary Care Programs

1. Choose a common condition that is amenable to a systems approach to care.
2. Identify a method for identifying patients in the primary care practice who have the selected condition.
3. Choose measurable outcomes that reflect best evidence-based medical or behavioral health practice for that condition.
4. Form a high-performance team to implement a system of care that improves outcomes.
5. Measure outcomes regularly and make changes as needed to improve outcomes.

evidence-based programs for primary care. These steps have proven useful in developing "vertical" integration programs that yield strong clinical, cost, and satisfaction outcomes (Katon et al., 1995, 1996; Von Korff et al., 1998).

Population-based care methods have provided structure for the development of most preventive medical programs. Many preventive medical problems involve risk-identification methods and behavioral counseling (U.S. Preventive Services Task Force, 1989). In fact, most preventive interventions can be classified as counseling interventions. These include educational programs aimed at risk factor modification as well as motivational interviewing strategies (e.g., tobacco use or unsafe sexual practices) (U.S. Preventive Services Task Force, 1996). Preventive behavioral activities occur in all areas of primary care medicine, including internal medicine, family medicine, pediatrics, and obstetrics and gynecology.

Taplin et al. (1998) have demonstrated that a population-based care program involving health-risk-factor screening and modification activities can be both feasible and practical when applied to an individual primary care physician's practice. This group of primary care researchers used a team model of care in a primary care practice to improve the proportion of eligible patients who achieved recommended levels of colon cancer screening and breast mammography. Behavioral health providers who plan to become primary-care team members need to anticipate possible applications of the population-based care model to prevent behavioral health problems and to treat intermittent, recurrent, and chronic behavioral disorders.

Evidence-Based Medicine

Among the behavioral health community, evidence-based medicine often is misconstrued as the process of using empirically validated treatments that are supported by clinical practice guidelines. This conception belies the true complexity of the evidence-based medicine model. Like population-based care, evidence-based medicine is rooted in clinical epidemiological and public health concepts. It involves the conscientious, explicit, and judicial application of current best evidence in making decisions about patient care. The practice of evidence-based care requires integration of clinical expertise with the best available external clinical evidence from systematic research. Within the context of everyday patient care, the provider that practices evidence-based medicine seeks to balance the factors of research evidence, clinical expertise, and patient preferences in providing care to the individual patient (Sackett et al., 1996). The steps in the clinical practice of evidence-based medicine include (1) selecting specific clinical questions from the patient's problem(s); (2) searching the literature or databases for relevant clinical information; (3) appraising the evidence for validity and usefulness to the patient and provider practice, and (4) implementing useful findings in everyday practice (Rosenberg & Donald, 1995).

In addition to assisting with the care of the individual patient, evidence-based medicine has the potential to inform and guide clinical decision-making concerning cost-effectiveness analyses and health policy development. Geyman (1998) suggests that evidence-based medicine consists of five components—each with an associated product. These component-product pairs include clinical epidemiological studies that produce practice guidelines, meta-analyses that produce care pathways, clinical trials that produce performance measures, cost-effectiveness analyses that produce process-based products, and decision analyses that produce outcome-based products.

A major product of evidence-based medicine is the development of a practice guide suggesting a quality hierarchy for guideline development (Eddy, 1996a; Eddy, Hasselblad, & Shachter, 1992). Guidelines have proliferated in recent years, as specialty organizations and governmental agencies have attempted to apply evidence-based medicine to conditions of concern. Unfortunately, the quality and value of early guidelines was variable, and a guideline is only as strong as the rigor of the scientific process involved in its development. A strong guideline is based on empirically validated clinical outcomes and patient preferences. Eddy (1996a; Eddy et al., 1992) suggested a quality hierarchy for guideline development that moved from the most basic level of global subjective judgment to the level of having an evidence base. The highest level in Eddy's quality hierarchy is the research-based practice guideline that is sensitive to patient preference. The Agency for Health Care Policy and Research (AHCPR) has created 19 practice guidelines and has established a group of evidence-based practice centers around the country to develop guidelines on a contractual basis (Practice Trends, 1997). AHCPR also created a national guideline clearinghouse on the Internet.

Use of evidence-based principles in primary care medicine has developed into an everyday reality for group and solo primary care providers, as they have begun to use Internet services on a daily basis. There are two major types of electronic databases used by physicians. One is bibliographic (e.g., MEDLINE), which retrieves relevant citations. The other provides direct access to evidence concerning specific clinical topics (e.g., the Cochrane Database of Systematic Reviews). Primary care providers may be employing evidence-based treatments in as many as 80% of their interventions (Ellis, Mulligan, Rowe, & Sackett, 1995; Gill et al., 1996). In one study, 53% of the treatments were supported by data from randomized clinical trials, while 29% were supported by convincing nonexperimental evidence (Gill et al., 1996).

Evidence-based medicine and population-based care methods empower providers to address the difficult issues related to resource allocation in a health-care system where needs often exceed resources. It should be noted that the growing emphasis on ESTs in the behavioral health industry has developed in relative isolation from the principles guiding evidence-based medicine. Evidence-based medicine is far more complicated than simply looking at the results of clinical trials and implementing a procedure based upon the empirical results alone. When implemented properly, this approach to medicine integrates cost considerations, risk-benefit to the consumer, existing variability in costs and outcomes, and strength of empirical evidence, as well as consumer preferences. Eddy offered the following 10 principles to guide the development of evidence-based models (Eddy, 1996b, pp. 252–265). Behavioral health providers need to familiarize themselves with these principles as they will wrestle an even larger monster of high needs and low resources when they work in primary care.

1. Consider financial costs of interventions.
2. Set priorities.
3. Understand that it is not feasible to provide every treatment that might have some benefit.
4. Know that the objective of health care is to maximize the health of the population served with available resources.
5. The priority of a treatment should not depend on whether a particular individual is our personal patient.
6. Priority-setting relies on estimates of benefits, harms, and costs.
7. Empirical evidence takes priority in assessing benefits, harms, and costs.
8. A treatment must meet three criteria before being promoted for use:
   a. Compared with no treatment, treatment is effective in improving health outcomes.
   b. Compared with no treatment, benefits outweigh harms of outcomes.
   c. Compared with next best alternative treatment, the treatment is a good use of resources for the population served (principle 5).
9. Patient preferences should be sought in making judgments of benefits, harms, and costs of a treatment.
10. In determining whether a treatment satisfies principle 8, the burden of proof is on those promoting its use.

These principles may seem obvious and unassailable, but there are many examples where they have not been followed in both medicine and behavioral health. Electronic fetal monitoring, for example, became widely applied with major impacts on perinatal care without satisfactory demonstration of criteria stated in principle 8 above. Behavioral health providers in primary care need to understand this larger set of decision rules when attempting to implement EST programs. Up to the present, there are few examples of EST programs being integrated within a system of primary care. This is due to the lack of onsite behavioral health services in most primary care clinics and to the rigor of the evidence-based model. The behavioral health provider who works in primary care is challenged to use the most relevant and valid data, as well as patient preferences, to create EST programs within the decision rule constraints imposed by evidence-based medicine.

The Primary Behavioral Health (PBH) Model

Several recent publications have described a Primary Behavioral Health Model (Strosahl, 1994, 1996a, 1996b, 1997, 1998; Strosahl, Baker, Braddick, Stuart, & Handley, 1997). This model involves managing the psychosocial aspects of chronic and acute diseases (i.e., behavioral medicine) and addressing lifestyle and health-risk issues (i.e., health psychology) through brief consultative interventions and temporary comanagement of certain behavioral health conditions. There is an emphasis on early identification and treatment, as well as long-term prevention and support of healthy lifestyles. Primary behavioral health services are delivered with a goal of increasing the effectiveness of primary care providers in addressing the behavioral health needs of patients. Behavioral health providers see patients in exam rooms or in offices nested in the primary care clinic. Behavioral health providers do not take charge of the patient's care, as would be the case in a specialty mental health approach. The goal is to manage the patient within the structure of the primary care team, with the behavioral health provider functioning as an integral member of this team.

Patients see behavioral health as a primary care service. Their care feels seamless. When a patient fails to respond to primary behavioral health care, or obviously needs specialized treatment, the patient is referred to a specialty mental health service (Strosahl, 1994). The Primary Behavioral Health Model also relieves patient concerns about receiving a "mental health" service. Consequently, many populations that have historically been reluctant to receive specialty mental health services (i.e., the elderly, male adults, ethnic and cultural minorities) accept care more readily from a behavioral health provider.

There are two distinct but complementary approaches to providing integrated behavioral health care. These have been described as horizontal and vertical models of integration (Strosahl, 1997). Horizontal integration is the most basic form of integrative care because almost any behavioral health problem can benefit from a well-organized general behavioral health service.

Horizontal Integration

Horizontal integration programs are designed to serve all comers. In this model, the goal is to deliver a large volume of brief psychosocial services that systematically improve the health of the entire primary care population. This model reflects the population-based care model used for primary medical services. Only small numbers of patients who require specialists are referred to specialty treatment centers and hospitals. This model is described extensively elsewhere (Strosahl, 1997). In the approach, the goal is to raise the skill level of primary care team members in treating behavioral health problems. Over time, primary care providers learn to handle routine problems more effectively in the context of 10-minute medical visits. Primary care providers learn quickly in a model that involves both consultation and the comanagement of cases. In this model, the behavioral health of the primary care population benefits from improvements in care delivered by primary care providers. As the primary behavioral health consultant "works him- or herself" out of the job of seeing less complex patients, more effort can be put into development of vertical behavioral health programs. In this sense, the horizontal integration provides a framework from which EST programs can be implemented successfully.

Vertical Integration

Vertical integration involves providing treatment according to a specific protocol to a defined subpopulation, for example, depressed primary care patients. Vertical integration programs are developed to serve highly prominent populations. Primary care populations may be prominent because they are prevalent, as is the case with depressed patients, or because they are high-profile patients, as may be the case with chronic-pain patients. Common vertical integration targets are high prevalence conditions, such as depression, panic disorder, or high-impact conditions, such as somatization and chronic pain. Vertical integration programs may be linked to clinical treatment pathways or practice guidelines. Vertical programs typically have both acute- and preventive-treatment foci. This allows the program to accommodate patients needing different levels of care and to prevent relapse. Successful vertical integration programs are developed through application of the principles of population-based and evidence-based medicine.

Relationship Between Horizontal and Vertical Integration Strategies

In most systems, the majority of primary care patients with behavioral health problems obtain benefit from primary care behavioral health services. These brief services focus on personal problem-solving, targeted skill development, and effective use of coping skills to respond to current psychosocial stresses. Patients with more complex problems benefit from more aggressive treatment, and these can be provided cost effectively in clinical pathways and in accordance with guidelines established by the employing organization or an independent body. To be fully integrated, a system should have a combination of targeted clinical pathways that address the needs of high frequency or high-impact subpopulations and a highly accessible horizontal integration service that serves as an easy access point for other patients.

Applying Vertical Integration Strategies to Behavioral Health Conditions in Primary Care

As discussed earlier, vertical integration programs are designed for high-frequency and high-impact behavioral health conditions. These programs need to include highly condensed, evidence-based interventions tailored to fit the fast pace of primary care. Temporary comanagement strategies with one or more medical team members often are key components of vertical programs. Although more behavioral health services are provided in vertical integration programs, the focus continues to be on patient education, self-management skills, medication adherence, and creation of a context where primary care team members reinforce each other's treatments. An example of an EST-based vertical integration program is the Integrated Care Program (Robinson, 1996; Robinson et al., 1996). In this program, a primary care provider and behavioral health consultant work together in a structured program that combines cognitive behavioral and pharmacotherapy treatments for patients with major depression or depressive symptoms secondary to life stresses and transitions (Robinson, 1996; Robinson et al., 1996). Compared with the usual care available in general medicine settings, randomized clinical trials have shown that the Integrated Care Program produced superior clinical outcomes, better medication adherence, increased use of coping strategies by patients, and significantly increased patient and provider satisfaction (Katon et al., 1996). Interestingly, the remission rates (approximately 70%) obtained in these studies compare very favorably with those reported in specialty field trials examining the effects of cognitive behavioral and medication treatments for depression (Elkin et al., 1989). This occurred even though the Integrated Care Program required only 3–4 total hours of behavioral health provider service. This is about a quarter of the treatment intensity observed in most clinical trials comparing treatments for depression.

Concepts, Problems, and Adaptation Targets for Redesigning ESTs for Primary Care

Given the radical differences in philosophies of care and patient populations, evidence-based mental health treatments are unlikely to transfer well to the primary care environment in their current form. Typically, they are too time-intensive, they cannot accommodate large patient flow, they lack a central patient-education or home-based, self-management focus, and they may not address the service preferences of primary care patients. Clinician researchers have attempted to deliver state-of-the-art mental health treatments for depression in a primary care setting without adaptation. Schulberg et al. (1996) have evaluated the effectiveness and feasibility of providing interpersonal therapy to depressed patients in a primary care setting. His team carefully followed a protocol determined to be effective in the mental-health-clinic setting. This study compared patients receiving interpersonal psychotherapy or pharmacotherapy with patients receiving usual medical care. Among treatment *completers*, approximately 70% of patients participating in the *full* pharmacotherapy or psycho-therapy protocol were judged as recovered at 8 months while only 20% of the usual care patients recovered. Unfortunately, only 33% of the pharmacotherapy and 42% of the psychotherapy patients completed active and continuation treatment phases, respectively. Less time-intensive versions of ESTs, such as brief interpersonal therapy, are required to retain and treat the high number of primary care patients who present for care. Careful attention to nine primary care program goals can help the behavioral scientist adjust ESTs for successful primary care implementation. Table 2.2 summarizes these goals, defines characteristics of ESTs that deserve evaluation, and suggests desired adaptations in ESTs for the primary care setting.

Embrace the Primary Care Service Philosophy

Most ESTs focus on provision of individual therapy in a specialist-based model of care. The orientation in mental health has always been to provide more intensive services to a smaller percentage of patients. In contrast, the philosophy of primary care is to provide much more abbreviated services to a much larger percentage of eligible patients. The mission is to improve the health of the community, not just the health of a few individuals in the community. This means that ESTs being reformulated for primary care must address the vast differences between programs designed for 3–5% of the population and those designed for 20–30%. In primary care, the mission is to serve the larger number of clients who do seek care for psychological problems, as well as those who do not seek care.

Expand the Population to Be Served

Most evidence-based mental health treatments are tested in clinical trials where subjects are required to meet stringent criteria for a specific mental disorder. Patients with co-morbid mental disorders, with subthreshold symptom complaints, or with problem drinking or drug abuse patterns are typically excluded. In primary care, patients will present with a much wider range of symptoms and co-occurring disorders or problematic behaviors, and they are the rule rather than the exception. In fact, patients with subthreshold symptoms are more common than patients with full-blown syndromes. For every patient who meets the criteria for major depression, there will be at least one to two primary care patients with subthreshold depressive symptoms (Katon et al., 1995 1996). Interestingly, losses in role functioning for patients with milder forms of depression may be

TABLE 2.2 EST Characteristics, Primary Care Goals, EST Adaptation Targets

Primary Care Goals	ESTs in Mental Health	Primary Care ESTs
1. Embrace the primary care service philosophy	Client-focused 3–5% penetration	Population focused 20–30% penetration
2. Expand the population to be served	Diagnostic syndromes only in homogenous protocol; subthreshold conditions excluded	All symptom levels treated within protocol; range of interventions available
3. Plan for population diversity	More educated; more females; better health; less ethnic and racial diversity; co-occurring disorders excluded in clinical trials; separate treatment of mental health and chemical dependency disorders	Less educated; more males; worse health; more seniors; more ethnic and racial diversity; less literacy; more co-occurring mental, chemical and medical disorders; high prevalence of drug and alcohol problems by adolescents, adults, and seniors
4. Use a patient-centered care approach	Patients expect longer sessions and more sessions over time	Patients expect very brief encounters that focus on advice and action
5. Deliver services in multiple formats	Predominantly one to one, couple, group, family therapy in solo provider model	Multiple service formats include consultation; temporary comanagement; flexible delivery models such as 1:1, telephone, group care clinic, classes
6. Reduce treatment length and intensity	Eight to 20 1-hour treatment sessions	Four to six 30-minute contacts
7. Convert to a patient education model	Specialist psychotherapy delivered in sequentially based protocol	Consultation and technical support to patient; patient education and home based self-management strategies taught in freestanding modules
8. Adopt a relapse prevention focus	Acute treatment focus; passive relapse prevention focus; patient to return to therapy if condition worsens	Risk monitoring and relapse prevention an integral part of longer term management protocol; risk monitoring is carried out by all medical team members
9. Build a team-based intervention	Solo practitioner focus; minimal, if any, relationship to patient's health-care team	Protocol designed to be delivered or supported by any member of the health-care team; team visits choreographed to create a seamless, consistent model of care

equal to those associated with major depression. Patients with subthreshold depressive symptoms have been found to have worse physical, social, and role functioning; worse perceived current health; and greater bodily pain than patients who have no behavioral health conditions (Wells et al., 1989). The primary care setting holds tremendous potential for addressing milder forms of common behavioral health conditions, thereby preventing the onset of more severe psychological problems. Delivery of components of EST programs for patients with subthreshold symptoms (e.g., patient education materials provided by the primary care provider) may enhance the realization of a medical cost offset associated with delivery of integrated behavioral health services (Von Korff et al., 1998). Behavioral health program designers need to redesign programs so that treatment protocols can be tailored to patients presenting with varying levels of symptoms and impairment in activities of daily living.

Plan for Population Diversity

In terms of demographic characteristics, primary care patients are a diverse group who differ from the typical group of subjects included in an EST research study. For example, depressed primary care patients are likely to be older and less educated than depressed patients who go to mental health specialists (Wells et al., 1989). They are also more likely to be married and of diverse ethnic backgrounds. There is a much higher percentage of monolingual patients and, in general, the education and literacy levels of primary care populations tend to be somewhat lower.

Medical co-morbidity is much more common in primary care than in mental health settings. Primary care patients with behavioral disorders often have multiple medical problems. The effects of medical conditions and psychological disorders, such as depression, on patient functioning appeared to be additive (Wells et al., 1989). For example, a patient with advanced coronary artery disease and depression may have twice the loss in social functioning compared with that associated with either condition alone. Patients with numerous medical conditions need to be treated alongside the multitude of other primary care patients with depressive symptoms.

The availability of EST programs for patients with co-occurring mental and chemical dependency problems needs to be improved. Most existing EST protocols are developed with patients who do not suffer from the mood, thought, and function-altering effects of ongoing substance abuse. Similar to the mental health population, most patients with chemical dependency issues are managed entirely within the primary care milieu, according to the Primary Behavioral Health Care Model (Strosahl, 1997). Many decline referral to chemical dependency treatment programs. EST programs need to anticipate and address the service needs of these more complicated patients. Sciacca and Thompson (1996) outline an example of the development of a dual or multiple disorder program that integrates diverse systems and provides comprehensive services within each of the programs within each delivery system. These types of programs can be cost-effective, can correct the issues of incompatible treatment interventions, and can end the dilemma of gaps in service systems and limited referral resources. The primary care setting is ideal for recasting chemical dependency as both a behavioral and physical health problem. Behavioral health consultants, along with primary care nurses, can take the lead roles in improving recognition of alcohol, tobacco, and other drug (ATOD) abuse problems in the primary care setting because this setting is fertile for cross-training among professionals, early detection, and ongoing relapse prevention efforts.

Use a Patient-Centered Care Approach

Most ESTs are designed for mental health clients, and their experiences in the mental health system have conditioned them to expect hour-long treatments that continue for months and, even years. Nevertheless, a significant percentage of mental health clients fail to adhere to typical EST protocols requiring only 10 to 20 sessions. When patients with behavioral health conditions present to the primary care setting, they expect brief treatments that provide them with education and self-management skills (e.g., medication information, problem-solving advice, educational pamphlets, etc.). Transferring EST protocols without significantly adjusting the service delivery model will result in significant patient adherence problems. Schulberg's (1996) reported excessive dropout rate likely occurred because the treatment length exceeded what primary care patients are willing to tolerate. In contrast, a highly condensed patient education approach yielded a treatment completion rate of over 90% (Katon et al., 1996). Mynors-Wallace et al. (1995) found that 93% of a group of depressed primary care patients completed treatment when offered a brief problem-solving treatment protocol for depression. In the same study, 81% of patients assigned to pharmacological treatment completed the protocol. In both the problem-solving and pharmacological treatment programs, patients were asked to attend six half-hour treatments over a 12-week period. These studies suggest that primary care patients tolerate around 3 hours of treatment over a 6-to-12-week period for a condition such as major depression.

Given the expectation of brief treatment, selection of effective therapeutic modalities and viable formats is critical. If properly "downsized," cognitive behavioral treatments for specific disorders are good candidates for implementation in primary care because they have an educational flavor, can be easily supported by educational materials, and are used by a significant number of primary care physicians (Robinson et al., 1995).

Deliver Services in Multiple Formats

Most ESTs are delivered in a 1:1 treatment format and, far less frequently, group or classroom models. The 1:1 modality is the service delivery model in the overwhelming majority of EST clinical trials. Unfortunately, the 1:1 modality is the unit of service with the least capacity and, if followed blindly, will jam the primary care behavioral health provider's calendar hopelessly in the first few weeks. This, of course, would result in frustration for both the primary care and behavioral health providers, and referrals likely would drop off rapidly. In primary care, treatments need to be offered in multiple formats. For example, a depression treatment program could be delivered in individual protocols, through telephone contacts, or in a group or classroom protocol. Group and classroom protocols must use freestanding content modules, to allow patients to enter the treatment program at any time. Sequentially, organized protocols that rely upon a series of consecutive visits to instill skills will be unsuccessful in primary care because they do not promote the immediate access required when patient volume is high. Finally, various medical team colleagues can also be enlisted to provide services such as making follow-up phone calls or leading groups or classes.

In all respects, flexibility in service delivery is absolutely essential in primary care. Using depression again as an example, a single prevention visit with the behavioral health consultant might be sufficient for a patient with mild symptoms, while pharmacological treatment by the primary care provider might be the choice for a patient who strongly preferred a solo medication treatment. An older, retired woman might select a 15-minute skill-building session in the morning, whereas several younger patients would attend a lunch-hour or after-work skill class. A brief behavioral skill-building booklet could provide the structure for a variety of contact options (Robinson et al., 1996). Collectively, these strategies maximize penetration into the population of primary care patients with a specified set of symptom complaints.

Reduce Treatment Length and Intensity

For the most part, evidence-based mental health treatments are developed in the context of an academically based research program where the probability of funding is greater when results are positive rather than negative. This paradigm encourages researchers to employ interventions that include "everything but the kitchen sink." As a result, evidence-based programs may be much more time and strategy intensive than is necessary for patient improvement. There is every reason to believe that the gestalt of primary care, with its emphasis on advice and action, favors the use of action-oriented, brief interventions. For example, Katon et al. (1996) found that a highly condensed package of "core" cognitive behavioral depression management skills produced robust treatment effects. Although there may be some ESTs that simply cannot be distilled into a home-based, self-management approach, clinical experience in primary care suggests that the majority can be rendered into this form. For example, anecdotal experience suggests that cognitive behavioral treatment for panic disorder can be accomplished in three to four 30-minute contacts when supported by patient education pamphlets, home-based practice, and on-demand telephonic consultation. Less-intensive treatments can be successful in primary care because they are supported and reinforced by a team of providers. In order to use members of the primary care team to extend the impact of brief treatments delivered by onsite behavioral health providers, treatment formats need to be packaged in an educational format and built around structures that support long-term skill change and increasing levels of patient self-efficacy in self-management. Further, the strategies need to be concrete, easy to understand, and supportable in the context of a 2-to-3-minute interaction between patient and medical provider.

Convert to a Patient Education Model

The specialty psychotherapy model practiced in mental health and chemical dependency encourages providers to take a great deal of responsibility for planning and implementing a treatment plan, often with minimal participation on the client's part. Although ESTs typically employ some psychoeducational strategies, the requirement for weekly or biweekly therapy sessions clouds the picture as to who is responsible for making change occur. Is it the therapist, through the accumulating influence of frequent therapy contacts? Or is the client, by practicing effective coping strategies outside the therapist's office, the active change agent? Most mental health providers will give the politically correct response, that is, the client is the active change agent. At the same time, the same providers will argue that reductions in session allotments in the era of managed care have harmed the quality of care. They argue that there is a well-documented "dose-effect" relationship between the number of sessions of psychotherapy and the amount of clinical gain observed. It seems implicit in these objections that most therapists believe a frequent presence is needed to guide and structure the process of behavior change. In primary care settings, that assumption gives way to what consumers consistently say they want in health care: to be given the information and skills necessary to manage their own problems with the minimum amount of assistance from a professional.

Primary care medicine is now characterized by an increasing emphasis on giving patients information about their conditions and then educating them in effective self-management skills. This is an essential feature of contemporary chronic-disease management programs that are proliferating in health-care settings across the county (Sobel & Ornstein, 1996). In a variety of medical studies, the patient education, self-management model has been shown to have a pronounced beneficial effect on health-care process and outcome measures. EST programs in primary care must develop condensed and informative educational materials, as well as provide an effective structure for the home-based practice of self-management skills. These education strategies are consistent with consumer preferences and will substitute for frequent visits with the behavioral health provider. In the modified EST approach, the primary behavioral health provider functions as a consultant and technical resource for the patient. The responsibility for practicing and assimilating new skills resides entirely with the patient.

Adopt a Relapse Prevention Focus

Currently, mental health specialists do not place a premium on prevention. Patients are usually experiencing moderate-to-severe levels of symptom distress and functional impairment when they access specialty mental health care. Treatment focuses on the reduction of acute symptoms and discharge occurs when the symptom picture improves. Most patients will leave the termination session without a written relapse prevention plan and no plan for follow-up "booster" visits. These patients will reenter the health-care system at greatly increased risk for relapse, without any particular plan for monitoring their functional and symptom status. In general, relapse prevention strategies are not widely practiced in mental health and are not required by managed care companies. Not surprisingly, there is also very little research on the clinical effect of relapse prevention strategies with recurrent conditions such as depression. In primary care, much of the cost containment and quality improvement potential with behavioral health conditions is related to the prevention of recurrences and the use of cost-effective procedures for doing so. For example, a large percentage of depressed primary care patients are left on antidepressants much longer than is indicated by the research. Although failing to provide any real prophylactic effect, these expensive medicines directly affect the pharmacy budget. In effect, an expensive, ineffective treatment is being employed to prevent recurrence. A far cheaper, effective alternative may be to construct EST programs so that they include relapse prevention plans, protocols for flagging at-risk patients, and a schedule of booster contacts with either the behavioral health provider or primary care provider.

The use of EST programs to take advantage of prevention opportunities should be well received in primary care. After all, the mission in primary care is to keep people healthy and to anticipate and thwart challenges to wellness. For example, in the study of the Integrated Care Program for Depression, primary care providers in the study began to formulate relapse prevention plans with 33% of their usual care patients after receiving brief training to support relapse prevention plans placed in the charts of the integrated care patients by behavioral health consultants. EST programs that systematize the use of relapse-prevention strategies might be very popular with primary care providers.

Build a Team-Based Intervention

In contrast to the solo office practice model of specialty mental health, primary care is evolving into a health-care-team service model. This means that physicians, midlevel providers, and nurses share a general responsibility for managing the patient's health care. To be sure, there are specific roles assigned to each team member based on discipline, experience, and specialized training. However, the message to the patient is that the team, rather than any one individual, is responsible for providing quality health care. During a typical medical visit, a patient might have contact with several members of the team, each performing a particular function. To adapt to this approach, behavioral health providers need to develop a wide range of "team-performance skills" that optimize the role of all team members in the patient's behavioral health care. EST interventions need to be couched in terms easily understood by the medical provider. Chart notes need to be shared with primary care providers on a same-day basis with the expectation that medical team members ask about and support the EST interventions being used with a particular patient. Behavioral health providers can assist the primary care physician in prescreening the weekly appointment schedule to identify patients eligible for the program. Visit protocols should be established that choreograph visits with the primary behavioral health provider and various health-care team members. During each medical visit, team members need to ask about the patient's progress toward behavior-change goals.

Finally, there is increasing evidence that primary care providers, with minimal training and consultative support, can be just as effective as behavioral health providers in managing certain mental health conditions. For example, Mynors-Wallace et al. (1995) went on to test the delivery of problem-solving therapy by nurses and demonstrated that primary care nurses and general physicians were as effective as psychiatrists in implementing and managing problem-solving interventions and antidepressant therapy with depressed primary care patients. Hunkler et al. (2000) have tested a nursing-based telephone intervention with depressed primary care patients that is designed to increase adherence to behaviorally based depression management skills. The results suggest this model of care produced better adherence, better use of self-management skills, and improved outcomes. Kent and Gordon (1997) have developed a group care clinic for unstable hypertensive patients, co-led by a psychologist and an internal medicine physician. This model of care reduced ambulatory outpatient medical costs, primarily through reductions in emergency room visits, and increased use of hypertension management strategies by patients. Robinson et al. (1998) have described a similar group care clinic for frail, elderly primary care patients, co-led by a family practice physician, psychologist, and nurse. Patients received this program positively, and findings suggested a change in utilization patterns among participants. A related project involved identification of elderly high utilizers of medical care and implementation of a nursing-based telephone intervention protocol that focused primarily on behavioral health issues. The results suggested that this intervention was extremely well received by patients and medical providers alike. The implications of these ground-breaking studies are clear. If one is to produce the volume of services needed to appreciably affect the behavioral health of the primary care population, EST protocols will have to be reorganized to permit the delivery of core services by medical personnel. Second, the primary behavioral health provider will need to assume responsibility for providing brief, effective training, as well as follow-up consultation to support the intervention activities of medical providers.

Primary care providers vary in their practice styles, and physician practice style does appear to be related to patient outcomes (Robbins et al., 1993). Providers seeking to develop behavioral health programs for specific populations in primary care need to address this variation by including provisions for variable levels of coparticipation by medically trained colleagues. Some physicians may prefer to implement EST protocols on their own and may succeed with only minimal curbside consultations. Other physicians will be reluctant to treat a specific disorder and may avoid an appreciable level of responsibility. However, as is true with all general physicians, they will want to be kept "in the loop" as the intervention progresses and will remain in charge of the patient's overall healthcare plan. The behavioral health provider needs to find a way to incorporate these differences, without compromising the integrity of the EST program or assuming the entire burden of care.

In any event, primary behavioral health providers need to develop proficiency in identifying the unique needs of any particular primary care population and the team-based resources that can be activated in a cost-effective way. Done properly, EST protocols have the potential to optimize the impact of primary care team members in addressing the burden of behavioral health problems in primary care.

Summary

The evolution of health care will most likely involve the integration of behavioral health services into the routine process of primary care medicine. This will provide the behavioral health industry with an unprecedented opportunity to reshape the way health is defined. Further, for the first time since the emergence of behavioral health as an industry, there is a real chance to dramatically impact the behavioral health of the general population. To achieve this lofty objective, behavioral health providers will need to adapt their best clinical technology to fit the demands of population care, evidence-based medicine, and the unique setting characteristics of primary care. The goal of this chapter has been to provide a framework for the successful translation of evidence-based mental health treatments into evidence-based, primary care behavioral health treatments. It is obvious that the process of translation will involve goring many a sacred cow, both in form and content. Behavioral health providers must be pragmatic, rather than paradigmatic, as they approach this daunting task. Direct experience suggests that thinking "out of the box" is a prerequisite for success in this endeavor. This mind-set allows us to first develop programs that are likely to work in primary care, then empirically test whether the results are acceptable. The process of design, test, and redesign is basic to nearly all models of quality improvement and will serve the primary behavioral health provider well.

References

Agency for Health Care Policy and Research (AHCPR). National Guideline Clearinghouse. Retrieved June 1, 2003, from www.guideline.gov.

Beeardsley, R., Gardocki, G., Larson, D., & Hidalgo, J. (1988). Prescribing of psychotropic medication by primary care physicians and psychiatrists. *Archives of General Psychiatry, 45*, 1117–1119.

Chambless, D. L., & Ollendick, T. H. (2001). Empirically supported psychological interventions: Controversies and evidence. *Annual Review of Psychology*, 685–716.

Eddy, D. M. (1996a). *Clinical decision making from theory to practice: A collection of essays from the journal of the American Medical Association*. Sudbury, MA: Jones & Bartlett.

Eddy, D. M. (1996b). Benefit language: Criteria that will improve quality while reducing costs. *Journal of the American Medical Association, 275*(8), 650–657.

Eddy, D. M., Hasselblad, V., & Shachter, R. (1992). *Meta-analysis by the confidence profile method: The statistical synthesis of evidence*. Boston: Academic Press.

Elkin, I., Shea, M. T., Watkins, J. T., Imber, S. D., Sotsky, S. M., Collins, J. F. et al. (1989). National Institute of Mental Health Treatment of Depression Collaborative Research Program: General effectiveness of treatments. *Archives of General Psychiatry, 46*, 971–982.

Elliot, R. E. (1998). Editor's introduction: A guide to the empirically supported treatments controversy. *Psychotherapy Research, 8*, 115–125.

Ellis, J., Mulligan, I., Rowe, J., & Sackett, D. L. (1995). Inpatient general medicine is evidence based. *Lancet, 346*, 407–410.

Epstein R. M. (1995). Communication between primary care physicians and consultants. *Archives of Family Medicine, 4*(5), 403–409.

Emmelkamp, P. M. G., Bouman, T., & Blaauw, E. (1994). Individualized versus standardized therapy: A comparative evaluation with obsessive-compulsive patients. *Clinical Psychology and Psychotherapy, 1*, 95–100.

Geyman, J. P. (1998). Evidence-based medicine in primary care: An overview. *Journal of the American Board of Family Practice, 11*(1), 46–56.

Gill, P., Dowell, A. C., Neal, R. D., Smith, N., Heywood, P., & Wilson, A. E. (1996). Evidence-based general practice: A retrospective study of interventions in one training practice. *British Medical Journal, 312*, 819–821.

Howard, K. I. (1992). The psychotherapeutic service delivery system. *Psychotherapy Research, 2*(3), 164–180.

Hoy, E., Curtis, R., & Rice, T. (1991). Change and growth in managed care. *Health Affairs, 10*, 18–36.

Hunkler, E. (2000). Nurse care by phone improves outcomes for depressed patients. *Archives of Family Medicine, 9*, 700–708.

Jacobson, N. S., Schmaling, K. B., Holtzworth-Munroe, A., Katt, J. L., & Wood, L. F. (1989). Research-structured vs. clinically flexible versions of social learning-based marital therapy. *Behavioral Research and Therapy, 27*, 173–180.

Katon, W., Robinson, P., Von Korff, M., Lin, E., Bush, T., Ludman, E. et al. (1996). A multifaceted intervention to improve treatment of depression in primary care. *Archives of General Psychiatry, 53*, 924–932.

Katon, W., Von Korff, M., Lin, E., Bush, T., Lipscomb, P., & Russo, J. (1992). A randomized trial of psychiatric consultation with distressed high utilizers. *General Hospital Psychiatry, 14*, 86–98.

Katon, W., Von Korff, M., Lin, E., Walker, E., Simon, G. E., Bush, T., Robinson, P., & Russo, J. (1995). Collaborative management to achieve treatment guidelines: Impact on depression in primary care. *Journal of the American Medical Association, 273*(13), 1026–1031.

Kent, J., & Gordon, M. (1997). Integration: A case for putting humpty dumpty together again. In N. Cummings, J. Cummings, & J. Johnson (Eds.), *Behavioral health in primary care: A guide for clinical integration* (pp. 103–120). Madison, CT: Psychosocial Press.

Knesper, D. J., & Pagnucco, D. J. (1987). Estimated distribution of effort by providers of mental health services to U.S. adults in 1982 and 1983. *American Journal of Psychiatry, 144*, 883–888.

Kroenke, K., & Mangelsdorff, A. (1989). Common symptoms in ambulatory care: Incidence, evaluation, therapy and outcome. *American Journal of Medicine, 86*, 262–266.

Magil, M. K., & Garrett, R. W. (1988). Behavioral and psychiatric problems. In R. B. Tayler (Ed.), *Family medicine* (3rd ed., pp. 534–562). New York: Springer-Verlag.

Mynors-Wallace, L., Gath, D. H., Lloyd-Thomas, A. R., & Tomlinson, D. (1995). Randomized controlled trial comparing problem solving treatment with amitriptyline and placebo for major depression in primary care. *British Medical Journal, 310*, 441–446.

Narrow, W., Reiger, D., Rae, D., Manderscheid, R., & Locke, B. (1993). Use of services by persons with mental and addictive disorders: Findings from the National Institute of Mental Health Epidemiologic Catchment Area Program. *Archives of General Psychiatry, 50*, 95–107.

Olfson, M., & Klerman, G. L. (1993). Trends in the prescription of psychotropic medications: The role physician specialty. *Medical Care, 31*, 559–564.

Practice Trends. (1997, April 15). AHCPR moves on. *Family Practice News*, 70.

Reiger, D. A., Goldberg, I. D., & Taube, C. A. (1978). The de facto US mental health services system: A public health perspective. *Archives of General Psychiatry, 41*, 934–941.

Reiger, D., Narrow, W., Rae, D., Manderschied, R., Locke, B., & Goodwin, F. (1993). The de facto US mental and addictive disorders service system: Epidemiologic Catchment Area prospective 1-year prevalence rates of disorders and services. *Archives of General Psychiatry, 50*, 85–94.

Rivo, M. L. (2000). It's time to start practicing population-based health care. American Academy of Family Physicians Family Practice Website. Retrieved October 12, 2002. from http://www.aafp.org.

Robbins, J. A., Bertakis, K. D., Helms, J. L., Azari, R., Callahan, E. J., & Crete, D. A. (1993). The influence of physician practice behaviors on patient satisfaction. *Journal of Family Medicine, 25*, 17–20.

Robinson, P. (1996). *Living life well: New strategies for hard times.* Reno, NV: Context Press.

Robinson, P., Bush, T., Von Korff, M., Katon, W., Lin, E., Simon, G. E. et al. (1995). Primary care physician use of cognitive behavioral techniques with depressed patients. *Journal of Family Practice, 40*(4), 352–357.

Robinson, P., Bush, T., Von Korff, M., Katon, W., Lin, E., Simon, G. E. et al. (1997). The education of depressed primary care patients: What do patients think of interactive booklets and a video? *Journal of Family Practice, 44*, 562–571.

Robinson, P., Del Vento, A., & Wischman, C. (1998). Integrated treatment of the frail elderly: The group care clinic. In S. Blount (Ed.), *Integrated care: The future of medical and mental health collaboration* (pp. 203–228). New York: Norton.

Robinson, P., Wischman, C., & Del Vento, A. (1996). *Treating depression in primary care: A manual for primary care and mental health providers.* Reno, NV: Context Press.

Roth, A. D., & Fonagy, P. (1996). *What works for whom? A critical review of psychotherapy research.* New York: Guilford.

Rosenberg, W., & Donald, A. (1995). Evidence-based medicine: An approach to clinical problem solving. *British Medical Journal, 310*, 1122–1126.

Sackett, D. L., Rosenberg, W. M. C., Muir Gray, J. A., Haynes, R. B., & Richardson, W. S. (1996). Evidence-based medicine: What it is and what it isn't. *British Medical Journal, 312*, 71–72.

Sackett, D. L., Richardson, W. S., Rosenberg, W., & Haynes, R. B. (1997). *Evidence-based medicine.* New York: Churchill Livingstone.

Schulte, D., Kunzel, R., Pepping, G., & Schulte-Bahrenberg, T. (1992). Tailor-made versus standardized therapy of phobic patients. *Advanced Behavioral Research and Therapy, 14*, 67–92.

Schulberg, H. C., Block, M. R., Madonia, M. J., Scott, C. P., Rodriquez, E., Imber, S. D. et al. (1996). Treating major depression in primary care practice: Eight-month clinical outcomes. *Archives of General Psychiatry, 53*, 913–919.

Sciacca, K., & Thompson, C. M. (1996). Program development and integrated treatment across systems for dual diagnosis: Mental illness, drug addiction and alcoholism (MIDAA). *Journal of Mental Health Administration, 23*(3), 10–15.

Shapiro, S., Skinner, E., & Kessler, L. (1984). Utilization of health and mental health services: Three epidemiologic catchment area sites. *Archives of General Psychiatry, 41*, 971–978.

Sobel, D. (1995). Rethinking medicine: Improving health outcomes with cost-effective psychosocial interventions. *Psychosomatic Medicine, 57*, 234–244.

Sobel, D., & Ornstein, R. (1996). *The healthy mind, healthy body handbook.* Los Altos, CA: DRx Publishing.

Spitzer, R., Kroenke, K., Linzer, M., Hahn, S., Williams, J., deGruy, F. et al. (1995). Health related quality of life in primary care patients with mental disorders. *Journal of the American Medical Association, 274*, 1511–1517.

Strosahl, K. (1994). New dimensions in behavioral health primary care integration. *HMO Practice, 8*, 176–179.

Strosahl, K. (1996a). Primary mental health care: A new paradigm for achieving health and behavioral health integration. *Behavioral Healthcare Tomorrow, 5*, 93–96.

Strosahl, K. (1996b). Confessions of a behavior therapist in primary care: The odyssey and the ecstasy. *Cognitive and Behavioral Practice, 3*, 1–28.

Strosahl, K. (1997). Building primary care behavioral health systems that work: A compass and a horizon. In N. Cummings, J. Cummings, & J. Johnson (Eds.), *Behavioral health in primary care: A guide for clinical integration* (pp. 37–68). Madison, CT: Psychosocial Press.

Strosahl, K. (1998). Integration of primary care and behavioral health services: The Primary Mental Health Care Model. In A. Blount (Ed.), *Integrative primary care: The future of medical and mental health collaboration* (pp. 43–56). New York: Norton.

Strosahl, K., Baker, N., Braddick, M., Stuart, M., & Handley, M. (1997). Integration of behavioral health and primary care services: The Group Health Cooperative Model. In N. Cummings, J. Cummings, & J. Johnson (Eds.), *Behavioral health in primary care: A guide for clinical integration* (pp. 61–86). Madison, CT: Psychosocial Press.

Taplin, S., Galvin, M. S., Payne, T., Coole, D., & Wagner, E. (1998). Putting population-based care into practice: Real option or rhetoric. *Journal of the American Board of Family Practice, 11*(2), 116–126.

U.S. Preventive Services Task Force. (1989). *The guide to clinical preventive services: An assessment of the effectiveness of 169 interventions.* Baltimore: Williams & Wilkins 125-128, 370-372.

U.S. Preventive Services Task Force. (1996). *Guide to clinical preventive services: report of the U.S. Preventive Services Task Force* (2nd ed.). Baltimore: Williams & Wilkins.

Von Korff, M., Katon, W., Bush, T., Lin, E., Simon, G. E., Saunders, K. et al. (1998). Treatment costs, cost offset, and cost-effectiveness of collaborative management of depression. *Psychosomatic Medicine, 60*, 143–149.

Wells, K., Steward, A., Hays, R., Burnam, M., Rogers, W., Daniels, M. et al. (1989). The functioning and well being of depressed patients: Results from the Medical Outcomes Study. *Journal of the American Medical Association, 262*, 914–919.

Chapter 3
The Role of the Behavioral Health-Care Specialist in the Treatment of Depression in Primary Care Settings

GLENN M. CALLAGHAN AND JENNIFER A. GREGG

Depression is a costly problem both psychologically and financially. This chapter presents an overview of depression as a biological, psychological, and social phenomenon to be treated in primary health-care settings. The utility of using an assessment-referral-treatment model makes use of all members of an interdisciplinary treatment team and focuses on the delivery of psychological interventions for depression as the primary treatment or adjunctively with medications. A cognitive behavioral therapy group intervention is described with respect to the necessary components for conducing the intervention and research evidence supporting its use. The chapter highlights a financial analysis of using this intervention in primary health-care settings.

Depression as a Biopsychosocial Phenomenon

Clinical depression and depressive disorders, including minor depression and dysthymia, comprise a set of psychological problems that are costly both emotionally and financially (American Psychiatric Association, 1994). The prevalence of these depressive disorders has been estimated to range between 6–20% in the general population (Budman & Butler, 1997; McGue & Christensen, 1997), and researchers have reported even significantly greater prevalence in primary and mental health-care settings as compared with community samples (Howland, 1993). For example, dysthymia is found among 22–36% of persons seeking services in mental health settings and between 5–15% of those seeking assistance with primary care providers (Sansone & Sansone, 1996).

A contemporary understanding of clinical depression conceptualizes the disorder as being caused and maintained by biological, psychological, and social factors. While serotonin and norepinepherine continue to be viewed as essential pathways (known as the biological amine hypothesis; see Buelow, Hebert, & Buelow, 2000), research in the past few decades has emphasized the shared role of behavioral influences in both the cause and treatment of depression (Charney, Miller, Licinio, & Salomon, 1995). Comprehensive approaches to the treatment of depression involve the assessment and treatment of all these factors. However, the medical treatment of psychological problems and the inappropriate or unwarranted prescription of medications (typically selective serotonin reuptake inhibitors, or SSRIs) can lead to unnecessary costs.

Overall, depressive disorders are associated with poor physical health. Patients suffering from depression tend to overutilize general and emergency medical services (Howland, 1993; McGue & Christensen, 1997). For example, Coulehan, Schulberg, Block, Janosky, and Arena (1990) reported that patients with depressive symptoms received more medical diagnoses (including diabetes and endrocrine, nutritional, musculoskeletal, and gastrointestinal problems), were prescribed more medications, and were more likely to have a history of surgical procedures than nondepressed patients. Depressive symptomology is also found to be higher in patients with connective tissue problems, gastrointestinal conditions, and cancer (Cavanaugh & Wettstein, 1989).

A key link between physical disorders and depression may be nonadherence to medical recommendations. The relationship between depression and nonadherence to medical treatment has been shown to be substantial, and depressed patients are up to three times more likely to be nonadherent to medical recommendations made by their physician than nondepressed patients (DiMatteo, Lepper, & Croghan, 2000). The issue of nonadherence to treatment recommendations also impacts depression treatment and is addressed in detail below.

Overall, patients with both physical problems and depressive symptoms tend to report a greater number of symptoms, receive medical treatment for their medical problems, but typically do not receive psychological treatment (Wells, Hays, Burnam, Greenfield, & Ware, 1989). Even if one corrects for the financial costs associated with medical co-morbidity, research indicates that providing treatments for patients with depressive disorders is more expensive than providing interventions to those without these problems (Simon, Ormel, VonKorff, & Barlow, 1995). Furthermore, somatic complaints (e.g., headache, fatigue, etc.) described by patients to primary care providers may be symptoms of depressive disorders, not of medical problems (Coulehan et al., 1990).

Major depression is reported to be one of the most common disorders found in medical practice (Coulehan et al., 1990). Despite the high prevalence in primary care settings, it is estimated that only one third of patients with depressive symptoms are properly diagnosed by primary care physicians (Budman & Butler, 1997; Muñoz, Hollon, McGrath, Rhem, VandenBos, 1994) and as many as 50% are incorrectly identified as depressed by primary care doctors (Perez-Stable, Miranda, Muñoz, & Ying, 1990). Even fewer patients who are correctly identified as clinically depressed receive treatment (Kupfer & Freedman, 1986). The prevalence of depressive disorders, coupled with the inaccuracy of identification and lack of effective care provision, indicates a clear need for the behavioral health-care specialist to address the problems of assessment and treatment of depression in primary care practice settings.

Psychosocial Treatments for Depression

The treatment of depression with psychosocial interventions has been considerably supported by the empirical literature with regard to efficacy (see for example Robinson, Berman, & Neimeyer, 1990). Typically, however, psychosocial treatments for depression in the primary care setting have not been considered as a first-line treatment. In a primary care setting, the first and predominant interaction for patients with depressive symptoms is with their physician, and physicians tend to employ pharmocotherapy (antidepressant medications) rather than psychosocial interventions (Attkisson & Zich, 1990). Primary care physicians have numerous classes of drug treatments at their disposal. Although pharmacological interventions are more often implemented in primary care, it is unclear whether these interventions are very effective when provided as a stand-alone treatment by physicians rather than part of a broader, team-based intervention (Lin et al., 1997).

Antidepressant medications have been demonstrated as an effective way to treat symptoms of depression, but posttreatment follow-up studies demonstrate that they are less efficacious in maintaining gain than psychosocial interventions (Shea et al., 1992) or interventions combining pharmacotherapy with psychological treatment (Simons, Murphy, Levine, & Wetzel, 1986; Wells et al., 2000). Despite the demonstrated long-term superiority of psychological treatment either alone or in combination with medications, patients with depression or depressive symptoms are primarily treated with antidepressants (Frank, Kupfer, Wagner, McEachran, & Cornes, 1991; Katon et al., 2001).

In primary care, other problems with the efficacy of pharmacotherapeutic interventions can be attributed to physician misdiagnosis, ineffective dosing of medications, insufficient treatment duration, or other factors related to the delivery of the pharmacological treatment (Katon, Von Korff, Lin, Bush, & Ormel, 1992). In addition to problems with prescribing medications, there are other reasons why the treatment of depression in the primary care setting may not be efficacious, including the limited time physicians have with each patient and their lack of training in effective assessment of depression.

Physician Collaboration

Given the difficulties in treating depression in primary care, multiple interventions have been developed and implemented to improve physician collaboration with mental health professionals in the primary care setting. One approach to improving physician practice with depressed patients has been to utilize interventions designed to educate physicians about the identification and treatment of depressive disorders. An exemplary study examined the effects of an extensive, 12-month educational program designed to enhance the primary care physician's diagnosis and treatment of depression (Lin et al., 1997). Although this program was more extensive than most interventions found in managed health-care settings, there were no lasting effects of the education intervention on changed physician behaviors such as prescribing patterns, medication and dosage selection, and depression outcomes.

The lack of success with this and earlier versions of education programs designed to improve physician treatment of depression in primary care has led researchers to shift their focus toward interventions designed to reorganize service delivery patterns. Katon and colleagues (1995, 2001) described several waves of interventions designed to target these domains by implementing organizational structure changes to facilitate improved detection and treatment of depression in primary care. The first wave of these interventions attempted to improve physician detection of depressive patients by implementing screening procedures in primary care. This wave resulted in more appropriate diagnoses of depressed patients, but it did not improve overall outcome (Katon et al., 1995). The second wave of programs, designed to improve collaboration between primary care physicians and mental health providers, consisted of interventions that required patients diagnosed with depression by primary care physicians to be randomly assigned to either an intervention group or a control group. In the intervention group, a psychiatrist performed a diagnostic interview and consulted with the physician on treatment selection. This intervention resulted in improved diagnosing, but it did not appreciably improve depression outcome treatment (Katon et al., 1992).

A third wave of programs, designed to improve depression care in primary care, has targeted these settings at a broader level through the use of disease management-quality improvement programs. These programs employ a number of methods, including local expert leaders, performance feedback, and workload shifting to enhance primary care providers' delivery of quality depression care within the existing setting and providers (e.g., Wells et al., 2000). This type of setting-level intervention has demonstrated improved outcomes in delivery of treatment and reduction in depressive symptoms, but no differences in medical visits or costs were discovered (Wells et al., 2000). There are drawbacks to this type of intervention as well, including the large amount of resources required to implement such a program and the buy-in required at both the administrative and physician levels to facilitate physicians performing such roles.

Due to the limited number of improved patient outcomes resulting from either improving depression screening procedures or structured consultation services with physicians and the complex buy-in required to implement quality improvement programs at an administrative level, the final wave of interventions targeted the integration of mental health professionals into the depression treatment in primary care. In order to fully integrate the mental health professionals, the treatment course began with the introduction of the mental health professional as part of the treatment team in the primary care setting. According to Strosahl (1996) the presence of the behavioral health-care specialist in the primary care setting is crucial because it avoids the necessity of the patient following up on a referral, reduces the stigma of seeing a mental health professional, and allows for time-efficient interventions for a primary care population who may have difficulties that do no warrant full-term psychosocial interventions. With the full integration of the mental health professional in this third wave of intervention, Katon and colleagues (1995) found better physician adherence to treatment recommendations, and 74% of patients diagnosed with major depression in the treatment condition showed significant improvement, compared with 44% of those in the control condition.

Cognitive Behavior Therapy for Depression

Among psychosocial treatments, there are a number of interventions that have been shown to be efficacious with depression in randomized controlled trials (Robinson et al., 1990). A review of these treatments is beyond the scope of this chapter. We will focus on one type of psychosocial intervention, cognitive behavior therapy (CBT; see for example Beck, Rush, Shaw, & Emery, 1979). CBT is a well-established and efficacious treatment for depression, with research findings indicating that CBT is an effective treatment for this disorder either in combination with pharmacotherapy or alone (see for example Antonuccio, Thomas, & Danton, 1997; Evans et al., 1992; Shea et al., 1992). In primary care settings, efforts have focused on providing both CBT and pharmacotherapy treatments for patients; both have been found to be somewhat effective (Schulberg, Katon, Simon, & Rush, 1998) and cost effective (Lave, Frank, Schulberg, & Kamlet, 1998). As discussed above, other researchers have argued that combined pharmacotherapy treatments or medication interventions alone are not as effective as psychosocial treatments such as CBT alone (Antonuccio, 1995), and given the dropout rates, side effects, and other issues with medication, psychotherapy is a better first-line choice for the treatment of depression (Wexler & Cicchetti, 1992).

CBT can be conducted in both individual and group formats, and both modalities are equally efficacious (e.g., Brown & Lewinsohn, 1984). The principles of this therapy are the same for both. There are considerable advantages to treating individuals in a group session, including the development of social skills for patients, the increased probability of building a social support network, and learning from other patients' experiences. Group therapy is also more cost effective and time efficient for health-care providers and agencies in that one therapist can see more patients during a 1-to-2-hour time block. For these reasons, we will focus our discussion on the group treatment approach.

The CBT group treatment developed by Organista and colleagues (1994) provides a structured treatment approach for using CBT for patient groups with depression. This treatment has been demonstrated to be empirically efficacious in reducing depression (Miranda & Muñoz, 1994; Wells et al., 2000). There are several advantages to using a manualized group treatment, such as the one described here. First, patients are treated in a limited number of sessions (typically 8 to 12). Second, the manual is given to patients to utilize as a treatment workbook. This allows patients to continue to work on the topics and strategies discussed in treatment on their own. Third, the manual offers a structured treatment strategy for therapists to utilize. Fourth, the manual assists therapists in accountability of treatment effectiveness by integrating ongoing assessment into the treatment process. This accountability practice is an activity essential in the changing face of psychological treatment provision in a managed, behavioral health-care industry (e.g., Cummings, 1995).

CBT treatments typically focus on three main areas of intervention. The first, or cognitive, area focuses on strategies to identify dysfunctional thinking, to generate alternatives to ineffective thought processes, and to have patients document their thoughts so that they might eventually alter their negative cognitions. The second and third areas typically focus on the behavioral component of the intervention. Interventions here focus on behaviorally activating the patient and improving his or her social skills. Focusing on the patients' level of activity helps them identify and engage in actions that are more likely to reduce depression and increase their opportunities to receive social reinforcers. Strategies to improve social interactions focus on teaching patients basic social skills so that they have the opportunity to engage in positive, rewarding contacts with other people, and to expand their social support systems.

CBT strategies focus heavily on the importance of requiring patients to complete assignments outside of the session. These assignments focus on having the patient work on tasks discussed during therapy sessions and then report back to the therapist or behavioral health-care specialist the next week. Problems and improvements encountered during the week are discussed and utilized as opportunities to work on the cognitive and behavioral areas described above.

Behavioral health-care specialists who provide CBT need to receive training in how to deliver an individual or group therapy protocol for the treatment of depression. The requirements for providing any psychological intervention vary from state to state but typically involve some licensure and supervision in a health-care specialty. Under the supervision of a trained doctoral-level clinical psychologist, other health-care providers can also provide the group CBT treatment (e.g., registered nurses, master's level psychotherapists).

Compliance

Whether a behavioral health-care specialist or other primary care support staff conducts the treatment, it is essential that patient adherence or compliance to the protocol be continually monitored. Compliance with depression treatment, whether pharmacological or psychological in nature, is viewed as a significant problem (DGP, 1993a, 1993b). Compliance rates have ranged from 4–90% in individuals diagnosed with mood disorders, depending on the method used for measuring compliance (DGP, 1993a, 1993b). Patient compliance with depression protocols can be challenging for several reasons.

First, patients may not understand the importance of addressing their problems from a psychological perspective. It is essential to address this barrier to compliance at the beginning of and *throughout* treatment by providing a thorough rationale for the use of a psychosocial intervention as an adjunct to or separate from pharmacotherapy. Ideally, these would be addressed both by the primary care physician and the behavioral health-care specialist. Research on patient compliance indicates that providing patients with information on the cause, symptoms, and natural progression of depression; options for treatment (including a discussion of the risks and benefits of each available treatment); and the outcome that can be reasonably anticipated greatly improves patient adherence to treatment (e.g., Altamura & Mauri, 1985; van Gent & Zwart, 1991).

Second, depressive symptomatology includes cognitive difficulties such as lack of concentration and problems with memory. These problems can produce noncompliance or nonadherence by patients simply owing to a lack of ability to comply at that moment, not a lack of motivation to comply. Provided this is not a neurological problem such as brain injury or dementia, behavioral health-care specialists can address this difficulty by helping patients develop better strategies to remember appointments, complete homework assignments, and ask for clarification when confused. These strategies will likely help the patient in other areas and will lend to the credibility of the service provider.

Third, the psychomotor retardation that sometimes accompanies depression can appear to be a lack of motivation. In these cases, it may be appropriate to modify the course of treatment to more quickly address the need for behavioral activation. Fourth, patients may be having difficulties with other areas of a multidisciplinary intervention, particularly medication. For example, patients may be experiencing side effects or may be not be dosed adequately. Research has shown that over 40% of patients prescribed antidepressant medication stop taking their medication after 3 months (Katon, 1995) despite recommendations for continuing medications 6–12 months after the resolution of the episode of major depression. This is a concern that should be anticipated and addressed, as it may be predictive of patients prematurely discontinuing a psychosocial intervention due to dissatisfaction with treatment.

Primary Prevention and Long-Term Management of Depression

Primary prevention of depression is an area that has received increased attention in the era of managed health-care organizations and population-based care (see chapter 2). Although this is an area that largely has not produced consistent outcomes, some studies have begun to illustrate that when prevention interventions target low-income, at-risk populations in a primary care setting, significant decreases in prevalence of depressive symptoms can be observed and maintained (e.g., Muñoz et al., 1995). These studies have utilized a cognitive-behavioral group treatment for depression discussed in more detail below.

Unlike primary prevention, there has been considerable attention paid to the long-term management and secondary prevention of depressive symptomology. Until recently, long-term medication use has been the most validated and utilized approach to prophylaxis in depression, with the best results obtained when patients are maintained on the dose and type of medication effecting clinical change in the acute phase of treatment (Kupfer et al., 1992). Within the past decade, researchers have begun examining the effects of psychosocial interventions with regard to the long-term management of depression, illustrating that continuation of psychosocial treatment in maintenance form can also significantly reduce recurrence of depression (e.g., Frank et al., 1990, 1991; Kupfer et al., 1992). CBT for depression (see description below), administered during depressive episodes, appears to be effective in reducing rates of relapse and recurrence of depressive symptoms (Simons et al., 1986; Wells et al., 2000). Additionally, studies comparing the long-term outcome of CBT-treated patients with medication-treated patients who were then withdrawn from medication have consistently found fewer relapses or need for further treatment in the CBT group (Blackburn, Eunson, & Bishop, 1986; Evans et al., 1992; Shea et al., 1992). Some researchers argue that these findings suggest that CBT's effectiveness in reducing depressive symptoms and risk for relapse lies in its ability to teach patients social skills and develop changes in their thinking (Teasdale et al., 2000).

Assessment of Depression

The need to assess for depressive symptoms in primary care has been documented above. That physicians are not especially equipped to accurately assess depressive symptomatology has also been addressed. In this section we discuss one basic assessment tool that can be used in primary care and offer a model for an assessment and referral process for the coordinated-care treatment of depression.

Assessment of Depressive Symptoms

There are numerous assessment tools for identifying and tracking depressive symptoms. Some of these are used in the context of making a formal research diagnosis, while others are tailored to different theoretical models for depression. The Beck Depression Inventory and Beck Depression Inventory-2 (BDI-2; Beck, Steer, & Brown, 1996; Beck, Ward, Mendelson, Mock, & Erbaugh, 1961) are commonly used, self-report instruments that measure the cognitive, affective, behavioral, and vegetative symptoms of depression (Beck et al., 1961, 1996). The assessment device consists of 21 items, each rated from 0 to 3, that assess the intensity of depressive symptoms experienced during the previous 2 weeks. Scores on the BDI range from 0 to 63, with higher scores indicating greater levels of depression. The BDI-2 typically takes less than 5 minutes to complete and 1 minute to score and interpret.

Research findings support the use of the BDI to screen for and diagnose depressive disorders by physicians in primary care settings (Zich, Atkisson, & Greenfield, 1990). There is evidence that using a depression screen is viewed favorably by primary care physicians, and that the use of these devices assists physicians in diagnosing and treating depression (Rucker, Frye, & Cygan, 1986). Although the BDI is not a structured clinical assessment device, it does provide a reliable assessment of the level of depressive symptomatology.

Scores on the BDI indicating depression vary, depending on the level of severity of depression as well as the purposes for which the assessment device is used. Scores of 16 and above on the BDI indicate that the patient is currently experiencing symptoms of depression (Beck, Steer, & Garbin, 1988). This cut-score has been established in the literature as being sensitive to detecting symptoms of depression without falsely identifying as depressed those individuals who report some sadness, but who are not experiencing clinical depression (Zich et al., 1990). Those individuals scoring above 30 (in the severe level range; Beck et al., 1988) tend to be severely depressed, often suicidal, and may need more intense care than is afforded in a group treatment approach. The research literature is unclear which type of treatment most benefits individuals with severe levels of depression, but it appears that they do not benefit from short-term psychotherapy interventions.

Physicians and their office administrative staffs, behavioral health-care specialists, and other members of a multidisciplinary care team can all provide and score a BDI when provided as a paper-and-pencil assessment device.

Model of Multistep Assessment and Referral Process

As described earlier, assessment is important, but not sufficient, to improve outcomes for depressive patients (e.g., Katon et al., 1995). We offer a model for collaborative care that has been developed based on suggestions from the empirical literature (Callaghan, Gregg, & O'Donohue, 2000). In an established relationship with primary care physicians we propose a three-step model of assessment, referral, and treatment.

In the first step, we suggest the assessment of any patient who has demonstrated an affective problem (e.g., evidences sad or depressed mood, reports decreased pleasure in activities) or self-reports difficulties with sad mood. The first phase of the assessment process begins with having physicians' office staff members administer and score BDIs for these patients. If the patient scores above 10 on the BDI, the staff then places the copy of the BDI at the front of the patient's chart flagged with a colored note to alert the physician.

In phase two of the assessment process, the physician then administers a brief screen to each of these patients (see Figure 3.1). This screen prevents those individuals from receiving a treatment for depression when it is not the correct diagnostic match for the patient, or it is not warranted.

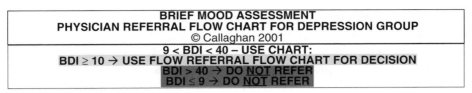

1. Have you been feeling **SAD, DOWN,** or like you are functioning at **LESS THEN YOUR OPTIMAL LEVEL** for more than **2 weeks**?

2. In the past several months, have there been several days at a time where you felt more **ELATED** (or really felt excited) even more than your normal feelings of being happy or excited or when you **DIDN'T NEED TO SLEEP** more than a few hours a night (for several nights in a row) but still had a **LOT OF ENERGY** the next day?

3. Have you been feeling sad, down, or at a suboptimal level for **MORE THAN 6 MONTHS**?

4. Have you experienced any **PERSONAL LOSS** or **DRAMATIC CHANGE** in your life in the last **six months** that has left you feeling sad, depressed, or at a suboptimal level?

5. Were you feeling like you were functioning at near your optimal level **BEFORE** **THIS PERSONAL LOSS OR DRAMATIC CHANGE**?

Fig. 3.1 Brief mood assessment physician referrral flow chart.

The physician-administered device includes questions to be asked by the physician about the quality of the patient's current distress. The screen will disqualify for referral to the CBT treatment all patients currently experiencing distress due to a recent interpersonal loss (adjustment disorder with depressed mood or bereavement) as well as those individuals who experience manic symptoms consistent with a diagnosis of bipolar affective disorder. Symptoms of depression in individuals with an adjustment disorder or who are grieving the loss of a loved one typically spontaneously remit within several months. Patients with bipolar affective disorder experience a variety of symptoms and problem behaviors not covered in a CBT treatment of depression. This screen is not designed to require the physician to make a formal diagnosis of major depressive disorder. Instead, it is designed to be sure that as many appropriate patients as possible are referred to a CBT group treatment.

Provided the patient meets the criteria for referral to the CBT group, the physician then informs the administrative staff member who, in turn, contacts the behavioral health-care specialist and refers the patient to the group. The behavioral care specialist then contacts the patient within 1 to 2 days to set the appointment to begin the group therapy. The group treatment can be conducted weekly for 90 minutes per session for 8 weeks. Our model requires several groups with rotating admission sessions for new members so that these newly referred patients need not wait longer than 1 week to begin treatment.

A Brief Economic Analysis of Depression

Not only do depressive disorders take an emotional toll on more than 11 million Americans each year (Budman & Butler, 1997), but studies indicate that depression has a tremendous financial impact. Estimated costs to the nation range from $2.7 billion to $5.6 billion annually in service provision (Rost, Zhang, Fortney, Smith, & Smith, 1998). These costs increase to as much as $30.4 billion to $44 billion annually, based on larger indices including work absenteeism, decreased productivity, treatment, and other factors (Antonuccio et al., 1997; Keller, 1994).

Much attention has been paid in the past decade to the cost of treating depression and the demonstration of cost-offset in the area of interventions for depression. Although some of the arguments for different interventions, particularly behavioral versus pharmacological, can be viewed as rhetoric, some recent empirical analyses have emerged. The difficulty in examining this literature lies with the equivocal nature of the data. Although some studies show demonstrable cost-offset and savings for depression (Dwight-Johnson, Unutzer, Sherbourne, Tang, & Wells, 2000), others indicate that this cannot be shown as clearly (Schulberg, Pilkonis, & Houck, 1998). One of the reasons for this lack of evidence for cost savings is the different types of interventions employed, the cost of these, the involvement of medications (particularly brand name SSRIs), and the time or intensity of the intervention (see for example, Antonuccio et al., 1997; Von Korff et al., 1998). Recent reviews of the medical cost-offset literature for the treatment of depression indicate both that depression is associated with increased use of medical services, and that treatment of depression can be expected to reduce medical expenditures (e.g., Simon & Katzelnick, 1997; Thompson et al., 1998).

On the optimistic side of the cost-offset literature, research indicates that psychoeducation in the form of cognitive behavioral therapies for somatic and medical disorders can prevent unnecessary physician visits and dramatically reduce costs for services (Friedman, Sobel, Myers, Caudill, & Benson, 1995). Ross, Hamilton, and Smith (1995) report that physicians can dramatically decrease medical utilization and medical costs by treating psychological problems directly or by referring to an appropriate mental health professional. In general, meta-analyses suggest that overall medical expenditures are reduced by an average of 20% for psychological interventions (Chiles, Lambert, & Hatch, 1999). However, no randomized controlled trials are currently available using only depressed patients.

Group psychotherapy is a highly cost-effective treatment for depression and is a great deal less expensive than providing medication. As discussed earlier, recent literature suggests that not only is CBT as effective as medication treatments, but that this therapy sustains decreased depressive symptomatology for longer periods, results in fewer relapses, and is much less expensive than pharmacotherapeutic treatments (Antonuccio et al., 1997). For this reason, we propose that behavioral health-care specialists encourage physicians to refer patients meeting criteria for depression to a group CBT treatment rather than prescribing medications as a first-line treatment. (If physicians determine that medication is the best strategy, this does not preclude the additional use of therapy, which can reduce relapse rates following medication discontinuation.)

As a basic illustration of the cost-effectiveness of an 8-week group treatment of depression compared with an 8-week course of pharmacotherapy alone (which we recognize is a substandard dosing period), we offer a financial breakdown of potential savings for 300 patients as shown in Table 3.1. These figures make specific assumptions about the cost of paying a therapist hourly for delivering the group treatment and writing session notes. The calculations for the therapist's per-hour rate assume a base salary of $55,000 per year or $26.44 per hour. We will use the generic form of Prozac (fluoxetine), which is estimated at $8.50 per week, based on an average of price quotes at national pharmacies for a standard dosage of this medication. Currently, SSRIs such as Prozac are most frequently prescribed for the treatment of depression. Only two SSRIs are available in the generic form (fluoxetine and fluvoxamine), while all other SSRIs and other atypical antidepressants are not available in the generic form. In the case where generic medications are unavailable, patients or managed health-care companies must pay full price for these name-brand medications. We have tried to make balanced conservative estimates of price for both treatment conditions.

Table 3.1 shows that if there are 10 patients per group in the therapy condition, and one therapist sees six groups per week, it would take five therapists to see 300 patients in 8 weeks. We have included the cost of the treatment manuals given to the patients and group leaders at an estimated $5 per manual. At these rates, 300 patients seen in the psychosocial intervention condition would cost $17,389 total, or $58 per patient. In contrast, 300 patients prescribed the SSRI (Prozac)

TABLE 3.1 Comparison of Psychosocial Intervention Versus Pharmacotherapy for 300 Patients for 8 Weeks

Group Treatment Costs		Medication Costs	
Therapist per hour rate (based on $55,000/yr)	$26	Physician rate per hour (based on $150,00/yr)	$75
Per session cost based on 2-hour sessions +.5 hr notes, etc.	$66	Two medication visits per patient in 8 weeks	$150
Per therapist per group of 10 patients with 8 sessions at 2.5 hrs	$529	Total cost for psychiatrist visits for 300 patients	$45,000
Per therapist cost for 60 patients in 6 groups run by 1 therapist	$3,173	Cost per week for fluoxetine (generic for Prozac)	$8.50
Total cost for all therapists with 5 therapists for all 8 sessions	$15,864	Cost per week for 300 patients on fluoxetine	$2,550
300 manuals for patients + 5 therapists	$1,525	Total cost for 300 pts for 8 weeks of fluoxetine	$20,400
Total cost for 300 patients for 8 weeks of treatment	$17,389	Total cost for 300 pts for 8 weeks of medication with physician visits	$65,400
TOTAL COST per patient for 8 weeks of treatment	$58	TOTAL COST per patient for 8 weeks of treatment	$218

for 8 weeks with two medication management visits with a physician (at $75 per hour based on a salary of $150,000 per year) would cost a total of $65,400, or $218 per patient.

Notice that these figures could range even higher for medication costs. At least two factors would greatly increase the costs of the pharmacotherapeutic intervention. First, the treatment duration is not likely sufficiently long. It is more likely that patients would take an SSRI for 16 weeks or longer, increasing the cost for 300 patients to $130,800, or $436 per patient using the generic drug, fluoxetine. Second, the most commonly prescribed antidepressant at the time of this printing was Zoloft (sertraline). Using these calculations for 8 weeks of treatment, the total cost for 8 weeks of treatment for 300 patients on Zoloft would be $87,000, or $290 per patient, a figure five times that of per-patient costs for psychotherapy.

Not all patients will be provided with only a psychosocial intervention. Some patients will desire a pharmacological intervention, and some physicians may feel it is a necessary part of the treatment. Still, if even a fraction of patients were referred to a group therapy intervention and not prescribed antidepressants, there would be substantial cost savings.

Quality Assurance

One of the advantages of using a cognitive behavioral intervention lies in the ongoing assessment of patient outcome. Many treatment outcome studies and manualized interventions advocate the continual assessment of progress as well as pre- and post-treatment assessments. We recommend that behavioral health-care specialists who provide a group or individual psychosocial treatment for depression employ weekly assessments of patient progress for all patients.

The BDI and BDI-2 as described above make excellent, easy to use, weekly assessment instruments. These devices are generic to patients and symptom-specific as well as sensitive to changes in depressive behaviors. We also advocate the use of weekly self-report ratings of mood such as the Daily Mood Scale developed by Muñoz and colleagues (Muñoz & Miranda, 1986). Patients are instructed to rate their mood each day on a scale of +5 to negative 5, with 0 being the patient's average, nondepressed day.

Obtaining consistent data for patients prior to, during, and following treatment serves multiple functions. First, it provides data to the patient about his or her progress in treatment. Second, the therapist can use these data to inform adjustments to the treatment as necessary. For example, if the patient made considerable progress in one area of treatment and then showed slowing in changes in the BDI scores, the behavioral health-care specialist could revisit these areas in an attempt to capitalize on changes made earlier (Callaghan, 2001). Third, these data can be used to directly communicate information about patient progress to physicians and managed care companies. Data can be presented as summary scores or graphically to indicate the direction of change over the course of treatment. Summaries of all patients could be averaged across time, providing information about the effectiveness of the intervention for a given population.

In the case of a lack of sufficient improvement, the therapist can consult with physicians to determine if an adjunctive pharmacotherapy intervention should be employed. If the patient is already taking a prescribed medication, an adjustment in dosage or type might be warranted. In any case, it is crucial that the therapist collect data to provide accountability for service provision to the patient, the physician with whom he or she is collaborating, and any managed behavioral health-care organization that requires information about the progress of patients.

Summary

We have described depression here as a complex biopsychosocial phenomenon. Despite the preponderance of antidepressants as a first-line treatment for depression, the empirical literature is clear that this is only one of many possible treatments, and that pharmacological treatments may not be the best choice of interventions for depression in a primary care setting. We advocate for the role of the behavioral health-care specialist as a central figure in the assessment and treatment of depressive disorders. This role will help ensure more accurate identification of depressed patients and a more effective treatment approach.

We have described a possible model for the integrated care of depressed patients. This model is one of many different options available to the behavioral health-care provider. Although we have emphasized a cognitive behavioral model for the psychosocial intervention, we suggest that any empirically supported therapy could easily be substituted. The key to this model is a group-based intervention that can be conducted over a relatively short period of time. Another essential ingredient to success is the ongoing collaboration between the behavioral health-care specialist and the primary care physician or other health-care agency. The consistent use of data provides important evidence for the success of the intervention and the necessary role of the behavioral care provider. Finally, continued focus on the cooperation of patients will help ensure that they are getting the most out of the intervention.

References

American Psychiatric Association. (1994). *Diagnostic and statistical manual of mental disorders* (4th ed.). Washington, DC: Author.

Altamura, A. C., & Mauri, M. (1985). Plasma concentrations, information and therapy adherence during long-term treatment with antidepressants. *British Journal of Clinical Pharmacology, 20,* 714–716.

Antonuccio, D. O. (1995). Psychotherapy for depression: No stronger medicine. *American Psychologist, 50,* 450–452.

Antonuccio, D. O., Thomas, M., & Danton, W. G. (1997). A cost-effectiveness analysis of cognitive behavior therapy and fluoxetine (Prozac) in the treatment of depression. *Behavior Therapy, 28,* 187–210.

Attkisson, C. C., & Zich, J. M. (1990). Depression screening in primary care: Clinical needs and research challenges. In C. C. Attkisson & J. M. Zich (Eds.), *Depression in primary care* (pp. 3–11). New York: Routlege.

Beck, A. T., Rush, A. J., Shaw, B. F., & Emery, G. (1979). *Cognitive therapy of depression.* New York: Guilford.

Beck, A. T., Steer, R. A., & Brown, G. K. (1996). *The Beck Depression Inventory-2.* New York: Harcourt-Brace.

Beck, A. T., Steer, R. A., & Garbin, M. G. (1988). Psychometric properties of the Beck Depression Inventory: Twenty-five years of evaluation. *Clinical Psychology Review, 8,* 77–100.

Beck, A. T., Ward, C. H., Mendelson, M., Mock, J., & Erbaugh, J. (1961). An inventory for measuring depression. *Archives of General Psychiatry, 4,* 53–63.

Blackburn, I. M., Eunson, K. M., & Bishop, S. (1986). A two-year naturalistic follow-up of depressed patients treated with cognitive therapy, pharmacotherapy, and a combination of both. *Journal of Affective Disorders, 10,* 67–75.

Brown, R. A., & Lewinsohn, P. M. (1984). A psychoeducational approach to the treatment of depression: Comparison of group, individual, and minimal contact procedures. *Journal of Consulting and Clinical Psychology, 52,* 774–783.

Budman, S. H., & Butler, S. F. (1997). The Lily family depression project: Primary care prevention in action. In N. A. Cummings, J. L. Cummings, J. N. Johnson, & N. J. Baker (Eds.), *Behavioral health in primary care: A guide for clinical integration.* (pp. 219–238). Madison, CT: Psychosocial Press/International Universities Press, Inc.

Buelow, G., Hebert, S., & Buelow, S. (2000). *Psychotherapist's resource on psychiatric medications.* Belmont, CA: Wadsworth.

Callaghan, G. M. (2001). Demonstrating clinical effectiveness for individual practitioners and clinics. *Professional Psychology: Research and Practice, 32,* 289–297.

Callaghan, G. M., Gregg, J. A., & O'Donohue, W. T. (2000, November). *Management of medical cost offset for the treatment of depression in a collaborative care setting.* Paper presented at the 34th annual meeting of the Association for the Advancement of Behavior Therapy, New Orleans, LA.

Cavanaugh, S. A., & Wettstein R. M. (1989). Emotional and cognitive dysfunction associated with medical disorders. *Journal of Psychosomatic Research, 22,* 505–514.

Charney, D., Miller, H., Licinio, J., & Salomon, R. (1995). Treatment of depression. In A. Schatzberg & C. Nemeroff (Eds.), *Textbook of psychiatry.* Washington, DC: American Psychiatric Press.

Chiles, J. A., Lambert, M. J., & Hatch, A. L. (1999). The impact of psychological interventions on medical cost offset: A meta-analytic review. *Clinical Psychology: Science and Practice, 6,* 204–220.

Coulehan, J. L., Schulberg, H. C., Block, M. R., Janosky, J. E., & Arena, V. C. (1990). Depressive symptomatology and medical comorbidity in a primary care clinic. *International Journal of Psychiatry in Medicine, 20,* 335–347.

Cummings, N. A. (1995). Impact of managed care on employment training: A primer for survival. *Professional Psychology: Research and Practice, 26,* 10–15.

Depression Guideline Panel (DGP). (1993a). *Depression in primary care: Vol. 1, Diagnosis and detection.* (Clinical Practice Guideline, No. 5, AHCPR Publication No. 93-0550). Rockville, MD: Department of Health and Human Services, Public Health Service, Agency for Health Care Policy and Research.

Depression Guideline Panel (DGP). (1993b). *Depression in primary care: Vol. 2, Treatment of major depression.* (Clinical Practice Guideline, No. 5, AHCPR Publication No. 93-0551). Rockville, MD: Department of Health and Human Services, Public Health Service, Agency for Health Care Policy and Research.

DiMatteo, M. R., Lepper, H. S., & Croghan, T. W. (2000). Depression is a risk factor for noncompliance with medical treatment: Meta-analysis of the effects of anxiety and depression on patient adherence. *Archives of Internal Medicine, 160,* 2101–2107.

Dwight-Johnson M., Unutzer J., Sherbourne C., Tang L., & Wells, K. B. (2000). Can quality improvement programs for depression in primary care address patient preferences for treatment? *Medical Care, 39,* 934–944.

Evans, M. D., Hollon, S. D., De Rubeis, R. J., Piasecki, J. M., Grove, W. M., Garvey, M. J. et al. (1992). Differential relapse following cognitive therapy and pharmacotherapy for depression. *Archives of General Psychiatry, 49,* 802–808.

Frank, E., Kupfer, D. J., Perel, J. M., Cornes, C., Jarret, J. B., Mallinger, A. G. et al. (1990). Three-year outcomes for maintenance therapies in recurrent depression. *Archives of General Psychiatry, 47,* 1093–1099.

Frank, E., Kupfer, D. J., Wagner, E. F., McEachran, A. B., & Cornes, C. (1991). Efficacy of interpersonal therapy as a maintenance treatment of recurrent depression. *Archives of General Psychiatry, 48,* 1053–1059.

Friedman, R., Sobel, D., Myers, P., Caudill, M., & Benson, A. (1995). Behavioral medicine, clinical health psychology, and cost offset. *Health Psychology, 14,* 509–518.

Howland, R. H. (1993). General health, health care utilization, and medical comorbidity in dysthymia. *International Journal of Psychiatry in Medicine, 23,* 211–238.

Katon, W. (1995). Collaborative care: Patient satisfaction, outcomes, medical cost-offset. *Journal of Family Systems Medicine, 13,* 351–365.

Katon, W., Rutter, C., Ludman, E., Von Korff, M., Lin, E., Simon, G. et al. (2001). A randomized trial of relapse prevention of depression in primary care. *Archives of General Psychiatry, 58,* 241–247.

Katon, W., Von Korff, M., Lin, E., Bush, T., & Ormel, J. (1992). Adequacy and duration of antidepressant treatment in primary care. *Medical Care, 30,* 67–76.

Katon, W., Von Korff, M., Lin, E., Walker, E., Simon, G., Bush, T. et al. (1995). Collaborative management to achieve treatment guidelines: Impact on depression in primary care. *JAMA, 273,* 1026–1031.

Keller, M. B. (1994). Dysthymia in clinical practice: Course, outcome and impact on the community. *Acta Psychiatrica Scandinavica* (supplement), *383,* 24–34.

Kupfer, D. J., Frank, E., Perel, J. M., Cornes, C., Mallinger, A. G., Thase, M. E. et al. (1992). Five-year outcomes for maintenance therapies in recurrent depression. *Archives of General Psychiatry, 49,* 769–773.

Kupfer, D. J., & Freedman, D. X. (1986). Treatment for depression. *Archives of General Psychiatry, 43,* 509–511.

Lave, J. R., Frank, R. G., Schulberg, H. C., & Kamlet, M. S. (1998). Cost-effectiveness of treatments for major depression in primary care practice. *Archives of General Psychiatry, 55,* 645–651.

Lin, E. H. B., Katon, W. J., Simon, G. E., Von Korff, M., Bush, T. M., Rutter, C. M. et al. (1997). Achieving guidelines for the treatment of depression in primary care: Is physician education enough? *Medical Care, 35,* 831–842.

McGue, M., & Christensen, K. (1997). Genetic and environmental contributions to depression symptomatology: Evidence from Danish twins 75 years of age and older. *Journal of Abnormal Psychology, 106,* 439–448.

Miranda, J., & Muñoz, R. (1994). Intervention for minor depression in primary care patients. *Psychosomatic Medicine, 56,* 136–142.

Muñoz, R. F., Hollon, S. D., McGrath, E., Rhem, L. P., & VandenBos, G. R. (1994). On the AHCPR depression in primary care guidelines: Further considerations for practitioners. *American Psychologist, 49,* 42–61.

Muñoz, R. F., & Miranda, S. (1986). *Group therapy for cognitive-behavioral treatment of depression.* Santa Monica, CA: San Francisco General Hospital Depression Clinic. [RAND (2000) Documnet MR-1198/4: available online at www.rand.org/publications.]

Muñoz, R. F., Ying, Y.-W., Bernal, G., Perez-Stable, E. J., Sorensen, J. L., Hargreaves, W. A. et al. (1995). Prevention of depression with primary care patients: A randomized controlled trial. *American Journal of Community Psychology, 23,* 199–222.

Organista, K. C., Muñoz, R. F., & Gonzalez, G. (1994). Cognitive-behavioral therapy for depression in low-income and minority medical outpatients: Description of a program and exploratory analysis. *Cognitive Therapy and Research, 18,* 241–259.

Perez-Stable, E. J., Miranda, J., Muñoz, R. F., & Ying, Y. W. (1990). Depression in medical outpatients. Underrecognition and misdiagnosis. *Archives of Internal Medicine, 150,* 1083–1088.

Robinson, L. A., Berman, J. F., & Neimeyer, R. A. (1990). Psychotherapy for the treatment of depression: A comprehensive review of controlled outcome research. *Psychological Bulletin, 108,* 30–49.

Ross, R. L., Hamilton, G. E., & Smith, G. R. (1995). Somatization disorder in primary care. *Mind/Body Medicine, 1,* 24–29.

Rost, K., Zhang, M., Fortney, J., Smith, J., & Smith, G. R. (1998). Expenditures for the treatment of major depression. *American Journal of Psychiatry, 155,* 883–888.

Rucker, L., Frye, E. B., & Cygan, R. W. (1986). Feasibility and usefulness of depression screening in medical outpatients. *Archives of Internal Medicine, 146,* 729.

Sansone, R. A., & Sansone, L. A. (1996). Dysthymic disorder: the chronic depression. *American Family Physician, 53,* 2588–2596.

Schulberg, H. C., Katon, W., Simon, G. E., & Rush, A. J. (1998). Treating major depression in primary care practice: An update of the Agency for Health Care Policy and Research Practice Guidelines. *Archives of General Psychiatry, 55,* 1121–1127.

Schulberg, H. C., Pilkonis, P. A., & Houck, P. (1998). The severity of major depression and choice of treatment in primary care practice. *Journal of Consulting and Clinical Psychology, 66,* 932–938.

Shea, M. T., Elkin, I., Imber, S. D., Sotksy, S. M., Watkins, J. T., Collins, J. F. et al. (1992). Course of depressive symptoms over follow-up: Findings from the National Institute of Mental Health treatment of depression collaborative research program. *Archives of General Psychiatry, 49*, 782–787.

Simon, G. E., & Katzelnick, D. J. (1997). Depression, use of medical services and cost-offset effects. *Journal of Psychosomatic Research, 42,* 333–344.

Simon, G., Ormel, J., VonKorff, M., & Barlow, W. (1995). Health care costs associated with depressive and anxiety disorders in primary care. *American Journal of Psychiatry, 152*, 352–357.

Simons, A. D., Murphy, G. E., Levine, J. L., & Wetzel, R. D. (1986). Cognitive therapy and pharmacotherapy for depression: Sustained improvement over one year. *Archives of General Psychiatry, 43*, 43–50.

Strosahl, K. (1996). Mind and body primary mental healthcare: New model for integrated services. *Behavioral Healthcare Tomorrow, 5*, 93–95.

Teasdale, J. D., Segal, Z.V., Williams, J. M. G., Ridgeway, V. A., Soulsby, J. M., & Lau, M. A. (2000). Prevention of relapse/recurrence in major depression by mindfulness-based cognitive therapy. *Journal of Consulting and Clinical Psychology, 68*, 615–623.

Thompson, D., Hylan, T. R., McMullen, W., Romeis, M. E., Buesching, D., & Oster, G. (1998). Predictors of a medical-offset effect among patients receiving antidepressant therapy. *American Journal of Psychiatry, 155*, 824–827.

van Gent, E. M., & Zwart, F. M. (1991). Psychoeducation of partners of bipolar-manic patients. *Journal of Affective Disorders, 21*, 15–18.

Von Korff, M., Katon, W., Bush, T., Lin, E. H. B., Simon, G., Saunders, K. et al. (1998). Treatment costs, cost offset, and cost-effectiveness of collaborative management of depression. *Psychosomatic Medicine, 60*, 143–149.

Wells, K. B., Hays, B. D., Burnam W. R., Greenfield, S., & Ware, J. E. (1989). Detection of depressive disorder for patients receiving prepaid or fee-for-service care: Results for the Medical Outcomes Society. *Journal of the American Medical Association, 262*, 3298–3302.

Wells, K. B., Sherbourne, C., Shoenbaum, M., Duan, M., Meredith, L., Unutzer, J. et al. (2000). Impact of disseminating quality improvement programs for depression in managed primary care: A randomized clinical trial. *Journal of the American Medical Association, 283*, 212–220.

Wexler, B. E., & Cicchetti, D. V. (1992). The outpatient treatment of depression: Implications of outcome research for clinical practice. *Journal of Nervous and Mental Disease, 180*, 277–286.

Zich, J. M., Atkisson, C. C., & Greenfield, T. K. (1990). Screening for depression in primary care clinics: The CES-D and the BDI. *International Journal of Psychiatry in Medicine, 20*, 259–277.

Suggested Reading/Websites for Depression

Suggested Reading

Burns, D. D. (1999). Feeling good: The new mood therapy. Avon.

Klein, D. F., & Wender, P. H. (1994). Understanding depression: A complete guide to its diagnosis and treatment. Oxford Press.

Papolos, D. (1997). Overcoming depression (3rd ed.). Quill Press.

Websites for Depression

Depression consumer information: http://www.depression.com/

National Alliance for Mentally Ill: http://www.nami.org/

National Institute of Mental Health: http://www.nimh.nih.gov/publicat/depressionmenu.cfm

Chapter 4
Anxiety Disorders in Primary Care

LAURA CAMPBELL-SILLS, JESSICA R. GRISHAM, AND TIMOTHY A. BROWN

Relevance, Epidemiology, and Cost of Anxiety Disorders in Primary Care

Individuals with anxiety disorders frequently seek medical care from a primary care physician for the treatment of their somatic symptoms (Katon, 1984; Kennedy & Schwab, 1997; Roy-Byrne, 1996). Because anxiety symptoms often resemble those associated with various medical conditions, patients may present with cardiac, neurological, or gastrointestinal complaints such as chest pain, palpitations, diarrhea, headache, or dizziness (see Table 4.1). Patients with anxiety disorders are also more likely to have specific co-morbid medical disorders such as angina, mitral valve prolapse, hypertension, peptic ulcer disease, or thyroid disease (Rogers et al., 1994). An anxiety disorder may exacerbate an underlying medical illness (e.g., coronary artery disease or asthma), or may mimic symptoms of a medical illness (Karajgi, Rifkin, Doddi, & Kolli, 1990; Kawachi et al., 1994; Rogers et al., 1994).

Recent epidemiological studies, such as the Epidemiological Catchment Area (ECA) Study and the National Comorbidity Study (NCS), have found 1-year prevalence rates of anxiety disorders of 12.6% and 17.2%, respectively (Kessler et al., 1994; Regier et al., 1993). With respect to primary care settings, a report from the World Health Organization on anxiety syndromes in five European primary care settings found that 15.6% of patients suffered from an anxiety disorder (Weiller, Bisserbe, Maier, & Lecrubier, 1998). A U.S. study found a similar current prevalence of 14.6% and a lifetime prevalence of 23.9% in primary care settings (Nisenson, Pepper, Schwenk, & Coyne, 1998).

Approximately 50% of patients with anxiety and mood disorders receive their mental health care in primary care settings (Harman, Rollman, Hanusa, Lenze, & Shear, 2002; Regier et al., 1993), and some evidence suggests that these patients receive suboptimal care. In a study of office visits for anxiety disorders from 1985 to 1998, Harman et al. (2002) found that treatment was offered by primary care clinicians in only 54% of visits that coded for a specific anxiety diagnosis. This statistic contrasted with the rate of treatment offered by psychiatrists who prescribed treatment in 95% of such visits. Furthermore, the rate of anxiety treatment in primary care is significantly lower than the rate of treatment that corresponds to depression-related visits (82%; Harman, et al., 2002).

Anxiety is often associated with considerable impairment and can affect the outcome and cost of medical treatment (Fifer et al., 1994; Ormel, Oldehinkel, Brilman, & van den Brink, 1993; Sherbourne, Jackson, Meredith, Camp, & Wells, 1996). Owing to the strong somatic component of

TABLE 4.1 Medical Conditions That May Cause or Resemble Anxiety

Type of Medical Condition	Examples of Specific Conditions
Endocrine	Hyper- and Hypothyroidism
	Pheochromocytoma
	Hypoglycemia
	Hyperadrenocorticism
Cardiovascular	Congestive Heart Failure
	Pulmonary Embolism
	Arrhythmia
	Mitral Valve Prolapse
Respiratory	Asthma
	Chronic Obstructive Pulmonary Disease
	Pneumonia
	Hyperventilation
Metabolic	Vitamin B12 Deficiency
	Porphyria
Neurological	Neoplasms
	Vestibular Dysfunction
	Encephalitis
	Seizure Disorders
Substance Intoxication	Alcohol, Amphetamine, Caffeine, Cannabis, Cocaine, Hallucinogens, Inhalants, Phencyclidine, and Others
Substance Withdrawal	Alcohol, Cocaine, Sedatives, Hypnotics, Anxiolytics, and Others
Other	Pregnancy
	Perimenopause

anxiety, the presence of an anxiety disorder may contribute to the development of certain medical conditions and may be a barrier to optimal care and treatment response (Klerman, Weissman, Ouellette, Johnson, & Greenwald, 1991; Ormel et al., 1993). Economic analyses suggest that patients with anxiety disorders tend to overutilize health-care services and resources (Roy-Byrne, 1996). Patients who are repeatedly evaluated or treated for a physical symptom that is a manifestation of an anxiety disorder (e.g., palpitations) may be inefficiently using health-care resources without achieving lasting relief from their illnesses.

A study by Kennedy and Schwab (1997) examined the utilization of medical specialists by 80 anxiety disorder patients and 14 nonanxious adults in a 5-year period. Interestingly, the type of medical care sought by anxiety patients depended somewhat on the type of disorder. Although patients with panic disorder (PD) frequently were seen in primary care family medicine and by neurology specialists, patients with generalized anxiety disorder (GAD) were often seen by gastroenterologists, presumably due to physical conditions, such as irritable bowel syndrome, that frequently accompany chronic tension and anxiety (Kennedy & Schwab, 1997). The results also suggested that medical utilization of patients with PD was particularly high, with 83% of these patients seeing their primary care physicians compared with 36% in the control group. Similarly, Leon, Portera, and Weissman (1995) analyzed data from the ECA Study (Regier et al., 1993) and found that nearly 30% of individuals with PD had used the general medical system for emotional, alcohol, or drug-related problems in the 6 months prior to the study interview. Furthermore, individuals with any anxiety disorder were more likely than nonanxious individuals to seek help from emergency rooms.

Simon, Ormel, VonKorff, and Barlow (1995) also examined the overall health costs associated with anxiety and depression among 2,110 primary care patients in a health maintenance organization (HMO). The results indicated that primary care patients with anxiety or depressive disorders had significantly higher baseline costs ($2,390) than patients with no anxiety or depressive disorder ($1,397). These cost differences reflected higher utilization of general medical services rather than higher mental health treatment costs and persisted after adjusting for medical morbidity.

In addition to costs associated with health-care overutilization, the prevalence of anxiety disorders in the community also results in substantial social costs. Patients with anxiety disorders are often impaired emotionally, physically, and economically, resulting in the social costs of decreased productivity and increased unemployment (Olfson et al., 1997). Leon et al. (1995) found that men with PD, phobias, or obsessive-compulsive disorder (OCD) were more likely to be chronically unemployed and to receive disability or welfare. In addition, Telch, Schmidt, Jaimez, Jacquin, and Harrington (1995) found that PD patients displayed significant impairment in quality of life.

Co-morbidity of anxiety with other mental disorders also affects health-care outcome and costs. Anxiety and depression often co-occur, with co-morbidity rates of major depression with PD and GAD in primary care settings that range up to 60% (Brown, Schulberg, Madonia, Shear, & Houck, 1996). Co-morbid depression and anxiety are associated with greater severity of depression, poorer psychosocial functioning, and poorer treatment outcomes (Coryell, Endicott, & Winokur, 1992), and may also be associated with particularly high health-care costs. Brown et al. (1996) showed that patients treated for depression with a co-morbid anxiety disorder took longer to recover, and those with lifetime PD showed a lack of response to pharmacotherapy and psychotherapy. To overcome the obstacles involved in treating depressed primary care patients with co-morbid anxiety, several researchers (Coplan & Gorman, 1990; Fawcett, 1990) have suggested evaluating and treating the symptoms of anxiety as soon as the patient begins treatment to improve compliance with antidepressant medication.

Successful treatment may produce not only significant medical cost offsets, but also meaningful improvements in quality of life. Salvador-Carulla, Segu, Fernandez-Cano, and Canet (1995) assessed the costs before and after the provision of effective treatment for PD. They measured lost workdays, health-care services used, and patients' assessment of general functioning, improvement, severity of symptoms, and level of disability. Overall, the authors found a 94% offset in these costs associated with PD with effective treatment.

Although more research is needed on treatment of anxiety disorders in primary care, timely recognition, accurate diagnoses, appropriate treatment, referral, and support are likely to reduce the financial burden of anxiety-related visits in primary care and to medical specialists. Moreover, the movement toward integrating mental health services into primary care settings may produce additional reductions in cost. A cost-effectiveness study of an English community mental health service based in primary care compared costs of services for patients with new episodes of anxiety and depression treated either in the mental health service or the traditional hospital-based service. The patients seen by the community primary care service incurred lower health services costs and were more satisfied with their treatment than patients seen by the hospital service, even when controlling for illness severity (Goldberg, Jackson, Gater, Campbell, & Jennett, 1996).

The integration of mental health services into primary care settings is often labeled *collaborative care*. Roy-Byrne, Katon, Cowley, and Russo (2001) tested a collaborative care intervention for PD against usual care in three primary care clinics. The collaborative care intervention consisted of sending educational materials about PD and medication to patients, scheduling two psychiatrist visits and two phone contacts in the first 8 weeks of medication treatment, and providing up to five additional phone calls within the 12-month follow-up period. Patients who received the collaborative care intervention were more likely to receive adequate medication and to comply with treatment recommendations. These patients also manifested greater symptom improvement and less disability, particularly in the first 3 to 6 months of the treatment phase. Furthermore, the collaborative care intervention was cost-effective (Katon, Roy-Byrne, Russo, & Cowley, 2002). Patients who received the intervention had an average of 74 fewer anxiety-free days and no significant differences in outpatient costs. There was a 70% probability that collaborative care was a "dominant" intervention (i.e., more effective *and* less expensive), with a savings of $4 per anxiety-free day (Katon et al., 2002).

In summary, the evidence demonstrating the high prevalence and cost of anxiety disorders in the community emphasizes the need for the accurate assessment, treatment, and prevention of anxiety disorders in primary care settings. Because of the close interaction between mental and physical components of anxiety, patients with anxiety disorders should be viewed from an integrative perspective that identifies psychological, social, and physiological vulnerabilities, stressors, and symptoms. Clinical research is beginning to elucidate strategies that are tailored to primary care settings that may help to achieve this ideal.

Assessment of Anxiety Disorders

The Challenges of Establishing a Diagnosis

Primary care settings are often the first point of assessment of a patient's anxiety difficulties. The task of assessment is complicated by the fact that patients vary considerably in their presentations and often emphasize somatic rather than psychological distress. Anxiety may be accompanied by symptoms such as heart-racing or palpitations, shortness of breath, dizziness, muscle tension, insomnia, and a variety of other physical sensations (see Table 4.2). Patients who experience panic attacks or generalized anxiety may attribute their symptoms to an underlying physical problem, and therefore they consult a medical doctor rather than a mental health clinician. The primary care clinician must often rule out possible medical problems before making a conclusive anxiety disorder diagnosis. A second level of differential diagnosis involves determining which anxiety disorder diagnosis best describes the patient's problems. Primary care providers may have difficulty with this second level of differential diagnosis, in that the majority of primary care visits for anxiety disorders are coded "anxiety state, unspecified" (Harman et al., 2002).

With regard to the first level of differential diagnosis (distinguishing anxiety from physical disorders), PD stands out as being particularly susceptible to interpretation by both patient and clinician as a physical problem. Indeed, one need only peruse the diagnostic criteria for a panic attack to understand why patients assume that something is wrong with them physically. The presence of sensations associated with autonomic arousal is compounded by the tendency of patients with PD to interpret these sensations in a catastrophic manner. Common interpretations of panic symptoms include beliefs that one is having a heart attack, stroke, or fainting spell. Thus, patients often present to the emergency room or to primary care facilities in extreme distress over what they perceive as a dangerous heart condition or neurological problem.

Primary care clinicians who encounter patients complaining of persistent bouts of uncomfortable physical sensations typically evaluate many aspects of the patient's physical functioning. Anxiety can produce symptoms resembling cardiac, respiratory, and neurological disorders as well as pregnancy (Spiegel & Barlow, 2000). At times, a physical condition can explain the patient's symptoms and be successfully treated via medical intervention. However, in many cases diagnostic test results are negative and an assessment of anxiety or other psychological problems is necessary.

TABLE 4.2 Somatic Symptoms Commonly Associated With Anxiety

Type of Anxiety	Specific Symptoms*
Panic Attack	Palpitations
	Accelerated Heart Rate
	Sweating
	Trembling
	Shortness of Breath
	Choking Sensations
	Chest Pain
	Nausea
	Abdominal Distress
	Dizziness, Lightheadedness, Imbalance
	Paresthesias
	Chills
	Hot Flushes
Generalized Anxiety	Insomnia
	Fatigue
	Muscle Tension
	Restlessness

*Both panic attacks and generalized anxiety can accompany the full range of anxiety disorders. These symptoms are not diagnostic of any specific anxiety disorder.

Although PD is the anxiety disorder with the most obvious physiological component, other anxiety disorders are also encountered in primary care. Empirical studies suggest that GAD is very frequently encountered in primary care settings (e.g., Shear & Schulberg, 1995). Associated symptoms of GAD include restlessness, fatigue, irritability, insomnia, concentration problems, and muscle tension. It has been noted that many anxious patients who present to primary care physicians do not meet full diagnostic criteria for GAD, but rather exhibit "subsyndromal" generalized anxiety or mixed anxiety-depression (Katon & Roy-Byrne, 1991; Olfson et al., 1996; Rickels & Schweizer, 1997). These individuals will likely emphasize physical problems when presenting to a primary care doctor, and it may take knowledgeable probing about psychological factors to determine if the problem is anxiety based.

Even when a diagnosable physical condition is present, this does not rule out the possibility of a coexisting anxiety disorder. Physicians must consider whether the patient's level of subjective distress or impairment exceeds that which would be expected given the medical diagnosis. For example, some patients with benign heart conditions experience considerable distress and life interference due to their *fear* of the physical sensations that arise on occasion. They may avoid activities or situations due to concerns about provoking symptoms, even though these symptoms are not harmful. In these cases, a co-morbid anxiety diagnosis may be appropriate.

Performing a Preliminary Assessment of Anxiety

An anxiety assessment should be part of the primary care evaluation when the patient's distress is either (1) not explained by any underlying physical problem, or (2) not *fully* explained by any underlying physical problem (e.g., in the case of a patient whose life is drastically altered by a benign medical condition). The first requirement for an adequate anxiety assessment is a thorough understanding of the criteria that define the various anxiety disorders in the *Diagnostic and Statistical Manual of Mental Disorders*, 4th edition (*DSM-IV*; American Psychiatric Association, 1994). Knowledge of the diagnostic criteria allows the primary care clinician to conduct an efficient preliminary assessment of the patient's problem.

The primary care clinician who is armed with knowledge about the characteristics of various anxiety disorders is prepared in one important sense. However, this technical knowledge may be to no avail if the topic of anxiety is not approached in a sensitive, nonthreatening manner. Indeed, patients who present to primary care clinicians rather than mental health professionals may be those who are most resistant to a psychological conceptualization of their problems. Although anxiety disorders are quite prevalent in the general population, the stigma associated with psychological problems remains, and it may influence patients' descriptions of their difficulties (Roy-Byrne & Katon, 2000). Primary care physicians must approach inquiry about psychological problems in a delicate and empathic manner. It is probably worth the time to spend a few minutes discussing the relationships between psychological stress and physical symptoms, as well as reassuring the patient that such problems are common and treatable. Doctors may also need to reinterpret psychological problems for patients who think that having an anxiety disorder means they are "crazy" or that their physical symptoms are not real. An example of this type of feedback follows:

> We have completed numerous tests for physical problems and each one has come back negative. I know this may be frustrating for you, since you are certainly experiencing physical discomfort. However, it does not appear that any cardiac or gastrointestinal disease is causing your unpleasant symptoms. Sometimes we think of mind and body as being completely separate, but in fact they are very intricately related. For example, sometimes people have stomach trouble or headaches when they are under stress or having personal problems. I wonder if some of your physical symptoms might be the result of stress or psychological factors. If they are, that would be important to know because there are effective treatments out there for such problems that could alleviate your symptoms. Would it be all right if I asked you some questions to find out if this type of treatment might be helpful for you?

Before moving into specific questions concerning anxiety or other psychological problems, the clinician should review the rules pertaining to doctor-patient confidentiality. Patients who understand the breadth and limits of confidentiality are more likely to feel at ease discussing psychological difficulties.

The *DSM-IV* diagnostic criteria can form the basis for the screening questions that are necessary for rapid assessment. Structured diagnostic interviews for anxiety disorders often include such questions, although their length precludes them from being fully administered in a primary care appointment. However, these interviews can be a useful source of ideas about how to ask patients about psychological problems and for choosing questions that are likely to lead to accurate diagnosis (Brown, Di Nardo, & Barlow, 1994; First, Gibbon, Spitzer, & Williams, 1996). For example, the patient who reports alternation between restlessness, headaches, and insomnia (symptoms of generalized anxiety) might be asked, "Do you tend to worry frequently about many different life matters?" or "Do you ever feel that it is hard to put your worries aside when you would like to focus on other things?" Excessive, uncontrollable worry is the defining feature of GAD and thus should be a subject of inquiry. Possible screening questions for all of the major anxiety disorders are presented in Table 4.3.

If a patient endorses a problem that seems to fit the criteria for an anxiety disorder, then two approaches may be taken. The first is to refer the patient for a comprehensive anxiety evaluation by

TABLE 4.3 Screening Questions for Commonly Diagnosed Anxiety Disorders

Disorder	Possible Screening Questions
Panic Disorder	"Do you experience sudden unexpected rushes of fear accompanied by uncomfortable physical sensations?" If yes: "When do you tend to have these feelings? In what kinds of situations?" If the patient reports attacks that are circumscribed to one type of situation (e.g., social situations): "Do the rushes of fear ever come unexpectedly or in situations that do not involve _____(e.g., public speaking)?" If yes, probe further for panic disorder. If no unexpected attacks, consider other diagnoses.
Agoraphobia	"Are you avoiding any situations or feeling apprehensive about doing certain things due to fears of becoming panicky or having uncomfortable sensations?" If yes: "Which types of situations?" Again, probe to determine if the avoidance is circumscribed enough to assign another diagnosis (e.g., social phobia).
Social Phobia	"Do you feel anxious or nervous about interacting with or speaking in front of other people?" "Do you often worry about embarrassing yourself in front of others?"
Generalized Anxiety Disorder	"Do you frequently worry about many aspects of your life?" "Do you often find yourself worrying about things that most people would call 'minor matters'?" "Is it difficult for you to stop worrying for a while to focus on other activities?"
Obsessive-Compulsive Disorder	"Do you ever have unwanted or intrusive thoughts or images that keep recurring to you?" "Do these thoughts or images bother you a great deal or seem inappropriate?" "Do you ever feel driven to repeat some behavior over and over again or until it feels 'just right'?"
Specific Phobia	"Do you have any strong fears of objects or situations, or do you feel the need to avoid anything at all costs?"
Posttraumatic Stress Disorder	"Have you ever experienced or witnessed a traumatic or life-threatening situation?" "Do you ever have intrusive memories, thoughts, or dreams about those experiences that upset you?"

a specialist. Alternatively, the primary care clinician can undertake the task of differentiating between the various anxiety diagnoses. This is an extremely important phase of diagnosis, because distinct empirically supported treatments exist for each anxiety disorder. Clinicians must also consider other psychological problems that share common features with anxiety, such as mood disorders and somatoform disorders. To illustrate the challenges of differential diagnosis, two apparently straightforward symptoms—panic attacks and worry—will be discussed in terms of their relation to various psychiatric diagnoses.

The Context of Panic Attacks

Establishing the context in which panic attacks occur is very important, because "panic attack" is not a psychiatric diagnosis. Panic attacks can be associated with any of the anxiety disorders (Barlow, Brown, & Craske, 1994), and in only a subset of cases is the diagnosis of PD appropriate. Clinicians must establish whether attacks occur unexpectedly across situations or if they occur exclusively in the context of a specific situation. For instance, individuals with social phobia or specific phobia often experience panic attacks, but these attacks are always cued by the presence of the feared stimulus (e.g., air travel, driving, public speaking). On the other hand, individuals who receive a diagnosis of PD experience at least some "out of the blue" panic attacks that are not predictable based on a specific feared situation.

Panic attacks can also occur in the context of GAD, and these attacks may be difficult to distinguish from the unexpected attacks that characterize PD. However, upon careful examination it becomes clear that the patient with generalized anxiety experiences attacks as the culmination of intense worry. Patients sometimes describe "working themselves into a panic attack" and emphasize the content of the worry rather than the panic symptoms as the key feature of the experience. Similarly, individuals with OCD may experience panic attacks when exposed to the content of their obsessions or when prevented from engaging in compulsive behaviors (e.g., when confronted with a contaminant or when prevented from checking an appliance). Once again, the focus of the patient's distress is likely to be the exposure to the obsessional content rather than the symptoms of anxiety.

It is also very important to determine if panic attacks are occurring in response to internal or external traumatic cues, as in the case of individuals with posttraumatic stress disorder (PTSD). Patients with a trauma history often experience autonomic arousal and even full-blown panic attacks when confronted with intrusive recollections or external cues that remind them of the traumatic event. Treatment for PD would not be helpful for most of these individuals because the provocative traumatic material would be left unaddressed.

In summary, it is important to recognize that panic attacks can be a feature of almost any anxiety disorder. Particularly when presenting to primary care, patients may focus on descriptions of panic-like symptoms because it is more culturally acceptable to discuss physical problems with a doctor. If it becomes clear that a patient is experiencing panic attacks, it is important to determine the greater context surrounding them to facilitate accurate diagnosis and appropriate treatment selection.

The Content of Worry

Like panic attacks, worry can be a characteristic of many anxiety disorders. Excessive, uncontrollable worry about many different life matters is the central feature of GAD and therefore clinicians may be inclined to assign this diagnosis if a patient describes him- or herself as a worrier. However, upon further inquiry it may become apparent that the focus of the patient's worry is too circumscribed to merit a diagnosis of GAD. Socially anxious individuals worry tremendously about upcoming social encounters, but may worry little about finances or health. People with PD may worry continually about when their next attack will occur; however, this should be considered a feature of PD rather than GAD. Clinicians will recognize that individuals who truly have GAD worry about many different areas of their lives, such as minor matters, health, relationships, work, and finances. If a patient reports worry about one aspect of his or her life, the clinician should probe further to achieve a picture of how diffuse the worry content is. If the worry can be better accounted for by a more specific anxiety disorder, then GAD should not be assigned.

Generalized anxiety also shares common features with mood disorders, which are also commonly encountered in primary care settings. In general, it is good practice to inquire about depressed mood if patients endorse anxiety symptoms, because mood and anxiety disorders are frequently co-morbid (Brown & Barlow, 1992; Brown, Campbell, Lehman, Grisham, & Mancill, 2001; Wittchen, Zhao, Kessler, & Eaton, 1994). This is particularly important in the case of GAD because many of its associated symptoms overlap with symptoms of depression. In fact, *DSM-IV* precludes assigning a diagnosis of GAD if the worry and tension occur exclusively during the course of a mood disorder. To facilitate selection of appropriate treatment, the primary care clinician should determine whether the patient's predominant mood involves worry and tension, or sadness and hopelessness.

Judging the Severity of the Problem

Depending on the severity of the anxiety problem, different levels of treatment may be indicated. For individuals in extreme amounts of distress, inpatient or intensive outpatient treatments may be the best option. For other patients, weekly outpatient sessions or self-directed therapy may be sufficient to treat the problem. Because efficient allocation of resources is a major issue in primary care, assessing the severity of the presenting problem is quite important. Patients who require intensive treatment should not be referred for brief, weekly outpatient therapy that is bound to fail. Likewise, it is important to recognize those patients who need a minimal amount of direct attention from the clinician, so that clinical hours are open for those who require more support. Appropriate allocation of resources begins with an accurate judgment of the severity of the patient's anxiety problem. The patient's level of subjective distress and the objective amount of life interference both contribute to an estimation of severity.

Primary care clinicians will likely get one sample of the patient's subjective distress in the consulting room. However, it is also important to ask how much the patient feels bothered by the problem on an ongoing basis. Does it cause him or her distress every day? For most of the day? Or does the problem only enter the patient's awareness occasionally? Patients with severe anxiety disorders often feel consumed by anxiety, and they report a tremendous amount of subjective distress. On the other hand, some patients feel that their anxiety is manageable for long periods of time and then becomes exacerbated (e.g., when under stress). These varying levels of distress influence the clinician's appraisal of the disorder severity.

Anxiety disorders frequently interfere with people's work, relationships, and leisure activities. Simply asking the patient, "In what ways has the anxiety interfered with your life?" is likely to provide useful information about the degree of life interference. Many patients function extremely well despite anxiety problems, and they typically describe few limits on their work and leisure. Others are truly debilitated by anxiety and are unable to sustain relationships or employment due to the severity of their disorders. Striking examples include the patient with agoraphobia who is housebound, and the individual with social phobia who must quit his or her job or drop out of school due to fear of interacting with others. Patients who do not elaborate spontaneously on the ways that anxiety affects their lives should be asked directly about the effects of anxiety on their work, relationships, leisure activities, and overall quality of life.

Tools That Aid in Anxiety Diagnosis

The financial and time pressures associated with primary care settings constrain the assessment process in important ways. Many useful forms of assessment, such as structured interviews and behavioral assessment, are simply not feasible in primary care settings. Therefore, this section of the chapter will focus on tools that aid in rapid assessment. When used in conjunction with a professional's carefully selected questions, these assessment tools should facilitate reliable and valid diagnosis. However, rapid assessment can be risky—particularly when dealing with a group of disorders that have overlapping features (see section above on differential diagnosis). Given that *distinct* empirically supported treatments exist for each of the anxiety disorders, accurate assessment results may truly mean the difference between effective and ineffective treatment. The best protection against misdiagnosis is an understanding of key features that differentiate among the disorders and a willingness to continue assessment beyond the initial meeting with the patient. As with any other diagnostic process, clinicians should be alert for further information that converges with or contradicts their initial impressions.

Once the primary care professional suspects that a patient's presenting problem is anxiety based, a preliminary conceptualization is developed through screening questions and unstructured questioning.

As noted above, the *DSM-IV* and structured clinical interviews may serve as resources for generation of screening and follow-up questions (see Table 4.3). In order to obtain additional evidence for diagnosis, clinicians may elect to utilize brief self-report inventories that target different types of anxiety symptoms. A number of self-report instruments have sound psychometric properties and are simple to administer and score. Table 4.4 presents a number of these questionnaires, as well as the anxiety disorders for which they are most relevant.

Some recent efforts have been focused on developing screening measures for anxiety that are specifically intended for use in primary care clinics. This approach envisions the screening process occurring in the waiting room before patients see their provider; in addition, the provider can use the information obtained in the screening to streamline their consultation. The Beck Anxiety Inventory for Primary Care (BAI-PC) is a seven-item scale that employs a cutoff score of 5 for detection of clinically significant anxiety (Beck, Steer, Ball, Ciervo, & Kabat, 1997). Using this cutoff score, the BAI-PC successfully identifies approximately 85% of patients with clinical anxiety disorders, while screening out about 80% of those individuals who do not have clinically significant anxiety (Beck et al., 1997; Mori et al., 2003). Mori et al. (2003) also report that the BAI-PC is a useful measure for detecting cases of depression and PTSD.

Questionnaire developers face a challenge in balancing brevity with diagnostic accuracy. Very brief questionnaires are often effective in detecting cases of a disorder, but tend to generate many false positives as well. For example, a two-question screen for PD was reported to have excellent sensitivity (catching 94–100% of true PD cases) but poor specificity (screening out only 25–59% of true negative cases; Stein et al., 1999). The finding that clinicians could be alerted to most true cases of PD on the basis of just two questions is impressive. However, the low specificity of the screen

TABLE 4.4 Self-Report Instruments for Measuring Anxiety

Questionnaire	# Items	Relevant Disorders*
Albany Panic and Phobia Questionnaire (Rapee, Craske, & Barlow, 1995)	27	PD, Social Phobia
Anxiety Sensitivity Index (Peterson & Reiss, 1992)	16	PD
Autonomic Nervous System Questionnaire (Stein et al., 1999)	2	PD
Beck Anxiety Inventory (Beck & Steer, 1990)	21	PD, GAD
Beck Anxiety Inventory for Primary Care (Beck, Steer, Ball, Ciervo, & Kabat, 1997)	7	PD, GAD
Depression Anxiety Stress Scales (Lovibond & Lovibond, 1995)	42	PD, GAD, Depression
Maudsley Obsessive-Compulsive Inventory (Hodgson & Rachman, 1977)	30	OCD
Penn State Worry Questionnaire (Meyer, Miller, Metzger, & Borkovec, 1990)	16	GAD
Posttraumatic Diagnostic Scale (Foa, Cashman, Jaycox, & Perry, 1997)	17	PTSD
PTSD Checklist (Weathers, Litz, Herman, Huska, & Keane, 1993)	17	PTSD
Social Interaction Anxiety Scale (Mattick & Clarke, 1998)	20	Social Phobia

*PD = panic disorder; GAD = generalized anxiety disorder; OCD = obsessive-compulsive disorder; PTSD = posttraumatic stress disorder.

creates an efficiency problem, in that providers will spend time assessing for PD in many patients who screened positive but do not actually have the disorder.

In addition to these disorder-specific questionnaires, general screening instruments for psychological problems have recently become available for use in primary care settings. Two of the more popular interviews are the Primary Care Evaluation of Mental Health Disorders (PRIME-MD; Spitzer et al., 1994) and the Mini-International Neuropsychiatric Interview (MINI; Sheehan et al., 1998). Each of these interviews includes a self-report symptom checklist that patients complete before meeting with their clinician. Brief clinician-administered interviews are used to follow up problem areas identified by the patient. The clinician-administered section can be administered quite rapidly, with an average of 8.4 minutes for the PRIME-MD and 15 minutes for the MINI (Sheehan et al., 1998; Spitzer et al., 1994). Closed-ended (yes or no) questions address symptoms of *DSM-IV* anxiety disorders, and diagnosis simply requires a symptom count.

In general, interviews such as the PRIME-MD and MINI have adequate reliability and validity. However, their sensitivity for detecting certain anxiety disorders is below the optimum level. With regard to the PRIME-MD, 57% of PD and GAD cases (as diagnosed by mental health professionals) were correctly identified by primary care clinicians using the PRIME-MD (Spitzer et al., 1994). The developers of the MINI also compared diagnostic results using their screening instrument to expert opinion. They found that 44% of PD cases and 67% of GAD cases identified by psychiatrists were detected using the MINI (Sheehan et al., 1998).

Although the PRIME-MD and MINI allow for diagnosis of psychological disorders in significantly less time than a full psychological evaluation, even a 10–15 minute interview may be too time-consuming to be employed in a typical primary care setting. To remedy this problem, studies are being conducted that investigate more time-efficient methods of administering these types of screens. For example, a self-report version of the PRIME-MD (Patient Health Questionnaire; PHQ) has been evaluated for use in primary care settings (Spitzer, Kroenke, & Williams, 1999). Initial results suggest that diagnoses obtained from physicians' reviews of PHQ were in good agreement with diagnoses made by independent mental health professionals. In addition, physicians were typically able to review the PHQ in less than 3 minutes, which represents a significant improvement in time-efficiency over the clinician-administered version.

Another diagnostic tool that aims to decrease the time burden of assessment for primary care providers is the Symptom Driven Diagnostic System for Primary Care (SDDS-PC; Weissman et al., 1998). The SDDS-PC can be reliably administered by health care professionals other than doctors (e.g., nurses). This tool first requires patients to complete a brief written questionnaire that screens for depression, GAD, PD, OCD, alcohol- and substance-use disorders, and suicidality. A nurse then administers a computerized diagnostic interview only for the disorders for which the patient screened positive. Preliminary investigation suggests that nurses take approximately 1.5 to 3.6 minutes to complete the diagnostic interview, depending on the diagnosis being queried (Weissman et al., 1998). The computerized interview subsequently produces a 1-page summary report with provisional diagnoses that aids the primary provider in probing efficiently for mental health problems.

Although use of the SDDS-PC produced moderate-to-excellent agreement between nurse and primary care physician diagnoses, agreement between physicians using the SDDS-PC and mental health professionals using a structured clinical interview was in the moderate-to-poor range for the anxiety diagnoses (Weissman et al., 1998). Typically, primary care physicians and mental health professionals agreed that the patient suffered *symptoms* of a particular diagnosis, but disagreed on whether the patient met full criteria for that specific diagnosis. The actual clinical implications of this type of disagreement remain unclear.

A final tool that may improve both efficiency and accuracy of primary care anxiety diagnoses is the Quick PsychoDiagnostics Panel (QPD; Shedler, Beck, & Bensen, 2000). The QPD is unique in that it is fully self-administered and therefore requires no clinician time for administration or scoring. Patients complete true/false questions on hand-held computer units that are programmed to screen for nine psychiatric disorders. The computer program is similar to a structured interview, in that the progression of questions is based on patients' answers to critical items (i.e., follow-up questions are only asked if the probe items are endorsed). Shedler et al. (2000) report that the QPD takes patients an average of 6.2 minutes to complete. A diagnostic report can be printed immediately after questionnaire completion, which provides the clinician with scores indicating the severity of disorder symptoms, provisional psychiatric diagnoses, and a list of the disorder symptoms that the patient endorsed.

The QPD assesses for GAD, PD, and OCD. Like the other primary care interviews, it is currently limited in that it does not assess for several other common anxiety disorders (e.g., PTSD, social phobia). However, an initial study of the reliability, validity, and utility of the QPD suggests that this instrument successfully assesses for GAD, PD, and OCD. The QPD demonstrated good sensitivity and specificity in identifying cases of these anxiety disorders, and manifested good agreement with diagnoses obtained by a well-validated structured clinical interview (Shedler et al., 2000).

The PRIME-MD, MINI, SDDS-PC, and QPD are promising steps toward adequate screening for psychological problems in primary care. Clinicians who utilize these instruments may improve their chances of accurate diagnosis by employing some of the other assessment strategies reviewed in this chapter. In particular, differential diagnosis requires probing beyond that which is included in basic screening instruments. If time permits, clinicians are advised to add questions to screening instruments that help them determine the true focus of the patient's anxiety problem.

Assessing Treatment Outcome and Quality Assurance

It is important to note that assessment does not end once the treatment phase begins. Some of the same assessment tools described above can be used for monitoring the patient's progress during treatment. Brief questionnaires can be completed by the patient in the waiting room before each appointment with the clinician. Scores from successive sessions can be plotted on graphs to provide objective information about progress to patients, other clinicians, and third-party payers.

Combining questionnaire results with patient self-monitoring provides a more comprehensive picture of progress throughout treatment. Patients may be asked to monitor variables such as levels of anxiety, percentage of the day spent worrying, and avoidance of feared situations on a daily basis. Patient's reports of these indicators of anxiety severity can also be graphed over time to provide another view of treatment outcome. Self-monitoring can also serve as a measure of treatment integrity. For example, different monitoring forms can be used as documentation of the skills that the patient is practicing as part of therapy (e.g., exposures, cognitive restructuring). The degree to which the patient records treatment-relevant activities also demonstrates the level of compliance with therapist instruction.

In summary, periodic use of objective measures and self-monitoring forms can aid in documentation of treatment integrity, the assessment of treatment compliance, and providing evidence of treatment efficacy. This serves to effectively communicate important aspects of treatment to other clinicians and third-party payers.

Treatment of Anxiety Disorders

Many useful options exist for primary care clinicians who discover that a patient's problems are anxiety related. Primary care clinicians overwhelmingly adopt a pharmacological approach to treatment of anxiety (Harman et al., 2002); indeed, there are numerous medications that have been shown to be efficacious for treating anxiety disorders (see Spiegel, Wiegel, Baker, & Greene, 2000, for a review). However, the value of equally efficacious psychosocial treatments for anxiety disorders is often unrecognized by primary care providers. For instance, cognitive-behavioral therapies that have been proven to be effective for treating anxiety disorders remain a very infrequent recommendation in primary care settings (Harman et al., 2002).

Efficacious psychosocial treatments now exist for all the major anxiety disorders, and handbooks that outline the major treatment strategies for different anxiety disorders are available (e.g., Barlow, 2001; Nathan & Gorman, 1998). The psychological treatments with the most demonstrated success in treating anxiety employ cognitive and behavioral techniques. The most recent list of empirically supported treatments assembled by an American Psychological Association taskforce contains 14 treatments for anxiety disorders that are considered "empirically validated" or "probably efficacious," as well as an efficacious treatment for coping with stress (Chambless et al., 1996). The empirically validated treatments are (a) cognitive-behavioral therapy for panic and agoraphobia, (b) cognitive-behavioral therapy for GAD, (c) group cognitive-behavioral therapy for social phobia, (d) exposure treatment for agoraphobia, (e) exposure treatment for social phobia, (e) exposure and response prevention for OCD, (f) stress inoculation training for coping with stressors, and (g) systematic desensitization for specific phobia. Probably efficacious treatments include two treatments for PTSD (exposure treatment and stress inoculation training), as well as other treatments for PD, GAD, specific phobia, and OCD.

Although the empirically supported therapies for anxiety disorders share a cognitive-behavioral approach, the implementation of cognitive-behavioral techniques differs depending on the disorder. This section of the chapter will outline the general techniques of cognitive-behavioral therapy, while integrating brief descriptions of the ways the techniques would be used when treating a particular anxiety disorder.

Most cognitive-behavioral therapies contain a significant psychoeducational component. Therapists obtain descriptions of patients' problems and conceptualize them within a cognitive-behavioral framework. Therapists often share their understanding of the nature and purpose of anxiety and break anxiety into components that will be important for treatment, such as thoughts, sensations, and behaviors. Throughout this process, it is important for therapists to solicit the opinions and interpretations of their patients, because the goal is to arrive at a common understanding of the anxiety problem that will underlie the remainder of treatment.

The psychoeducational component differs depending on which anxiety disorder is the focus of treatment. For instance, the clinician might spend more time explaining the physiological basis of anxiety with a patient who has PD than with individuals who have other anxiety disorders. Because patients with PD are very fearful about the implications of their physical symptoms, it is helpful to explain the origins of their symptoms in the sympathetic nervous system, and to point out that these symptoms are not harmful. On the other hand, individuals with OCD are frequently taught about the paradoxical effects of thought suppression, whereas patients with phobias learn that escape and avoidance of feared situations serve to maintain their fear.

It should be apparent that the content of the psychoeducational component of treatment varies depending on the particular anxiety problem. The important common factor is that patients adopt a new way of thinking about their problems that is more likely to lead to change. Explanation of treatment strategies and providing a rationale for each of them also contribute to increasing the patient's understanding of and motivation for treatment.

The psychoeducational aspect of cognitive-behavioral therapy renders treatment relatively "transparent" to patients, which allows them to be active participants in their own attempt to change. Another aspect of cognitive-behavioral therapy that increases patient participation is assignments completed outside of therapy sessions, sometimes called the homework of therapy. Homework serves to apply and reinforce what the patient learns in sessions and allows the patient to develop anxiety management skills to a much greater degree. It is unlikely that patients will be able to master new ways of thinking and behaving without considerable practice between sessions, and therefore most cognitive-behavioral therapists emphasize monitoring and other exercises as an essential part of treatment. For homework, a patient with PTSD might be asked to write paragraphs about his or her traumatic experience in order to facilitate processing of the traumatic material (e.g., Calhoun & Resick, 1993). In contrast, a patient with a specific phobia might be required to gradually confront feared situations of increasing difficulty over the course of treatment. Finally, patients with GAD could be assigned exercises that help them identify and challenge their worrisome thoughts. These assignments not only help to transfer the benefits of therapy from the consulting room to the real world, but they also provide an ongoing indication of the patient's understanding of and commitment to treatment.

Techniques that are taught to patients during the course of anxiety treatment help them to change maladaptive patterns of thinking and behavior. Changing thought patterns usually entails teaching the patient the technique of cognitive restructuring. Patients must first learn to identify the thoughts associated with their emotions, which is sometimes difficult because of the automatic or habitual nature of anxious thinking. Once they are able to stop themselves in an anxious moment and identify what their concerns are, patients can begin to alter their patterns of thinking. Under certain circumstances, patients are taught to recognize specific types of distorted thinking that are common during anxious episodes. These distorted ways of thinking include patterns such as "all or nothing thinking," "jumping to conclusions," and "magnification" (Burns, 1999).

Challenging anxious thoughts also entails considering the evidence that supports and refutes anxious thoughts, as well as evaluating the real impact and importance of feared outcomes. Patients are taught to ask questions in response to their anxious thoughts and to introduce some logical thinking into their emotional reasoning. Patients may ask themselves, "What evidence do I have that _____ will happen?" or "How important is it really if _____ does happen?" Once they answer these questions, they may be able to come up with a more balanced or rational way of thinking about the situation, which is reinforced the more the patient practices. Over time, introducing more balanced thinking into anxiety-provoking situations serves to alleviate patients' distress. The goal of cognitive restructuring is for the patient to learn that his or her anxious assumptions are not necessarily true, and that alternate ways of thinking may lead to less aversive emotional reactions.

Clinicians also incorporate behavioral exercises to promote cognitive change. For instance, while focusing on changing patterns of thinking, patients are often asked to perform experiments to test their anxious beliefs. When anticipating an anxiety-provoking situation, patients typically make numerous predictions about negative and even disastrous outcomes. They can learn a great deal by facing the situation and obtaining objective evidence that often completely contradicts their anxious predictions. For example, patients with GAD often worry about turning in work that is not perfect, which leads to extensive reviewing and reworking of projects. When anxious, they may predict that imperfect work would lead to being chastised by their superiors or even being fired. To test these beliefs, the patient might be asked to hand in a report that includes a misspelling or a minor omission. The patient might find that small errors have little consequence and certainly do not lead to catastrophe. These learning experiences may lead to less worry about task completion and reinforce cognitive change.

The behavioral experiments used to help change maladaptive thought patterns resemble an important behavioral approach called exposure. *Situational exposure* entails confronting a feared situation and refraining from attempts to avoid the anxiety that is provoked. The content of exposure varies depending on a patient's presenting problem, but might include driving on a highway (driving phobia), recounting a traumatic experience (PTSD), or asking a stranger for directions (social phobia). In the case of PD, patients also undergo *interoceptive exposure*, which involves deliberate provocation of the sensations that they fear (e.g., hyperventilating to induce shortness of breath and dizziness). The common element of each form of exposure is that patients allow the anxiety or fear process to take its natural course, without trying to avoid the emotion. This allows patients to experience the process of habituation, in which anxiety diminishes over time as the situation becomes more familiar and the patient's worst-feared consequences do not eventuate. Over time, patients usually find that habituation occurs more quickly, and that their initial level of anxiety is not as intense. Exposure must be practiced repeatedly in order to achieve its therapeutic effects, so a significant portion of session time and homework may be devoted to such activities.

Exposure is a treatment strategy that counteracts the detrimental effects of avoidance, which is associated to varying degrees with each anxiety disorder. Another behavioral component of many anxiety disorders involves problematic behaviors, such as excessive cleaning in OCD or the "safety behaviors" associated with PD. During cognitive-behavioral treatment, patients are helped to decrease and eventually eliminate these problematic behaviors. Clinicians explain that such behaviors, which are initially perceived as alleviating anxiety, actually maintain the anxiety problem in the long term. Patients experiment with phasing out problematic behaviors (e.g., decreasing lock-checking from 10 times a day to 3 times a day) or make a commitment to eliminating them altogether from the start of treatment (e.g., the response prevention component of intensive treatment for OCD).

The treatment components described above comprise the basic strategies of most cognitive-behavioral therapies for anxiety disorders. A multitude of other techniques may be incorporated depending on the specific problem. Some examples include relaxation training, problem solving, time management, and social skills training. For more detailed information about the procedures for treating a particular anxiety problem, readers are referred to disorder-specific treatment manuals, which are listed in Suggested Reading.

Practical Issues Related to the Administration of Treatment

Psychologists, psychiatrists, licensed social workers, and clinicians under their supervision typically conduct cognitive-behavioral treatment for anxiety. Individuals who administer this form of therapy should have had extensive training in both general therapeutic techniques as well as specific treatment protocols. This training may occur in the form of some combination of supervision by an experienced clinician, formal education, or workshops led by reputable experts in the field. Mental health professionals who have not received formal training in a specific form of therapy should seek appropriate supervision before and during their first attempts to utilize cognitive-behavioral techniques.

Primary care clinicians have important roles to play in the delivery of mental health treatment, even though most patients are referred to a mental health professional when psychosocial treatment is indicated. As noted above, primary care settings are often the first point of contact for anxious patients, and therefore the early phases of assessment will occur there. Primary care clinicians can greatly improve their patients' chances of receiving effective treatment by familiarizing themselves with community resources for anxiety treatment. Unfortunately, many patients with anxiety disorders receive suboptimal treatment because they are referred to "generalist" psychotherapists who are not trained in the empirically supported treatments for anxiety disorders. Primary care physicians should make efforts to determine a therapist's specialties and approach to treatment before making a referral. Given the research literature, it is recommended that referrals be provided to cognitive-behaviorally oriented clinicians who have substantial experience with anxiety disorders.

If patients opt to search for a therapist on their own, the primary care clinician can educate the patient about which treatment approaches have been found effective so that the patient is an informed consumer.

A recent development that may streamline the referral process for primary care clinicians is the integration of mental health services into some primary care settings (Dea, 2000; Nickels & McIntyre, 1996; Price, Beck, Nimmer, & Bensen, 2000). The presence of qualified mental health professionals in the primary care setting would simplify the referral process greatly and might also increase the likelihood of patients pursuing more specialized treatment for their anxiety difficulties. Integration of primary and mental health care could also facilitate communication among providers and produce medical cost offsets (Dea, 2000; Katon et al., 2002). Initial studies of integrated care for PD and GAD suggest that this form of treatment produces better outcomes for patients, along with the possibility of reduced health-care costs (Katon et al., 2002; Price et al., 2000).

Once the patient finds a suitable therapist for anxiety treatment, the primary care clinician may continue to support the patient by collaborating with the mental health clinician. Communication between treatment providers is strongly recommended, particularly if the primary care clinician is prescribing medication for anxiety. Primary care clinicians can facilitate mental health treatment by scheduling follow-up appointments to check on the patient's progress. This conveys to patients that treatment for anxiety is important, and it may enhance their motivation to comply with recommendations. Because overcoming anxiety often involves difficult tasks (e.g., facing feared situations), additional support for the patient's efforts is always helpful and may even improve compliance. Meeting with the patient after the referral process is complete also provides a forum for the patient to discuss other options if he or she is dissatisfied with the treatment.

The role of the primary care clinician may be expanded under some circumstances. For instance, clinicians who are prescribing medications for anxiety will have more frequent contact with the patient's psychotherapist to coordinate care. In some cases, patients want to decrease or stop medication use as they acquire new skills for managing anxiety. Primary care clinicians will be involved in advising them of an appropriate taper schedule and informing them about any expected withdrawal effects. Primary care physicians can consult a recent chapter by Spiegel, Wiegel, Baker, and Greene (2000) for more detailed guidelines on the pharmacological treatment of anxiety disorders.

Primary care clinicians may also play an important role for patients whose anxious behaviors include seeking reassurance from their doctors (e.g., the patient with PD who calls his or her doctor every time a heart palpitation occurs). Providers of psychological treatment should enlist primary care clinicians to help decrease these safety behaviors and to selectively reinforce appropriate use of primary care resources.

The availability of self-directed treatment manuals for many anxiety disorders introduces the possibility that primary care clinicians will play a more direct role in anxiety treatments. As mentioned above, patients with milder anxiety problems may benefit from simple psychoeducation and manuals describing exercises they can complete on their own. Self-directed treatment manuals exist for virtually every anxiety disorder, and many patients may choose this form of treatment for its flexibility and convenience (see Suggested Reading/Websites for Anxiety on p. 107). In cases where patients are attempting self-help, primary care clinicians should make follow-up meetings can even greater priority. These meetings can consist of helping to maintain the patient's focus on the program and troubleshooting any difficulties that arise.

Prevention

In addition to treatment options for anxiety disorders, prevention or early intervention in primary care may stop progression and the development of complications and subsequent relapses.

Prevention efforts may include empathic responses to major life events, provision of social support, identification of at-risk individuals, and the promotion of mental health through self-help manuals and education (Murray & Jenkins, 1998). Psychoeducation, which is a key component of cognitive-behavioral treatment, may be particularly beneficial for preventing the development of an anxiety disorder in individuals who exhibit subclinical anxiety symptoms. Patients presenting to primary care settings with physical symptoms having no underlying medical condition, or are in excess of a medical condition, should be educated about the nature of anxiety and the potential misinterpretation of symptoms of anxiety. This psychoeducation may prevent the development of a clinical anxiety disorder and its concomitant emotional, financial, and social costs.

Case Example

Ms. A is a 36-year-old, married, African-American female who works as a school teacher. In a 12-month period she had several appointments with her primary care physician, Dr. B. Ms. A was diagnosed with asthma and hypertension; both conditions are well-controlled with medication. However, Ms. A reported symptoms of nausea, intestinal distress, and hot flushes at her first two primary care visits of the year. Although they never fully resolve her symptoms, Ms. A stated that she "never goes anywhere" without numerous over-the-counter medications for nausea and intestinal distress. At her third visit, Ms. A was given a referral to a gastroenterologist for a full evaluation of her symptoms. The results of testing for gastrointestinal diseases were negative.

For her fourth appointment with Dr. B, Ms. A was asked to arrive 20 minutes early. In the waiting room, she completed the QPD on a hand-held computer. A nurse printed out the QPD diagnostic summary report and placed it in Ms. A's chart for Dr. B's review. The QPD report suggested that Ms. A could be suffering from both PD and GAD. She had endorsed unexpected attacks characterized by chest discomfort, shortness of breath, stomach distress, hot flushes, and feelings of unreality. Ms. A reported that she feared she would lose control during these attacks, and that she was very worried about having more of them. In addition, Ms. A had endorsed excessive worry about several different areas of her life. She reported that the worry was hard to control and that she had associated symptoms of restlessness, irritability, and muscle tension.

In the consultation room, Ms. A spoke about her continued problems with nausea and intestinal discomfort. Dr. B asked if she would be willing to discuss the results of the QPD in order to better understand her symptoms. Ms. A agreed to this plan and acknowledged that she had been feeling very worried about both her physical symptoms and other areas of her life (e.g., work, finances, her marriage). Ms. A indicated that she frequently felt "keyed up" and that she became especially upset when she had sudden nausea, hot flashes, and other symptoms that made her feel like she was going to "lose it." She reported that she was beginning to refrain from taking long car trips and from going to church because she did not want to be "trapped anywhere for too long" or to embarrass herself by having to exit a situation suddenly.

Ms. A and her physician talked about the possibility that her symptoms might be related to anxiety. Her physician provided educational pamphlets on PD and GAD. Ms. A glanced at the pamphlets and stated, "This looks like me." When asked why she had not disclosed her anxiety symptoms before, Ms. A replied that she had only discussed her somatic symptoms because she did not think it was appropriate to discuss "mental problems" with her primary care doctor. Her physician replied that disclosing emotional symptoms was appropriate and in fact helped to determine the best course of treatment.

Ms. A discussed several different treatment options with her doctor including pharmacotherapy, referral to a cognitive-behavioral therapist, and self-directed therapy. Dr. B reviewed the potential benefits and side effects of selective serotonin reuptake inhibitors (SSRIs), and Ms. A decided that she would try a low dose of one of these medications. She was concerned about side effects, but also felt that medication would be more manageable for her than regular psychotherapy appointments.

Ms. A also expressed interest in reading more about cognitive-behavioral techniques for managing anxiety. Dr. B referred her to the client workbooks *Mastery of Your Anxiety and Panic* and *Mastery of Your Anxiety and Worry* (see Suggested Reading/Websites for Anxiety on p. 107). At her follow-up appointment 1 month later, Ms. A reported that her anxiety and physical symptoms had improved. She noted that simply learning more about anxiety and its physical manifestations had been helpful, and seemed to prevent her panic symptoms from escalating. Ms. A also thought that improvement in her anxiety symptoms had reduced the frequency and intensity of her asthma attacks and gastrointestinal problems. She reported using her inhaler and her over-the-counter stomach medications less frequently.

Ms. A had attempted some of the cognitive-behavioral strategies such as cognitive restructuring and exposure to feared situations (e.g., she had resumed going to church). However, she was unsure about trying the interoceptive exposure practices because of her other medical issues. Dr. B reassured her that she could perform most of the symptom-induction exercises, but offered a few modifications based on Ms. A's history of asthma (Feldman, Giardino, & Lehrer, 2000). Ms. A planned to try other techniques in the workbook, and also decided to increase her SSRI to a therapeutic dose.

Summary

Individuals with anxiety disorders frequently seek treatment from primary care clinicians, and indeed may overutilize primary care resources. Inefficient treatment of anxiety disorders results in strain on the primary care setting, as well as prolonged distress and life interference for the patient. Efficacious treatments now exist for all the major anxiety disorders, and with adequate assessment and treatment most patients whose problems are anxiety related can attain substantial alleviation of symptoms and improvement in overall functioning. There are a number of tools that can help the primary care clinician discern whether a patient's problems are due to an anxiety disorder. Possible screening questions, self-report inventories, and comprehensive screens developed for primary care settings were reviewed in this chapter. Primary care clinicians should also familiarize themselves with treatments that have demonstrated efficacy for alleviating anxiety disorders, and should be prepared to make referrals to appropriate specialists. The major techniques employed by cognitive-behavioral therapists were summarized in this chapter for the benefit of primary care clinicians who might offer different forms of support to patients attempting this type of treatment. With improved recognition of anxiety disorders and increased referrals to appropriate treatment, the impact of these prevalent disorders on both individual patients and overburdened primary care facilities may be substantially reduced.

References

American Psychiatric Association. (1994). *Diagnostic and statistical manual of mental disorders* (4th ed.). Washington, DC: Author.

Barlow, D. H. (2002). *Anxiety and its disorders: The nature and treatment of anxiety and panic* (2nd ed.). New York: Guilford.

Barlow, D. H. (Ed.). (2001). *Clinical handbook of psychological disorders* (3rd ed.). New York: Guilford.

Barlow, D. H., Brown, T. A., & Craske, M. G. (1994). Definitions of panic attacks and panic disorder in *DSM-IV*: Implications for research. *Journal of Abnormal Psychology, 103*, 553–564.

Barlow, D. H., Esler, J. L., & Vitali, A. E. (1998). Psychosocial treatments for panic disorders, phobias, and generalized anxiety disorder. In P. E. Nathan & J. M. Gorman (Eds.), *A guide to treatments that work* (pp. 288–317). Oxford, England: Oxford University Press.

Beck, A. T., & Steer, R. A. (1990). *Manual for the Beck Anxiety Inventory.* San Antonio, TX: Psychological Corporation.

Beck, A. T., Steer, R. A., Ball, R., Ciervo, C. A., & Kabat, M. (1997). Use of the Beck Anxiety and Beck Depression Inventories for primary care with medical outpatients. *Assessment, 4,* 211–219.

Brown, C., Schulberg, H. C., Madonia, M. J., Shear, K., & Houck, P. R. (1996). Treatment outcomes for primary care patients with major depression and lifetime anxiety disorders. *American Journal of Psychiatry, 153,* 1293–1300.

Brown, T. A., & Barlow, D. H. (1992). Comorbidity among anxiety disorders: Implications for treatment and *DSM-IV. Journal of Consulting and Clinical Psychology, 60,* 835–844.

Brown, T. A., Campbell, L. A., Lehman, C. L., Grisham, J. R., & Mancill, R. B. (2001). Current and lifetime comorbidity of the *DSM-IV* anxiety and mood disorders in a large clinical sample. *Journal of Abnormal Psychology, 110,* 585–599.

Brown, T. A., Di Nardo, P. A., & Barlow, D. H. (1994). *Anxiety disorders interview schedule for* DSM-IV: *Adult version.* San Antonio, TX: Psychological Corporation.

Calhoun, K. S., & Resick, P. A. (1993). Posttraumatic stress disorder. In D. H. Barlow (Ed.), *Clinical handbook of psychological disorders* (2nd ed., pp. 48–98). New York: Guilford.

Chambless, D. L., Sanderson, W. C., Shoham, V., Johnson, S. B., Pope, K. S., Crits-Christoph, P. et al. (1996). An update on empirically validated therapies. *Clinical Psychologist, 49,* 5–18.

Clark, D. M. (1986). A cognitive approach to panic. *Behaviour Research and Therapy, 24,* 461–470.

Coplan, J., & Gorman, J. (1990). Treatment of anxiety disorders in patients with mood disorders. *Journal of Clinical Psychiatry, 51,* 9–13.

Coryell, W., Endicott, J., & Winokur, G. (1992) Anxiety syndromes as epiphenomena of major depression: Outcome and familial psychopathology. *American Journal of Psychiatry, 149,* 100–107.

Dea, R. A. (2000). The integration of primary care and behavioral health care in northern California Kaiser-Permanente. *Psychiatric Quarterly, 71,* 17–29.

Fawcett, J. (1990). Targeting treatment in patients with mixed symptoms of anxiety and depression. *Journal of Clinical Psychiatry, 51,* 40–43.

Feldman, J. M., Giardino, N. D., & Lehrer, P. M. (2000). Asthma and panic disorder. In D. I. Mostovsky & D. H. Barlow (Eds.), *The management of stress and anxiety in medical disorders* (pp. 220–239). Boston: Allyn and Bacon.

Fifer, S. K., Mathias, S. D., Patrick, D. L., Mazaonson, P. D., Lubeck, D. P., & Buesching, D. P. (1994). Untreated anxiety among adult primary care patients in a health maintenance organization. *Archives of General Psychiatry, 51,* 740–750.

First, M. B., Gibbon, M., Spitzer, R. L., & Williams, J. B. W. (1996). *User's guide for the structured clinical interview for* DSM-IV *Axis I disorders: Research version.* New York: Biometrics Research.

Foa, E. B., Cashman, L., Jaycox, L., & Perry, K. (1997). The validation of a self-report measure of posttraumatic stress disorder: The posttraumatic diagnostic scale. *Psychological Assessment, 9,* 445–451.

Goldberg, D., Jackson, G., Gater, R., Campbell, M., & Jennett, N. (1996). The treatment of common mental disorders by a community team based in primary care: A cost-effectiveness study. *Psychological Medicine, 26,* 487–492.

Harman, J. S., Rollman, B. L., Hanusa, B. H., Lenze, E. J., & Shear, M. K. (2002). Physician office visits of adults for anxiety disorders in the United States, 1985–1998. *Journal of General Internal Medicine, 17,* 165–172.

Hodgson, R. J., & Rachman, S. J. (1977). Obsessive-compulsive complaints. *Behaviour Research and Therapy, 15,* 389–395.

Karajgi, B., Rifkin, A., Doddi, S., & Kolli, R. (1990). The prevalence of anxiety disorders in patients with chronic obstructive pulmonary disease. *American Journal of Psychiatry, 147,* 200–201.

Katon, W. (1984). Panic and somatization: A review of 55 cases. *American Journal of Medicine, 77,* 101–106.

Katon, W., & Roy-Burne, P. (1991). Mixed anxiety and depression. *Journal of Abnormal Psychology, 100,* 337–345.

Katon, W. J., Roy-Byrne, P., Russo, J., & Cowley, D. (2002). Cost-effectiveness and cost offset of a collaborative care intervention for primary care patients with panic disorder. *Archives of General Psychiatry, 59,* 1098–1104.

Kawachi, I., Colditz, G. A., Ascherio, A., Rimm, E. B., Giovannucci, E., Stampfer, M. J. et al. (1994). Prospective study of phobic anxiety and risk of coronary artery disease in men. *Circulation, 89,* 299–302.

Kennedy, B. L., & Schwab, J. J. (1997). Utilization of medical specialists by anxiety disorder patients. *Psychosomatics, 38,* 109–112.

Kessler, R. C., McGonagle, K. A., Zhao, S., Hughes, M., Eshleman, S., Wittchen, H. U. et al. (1994). Lifetime and 12-month prevalence of *DSM-III-R* psychiatric disorders in the United States. *Archives of General Psychiatry, 51,* 8–19.

Klerman, G. L., Weissman, M. M., Ouelette, R., Johnson, J., & Greenwald, S. (1991). Attacks in the community: Social morbidity and health care utilization. *Journal of the American Medical Association, 265,* 742–746.

Leon, A. C., Portera, L., & Weissman, M. M. (1995). The social costs of anxiety disorders. *British Journal of Psychiatry, 166* (suppl. 27), 19–22.

Lovibond, S. H., & Lovibond, P. F. (1995). *Manual for the depression anxiety stress scales.* Sydney, Australia: Psychological Foundation of Australia.

Mattick, R. P., & Clarke, J. C. (1998). Development and validation of measures of social phobia scrutiny fear and social interaction anxiety. *Behaviour Research and Therapy, 36,* 455–470.

Meyer, T. J., Miller, M. L., Metzger, R. L., & Borkovec, T. D. (1990). Development and validation of the Penn State Worry Questionnaire. *Behaviour Research and Therapy, 28,* 487–495.

Mori, D. L., Lambert, J. F., Niles, B. L., Orlander, J. D., Grace, M., & LoCastro, J. S. (2003). The BAI-PC as a screen for anxiety, depression, and PTSD in primary care. *Journal of Clinical Psychology in Medical Settings, 10,* 187–192.

Murray, J., & Jenkins, R. (1998). Prevention of mental illness in primary care. *International Review of Psychiatry, 10,* 154–157.

Nathan, P. E., & Gorman, J. M. (1998). *A guide to treatments that work.* Oxford, England: Oxford University Press.

Nickels, M. W., & McIntyre, J. S. (1996). A model for psychiatric services in primary care settings. *Psychiatric Services, 47,* 522–526.

Nisenson, L. G., Pepper, C. M., Schwenk, T. L., & Coyne, J. C. (1998). The nature and prevalence of anxiety disorders in primary care. *General Hospital Psychiatry, 20,* 21–28.

Olfson, M., Broadhead, W., Weissman, M., Leon, A., Farber, L., Hoven, C. et al. (1996). Subthreshold symptoms in a primary care group practice. *Archives of General Psychiatry, 53,* 880–886.

Olfson, M., Fireman, B., Weissman, M. M., Leon, A. C., Sheehan, D. V., Kathol, R. G., Hoven, C., & Farber, L. (1997). Mental disorders and disability among patients in a primary care group practice. *American Journal of Psychiatry, 154,* 1734–1740.

Ormel, J., Oldehinkel, T., Brilman, E., & van den Brink, W. (1993). Outcome of depression and anxiety in primary care: A three-wave 3 ½ year study of psychopathology and disability. *Archives of General Psychiatry, 50,* 759–766.

Peterson, R. A., & Reiss, S. (1992). *Anxiety sensitivity index manual* (2nd ed.). Worthington, OH: IDS Publishing.

Price, D., Beck, A., Nimmer, C., & Bensen, S. (2000). The treatment of anxiety disorders in a primary care HMO setting. *Psychiatric Quarterly, 71,* 31–45.

Rapee, R. M., Craske, M. G., & Barlow, D. H. (1995). Assessment instrument for panic disorder that includes fear of sensation-producing activities: The Albany Panic and Phobia Questionnaire. *Anxiety, 1,* 114–122.

Regier, D. A., Narrow, W. E., Rae, D. S., Manderscheid, R. W., Locke, B. Z., & Goodwin, F. K. (1993). The de facto U.S. mental and addictive disorders service system: Epidemiological Catchment Area prospective 1-year prevalence rates of disorders and services. *Archives of General Psychiatry, 50,* 85–94.

Rickels, K., & Schweizer, E. (1997). The clinical presentation of generalized anxiety in primary-care settings: Practical concepts of classification and management. *Journal of Clinical Psychiatry, 58* (suppl. 11), 4–10.

Rogers, M. P., White, K., Warshaw, M. G., Yonkers, K. A., Rodriguez-Villa, F., Chang, G. et al. (1994). Prevalence of mental illness in patients with anxiety disorders. *International Journal of Psychiatry in Medicine, 24,* 83–96.

Roy-Byrne, P. (1996). Generalized anxiety and mixed anxiety-depression: Association with disability and health care utilization. *Journal of Clinical Psychiatry, 57,* 86–91.

Roy-Byrne, P. P., & Katon, W. (2000). Anxiety management in the medical setting: Rationale, barriers to diagnosis and treatment, and proposed solutions. In D. I. Mostofsky & D. H. Barlow (Eds.), *The management of stress and anxiety in medical disorders* (pp. 1–14).

Roy-Byrne, P. P., Katon, W., Cowley, D. S., & Russo, J. (2001). A randomized effectiveness trial of collaborative care for patients with PD in primary care. *Archives of General Psychiatry, 58,* 869–876.

Salvador-Carulla, L., Segu, J., Fernandez-Cano, P., & Canet, J. (1995). Costs and offset effect in panic disorders. *British Journal of Psychiatry, 166,* 23–28.

Shear, M. K., & Schulberg, H. C. (1995). Anxiety disorders in primary care. *Bulletin of the Menninger Clinic, 59*(suppl. A), 73–85.

Shedler, J., Beck, A., & Bensen, S. (2000). Practical mental health assessment in primary care: Validity and utility of the Quick PsychoDiagnostics Panel. *The Journal of Family Practice, 49,* 614–621.

Sheehan, D. V., LeCrubier, Y., Sheehan, K. H., Amorim, P., Janavs, J., Weiller, E. et al. (1998). The Mini-International Neuropsychiatric Interview (MINI): The development and validation of a structured diagnostic interview for *DSM-IV* and *ICD-10. Journal of Clinical Psychiatry, 59*(suppl. 20), 22–33.

Sherbourne, C. D., Jackson, K. B., Meredith, L. S., Camp, P., & Wells, K. B. (1996). Prevalence of comorbid anxiety in general medical and mental health specialty outpatients. *Archives of Family Medicine, 5,* 27–34.

Simon, G., Ormel, J., VonKorff, M., & Barlow, W. (1995). Health care costs associated with depressive and anxiety disorders in primary care. *American Journal of Psychiatry, 152,* 352–357.

Spiegel, D. A., & Barlow, D. H. (2000). Generalized anxiety disorder. In M. G. Gelder, J. J. López-Ibor, & N. C. Andreasen (Eds.), *New Oxford textbook of psychiatry* (pp. 785–794). Oxford, England: Oxford University Press.

Spiegel, D. A., Wiegel, M., Baker, S. L., & Greene, K. A. (2000). Pharmacological management of anxiety disorders. In D. I. Mostovsky & D. H. Barlow (Eds.), *The management of stress and anxiety in medical disorders* (pp. 36–65). Boston: Allyn & Bacon.

Spitzer, R. L., Kroenke, K., & Williams, J. B. (1999). Validation and utility of a self-report version of the PRIME-MD: The PHQ primary care study. *Journal of the American Medical Association, 282*(18), 1737–1744.

Spitzer, R. L., Williams, J. B. W., Kroenke, K., Linzer, M., deGruy, F. V., Hahn, S. R. et al. (1994). Utility of a new procedure for diagnosing mental disorders in primary care: The PRIME-MD study. *Journal of the American Medical Association, 272,* 1749–1756.

Stein, M. B., Roy-Byrne, P. P., McQuaid, J. R., Laffaye, C., Russo, J., McCahill, M. E., Katon, W., Craske, M., Bystritsky, A., & Sherbourne, C. D. (1999). Development of a brief diagnostic screen for PD in primary care. *Psychosomatic Medicine, 61,* 359–364.

Telch, M. J., Schmidt, N. B., Jaimez, T. L., Jacquin, K. M., & Harrington, P. J. (1995). Impact of cognitive behavioral treatment on quality of life in panic disorder patients. *Journal of Consulting and Clinical Psychology, 63,* 823–830.

Weathers, F. W., Litz, B. T., Herman, D. S., Huska, J. A., & Keane, T. M. (1993, October). *The PTSD checklist: Reliability, validity, and diagnostic utility.* Paper presented at the annual meeting of the International Society for Traumatic Stress Studies, San Antonio, TX.

Weiller, E., Bisserbe, J. C., Maier, W., & Lecrubier, Y. (1998). Prevalence and recognition of anxiety syndromes in five European primary care settings: A report from the WHO study on psychological problems in general health care. *British Journal of Psychiatry, 173*(suppl. 34), 18–23.

Weissman, M. M., Broadhead, E., Olfson, M., Sheehan, D. V., Hoven, C., Conolly, P., Fireman, B. H., Farber, L., Blacklow, R. S., Higgins, E. S., & Leon, A. C. (1998). A diagnostic aid for detecting (DSM-IV) mental disorders in primary care. *General Hospital Psychiatry, 20,* 1–11.

Wittchen, H. U., Zhao, S., Kessler, R. C., & Eaton, W. W. (1994). *DSM-III-R* generalized anxiety disorder in the National Comorbidity Survey. *Archives of General Psychiatry, 51,* 355–364.

Suggested Reading/Websites for Anxiety

Suggested Reading

Textbooks

The following textbooks provide theoretical perspectives and information regarding the assessment and treatment of anxiety.

Barlow, D. H. (2002). *Anxiety and its disorders: The nature and treatment of anxiety and panic* (2nd ed.). New York: Guilford Press.

Clark, D. M., & Fairburn, C. G. (1997). *Science and practice of cognitive behaviour therapy.* Oxford, England: Oxford University Press.

Rapee, R. M., Wignall, M., Hudson, J. L., & Schneier, C. A. (2000). *Treating anxious children and adolescents. An evidence-based approach.* Oakland, CA: New Harbinger Publications.

Self-Directed Therapy Manuals

The texts below can be utilized by clients for self-directed therapy. Most of these workbooks have companion therapist guides.

Antony, M. M., Craske, M. G., & Barlow, D. H. (1995). *Mastery of your specific phobia: Client workbook.* San Antonio, TX: Psychological Corporation.

Antony, M. M., & Swinson, R. P. (2000). *The shyness and social anxiety workbook: Proven techniques for overcoming your fears.* Oakland, CA: New Harbinger Publications.

Barlow, D. H., & Craske, M. G. (2000). *Mastery of your anxiety and panic: Client workbook* (3rd ed.). San Antonio, TX: Psychological Corporation.

Burns, D. D. (1999). *The feeling good handbook.* New York: Plume.

Craske, M. G., Barlow, D. H., & O'Leary, T. A. (1992). *Mastery of your anxiety and worry.* San Antonio, TX: Psychological Corporation.

Foa, E. B., & Kozak, M. J. (1997). *Mastery of obsessive-compulsive disorder.* San Antonio, TX: Psychological Corporation.

Rapee, R. M., Spence, S. H., Cobham, V., & Wignall, M. (2000). *Helping your anxious child: A step-by-step guide for parents.* Oakland, CA: New Harbinger Publications.

Websites for Anxiety

The following websites provide resources for practitioners and consumers.

Anxiety Disorders Association of America: includes professional referral listings, educational information, self-help tools, and an online bookstore. Visit www.adaa.org

National Institute of Mental Health Website: provides fact sheets, references, press releases, and links to other resources. Visit www.nimh.nih.gov/anxiety

Chapter 5
Suicide and Parasuicide Management in the Primary Care Setting

ELIZABETH A. LILLIS AND ALAN E. FRUZZETTI

Suicidal people commonly present in integrated care settings, and primary care is often the only point of contact with professionals for this population. Although comprehensive treatment of suicidal patients is outside the scope of primary care settings, guidelines for assessment and brief intervention are necessary for stabilization of these patients and to make appropriate referrals for comprehensive treatment. This chapter provides a set of guidelines for how to assess and manage suicidality and parasuicidality in an integrated care setting. Assessment includes not only identifying suicide risk factors, but also differentiating between acutely and chronically suicidal individuals. Further, given the challenging nature of working with highly emotionally dysregulated patients, methods of reducing the suicidal patient's emotional arousal will also be addressed. Then, assessment and brief interventions can be integrated, which may reduce immediate risk and also facilitate more accurate assessment. This, in turn, may make referrals and subsequent treatment better matched and more effective. Specific steps in conducting a risk assessment and interventive assessment will be addressed, and issues related to referring suicidal patients to appropriate treatment will also be discussed.

Suicide is the 11th-leading cause of death in the United States, and the 8th-leading cause of death among males (National Institute of Mental Health, 2001). There are an average of 84 reported suicides per day, one every 17 minutes, or about 30,622 completed suicides per year (National Institute of Mental Health, 2001; Westefeld et al., 2000). Of course, the total number of actual deaths by suicide is likely higher; a substantial number of deaths that are likely suicides are officially listed as "accidents." For young adults between the ages of 15 and 24, suicide is the 3rd-leading cause of death (National Institute of Mental Health, 2001). Every year, approximately 186,000 Americans are affected when a close friend or family member commits suicide (American Association of Suicidology, 1998). Moreover, for every completed suicide, many times that number of people engage in unsuccessful suicide attempts, make suicide plans, or are disturbed by suicidal thoughts. Moreover, individuals who ultimately do kill themselves are two to three times more likely to have had recent contact with primary care providers (PCPs) than with mental health providers (Luoma, Martin, & Pearson, 2002). In fact, the primary care setting is the de facto setting for mental health

109

services for a large number of patients in the United States (Regier, Goldberg, & Taube, 1978). Despite the high prevalence of suicidal behavior, there have been few advances in how to predict suicide attempts, or how to discriminate between those with suicidal thoughts or plans who will not act on them and those who will. Even though health-care professionals encounter suicidal patients every day, suicide assessment remains unstandardized and effective prevention strategies elusive.

Accurately identifying those who will attempt suicide is extremely difficult because of the problems of base rates and false positives. That is, it is likely that 95% of the general population has thoughts about suicide in their lifetime (Chiles & Strosahl, 1995). Chiles and Strosahl (1995) investigated suicidal ideation in the general population and found that 20% of those surveyed had at least one episode of moderate to severe suicidal ideation (with a formed plan) over a 2-week time period, and 20% had at least one episode of troublesome suicidal ideation (without a formed plan) over a 2-week time period. Approximately 500,000 individuals are treated for attempted suicide each year (U.S. Public Health Service, 1999). Thus, engaging in suicidal thoughts is extremely common in the general population, although completed suicide is extremely rare. Thus, suicidal thoughts are poor predictors of suicide attempts and completion. This may also be considered a problem of base rates: only one out of the thousands that engage in this behavior will end up completing suicide. Consequently, most indices of risk based on suicidal ideation alone result in very high rates of false positives.

This chapter will serve several functions. It will primarily address the function and role of the primary care provider in suicide assessment and response. We will discuss the distinctions between acute versus chronic suicidal patients, and short-term versus long-term assessment and treatment strategies. We will then highlight risk factors in different populations. Furthermore, we will provide a rationale and overview for conducting a brief behavioral analysis and "interventive interview" with suicidal and parasuicidal patients, which will serve as a core patient management strategy in primary care settings in order to reduce risk, improve assessment, and facilitate appropriate referrals when needed.

Models of Suicide

Many factors have been identified that statistically increase the risk of a suicide attempt. However, these factors are found at high rates in individuals who do not commit suicide. Thus, it is clear that some individuals will commit suicide and some will not, but the factors that discriminate between these two groups are not clear.

Social learning theories have been proposed for suicidal behavior; for example, it has been proposed that completed suicide is more common in societies where condemnation of suicide is low (Lester, 1988). Durkheim (1951) hypothesized that this factor may account for the low suicide rates among Catholic, Greek Orthodox, and Jewish populations. Linehan (1973) also investigated sex differences in society. She proposed that if attempted suicide is seen as a "weak" or "feminine" behavior, then men may be less likely to choose that alternative until emotional dysregulation leads to more lethal attempts.

Suicide has also been theorized as a learned problem-solving technique (Carr, 1977; Chiles and Strosahl, 1995; DeCatanzaro, 1981; Ferster, 1961; Linehan, 1993, 1999). This model posits that suicidal acts are a learned means of alleviating painful internal states or aversive external problems. Feelings such as sadness, anxiety, shame, guilt, or other intense negative emotions can be an integral part of a suicidal crisis, as can an external event such as the loss of a loved one or a recent divorce. Essentially, engaging in suicidal behavior might sometimes be effective, at least in the immediate sense of escaping from suffering; other people might respond with increased attention or soothing, or they may stop criticizing or aggressive acts. Privately, the patient is likely seeking relief from a difficult emotional state. The hypothesis is that the self-injurious and suicidal behavior of a chronically suicidal individual is being reinforced. This is one premise of dialectical behavior therapy (DBT), the only empirically supported therapy to date for treating chronically suicidal and parasuicidal patients with borderline personality disorder (Linehan, 1993).

Demographics of Suicide

As noted earlier, most people have had or will have suicidal thoughts during their lifetime. About 40% of people have serious thoughts of suicide consistently for 2 or more weeks, 20% of these people will form a plan, and ultimately, 1–2% of those who form a plan will carry through with the plan and take their own life (Chiles & Strosahl, 1995). However, the magnitude of this problem has not made predictions accurate or interventions successful. There are some epidemiological data that identify subgroups of people who are at higher risk for suicide. However, these kinds of nomothetic (group) data do not provide information regarding an *individual's* risk for suicide. What is known is that being human is itself an individual risk factor for suicidality. Available epidemiological data are presented below. It is important to keep in mind that when an individual presents in the clinic with suicidal thoughts, the following factors point to a level of risk but cannot replace an idiographic assessment and do not predict patient response to intervention. Despite this, risk-factor information is useful because it identifies individuals who are at higher risk to treatment providers. These individuals require a lower threshold for aggressive intervention.

Social Risk Factors

Certain social factors influence suicide risk. In general, unmarried people (single, divorced, widowed) commit suicide more than those who are married (Statham et al., 1998). This is especially true in the elderly population (McIntosh, Hubbard, & Santos, 1994). In a study of one Maryland county linking state death records, Li (1995) reported that suicide rates of widowed men were three times higher than that of married men. However, older widowed women showed no increase in suicide rate as compared to older married women. Duberstein, Conwell, and Cox (1998) found that widowed older individuals were at greater suicide risk within 4 years following the death of a spouse. Being unemployed also accounts for a higher risk of suicide (Reinecke, 2000). Also, in the case of the elderly, the suicide rate is known to increase after retirement (McIntosh, 1995).

Family Risk Factors

Family history also plays a role in suicidal behavior, and suicide tends to cluster in families. There are at least two explanations for this risk. The first is social learning theory (Diekstra, 1973), which states that suicidal behavior is a learned coping method and depends on suicidal behaviors in a person's existing repertoire. Modeling has been hypothesized to play a role in influencing an individual's suicidal behavior (Bandura, 1969). That is, if an individual observes suicidal behavior, this individual can acquire those modeled responses him- or herself. Diekstra (1973) stated that suicidal behavior is acquired through socialization and that family and friends provide both the motives for suicidal behavior and the expectations about the outcome of suicidal behavior. This and other similar findings (Perlin & Schmidt, 1975) suggest that suicidal behavior is not simply mimicked by the observer, but that some sort of cognitive appraisal of the behavior occurs and then mediates the response. However, a 1985 study demonstrated that individuals recently hospitalized for a suicide attempt reported fewer suicidal models than did suicidal ideators, nonsuicidal psychiatric patients, and medical controls (Chiles, Strosahl, McMurtray, & Linehan, 1985). Other studies looking at suicidal modeling effects have found the opposite: attempters often have relatives who have engaged in suicidal behavior (Maxmen & Tucker, 1973; Murphy & Wetzel, 1982). Thus, the findings are mixed, and it is unclear what impact modeling has on suicidal behavior.

Genetics has been proposed as a second explanation for familial risk of suicide. Some studies of monozygotic and dizygotic twins have found that the clustering may represent genetic loading for those psychiatric disorders associated with suicide (but not for suicide per se). Data are mixed with respect to the impact of family environmental factors on suicide (Chiles & Strosahl, 1995; Roy, Segal, Centerwall, & Robinette, 1991; Keitner et al., 1987). For example, a study by Statham et al. (1998) using monozygotic and dizygotic twins supported the view that suicidal loss of a close relative may trigger suicide in other family members only if they share the relevant genetic predispositions.

Given these two explanations, it can further be hypothesized that familial risk factors are mediated through shared biological vulnerability and a shared environment (Moscicki, 1997). Whether environmental, genetic, or both, a family history of psychopathology or suicidal behavior is an essential part of risk assessment of the suicidal individual.

Age

Suicidal risk increases with age, with the highest risk being in elderly males (Pearson, 2000). The overall suicide rate among those over 65 is approximately 19 per 100,000, and approximately 23 per 100,000 for those between 75 and 84 (Kochanek & Hudson, 1995). Given the varying processes of completing death certificates for the elderly, this may even be an underestimate for this population. Death certificates, depending on the state, may be completed by any number of people including an appointed layman, lawyer, sheriff, mortician, general practitioner, or a forensic pathologist (Pearson, 2000). For isolated elderly patients whose death certificate is being handled by unfamiliar people, a suicide attempt such as a medication overdose or a fall could be mistaken for an accident or as resulting from dementia. Another consideration for the elderly is that even though the death rate by suicide is higher than for all other age groups, it is not the most common form of death. Heart disease, malignancies, and cerebrovascular diseases are more common forms of death than suicide in this cohort (Morgan, 1989). Therefore, treatment providers working with the elderly may overlook suicide risk while assessing physical ailments, perhaps leading to suicides that could have been prevented or suicides that are believed to have resulted from accidental overdoses.

Chronic Pain and Medical Illness

Individuals suffering from chronically painful conditions such as migraine headaches (Breslau, Davis, & Andreski, 1991), low back pain (Penttinen, 1995), and cancer (Breitbart, 1993) have elevated rates of suicidal ideation and attempts. Depression in pain patients has been associated with greater pain intensity and pain-related disability (Haythornthwaite, Sieber, & Kerns, 1991), higher levels of catastrophizing (Geisser, Robinson, Keefe, & Weiner, 1994), and lower levels of social support (Kerns, Haythornthwaite, Southwick, & Giller, 1990), all of which may contribute to increased suicidal ideation.

The relationship between chronic pain and illness is not a simple one (Breitbart, 1993). Studies suggest that patients with chronic pain are at increased risk for suicidal intent, possibly due to elevated rates of depression (Fisher, Haythornthwaite, Heinberg, Clark, & Reed, 2001). For example, in a study of cancer patients, suicidal ideation was not related to the intensity of the cancer, but rather to the degree of depression (Saltzberg et al., 1989). Among individuals with chronically painful conditions, there is a shortage of studies that control for depressive symptomotology (Fisher et al., 2001), making conclusions about increased risk with this population difficult. However, it can be concluded that individuals with chronic pain compounded with depression are at greater risk for suicidal ideation and attempts.

Psychological Risk Factors

Suicidality is not exclusive to any one mental disorder. Studies demonstrate that many different diagnoses include the symptomotology of suicidality, with suicide rates within these diagnoses ranging from 5–15% (Chiles & Strosahl, 1995). However, suicide rates are much higher in the psychiatric population than in the general population. The base rate of suicide in the general population is approximately 12 per 100,000 versus 60 per 100,000 in the psychiatric population (Hilliard, 1995; Murphy, 1984; Tanney, 1992). A large retrospective study with veterans showed completed suicides were most often associated with depression (present in 50% of completed suicides), alcohol and drug abuse (present in about 20–25%), and schizophrenia (present in about 10%) (Pokorny, 1992). Inskip, Harris, and Barraclough (1998) have presented a more recent risk estimate of 6% for affective disorders, 7% for alcohol dependence, and 4% for schizophrenia. Similarly, bipolar disorder has also been demonstrated to be associated with suicidality, particularly bipolar II. In fact, a history of suicide attempts was highest, as was death by suicide, among bipolar II patients over bipolar I, or even those with unipolar depression (Dunner, 1998).

Some clarification is needed regarding suicide prevalence data. Although the correlation between depression and suicide is high, the correlation is not as simple as it is often described. For example, although half of those who have completed suicide have had a diagnosable depressive disorder, the disorder itself is *not* a valid predictor of suicidality because of its significantly higher base rate, especially in primary care settings. In fact, the vast majority of depressed patients never engage in suicidal behaviors. Although the base rates of suicide in the United States are 12 per 100,000 people (Hilliard, 1995; Murphy, 1984; Tanney, 1992), it is estimated that between 230 and 566 per 100,000 of the population have a depressive disorder (Clark, Young, Scheftner, Fawcett, & Fogg, 1987; Fremouw, de Perczel, & Ellis, 1990). Thus, although a very substantial portion of suicidal patients are depressed, the reverse is not true. Thus, it is faulty to infer that depression per se is a more substantial risk factor than a host of other diagnoses that similarly carry high risk, such as schizophrenia, substance dependence, and borderline personality disorder.

Also relevant are other factors that potentiate suicide risk in those individuals with affective disorders, schizophrenia, and alcohol dependence. Just having the disorder does not necessarily increase risk, but having the disorder in addition to other environmental influences seems to increase risk. These factors will be discussed along with the disorders themselves.

Psychiatric Disorders

As previously stated, depression is the most common diagnosis associated with suicide. Again, this is not to say that most depressed individuals are suicidal, but that suicidal individuals also tend to have diagnoses of depression. A study by Fawcett, Scheftner, Clark, and Hedeker (1987) indicated that severe anhedonia, global insomnia, diminished concentration, severe anxiety, panic attacks, obsessive-compulsive features, and acute use of alcohol significantly increased acute risk of suicide within 6–12 months of the reference diagnosis of depression. Short-term risk in this sample increased if (1) the current episode of depression was one of three or fewer lifetime episodes; (2) the individual had no children under age 18 in the home; and (3) she or he also demonstrated a current episode of cyclic affective disorder (such as bipolar I or II).

Suicide among those diagnosed with schizophrenia tends to occur earlier in the lifespan, with the modal age of suicide in early adulthood (relatively early in the course of the disorder). Follow-up studies have estimated that approximately 10% of individuals with schizophrenia die by suicide, which is the main cause of death among these patients (Andreasen, 2000). Typically, schizophrenic patients who commit suicide are white males who have never married and who have not experienced a full recovery after the first few psychotic episodes. The risk is even higher for those who are better educated and have higher expectations for themselves, as well as for those who had higher premorbid functioning (Cohen, Test, & Brown, 1990). Relative to acute risk, Peuskens et al. (1997) found that concurrent depression increased the prevalence of schizophrenic suicide. For young, white schizophrenic males who have higher levels of intelligence, severe co-morbid depression is a short-term risk factor that should be assessed.

Survivors of highly traumatic isolated events or chronic traumatization are at high risk for a variety of psychiatric syndromes, including posttraumatic stress disorder (PTSD); dissociative disorders; severe personality disorders; and substance abuse, depression, and eating disorders (Chu, 1999). Many trauma patients have attempted suicide or engaged in parasuicidal behavior, and many have chronic suicidal ideation and impulses. Traumatic events that often result in these symptomologies are wartime combat, physical or sexual assault, psychological terror, accidents, and natural disasters (Chu, 1999). Not surprisingly, borderline personality disorder (BPD) patients frequently have some form of trauma in their histories, most often childhood physical or sexual abuse (Linehan, 1993).

PTSD has been shown to increase suicide risk. For example, combat veterans are seven times more likely than the general population to commit suicide (Bullman & Kang, 1994). These researchers also demonstrated that combat veterans with PTSD *and* another concurrent psychiatric diagnosis were 10 times more likely to commit suicide than those without PTSD. Substance abuse and depression were also highly correlated with completed suicides and PTSD.

Duberstein and Conwell (1997) estimated that 30–40% of individuals who complete suicide have an Axis II personality disorder. One of the most frequent personality disorders associated with elevated suicide risk is BPD. In a study of BPD inpatients followed from 10–23 years after discharge (Stone, 1989), patients meeting all eight *DSM-III* criteria for BPD at admission had a suicide rate of 36% compared with a rate of 7% for those who met five to seven of the criteria. The same study showed that BPD individuals who had a history of self-injury had double the suicide rates of those without previous self-injury; 70% of BPD patients have a history of at least one act of self-injurious behavior (Cowdry, Pickar, & Davies, 1985), thus highlighting the difficulty in accurately identifying the approximately 9% of BPD patients that will complete suicide (Stone, 1989).

These are complicated data, however, because the co-morbidity of BPD with affective disorders or substance abuse is high (Kleespies & Dettmer, 2000). Tanney (1992) found that in several studies that examined serious suicide attempts (those attempters with clear intent to die, yet their method was unsuccessful) there was a co-morbid affective or substance abuse disorder diagnosed along with BPD. Another study demonstrated that 48% of substance abuse suicide completers also met the criteria for borderline personality disorder (Murphy & Robins, 1967). Thus, individuals with BPD and multiple Axis I disorders constitute a high-risk group for suicide.

Individuals with antisocial personality disorder also have a high rate of suicidal behavior, especially in adolescents (Hawton, 1986; Shaffer, 1974). Antisocial symptoms (e.g., bullying, stealing) have been shown to be just as common as emotional symptoms (e.g., depression) in suicidal adolescents (Shaffer, 1974). In one study, 45% of adolescents diagnosed with conduct or substance abuse and depressive disorders made suicide attempts, compared with only 22% of adolescents with depressive disorders alone and 10% of adolescents with no depressive disorders (Kovacs, Goldston, & Gatsonis, 1993). Again, Axis II co-morbidity plays an important role when assessing for suicidal behavior in those individuals diagnosed with an Axis I disorder.

It has also been proposed that risks associated with certain psychiatric diagnoses vary across the lifespan. In a study by Conwell, Duberstein, Cox, and Hermann (1996) involving 141 suicide completers, it was found that those in middle age were more likely to have co-morbid affective and substance abuse disorders, while elderly suicide completers were more likely to have late onset unipolar depression. In an earlier study by Dorpat and Ripley (1960), it was reported that for suicide completers under 40 years of age, schizophrenia was the most common diagnosis; for ages 40–60, alcoholism was the most common diagnosis; and for those over 60, depression with psychotic features was the most common diagnosis.

Individuals having any of the mentioned psychiatric diagnoses have a higher risk of completing suicide within 2 years of the patient's hospitalization for a suicide attempt (Davis, Gunderson, & Myers, 1999). For those individuals diagnosed with BPD, this risk is elevated for 5 years after the hospitalization. A history of multiple hospitalizations has also been associated with a higher rate of completed suicides (Kullgren, Renberg, & Jacobson, 1986). Therefore, assessing for the client's history of psychiatric hospitalizations, perhaps reflecting on instability and severity, is crucial in determining greater risk for completed suicide.

Alcohol and Substance Abuse

In a study of alcohol intake and premature death, it has been reported that for those who consume six or more drinks daily, there is a sixfold increase in suicide risk relative to nondrinkers (Klatsky & Armstrong, 1993). Murphy and Robins (1967) found that 48% of alcoholics who completed suicide had experienced the loss of an important relationship within 1 year of their suicides, while only 15% of the depressed suicide cases had comparable losses. Duberstein, Conwell, and Caine (1994) extended these studies to include not only losses, but also interpersonal conflicts. That is, recent conflicts with spouses or close friends increased the risk of suicide. It appears, in summary, that interpersonal disruption is a large risk factor for suicidal vulnerability in alcoholics. Further, the alcoholic patient is typically in an active period of drinking when he or she commits suicide (Conwell et al., 1996).

Those who abuse other drugs are also at elevated suicidal risk. In a study by Marzuk, Tardiff, Leon, and Morgan (1992), one in five individuals under the age of 60 who committed suicide had used cocaine in the days prior to their deaths. Fifty percent of the cocaine users also used alcohol. In studies investigating alcohol abuse alone, suicides tended to occur in middle age, while polysubstance abuse and solely drug suicides tend to occur earlier in life (Kleespies & Dettmer, 2000; Rich, Sherman, & Fowler, 1989), with the mean age at suicide for alcoholics being 50 and the mean age at suicide for polysubstance abusers being 31 (Porsteinsson et al. 1997).

Thus, psychiatric diagnoses, and in particular multiple co-morbid diagnoses, increase the risk of suicide. Depression, substance abuse, and schizophrenia, as well as the relevant Axis II diagnoses should be assessed when determining risk.

Differentiating Between the Suicidal and Parasuicidal Patient

In general, *acutely suicidal* individuals have not frequently engaged in suicidal or parasuicidal acts previously and have recently suffered an extremely difficult event or loss, or an exacerbation of an ongoing stressor. In contrast, *chronically suicidal* individuals typically have a history of suicidal and parasuicidal activities, have had multiple treatments, and likely have been hospitalized in the past for this behavior. For many reasons, quite different treatment protocols may be indicated for these two subtypes of suicidal patients, so accurate assessment is needed to make an appropriate referral. Treating the chronically suicidal patient as though he or she is not chronically suicidal could exacerbate suicidality or perpetuate chronicity, just as treating the first-time, acutely suicidal patient as chronically suicidal could present unnecessary risks.

Discriminating between suicidal and parasuicidal (chronically suicidal and self-injurious) patients is an important distinction to make owing to its implications for treatment. Certain kinds of data help make this distinction. For example, the chronically suicidal patient often engages in parasuicidal behaviors that distinguish them from acutely suicidal patients. The word "parasuicide" was first defined by Kreitman (1977) to mean nonfatal, self-injurious behavior with clear intent to cause bodily harm or death. This could be self-injurious behavior resulting in tissue damage or other life-threatening bodily harm, or ingesting substances in amounts greater than the prescribed dose in order to cause harm or death. Thus, the chronically suicidal, or parasuicidal, patient often presents with a distinctive history of self-injury that is not characteristic of a patient who is experiencing an acute and limited period of suicidality. By recognizing these risk factors early on, proper treatment can be expedited while circumventing unnecessary assessment.

Certain demographic factors may also be relevant in discriminating between the acutely and chronically suicidal individual. For example, being female increases the risk of parasuicide and decreases the risk of suicide (Linehan, 1993). In particular, meeting the criteria for BPD, which is diagnosed more significantly in females than in males (Grilo, Becker, Fehon, & Walker, 1996), increases the risk for parasuicidal acts. Women are more likely to use overdosing or poisoning, cutting, burning, and other harmful acts with low risk of fatality. Males, on the other hand, complete suicide more often than females, but are at a lower risk for parasuicide than females. The methods typically used by males involve hanging or firearms (Canetto & Lester, 1995). Thus, though BPD per se is a risk factor for suicide, males are generally more likely to complete suicide than females. For primary care purposes, a female with a parasuicidal history is generally at lower risk for a lethal suicide attempt than a male, whereas a male is typically considered at higher risk for a lethal attempt with or without a parasuicidal history. In general, women attempt suicide more often and men complete suicide more often (Fremouw et al., 1990).

Assessing affect also aids in distinguishing the chronically and acutely suicidal. Both acutely and chronically suicidal patients may be depressed at the time of the act of parasuicide or suicide, but nonchronic, acutely suicidal patients generally have a more "numb" depression, whereas the chronically suicidal and parasuicidal is typically more angry or has other intense emotions (e.g., shame). That is, the acutely suicidal patient appears more apathetic than openly hostile or upset. Therefore, it is crucial to attend to affect with chronically suicidal patients (Linehan, 1993, 1999). If the care provider sees the patient becoming more depressed and apathetic over the course of assessment, this may indicate an exacerbation of risk for a suicide attempt.

Assessing for risk factors is only the first step in understanding suicidal risk and cannot replace an individual assessment in guiding assessment strategies and treatment plans. The following sections will discuss two useful, comprehensive assessment options available in primary care and how and when to use each one. The epidemiological information discussed above provides the backdrop for individualized assessment, and we will return to it as we consider intervention and treatment options. There are also some clinical issues that arise when dealing with such a high-risk population, which are important for effective assessment and treatment planning.

Considerations for Assessment

Many primary care physicians understandably believe it is difficult (if not impossible) to conduct a sufficiently effective suicide assessment to make an accurate referral or intervention in the less-than-10-minute average time they have with each patient. However, a caring and thorough suicidal assessment can often be reasonably brief as well as fit to be integrated into the treatment or intervention procedure. To start with, establishing an accurate patient history via suicide self-report questionnaires and communicating with other mental health professionals can be completed before a crisis. This, along with routine diagnostic screening for mental disorders, can prevent suicidal behavior on the front end by facilitating appropriate treatment referrals. Because between 50 and 90% of suicidal individuals meet the criteria for one or more psychiatric disorders, (Chiles & Strosahl, 1995) these patients can be monitored for suicidality (and assessed on other dimensions) more closely once they are screened. It is imperative that the primary health-care practitioner has the patient's mental health history data on hand (i.e., not just kept in a separate mental health facility). Having the information in multiple locales is fine, but it is important that the primary care physician has ready access to the mental health history of his or her patients.

There are several indications that a particular patient may need to be assessed for suicidality. The first is when the patient him- or herself reports feeling suicidal. The second is when there is known parasuicidal or suicidal behavior in the patient's history; this behavior should be assessed at fixed intervals or during routine care. The third is if there are any indications of recent parasuicidal behaviors (e.g., cuts, burns). The fourth is when the patient's affect seems different from his or her usual level of emotion, or when any of the aforementioned demographic or psychological factors are present. Fifth is if the patient seems depressed, anxious, or numb. If any of these criteria are met, a Beck Depression Inventory II (BDI-II; Beck, Steer, & Brown, 1996) can be given to the patient as a brief screening device. If the answer to question 9 (Suicidal Thoughts or Wishes) is a 2 "I would like to kill myself" or a 3 "I would kill myself if I had the chance," further assessment is necessary. The BDI-II takes only about 5 minutes for the patient to complete and has the benefit of also measuring general psychological distress (Beck, Steer, & Garbin, 1988). Of course, the primary care provider can also simply ask the patient if he or she feeling suicidal.

As mentioned earlier, there are two types of suicide assessment: risk assessment and treatment-oriented (interventive) assessment. An empathic assessment of history and risk can be the first step in any treatment for the suicidal patient, but treatment-oriented assessment capitalizes on this approach by focusing time and resources efficiently when presented with a suicidal individual. Available resources (time and staff) will determine which type of assessment is employed in any given primary care setting. Both of these assessment approaches will now be discussed in more detail.

Risk Assessment

Risk assessment is primarily an assessment of short-term risk of imminent suicide, which is also informed by longer-term risk factors. The goal of risk assessment traditionally has been to determine whether to hospitalize a patient. High-risk patients are hospitalized, and low-risk patients are sent home, often with a referral to a mental health practitioner. Risk assessment can generally be conducted by a wide range of staff and may require less time than an interventive assessment. Given the current state of many managed health-care systems, it is important to note how system issues affect the risk assessment and subsequent hospitalization of suicidal patients.

Feldman and Finguerra (2001) discuss several advantages and disadvantages of the managed care system in terms of immediate response to suicidal patients. An advantage is that a managed care, system is likely to contract with a wide spectrum of services for its members. They may include partial hospitalization programs, acute residential treatment centers, crisis centers, respite care, shelters, outpatient clinics, and many others. Effective managed care will have an advanced triage system to place patients in the most appropriate setting. Also, the larger and better the system of care, the more likely specialists will be available to manage crises, such as family therapists, behavior therapists, addiction specialists, crisis teams, and so forth. Large systems also dilute responsibility for the suicidal patient, reducing the burden for practitioners. Finally, record keeping in an efficient system makes it easy to look up a patient's previous crisis history.

Disadvantages to managed care are that in general, patients receive less treatment overall, are discharged too early, or are placed in a less-intensive level of care than may be needed for safety (Feldman & Finguerra, 2001). However, for the chronically suicidal individual, this could be beneficial (they are more likely to be placed in a less-regressive outpatient setting). Given the issues involved in hospitalization in the managed health-care era, risk assessment is crucial in determining whether to refer a patient for inpatient treatment. Conducting risk assessment is a difficult task because it is unstandardized, and risk assessment systems in general are not always applied reliably to the individual patient. Most importantly, there are no valid algorithms for determining what level of perceived risk necessitates hospitalization. Balancing costs, liability, and effective treatment is the goal, but the various methods employed to achieve this balance have not yet received empirical support.

One problem with risk-prediction systems is that they have become highly statistical (Chiles & Strosahl, 1995). Prediction equations have emerged that take into account key environmental, personality, and historical characteristics of suicide. This has left us with many suicide prediction instruments fundamentally unable to do anything but identify that a patient is in a higher risk group. This is not the same thing as assessing short-term risk for the individual. The problem is that the prediction systems identify groups of people with higher risk of suicide, but not individuals. For example, if it is known that on a certain questionnaire one item has been shown to be correlated with more completed suicides, and if a patient marks that answer, we know that he or she might be in a group tending to have a higher rate of completed suicides. However, most members of that group are not eventually going to attempt, much less complete, suicide. Knowledge of risk factors per se still does not lead to effective treatment or referral, which must be determined on an individual basis.

In order to conduct a risk assessment efficiently, focus should be placed on clinically relevant information. Simply interviewing the client about every risk factor known will probably result in the patients feeling misunderstood and taking an unnecessarily long time. In general, with exception to previous suicide attempts and a family history of suicide, the assessment should focus on the current problem and suicidality. A more positive atmosphere is created by not linking this episode to an entire lifetime of possibly misunderstood suffering.

The assessment of demographic variables, available means for completing suicide, intensity of intent (urges), deterring factors, and a plan are all parts of risk assessment. The goal is to prevent suicidal behavior. No treatment is conducted during a typical risk-assessment session, and in general the two possible outcomes are: (1) the patient is deemed safe enough to leave from immediate medical and psychological care (perhaps to return for mental health care at a later time) or (2) hospitalization. Hospitalization plays a key role in risk assessment and should be considered carefully. However, inpatient hospitalization is often unnecessary for safety, it incurs high costs, and it may have (in some populations) iatrogenic effects. Hospitalization may also be overutilized to limit primary care liability or because many providers have not learned alternative approaches.

Inpatient hospitalization has long been considered a standard of care for suicidal patients, and given the legal and ethical responsibilities of a psychotherapist or other mental health-care provider, it is sometimes necessary. However, one of the top five reasons for psychiatric malpractice suits in the United States is *unnecessary* hospitalization (Hirsh & Lielbreidis, 1983). Therefore, it is always preferable to obtain voluntary hospitalization; however, if the situation demands it, involuntary detention may be necessary. According to Beutler, Clarkin, & Bongar (2000):

> Risk and retention are optimized if the patient is realistically informed about the probable length and effectiveness of the treatment and has a clear understanding of the roles and activities that are expected of them during the course of treatment (p. 182).

There are several points to keep in mind when deciding whether to hospitalize (Linehan, 1993, 1999). The first is the presence of a serious psychiatric state along with suicidal threats. For diagnoses like schizophrenia, psychotic depressions, or severe affective disorders, hospitalization may provide the around-the-clock management that only a hospital can provide. A second consideration for hospitalization is if the patient has overwhelming acute problems and no social support. The second consideration is whether the person lives in a home or social environment so destructive that they cannot manage in it, and there are no other available refuges. A third consideration is to monitor psychotropic medications when overdose risk is high. A fourth consideration for hospitalization is when admissions are planned as a long-term treatment plan. This could include conducting exposure treatment of posttraumatic stress in a safe environment and planning a hospital stay when the primary therapist is on vacation, among other, nonacute therapeutic reasons. The fifth consideration is whenever suicide risk outweighs the risk of inappropriate hospitalization. This consideration is especially important in the hospitalization of chronically suicidal individuals, for whom unnecessary hospitalization could be reinforcing suicidal behavior (Linehan, 1993).

There are alternatives to hospitalization that provide necessary intensive treatment but without the inpatient status. Partial hospitalization typically involves a day-treatment program for several days or weeks and usually follows a period of inpatient hospitalization. For example, a suicidal individual could spend several days in inpatient care and then go home with the regimen of attending the partial hospitalization program every day for 8 hours for 2 weeks. Basically the patient eats an evening meal and sleeps at home, and spends the rest of the time in treatment. Acute residential treatment involves 24-hour care that is not typically held in a contained facility. They are generally viewed as a kind of respite care and are less costly than inpatient admission. Observation or holding beds allows extended assessment or 24-hour supervision while more triaging options are entertained. Thus, there are more options than inpatient hospitalization that are sometimes overlooked when a patient is deemed a danger to go home alone. It is important for primary care providers to be aware of local resources for comprehensive mental health treatment for suicidal patients.

Interventive Assessment

Risk assessment does not try to reduce present risk, only to assess it. An alternative approach to assessment, what we call *interventive assessment*, focuses instead on risk reduction and generally requires a more highly trained professional (many primary care providers could be trained to do this) with sufficient time (up to 30 minutes) available. Interventive assessment is extremely useful for the chronically suicidal patient in reducing both short-term and long-term risk, and it may lower the incidence of unnecessary hospitalization or hospitalization that could have iatrogenic effects. It is to interventive assessment that we will now turn. This approach to suicidal patients has gained evidence to support its use, and with that have come respect and popularity in recent years (Chiles & Strosahl, 1995; Linehan, 1993).

Chronic and multiproblem patients are typically good candidates for interventive assessment because they often present in the clinic with parasuicidal self-injuries that are sometimes mistaken for suicide attempts. The multiproblem patient is a patient who is regularly in crisis and for whom suicidal behavior may be reinforced in multiple ways. BPD patients fit the profile of a multiproblem patient. Their behavior is typically characterized by emotional reactivity or emotion dysregulation, and interpersonal turmoil. Parasuicide or nonlethal suicide attempts (as well as possible lethal suicide attempts) may function to alleviate misery temporarily in a variety of ways (Fruzzetti, 2002; Linehan, 1993).

The goals of interventive assessment are to validate the patient's emotional pain, teach acceptance of that pain, help the patient tolerate the pain, and help the patient make significant life changes and reduce pain in the long term. Interventive assessment may be sufficient treatment for some problems, or may simply help the PCP get an accurate assessment that facilitates making a referral to an appropriate treatment program. The first step is to reframe the suicidality as an implicit (or explicit) problem-solving technique that has been useful in the past (mostly as an escape) but clearly has not solved the person's life problems. Risk factors and information surrounding the current episode are then gathered in a problem-solving context, with the participation and collaboration of the patient. The key to interventive assessment is that the suicidality is not labeled as the problem, but rather the present triggers or current (temporary) life circumstances or recent problematic events are identified as the problem(s) to be ameliorated. Some clients may break up with a partner or lose a job and manage their distress unproductively by slashing tires or by aggressing against the person they feel is responsible for their pain, withdrawal, or other ineffective acts. The multiproblem patient may feel so much emotional pain and have such difficulty tolerating or ameliorating it that suicide seems the only solution. Thus, suicidal behaviors may serve as an escape route from severe emotional pain, or paradoxically, may provide relief from emotional pain. After identifying and validating the patient's emotion, interventive assessment focuses on the problem at hand, rather than on the ineffective ways in which the patient has tried to manage it.

Reducing Emotional Arousal in Dysregulated Patients

The most common reason patients are difficult to manage is that there are high levels of emotional arousal that can interfere with their normal capacity to think and problem solve (Fruzzetti, 2002; Fruzzetti & Nilsonne, 2004; Linehan, 1993). Linehan (1993) describes this as *emotion dysregulation.* What often happens in health-care settings is that patients become more dysregulated as a result of the ways that the "system" responds to them, and this high arousal can result in crisis exacerbation. For a sensitive and reactive suicidal patient, being told "you'll just get another boyfriend/girlfriend" may invalidate the person's high levels of fear, anguish, or other emotion. Thus, by using brief validating statements instead, and then helping patients reorient their attention, patient emotional arousal can be reduced to a reasonable level, which in turn allows them to behave more effectively (Fruzzetti & Nilsonne, 2004). Often, strategies to enhance emotion self-management should be targeted before other problem-solving strategies to help patients de-escalate closer to their baseline levels of emotional arousal; thus, interventions will be more effective and manageable for care providers.

There are several reasons why reducing a patient's emotional arousal can help bring about positive consequences in the health-care setting (Fruzzetti & Nilsonne, 2004). These include:

1. *Increases patient satisfaction with his or her health care.* Satisfied patients are more willing to cooperate with treatment goals. This could hopefully result in improved mood, more collaboration, and less suicidal behaviors. It is also important legally because, according to Gutheil (1998), malpractice lawsuits often arise from a "malignant synergy" of bad outcomes and bad feelings, not necessarily failure to provide appropriate treatment. Thus, by improving patient satisfaction, there will be less likelihood for malpractice lawsuits.
2. *Increases the accuracy and relevance of information collected.* An upset or agitated patient is less likely to cognitively process in a way that allows for accurate assessment of information necessary for effective problem solving.
3. *Improves treatment and/or referral.* More accurate assessment data will naturally lead to better treatment and a better-matched referral for appropriate treatment.
4. *Decreases agitation, resulting in fewer negative staff reactions and less staff burnout.* The high emotional arousal of suicidal patients can be frightening and frustrating to staff. By decreasing the emotional arousal in patients, staff will be more motivated to help these patients over a longer period of time.

5. *Increases compliance with treatment protocols.* By reducing a patient's arousal, not only will the patient be satisfied with his or her health care (number 1), but also will be more likely to comply with the prescribed treatment regimen.
6. *Decreases health-care utilization and costs.* Compliance is heightened and costs are lowered by giving patients instructions and treatment protocols when they are more able cognitively to process them in a baseline emotional state as opposed to a dysregulated state.

There are several steps to managing emotional arousal in suicidal patients (Fruzzetti & Nilsonne, 2004). They include:

1. *Identify goals and targets.* This requires the provider to stay emotionally regulated him- or herself and to adopt a nonjudgmental stance toward the patient.
2. *Identify targets to validate.* These can be the patient's emotional pain, the patient's goals, or problems that are getting in the patient's way.
3. *Redirect the patient to pay attention to some neutral stimulus.* If he or she is becoming dysregulated, direct the patient to the provider's face ("Look at me."), an inanimate object in the room such as a picture, their own breathing, and so forth.
4. *Continue to validate as needed.* This is to keep the patient feeling understood and focused.
5. *When the patient is re-regulated, problem solve.* After the patient's emotional arousal is down, the original purpose of the visit can be addressed. This may, of course, include making a referral to specialists, including an appropriate comprehensive mental health treatment program.

Staff Issues

Many staff issues and reactions can get in the way of effective patient management, especially when providing care to dysregulated patients who can be hostile and out of control (Fruzzetti & Nilsonne, 2004). The first are the emotions of the staff member. Staff will no doubt have feelings of frustration, fear, anger, and sadness, among others when dealing with difficult patients. Staff can also make negative or critical judgments about the patient's behavior, or about the staff's own reactions to the patient. It is important to remember that the patient is struggling and is doing the best he or she can under the circumstances. Also, emotional arousal is typically getting in the way of the patient behaving effectively and anyone, given the right circumstances (e.g., few personal resources coupled with extraordinary life stress), could be a difficult patient. It is crucial to focus on being effective, not belaboring a point so the patient agrees. It is easy to become judgmental about patients with high emotional arousal and immediately feel frustration when they will not do what you want them to do. By being effective instead of focusing on being frustrated, you can more easily and quickly discontinue approaches that do not work and move on to more effective ones.

For the chronically suicidal patient, it is important to assess immediate short-term versus long-term risk. Linehan (1993) states that active intervention is used to prevent suicide with these types of patients, but parasuicide per se is not specifically targeted at that moment unless the parasuicidal act will lead to serious harm. The "life worth living" goal of DBT, pioneered by Linehan, is an interesting agenda to keep in mind while working with the chronically suicidal patient. A life worth living generally does not involve continual hospitalization.

Interventive assessment directly dictates the course of treatment. Interventive assessment is useful because of its targets of re-regulating and reorienting the patient. By reducing emotional arousal and providing a plan for soothing the patient or solving one or more problems, hospitalization may not be needed. By staying focused on the aforementioned targets *until the present risk is reduced,* the patient can then be referred to appropriate outpatient care. Interventive assessment can be a vital part of treatment but, of course, hospitalization (or additional intervention) is sometimes needed as well.

Clinical Examples. The relative utility of interventive assessment and risk assessment is illustrated in the following alternative ways to handle common presentations in a primary care setting.

Example A: Mary. Mary presented to her PCP for a routine visit. Mary had self-injured (superficial cutting that did not require medical attention) in the prior 48 hours and reported current suicidal ideation.

Risk assessment approach. Upon learning of the recent parasuicide, the PCP inquired about suicidal thoughts (they were present) and did a brief risk assessment that determined that Mary was at high risk for attempting suicide (i.e., she met criteria for several risk factors including substance abuse, depression, recent loss, and a history of self-injury). The PCP promptly referred Mary to inpatient treatment.

Interventive assessment approach. After identifying the parasuicide and current suicidal ideation, the PCP began to assess for current events in Mary's life that may have been exacerbating her suicidality. The PCP learned that she had broken up with her boyfriend, which precipitated her self-injury. However, her suicidal thoughts were no higher than usual for Mary, and Mary was not particularly disturbed by them. Moreover, "breaking up" seemed to be a frequent occurrence in their relationship, followed within days of getting back together. The PCP supported and validated Mary's sadness about the loss and fears that they would stay broken up and then quickly began to problem solve with Mary regarding how to manage either getting back together with her boyfriend successfully or how to tolerate the loss and seek social support from others in the next 24–48 hours. Together they made a brief plan for what Mary would do if her suicidality increased. The PCP referred Mary to appropriate *outpatient* mental health service personnel, who arranged an appointment within 72 hours with a local couples therapist to help Mary and her boyfriend with their relationship, assuming that the current breakup was not, in fact, permanent.

Of course, if the PCP had not been able to develop a collaborative plan that de-escalated the patient's immediate risk for suicide fairly quickly (or clearly established that safety could be achieved in some other way), inpatient treatment could have become an important part of Mary's treatment plan.

In this scenario, the chronicity (and predictability) of the patient's suicidality informed the PCP's assessment and intervention strategies. Rather than focusing solely on Mary's present suicidal ideation and other relevant risk factors, the PCP was able to reduce the risk to a lower (and more acceptable) level by focusing on the present emotion and events that were contributing to Mary's suicidal thoughts and urges. In addition, the additional assessment made the referrals much more likely to address and resolve Mary's pattern of suicidality.

Furthermore, this assessment could have been provided by any number of health-care professionals, including physicians, nurses, physician's assistants, onsite therapists, or social workers. In this case the PCP, on discovering Mary's recent parasuicide and current suicidal ideation, could have called in a staff therapist or other mental health practitioner to complete a similar interventive assessment.

Example B: Brian. Brian's chief complaints were fatigue, sleeplessness, and depressed mood. The primary care provider, of course, assessed further for depression and Brian disclosed that he also has been drinking alcohol nightly to intoxication, using methamphetamines several times per week, and recently was kicked out of his apartment by his girlfriend. He has been staying for the past several weeks in a room over his brother's garage. When asked directly about suicidal thoughts or intentions, Brian was initially evasive, but when pressed he disclosed that he has had thoughts about shooting himself (his brother keeps several guns in the house).

Risk-assessment approach. The PCP immediately referred Brian for inpatient assessment and treatment due to the combination of risk status, suicidal thoughts, and access to suicide means.

Interventive assessment approach. The PCP discussed briefly with Brian whether he was willing and able to stop all substance use and willing to involve his brother in a safety plan. Brian was ambivalent about his own safety, not willing to commit to getting rid of drugs or alcohol, and did not want to call his brother. After the PCP spent several minutes trying to understand and validate Brian's experiences, Brian continued to seem detached and continued to be unwilling to collaborate in any kind of safety planning. Consequently, the PCP referred Brian immediately for inpatient assessment and treatment.

In this example, given the high-risk situation, involvement of substances, access to weapons, and the unwillingness of the patient to commit strongly to an alternative course all conspired to reduce effective options. Simply letting the patient go with a referral for outpatient services would not be advisable in this type of high-risk–low-collaboration situation.

Example C: Christina. This patient presented to her PCP in a mildly agitated state, asking for medications to help her calm down and sleep. Christina described fits of crying, a lot of fear and sadness, trouble sleeping, binge eating, and social isolation. A couple of days ago her boyfriend had left her after finding out that she had been having an affair. Christina reported a lot of shame even disclosing this to the PCP, and acknowledged that she had not told anyone else about it. When asked directly about suicidal thoughts she acknowledged having fleeting thoughts about driving off a bridge or "just dying" when she was feeling overwhelmed, ashamed, and alone, and had cut herself superficially on the back of her arm twice in the past couple of days (with a history of having done this several times in the past couple of years).

Risk assessment approach. Based on her risk status, suicidal thoughts, high levels of emotion, and impulsivity, the PCP referred Christina for inpatient assessment and treatment.

Interventive assessment approach. The PCP validated her feelings, while challenging her suicidality (e.g., "Of course, when anybody does things that she's not proud of, and those things mess up our relationships or hurt others, we feel awful about it. Killing ourselves doesn't really solve the problem, however."). After a few minutes Christina reported feeling a lot better "just having someone know about her pain." She did not want to go to a hospital, but was willing to make an appointment at the local community mental health center having a specialized program for parasuicidal patients (DBT, see below) for the next day. Because her emotional arousal had abated, Christina was willing to engage in collaborative problem solving concerning her safety. She agreed, while still with the PCP, to call her sister, who in turn agreed to have Christina come and spend the night with her and to go with her to her appointment the next day. The PCP asked Christina and her sister to commit to calling the ER should her suicidal thoughts or urges return before the next day's appointment, to which they agreed.

The possible advantages of the interventive approach include (a) patient empowerment (reinforcing patient collaborative problem solving rather than external control); (b) lower health-care costs; (c) more immediate involvement of the patient's social and family network; (d) integrating the patient's mental health treatment into the managed care setting, facilitating coordination, communication, and effective treatment; and (e) likely matching of response to risk. Of course, risk is not zero, and this approach likely would take 10–15 minutes of a health-care provider's time. Thus, it may not always be possible or desirable.

Treating Psychiatric Disorders Associated With Suicidality

As discussed earlier, one of the major factors associated with suicide is a psychiatric condition, in particular, depression, schizophrenia, substance abuse, or borderline personality disorder. The first treatment consideration is dealing with these disorders. As soon as the initial crisis has passed, long-term treatment can begin. Reinecke (2000) quotes Bongar (1991) describing this target of longer-term care:

> If the clinician becomes preoccupied with the issue and threat of a patient's suicide, it can divert the clinician from the primary task of attending to more disposition-based treatment-therapeutics that are solidly grounded in an understanding of the power of a sound therapeutic alliance and on a well-formulated treatment plan (p. 104).

If depression is the primary disorder, cognitive-behavior therapy could be considered with possible treatment goals being developing stable and supportive interpersonal relationships and effective communicating (Reinecke, 2000). Family or marital counseling may also be effective in reducing depression and resolving interpersonal problems (e.g., Jacobson, Dobson, Fruzzetti, Schmaling, & Salusky, 1991).

In the case of BPD, dialectical behavior therapy (DBT) has been shown to be effective in reducing suicidal crises. DBT was first evaluated with a 1-year clinical trial involving 47 chronically parasuicidal women meeting criteria for BPD (Linehan, Armstrong, Suarez, Allmon, & Heard, 1991) who were randomly assigned to either DBT or treatment as usual (TAU). Results indicated that TAU participants engaged in significantly more parasuicides than did DBT clients during the year of treatment. Looking at only those participants who were parasuicidal, parasuicides in the TAU group were of significantly higher medical risk and required significantly more medical treatment than those participants in the DBT group. Results further indicated that 58% of TAU group participants dropped their first therapist in the first year, compared with only 17% of those in the DBT group. Participants in the DBT group also spent significantly fewer days in psychiatric inpatient units and incurred substantially fewer costs. Further studies of DBT's effectiveness in treating chronically suicidal women and reducing hospitalization and therapist costs can be found in Koerner and Dimeff (2000) and Fruzzetti (2002).

Of course, many treatments have also proven to be effective in reducing depression and suicidal ideation. These include cognitive-behavioral therapies and other approaches specific to certain conditions such as trauma, panic, and posttraumatic stress. Again, depending on the specific disorder, the treatment should be determined during assessment (see Chambless & Hollon, 1998; Nathan & Gorman, 1998).

After the short-term crisis has been handled, long-term treatment can consider other factors besides safety. What are the client's problem-solving deficits? What is the patient's psychiatric disorder? Is the patient receiving good, evidence-based treatment? Are the family and social environments stable, or instead reinforcing suicidality or contributing to suicidality? Without attending to these questions, long-term treatment could quickly turn into long-term crisis management. It is crucial to treat the thoughts, emotions, behaviors, and life problems leading to suicidality, and these should be the essence of effective treatment. There are, of course, many empirically supported psychotherapies and pharmacotherapies to treat depression, schizophrenia, substance abuse, and other disorders, but appropriate treatment is predicated on thorough assessment, starting with safety.

Summary

Suicidal crises in a primary care setting are difficult, yet manageable tasks given clear goals and appropriately trained staff. Two approaches were highlighted: (1) risk assessment, with a focus on identifying relevant risk factors leading to either hospitalization (higher risk) or outpatient referral (lower risk), and (2) interventive assessment, with a focus on validation of emotion, problem solving, and risk reduction, with a target of reducing risk to the point that outpatient treatment or management is appropriate (lower risk). Also noted was the value of distinguishing between an acute suicidal crisis that follows a long period of higher functioning without ongoing suicidality, and an acute exacerbation of suicidality in the context of a long history of chronic suicidality.

The importance of not exacerbating a suicidal crisis or reinforcing a problematic pattern of crisis behavior in the primary care setting was highlighted. The primary care setting is also an essential nexus to appropriate referrals, matching referrals to the presenting problems. Consultation among primary care providers was stressed to alleviate provider burnout, help make balanced decisions in crises, and limit patient risk and provider liability. Thus, the primary care clinician plays a key role in the serious clinical presentation of suicidal patients.

References

American Association of Suicidology. (1998). *U.S.A. suicide: 1996 official data.* Washington, DC: Author.

Andreasen, N. C. (2000). Schizophrenia: The fundamental questions. *Brain Research Reviews, 31,* 106–112.

Bandura, A. (1969). *Principles of behavior modification.* New York: Holt, Rinehart, & Winston.

Beck, A. T., Steer, R. A., & Brown, G. K. (1996). *Manual for Beck Depression Inventory-II.* San Antonio, TX: Psychological Corporation.

Beck, A. T., Steer, R. A., & Garbin, M. G. (1988). Psychometric properties of the Beck Depression Inventory: Twenty-five years of evaluation. *Clinical Psychology Review, 8,* 77–100.

Beutler, L. E., Clarkin, J. F., & Bongar, B. (2000). *Guidelines for the systematic treatment of the depressed patient.* New York: Oxford University Press.

Bongar, B. R. (1991). *The suicidal patient: Clinical and legal standards of care.* Washington, DC: American Psychological Association.

Breitbart, W. (1993). Suicide risk and pain in cancer and AIDS patients. In C. R. Chapman & K. M. Foley (Eds.), *Current and emerging issues in cancer pain: Research and practice* (pp. 49–65). New York: Raven Press.

Breslau, N., Davis, G. D., & Andreski, P. (1991). Migraine, psychiatric disorders, and suicide attempts: An epidemiologic study of young adults. *Psychiatry Research, 37,* 11–23.

Bullman, T. A., & Kang, H. K. (1994). Posttraumatic stress disorder and the risk of traumatic deaths among Vietnam veterans. *Journal of Nervous and Mental Disease, 182,* 604–610.

Cannetto, S. S., & Lester, D. (1995). Gender and the primary prevention of suicide mortality. *Suicide and Life-Threatening Behavior, 25,* 58–69.

Carr, E. G. (1977). The motivation of self-injurious behavior: A review of some hypotheses. *Psychological Bulletin, 84,* 800–816.

Chambless, D. L., & Hollon, S. D. (1998). Defining empirically supported therapies. *Journal of Consulting and Clinical Psychology, 66,* 7–18.

Chiles, J. A., & Strosahl, K. D. (1995). *The suicidal patient: Principles of assessment, treatment, and case management.* Washington, DC: American Psychiatric Press.

Chiles, J., Strosahl, K. D., McMurtray, L., & Linehan, M. M. (1985). Modeling effects on suicidal behavior. *Journal of Nervous and Mental Disease, 173,* 477–481.

Chu, J. A. (1999). Trauma and suicide. In D. G. Jacobs (Ed.), *The Harvard Medical School guide to suicide assessment and intervention* (pp. 332–354). San Francisco: Jossey-Bass.

Clark, D. C., Young, M. A., Scheftner, W. A, Fawcett, J., & Fogg, L. (1987). A field test of Motto's risk estimator for suicide. *American Journal of Psychiatry, 144,* 923–926.

Cohen, L., Test, M., & Brown, R. (1990). Suicide and schizophrenia: Data from a prospective community study. *American Journal of Psychiatry, 147,* 602–607.

Conwell, Y., Duberstein, P. R., Cox, C., & Hermann, J. H. (1996). Relationship of age and Axis I diagnoses in victims of completed suicide: A psychological autopsy study. *American Journal of Psychiatry, 153,* 1001–1008.

Cowdry, R. W., Pickar, D., & Davies, R. (1985). Symptoms and EEG findings in the borderline syndrome. *International Journal of Psychiatry in Medicine, 15,* 201–211.

Davis, T., Gunderson, J. G., & Myers, M. (1999). Borderline personality disorder. In D. G. Jacobs (Ed.), *The Harvard Medical School guide to suicide assessment and intervention* (pp. 311–331). San Francisco: Jossey-Bass.

DeCatanzaro, D. (1981). *Suicide and self-damaging behavior.* New York: Academic Press.

Diekstra, R. (1973). *A social learning approach to the prediction of suicidal behavior. Proceedings of the 7th International Congress for Suicide Prevention.* Amsterdam: Swets & Zeitlinger.

Dorpat, T. L., & Ripley, H. L. (1960). A study of suicide in the Seattle area. *Comprehensive Psychiatry, 1,* 349–359.

Duberstein, P. R., & Conwell, Y. (1997). Personality disorders and completed suicide: A methodological and conceptual review. *Clinical Psychology: Science and Practice, 4,* 359–376.

Duberstein, P. R., Conwell, Y., & Caine, E. R. (1994). Age differences in the personality characteristics of suicide completers: Preliminary findings from a psychological autopsy study. *Psychiatry: Interpersonal & Biological Processes, 57,* 213–224.

Duberstein, P. R., Conwell, Y., & Cox, C. (1998). Suicide in widowed persons: A psychological autopsy comparison of recently and remotely bereaved older participants. *American Journal of Geriatric Psychiatry, 6,* 328–334.

Dunner, D. L. (1998). Bipolar disorders in *DSM-IV*: Impact of inclusion of rapid cycling as a course modifier. *Neuropsychopharmacology, 19*, 189–193.

Durkheim, E. (1951). *Suicide*. New York: The Free Press.

Fawcett, J., Scheftner, W., Clark, D., & Hedeker, D. (1987). Clinical predictors of suicide in patients with major affective disorders: A controlled prospective study. *American Journal of Psychiatry, 144*, 35–40.

Feldman, J., & Finguerra, L. (2001). Managed crisis care for suicidal patients. In J. M. Ellison (Ed.), *Treatment of suicidal patients in managed care* (pp. 15–38). Washington, DC: American Psychiatric Press.

Ferster, C. (1961). Positive reinforcement and behavioral deficits of autistic children. *Child Development, 32*, 437–456.

Fisher, B. J., Haythornthwaite, J. A., Heinberg, L. J., Clark, M., & Reed, J. (2001). Suicidal intent in patients with chronic pain. *Pain, 89*, 199–206.

Fremouw, W. J., de Perczel, M., & Ellis, T. E. (1990). *Suicide risk: Assessment and response guidelines*. Elmsford, NY: Pergamon.

Fruzzetti, A. E. (2002). Dialectical behavior therapy for borderline personality disorder and related disorders. In T. Patterson (Ed.), *Comprehensive handbook of psychotherapy, Vol. 2: Cognitive-behavioral approaches* (pp. 215–240). New York: Wiley.

Fruzzetti, A. E., & Nilsonne, A. (2004). *Patient management: Skills for healthcare professionals*. Unpublished manuscript.

Geisser, M. E., Robinson, M. E., Keefe, F. J., & Weiner, M. L. (1994). Catastrophizing, depression, and the sensory, affective, and evaluative aspects of chronic pain. *Pain, 59*, 177–184.

Grilo, C. M., Becker, D. F., Fehon, D. C., & Walker, M. L. (1996). Gender differences in personality disorders in psychiatrically hospitalized adolescents. *American Journal of Psychiatry, 153*, 1089–1092.

Gutheil, T. (1998). The wellsprings of litigation. In L. Lifson & R. Simon (Eds.), *The mental health practitioner and the law* (pp. 250–261). Cambridge, MA: Harvard University Press.

Hawton, K. (1986). Suicide in adolescents. In A. Roy (Ed.), *Suicide* (pp. 135–150). Baltimore: Williams & Wilkins.

Haythornthwaite, J. A., Sieber, W. J., & Kerns, R. D. (1991). Depression and the chronic pain experience. *Pain, 46*, 177–184.

Hilliard, J. R. (1995). Predicting suicide. *Psychiatric Services, 46*, 223–225.

Hirsh, H. L. & Lielbreidis, P. (1983). Psychiatric malpractice: Liability for suicide and attempted self-destruction. *Urban Health*.

Inskip, H. M., Harris, E. C., & Barraclough, B. (1998). Lifetime risk of suicide for affective disorder, alcoholism and schizophrenia. *British Journal of Psychiatry, 172*, 35–37.

Jacobson, N. S., Dobson, K., Fruzzetti, A. E., Schmaling, K. B., & Salusky, S. (1991). Marital therapy as a treatment for depression. *Journal of Consulting and Clinical Psychology, 59*, 547–557.

Keitner, G. I., Miller, I. W., Fruzzetti, A. E., Epstein, N. B., Bishop, D. S., & Norman, W. H. (1987). Family functioning and suicidal behavior in psychiatric inpatients with major depression. *Psychiatry, 50*, 242–255.

Kerns, R. D., Haythornthwaite, J. A., Southwick, S., & Giller, E. L. (1990). The role of marital interaction in chronic pain and depressive symptom severity. *Journal of Psychosomatic Research, 34*, 410–418.

Klatsky, A., & Armstrong, M. (1993). Alcohol use, other traits, and risk of unnatural death: A prospective study. *Alcoholism: Clinical and Experimental Research, 17*, 1156–1162.

Kleespies, P. M., & Dettmer, E. L. (2000). An evidence-based approach to evaluating and managing suicidal emergencies. *Journal of Clinical Psychology, 56*, 1109–1130.

Kochanek, K. D., & Hudson, B. L. (1995). Advance report of final mortality statistics. *Monthly Vital Statistics Report, 43*.

Koerner, K., & Dimeff, L. A. (2000). Further data on dialectical behavior therapy. *Clinical Psychology Science and Practice, 7*, 104–112.

Kovacs, M., Goldston, D., & Gatsonis, C. (1993). Suicidal behaviors and childhood-onset depressive disorders: A longitudinal investigation. *Journal of the American Academy of Child and Adolescent Psychiatry, 32*, 8–20.

Kreitman, N. (1977). *Parasuicide*. Chinchester, England: Wiley.

Kullgren, G., Renberg, E., & Jacobsson, L. (1986). An empirical study of borderline personality disorder and psychiatric suicides. *Journal of Nervous and Mental Disease, 174*, 328–331.

Lester, D. (1988). *Suicide from a psychological perspective*. Springfield, IL: Charles C Thomas.

Li, G. (1995). The interaction effect of bereavement and sex on the risk of suicide in the elderly: An historical cohort study. *Social Science and Medicine, 40*, 825–828.

Linehan, M. M. (1973). Suicide and attempted suicide: Study of perceived sex differences. *Perceptual and Motor Skills, 37*, 31–34.

Linehan, M. M. (1993). *Cognitive-behavioral treatment of borderline personality disorder*. New York: Guilford.

Linehan, M. M. (1999). Standard protocol for assessing and treating suicidal behavior for patients in treatment. In D. G. Jacobs (Ed.), *The Harvard Medical School guide to suicide assessment and intervention* (pp. 146–187). San Francisco: Jossey-Bass.

Linehan, M. M., Armstrong, H. E., Suarez, A., Allmon, D., & Heard, H. L. (1991). Cognitive behavioral treatment of chronically suicidal parasuicidal borderline patients. *Archives of General Psychology, 48*, 1060–1064.

Luoma, J. B., Martin, C. E., & Pearson, J. L. (2002). Contact with mental health and primary care providers before suicide: A review of the evidence. *American Journal of Psychiatry, 159*, 909–916.

Marzuk, P. M., Tardiff, K., Leon, A. C., & Morgan, E. B. (1992). Prevalence of cocaine use among residents of New York City who committed suicide during a one-year period. *American Journal of Psychiatry, 149*, 371–375.

Maxmen, J. E., & Tucker, G. J. (1973). No exit: The persistently suicidal patient. *Comprehensive Psychiatry, 14*, 71–79.

McIntosh, J. (1995). Suicide prevention in the elderly (age 65–99). *Suicide and Life-Threatening Behavior, 25*, 180–192.

McIntosh, J. L., & Hubbard, R. W., with Santos, J. F. (1994). *Elder suicide: Research, theory, and treatment*. Washington, DC: American Psychological Association.

Morgan, D. L. (1989). Adjusting to widowhood: Do social networks really make it easier? *Gerontologist, 29*, 101–107.

Moscicki, E. K. (1997). Identification of suicide risk factors using epidemiologic studies. *Psychiatric Clinics of North America, 20*, 499–517.

Murphy, G., & Robins, E. (1967). Social factors in suicide. *Journal of the American Medical Association, 199*, 341–349.

Murphy, G. E., & Wetzel, R. D. (1982). Family history of suicidal behavior among suicide attempters. *Journal of Nervous & Mental Disease, 170*, 86–90.

Murphy, J. L. (1984). Stability of prevalence: Depression and anxiety disorders. *Archives of General Psychiatry, 41*, 990–997.

Nathan, P. E., & Gorman, J. M. (Eds.). (1998). *A guide to treatments that work.* Oxford: Oxford University Press.

Narrow, W., Regier, D., & Rare, D. (1993). Use of services by persons with mental health and addictive disorders. *Archives of General Psychiatry, 50*, 95–107.

National Institute of Mental Health. (2001). Suicide fact sheet. Retrieved May 5, 2002, from http://www.nimh.nih.gov/research/suifact.cfm.t

Pearson, J. L. (2000). Suicidal behavior in later life: Research update. In R. W. Maris, S. S. Canetto, J. McIntosh, & M. M. Silverman (Eds.), *Review of suicidology* (pp. 202–205). New York: Guilford.

Penttinen, J. (1995). Back pain and risk of suicide among Finnish farmers. *American Journal of Public Health, 85*, 1452–1453.

Perlin, S., & Schmidt, C. (1975). Psychiatry. In S. Perlin (Ed.), *A handbook for the study of suicide* (pp. 147–163). New York: Oxford University Press.

Peuskens, J., DeHert, M., Cosyns, P., Pieters, G., Theys, P., & Vermote, R. (1997). Suicide in young schizophrenic patients during and after inpatient treatment. *International Journal of Mental Health, 25*, 39–44.

Pokorny, A. (1992). Prediction of suicide in psychiatric patients: Report of a prospective study. In R. Maris & A. Berman (Eds.), *Assessment and Prediction of Suicide* (pp. 105–192). New York: Guilford.

Porsteinsson, A., Duberstein, P. R., Conwell, Y., Cox, C., Forbes, N., & Caine, E. R. (1997). Suicide and alcoholism: Distinguishing alcoholic patients with and without comorbid drug abuse. *American Journal on Addictions, 6*, 304–310.

Regier, D. A., Goldberg, I. D., & Taube, C. A. (1978). The de facto U.S. mental health services system: A public health perspective. *Archives of General Psychiatry, 35*, 685–693.

Reinecke, M. A. (2000). Suicide and depression. In F. M. Dattilio & A. Freeman (Eds.), *Cognitive-behavioral strategies in crisis intervention* (2nd ed.) (pp. 84–125). New York: Guilford.

Rich, C. L., Sherman, M., & Fowler, R. C. (1989). San Diego suicide study: The adolescents. *Adolescence, 25*, 855–865.

Roy, A., Segal, N. L., Centerwall, B. S., & Robinette, C. D. (1991). Suicide in twins. *Archives of General Psychiatry, 48*, 29–32.

Saltzberg, D., Breitbart, W., Fishman, B., Stiefel, F., Holland, J., & Foley, K. (1989, May). *The relationship of pain and depression to suicidal ideation in cancer patients.* Abstract presented at the annual meeting of the American Society of Clinical Oncologists, San Francisco.

Shaffer, D. (1974). Suicide in childhood and early adolescence. *Journal of Child Psychology and Psychiatry & Allied Disciplines, 15*, 275–291.

Statham, D. J., Heath, A. C., Madden, P. A., Bucholz, K. K., Bierut, L., Dinwiddie, S. H. et al. (1998). Suicidal behaviour: An epidemiological and genetic study. *Psychological Medicine, 28*, 839–855.

Stone, M. H. (1989). Long-term follow-up of narcissistic/borderline patients. *Psychiatric Clinics of North America, 12*, 621–641.

Tanney, B. L. (1992). Mental disorders, psychiatric patients, and suicide. In R. W. Maris & A. L. Berman (Eds.), *Assessment and prediction of suicide* (pp. 277–320). New York: Guilford.

U.S. Public Health Service. (1999). *The surgeon general's call to action to prevent suicide.* Washington, DC: Author.

Westefeld, J. S., Range, L. M., Rogers, J. R., Maples, R., Bromley, J. L., & Alcorn, J. (2000). Suicide: An overview. *Counseling Psychologist, 28*(4), 445–510.

Suggested Reading

Chiles, J. A., & Strosahl, K.D. (1995). *The suicidal patient: Principles of assessment, treatment, and case management.* Washington, DC: American Psychiatric Press.

Ellison, J. M. (2001). *Treatment of suicidal patients in managed care.* Washington, DC: American Psychiatric Press.

Feldman, J., & Finguerra, L. (2001). Managed crisis care for suicidal patients. In Ellison, J. M. (Ed.) *Treatment of suicidal patients in managed care.* (pp. 15-38). Washington, DC: American Psychiatric Press.

Hilliard, J.R. (1995). Predicting suicide. *Psychiatric Services, 46*, 223-225.

Kleespies, P.M., & Dettmer, E.L. (2000). An evidence-based approach to evaluating and managing suicidal emergencies. *Journal of Clinical Psychology, 56*, 1109-1130.

Linehan, M.M. (1993). *Cognitive-behavioral treatment of borderline personality disorder.* New York: Guilford.

Linehan, M.M. (1999). Standard protocol for assessing and treating suicidal behavior for patients in treatment. In D.G. Jacobs (Ed.). *The Harvard Medical School guide to suicide assessment and intervention* (pp. 146-187). San Francisco: Jossey-Bass.

Tanney, B.L. (1992). Mental disorders, psychiatric patients, and suicide. In Maris, R.W., & Berman, A. L. (Eds.). *Assessment and prediction of suicide* (pp. 277-320). New York: Guilford.

Chapter 6
Integrating PTSD Services: The Primary Behavioral Health Care Model

GREGORY A. LESKIN, LESLIE A. MORLAND, AND TERENCE M. KEANE

This chapter provides an overview of current diagnostic strategies and clinical treatment approaches for primary care patients suffering from the aftermath of emotional trauma. We provide a rationale to define patients with posttraumatic stress disorder (PTSD) as a clinically special target population. By doing so, primary care providers (PCPs) and primary care teams (PCTs) can identify, provide treatment for, and evaluate outcomes for PTSD patients using both a population-based approach as well as empirically validated treatments. Further, we provide a theoretical model for implementing PTSD services within an integrated behavioral health program (as described by Strosahl, Baker, Braddick, Stuart, & Handley, 1997; Strosahl, 1998) that includes delivery of care and monitoring of outcomes. In addition, information is presented about educational and skills-based approaches with an emphasis on coping skills and patient self-management. Finally, we describe a clinical protocol for treatment of PTSD in a primary care setting, including an analysis of cost issues for implementing such an integrative approach.

Survivors of trauma often seek care from primary care and emergency room settings for life-saving and palliative medical attention. However, the traumatic events suffered by these patients may extend beyond physical injuries and disease states. Many patients seeking treatment in medical settings also suffer from psychological impairment directly related to the emotional consequences of a traumatic event. For example, patients injured in vehicular accidents, burned in residential or industrial fires, shot during crimes, or violated by sexual assault may develop PTSD. PTSD is a psychiatric condition resulting from exposure to these types of highly stressful and life-threatening situations. In order to qualify for a diagnosis of PTSD, the individual's emotional response to the traumatic event must include intense fear, helplessness, or horror. Acute PTSD is diagnosed if the duration of symptoms has been less then 3 months, whereas a diagnosis of chronic PTSD is made if symptoms persist longer than 3 months. If the symptoms emerge in the first month following the event the clinician is urged to consider a diagnosis of acute stress disorder. The onset of PTSD symptoms can promote a substantial impairment in physical, occupational, or social functioning.

The symptoms of PTSD, as defined in the *DSM-IV* (American Psychiatric Committee on Nomenclature and Statistics, 1994), include reexperiencing symptoms such as (a) recurrent and intrusive recollections of the event, (b) recurrent anxious dreams or trauma-related nightmares of the event, (c) perceptions of the event reoccurring, (d) intense distress or anxiety at exposure to cues related to the trauma, and (e) physiological reactivity (increased heart rate, sweating) to cues or reminders of the event. These symptoms are commonly referred to as *traumatic memories* for these events (Leskin, Kaloupek, & Keane, 1998).

PTSD is also characterized by continued avoidant behaviors and emotional numbing (Foa, Riggs, & Gershuny, 1995; King, Leskin, King, & Weathers, 1998). These symptoms include (a) efforts to avoid thoughts or feelings related to the trauma, (b) efforts to avoid verbalizing details about the trauma, (c) efforts to avoid people, places, or activities related to the event, (d) loss of interest in normal, everyday activities, (e) feeling detached or alienated from others, (f) restricted range of emotions (i.e., feeling numb), and (g) severe limitations to conceptualize a future that includes positive life experiences. These particular symptoms can adversely affect a patient's health care due to his or her inconsistent adherence to medical services or psychotherapy (Shemesh et al., 2000).

In addition, hallmark symptoms of PTSD include difficulties modulating physiological or emotional arousal. Arousal symptoms include (a) consistent problems initiating and maintaining sleep, (b) inappropriate and intense anger at self and others, (c) concentration problems, (d) hyper-vigilance or scanning for danger cues, and (e) highly responsive startle reactions (i.e., jumping at loud noises) (Prins, Kaloupek, & Keane, 1995).

The presence of these symptoms after a traumatic event may suggest that the individual continues to fear the occurrence of additional trauma; that the world feels dangerous, highly unpredictable, and completely uncontrollable. By addressing these symptoms in the primary care setting, the patient will be able to increase his or her sense of safety and trust, and, thereby, improve his or her adherence to medical and mental health treatment. For these reasons, we recommend a more focused, vertical approach in primary care settings to improve the overall health care of PTSD patients. Since prior traumatic experience and PTSD may significantly impair the patient's physical and mental functioning and adherence to medical care, we recommend *PTSD critical pathways* be integrated into primary care settings. According to this model, prior traumatic experiences and PTSD are routinely screened for and interventions provided in the primary care setting. As we demonstrate in the following sections, by integrating PTSD critical pathways into primary care settings, patients with PTSD are provided with psychotherapeutic case management, which includes psychoeducation about the relationship between trauma and PTSD, coping skills to alleviate associated distress, and brief cognitive-behavioral interventions. We believe such an approach can improve these patients' overall mental health status, as well as help to prepare them for subsequent medical care interventions.

In the sections that follow, we describe the population prevalence rates of PTSD in the community and with selected at-risk medical populations. Some of these patients will present with undetected PTSD and overutilize medical services with specific somatic complaints, such as gastrointestinal upset and pain sensitivity. Further, we suggest that patients with PTSD are frequently diagnosed with co-morbid and chronic medical disorders, such as arterial, lower gastrointestinal, dermatological, and musculoskeletal disorders (Schnurr, Spiro, & Paris, 2000).

Prevalence Rates of Exposure to Trauma and PTSD

Epidemiological studies examining prevalence rates of exposure to extreme trauma have consistently demonstrated that exposure to a variety of traumatic events is far more common than once thought. In recent studies examining civilian-related trauma exposure, lifetime exposure to traumatic events was reported to be as high as 70% in the general adult population (Norris, 1992;

Resnick, Kilpatrick, Dansky, Saunders, & Best, 1993). Similarly, Kessler, Sonnega, Bromet, Hughes, and Nelson (1995) describe findings from the National Comorbidity Survey that 60% of men and 51% of women (15–54 years) experienced at least one traumatic event in their lifetime. In the Detroit HMO study, Breslau, Davis, Andreski, and Peterson (1991) found that 39.1% of a sample of young adults (aged 21–30) had been exposed to traumatic events during their lifetime.

Two of the most widely studied trauma populations are combat veterans and survivors of sexual assault. With respect to exposure to combat, Kulka et al. (1990) conducted the National Vietnam Veterans Readjustment Study (NVVRS), a national epidemiological survey of PTSD among Vietnam veterans. They found that 64.2% of male veterans who served in Vietnam had been exposed to one or more traumatic events in their lifetime, compared with 47.8% of men who served in the military but not in Vietnam and 44.5% of the men who never served in the military. Estimates of lifetime exposure among women were 70.8% for those who served in Vietnam, 49.5% for other women veterans, and 37.2% for the nonveteran women.

A national survey of exposure to violence among adult women in the United States (Resnick et al., 1993) found that 35.6% reported that at some point in their lives they had been the victims of a crime. Of those exposed to criminal violence, 51.8% of the sample reported they had experienced more than one type of crime or multiple criminal episodes. With regard to sexual trauma, among women in the United States, approximately 13% have experienced a completed rape (Kilpatrick, Edmonds, & Seymour, 1992). Lifetime prevalence rates for sexual assault have ranged from 13–20% (Koss, 1993).

The prevalence of PTSD is much lower than the prevalence of exposure to potentially traumatic experiences. That is, a relatively small number of individuals who are survivors of violence, accidents, and disaster actually develop the full set of PTSD diagnostic features. Several well-planned epidemiological studies have examined the rates of trauma exposure and PTSD in the community and in primary care settings. In the early 1990s, the National Comorbidity Survey (NCS; Kessler, 1995) conducted face-to-face diagnostic interviews to determine the prevalence of a wide range of potentially traumatic stressors and mental health disorders in a large nationally representative sample. The NCS found that 7.8% of respondents were diagnosed with a lifetime history of PTSD. This prevalence rate is comparable to the PTSD rates of 6% among men and 11% among women found in the Detroit Health Maintenance survey (Breslau et al., 1991).

Gender Differences

Examination of the rates of trauma exposure across studies does support the presence of significant gender differences. Much of the research suggests that while males report higher rates of trauma exposure, females report higher rates of PTSD (Breslau, Chilcoat, Kessler, Peterson, & Lucia, 1999). One possible reason is that females may be more vulnerable to developing PTSD due to the types of stressors to which they are differentially exposed. For example, women are exposed more frequently to sexual assault, which may be more strongly related to the development of PTSD (Boudreaux, Kilpatrick, Resnick, Best, & Saunders, 1998).

Co-Morbidity of PTSD and Other Psychiatric Disorders

In addition to considering the high rates of PTSD and trauma exposure, patients with PTSD frequently meet diagnostic criteria for other major psychiatric conditions (Keane & Kaloupek, 1997; Keane & Wolfe, 1990). It is not uncommon for these patients to present with co-morbid major depression, another anxiety disorder (i.e., panic attacks), and also substance abuse.

The NVVRS found that 50% of veterans with PTSD had a least one other psychiatric disorder. According to this survey, veterans with PTSD had the following lifetime prevalence rates for co-morbid psychological conditions: major depression (20%), alcohol abuse (75%), drug abuse (23%), and personality disorders (20%). According to the NVVRS, males diagnosed with PTSD were twice as likely to have alcohol-related problems, while women with PTSD were five times more likely to have alcohol-related problems (Jordan et al., 1991).

Sierles, Chen, Messing, Besyner, and Taylor (1986) at the North Chicago Veterans Affairs (VA) Medical Center studied co-morbidity in samples of Vietnam veterans with PTSD being treated as inpatients and outpatients. In both of these groups, more than 80% of the patients were found to have one or more co-morbid psychiatric disorders. Community studies examining PTSD have also demonstrated high rates of co-morbid psychiatric disorders. In the NCS, Kessler et al. (1995) reported 79% of women and 88.3% of the men with PTSD met criteria for another lifetime psychiatric disorder. The disorders more prevalent for men with PTSD were alcohol abuse or dependence and history of a major depressive episode.

In sum, PTSD patients frequently present with other psychiatric conditions. These patients may have had preexisting behavioral disorders prior to their traumatic experiences or developed other mental disorders (i.e., panic) in reaction to the trauma. Additionally, patients may develop co-morbid disorders (i.e., substance abuse) as a method to cope or quell the intense emotional affect related to PTSD.

Traumatic Stress, PTSD, and Physical Health

There is growing acceptance that traumatic exposure and PTSD are linked to poor physical health, greater utilization of medical care, and higher overall morbidity (Rosenberg et al., 2000; Taft, Stern, King, & King, 1999). For example, a recent meta-analysis compared the results of seven studies examining sexual assault history and health perceptions (Golding, Cooper, & George, 1997). A history of sexual assault was associated with a 46% increased likelihood of poor subjective health, even after controlling for the effects of major depression. Friedman and Schnurr (1995) investigated health functioning in combat veterans, sexual assault victims, and disaster survivors. Traumatic exposure was related to poor outcomes in four categories: self-reported physical health and symptoms, utilization, morbidity as indicated by physician diagnosis, and mortality. Accordingly, PTSD was proposed as a primary mediator between traumatic life experiences and these poor physical health outcomes.

Several investigations have demonstrated relationships between lifetime trauma histories and specific medical diagnoses, even years after the trauma occurred. Some examples include cardiovascular disease (Falger et al., 1992), gastrointestinal disorders such as irritable bowel syndrome (Drossman, Li, Leserman, Toomey, & Hu, 1996; Leserman et al., 1996), chronic pelvic pain (Reiter, Shakerin, Gambone, & Melburn, 1991), and fibromyalgia (Lutgendorf et al., 1995). In addition, recent research indicates that male Vietnam veterans with PTSD were at higher risk for atrioventricular conduction defects and infarctions (Boscarino & Chang, 1999).

A possible explanation for these reductions in physical health status in PTSD patients is that hormones released in the brain (e.g., glucocorticoids, catecholamines) during stressful events can damage bodily systems (Sapolsky, 1996). During stress, these hormones mediate the activation and regulation of central and peripheral nervous system processes in order to respond to environmental demands. According to the theory of allostatic load (McEwen, 2000), continued activation of these brain processes, such as in PTSD, may result in atrophy of biological systems, leading to disease states.

Life-threatening medical conditions, including heart attack, cancer, and asthma, may also contribute to the causation or worsening of PTSD. For example, research now exists suggesting that invasive types of medical procedures, such as bone marrow and liver transplantation (Walker et al., 1999) and breast cancer (Mundy et al., 2000), can meet criteria as traumatic stressors. Jacobsen and colleagues (1998) found that about 15% of females undergoing autologous bone marrow transplantation (ABMT) for breast cancer met criteria for a current diagnosis of PTSD. Follow-up studies suggest that these women continued to suffer from PTSD 12 months after their surgeries (Andrykowski, Cordova, McGrath, Sloan, & Kenady, 2000).

Population-Based Care for PTSD

A population-based management approach starts with a basic understanding of the prevalence rates of trauma and PTSD in primary care settings. Recent epidemiological studies of PTSD in outpatient medical settings have found high rates in both general community settings, as well as with patients known to be at risk due to prior trauma exposure. Samson, Bensen, Beck, Price, and Nimmer (1999) examined the prevalence of PTSD in patients at Kaiser Permanente in Denver, CO, with histories of anxiety or depression. Among those patients, 38% were diagnosed with PTSD. Stein, McQuaid, Pedrelli, Lenox, and McCahill (2000) examined 1-month rates of PTSD in a community primary care clinic. About 12% of primary care enrollees were diagnosed with PTSD. This study also determined that over 60% of patients who complained of depression, also met criteria for PTSD.

In another recent study conducted in Israel, Taubman-Ben-Ari, Rabinowitz, Feldman, and Vaturi (2001) screened for PTSD in a representative sample of patients from 26 Israeli primary care clinics. Of 2,975 patients, 37% of males and 40% of females met criteria for current PTSD diagnosis. In the Veterans Health Study, Hankin, Spiro, Miller, and Kazis (1999) screened for PTSD in a large random sample of males seeking care from a VA ambulatory care clinic in the northeastern United States. Twenty percent of the sample met diagnostic criteria for lifetime PTSD. Further, 82% of those patients with PTSD also met criteria for a depressive disorder. These two groups may represent at-risk groups for PTSD because of the patient's higher potential for exposure to combat or wartime violence.

Assessment

Compelling evidence suggests that PTSD is one of the most common anxiety disorders in primary care (Fifer et al., 1994; Sampson et al., 1999). It also appears that patients with a history of trauma and PTSD have a greater preference to seek help from a primary care practitioner rather than a mental health provider (Druss & Rosenheck, 1997; Murdoch & Nichol, 1995). Further, there are multiple studies indicating that individuals exposed to trauma have an increased likelihood of poor self-reported health possibly leading to increased utilization of medical services (Rosenberg et al., 2000). In a recent set of analyses, Deykin et al. (2001) found that high users of VA medical services are almost twice as likely to have a diagnosis of PTSD than those who use primary health-care services less frequently. Further, the veterans with the most severe PTSD tended to have the highest mean number of physician-diagnosed medical conditions. Despite these findings, most medical and community mental health settings do not routinely screen for trauma exposure or PTSD (Leskin, Ruzek, Friedman, & Gusman, 1999).

Several barriers may account for the lack of attention paid to the assessment of trauma exposure and PTSD in primary care. Many clinicians are not trained to ask about recent or lifetime trauma exposure or specifically about PTSD. Some clinicians assume patients will readily disclose trauma exposure or symptoms of PTSD. However, PTSD patients may be waiting to be asked about these experiences or they are socialized to focus on medical symptoms during a physician examination. Clinicians may feel uncomfortable, embarrassed, or intrusive asking patients about the patient's trauma exposure or PTSD symptoms. However, a majority of primary and specialty care patients indicate that they would like to be asked about their traumatic events more directly (Friedman, Samet, Roberts, Hudlin, & Hans, 1992; Robohm & Buttenheim, 1996).

Providers may think that asking about previous trauma will cause the patient to become unnecessarily distressed or agitated. Also, primary care providers may decide that encouraging disclosure about traumatic experiences will lead to additional staff resources and work to assist the patients with their life circumstances. All these potential barriers may certainly play a role in the decision about whether or not to routinely screen for trauma and PTSD in primary care settings. However, actively screening for trauma, PTSD symptomatology, and associated risk factors can aid in implementing both primary and secondary prevention within an integrated health-care service delivery model.

Brief Measures

One approach to screening PTSD in the primary care setting is to embed a brief trauma exposure measure and PTSD symptom screen into a primary care self-report evaluation. These measures can be used to quickly identify PTSD symptoms as well as unhealthy or risky behaviors. This approach may be appealing because of the previously discussed relationship between PTSD and health risks.

The Education Division of the National Center for PTSD has developed a PTSD screen, the Primary Care PTSD (PC-PTSD) screen (see Table 6.1), which can be embedded within the original PRIME-MD patient problem questionnaire (Prins, 2004) or other patient health questionnaires. This 4-item screen assesses for current PTSD without a specific trauma probe question. Using a sample of mostly female VA patients ($N = 70$) and the Clinician Administered PTSD Scale (CAPS) as a diagnostic "gold standard," endorsement of any two items resulted in adequate sensitivity and positive predictive power (.68 and .60, respectively) and excellent specificity and negative predictive power (.91 and .93, respectively). The overall efficiency of this screen was very good (.88). Based on these findings, it is recommended that when administering the PC-PTSD the results of the screen should be considered "POSITIVE" if a patient responds "YES" to two or more of the screening items. A positive response to the screen does not necessarily indicate that the patient has PTSD, but rather it indicates that a patient *may* have PTSD and that further investigation is warranted.

The Pacific Island Division of the National Center has investigated the use of a trauma measure—Traumatic Life Events Questionnaire (TLEQ)—and a PTSD measure—Distressing Event Questionnaire (DEQ)—in various settings, including family practice, outpatient psychiatry, and a substance abuse program. Both measures have demonstrated good validity and reliability across trauma populations (Kubany, Haynes et al., 2000; Kubany, Leisen, Kaplan, & Kelly, 2000). Using a sample of male veterans ($N = 120$) and the CAPS as a diagnostic gold standard and employing a cutoff score of 26, the DEQ demonstrated adequate sensitivity and positive predictive power (.87 and .78, respectively) and excellent specificity and negative predictive power (.85 and .91, receptively). The overall efficiency of the screen was again very good (.86). Using female trauma survivors ($N = 255$) and the CAPS as a diagnostic gold standard (a cutoff score of 26), the DEQ

TABLE 6.1 PTSD Primary Care Screen

Have you ever had an experience that was so frightening, horrible, or upsetting that, *in the past month*, you …		
a. Have had nightmares about it or thought about it when you did not want to?	YES	NO
b. Tried hard not to think about it or went out of your way to avoid situations that reminded you of it?	YES	NO
c. Were constantly on guard, watchful, or easily startled?	YES	NO
d. Felt numb or detached from others, activities, or your surroundings?	YES	NO

demonstrated adequate sensitivity and positive predictive power (.90 and .88, respectively) and adequate specificity and negative predictive power (.58 and .88, respectively). The overall efficiency of the screen was good (.90). Although these measures cannot be considered screens because of their length, they do offer a comprehensive, self-reporting assessment of various events and PTSD symptomotology.

The TLEQ should be used in combination with the DEQ. When used together, the questionnaires constitute a trauma history and PTSD screening protocol. Both measures are purposefully brief to be used in both mental health and medical settings. In addition, the utility of abbreviated versions of these measures is currently being investigated.

The most widely used measure of PTSD is the CAPS (Blake et al. 1995; Weathers, Keane, & Davidson, 2001). The CAPS uses a structured interview process to assess the frequency and intensity of the 17 *DSM-IV* core symptoms of PTSD and associated symptoms. Through repeated psychometric studies, the CAPS has demonstrated sound reliability and validity, and it provides a highly accurate diagnosis of PTSD. Although clearly more time intensive than the TLEQ and DEQ, the CAPS does provide the clinician with more clinically rich data about the specific symptoms and their course over time.

Although a complete overview of PTSD diagnostic assessment is not possible here, several excellent texts are available that detail these issues (for reviews see Blanchard & Hickling, 1997; Briere, 1997; Wilson & Keane, 1997). It is recommended that a brief screen for PTSD, such as the four-item Primary Care PTSD Screen, be integrated into an initial patient assessment packet in order to routinely assess for the presence of PTSD symptoms. If necessary, a complete psychological assessment would reduce false positives from the screening procedure so that psychological interventions can proceed with patients who have subthreshold or acute PTSD. This psychological assessment should incorporate an assessment of traumatic exposure (e.g., TLEQ) and a structured interview for PTSD (e.g., CAPS).

Acute Stress Disorder

Once trauma and PTSD have been screened, several options exist for clinicians within the primary care setting to use psychotherapeutic methods to minimize trauma-related distress. Immediately following trauma, critical incident stress debriefing (CISD) may be a viable treatment to reduce the likelihood of developing PTSD among certain patients. CISD consists of a single retelling of facts (usually within a group format) related to the traumatic incident soon after the individual is within a safe and comforting environment to discuss these details. This approach has been widely used following natural and technological disasters, airplane and automobile accidents, and mass shootings (Everly, Flannery, & Mitchell, 2000). Although there is a lack of controlled, randomized trials of CISD, the research suggests that CISD may be most effective for those with less direct exposure to the trauma, for example, emergency care personnel exposed to the death of others (Bisson, McFarlane, & Rose, 2000). One potential use of the CISD approach is to identify those individuals at most risk for developing PTSD who require more intensive and direct intervention. Others have recommended that psychological debriefing be integrated within a comprehensive traumatic stress management program (Dyregrov, 1997).

There is evidence that more intensive treatment may be necessary for victims of severe and direct trauma. Foa, Rothbaum, Riggs, and Murdock (1991) provided four sessions of psychotherapy to female rape victims and nonsexual assault victims about 3 weeks following their assault. This intervention included education about the connection between trauma and PTSD, relaxation exercises, imaginal and in vivo exposure, and cognitive restructuring. When compared with the matched controls, individuals receiving this preventative care had fewer complaints about traumatic memories and were significantly less depressed 5 months postassault. Similarly, Bryant, Moulds, and

Guthrie (2001) used cognitive behavioral therapy immediately following moving vehicle accidents. There were fewer cases of PTSD among patients who received a five-session package consisting of prolonged exposure therapy, anxiety management, and cognitive restructuring exercises. In the sections below, we describe some of these treatment techniques in greater detail for use in primary care management of traumatized patients.

Primary care providers in traditional medical settings can conduct debriefings or acute interventions following acute traumatization. The physician or mental health provider can incorporate brief, one-session individual, family, or group debriefings into a medical examination. The focus of these sessions should be on assessment for continued treatment, providing psychological first aid(e.g., ensuring the patient's safety), psychoeducation about trauma, and information about treatment options (Litz, Gray, Bryant, & Adler, 2002).

Treatment Options for PTSD

A number of different psychological and pharmacological treatments have been recommended for PTSD (see reviews by Foa, Keane, & Friedman, 2000; Friedman, 2000; Leskin et al., 1998). Some patients with more disabling forms of PTSD will require a more intensive treatment approach that includes both types of interventions. Cognitive-behavioral treatment interventions have received the most empirical study and include methods such as exposure therapy, cognitive therapy, anxiety management training (e.g., breathing exercises), and social skills training.

Here, we provide an overview of those elements of CBT and psychosocial interventions that may be useful in a brief treatment model for patients seen in primary care settings. Some PTSD patients require a referral for more intensive treatment in a specialized mental health setting for reduction of their PTSD; for these individuals a lengthier course of treatment may be required. For example, patients with chronic forms of PTSD, multiple lifetime traumatic events, or poor adherence to treatment plans may require more intensive, specialized PTSD treatment.

Cognitive-Behavioral Treatment for PTSD

The current treatment of choice for chronic and severe cases of PTSD is behavioral and cognitive-behavioral methods, including exposure-based approaches (Solomon, Gerrity, & Muff, 1992; Keane, 1998; Tarrier et al., 1999). During an imaginal exposure therapy session, the patient recalls their traumatic experience in detail while also processing their emotional reactions during the event (for a detailed explanation of this therapeutic intervention, see Keane, 1998, and Foa & Rothbaum, 1997). Through repeated therapy sessions, exposure therapy provides a structured approach to directly reduce the distress related to the reprocessing of traumatic memories. Several recent studies have found that exposure-based therapy is a safe and effective therapy for treating the chronic forms of PTSD (Tarrier et al., 1999; Tarrier & Humphreys, 2000). Tarrier et al. (1999) have demonstrated that PTSD patients improved from exposure therapy on multiple outcome measures even after a 12-month follow-up assessment.

In addition, cognitive therapy can assist patients in reinterpreting the meaning of the traumatic events, in order to assist the patient to reestablish a sense of safety and control in his or her life and reduce guilt or shame related to the trauma (see Ehlers & Clark, 2000; Kubany, 1998 for descriptions of cognitive therapy for PTSD). Strategically, the main purposes of the cognitive interventions are to reappraise the traumatic event in terms of personal responsibility and develop adaptive self-talk to regain a sense of calm and safety. In addition, cognitive therapy can be helpful to reduce distorted or unhealthy cognitive coping strategies, such as harsh self-punishment or thinking of oneself as undesirable or defenseless (Resick & Schnicke, 1992).

Psychosocial Intervention

Psychosocial interventions are techniques focused on improving daily living skills and interpersonal interaction. Psychosocial rehabilitation is often appropriate for individuals with disorders that impact daily living and who demonstrate needs in social functioning related to day-to-day living. Most psychosocial interventions are general in nature and not specific to symptoms of a disorder but rather target the by-products of the disorder. Owing to the impact PTSD can have on daily living, such as health, social, and occupational functioning, psychosocial techniques are recommended as an adjunct to accompany the cognitive and behavioral treatments for PTSD.

The approach taken with psychosocial intervention is often problem-focused, when an individual identifies a problem associated with the PTSD, then together the individual and the clinician can generate behavioral strategies to resolve the problem. Techniques typically include (a) health education and psychoeducation, (b) self-care and independent-living skills training, (c) supportive housing, (d) family skills training, (e) social skills training, (f) vocational rehabilitation, and (g) case management (Penk & Flannery, 2000).

Psychosocial interventions may be most appropriate in the cases of chronic PTSD where the symptoms over time have created difficulty in day-to-day living. Psychosocial interventions are also appropriate in the later stages of PTSD treatment in which the individual is prepared to reestablish social interactions and positive emotional experiences that have been adversely affected by the traumatic event.

Integrated PTSD Services Into Primary Care Settings

According to the Primary Behavioral Health Care Model (Robinson, Wischman, & Del Vento, 1996; Strosahl, 1998) defined target populations with specific mental health disorders are screened and treated by the primary care team within the primary care clinic. Behavioral health-care specialists work together with the medical staff to develop critical pathways for routine screening, collaborative case management, treatment, and follow-up of those screened positive for disorders requiring selective staff attention. In addition, this integrated model requires rapid turnover of cases using brief interventions. Those cases that require more intensive secondary treatment are referred to specialized behavioral health-care treatment specialists. Table 6.2 demonstrates a PTSD model integrated into primary care settings based on the Primary Behavioral Health Care Model.

Because PTSD is a relatively new clinical diagnosis, less empirical research is available to evaluate the effectiveness of treating PTSD within the Primary Behavioral Health Care Model. In fact, the majority of PTSD treatment services to date have been in traditional outpatient and inpatient mental health settings, such as those at the Department of Veterans Affairs (Fontana & Rosenheck, 1997). However, several brief treatment strategies for PTSD may be incorporated using the approach proposed herein. For example, it seems plausible that patients screened positive for PTSD can receive educational materials, self-management exercises, and even instructions to write out the details of the trauma at home as an exposure-type treatment.

Costs and Value

There is increasing evidence that PTSD is associated with the highest rate of mental health service use and has one of the highest per capita costs of any mental health disorder (Kessler, 2000) In addition, Walker, Harris, Baker, Kelly, and Houghton (1999) found substantially increased overall health-care costs associated with female patients who reported histories of childhood abuse and neglect. In their study of 1,225 randomly selected women from an HMO, those women who reported prior trauma histories had median annual health-care costs that were $97 more than

TABLE 6.2 A Framework for Integrated Primary Care Behavioral Health: PTSD Critical Pathways

Approach	General Goals	Specific PTSD Goals
1. Program planning approach	Population-based care planning framework based in epidemiological assessments; priority behavioral health needs addressed in resource allocations	Trauma, PTSD, and co-morbid diagnosis routinely screened for and treated in primary care settings
2. Integration models employed	System employs at least one critical pathway (vertical) and general behavioral health services (horizontal)	PTSD assigned "critical pathway status"
3. Predicted population impact	High population impact; services target high areas of behavioral health needed; service density great enough to service a variety of behavioral health needs; large cost returns possible because of multiple population targets	High impact on traumatized populations (i.e., veterans, domestic violence, sexual abuse); increase in number of patients identified with PTSD; potential for cost returns because of high utilization of this patient population
4. Service locations	Onsite services delivered within medical practice area as part of general health-care processes	Use of both primary care and specialty PTSD treatment settings
5. Service philosophy	Behavioral health-care integrated into primary medical practice; both services integrated in primary care team; goals consistent with primary mental health-care model	Patients provided with treatment in primary care (psychoeducation, coping skills, psychopharmacology); chronic, complex, and difficult cases referred to specialty care settings
6. Service characteristics	Behavioral health delivered in consultation model; physician remains in charge; visit pattern designed to integrate activities of both providers seen by patient as adjunct to primary care teams; service length is short by program design; primary care access standard used	Practice guidelines for PTSD screening, diagnosis, referral, and education in primary care settings; brief interventions employed
7. Service penetration	20% or more; program capacity great due to consultative services and multiple critical pathways	Same as general goals
8. Referral and case finding impacts	Program reduces physician referrals for specialty mental health by at least 50%; 20% or fewer patients enrolled in program referred on to specialty care	Same as general goals
9. Ongoing evaluation and training	Physicians, mental health providers, and staff continue ongoing evaluations and training for integration practices; patients and other consumers provided with education about system changes	Continued evaluation of services and population impact (i.e., costs, service utilization, clinical outcomes); patient/ staff satisfaction determined

Note. Adapted from Strosahl, 1998 and Strosahl et al., 1997.

women without childhood abuse and neglect. For those women with histories of prior sexual victimization, the median annual health-care costs were as much as $245 greater even after controlling for the effect of chronic disease burden. Although the goal of any health-care organization should be on quality of care rather than costs, these figures do illustrate the direct financial burden that trauma histories play on the provider and, more broadly, on health-care systems. The empirical literature has, to date, not considered whether brief interventions in the primary care setting would actually reduce the overall health-care costs of these patients. However, the available research does suggest that psychotherapeutic interventions can reduce the pain and distress associated with PTSD (Foa et al., 2000).

Summary

In this chapter we have demonstrated a rationale for the development and implementation of PTSD services integrated into primary care settings. PTSD is a debilitating emotional disorder that results from exposure to traumatic experiences. In its more chronic forms, PTSD can adversely impact an individual's physical and mental functioning. Effective psychotherapeutic treatments are available to reduce the patient's suffering and improve adherence to medical care. More empirical research is necessary, however, to determine the effectiveness on long-term clinical outcomes by using such an integrated behavioral health-care model.

References

American Psychiatric Committee on Nomenclature and Statistics. (1994). *Diagnostic and statistical manual of mental disorders* (4th ed.). Washington, DC: American Psychiatric Association.

Andrykowski, M. A., Cordova, M. J., McGrath, P. C., Sloan, D. A., & Kenady, D. E. (2000). Stability and change in posttraumatic stress disorder symptoms following breast cancer treatment: A 1-year follow-up. *Psycho-Oncology, 9*, 69–78.

Bisson, J. I., McFarlane, A. C., & Rose, S. (2000). Psychological debriefing. In E. B. Foa, T. M. Keane, & M. J. Friedman (Eds.), *Effective treatments for PTSD: Practice guidelines from the International Society for Traumatic Stress Studies* (pp. 39–59). New York: Guilford.

Blake, D. D., Weathers, F. W., Nagy, L. M., Kaloupek, D. G., Gusman, F. D., Charney, D. S. et al. (1995). The development of a clinician-administered PTSD scale. *Journal of Traumatic Stress, 8*, 75–90.

Blanchard, E. B., & Hickling, E. J. (1997). *After the crash: Assessment and treatment of motor vehicle accident survivors.* Washington, DC: American Psychological Association.

Boscarino, J. A., & Chang, J. (1999). Electrocardiogram abnormalities among men with stress-related psychiatric disorders: Implications for coronary heart disease and clinical research. *Annals of Behavioral Medicine, 21*, 227–234.

Boudreaux, E. D., Kilpatrick, D. G., Resnick, H. S., Best, C. L., & Saunders, B. E. (1998). Criminal victimization, posttraumatic stress disorder, and comorbid psychopathology among a community sample of women. *Journal of Traumatic Stress, 11*, 665–678.

Breslau, N., Chilcoat, H. D., Kessler, R. C., Peterson, E. L., & Lucia, V. C. (1999). Vulnerability to assaultive violence: Further specification of the sex difference in post-traumatic stress disorder. *Psychological Medicine, 29*, 813–821.

Breslau, N., Davis, G. C., Andreski, P., & Peterson, E. (1991). Traumatic events and posttraumatic stress disorder in an urban population of young adults. *Archives of General Psychiatry, 48*, 216–222.

Briere, J. N. (1997). *Psychological assessment of adult posttraumatic states.* Washington, DC: American Psychological Association.

Bryant, R. A., Moulds, M., & Guthrie, R. M. (2001). Cognitive strategies and the resolution of acute stress disorder. *Journal of Traumatic Stress, 14*, 213–219.

Deykin, E. Y., Keane, T. M., Kaloupek, D., Fincke, G., Rothendler, J., Siegfried, M. et al. (2001). Posttraumatic stress disorder and the utilization of health services. *Psychosomatic Medicine, 63*(5), 835–841.

Drossman, D. A., Li, Z., Leserman, J., Toomey, T. C., & Hu, Y. J. (1996). Health status by gastrointestinal diagnosis and abuse history. *Gastroenterology, 110*, 999–1007.

Druss, B. G., & Rosenheck, R. A. (1997). Use of medical services by veterans with mental disorders. *Psychosomatics, 38*, 451–458.

Dyregrov, A. (1997). The process in psychological debriefings. *Journal of Traumatic Stress, 10*, 589–605.

Ehlers, A., & Clark, D. M. (2000). A cognitive model of posttraumatic stress disorder. *Behaviour Research and Therapy, 38*, 319–345.

Everly, G. S., Flannery, R. B., & Mitchell, J. T. (2000). Critical incident stress management (CISM): A review of the literature. *Aggression and Violent Behavior, 5*, 23–40.

Falger, P. R., Op den Velde, W., Hovens, J. E., Schouten, E. G., De Groen, J. H., & Van Duijn, H. (1992). Current posttraumatic stress disorder and cardiovascular disease risk factors in Dutch Resistance veterans from World War II. *Psychotherapy Psychosomatics, 57*, 164–171

Fifer, S. K., Mathias, S. D., Patrick, D. L., Mazonson, P. D., Lubeck, D. P., & Buesching, D. P. (1994). Untreated anxiety among adult primary care patients in a health maintenance organization. *Archives of General Psychiatry, 51*, 740–750.

Foa, E. B., Keane, T. M., & Friedman, M. J. (2000). *Effective treatments for PTSD: Practice guidelines from the International Society of Traumatic Stress Studies.* New York: Guilford.

Foa, E. B., Riggs, D. S., & Gershuny, B. S (1995). Arousal, numbing, and intrusion: Symptom structure of PTSD following assault. *American Journal of Psychiatry, 152*, 116–120.

Foa, E. B., & Rothbaum, B. O. (1997). *Treating the trauma of rape.* New York: Guilford.

Foa, E. B., Rothbaum, B. O., Riggs, D. S., & Murdock, T. B. (1991). Treatment of posttraumatic stress disorder in rape victims: A comparison between cognitive behavioral procedures and counseling. *Journal of Consulting and Clinical Psychology, 59,* 715–723.

Fontana, A., & Rosenheck, R. A. (1997). Effectiveness and cost of the inpatient treatment of posttraumatic stress disorder: Comparison of three models of treatment. *American Journal of Psychiatry, 154,* 758–765.

Friedman, L. S., Samet, J. H., Roberts, M. S., Hudlin, M., & Hans, P. (1992). Inquiry about victimization experiences. A survey of patient preferences and physician practices. *Archives Internal Medicine, 152,* 1186–1190.

Friedman, M. J. (2000). *Post traumatic stress disorder: The latest assessment and treatment strategies.* Kansas City, MO: Compact Clinicals.

Friedman, M. J., & Schnurr, P. P. (1995). The relationship between trauma, post-traumatic stress disorder, and physical health. In Friedman, Charney, & Deutch (Eds.), *Neurobiological and clinical consequences of stress: From normal adaptation to post-traumatic stress disorder.* Philadelphia, PA: Lippincott-Raven.

Golding, J. M., Cooper, M. L., & George, L. K. (1997). Sexual assault history and health perceptions: Seven general population studies. *Health Psychology, 16,* 417–425

Hankin, C. S., Spiro, A., Miller, D. R., & Kazis, L. (1999). Mental disorders and mental health treatment among U.S. Department of Veterans Affairs outpatients: The Veterans Health Study. *American Journal of Psychiatry, 156,* 1924–1930.

Jacobsen, P. B., Widows, M. R., Hann, D. M., Andrykowski, M. A., Kronish, L. E., & Fields, K. K. (1998). Posttraumatic stress disorder symptoms after bone marrow transplantation for breast cancer. *Psychosomatic Medicine, 60,* 366–371.

Jordan, B. K., Schnurr, W. E., Hough, R., Kulka, R. A., Weiss, D., Fairbank, J. A., & Marmar, C. R. (1991). Lifetime and current prevalence of specific psychiatric disorders among Vietnam veterans and controls. *Arch Gen Psychiatry, 48,* 207–215.

Keane, T. M. (1998). Psychological and behavioral treatments of post-traumatic stress disorder. In P. E. Nathan & J. M. Gorman (Eds.), *A guide to treatments that work* (pp. 398–407). New York: Oxford University Press.

Keane, T. M., & Kaloupek, D. G. (1997). Comorbid psychiatric disorders in PTSD: Implications for research. *Annals of the New York Academy of Sciences, 821,* 24–34.

Keane, T. M., & Wolfe, J. (1990). Comorbidity in post-traumatic stress disorder: An analysis of community and clinical studies. *Journal of Applied Social Psychology, 20,* 1776–1788.

Kessler, R. C. (2000). Posttraumatic stress disorder: The burden to the individual and to society. *Journal of Clinical Psychiatry, 61,* 4–12.

Kessler, R. C., Sonnega, A., Bromet, E., Hughes, M., & Nelson, C. B. (1995). Posttraumatic stress disorder in the National Comorbidity Survey. *Archives of General Psychiatry, 52,* 1048–1060.

Kilpatrick, D. G., Edmonds, C. N., & Seymour, A. (1992). *Rape in America: A report to the nation.* Arlington, VA: National Victim Center.

King, D. W., Leskin, G. A., King, L. A., & Weathers, F. W. (1998). Confirmatory factor analysis of the clinician-administered PTSD scale: Evidence for the dimensionality of posttraumatic stress disorder. *Psychological Assessment, 10,* 90–96.

Koss, M. P. (1993). Rape: Scope, impact, interventions, and public policy responses. *American Psychologist, 48,* 1062–1069.

Kubany, E. S. (1998). Cognitive therapy for trauma-related guilt. In V. M. Follette, J. I. Ruzek, & F. R. Abueg (Eds.), *Cognitive-behavioral therapies for trauma* (pp. 124–161). New York: Guilford.

Kubany, E. S., Haynes, S. N., Leisen, M. B., Owens, J. A., Kaplan, A. S., Watson, S. B. et al. (2000). Development and preliminary validation of a brief broad-spectrum measure of trauma exposure: The Traumatic Life Events Questionnaire. *Psychological Assessment, 12,* 210–224

Kubany, E. S., Leisen, M. B., Kaplan, A. S., & Kelly, M. P. (2000). Validation of a brief measure of posttraumatic stress disorder: The Distressing Event Questionnaire (DEQ). *Psychological Assessment, 12,* 197–209.

Kulka, R. A., Schlenger, W. E., Fairbank, J. A., Hough, R. L., Jordan, B. K., Marmar, C. R. et al. (1990). *Trauma and the Vietnam war generation: Report of findings from the National Vietnam Veterans Readustment Study.* New York: Brunner/Mazel.

Leserman, J., Drossman, D. A., Li, Z., Toomey, T. C., Nachman, G., & Glogau, L. (1996). Sexual and physical abuse history in gastroenterology practice: How types of abuse impact health status. *Psychosomatic Medicine, 58,* 4–15.

Leskin, G. A., Kaloupek, D. G., & Keane, T. M. (1998). Treatment for traumatic memories: Review and recommendations. *Clinical Psychology Review, 18,* 983–1001.

Leskin, G. A., Ruzek, J. I., Friedman, M. J., & Gusman, F. D. (1999). Effective clinical management of PTSD in primary care settings: Screening and treatment options. *Primary Care Psychiatry, 5,* 3–12.

Litz, B. T., Gray, M. J., Bryant, R. A., & Adler, A. B. (2002). Early intervention for trauma: Current status and future directions. *Clinical Psychology: Science and Practice, 9,* 112–134.

Lutgendorf, S. K., Antoni, M. H., Ironson, G., Fletcher, M. A., Penedo, F., Baum, A., Schneiderman, N., & Klimas, N. (1995). Physical symptoms of chronic fatigue syndrome and exacerbated by the stress of Hurricane Andrew. *Psychosom Med., 57,* 310–323.

McEwen, B. S. (2000). Allostasis and allostatic load: Implications for neuropsychopharmacology. *Neuropsychopharmacology, 22,* 108–124.

Mundy, E. A., Blanchard, E.B., Cirenza, E., Gargiulo, J., Maloy, B., & Blanchard, C. G. (2000). Posttraumatic stress disorder in breast cancer patients following autologous bone marrow transplantation or conventional cancer treatments. *Behaviour Research and Therapy, 38,* 1015–1027.

Murdoch, M., & Nichol, K. L. (1995). Women veterans' experiences with domestic violence and with sexual harassment while in the military. *Archives of Family Medicine, 4,* 411–418.

Norris, F. H. (1992). Epidemiology of trauma: Frequency and impact of different potentially traumatic events on different demographic groups. *Journal of Consulting and Clinical Psychology, 60,* 409–418.

Penk, W. E., & Flannery, R. B. (2000). Psychosocial rehabilitation. In E. B. Foa, T. M. Keane, & Friedman, M. J. (Eds.), *Effective treatments for PTSD: Practice guidelines from the International Society for Traumatic Stress Studies* (pp. 224–246). New York: Guilford.

Prins, A., Kaloupek, D. G., & Keane, T. M. (1995). Psychophysiological evidence for autonomic arousal and startle in traumatized adult populations. In M. Friedman, D. S. Charney, & A. Deutch (Eds.), *Neurobiological and clinical consequences of stress: From normal adaptation to PTSD* (pp. 315–334). Philadelphia: Lippincott-Raven.

Prins, A., Ouimette, P. C., Kimerling, R., Cameron, R., Hugelshofer, D. S., Shaw-Hegwer, J., Thrailkill, A., Gusman, F., & Sheikh, J. (2004). The primary care PTSD screen (PC-PTSD): Development and operating characteristics. *Primary Care Psychiatry, 9*, 9–14.

Reiter, R. C., Shakerin, L. R., Gambone, J. C., & Milburn, A. K. (1991). Correlation between sexual abuse and somatization in women with somatic and nonsomatic chronic pelvic pain. *American Journal of Obstetrics and Gynecology, 165*, 104–109.

Resick, P. A., & Schnicke, M. K. (1992). Cognitive processing therapy for sexual assault victims. *Journal of Consulting and Clinical Psychology, 60*, 748–756.

Resnick, H. S., Kilpatrick, D. G., Dansky, B. S., Saunders, B. E., & Best C. L. (1993). Prevalence of civilian trauma and posttraumatic stress disorder in a representative national sample of women. *Journal of Consulting and Clinical Psychology, 61*, 984–991.

Robinson, P., Wischman, C., & Del Vento, A. (1996). *Treating depression in primary care: A manual for primary care and mental health providers.* Reno, NV: Context Press.

Robohm, J. S., & Buttenheim, M. (1996). The gynecological care experience of adult survivors of childhood sexual abuse: A preliminary investigation. *Women's Health, 24*, 59–75.

Rosenberg, H. J., Rosenberg, S. D., Wolford, G. L., Manganiello, P. D., Brunette, M. F., Boynton, R. A. (2000). The relationship between trauma, PTSD, and medical utilization in three high risk medical populations. *International Journal of Psychiatry and Medicine, 30*, 247–259.

Samson, A. Y., Bensen, S., Beck, A., Price, D., & Nimmer, C. (1999). Posttraumatic stress disorder in primary care. *Journal of Family Practice, 48*, 222–227.

Sapolsky, R. M. (1996). Why stress is bad for your brain. *Science, 273*, 749–750.

Schnurr, P. P., Spiro, A., & Paris, A. H. (2000). Physician-diagnosed medical disorders in relation to PTSD symptoms in older male military veterans. *Health Psychology,19*, 91-97.

Shemesh, E., Lurie, S., Stuber, M.L., Emre, S., Patel, Y., Vohra, P. et al. (2000). A pilot study of posttraumatic stress and non-adherence in pediatric liver transplant recipients. *Pediatrics, 105*, 29–30.

Sierles, F. S., Chen, J. J., Messing, M. L., Besyner, J. K., & Taylor, M. A. (1986). Concurrent psychiatric illness in non-Hispanic outpatients diagnosed as having posttraumatic stress disorder. *Journal of Nervous and Mental Disease, 174*, 171–173.

Solomon, S. D., Gerrity, E. T., & Muff, A. M. (1992). Efficacy of treatments for posttraumatic stress disorder: An empirical review. *Journal of the American Medical Association, 268*, 633–638.

Stein, M. B., McQuaid, J. R., Pedrelli, P., Lenox, R., & McCahill, M. E. (2000). Posttraumatic stress disorder in the primary care medical setting. *General Hospital Psychiatry, 22*, 261–269.

Strosahl, K. (1998). Integrating behavioral health and primary care services: The primary mental health care model. In A. Blunt (Ed.), *Integrated primary care: The future of medical and mental health collaboration* (pp. 61–86). New York: Norton.

Strosahl, K., Baker, N. J., Braddick, M., Suart, M. E., & Handley, M. R. (1997). Integration of behavioral health and primary care services: The group health cooperative model. In N. A. Cummings, J. L. Cummings, & J. N. Johnson (Eds.), *Behavioral health in primary care: A guide for clinical integration.* Madison, CT: Psychosocial Press.

Taft, C. T., Stern, A. S., King, L. A., & King, D. W. (1999). Modeling physical health and functional health status: The role of combat exposure, posttraumatic stress disorder, and personal resource attributes. *Journal of Traumatic Stress, 12*, 3–23.

Tarrier, N., & Humphreys, L. (2000). Subjective improvement in PTSD patients with treatment by imaginal exposure or cognitive therapy: Session by session changes. *British Journal of Clinical Psychology, 39*, 27–34.

Tarrier, N., Pilgrim, H., Sommerfield, C., Faragher, B., Reynolds, M., Graham, E. et al. (1999). A randomized trial of cognitive therapy and imaginal exposure in the treatment of chronic posttraumatic stress disorder. *Journal of Consulting and Clinical Psychology, 67*, 13–18.

Taubman-Ben-Ari, O., Rabinowitz, J., Feldman, D., & Vaturi, R. (2001). Post-traumatic stress disorder in primary-care settings: prevalence and physicians' detection. *Psychological Medicine, 31*, 555–560.

Walker, A. M., Harris, G., Baker, A., Kelly, D., & Houghton, J. (1999). Post-traumatic stress responses following liver transplantation in older children. *Journal of Child Psychology and Psychiatry and Allied Disciplines, 40*, 363–374.

Walker, E. A., Unutzer, J., Rutter, C., Gelfand, A. N., Saunders, K., Von Korff, M. et al. (1999). Costs of health care use by women HMO members with a history of childhood abuse and neglect. *Archives of General Psychiatry, 56*, 609–613.

Weathers, F. W., Keane, T. M., & Davidson, J. R. (2001). Clinician-administered PTSD scale: A review of the first ten years of research. *Depression and Anxiety, 13*, 132–156.

Wilson, J. P., & Keane, T. M. (1997). *Assessing psychological trauma and PTSD.* New York: Guilford.

Chapter 7
Identification and Treatment of Substance Abuse in Primary Care Settings

JANET L. CUMMINGS

The Impact of Substance Abuse on Medical Treatment

In the late 1970s, a 45-year-old longshoreman underwent simple surgery in a California Kaiser Permanente hospital. What should have been a 3-day hospital stay instead lasted over 3 weeks. Shortly after the surgery, the patient began hallucinating and, as a result, tried to jump out the window. He ripped open his incisions several times, tearing himself out of restraints each time. Severe infection resulted, which required intravenous antibiotics and constant monitoring by nursing staff. A treatment team consisting of physicians, nurses, and mental health professionals determined that the patient was an alcoholic, and that anesthesia medications in combination with alcohol withdrawal had precipitated the hallucinations. The hallucinations, in turn, prompted the patient's self-destructive behavior, which jeopardized his healing and caused his hospital stay to become so protracted.

This case prompted an in-house research project to assess the effects of substance abuse on medical conditions, surgery outcomes, and hospitalizations for medical problems (Kaiser Permanente Health Plan, 1981). The study found that substance abuse significantly affected all these medical arenas.

For example, the study looked at patients hospitalized for medical conditions and found that the hospital costs for substance abusers were 2 ½ times the hospital costs for nonsubstance abusers hospitalized for the same condition. Two factors accounted for the increased costs: (1) the substance-abusing patients stayed in the hospital significantly longer than the nonsubstance-abusing patients hospitalized with the same condition; (2) the substance-abusing patients required more medical interventions during their stays owing to significantly increased rates of both medical complications and healing time. Following the hospital stays, substance-abusing patients continued to utilize more medical services than nonsubstance-abusing patients with the same condition. Two factors accounted for these increased posthospitalization costs: (1) the substance abusers were notoriously noncompliant with medical treatment, often ignoring the directions of their physicians and failing to keep follow-up appointments until problems became severe enough to require much more costly

143

interventions; (2) substance abuse greatly retarded the healing process, often creating additional medical problems to compound the original problems.

The Kaiser Permanente study also determined that alcoholism was the most costly complication of diabetes in the population studied. Alcoholic diabetics had far more complications than nonsubstance-abusing diabetics, because of both the direct effects of the alcohol on blood sugar levels and the patients' noncompliance with their physicians' directives.

The study also found that 6% of the patient population accounted for 73% of physician visits for nasopharyngitis. These 6% were cocaine abusers experiencing irritation and inflammation of the nasal passages and pharynx from their "snorting."

Heroin addicts who underwent surgery, even simple surgery, were even more costly to manage during the recovery period than were the alcoholics who had surgery. These individuals had developed a high tolerance to the most potent analgesic known (heroin), so the Demerol or even morphine administered at proper dosages had little or no effect on these patients' pain. They were very demanding patients, requiring excessive time from physicians and especially nurses. Many threatened physical violence or litigation, blaming the medical staff for their inability to alleviate the postsurgical pain.

The 7-year study known as the Hawaii Project also looked at the added costs of treating substance abusers for medical conditions using a 36,000 Medicaid population and 90,000 population of federal employees (Cummings, Dorken, Pallak, & Henke, 1991, 1993). The prospective, randomized study looked at three groups of subjects: (1) patients receiving no treatment, (2) patients receiving targeted and focused psychotherapy, and (3) patients receiving other mental health treatment. The greatest cost savings found in the project were among substance abusers who received appropriate substance-abuse treatment. The medical savings here was significantly greater than for the chronically medically ill, phobics, somatizers, or any other group studied.

Appropriate treatment for substance abusers resulted in a savings of $700 per patient per year. However, inappropriate treatment for substance abusers actually increased medical costs by close to $1,000 per patient per year. The cost of medical treatment for no treatment controls increased only slightly. The cost savings for the chronically medically ill subjects receiving focused and targeted psychotherapy was quite impressive, but less than for the substance-abusing subjects. For the chronically medically ill, targeted and focused psychotherapy resulted in a savings of about $500 per patient per year, with other (inappropriate) mental health treatment increasing medical costs by about $800 per patient per year and no treatment, resulting in a very slight increase in costs.

As these and other studies demonstrate, the potential savings in health-care dollars by the appropriate assessment and treatment of substance-abusing patients is enormous. Add to this the savings that could result from decreasing injuries and deaths from auto and industrial accidents, decreasing lost workdays, and increasing productivity. The amount of money potentially saved by appropriately assessing and treating substance abuse becomes incalculable.

Prevalence Rates: Who Is the Substance Abuser?

Hard-core addicts are generally easy to spot. Most health-care providers are trained to recognize the bulbous nose and pasty skin characteristic of hard-core alcoholics and the track marks characteristic of longtime intravenous drug abusers. However, most addicts are not this easy to recognize, especially when the addict is a neighbor, a coworker, or a colleague.

According to the National Institute on Drug Abuse (NIDA) and the National Institute on Alcoholism and Alcohol Abuse (NIAA), about 35 million Americans abuse alcohol. About half that number (or 17 million) abuse marijuana. A startling 40 million abuse legal drugs (both prescription and over-the-counter varieties). Following a period of decline, heroin abuse is on the rise, with about 3 million heroin addicts in the United States at this time. About 4 million Americans regularly abuse cocaine (including crack cocaine) and about 5 million regularly abuse amphetamines (including methamphetamines). About 11 million regularly abuse barbiturates (Cummings & Cummings, 2000; NIDA & NIAA, 1999).

Attempting to add these numbers would lead to an overestimation of the number of substance abusers. There is considerable overlap, as most substance abusers these days engage in polysubstance abuse (NIDA & NIAA, 1999). In fact, pure alcoholics (those who only abuse alcohol) are seen less and less frequently and are 45 and older. Although exact numbers are difficult to obtain, estimates place chemical abuse and chemical dependency in America at a low figure of 15% and a high figure of 20% of the total population. In other words, one in six or one in five Americans is a substance abuser (Cummings & Cummings, 2000; Falco, 1992; NIDA & NIAA, 1999).

Surprisingly, NIDA and NIAA report that 71% of substance abusers are employed (NIDA & NIAA, 1999). Most of these have health insurance and are therefore potential patients in both behavioral health and primary care settings. Only about 21% of substance abusers are unemployed, marginally employed, homeless, or in prison (U.S. Department of Labor, 1998).

The implications of these figures for primary care practice are astounding. In settings where only patients with employer health insurance are seen, probably as many as one in five or one in six are substance abusers. In settings that serve persons covered by Medicaid, Social Security Disability, and Medicare, the figure will be even higher, with as many as one in two or one in three patients being substance abusers (Cummings & Cummings, 2000; NIDA & NIAA, 1999).

In this chapter the terms "abuse," "addiction," and "dependency," as well as the terms "addict" and "substance abuser," are used interchangeably. Physical craving for the substance upon withdrawal is not the defining characteristic of addiction, as many believe, since not all abused substances produce such physical cravings. The unfortunate consequence of the erroneous belief that addiction is defined by physical cravings is that it has led much of the medical profession and public to believe that any substance yet to be declared medically addictive carries no potential for addiction. Nor is heavy use over long periods of time the defining characteristic of addiction, as some nonaddicts can engage in heavy use over a period of time. (For example, the amount of alcohol consumed at some college parties can be alarming enough to look like incipient alcoholism in many of the participants, although many who engage in such behavior in college do not go on to become alcoholics.) (Cummings & Cummings, 2000).

Rather, the "addict" or "substance abuser" is someone who continues to imbibe after a series of consequences, any one of which would lead the nonaddict to decide that the chemical simply is not worth it. In other words, the defining characteristic of substance abuse or addiction is *trouble*—the kind of trouble that would not occur without the substance abuse. If a person continues to use a substance despite recurring trouble (legal, marital, occupational, health-related, etc.), it is an indication that he or she is addicted. Characteristically, the addict is the last to realize that the trouble is the result of the substance abuse. Since continued frequent intoxication will inevitably result in trouble sooner or later, the terms "addiction," "substance abuse," and "chemical dependency" become interchangeable rather than somehow defining the degree of abuse. Again, it is the trouble that defines the abuse (Cummings & Cummings, 2000).

Who Is Supplying Substances to Addicts?

The term "pusher" conjures up stereotypic images of shady characters lurking just outside fenced schoolyards or of thugs waiting in secret inner-city meeting places (such as crack houses) to sell their wares. These are not the most common pushers in the United States today, nor the most worrisome. The real pushers, the ones who should cause the most concern, look like our neighbors, coworkers, classmates, friends, and colleagues. The drug lord or mafioso is many steps removed, so that in many cases the addict is also the pusher. Addicts often become pushers or dealers of street drugs in order to supply their own habits. Each obtains a supply, removes what he or she needs for personal use, then dilutes the remainder to sell in order to have money to purchase the next supply. (Thus, the purity and potency of street drugs depends on how many times they have been diluted.)

The number of prescription drugs being resold is alarming. Nearly one third of Ritalin prescribed to school children is being resold by these same children, who often use the money to purchase amphetamines or crack cocaine for themselves. Pain patients who have "graduated" from prescription codeine to more highly refined street opiates often sell their prescription medications on the streets (at inflated prices) in order to pay for their more potent narcotics (Cummings & Cummings, 2000; Moore, 1998).

With all due respect to the medical profession, the pusher is often a physician. Although physicians are generally well meaning, a small minority of unscrupulous physicians are knowingly dealing drugs. Because such a physician issues an enormous number of prescriptions for a certain type of drug, he or she needs to present the appearance that these prescriptions are legitimate. For example, he or she may claim to specialize in weight reduction so as to explain the large number of prescriptions for amphetamines being issued. Some physicians are so unscrupulous that they knowingly addict their patients to drugs in order to have them provide a steady income stream (Cummings & Cummings, 2000).

More commonly, the physician pusher is kindly and well meaning. He or she wants to alleviate all pain and discomfort. This physician overly prescribes narcotic pain killers, sleeping pills, and other mind-altering drugs. He or she is too naive to recognize the addicted patient, who always comes in requesting a specific drug and yet obtaining the same drug from a number of other physicians so that no one physician is aware of the full extent of the patient's drug use. The pusher may also be an "impaired" (addicted) physician who, because of his or her own chemical dependency, cannot stand to see a patient in withdrawal. Such physicians fail to recognize that their addicted patients typically present themselves as suffering far more than they actually are (Dejong & Doot, 1999; Earl, 1988; Green, Carroll, & Buxton, 1978). Thus, they are quick to provide a prescription to carry the patient until he or she can obtain the illegal drug of choice or to continue issuing prescriptions for drugs that no longer have a legitimate medical use rather than see these patients suffer the discomfort of withdrawal (Earl, 1988; Moore, 1998).

One factor that contributes to some well-meaning physicians' drug pushing is the fact that an addict is addicted to an entire class of drugs rather than to a single drug within that class. The addiction is perpetuated rather than alleviated when other drugs belonging to the same class are administered in an attempt to treat the addiction. For example, abuse of alcohol (a central nervous system depressant) has traditionally been treated using other types of central nervous system (CNS) depressants, particularly the benzodiazepines (such as Valium, Xanax, and Librium). With such treatment, the patient does not learn to live without alcohol, but simply learns to accept an "alcohol equivalent" instead. In many cases, the alcoholic uses his or her prescription medication in addition to alcohol rather than instead of it, which is a potentially lethal combination. Many patients who were addicted to older barbiturate medications have been switched to newer benzodiazepines, but these serve only to perpetuate the addiction to CNS depressants. Methadone clinics attempt to treat heroin addiction by substituting methadone for heroin, even though methadone withdrawal is more difficult than heroin withdrawal and recovery from methadone addiction is more difficult than recovery from heroin addiction (Cummings & Cummings, 2000).

Another factor that contributes to prescription drug-pushing by well-meaning physicians is that addicts present as anything but addicts, both in mental health settings and in primary care. In mental health settings, the addict who has been sent to treatment by a spouse, employer, or judge may mention the substance abuse but deny that it really exists. Those who self-refer for mental health services present with everything except substance abuse, generally reporting the consequences of the abuse (marital problems, occupational problems, legal problems, etc.) but never mentioning the abuse itself. In primary care settings, some substance-abusing patients mention these same consequences to their physicians, who quickly change the subject to a discussion of physical symptoms.

Other substance-abusing patients fail to mention such consequences to their physicians. Rather, they present with purely physical symptoms. These symptoms, on the surface, often seem like just that—symptoms of some physical illness. However, they are ploys used by addicted patients to obtain the drugs they want. For example, a patient may complain of anxiety or insomnia in order to obtain a prescription for benzodiazepines. The reported symptoms may be contrived or due to a rebound effect from using the very drug desired. A patient may complain of chronic, debilitating pain in order to secure a prescription for narcotics. Again, the reported symptoms may be contrived or due to pain that began as a physical problem but is being perpetuated by the addiction and psychological factors.

The elderly are most vulnerable to becoming addicted to prescription medications, and most chemical dependency among the elderly is iatrogenic (Hartman-Stein, 1998; Kaplan & Sadock, 1993). Physicians do not consistently warn patients not to use alcohol in combination with prescription medications where alcohol use would be contraindicated (Hartman-Stein, 1998; Joseph, 1997). Older adults have less tolerance for alcohol than younger adults, and may need less prescription medication (often less than what would be indicated by standard dosage ranges) to be effective. Physiological differences in the elderly (including slowed absorption rates, decreased availability of plasma proteins, declining liver functioning, and decreased kidney function) can cause them to react differently than do younger people to certain medications (Gitlin, 1996; Kaplan & Sadock, 1993). The elderly sometimes take extra doses of medication because they forget they had already taken it. Some physicians may be too quick to inappropriately medicate the elderly for grief or other psychological conditions, thinking they cannot really do very much for older persons (Cummings & Cummings, 2000; Hartman-Stein, 1998).

Assessing Substance Abuse

Most psychotherapists are able to identify only about one in ten patients with significant substance abuse problems (Cummings & Cummings 2000). Because most physicians have received little education on substance abuse (generally a few hours in most training programs, with little emphasis on the management of such patients beyond initial detoxification), they are able to identify significantly fewer of their substance-abusing patients than psychotherapists (Horst, 1997). The identification rate in both psychotherapy and primary care is abysmal (Cummings & Cummings, 2000).

For this reason, and because primary care physicians have neither the time nor the training to conduct long clinical interviews to screen for substance abuse, a number of screening devices have been developed in attempts to increase the number of substance abusers identified in primary care settings. Physicians find some to be too long and cumbersome to use regularly. For example, the 25-item Michigan Alcoholism Screening Test has been studied in primary care practices, but most physicians find even the briefer versions too cumbersome (Horst, 1997). Other screening devices are not sensitive enough to identify many substance abusers, resulting in too many false negatives. For example, the four-question (CAGE) instrument has also been studied in primary care settings, but research indicates that it fails to identify many alcoholics and most patients who abuse other substances (Horst, 1997).

When physicians or psychotherapists ask a substance-abusing patient about his or her drug and alcohol use during clinical interviews, the patient's denial will invariably cause him or her to grossly minimize the amount. My own clinical experience suggests that a more accurate assessment can be obtained by multiplying the patient's answer by two, four, or even ten (Cummings & Cummings, 2000). Patients will sometimes ask a matter-of-fact question or make a statement (as an aside) that both hides and discloses the facts. For example, an aside might be, "By the way, doctor, I sometimes have a shot of whiskey at bedtime to help me sleep." The physician generally responds, "That's fine. One shot of whiskey occasionally at bedtime never hurt anyone." It may be, however, that the patient is going to bed with a bottle every night. The patient mentions the "one shot" because he or she is worried and seeks reassurance. Another patient might ask, "Having a glass of wine with dinner is okay, isn't it?" The physician generally responds to such a question by reassuring the patient that a glass of wine is fine, not realizing that the patient's "glass" actually holds 32 or even 64 ounces of wine. By throwing out the aside and receiving the physician's response, the patient can reassure him- or herself, "I told the doctor, and he (or she) doesn't think I drink too much."

Interestingly, at least 80% of substance abusing patients will candidly answer questions regarding their drug and alcohol behavior on written questionnaires or scales presented within the health system. These same patients will lie at least 90% of the time when asked face-to-face about their drug and alcohol use, and will even contradict their written statements in a face-to-face interview (Cummings & Cummings, 2000). Most primary care practices include questions on alcohol and drug use in their medical history forms, which each patient is required to complete. These health screening devices include such questions as, "Most days I have none, one, two or three, more than five drinks in a day [indicate number]" or "I use the following recreational drugs," with choices after each [never, rarely, occasionally, frequently, regularly]. The numbers reported on such written questionnaires are far more accurate than those elicited during a face-to-face interview. The patient answers accurately so that he or she can then reassure him- or herself that the doctor knows the truth and is not concerned. Amazingly, this is usually the case, as physicians seldom pay much attention to the drug and alcohol information on the very questionnaire they demand that each patient complete (Cummings & Cummings, 2000). These same physicians do take into account information on disease or family medical history revealed on the same questionnaire. The portion of medical questionnaires dealing with drug and alcohol use provides useful therapeutic information to physicians and should not just be treated as filler for the chart.

A number of good screening devices are currently being used in primary care settings. These include the four-question CAGE instrument (Ewing, 1984), the 25-question Michigan Alcoholism Screening Test (Selzer, 1971), and the 10-question Alcohol Use Disorders Inventory Test (AUDIT) (Saunders, Aasland, & Babor, 1993). These and other similar instruments can be helpful in assessing substance abuse in primary care settings. However, many physicians find the longer instruments (those with 11 or more questions) to be too lengthy (Horst, 1997). Some primary care practices have found it helpful to embed the substance-abuse questions within other general medical questions, rather than on a separate form, to increase the truthfulness of patient responses (Horst, 1997).

Cummings and Cummings (2000) list a number of signposts that can alert the psychotherapist or physician to the possibility of substance abuse. The patient exhibiting such signs may or may not be an addict, but it is prudent to explore the possibility. No one signpost is conclusive, but each serves to raise a red flag. These signs should never be ignored or glossed over, as taking them seriously will significantly increase the number of substance-abusing patients properly identified. The signposts most likely to become apparent in a primary care setting are

1. *Frequent auto accidents.* The injuries sustained often require medical care.
2. *Two or more bone fractures in a 3-to-5-year period.* The patient may be a falling-down drunk.

3. *Spousal battery, physical abuse of children, or both.* Men who batter their spouses and beat their children are usually heavy drinkers or drug users. Since a physician or group practice may provide medical care to entire families, the medical problems of some family members may indicate substance abuse on the part of another family member.
4. *Tweaking (picking the face or the skin on the forearm).* This can be a sign of drug abuse, particularly in women.
5. *Unusual physique.* Amphetamine users will be very thin, even emaciated. Some cases of obesity, particularly a sudden occurrence in a younger patient, may be due to "marijuana munchies."
6. *Paranoia.* Prolonged, heavy use of amphetamines can result in sudden and severe paranoia, even in patients with no history of psychotic symptoms. The paranoia is often accompanied by tactile and visual hallucinations. Unlike the auditory hallucinations common to schizophrenics, tactile and visual hallucinations are due to organicity.
7. *Stains on clothing, red eyes or nose, sores around the mouth, poor muscle control, and loss of appetite.* These are seen in children who abuse inhalants.
8. *Missed adolescence.* Many addicts missed going through their own adolescence, and therefore have never resolved the adolescent authority struggle. They reject any of life's demands. In primary care settings, these patients often present as demanding, argumentative, and noncompliant with the physician's recommendations.

Other signposts are commonly seen in mental health settings, but may also be reported on occasion in primary care settings.

1. *DUI* (driving under the influence) or *DWI* (driving while intoxicated).
2. *Frequent traffic violations.*
3. *"I've lost everything!"* (a frequent complaint among addicts who are upset by the consequences of their addiction but fail to recognize that their addiction has contributed to their troubles).
4. *Amotivational syndrome.* Chronic marijuana users eventually lose interest in life. They often express a general, vague dissatisfaction, but are not really depressed.

Most physicians are, understandably, reluctant to probe for more information on substance use when they notice reports of high usage on a questionnaire, hear an aside that alerts them to the possibility of substance abuse, or observe another signpost of substance abuse. In integrated settings, however, the nurse or physician who first notices a report of heavy substance use on a questionnaire can alert the behavioral health-care specialist onsite and ask him or her to participate in the patient interview along with the physician. Should an aside or other signpost become apparent during the interview, the behavioral health-care specialist can then be brought in. (For detailed interviewing strategies, the reader is referred to chapter 6, "Establishing a Therapeutic Alliance" and chapter 7, "Further Interviewing Strategies" in Cummings and Cummings, 2000). Should the discussion become protracted or should the patient need further substance-abuse assessment or intervention, the physician can seamlessly leave the patient with the behavioral health-care specialist and continue tending to other patients.

In carve-out systems, where behavioral health care is not colocated with primary care, the physician is left with several options when he or she notices a report of high substance usage on a questionnaire, an aside, or other signpost: (1) ignore the information, (2) attempt to interview the patient to further assess for substance abuse, even though he or she may have neither the time nor skills to do so, (3) refer the patient for assessment in a behavioral health-care setting, accepting the fact that few patients (at most 10–15%) will then present to be assessed in behavioral health care (Cummings, Cummings, & Johnson, 1997).

Models of Substance Abuse Treatment

Cummings and Cummings (2000) list three treatment models in the field of chemical dependency. Each makes important contributions to the field, but each has its own inherent limitations. They are the medical model, the behavioral model, and the abstinence model.

The Medical Model

The medical model asserts a physiologic basis for addiction and further holds that treatment is medical. In its purest form, this model refuses to acknowledge any psychological basis for addiction, which is always viewed as physiological. The medical model acknowledges the growing body of evidence regarding the role of genetics in addiction, provides a basis for the tissue changes that occur with addiction, and explains the phenomenon of tolerance in light of these tissue changes (Bloom, Lazerson, & Hofstadter, 1985; Carlson, 1986; Murray & Stabenau, 1982).

The medical model has two forms of treatment: withdrawal by substituting another drug and slow withdrawal by titration. Because the addict is addicted to a class of drugs rather than to just one member of the class, the substitution approach fails to treat the addiction. Although the abrupt withdrawal of CNS depressants can result in seizures and other medical complications and must be titrated, the concept has been extended to withdrawal from drugs in which seizures or other complications are not a threat. Physicians use titration even when it is medically unnecessary in order to make withdrawal comfortable, a concept that may actually encourage addiction. Unfortunately, the medical model has contributed to a culture that believes a solution to any problem can be found in a pill or potion. In turn, the model seems acceptable to many patients in light of the current culture.

The Behavioral Model

The behavioral model is a psychological approach to addiction treatment that regards addictive behavior as a learned response (L'Abate, Farrar, & Serritella, 1991; Miller, Smith, & Gold, 1996). Most psychologists adhere to this model and use cognitive behaviorism and other approaches to change the set of learned behaviors (or habit patterns) regarded as addiction.

Although addictive behavior is a learned response and the comprehensive treatment of addiction relies heavily on behavioral therapy, the model is based on an erroneous basic premise. The premise is that addicts can learn to become social users. Although many substance abusers can control their use and appear to be social users for a limited period of time, relapse is inevitable (Cummings & Cummings, 2000).

The Abstinence Model

The abstinence model incorporates the physiological aspects of the medical model with the best in the behavioral treatment of addiction. It asserts that substance abuse brings about permanent cellular changes, which constitute the drug tolerance of the addict and make it impossible for the person to go back to a level of social use. This model is the most used conceptualization of addiction, as it is espoused by Alcoholics Anonymous, Narcotics Anonymous, and other 12-step programs.

It is axiomatic in this model that the highest level of drug tolerance achieved becomes the minimum daily requirement for that drug. According to this model, the only alternative to a life of increasing dosage is total abstinence. The model acknowledges that addiction can be predisposed by genetics, that it is acquired physiologically by use and abuse, and that it can be learned and acquired through life experiences. However, it avoids futile attempts to weigh the contribution of each of these factors toward the resulting addiction in a particular individual.

Research has shown that the behavioral and abstinence models are about equally effective for up to 2 years posttreatment. However, through the 3rd and 4th years, the abstinence model clearly prevails over the behavioral model (Cummings & Cummings, 2000; Quimette, Finney, & Moos, 1997).

The critical feature that increases the likelihood of a successfully clean lifestyle is the drugless detoxification of the patient in which he or she undergoes withdrawal or detoxification without the use of alternative or substitute medications. For those patients in danger of convulsions, a sufficient dose of the drug is available if necessary. However, the patient is not so advised due to the likelihood that he or she would bring on a convulsion in order to get the medication. This drugless detoxification is certainly rough on patients, but they never forget the horrendous discomfort, which becomes a constant deterrent to recidivism. There is considerable evidence that patients who are offered relief from the symptoms of withdrawal will experience an escalation of these symptoms in order to be given the substitute medication (Center for Substance Abuse Treatment, 1997; Cummings & Cummings, 2000). This has led to an axiom that addicts easily understand: the degree of pain on withdrawal is directly proportional to the proximity of a sympathetic physician.

The abstinence model does have one intrinsic limitation. The requirement of abstinence is quite stringent, and it is usually demanded of the addict long before he or she is ready to contemplate a lifestyle totally free of chemical abuse (Gould, 1999; Narcotics Anonymous Worldwide Services, 1988). In other words, the patient is confronted with the requirement of abstinence in the absence of sufficient motivation, or long before he or she has hit bottom. Very few patients referred for substance-abuse treatment have actually hit bottom. Rather, the referrals usually reflect the exasperation of others in the addicts' lives. In the medical and behavioral models, the patient cooperates with treatment because of the belief that treatment will enable him or her to be a social user. The failure of this type of treatment is evident only after the treatment is concluded and the patient's use escalates to the pretreatment level, whereas the demand for abstinence is immediate in the abstinence model (Gould, 1999; Alcoholics World Services, 1986).

Treatment Strategies That Work

Inpatient Versus Outpatient Care

In the past 15 years, there has developed a multibillion-dollar, for-profit, inpatient-addiction treatment industry. Addiction treatment has cost employers billions of dollars per year. Even though employers have balked at paying for the treatment of emotional and mental disorders, they have in the past been eager to pay for inpatient addiction treatment in anticipation of saving money in the long run by reducing absenteeism, job injuries, poor productivity, and lawsuits. The results of expensive inpatient addiction treatment have been most disappointing (Cummings & Cummings, 2000).

The research overwhelmingly indicates that inpatient treatment of substance abuse is not significantly more effective than outpatient treatment to the point where this conclusion is inescapable (Saxe & Goodman, 1988). In the United States, misallocation of resources has led to drastic overspending to treat addiction. Unfortunately, however, spouses, families, employers, and society (through its overcrowded courts) are clamoring for inpatient care in order to have someplace to send the addict. Later these same people complain that hospitalization is too costly in view of its disappointing results.

The determination to hospitalize a patient should not be based on psychological need, but rather on two factors: medical necessity and social instability. The need to detoxify in a hospital setting has often been cited by hospital-based practitioners, but research has clearly demonstrated that the number of patients needing to do so is much smaller than previously believed (Saxe, Dougherty, Esty, & Fine, 1983; Saxe & Goodman, 1988). If a patient is in danger of convulsions or other dangerous medical complications, he or she should be detoxified in a hospital. However, the decision is usually based on patient comfort or the existence of insurance that will pay for the hospitalization. Even for a patient in danger of medical complications, it is usually feasible to hospitalize him or her only briefly, often in a system less intensive than the full hospital. A well-trained addiction nurse practitioner is present to monitor the patient for prodromal signs of medical complications for the first 48 to 72 hours, after which the patient is seamlessly transferred to outpatient care within the same program.

Very skilled psychotherapists are able to successfully employ outpatient drugless detoxification of most patients, including heroin addicts, by sending them home with a drug-free friend who babysits them through 72 hours of withdrawal. In such cases, the psychotherapist gives the "babysitter" about 2 hours of training prior to the detoxification process and telephones the patient and "babysitter" every 2 or 3 hours, day and night, throughout the withdrawal process (Cummings, 1979; Cummings & Cummings, 2000). Since less-skilled psychotherapists may not be equipped to handle their patients' detoxifications in this manner, the next-best approach is to admit the patient to a hospital or less-intensive facility for up to 72 hours. The patient is monitored by a nurse practitioner. The hospital or other facility must agree beforehand, however, that medications will not be administered to the patient unless a small amount is medically necessary to prevent medical complications.

As was previously stated, social instability (lack of social support) may be a reason to consider inpatient treatment for a particular patient. Research has suggested that more severely addicted and less socially stable patients often do better in either inpatient care or more intensive outpatient treatment, whereas less severely addicted and more socially stable patients do better in less-intensive outpatient programs (Saxe, Dougherty, Esty, & Fine, 1983; Saxe & Goodman, 1988).

It is quite common to find patients who have repeatedly failed inpatient programs to go on to succeed in outpatient treatment (Cummings, 1991). In the hospital, the patient has not given up the chemical. Rather, the chemical is being temporarily withheld or, worse yet, a substitute chemical is being administered. Hospitalized patients do not develop the coping skills necessary for success outside the hospital. On the other hand, the patient who becomes abstinent outside the hospital is already establishing the skills needed to maintain abstinence (Cummings & Cummings, 2000; Quimette et al., 1997; Saxe et al., 1983; Saxe & Goodman, 1988).

Intensive Outpatient Programs

The intensive outpatient program (IOP) has been devised to increase patients' motivation to seriously consider an abstinent lifestyle as the best solution to addiction. In its ideal form, the IOP combines the best of outpatient treatment with the intensity of partial residential care. The IOP typically is several hours of outpatient care daily for a specified number of weeks or for a number of weeks specifically tailored for each individual case. Patients are required to meet criteria of attendance, abstinence, and family involvement. For most of the severely addicted and socially unstable patients, the IOP is more effective than hospitalization. It is, however, too intensive for less severely addicted and more socially stable patients. They will respond better to a fully outpatient program (Cummings & Cummings, 2000; Quimette, Finney, & Moos, 1997; Saxe et al., 1983; Saxe & Goodman, 1988).

Preaddictive Group Programs

The preaddictive group is a program developed for patients who are likely substance abusers but who are not ready to enter an outpatient addiction group or IOP. Like the IOP, the preaddictive group was devised to increase the patient's motivation to embrace an abstinent lifestyle. It satisfies the objection that by going directly into an addictive program the patient is being erroneously labeled an addict. The program is designed to soften the resistance of addicts who are far from hitting bottom and who object to an abstinence-based program. The addict who resists referral to an outpatient addiction group or IOP is invited to join a psychoeducational program and then be the judge of whether he or she is addicted. The patient is assured that there will be no pressure if he or she decides not to go into a treatment program. Even more provocatively, the patient can be challenged, "Why not spend five sessions and prove you are not an addict just like you say?"

The preaddictive group meets for 2 hours daily, usually in the evening to accommodate patients' work schedules, with five consecutive daily meetings in each series. Follow-up studies indicate a 50% increase in the number of addicts who enter an outpatient addiction treatment program and a similar increase in the number who complete the program (American Biodyne, 1985–90; Cummings, 1979). The group also serves to reduce the number of complaints by addicts who are required to be abstinent (Cummings & Cummings, 2000).

In larger group practices, a preaddictive group can be offered onsite. Patients may be more willing to attend such a group in the primary care setting than in a separate behavioral health-care setting (Cummings, Cummings, & Johnson, 1997). However, smaller practices may not have a large enough patient population to offer such a program onsite. In such cases, a significant number of patients properly assessed and challenged by a behavioral health-care specialist onsite will attend the preaddictive group even though they must go to a separate behavioral health-care setting in order to do so.

Group Versus Individual Therapy

Abstinence-based group treatment for substance abuse is overwhelmingly more effective than individual treatment (Cummings, 1991; Cummings & Cummings, 2000) and generally graduates into recovery about 60% of those who begin (Cummings, 1982; Cummings & Cummings, 2000). The behavior of substance abusers in their denial resembles that of adolescents more than that of adults. They tend to be antiauthority (antiparental) and are generally more influenced by peers (fellow adolescent-like addicts) than by their physician or psychotherapist, who are seen as parent figures. Patients in a group setting can say things to each other that the therapist could never say, because the patient would either take umbrage or simply dismiss what the authority figure said. In group substance-abuse treatment, the role of the therapist is to create a group culture committed to abstinence and subsequent change of lifestyle. Once such a culture has been created, the milieu allows patients to challenge and confront each other with a directness that would never be tolerated from a therapist. Addicts are often able to "con" their physicians and even their psychotherapists, but rarely can they fool their fellow patients.

A typical successful outpatient addictive group is composed of 10 to 12 patients who have all undergone withdrawal and are abstinent (Cummings, 1982; Cummings & Cummings 2000). The patients are addicted to various substances, as this variety helps to emphasize the nature of addiction: an addict is not defined by what he or she ingests, shoots, or inhales but by his or her lifestyle. This type of mixed group may be particularly eye-opening for the patient addicted to prescription medications. Such a patient may self-righteously believe that he or she is not a real addict, and finding him- or herself in a group program alongside patients addicted to hard-core street drugs may cut through a patient's strong denial.

The group meets once a week for 2 hours, usually in the evening because it is a requirement that patients return to work as soon as possible. The program can take place in the primary care setting or separate behavioral health-care setting. All group members start on the same first session, and once the group begins no one else is allowed to join. The program lasts 20 weeks, during which time the patient has recourse to five individual sessions, but only in response to need. Thus, the approach allows for individual attention in a severe crisis, without detracting from the group process. Attendance and abstinence are both required. At the beginning of each session, each patient is asked whether he or she has remained sober since the last session. Any patient that has not remained sober is assigned a "fall." A fall is also assigned to any patient who was absent from the previous session, and whose absence the group votes to be unexcused. Patients receiving a fall for failing to maintain sobriety are required to leave and forfeit the remainder of the session. Each patient is allowed three falls, and on the fourth fall the patient has failed the program and is excluded from the group (Cummings, 1982; Cummings & Cummings, 2000).

Aftercare

Addiction cannot be cured, although recovery is possible. Therefore, most addicts who complete an addiction treatment program need to continue in some type of aftercare in order to maintain sobriety. Although some substance-abuse programs offer an aftercare program, many utilize 12-step programs available in most communities for aftercare. Addicts can be encouraged to join 12-step programs while in the IOP or other outpatient addiction treatment program. On completion of the program, they can be encouraged to continue in their 12-step program for as long as necessary.

Countering Resistance and Motivating the Patient for Appropriate Treatment

The difficulty in treating substance abuse using the abstinence model is that there are great individual differences in what constitutes "bottom" (a set of adverse circumstances under which an addict is motivated to give up his or her addiction), and some addicts do not have a bottom. Furthermore, the physician may assess substance abuse in a patient long before that patient has hit bottom. He or she must then refer the patient to an appropriate behavioral health-care specialist long before the patient would be motivated to seek such treatment. The behavioral health-care specialist must in turn encourage the patient to enter a treatment program that requires a commitment to abstinence when the patient still believes he or she can become a social drinker (Cummings & Cummings, 2000).

There are a number of techniques a skilled behavioral health-care provider can use to increase the patient's motivation for appropriate treatment. In integrated systems, the physician should involve the behavioral health-care specialist in the treatment of the patient suspected of being an addict. In a carve-in or fully integrated system, the physician can introduce the patient to his or her "colleague," the behavioral health-care specialist in the office, for a seamless transition with nearly 100% of patients having at least a brief initial encounter with the behavioral health-care specialist. In a carve-out system, the physician must refer the patient to a separate location in order to see the behavioral health-care professional. In such a case, only about 10% of patients referred will actually present (Cummings et al., 1997).

Some of the techniques that skilled behavioral health-care providers use to motivate addicted patients are paradoxical and may look uncompassionate or be otherwise misunderstood by the untrained observer. Even though most physicians will never be called upon to deliver such interventions, it is imperative that they become familiar with the basic types of paradoxical interventions used in order to avoid becoming alarmed at seeing the interventions implemented and inadvertently sabotaging the efforts of the behavioral health-care provider. Physicians can receive this level of training in brief (1 or 2 hours) in-service programs. At the very least, physician training should emphasize that successfully motivating the patient rests on two important therapeutic principles of addiction: (1) the addicted patient is not really ready to change even if he or she asks for substance abuse treatment; (2) the secret to reaching the patient is through the obstinacy that is part and parcel of the addict's denial. A brief description of the major interventions for reaching the patient through his or her obstinacy, outlined by Cummings and Cummings (2000), follows.

The Preaddictive Group

The preaddictive group, described previously in this chapter, is a means for reducing the resistance of addicts with very intense denial about their addiction. Information on addiction will be presented, and the addict can decide for him- or herself whether it applies. Attending the preaddictive group increases the addict's chance of entering the addiction program by 50% (American Biodyne, 1985–90). Once he or she has entered the addiction program, the addict has a 50% greater chance of successfully completing the program (American Biodyne, 1985–90).

Axioms

Another way of countering the denial of the patient who is not ready to consider a life of abstinence is by strategic paradoxical interventions termed "axioms." Twelve-step programs use a number of axioms, which are readily understandable to the addict. For example, 12-step participants who try to justify ongoing substance abuse by saying they have a "disease" will often hear their fellow addicts say in unison, "You are not responsible for your disease, but you are responsible for your recovery." Axioms can also be used when interviewing or treating addicts in medical or mental health settings. For example, when a highly resistant patient demands a practitioner who will provide a substitute drug to ease the ordeal of withdrawal, such a referral is offered, along with the axiom that "the degree of pain on withdrawal is directly proportional to the availability of pain killers." As another example, when a resistant patient insists that he or she will be able to dry out once there has been sufficient psychoanalysis, the skilled therapist offers an axiom by asking the patient if he or she has noticed that "all insight is soluble in alcohol and drugs."

The Challenge

Many of our addicted patients will vehemently deny that they are addicted. Others will admit to their addiction and express the sincere desire to quit. However, once this addict sees some success in convincing the psychotherapist of sincere intent, denial takes over once again. The psychotherapist is quick to reassure the pleading patient that all will be well because the patient really wants to get well, and this reassurance results in the patient's concluding that all is well *right now*.

A preferable alternative is to challenge the patient's sincerity, and this must be done firmly, resolutely, and consistently. The therapist plays "devil's advocate" and gives the patient reasons why he or she really does not want or need to quit. In response, the patient generally will counter the therapist's points with reasons that he or she really does need to quit. Then, the therapist challenges the patient's ability to quit for a specified period of time (which is generally the longest interval of sobriety that the patient has experienced in the past 6 months).

When the patient returns after the specified period of sobriety, the therapist challenges the patient's willingness and ability to sustain sobriety long term. The patient will generally argue that he or she is indeed willing and able. The therapist then suggests that the patient prove it by entering an addiction group or IOP. (For a more detailed discussion of "The Challenge," the reader is referred to chapter 6, "Establishing the Therapeutic Alliance," in Cummings and Cummings, 2000.) Even if the patient's intentions seem nefarious at this point, he or she is going to spend 20 weeks in a firm, continuously challenging, and successful program based on abstinence. The longer the patient is abstinent, the greater the inroad of therapy.

A Variation of the Challenge

It is sometimes possible to elicit a long-lost wish from the patient and then to reignite it in the service of motivating him or her. This wish can be almost anything, such as the ambition to obtain a college degree or return to the pursuit of a career that was long-ago abandoned, or the desire to be reunited with one's children. At this point, the therapist gives an example of a former patient (or two) who had just such a longing and who, by cleaning up, fulfilled the desire. Then, just as the patient begins to show excitement at the prospect, the therapist becomes discouraging, focusing on the patient's degree of addiction and lack of desire to give up the chemical dependency. As in the previously described challenge, the patient insists that it is possible to try. The therapist can then go into the standard challenge, "Well, I'm not convinced. But there is a way that would prove me wrong."

"You're Not an Addict"

Patients try to convince their physicians and psychotherapists that they are not addicted. After establishing the necessary rapport and therapeutic alliance with the patient, the therapist can begin this paradoxical strategy when the patient resorts to denial. Consider the following example:

Patient: My wife is threatening to leave me. I've got to get off the dope.

Therapist: How many times has she threatened to leave? She always comes back to you when you've laid off for a while. This is no different.

Patient: No. She really means it this time. She says I neglect her and the kids, and she's had enough.

Therapist: Don't give up so easily. Let's spend a little time figuring out how you might con her again. Just think of what you're saying, that you'll give up drinking forever. No way!

Patient: No. I don't think it would work. I think it's time to really shape up.

Mobilizing Rage to Support Health

Rage is the most galvanizing emotion in the human experience. Although love may be the greater emotion in the long run, rage is immediate and directed (Cummings & Sayama, 1995; Fromm-Reichman, 1950). Addicts generally have trouble with hostility. Although many are mild, lovable people when sober, many become hostile and mean when stoned or drunk. The previous examples have shown how a therapist can skillfully mobilize the patient's rage against the therapist, but in the direction of a healthy outcome. The mobilization of rage in the interest of health enables the therapist to cut through a wall of denial that otherwise would be impenetrable (Cummings & Cummings, 2000).

Leveraging the Blackout

It is important to ask whether the patient has experienced blackouts. If not asked, the patient will not think to mention it because his or her denial has already relegated the blackouts to the realm of insignificance. In fact, blackouts are extremely important because they are an early sign of brain damage (Lezak, 1983).

Patients are horrified to be told that the blackout is early alcoholic brain damage. The therapist can use this knowledge to increase the patient's motivation, but only indirectly. As soon as the patient begins getting over the realization that his or her brain has been damaged, denial kicks in to minimize the importance of the damage. At this point, the therapist can begin a paradoxical strategy by impressing on the patient that the brain damage is irreversible and progressive, and at the same time grossly minimizing the importance of the central nervous system involvement for him or her.

The therapist may then state that there are great individual differences, and the patient may be one who is only slightly affected. The patient will generally protest that he or she does not want to take that chance because one in two odds are not very good and he or she needs all his or her brain cells. From here, the therapist expresses doubt as to the patient's sincerity and leads him or her through the challenge.

This particular intervention lends itself especially well for use in an integrated primary care setting with a physician and a behavioral health-care specialist working together. The physician can explain the physiological basis for blackouts, thus giving credence to the behavioral health-care specialist's strategic intervention.

Challenging the Group

During the first session of the 20-session substance-abuse group program, the therapist tells the group that the ideal group size is eight patients, but that ten have been accepted because two will flunk out. (If twelve have been accepted, then the expectation is given that four will fail.) This is a challenge that no addict can resist: to show the therapist and the rest of the group that he or she will not be the one who flunks out of the group.

Confronting the Games

There are a number of behaviors stemming from the addict's denial that are so consistent and enduring that they have been termed "the games" (Berne, 1964; Cummings & Cummings, 2000). The games are simply derivatives of denial or, in other words, the vehicles through which denial operates. It is helpful to assign names to each of the 11 games to provide a shorthand for confronting the addict during the group process in the addiction group. It is helpful for the physician or psychotherapist to become familiar with these games, as recognizing them in patients will increase the practitioner's ability to recognize the substance-abusing patient.

The Woe-Is-Me Game. The woe-is-me game is a form of self-pity that the patient's denial has adopted in the service of the addiction. The patient rationalizes his or her addiction, believing he or she has been driven to addiction by life's unfortunate circumstances. This game is used as an excuse to resume alcohol and drug activity after a brief period of sobriety. For example, an addict may rationalize a relapse because he or she was denied a promotion at work, because his or her car broke down, or because of a nagging spouse.

The Victim Game. This is similar to the woe-is-me game, except that the addict sees the cause of his or her addiction as stemming from a more permanent or pervasive source than the sudden annoyances that beset everyone. For example, the addict may rationalize his or her addiction because he or she grew up in poverty. It is important for the physician or psychotherapist to remember that the majority of persons growing up in such circumstances do not become addicts, and that there is a significant percentage of those growing up with privilege that do become addicted.

The Rescue Game. The addict spends a great deal of time rescuing anyone and everyone else who may want help. The more unworthy the prospective recipient the greater the likelihood the addict will expend energy to rescue that person. Because the addict believes in some kind of magical score-keeping, he or she behaves as though there were a depository of owed rescues. The belief is that when he or she requires rescuing, no matter how much he or she has messed up, someone will ride to the rescue.

The Blame Game. The blame game differs from the victim game in that the addict holds someone else directly responsible for an unfortunate event that happened. For example, if a diagnostic workup shows chronic pancreatitis, the addict will blame poor medical care, not chemical dependency.

The Feeling Game. The addict is adroit at counterfeiting feelings such as genuine understanding and contrition. Tears of remorse are common, yet the remorse quickly disappears as the addict then plunges into defending his or her behavior. Because chronic inebriation breeds irritability and a short temper, not warmth and kindness, be wary of the patient who presents as just too wonderful. His or her family or coworkers may present a completely different picture.

The Insight Game. Addicts enjoy talking about everything in their lives except their addictions, showing impressive insights, yet continuing their addictive behavior. The physician or psychotherapist must avoid being seduced by such a patient's "insight," remembering that it is meaningless in light of continued substance abuse.

The Rubber Yardstick Game. The rubber yardstick game is used by the addict to measure his or her substance abuse. The addict may greatly underestimate the amount of drugs or alcohol used, or may greatly overestimate the period of sobriety. A frequently overlooked manifestation of the rubber yardstick game, particularly pertinent to primary care settings, is seen in the patient who is purposely seeing multiple physicians and obtaining prescriptions from each for the drug to which he or she is addicted. The patient may be seeing five or even as many as ten doctors, but on inquiry will recall only two or at most three.

The Vending Machine Game. The addict believes that if he or she puts enough coins in the vending machine (e.g., stays clean for 2 months), then the desired item will automatically be dispensed (e.g., the estranged spouse will return).

The File Card Game. The file card game is a mnemonic device, but the addict sets it up and uses it unconsciously. The patient decides that if a certain thing happens, he or she has the right to resume substance abuse. Once he or she has determined what this crucial thing is, the addict develops amnesia with regard to this decision.

The Musical Chairs Game. Addicts sometimes try to beat the consequences of their substance abuse by switching among comparable drugs (those in the same class). When the original substance produces side effects, interpersonal problems, or legal problems, the addict invokes the same high from another drug to continue the addiction. Alcoholics playing the musical chairs game will generally seek prescription central nervous system depressants from their physicians. They think, for example, that they can remain high yet avoid having their substance abuse detected on a breathalizer test.

The Special Person Game. Down deep inside, all addicts believe that they are special persons and that some day this fact will manifest itself to the world. This game may seem innocuous, but really is dangerous in that it perpetuates the addictive lifestyle. As long as the addict believes that any day now the special person will make his or her appearance, it is not important to change the addictive behavior.

Physicians who learn to adeptly recognize these games in their patients will greatly increase the number of appropriate referrals made to behavioral health-care specialists for further assessment of substance abuse. Further, such physicians will be significantly less likely to become well-meaning "pushers" who inadvertently perpetuate their patients' addictions.

Summary

Even though most physicians will not readily be able to properly identify all their substance abusing patients, they will likely be able to identify many of them. With practice in the assessment skills presented here, physicians can become increasingly adept at spotting the red flags that indicate the possibility of substance abuse so that they can appropriately refer these patients to a behavioral health-care specialist. Needless to say, the onsite behavioral health-care specialist must be an individual who is quite adept at identifying substance-abusing patients and very skilled at implementing the interventions outlined in this chapter.

References

Alcoholics Anonymous World Services. (1986). *Alcoholics anonymous.* New York: Author.

American Biodyne. (1985–1990). Various in-house studies.

Berne, E. (1964). *Games people play: The psychology of human relationships.* New York: Ballantine.

Bloom, F. E., Lazerson, A., & Hofstadter, L. (1985). *Brain, mind, and behavior.* New York: W. H. Freeman.

Carlson, N. R. (1986). *Physiology of behavior* (3rd ed.). Boston: Allyn & Bacon.

Center for Substance Abuse Treatment. (1997). *Recovery from substance abuse and addiction: Real people tell their stories.* Rockville, MD: Substance Abuse and Mental Health Services Administration.

Cummings, N. A. (1979). Turning bread into stones: Our modern anti-miracle. *American Psychologist, 34*(12), 1119–1129.

Cummings, N. A. (1982). *Biodyne training manual* (2nd ed.). South San Francisco, CA: Foundation for Behavioral Health.

Cummings, N. A. (1991). Inpatient versus outpatient treatment of substance abuse: Recent developments in the controversy. *Contemporary Family Therapy, 13*(5), 507–520.

Cummings, N. A., & Cummings, J. L. (2000). The first session with substance abusers: A step-by-step guide. San Francisco: Jossey-Bass.

Cummings, N. A., Cummings, J. L., & Johnson, J. N. (Eds.). (1997). *Behavioral health in primary care: A guide for clinical integration.* Madison, CT: Psychosocial Press.

Cummings, N. A., Dorken, H., Pallak, M. S., & Henke, C. J. (1991). *The impact of psychological intervention on health care costs and utilization: The Hawaii Medicaid Project.* (HCFA Contract Report #11-C-983344/9).

Cummings, N. A., Dorken, H., Pallak, M. S., & Henke, C. J. (1993). The impact of psychological intervention on health care costs and utilization: The Hawaii Medicaid Project. In N. A. Cummings & M. S. Pallak (Eds.), *Medicaid, managing behavioral health and implications for public policy, Vol. 2: Healthcare and utilization cost series* (pp. 3–23). South San Francisco, CA: Foundation for Behavioral Health.

Cummings, N., & Sayama, M. (1995). *Focused psychotherapy: A casebook of brief, intermittent psychotherapy throughout the life cycle.* New York: Brunner/Mazel.

Dejong, A., & Doot, M. (1999). *Dying for a drink: A pastor and a physician talk about alcoholism.* Grand Rapids, MI: Eerdmans.

Earl, M. (1988). *Physician heal thyself.* Minneapolis, MN: Hazelden.

Ewing, J. A. (1984). Detecting alcoholism: The CAGE questionnaire. *Journal of the American Medical Association, 252,* 1905–1907.

Falco, M. (1992). *The making of a drug-free America: Programs that work.* New York: Times Books.

Fromm-Reichman, F. (1950). *Principles of intensive psychotherapy.* Chicago: University of Chicago Press.

Gitlin, M. J. (1996). *The psychotherapist's guide to psychopharmacology.* New York: Free Press.

Gould, M. (1999). *Staying sober: Tips for working a twelve step program of recovery.* Minneapolis, MN: Hazelden.

Green, R., Carroll, G. J., & Buxton, W. D. (1978). *The care and management of the sick and incompetent physician.* Springfield, IL: Charles C Thomas.

Hartman-Stein, P. E. (1998). *Innovative behavioral healthcare for older adults.* San Francisco: Jossey-Bass.

Horst, T. (1997). Clinical presentation, screening, and treatment of substance abuse in the primary care setting. In J. D. Haber & G. E. Mitchell (Eds.), *Primary care meets mental health: Tools for the 21st century* (pp. 167–177). Tiburon, CA: CentraLink.

Joseph, S. (1997). *Symptom-focused psychiatric drug therapy for managed care.* New York: Haworth Medical Press.

Kaiser Permanente Health Plan. (1981). *The differential cost for the treatment of medical conditions for substance abusers and non-substance abusers.* Oakland, CA: Author.

Kaplan, H. I., & Sadock, B. J. (1993). *Pocket handbook of psychiatric drug treatment.* Baltimore: Williams & Wilkins.

L'Abate, L. L., Farrar, J. E., & Serritella, D. (1991). *Handbook of differential treatments for addictions.* Boston: Allyn & Bacon.

Lezak, M. D. (1983). *Neuropsychological assessment* (2nd ed.). New York: Oxford University Press.

Miller, N. S., Smith, D. E., & Gold, M. S. (1996). *Manual of therapeutics for addictions.* New York: Wiley.

Moore, T. J. (1998). *Prescription for disaster.* New York: Simon & Schuster.

Murray, R. M., & Stabenau, J. R. (1982). Genetic factors in alcoholism predisposition. In E. O. Pattison & E. Kaupman (Eds.), *Encyclopedic handbook of alcoholism* (pp. 135–143). New York: Gardner.

Narcotics Anonymous World Services. (1988). *Narcotics anonymous.* Van Nuys, CA: Author.

National Institute on Drug Abuse and National Institute on Alcohol and Alcohol Abuse (NIDA & NIAA). (1999). *NIDA and NIAA 1998 statistics.* Rockville, MD: Author.

Quimette, P. C., Finney, J. W., & Moos, R. H. (1997). Twelve-step and cognitive-behavioral treatment for substance abuse: A comparison of treatment effectiveness. *Journal of Counseling and Clinical Psychology, 65,* 230–240.

Saunders, J. B., Aasland, O. G., & Babor, T. F. (1993). Development of the Alcohol Use Disorders Identification Test (AUDIT): WHO collaborative project on early detection of persons with harmful alcohol consumption—II. *Addiction, 88,* 791–804.

Saxe, L., Dougherty, D., Esty, K., & Fine, M. (1983). *The effectiveness and costs of alcoholism treatment* (Health Technology Case Study 22). Washington, DC: Office of Technology Assessment.

Saxe, L., & Goodman, L. (1988). *The effectiveness of outpatient versus inpatient treatment: Updating the OTA Report* (Health Technology Case Study 22 Update). Washington, DC: Office of Technology Assessment.

Selzer, M. L. (1971). The Michigan Alcoholism Screening Test: The quest for a new diagnostic instrument. *American Journal of Psychiatry, 127,* 1653–1658.

U.S. Department of Labor. (1998). *Facts and figures about drugs and alcohol in the workplace.* Washington, DC: Author.

Chapter 8
Identifying and Treating the Somatizer: Integrated Care's Penultimate Behavioral Intervention

NICHOLAS A. CUMMINGS

Those few health-care delivery systems that are striving to integrate behavioral health into primary care tend to approach the task in a piecemeal fashion. Usually one, and sometimes two protocols are parachuted into an otherwise conventional delivery system, yielding disappointing results. Most frequently a single disease management program (e.g., diabetes, asthma, rheumatoid arthritis) is partially infused into the delivery system, and it has as much impact on the total system as one drop of red dye in a five-gallon bucket of white paint. A favorite single program is a depression protocol, ostensibly justified because as many as a third or more of primary care patients reveal some level of depression (Strosahl, Baker, Braddick, Stuart, & Handley, 1997). A truly integrated program is a complex of seamless behavioral interventions comprising an indistinguishable part of a multifaceted health-care delivery system (Cummings, 1997; Strosahl, 1997). The possible effective exception to the single program approach is that of identifying and treating the somatizer. Because of the remarkably skewing effect somatization has on a health-care system, its alleviation has an equally remarkable positive impact. This positive effect has been demonstrated in such extensive demonstration/research projects as the 20-year Kaiser Permanente experience (Cummings & VandenBos, 1981) and the 7-year Hawaii Medicaid project (Cummings, Dorken, Pallak & Henke, 1993). A description of how such a program works is important, as it is potentially the most rewarding single beginning in an otherwise conventional (nonintegrated) delivery system. A caveat must be noted, however; in spite of its rewards it does not replace or even approach the potential effectiveness of a fully integrated system.

Historical Perspective

Somatization was identified in the late 1950s at Kaiser Permanente where it was discovered that 60% of physician visits were by patients who either manifested no diagnosable physical illness that would account for their symptoms, or whose chronic illness was exacerbated by psychological factors (Cummings & VandenBos, 1981). In that era the relationship between stress and physical symptoms was not clearly understood, and the patients for whom no medical diagnosis could be determined were identified in their medical charts as hypochondriacs. Being capitated they did not have to submit a diagnosis on a reimbursement claim, so Kaiser Permanente physicians had no necessity to render a provisional diagnosis when no definitive diagnosis could be found. This was the origin of the diagnosis of hypochondriac, believed to constitute a reflection of absence of physical disease. When I joined the staff of Kaiser Permanente in San Francisco in the late 1950s, I found the term to be pejorative at best. It implied that the patient was at fault, doing something purposely to cause his or her own misery, as well as that of the overworked and baffled physician. Since physicians were trained to persevere in looking for an organic cause to the symptoms, laboratory work, x-rays, electrocardiograms, and other tests were repeated ad infinitum, imposing a financial strain on the medical system along with the strain stemming from physician overload. Furthermore, since the Kaiser Permanente physicians were capitated, as opposed to fee-for-service, the high utilizers of health care added no revenue and deflected the overworked physician from time that might be devoted to the seriously medically ill. These severe strains on the medical system are what prompted Kaiser Permanente to create a mental health department that would address the issue. It must be noted that this was during a period when no insurer or third-party payer included psychotherapy as a covered benefit. To incorporate psychotherapy within the medical care system was a radical step, indeed, and one that eventually led to the inclusion of psychotherapy not only at Kaiser Permanente, but also in indemnity health insurance in general (Cummings & VandenBos, 1981).

Several methods were used at Kaiser Permanente to identify and treat the overutilizers of medical care, but first it was necessary to purge the system of the concept of hypochondria. I tried a number of substitutes, all of which were rejected, until at a late-night brainstorming session I suggested that these patients were somaticizing stress, and could be referred to as somaticizers. Both Drs. Sidney Garfield and Morris Collen, cofounders of Kaiser Permanente, liked the terms, suggesting they sounded medical enough to be acceptable to the physicians. Thus were born the terms, which later were shortened by grammarians to somatizing and somatizers, and ended use of the offensive term *hypochondria* as standard diagnostic label in medical charts.

Recently some health psychologists have begun using the term "somatically focused patient," believing this to be more politically acceptable because *somatizer* is a pejorative term among physicians. Experience has shown that physicians are not hostile toward somatizers, but baffled as to how to manage these patients who require so much of their time and do not respond to medical attention. When a colocated behavioral care provider is available, however, physicians reveal their interest and intense concern for the somatizer. The substitution of an ostensibly more politically correct term that physicians would find awkward and unusable provides a verbal varnish at best, and does not begin to address the real problem of population management that requires the implementation of integrated care.

Several years after a system of triage for the somatizers had been in operation, there emerged a series of studies that established the impressive reduction in medical overutilization through brief, focused behavioral interventions (Cummings & Follette, 1968; Cummings, Kahn, & Sparkman, 1962; Follette & Cummings, 1967). These studies captured the attention of the National Institute of Mental Health (NIMH), and a series of two dozen replications emerged within a decade (Jones & Vischi, 1979). In all but one study the savings in medical costs far exceeded the cost of providing the behavioral services, and the NIMH dubbed the phenomenon as the "medical cost offset" effect. A subsequent consensus conference attended by all the researchers in medical cost offset indicated that the effect was present only in organized systems of care that had the capacity to identify and treat the somatizer, and it was not present in solo-practice, fee-for-service settings where the somatizers increased revenue and thus removed any incentive to address medical overutilization. (These findings are discussed in the Results section below.) Suffice it to say that the insurance community and the federal government were impressed enough to begin considering psychotherapy as a covered benefit.

The Definition of Somatization

Somatization is simply the translation into physical symptoms of any psychological stress, emotional distress, or conflicts in living. In this way the source of the original stress is masked and not immediately identifiable by the physician who regards physical symptoms as indicative of medical illness. It has nothing to do with the diagnostic category of somatization disorder, introduced by the American Psychiatric Association into the *Diagnostic and Statistical Manual (DSM-IV)* many years after the original term was coined at Kaiser Permanente (American Psychiatric Association, 1994). In the so-called somatization disorder the patient manifests symptoms from at least three of several categories, reminiscent of choosing a Chinese dinner with two dishes from column A, three from column B, and one from column C. In half a century of practice I have seen less than a half-dozen patients who would qualify for this esoteric diagnosis, and these were eventually rediagnosed as latent schizophrenics who were defending against the disintegration of their thought disorder by a plethora of somatizations, somewhat akin to the manner persons with Munchausen syndrome manifest symptoms to obtain medical procedures, particularly extensive surgery.

There exists a plethora of models as how stress is translated into physical symptoms. Among these are alexithymia, the inability to verbalize emotions (Peter Sifneos), displacement of unconscious conflict (Sigmund Freud), culturally determined idioms of distress, operant conditioning (B. F. Skinner), learned behaviors (Aaron Beck), and many others. All of these are pertinent, but beyond the scope of this chapter, which is constrained to present the utility, outreach, and methodology (i.e., the nuts and bolts, not the theory) of directly addressing somatization once it has occurred.

Data From the Hawaii Medicaid Project

Under the auspices of the Health Care Financing Administration (HCFA), 36,000 Medicaid-eligible recipients and 90,000 federal employees on the Island of Oahu (Honolulu) were randomized into a control group (receiving the Medicaid/federal employees' mental health benefit through privately practicing psychiatrists and psychologists) and an experimental group. The latter received all behavioral care through a new delivery system known as the Biodyne Centers, created jointly by the state of Hawaii and the Foundation for Behavioral Health, specifically for this research project.

The Biodyne Centers provided all mental health services for the experimental group, but made extensive use of the focused, targeted interventions known as *focused, intermittent psychotherapy* throughout the life cycle (Cummings & Sayama, 1995). The control group was eligible for 52 sessions of individual psychotherapy a year with a practitioner of their choice in the community, and these 52 sessions were renewable annually. In addition, the Biodyne Centers outreached (using the method described below) each month the 15% highest utilizers of medical care by frequency of services, not by total dollar amount. The project permitted further delineation of the patients into those who had psychological problems only, those who had chronic medical conditions (asthma, diabetes, emphysema, hypertension, ischemic heart disease, and rheumatoid arthritis), and those who manifested substance-abuse problems.

The Hawaii project for the first time compared organized mental health care employing targeted interventions with the far less effective and apparently inefficient solo practice, fee-for-service psychotherapy model (Cummings, 1997; Cummings et al., 1993). (These results are discussed in the Results section below.)

The Essence of Medical Cost Offset

Although there is tremendous pressure in the current health-care economy to save dollars, medical cost offset is not about money. It is about effective care. First, for care to be effective, it must be the right care. No amount of medical overutilization will bring relief to the patient if it is inappropriate care. The patient is reflecting psychological, not medical, problems and needs to be treated by effective behavioral interventions. Redundant medical tests only reinforce the patient's notion that his or her condition is medical, and all that is needed is another series of tests to establish this. But the research also demonstrates that not all behavioral interventions are effective, and somatization is reduced only by appropriate care. The appropriate care is effective care, and effective care saves money. But more important than medical savings is the amelioration of the patient's suffering. Often this suffering has existed for years because the real (behavioral) condition has not been addressed by either the medical system or the traditional psychological system.

It is to the description of one such system, the identification and treatment of the somatizer, that we now turn. It is emphasized that this falls short of a system in which behavioral health and primary care are fully integrated, but it is a rewarding beginning because it addresses the largest unnecessary drain on the medical system and is in contrast to the usual one or two programs within a traditional health-care model that have yielded disappointing results.

The Model

Outreach

There are two approaches to the computer selection of the somatizer. In each, 15% of the highest utilizers of health care are selected by *frequency of visits*, not by dollar amounts expended. The somatizer is identified by constantly seeking medical services, regularly through a large number of repeat visits, but when these are not sufficient, often through nonappointment (drop-in) clinics or, if these are not available, through recourse to emergency rooms. Selecting high utilizers by dollar amount, on the other hand, merely elicits the organ transplants and other costly medical heroics, patients who are not necessarily somatizers.

Outreach Method 1 was the earliest approach employed. It was more cumbersome because it sought to acknowledge medical prerogatives and the preeminence of the physician in the referral process. After eliciting 15% of the highest utilizers by frequency, these patients' names were sent to their respective physicians accompanied by a request that the physician consider referring them for psychotherapy, or behavioral intervention. What was termed a "consider rule" was used in lieu of advising the physician to refer, or what is known among the various medical specialties in collaborating with each other as an "advice rule." Because this was the earliest approach to the triage of the somatizer, utmost care was taken so it would not appear as if the computer were advising the physician. Along with attention to these professional sensitivities, there was extensive training of the primary care physicians with strong apparent "buy-in" to the procedure.

The patients were randomized, with the experimental condition receiving the consider rule, while the control condition became the existing collaboration with behavioral care specialists by physicians who had received extensive training in identifying behavioral problems in their patients. The results were disappointing in that the computer consider rule did not elicit any more referrals than did the usual primary care practice (Cummings & Follette, 1968). The results were interpreted that in a system in which primary care physicians (PCPs) are optimally referring behavior problems, the addition of a computer-generated consider rule did not increase referrals. Both methods resulted in referral of less than 40% of those who would be identified as somatizers by tabulating 15% of the highest utilizers resulting from frequency of visits.

On reconsideration, the elicitation of only 40% of the somatizers, either directly by the PCPs or through computer prompting, was far from optimal. The research was redesigned so there was even more extensive training of the PCPs. This included the validation of 38 criteria of distress derived from the PCPs' own work samples as recorded by them in their patients' charts, and without recognizing that these were, indeed, signs that these patients were somatizers. These chart samples were also validated into those that scored either 3 or 2 points, while most received a score of 1. A score of 9 or more indicated sufficient emotional distress to warrant behavioral care interventions. By accompanying the computer consent rule with each individual patient's score on these quickly recognizable work samples, the physicians could immediately identify with the need for referral. The number of referrals in the experimental group increased by 50% to almost 60% of the possible number, while the control group declined to 35% (Cummings, 1977; Cummings & Follette, 1976). The PCPs uniformly expressed professional comfort in referring these patients, and often followed with the addendum, "I always knew there was something psychologically wrong with this patient." This latter response to our referring physician survey made us uncomfortable and prompted further research the following year that was not published for several years after its completion (Cummings, 1985).

A group of 10,667 patients were assessed with the Neuromental Questionnaire (NMQ) and the 38 criteria of distress in a 6-month period in an automated multiphasic health screening. Both the NMQ and the Kaiser automated multiphasic health screening employing 29 computer leads testing various medical functions (e.g., blood sugar, electrocardiogram, blood pressure, vital lung capacity, and so forth, along with the NMQ) in a 2-hour assembly-line procedure have been extensively reported (see, for example, Friedman, Ury, Klatsky, & Siegelaub, 1974), and will not be repeated here. Suffice it to say that there was a follow-up over a 6-month period of missed medical diagnoses by the same 34 PCPs for their patients and for whom they received the consider rule (experimental group) versus those for whom they did not (control group). The experimental patients were randomly divided further into three subgroups: (1) those patients for whom the PCP received only a cryptic consider rule stating, "The patient may have significant emotional distress; consider a referral to a psychologist," (2) those patients for whom the PCP received, along with the consider rule, a paragraph describing somewhat the nature of their emotional distress, and (3) those patients for whom the PCP received not only the consider rule, but also a two-page computer-generated description of the patient based on his or her NMQ results. It was anticipated that increasing levels of psychological information would correspondingly increase the comfort level and incentive for the PCPs to refer for behavioral care.

In this study (Cummings, 1985), there was a tabulation of the number of symptoms initially ascribed by the physician to emotional distress that were later (within 6 months) rediagnosed as physical illness. Using the control group as the baseline for the number of missed diagnoses of physical illness, it was found that the number of missed diagnoses increased significantly in proportion to the amount of psychological assessment information rendered to the PCP. It was as if the increasing amount of information not only increased the likelihood of psychological referral, but it also increased the likelihood that physical illness would be overlooked in a population that was labeled as having emotional distress.

The function of computer-based elicitation of somatization is to enhance the quality of care and ensure that individuals who translate emotional distress into physical symptoms receive the behavioral care they need. Researchers may be meticulous in establishing the validity and reliability of computer-based programs, in this case the NMQ and the 38 criteria of distress, but it is important that "treatment validity," or the effect on a delivery system, also be established. Efforts to address medical prerogatives and sensitivities backfired and led to the discontinuance of having the PCPs serve as intermediaries in the computer referral to behavioral care of the 15% of highest utilizers (as defined by the number of physician visits per year).

Outreach Method 2 was employed in the aforementioned 7-year Hawaii-HCFA-Medicaid study with considerable success and without the limitations and difficulties experienced in the use of Outreach Method 1. It is the method recommended unless political or sensitivity problems plague the relationship of PCPs to behavioral care providers. In those instances Method 1 may be the only consideration, but it should be undertaken with the knowledge that results will be limited and even complicated by the cumbersome involvement of PCPs as middle step in the referral procedure. For the use of Method 2 the setting should meet the criterion of PCP willingness to be informed after the elicitation, referral, outreach, and initial behavioral intervention have all occurred. A slight modification of Method 2 may be communication to the PCP after the step of outreach and before the initial behavioral intervention. In all instances, PCP approval and cooperation are vital in the success of Method 2, with the ultimate aim being collaboration with the PCP in the care of the somatizer.

Method 2 simply elicits the 15% of patients within a health system that account for the highest utilization of services by physician visits, not dollar amount. This presupposes that the health plan has the electronic information systems in place where this is easily accomplished, something that is far from always the case. The informatics age has been upon us now for over two decades, and the fact that most health delivery systems do not have in place sufficient medical informatics (MI) technology attests to the snail's pace at which health care typically progresses. It is especially troubling to me, who in working at Kaiser Permanente was able to readily access this kind of information as early as the mid-1960s.

Elicitation of the 15% highest utilizers is done monthly, and the patients are contacted by a well-trained outreach worker, usually a nurse practitioner, by telephone. A medical social worker possessing the same skills and knowledge is an acceptable substitute for the nurse practitioner. The patient's belief that her or his condition is caused by physical illness is never challenged. Rather, the outreach worker empathizes with the patient, "Someone who has had as much illness as you have had certainly must be upset about it." This statement usually elicits an immediate reaction, ranging from an exposition of symptoms to the complaint that physicians don't seem to understand or to be sympathetic to the patient's plight. After hearing the patient out sufficiently to permit the development of some initial trust, the patient is invited in to explore how the health system might be of help. The service is free, and perhaps there can be an investigation of the possibility of alternative treatments to those that have not seemed to work; or perhaps the patient, once the difficulty is better appraised, may be put in touch with a more sympathetic physician. Then an initial appointment is made. The entire process has been between patient and outreach worker, with an initial appointment made directly with a psychologist without the cumbersome and often discouraging intervening step of conveying the patients' names to their physicians who then may or may not refer. The well-meaning physician who does refer may do so with far less finesse than an outreach worker, often inadvertently challenging the patient's somatizing.

In contrast, Method 2 successfully elicits initial appointments with most of the high utilizers who are outreached. It should not be surprising that offering a high utilizer another appointment with still another doctor (this time a psychologist) is readily accepted, especially when it is accompanied by such an empathic attitude. This method was not only used in the Hawaii project, but was also used with considerable success at American Biodyne, a practitioner-driven, national managed, behavioral health-care organization (MBHO) from 1985 to 1992, after which the company changed hands and much of the clinical focus was abandoned by the business interests that constituted the new ownership. Outreach Method 2 has been extensively described by Cummings and Bragman (1988) and will not be delineated further here.

Extreme Outreach

The telephone outreach is but one approach used to bring the somaticizing patient into therapy. In both the Hawaii project and at American Biodyne, there were periodic mailings of brochures and newsletters to remind these high utilizers of the services offered. Additionally, the monthly newsletter highlighted a specific somatic complaint in each issue, emphasizing the physician's inability to help the patient, and again carefully avoiding challenging the patient's conviction that the condition is a physical malady.

In spite of all efforts, 8–10% of those outreached consistently resisted making the initial appointment. A house call seemed indicated, but a psychologist or outreach worker showing up at the door was invariably refused entrance. A number of approaches were attempted without success, until we stumbled upon a unique one. A nurse appearing at the door in full regalia, which included cap, nurse's gown, cape, and black bag, was not refused admittance to the home even once. She then typically conducted an interview around the kitchen table, usually with the entire family gathered, that resulted in the initial appointment being accepted by the somatizer. What was termed extreme outreach succeeded over time in bringing in, for at least the initial interview, a remarkable 96.3% of the high utilizers outreached (Cummings & Bragman, 1988).

The Treatment

Assignment of Treatment

One of the primary tasks of the initial appointment with the high utilizer is matching the patient's condition with the appropriate treatment. Within the 15% highest utilizers every conceivable psychological condition will be found, requiring a menu consisting of a large number of targeted and focused interventions. It is the task of the psychologist conducting the initial interview to (1) arrive at which treatment would most benefit each patient, and (2) motivate the patient to enter that program. In the delivery systems Kaiser Permanente, Hawaii project, and American Biodyne as reported here, there were ultimately 68 program protocols available. Most of the protocols were psychoeducational treatment group programs, and experience demonstrated that the psychotherapist's time in this kind of delivery system is divided 50% for these psychoeducational groups, 25% in time-limited groups, and only 25% in individual time-sensitive therapy. Considering that the group programs had 5 to 12 patients in each, it is apparent that as many as 90% of the 15% highest utilizers seen would enter a group, rather than an individual treatment program.

A majority of the patients outreached demonstrate some modicum of depression, reflecting a response to their "physical" symptoms with understandable emotional distress. This does not mean that all these patients should be assigned to depression treatment; rather, the depression protocols should be restricted to those manifesting primarily depression, or whose depression is debilitating enough to be the center of focus. Addressing the depression that might accompany the primary psychological condition is a part of all 68 protocols. Another significant portion of these high utilizers will manifest substance-abuse problems. Addicts are high utilizers, ranging from the frequent injuries of "falling down drunks" to the persistent diagnosis of nasopharyngitis for those who snort cocaine. It is important to motivate the substance abuser to enter a chemical dependency program, and this may require several individual appointments. In fact, the number of individual initial sessions required to successfully assign the patient to the right treatment modality is bimodal, in that both one and three sessions are equal in number.

Offering a somatizer another health-care service constitutes an offer that is rarely refused. These are patients whose number of physician visits a year frequently exceeds 100, with a mean of 58. Even then, they would like to have more visits if access were easier. One patient, a research psychologist, set what for us has been a record: 643 physician visits in one 12-month period, although we have treated a number whose physician visits exceeded 400. This was a man in his late 40s who was convinced he was suffering heart attacks, and negative electrocardiograms seldom reassured him for more than a few hours or a couple of days at maximum. He would often present himself to the emergency room (ER) before 6:00 A.M., leave reassured, only to return to the drop-in clinic by 11:00 that same morning. This rushing to the doctor was often repeated again in the afternoon or evening. On his "bad days," as he called them, six or more physician visits was standard behavior. He was on the research staff of his health plan and knew personally all the cardiologists and ER physicians, who accorded him unwarranted courtesy and deference. He was aware of the goals and purpose of our somatization program, but he nonetheless eagerly signed on and typically never missed a session.

The Somatization Treatment Protocol

Following the individual preparatory sessions, the somatizers enter a group program of 8 to 12 patients, depending on the traffic flow. A total of 20 group sessions are spaced over a 6-month period as follows: 4 semiweekly sessions, followed by 14 weekly sessions, and culminating with 2 monthly sessions. Each group session is 2 hours in length. The patient has recourse to three individual sessions that may be used at any time during the 6 months as needed, or not used at all. This number has been found sufficient to provide access in an emotional crisis or when the patient's progress seems stymied and in need of individual attention, but without fostering the patient's ingrained desire for more and more visits.

The somatization protocol embodies all of the features present in all of the 68 Biodyne group programs, and these elements have been extensively described (see Cummings & Cummings, 1997, pp. 336–345). An important feature is that mixing and matching of these elements is readily accomplished as might be appropriate to the condition being treated, and only the unique features of the somatization protocol will be delineated here. It should be stated that many interventions make use of a broad range of cognitive behavior therapies (CBTs), but these are tailored to fit the somatizer. This accommodation is the result of many years of field testing in actual delivery systems, so that the limitations of CBT are alleviated. One of these limitations is that CBT does not pay enough attention to basic characteristics, other than the problem presented, which define the differences among the persons presenting. For example, a somatizer who is also a borderline personality disorder must be addressed differently from those who are chronically depressed, obsessive-compulsively disordered, or addicted to prescription drugs.

Requirements. Patients are expected to attend every group session and to complete their homework. Failure to complete the homework results in the patient's being sent home and forfeiting that session. When symptoms tempt the patient to seek a medical appointment, or to rush to a nonappointment visit with a physician (defined as including all physician extenders such as a physician assistant, nurse practitioner, etc.), the patient is required to first call the "buddy" assigned to him or her as described below.

Buddy System. Patients are randomly paired off as buddies. They are encouraged to phone each other whenever they have a need to talk, but they are not permitted to call the psychotherapist. If a patient breaks this rule and does call the therapist, it counts as one of the three individual visits permitted during the 6 months. Patients are required to call each other before seeking a visit with a physician, and they are further required to obtain the buddy's agreement before seeing the physician.

Tokens. Each patient at the first group session is given 10 coupons, each good for a visit with a physician anytime during the 6-month treatment period. The patient is free to spend these on physician visits with or without the agreement of the buddy, but once all 10 coupons are spent, there are no more. If the patient is found on examination by the physician to have at that moment a physical disease necessitating medical attention, neither the patient nor the buddy forfeits one of their respective 10 coupons. If there is no such condition, the patient forfeits one coupon, and if the buddy had agreed to the visit, the buddy also forfeits a coupon. If the buddy did not agree with seeking the visit and did her or his best to dissuade the patient, the buddy does not forfeit a coupon. This is designed to aid both patient and buddy to begin learning to differentiate between real sickness and somatization, something the general population does routinely when deciding whether they are sick enough to go to the doctor. The therapist may need reassurance here, and must be reminded that these patients have been medically explored beyond all reason, and have been found to have no medical disease, and certainly no life-threatening disease. In several decades of using this protocol, there has never been an untoward medical event in which a patient who really needed the doctor chose not to seek one. The invariable decision is in the opposite direction of seeing a physician when it was not necessary.

Psychoeducation. Information on how the body translates stress into physical symptoms is important, but it is even more important to include simple psychodynamics tailored and woven into each individual patient's personal verbalizations, exquisitely timed and expertly interpreted, to help the patient see how this goes on within his or her own life. In presenting the psychoeducational portion, however, a patient who insists "I am not somatizing" is never challenged directly. The therapist will get a rapid assist from the other group members who will challenge the patient. For these patients parental attention came essentially only when the child was ill, and very likely the excuse worked: "Mommy, my tummy hurts too much to go to school today even if I do have a spelling test." There are many examples of a learned response to stress that results in somatization, a pattern that follows the patient throughout life.

Homework. There is homework, tailored to what should be the next progressive step for the patient, given at the end of each session. This may include readings, charting the events and feelings that precede the urge to see a physician, putting into practice "antidotes" to running to the doctor, and later in the sequence of treatment finding long-term alternatives to seeking medical attention at times of stress. Toward this end, relaxation and guided imagery exercises are assigned as homework. As mentioned earlier, the homework is enforced, and the patient who has not done the homework forfeits the session. The therapist must be prepared for the patient's outcry, "I need therapy more than ever this week and you are sending me home," by replying, "Then do your homework so you can get help from both yourself and the group." More than anything else, the homework drives home the concept that the patient, not the physician, is ultimately responsible for his or her own health, and that the patient must partner with the physician toward wellness.

Veterans. At the end of the 6 months, one or two patients who have done well may express a desire for more therapy, and they are allowed to enter a new group with an entirely new cast of patients. The presence of one of these "veterans" in a group is a great aid to the therapist. Patients listen when one of these veterans states, "I remember when I felt like you do, and here is what I did about it."

Self-efficacy and *learned helplessness*, as described respectively by Bandura (1991) and Seligman (1975, 1994), are of particular importance to these patients. They need the self-efficacy that comes from accomplishing specific, and often small, tasks toward their own well-being, and they have to overcome their learned helplessness, feeling there is nothing they can do in the face of scary physical symptoms other than run to the doctor.

All the elements listed by Cummings and Cummings (1997, pp. 336–345) are woven into the protocol, but special mention must be made of physical exercise because patients resist this important antidote to anxiety and depression, and therapists, perhaps because of their own more or less sedentary lifestyles, do not enforce it by making it part of the homework. Throughout the 6 months the psychologist must be skilled in group dynamics, interpreting and interceding as necessary, but allowing the group to drive home to each member the processes in their own somatization. Patients accept a degree of directness and even bluntness from peers that they would dismiss if proffered even tactfully by the therapist.

The Extreme Protocol

There are somatizers deemed so recalcitrant that some health plans have resorted to an extreme procedure that has been termed a "lock-in." The patient is assigned a PCP and the patient cannot see any other physician or go to a specialist unless this lock-in physician approves it. This PCP is usually highly trained in somatization, but unfortunately there often ensues a standoff between patient and lock-in physician. In the method described in this chapter, there has never been an experience where resorting to such a desperate measure was even considered. We have been confronted with two situations, however, when our triaging of the somatizer came after the health plan had instated a lock-in system. In both instances we worked with the lock-in physicians and adapted our protocol to accommodate this extreme measure. It is not surprising that the patients came to the group program hostile and resentful. There was also resistance from the lock-in physicians to the 10-coupon freebies, inasmuch as under our system the patient was free to spend these coupons after consulting with the buddy, but had to accept the fact that once these were spent, there would be no more coupons until the end of the 6 months of treatment. The lock-in PCPs saw themselves as the gatekeeper, not the coupons, and complained they would be subordinated by both a piece of paper (the coupon) and the patient's buddy.

An accommodation was reached in which the patient was given 15 coupons, but could redeem them only with the lock-in physician. The increased number of coupons was to give the lock-in PCPs the added discretion they wanted, rather than granting the patients more leeway. In both instances where a lock-in system was in place before our arrival, it was abandoned within the first year after this protocol had been instituted. Both the health plan, which was ever mindful of patient complaints and even potential lawsuits, and the lock-in physicians, who had tired of being the bad guys, heaved a noticeable sigh of relief.

Results

This method has been employed on a large scale by a number of settings for several decades with uniformly positive results. The NIMH early on was so impressed that it funded 20 replications that it reported in summary (Jones & Vischi, 1979). A year later it sponsored the Bethesda Consensus Conference where all the experts in medical cost offset addressed over 3 days the wide ranging cost savings within the uniformly positive findings. This conference concluded that the more closely the treatment replicated our Group Method 2, the greater was the reduction in somatization (Jones & Vischi, 1980).

The Kaiser Permanente Studies

It was at Kaiser Permanente that the term somaticizer was coined in the early 1960s and the method of triaging them into a behavioral care system was developed (Cummings & VandenBos, 1981).

The typical reduction in somatization is illustrated in Figure 8.1, demonstrating a steady reduction in somatization in a 5-year period, which resulted in a somatization rate for the experimental group to a baseline that resembles the usual utilization rate of healthy, nonsomaticizing patients. The difficulty with a long line of such researches is that they were retrospective studies with a comparison, rather than a control group. Nonetheless, these early studies were important in piquing the interest of both researchers and program planners who were interested in health-care delivery models.

The Hawaii-HCFA-Medicaid Project

The HCFA funded in 1981 a 7-year project in Honolulu involving 36,000 Medicaid recipients and 90,000 federal employees, in which a new delivery system was created for the first time as a behavioral care carve-out that interfaced with a traditional medical system under the sponsorship of the Hawaii Medical Services Association (HMSA), the Blue Cross/Blue Shield affiliate in Hawaii.

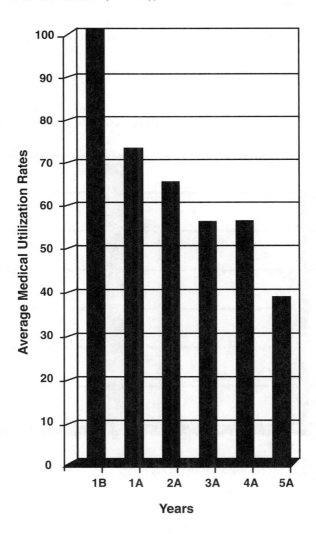

Fig. 8.1 Average medical utilization for the year before (1B) and the 5 years after (1A, 2A, 3A, 4A, and 5A) behavioral intervention was instituted (from Follette & Cummings, 1967).

The Hawaii project had the advantage of being a large-scale (126,000 eligible patients) prospective study with a randomized design. As with the Kaiser Permanente experience, psychologists were trained in the model of addressing somatization with targeted programs and without challenging the somatization directly.

The prospective, randomized Hawaii project confirmed the results derived from years of retrospective studies and added a number of dimensions. First, it demonstrated that the Somatizer Program Method 2 was instrumental in significantly reducing medical utilization in the experimental group (the Biodyne model), while the traditional private practice, fee-for-service sector (control group) significantly raised medical utilization, in most instances by as much as 30%. Second, the reduction in medical utilization by those patients suffering from six chronic medical conditions (asthma, diabetes, emphysema, hypertension, ischemic heart disease, and rheumatoid arthritis) was even more dramatic than that of the simple somaticizers inasmuch as the protocol dramatically increased compliance and reduced the emotional component that accompanies chronic physical disease. The control group (treated by the private practice, fee-for-service sector) demonstrated equally greater increases in the opposite direction: an increase in overutilization (Cummings, Dorken, Pallak, & Henke, 1991, 1993). These findings are illustrated in Figures 8.2 and 8.3.

The Fort Bragg Study

An initially highly touted experiment with a government CHAMPUS population in North Carolina purported that it was unlimited access to privately practicing, fee-for-service psychologists, not the

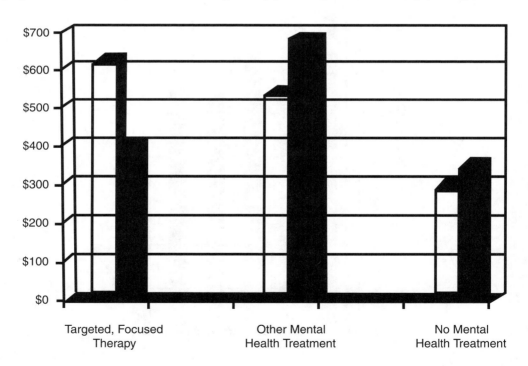

Fig. 8.2 Chronically ill group. Average medical utilization in constant dollars by the Hawaii project chronically ill group for the year before treatment (lightly shaded columns) and the year after treatment (darkly shaded columns) for those receiving targeted and focused treatment in the private practice community, and no mental health treatment (from Cummings, Dorken, Pallak, & Henke, 1993).

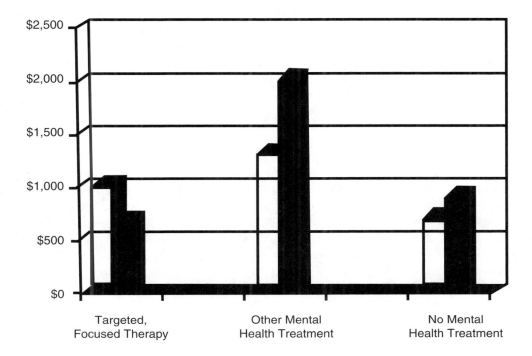

Fig. 8.3 Nonchronic group. Average medical utilization in constant dollars for the Hawaii Project Nonchronic Group for the year before treatment (lightly shaded columns) and the year after treatment (darkly shaded columns) for those receiving targeted and focused treatment, other mental health treatment in the private practice community, and no mental health treatment (from Cummings, Dorken, Pallak, & Henke, 1993).

targeted programs, that would reduce medical/surgical utilization. Congress funded $8 million to provide unlimited psychotherapy for the study and found to its dismay that (1) it cost $80 million and (2) it did not decrease medical/surgical utilization below that of the conventional managed care system, which did not use targeted group programs (Bickman, 1996). In other words, a study that cost 10 times that of the Hawaii project ($80 million versus $8.2 million) confirmed that targeted programs, not unlimited traditional individual psychotherapy, are crucial in deriving results. The American Psychological Association "embalmed" the findings in a special issue of the *American Psychologist* and has not referred to the study since (Bickman, 1996).

Discussion

Medical Confidentiality

The health-care system changes slowly and in its reluctance to move forward it is likely to raise issues that are tangential or irrelevant. One such issue is the matter of medical confidentiality and whether it is compromised or even violated in the computerized identification of the 15% highest utilizers of health care by number of physician visits. The answer is no because no information other than utilization data are conveyed, a practice common within health systems. Whether used for third-party reimbursement or, as in our case, for outreach, nothing more than utilization data is exchanged. Once outreached, the patient can participate voluntarily or refuse to do so, and until the patient is seen and discusses her- or himself with the practitioner, no medical or psychological information is available. No health system can operate without utilization information flowing freely *within the health system* that is being used by the patient. The method and protocol described in this chapter become integral parts of that health delivery system and are of no greater or less consequence than a PCP referring a patient to a specialist within the same medical system. It must be emphasized that the monthly listing of the patients manifesting the 15% highest number of physician visits is not accompanied by any information beyond frequency and dates of visits to physicians. Once the patient elects to come in after the outreach, then the patient's medical chart becomes available by patient consent and participation in the treatment modality.

Wither Integration?

Shaffer (2001) identifies three levels on the ladder to full integration of behavioral health in primary care: (1) communication, (2) collaboration, and (3) integration. In the first there is communication between PCPs and behavioral providers, a procedure that would seem at minimum to be a necessity in adequate health care, but which is surprisingly absent to a significant degree in most health delivery systems. Amazingly, it is common for PCPs to refer a patient for psychotherapy and receive no follow-up response other than a statement of whether the patient did or did not make an appointment with the psychologist. The reason given is that psychological information deserves the utmost in confidentiality, but this is an irrelevant argument. The PCP neither cares about nor needs the kind of information that the psychotherapist guards so zealously. Rather, the PCP needs information upon which to base medical treatment decisions, such as which medication to prescribe, and without adequate communication between PCP and psychologist, the patient is being short-changed.

A simple yet valuable form of communication is a 24-hour, toll-free telephone number where a PCP can obtain quick consultation with a behavioral provider about a patient manifesting psychological problems. This important communication has been shown to prevent more costly procedures or preclude treatment errors, including psychiatric hospitalization, medication miscalculations, and suicidal activity. The facility with which communication occurs can be a progression that is characteristic of a system, or it can be no more than a regular communication that might exist between one or two PCPs and a nearby behavioral care provider with whom they have formed a special relationship. When one considers how absent or primitive mere communication often is within a system, one is struck with how far off integration is. This is such an apparent lack in health systems that MedCo/Merck was prompted to allocate $100 million to help foster communication within a health system (Gilmartin, 2001).

Collaboration involves the active participation of a PCP and a behavioral care provider in the treatment of a patient. Usually the behavioral care provider is a specialist who is not part of the PCPs' health-care system (e.g., private practitioner, group practice, separate psychiatric clinic), or if he or she is a part of the same system, it is still as a specialist in the department of psychiatry. There are instances in which collaboration masquerades as integration inasmuch as the psychiatric (psychological) specialist is on colocation, giving the aura of integration.

An integrated program not only has the behavioral care provider on colocation, but the psychologist is not involved in specialty care. Rather, the psychologist is a member of the primary care team and is no longer affiliated with specialty care, defined as a department of psychiatry or psychology doing psychotherapy. Integration is a seamless primary care system employing a wide range of disease and population-based programs, and may on occasion refer perhaps as many as 10% of the patients to specialty psychiatric care as needed.

Program Matters

The somatizer cannot be addressed in a traditional system offering the usual fare of psychotherapy. The two studies previously cited make this crystal clear. The Hawaii project, with its targeted outreach and treatment, not only reduced somatization, but through the attendant medical cost savings, the government recouped within 18 months the expenditure that created a new delivery system (Cummings et al., 1991, 1993). In the Fort Bragg study, where it was thought unlimited access would do better than targeted programs, the expected reduction in somatization did not occur, the government recovered nothing, and Congress experienced a devastating tenfold overrun (Bickman, 1996).

The method for the identification and treatment of the somatizer as described in this chapter falls considerably short of being an integrated program. But it is important that it is the only single-thrust targeted program that will yield substantial results where other single-targeted protocols (e.g., depression pathways) fall far short of making an impact in an otherwise traditional delivery system. Even more important, it is applicable in a carve-out relationship, which is the main form of behavioral care delivery today, and where no significant form of integration is possible. In implementing the program, however, it is important to avoid the cumbersome middle step of the physician who receives the computer printout and makes the actual referral. The results of this procedure are disappointing, even when physicians sincerely believe they are cooperating fully. The computer elicitation, followed by a direct and immediate outreach, will reap several times more somaticizers in treatment than the physician-intermediary model. Furthermore, this direct outreach program is the most adaptable to an existing carve-out system.

References

American Psychiatric Association. (1994). *Diagnostic and statistical manual of mental disorders* (4th ed.) (DSM-IV). Washington, DC: American Psychiatric Press.

Bandura, A. (1991). Self-efficacy mechanism in psychological activation and health-promoting behavior. In J. Madden (Ed.), *Neurobiology of learning, emotion and affect* (pp. 90–111). New York: Raven Press.

Bickman, L. (1996). A continuum of care: More is not always better. *American Psychologist, 51,* 689–701.

Cummings, N. A. (1977). Prolonged (ideal) versus short-term (realistic) psychotherapy. *Professional Psychology, 8,* 491–501.

Cummings, N. A. (1985). Assessing the computer's impact: Professional concerns. *Computers in Human Behavior, 1,* 293–300.

Cummings, N. A. (1997). Behavioral health in primary care: Dollars and sense. In N. A. Cummings, J. L. Cummings, & J. N. Johnson (Eds.), *Behavioral health in primary care: A guide for clinical integration* (pp. 3–35). Madison, CT: Psychosocial Press/International Universities Press.

Cummings, N. A., & Bragman, J. I. (1988). Triaging the "somaticizer" out of the medical system into a psychological system. In E. M. Stern & V. F. Stern (Eds.), *The somatizing patient* (pp. 109–112). New York: Haworth.

Cummings, N. A., & Cummings, J. L. (1997). The behavioral health practitioner of the future: The efficacy of psychoeducational programs in integrated primary care. In N. A. Cummings, J. L. Cummings, & J. N. Johnson (Eds.), *Behavioral health in primary care: A guide for clinical integration* (pp. 325–346). Madison, CT: Psychosocial Press/International Universities Press.

Cummings, N. A., Dorken, H., Pallak, M. S., & Henke, C. J. (1991). *The impact of psychological intervention on health care costs and utilization. The Hawaii Medicaid Project.* (HCFA Contract Report #11-C-983344/9).

Cummings, N. A., Dorken, H., Pallak, M. S., & Henke, C. J. (1993). *The impact of psychological intervention on health care costs and utilization: The Hawaii Medicaid Project.* In N. A. Cummings & M. S. Pallak (Eds.), *Medicaid, managed behavioral health and implications for public policy, Vol. 2: Healthcare and utilization cost series* (pp. 3–23). South San Francisco, CA: Foundation for Behavioral Health.

Cummings, N. A., & Follette, W. T. (1968). Psychiatric services and medical utilization in a prepaid health plan setting: Part 2. *Medical Care, 6,* 31–41.

Cummings, N. A., & Follette, W. T. (1976). Brief psychotherapy and medical utilization: An eight-year follow-up. In H. Dorken (Ed.), *The professional psychologist today* (pp. 126–142). San Francisco: Jossey-Bass.

Cummings, N. A., Kahn, B. I., & Sparkman, B. (1962). *Psychotherapy and medical utilization: A pilot study.* Oakland, CA: Annual Reports of Kaiser Permanente Research Projects.

Cummings, N., & Sayama, M. (1995). *Focused psychotherapy: A casebook of brief, intermittent psychotherapy throughout the life cycle.* New York: Brunner/Mazel.

Cummings, N. A., & VandenBos, G. R. (1981). The twenty year Kaiser Permanente experience with psychotherapy and medical utilization: Implications for national health policy and national health insurance. *Health Policy Quarterly, 1,* 159–175.

Follette, W. T., & Cummings, N. A. (1967). Psychiatric services and medical utilization in a prepaid health plan setting. *Medical Care, 5,* 25–35.

Friedman, G. D., Ury, H. D., Klatsky, A. L., & Siegelaub, A. B. (1974). A psychological questionnaire predictive of myocardial infarction: Results from the Kaiser Permanente epidemiologic study of myocardial infarction. *Psychosomatic Medicine, 36,* 72–91.

Gilmartin, R. (2001, April 24). *CEO's report to the annual meeting of the Merck stockholders.* Whitehouse, NJ.

Jones, K. R., & Vischi, T. R. (1979). The impact of alcohol, drug abuse, and mental health treatment on medical utilization: A review of the literature. *Medical Care, 17*(suppl.), 43–131.

Jones, K. R., & Vischi, T. R. (1980). *The Bethesda Consensus Conference on Medical Offset. Alcohol, drug abuse, and mental health administration report.* Rockville, MD: Alcohol, Drug Abuse and Mental Health Administration.

Seligman, M. E. P. (1975). *Helplessness: On depression, development and death.* San Francisco: Freeman.

Seligman, M. E. P. (1994). *What you can change and what you can't.* New York: Knopf.

Shaffer, I. A. (2001). Managed care: Cost and effectiveness. In N. A. Cummings, W. O'Donohue, S. C. Hayes, & V. Follette, *Integrated behavioral healthcare: Positioning mental health practice with medical/surgical practice* (pp. 187–206). San Diego, CA: Academic Press.

Strosahl, K. (1997). Building primary care behavioral health systems that work: A compass and a horizon. In N. A. Cummings, J. L. Cummings, & J. N. Johnson (Eds.), *Behavioral health in primary care: A guide for clinical integration* (pp. 37–58). Madison, CT: Psychosocial Press/International Universities Press.

Strosahl, K., Baker, N. J., Braddick, M., Stuart, M. E., & Handley, M. R. (1997). Integration of behavioral health and primary care services: The Group Health Cooperative Model. In N. A. Cummings, J. L. Cummings, & J. N. Johnson (Eds.), *Behavioral health in primary care: A guide for clinical integration* (pp. 61–86). Madison, CT: Psychosocial Press/International Universities Press.

Chapter 9
Treating Attention Deficit Hyperactivity Disorder and Oppositional Defiant Disorder in the Primary Care Setting

WILLIAM E. PELHAM, JR., DAVID MEICHENBAUM, AND GREGORY A. FABIANO

Children with attention deficit/hyperactivity disorder (ADHD) and oppositional defiant disorder (ODD) are typically treated within the primary care setting, though there is often a discord between the current evidence-based treatment recommendations for these disorders and current practice. Effective interventions will include a standard assessment using validated rating scales, psychosocial treatment components including school-based behavioral and academic interventions, parenting programs, and child-focused programs that improve peer relationships and academic achievement. After psychosocial programs are established, a stimulant medication trial may be initiated and adjunctive medication used, if necessary. Treatment approaches will need to be chronic and comprehensive to be effective for most children with ADHD/ODD.

Externalizing behavior disorders, also known as disruptive behavior disorders (DBDs), are the most commonly occurring childhood mental health problem faced by mental health professionals, educators, and primary care physicians (Lahey, Miller, Gordon, & Riley, 1999; Rushton, Bruckman, & Kelleher, 2002). Of these disorders, ADHD, affecting 3–7% of the school-age population (American Academy of Pediatrics, 2000; American Psychiatric Association, 1994), attracts the most attention in popular media. ADHD is characterized by difficulties in core symptoms of inattention, hyperactivity, and impulsivity. The other DBDs—ODD and conduct disorder (CD)—are also common childhood problems seen in primary care settings with rates of diagnosis as high as ADHD (American Psychiatric Association, 1994; Lahey et al., 1999). ODD is characterized by oppositional and defiant behavior directed at adults. Children with CD exhibit serious antisocial behavior, including aggression, stealing, lying, and property destruction. It is useful to think of ODD and CD as a continuum, with CD being the more extreme variant of antisocial behavior and emerging in childhood later than ODD.

These disorders are highly co-morbid. In preschool children it is difficult to discriminate among them (e.g., Campbell, Szumowski, Ewing, Gluck, & Breaux, 1982). In school-age epidemiological samples, up to 50% of children with ADHD have co-morbid ODD and 15% have co-morbid CD, with widely varying rates across studies (see Lahey et al., 1999, for a review). In clinical populations, co-morbidity between ADHD and ODD/CD is even higher, with 75% of clinical study ADHD samples having co-morbid ODD and 25% CD (e.g., Pelham, Waschbusch et al., 2001; Pelham, Hoza et al., 2002). Comorbidity of ADHD in clinic samples selected for ODD and CD are similarly high (Schuhman, Foote, Eyberg, Boggs, & Algina, 1998). Further, there is a developmental sequence for the relationship among these disorders, with ADHD beginning earliest, a proportion of ADHD children later developing ODD, and a proportion of those individuals later developing CD (Chamberlain & Patterson, 1995). Further, a proportion of the CD individuals continue into adolescence to develop delinquent behaviors.

Children with externalizing disorders experience serious social, emotional, and academic problems across the multiple settings of school, home, and peer network. It has become well established that impairments in functioning associated with childhood DBDs persist throughout one's life. Risk for negative outcomes in adolescents and adults with ADHD, ODD, and CD include school and vocational failure, dysfunctional interpersonal relationships, criminal behavior, and alcohol or other substance abuse (Frick & Loney, 1999; Mannuzza & Klein, 1999). If a child has concurrent ADHD *and* ODD/CD, the risks of such negative outcomes increase dramatically relative to the single disorders (Lynam, 1996). The costs to the individual and society of the adult outcomes of children with DBDs are enormous. Thus, the development and implementation of effective childhood interventions is critical both to offset the costs to our society associated with *childhood* DBDs and to *prevent* the development and expense of ever more serious outcomes in adolescence and adulthood.

The etiology of ADHD and ODD/CD is still unknown; however, many view ADHD as being a biopsychosocial phenomenon. First, while no biological markers have been reliably identified in probands, there is a greater rate of concordance among biological relatives (Epstein et al., 2000) and in twin studies, and molecular genetic studies provide strong evidence for a genetic role in ADHD (Castellanos, 1999; Castellanos et al., 2002). At the same time, environmental and familial stressors have also been linked to elevated risk for and exacerbation of ADHD symptoms. A reciprocal relationship has been established between ADHD in children and parental psychopathology (e.g., depression), dysfunctional marital relations, parental use of alcohol or substances, and elevated parent-child conflict (Mash & Johnston, 1990; Pelham & Lang, 1999). Finally (as will be noted below), the symptoms and impairment associated with ADHD are effectively treated in the short term by *either* pharmacological *or* behavioral treatments. Thus, with respect to etiology and mechanism, as well as intervention, ADHD is a biopsychosocial phenomenon.

In contrast, it is generally thought that aggressive disorders, such as ODD and CD, are more affected by environmental circumstances such as poverty and poor parenting than by biological influences (McGee & Williams, 1999). Robin (1998) goes so far as to describe ODD as being "an interactional problem of a family system, not a disorder that resides inside a child/adolescent" (p. 62). At the same time, biological factors have been argued to play a role in ODD and CD, though the evidence is not as strong as for ADHD (Pliszka, 1999; Sanson & Prior, 1999). ODD and CD are treated primarily and effectively with psychosocial treatments. Although there has long been interest in discovering a medication to treat aggressive behavior in children, there is no FDA-approved medication for ODD or CD. At the same time, it is important to emphasize that for a given child, the co-morbidities among ADHD, ODD, and CD are so high that a child in primary care is more likely than not to have both ADHD and ODD or CD. In such cases, medication for ADHD is as effective as for ADHD children without co-morbid ODD/CD, and ODD/CD–related symptoms are diminished.

Thus, ADHD and ODD/CD are thought to have, at least in part, biological bases. At the same time, it is clear that psychosocial factors influence the development of the disorders and offer the most studied evidence-based treatment.

Evidence-Based Treatments for ADHD and ODD/CD

ADHD and ODD/CD have been treated in a variety of settings in a broad variety of ways, including traditional one-to-one therapy, cognitive therapy, play therapy, restrictive or supplemental diets, biofeedback, treatment for inner ear problems, allergy treatments, chiropractics, pet therapy, and sensory integration training, among others. *None* of these interventions, however, have been demonstrated to be effective in treating ADHD and ODD/CD. Only three treatments have been validated as being effective, *short-term* treatments for these disorders: (1) central nervous system (CNS) stimulant medication (for any child with ADHD), (2) behavior modification (i.e., parent training, classroom interventions, peer interventions; for any child with either ADHD or ODD/CD), and (3) the combination of stimulant medication and behavior modification (for any child with ADHD). The large research base demonstrating the effectiveness of these three treatments (e.g., Barkley, 1998; McMahon & Wells, 1998) has led to the endorsement of these interventions by the Society for Clinical Child and Adolescent Psychology (Brestan & Eyberg, 1998; Pelham, Wheeler, & Chronis, 1998), the National Institutes of Health (NIH; NIH, 2000), the American Medical Association (AMA; Goldman, Genel, Bezman, & Slanetz, 1998), the American Academy of Pediatrics (AAP; AAP, 2001), and the American Academy of Child and Adolescent Psychiatry (AACAP; AACAP, 1997a, 1997b). It is notable that the AAP and AMA guidelines apply only to ADHD; ODD and CD have not been addressed by these groups.

As noted above, there is high diagnostic overlap among ADHD, ODD, and CD. Fortunately, this overlap does not create difficulties in deciding which treatments to utilize. Effective psychosocial treatments for ADHD and ODD/CD are identical, and response to treatment does not vary as a function of co-morbidity (Conduct Problems Prevention Research Group, 1999; Kolko, Bukstein, & Barron, 1999; MTA Cooperative Group, 1999b; Pelham et al., 1993). Children with co-morbid disorders may be more severely impaired and require more intensive or comprehensive behavioral treatments, including stimulant medication; however, the co-morbidity does not mean that alternative treatments are needed beyond those indicated.

Despite a large evidence base documenting the effective treatments for ADHD and ODD/CD, and published guidelines endorsing the use of these treatments, a review of current practice in primary care settings reflects a discord between what is recommended and what is implemented. Before we turn our attention to evidence-based assessment and treatment in primary care settings, we first address the occurrence and typical treatment of ADHD and ODD/CD in these settings.

ADHD and ODD/CD in the Primary Care Setting

Although ADHD and ODD/CD are mental health disorders, it is often primary care physicians who are responsible for diagnosing, treating, or referring the child (Costello, 1986; Kwasman, Tinsley, & Lepper, 1995; Rushton et al., 2002). ADHD and related disruptive behavior disorders have become a prevalent and escalating problem within primary care settings. Data from the Child Behavior Study (CBS), a data set compiled from two large international practice-based primary care networks consisting of more than 2,000 clinicians from more than 600 practices, indicate that 19% of children have a psychosocial problem on presentation at the physician's office—half for ADHD, and 37% for "behavioral or conduct problems"—that is, ODD or CD (Rushton et al., 2002). Similarly, data from the National Ambulatory Medical Care Survey (NAMCS) indicates that about 60% of all children's visits to physicians, where a mental health problem was identified as the primary reason for the visit, were a result of the child's having ADHD (Hoagwood, Kelleher, Feil, & Comer, 2000). Moreover, there was a threefold increase between 1989 and 1996 in the number of office-based visits resulting in a diagnosis of ADHD. It is interesting to note that diagnostic differences in ADHD were not found across racial, economic, and familial status, highlighting the pervasiveness of the disorder across demographic groups (Wasserman et al., 1999). Despite the increase in diagnosis rates, there is evidence that ADHD, and childhood psychopathology in general, is underdiagnosed and untreated within the community and pediatric primary care (Angold, Costello, Farmer, Burns, Erkanli, 1999; Costello, 1989).

A common practice among primary care physicians is to make referrals to other professionals (e.g., child psychiatrists, psychologists, counselors, social workers) to develop and implement treatments. Moser and Kallail (1995) conducted a survey indicating that 43% of family physicians referred children they suspected to have ADHD to other professionals in the community. Making referrals to other professionals, however, may not always be a viable or preferred option. The CBS study discussed above found that only 17% of the identified ADHD cases were referred for other interventions, with half of these referrals to psychologists. Further, fewer than half of referred patients actually followed through with contact with a mental health specialist (Rushton et al., 2002). The CBS participants cited the availability of an expert as the primary stumbling block to referrals. In place of referring out for services, the primary care providers reported their two most common "treatment" strategies were watchful waiting (38%) and nonspecific counseling (33%)—both contraindicated for treating externalizing behavior disorders. For children with ADHD, nonspecific, in-practice counseling was often combined with medication. However, for behavior or conduct problems, no medication was being used. Clearly, this raises the question of the quality of treatment for ADHD and ODD/CD that is being delivered in these settings.

In summary, given the prevalence of ADHD and ODD/CD in primary care settings, along with the impairing nature, chronicity, and cost associated with the disruptive disorders, it is imperative to explore ways to implement effective evidence-based treatments for ADHD and ODD/CD within primary care settings.

Pharmacological Treatment Practices for ADHD

The most widely used and studied treatment for ADHD is stimulant medication (Spencer et al., 1996; Swanson, McBurnett, Christian, & Wigal, 1995). Stimulants are clearly effective in suppressing the symptoms of ADHD in the short term. With one recent exception (Biederman, Heiligenstein, et al., 2002) stimulant medications are the *only* pharmacological agents with strong empirical support for effectively treating ADHD. Other psychotropic medications are *not* validated for use in children with ADHD, even though many physicians prescribe these medications off label (Guevara, Lozano, Wickizer, Mell, & Gephart, 2002; Jensen et al., 1999). Given that the efficacy and side effect profiles of nonstimulant drugs are not sufficiently documented, either alone or in combination with stimulants, we will only discuss the use of stimulants.

Stimulants are relatively inexpensive, are easy to administer, and result in significant acute improvements in key domains of functioning for approximately 70% of children with ADHD (Swanson et al., 1995). Typical beneficial effects of stimulant medication include increased academic task completion, decreased disruption and aggression, and increased compliance with adult directions. As a result, administering stimulant medication to children with ADHD is the overwhelming treatment practice adopted by primary care physicians. Data from the NAMCS indicate an increase in stimulant prescriptions from 54.8% of primary care visits in 1989 to 75.4% in 1996 (Hoagwood et al., 2000), and stimulant prescription has continued to increase dramatically in the 8 years since (Zito et al., 2003).

Despite the widespread use of CNS stimulants and the fact that they are an evidence-based treatment for ADHD, one must be cognizant of their limitations as a sole intervention. First, the effects of medication are not uniform. That is, approximately one third of all children show either no response or an adverse response to medication (Pelham & Smith, 2000). Second, like all medications, stimulants have side effects—primarily insomnia and appetite suppression, but they may also result in other problems such as headaches, stomachaches, anxiety, and irritability, and they may exacerbate motor tics (Kurlan et al., 2002). At times these side effects may preclude the use of a high dose of medication or give physicians and families cause to discontinue medication altogether. For example, although evidence from early studies suggested that growth suppression was not a problem with stimulant therapy, more recent evidence suggests that stimulant therapy lasting 2–3 years may result in permanent effects on growth (Kramer, Loney, Ponto, Roberts, & Grossman, 2000; MTA Cooperative Group, 2004). Third, despite the short-term benefits of stimulants, there is no evidence that documents the long-term efficacy of stimulants in improving areas of impairment and outcome (Swanson et al., 1995). Fourth, even with the increase in longer acting medications, the effects of the medication are only evident 30–60 minutes after administration and the effects are only present while the medication is active. Given that the side effect of insomnia precludes use of stimulants for many children during the evening hours, parents are often left to deal with their child in the morning and evenings when they are unmedicated. Fifth, medication alone is often not sufficient in bringing the child back to a normal range of functioning (Swanson et al., 2001), likely because important functional domains, such as academic and social skills, parent-child interactions, teacher- and parent-child management skills, reduced self-esteem, and co-morbid problems such as oppositional and conduct behavior, specific learning disabilities, anxiety, and depression are not directly addressed with stimulant medication treatment. Furthermore, administering medication may reduce the motivation and likelihood that parents and teachers will initiate and employ psychosocial treatments that may address the remaining impaired areas of functioning.

Perhaps the most important limitation of stimulant medication as a treatment for ADHD is the lack of parent satisfaction with the treatment. There is a general dissatisfaction among parents and teachers for the use of pharmacological treatments with children, and a very strong preference for behavioral treatments (Liu, Robin, Brenner, & Eastman, 1991). For example, in the multimodal treatment study for ADHD (MTA), parents were 15 times more likely to drop out of or be dissatisfied with the medication group compared with the behavior therapy group, and only half as likely (34% versus 64%) to be strongly satisfied with the treatment (Pelham, Gnagy, Greiner, & MTA Cooperative Group, in press). Given the chronicity of the disorder, it is critical that treatments for ADHD and ODD/CD be sufficiently palatable to families that they will be continued in the long run; it does not appear that medication employed as the sole intervention is a palatable treatment for families.

Finally, negative attitudes of children and adolescents about medication may result in poor compliance with medication regimens (Sleator, Ullmann, & von Neumann, 1982). A number of studies have shown that ADHD children do not believe that their medication has a beneficial effect on their functioning (Pelham, Hoza, Kipp, Gnagy, & Trane, 1997; Pelham, Hoza et al. 2002; Pelham, Waschbusch et al., 2001). This fact may mean that ADHD children, with or without ODD/CD, will not continue taking medication when they reach the age at which they have a voice in their treatment. Recently we have examined the long-term medication practices of children as they have moved into adolescence and young adulthood and found that 49% of children who were ever medicated stopped using medication between the ages of 11 and 15 (Meichenbaum, Gnagy, Flammer, Molina, & Pelham, 2001). This is troubling given that preadolescence and early adolescence are critical transitional periods where developmental, social, and academic demands warrant the continued use of medication, and medication is acutely effective at these ages (Evans et al., 2001; Smith et al., 1998).

In recent years a new generation of stimulants that can be taken once a day and have effects into the evening has been developed to deal with some of these limitations (e.g., Biederman, Lopez, Boellner, & Chandler, 2002; Pelham, Gnagy et al., 2001). They have shown improved coverage during school (without midday doses) and into the evening hours, and they are effective in that role. At the same time, this advantage comes at a cost. The typical ADHD child who was previously medicated with 15 or 20 mg methylphenidate per day must take, for example, 36 mg of Concerta to have the same effect—an 80–140% increase in total daily dose. Since total daily dose predicts growth retardation (Kramer et al., 2000), this is a decided limitation of the new agents.

In summary, stimulant medication is a useful treatment for the majority of ADHD children. At the same time, its limitations mean that treatment plans for children with ADHD, with or without ODD/CD, must be more comprehensive in scope than medication alone (AAP, 2001). Since there is no effective medication for ODD or CD, it is clear that psychosocial treatments form the basis of treatment for them. Because these practice parameters include behavior modification treatment as an important component of treatment, practitioners of behavior modification are integral contributors to treatment in the primary care setting.

Diagnosing and Assessing ADHD and ODD/CD in Primary Care

The American Academy of Pediatrics (2000) notes that the initial evaluation for an ADHD patient will often take two to three visits. In practice, however, the majority of pediatricians spend 50 to 60 minutes on an initial ADHD consultation, whereas family practitioners spend on average between 23 and 29 minutes (Kwasman et al., 1995; Wolraich et al., 1990). Given the financial pressure in primary care, the typical pediatric office visit lasts 10 minutes. Thus, it is not surprising that the major problem identified by pediatricians in having children with ADHD in their practice is the amount of time required to work with them.

Since time is a major barrier in both primary care and mental health settings, it is critical that the assessment techniques being employed are both effective and efficient. At this point the assessment of ADHD and ODD in primary care settings lacks standardization (Wasserman et al., 1999). There is no medical, neurological, or psychological test that provides a valid diagnosis of ADHD or ODD/CD (AACAP, 1997a and 1997b; AAP, 2000). ADHD and ODD/CD are instead defined by a group of behavioral symptoms. Although these are observable characteristics (e.g., short attention span, defiance), it has been well established and well communicated that ADHD and ODD cannot be validly diagnosed by observing a child during an office visit. In addition, ADHD children and ODD children are not veridical reporters of their own functioning (Hoza, Pelham, Dobbs, & Owens, 2002), so interviewing them regarding their symptoms and impairment is not useful in diagnosis. Rather, diagnosis must evaluate the child's behavioral symptoms and associated impairment in the settings of interest—the home and school.

Over the past several decades, many researchers and clinicians have emphasized the importance of making an accurate diagnosis for ADHD and ODD using symptoms identified in the *Diagnostic Statistical Manual of Mental Disorders* (*DSM-IV*; American Psychiatric Association, 1994). Some primary care physicians may be using the *DSM-PC*, an AAP modification of the *DSM* (American Academy of Pediatrics, 1996). Criteria for diagnosis of a disorder are identical in the two manuals; the *DSM-PC* introduces a subdiagnostic level of problematic behavior that has face-validity but has not been the focus of research.

Although the *DSM* system has improved the reliability of diagnosis and is useful in screening for ADHD and ODD, its utility is limited because the presence of *DSM* symptoms alone does not provide any useful information about treatment (Scotti, Morris, McNeil, & Hawkins, 1996). In addition to symptom presence, impairment is required to diagnose both ADHD and ODD in the *DSM*. For ADHD, impairment is required in home, school, or peer functioning in at least two settings. It is these impairments in daily life functioning (e.g., a child is failing a class because he or she fails to hand in completed homework assignments a family cannot take a child out in public because of embarrassing temper tantrums) that are far more important in the assessment process than are *DSM* symptoms. This is true for several reasons. First, problems in daily functioning become the natural targets of treatment, and improvement in these areas is the natural index of treatment outcome (Pelham & Fabiano, 2000). Second, the importance of impairment is underscored by the finding that the use of clinical services is precipitated by impairment, not symptoms (Angold et al., 1999). Children are not referred to physicians or psychologists because of *DSM* symptoms; instead they are referred because of their problems in daily activities at school, with peers, or at home. Finally, the most important predictor of negative long-term outcomes for the disruptive behavior disorders is the initial severity of *behavioral impairment, not diagnosis* (Pierce, Ewing, & Campbell, 1999). The three domains most predictive of long-term outcomes for children with disruptive behavior (including ADHD and ODD) are academic achievement and school functioning, parent-child relationships and parenting skills, and peer relationships (Chamberlain & Patterson, 1995; Coie & Dodge, 1998; Hinshaw, 1992). Indeed, functioning in these domains *mediates* outcome, and improvement in the impaired domains must be achieved to avoid continued problems throughout development.

Table 9.1 presents a set of guidelines to facilitate and foster the timely, thorough, and valid assessment of ADHD and ODD/CD children in primary care. The guide incorporates a behavioral approach to assessment (Mash & Terdal, 1997), the AAP guidelines for ADHD (AAP, 2000), and a well-validated approach for assessing ODD/CD (McMahon & Wells, 1998). The table also includes, when possible, the sites on the World Wide Web from which useful assessment instruments can be downloaded at no cost.

Given the discussion above, it should be clear that the focus of assessment should be on problems in daily life functioning and adaptive skill deficits rather than on *DSM* symptoms. The assessment typically takes more than one session. In part, establishing this phase of treatment as requiring more than the initial contact serves as a control for the physician's tendency to diagnose and prescribe medication in the first visit. Assessment should involve a clinical interview with the parent regarding the child's functioning across important domains (home, school, peer), with a detailed listing of the target behaviors, antecedents, and consequences, and a functional analysis of the relationships among these. A comprehensive interview will facilitate the conceptualization of the case and lay the groundwork for intervention. Because this interview will take more time than a primary care physician will be able to spend, a collaborating mental health professional or nurse in the doctor's office is the best person to perform this task. A comparable interview should be conducted with the child's teacher either face to face, via phone, or via questionnaire.

In addition to identifying targets for treatment and developing the intervention—both activities that focus on impairment and adaptive skills—the assessment will involve making a diagnosis. Diagnosis must typically be given for third-party payments and administrative purposes, including eligibility for special educational services under the "other health impaired" category of the Individuals with Disabilities Education Act (IDEA). Although the gold standard in psychiatry is to make diagnoses using a formal structured interview (e.g., DBD Structured Interview, wings.buffalo.edu/adhd; K-SADS, www.wpic.pitt.edu/ksads/default.htm), such instruments are lengthy, staff-time intensive, and therefore very costly compared to rating scales that yield the same information. Thus, ratings from parents and teachers on standardized rating scales of *DSM* symptoms are more appropriate for a primary care context (AAP, 2000).

There are two types of rating scales. The first type comprises broad-band, empirically derived parent and teacher rating scales (e.g., Child Behavior Checklist, Achenbach, 1991; Revised Conners Rating Scales, Conners, Sitarenios, Parker, & Epstein, 1998). These screen for many problem areas and do not use *DSM* symptoms but instead empirically derived items and factors. More appropriate for the present purposes are the rating scales specific to the disorders of ADHD and ODD/CD

TABLE 9.1 Assessment Guidelines for Practitioners Working in Primary Care for a Child With ADHD, ODD, or CD

1. Send parents and teachers *standardized rating scales* assessing DSM symptoms of ADHD, ODD, and CD to be completed and reviewed prior to intake evaluation. Use the following for diagnosis:
   • Disruptive Behavior Disorders Rating Scale (Pelham, Gnagy, Greenslade, & Milich, 1992, http://wings.buffalo.edu/adhd)
   • Vanderbilt Rating Scale (AAP & NICHQ Toolkit, 2002, http://www.nichq.org/resources/toolkit/)
   • ADHD Rating Scale (DuPaul et al., 1998)
   • SNAP rating scale (Atkins, Pelham, & Licht, 1985, http://adhd.net)

2. Send parents and teachers standardized scales to assess *impairment* in daily life functioning and adaptive skills (e.g., Children's Impairment Rating Scale; Fabiano et al., 1999, http://wings.buffalo.edu/adhd).

3. Conduct a clinical interview (e.g., CCF Intake Outline, http://wings.buffalo.edu/adhd) with parents to determine areas of impairment, age of onset, duration of problem, the settings where symptoms occur; inquire about antecedents and consequences to behavior and functions of behavior; identify targeted behaviors for treatment; gather other information relevant to case conceptualization.

4. Ask parents and teachers to describe parenting and disciplining strategies and their effectiveness (e.g., Teacher Behavioral Practices Interview, http://wings.buffalo.edu/adhd).

5. If suspect co-morbid diagnoses other than disruptive behavior disorders, screen with broad-band rating scales (e.g., Child Behavior Checklist; Achenbach, 1991).

6. Determine presence of other familial conditions that may exacerbate impairment and/or compromise treatment (e.g., parental psychopathology, parental substance use, marital distress, socioeconomic status, single parent).

7. Complete a physical to ensure that, if needed, there are no medical reasons to preclude the use of stimulant medication.

8. Do not use broad-band rating scales, neuropsychological tests, attentional tasks, tests for soft or hard neurological signs, biological laboratory tests, psychoeducational tests, or observations of office behavior in making a diagnosis.

9. Refer for other specific evaluation if necessary (e.g., psychoeducational testing for school placement/determination of eligibility for school services, speech and language evaluation).

(e.g., ADHD Rating Scale, DuPaul, Power, McGoey, Ikeda, & Anastopoulos, 1998; Disruptive Behavior Disorder Rating Scale, Pelham Gnagy, Greenslade, & Milich, 1992; SNAP Rating Scale, Atkins, Pelham, & Licht, 1985; and the Vanderbilt Rating Scale, AAP & NICHQ, 2002). These scales typically include the *DSM* items for the disruptive behavior disorders (ADHD, ODD, and CD), are used with both parents and teachers, have excellent (and comparable) psychometric properties, and are available without charge on the World Wide Web (see Table 9.1). For the purpose of diagnosis of ADHD and ODD, only these scales are necessary. For the purposes of screening for other potential problematic behaviors and domains, broad-band scales are complementary to the *DSM*-based scales.

Thus far, rating scales have not been routinely used as a primary component of assessment in primary practices (Goldman et al., 1998; Moser & Kallail, 1995), and are only recommended, not required, in the AAP diagnostic guidelines (AAP, 2000). This is surprising because rating scales offer a quick and effective method to assess *DSM* symptomatology. We recommend that parents and teachers complete all rating scales prior to their first meeting with the clinician in order to maximize the efficiency of the diagnostic process. This can be accomplished through prior mailing or Web-based procedures. The newly released ADHD toolkit for primary care physicians (AAP & NICHQ, 2002; www.nichq.org/resources/toolkit/) includes a *DSM*-symptom–based rating scale that assesses both ADHD and ODD items, so it is likely that use of these rating scales in primary care will increase.

Although DSM-based standardized rating scales provide information about the presence of symptoms, impairment must also be assessed to make a diagnosis and particularly to identify domains for target behaviors. The ADHD toolkit includes a brief scale for assessing impairment. Another one that has better psychometric properties, is well validated, sensitive to treatment effects, and widely used is the Children's Impairment Rating Scale (CIRS; Fabiano et al., 1999; see Table 9.1). The CIRS uses a simple format to assess functioning in several key domains—relationships with adults and peers/siblings, academic functioning, disruptive behavior, self-esteem, and overall functioning—and allows parents and teachers to include a narrative about the child in each of these domains. Scales assessing impairment are essential components of a comprehensive assessment that will directly inform treatment planning and evaluation.

The mental health clinician should also routinely assess for other potentially coexisting conditions within the child (e.g., learning disabilities, language difficulties) and family (e.g., parental depression or substance use, marital distress), along with barriers (e.g., single-parent household, poverty) that may be contributing to the child's dysfunction and compromising treatment. When identified, referrals should be made to practitioners who implement evidence-based treatments for the appropriate disorder, and modifications to the treatment plan should be made.

The AAP guidelines for diagnosing ADHD (AAP, 2000) are useful for identifying aspects of assessment that are *not* useful for children with disruptive behavior disorders. Specifically, neuropsychological assessments, continuous performance tests, tests of executive functioning, psychoeducational evaluation, personality or projective testing, neurological examinations, EEG, and other biological laboratory assessments (e.g., tests of thyroid function) have not been shown to be useful in diagnosing or assessing children with disruptive behavior problems.

In summary, a comprehensive assessment is the first step in developing an effective individualized treatment plan. By replacing inefficient and ineffective evaluation methods (e.g., interviewing children, neuropsychological evaluations, structured interviews with parents) with efficient and effective assessment methods, clinicians can reduce the amount of time necessary for assessment and diagnosis, allowing for a greater portion of contact time to be spent on treatment.

Behavior Modification

Behavioral treatments have a long history of documented effectiveness as an intervention for disruptive behavior disorders and their associated problems (e.g., poor peer relationships, conflictual parent-child relations, aggression, and low academic achievement), and they clearly result in clinically meaningful behavior change (Brestan & Eyberg, 1998; DuPaul & Eckert, 1997; Pelham, Wheeler et al., 1998). The goals of behavioral treatments for these disorders are to minimize the child's impairment and maximize his or her adaptive functioning and to teach skills to parents and teachers (Pelham & Fabiano, 2000).

Table 9.2 provides management guidelines for working with ADHD and ODD/CD in primary care settings. Table 9.3 provides the specifics of behavioral interventions for parents, schools, and children with these difficulties.

The first issue to consider is where behavior modification falls in the comprehensive treatment plan for the child. For a child with only ODD or CD, this is not an issue. Since medication is used with far more ADHD children than is behavior modification, behavior modification is typically not the first-line treatment for children with ADHD, whether co-morbid or not. Indeed, based primarily

TABLE 9.2 Management Guidelines for Practitioners Working in Primary Care for a Child With ADHD, ODD, or CD

Treatment Planning

1. Integrate parent and teacher reports from assessment.

2. Establish *target behaviors* (e.g., completes academic work on time, is not aggressive during recess), focusing on areas of impairment (i.e., classroom behavior, academic functioning, parent-child and parent-teacher interactions, peer relationships), from which treatment outcome will be judged.

3. Introduce and describe to parents school-based support for ADHD, such as Section 504 behavioral plans or classification as a special education student and the development of an IEP (ADHD Toolkit, AAP, 2002; also available at http://www.ed.gov.index.jsp, http://www.nichq.org/resources/toolkit/).

4. Offer or refer child for services to manage problems that cannot be dealt with in a mental health or primary care setting (e.g., intervention for a reading disability).

5. Offer or refer family for services to manage coexisting problems (e.g., ADHD, marital conflict, anger-management problems, paternal substance use, maternal depression).

6. Inform parents of community based support groups (e.g., CHADD; http://www. chadd.org).

Treatment

1. Treatment always begins with behavior modification (see Table 9.3) first to determine the effectiveness of this approach alone and avoid medication if possible ("first, do no harm"), and behavioral interventions will double as indicators of treatment response (e.g., percentage of daily report card targets met—see Table 9.4 for a sample).

2. If behavior modification alone is insufficient to normalize functioning, determine if a double-blind, randomized, placebo-controlled, school-based medication assessment should be *combined* with the ongoing behavior modification treatment. If yes, see Table 9.5.

Maintenance, Monitoring, and Follow-Up

1. Reemphasize to parents and teachers that ADHD is a chronic disorder in need of chronic treatment and that treatment effects will not be maintained without continued treatment. Therefore, establish a comprehensive, chronic treatment plan and evaluate and modify it on an ongoing basis.

2. Adherence to treatment components is regularly checked, and treatment goals are continually added, deleted, or modified based on an ongoing functional analysis of behavior.

3. Schedule periodic follow-up visits to evaluate changes in functioning and emerging problems.

4. Assist in troubleshooting failed treatment strategies.

5. Offer continued support and make self available for questioning for as long as necessary.

6. Reestablish contact for major developmental transitions (e.g., school entrance at kindergarten, adolescence).

on one recent NIMH collaborative trial, the Multimodal Treatment Study for ADHD (MTA Cooperative Group, 1999a), medication is being increasingly widely recommended as the first-line intervention for children with ADHD (AACAP, 2002; MTA Cooperative Group, 1999a). In addition and also based on this study, current medication guidelines recommend that dosages for ADHD children be "pushed" to the maximally effective dose (AAP, 2001; AACAP, 2002). However, there is good reason to avoid medication and to use low dosages of stimulants. The most salient reason is "first, do no harm." If we know that we can avoid medication and offer an effective treatment alternative, then primary care practitioners should be doing that routinely—or at least informing parents of that alternative and letting parents choose. The data on parent preference suggests

TABLE 9.3 Behavior Modification Treatment Guidelines for Practitioners Working in Primary Care for the Management of a Child With ADHD, ODD, or CD

General Guidelines

1. Treatment always begins first with behavior modification to determine the effectiveness of this approach alone and avoid medication if possible, and behavioral interventions will double as measures of treatment response (e.g., percentage of daily report card targets met).

2. Behavioral approach; therapist teaches parents and teachers contingency management techniques and other behavior management skills to use with the child and the parent, and teacher implements the treatment. An expansive list of helpful readings and resources is available in the "ADHD psychosocial treatment information sheet for parents and teachers" located at http://wings.buffalo.edu/adhd.

3. Focus on specific target behaviors that reflect impairment in key domains of functioning (e.g., peer relationships, parenting skills and family relationships, academic and school functioning); maladaptive behaviors are targeted for reduction and adaptive skills are targeted for development.

Parent Training

1. Educate parents about the diagnosis, causes, prognosis, and treatments of ADHD (e.g., "What Parents and Teachers Should Know About ADHD/ODD/CD," available at http://wings.buffalo.edu/adhd; http://www.chadd.org).

2. Use standard, manualized *group* parent training procedures for 8–16 sessions (e.g., Barkley, 1998; Cunningham, Bremner, & Secord-Gilbert, 1998; Forehand & Long, 1996; Robin, 1998; Sanders et al., 2000; http://www.pfsc.uq.edu.au/02_ppp/ppp.html; Webster-Stratton, 1992, http://www.incredi bleyears.com).

3. Focus on teaching parents appropriate positive behavior management strategies (e.g., praise, reward programs) and effective nonphysical discipline strategies (e.g., time out).

4. Help parents establish, monitor, and modify as needed a home-based daily report card and reward system; see "Creating a Daily Report Card for the Home" at http://wings.buffalo.edu/adhd.

5. Supplement with individual parent sessions as necessary to individualize programs to the child's problems, provide further instruction/coaching, or modify existing behavioral programs.

School Intervention

1. Educate teachers about the diagnosis, causes, prognosis, and treatments of ADHD (e.g., ADHD Toolkit, AAP, 2002, http://www.nichq.org/resources/toolkit/; "What Parents and Teachers Should Know About ADHD" available at http://wings.buffalo.edu/adhd; http://www.chadd.org).

2. Use standard, manualized teacher training procedures (e.g., Pelham, 2002; Pfiffner, 1996; Walker, Colvin, & Ramsey 1995; Walker & Eaton-Walker, 1991; http://www.pbis.org/).

3. Focus on teaching teachers appropriate positive behavior management strategies (e.g., praise, reward programs) and effective nonphysical discipline strategies (e.g., time out).

4. Work with the teacher to construct a *daily* school-home report card that lists the child's target behaviors (see Table 9.4; see "How To Establish a Daily Report Card" at http://wings.buffalo.edu/adhd). The daily report card is sent home to the child's parents each day, and the parents provide a positive consequence at home for each goal met.

Child Intervention

1. Behavioral and developmental approach—involving direct work in natural or analogue settings—*not* clinic settings.

2. Focus on specific target behaviors that reflect impairment in multiple domains of functioning (e.g., peer relationships, interactions with adults, sibling relationships, academic skills, classroom and family functioning, self-esteem); maladaptive behaviors are targeted for reduction and adaptive skills (e.g., social skills, sports skills, academic skills) are targeted for development.

TABLE 9.3 (continued)

> 3. Typically paraprofessional implemented.
>
> 4. Intensive treatment settings such as summer treatment programs (9 hours daily for 8 weeks), and/or school year, after-school, and Saturday (3 hours) sessions. See http://www.summertreatmentpro gram.com for description.
>
> 5. Behavioral (contingent rewards and negative consequences) and cognitive behavioral (e.g., social skills training, problem-solving training) integrated in the context of recreational activities.

strongly that parents will almost uniformly choose a nonpharmacological intervention as the first treatment, and that they prefer low doses to higher doses (Pelham et al., 2000). In the MTA study, 75% of the children assigned to the behavioral treatment group (which got the kind of comprehensive behavioral treatment shown in Table 9.3) were maintained without medication for the 14 months of the study and made dramatic improvements in functioning—improvements as great as children who were medicated by their family physicians (Conners et al., 2001; MTA Cooperative Group, 1999a; Pelham, 1999). Further, 62% of this group were being maintained by their parents without medication and with continued positive functioning 1 year later—a full 18 months after their behavioral treatment had ended (MTA Cooperative Group, 2004). For those who were being medicated, the dose on which they were maintained was 43% lower than children in the medication-only group of the study, 95% of whom were continually medicated. In contrast, children in the combined treatment group—for whom medication was begun at the same time as behavior therapy—were also medicated at a higher rate (95%) and at a dose approximately 37% higher.

Thus, when behavioral intervention is begun before medication in ADHD children, a substantial portion of the population will be able to avoid medication, and those medicated will receive lower doses. Given parental preferences for this approach, lowered risk of side effects, and the "do no harm" credo, this would appear to be the sequence of choice.

Behavior modification needs to be multifaceted, involving parents, school, and child. Behavioral interventions are conceptualized as the application of social learning theory to modify children's behavior by training *parents and teachers* to manipulate environmental antecedents (e.g., commands), consequences (e.g., rewards, punishments), and contingencies (the relationship among target behaviors, antecedents, and consequences) (Jacob & Pelham, 1999). Operant procedures, that is, using negative (e.g., punishment) and positive (e.g., rewards) contingencies to reduce problem behaviors and increase adaptive behaviors, are behavioral strategies commonly used to modify children's behavior. Training parents and teachers to implement contingency management programs is a clinical behavioral intervention that can be initiated and coordinated by primary care practitioners or mental health practitioners working in collaboration with them. These treatments range on a continuum of intensity from relatively lower (e.g., praise, daily report card) to higher intensity (e.g., special education placement, time out). Comprehensive treatment must also include a child-focused component—difficult to do in a primary care setting, but necessary for the important domains of academic functioning and the development of appropriate peer relationships.

Behavioral Parent Training

The purpose of parent training is to help parents manage their child's behavior problems and improve the family relationship. Table 9.3 lists the components of comprehensive parent training. The procedures are flexible enough to enable parent training to be conducted by a trained paraprofessional, nurse, or mental health or school professional. Sessions are typically held in groups in the evening or on weekends. Parents can meet in primary care offices, mental health clinics, or schools. There are a number of existing comprehensive and effective parent-training programs (e.g., Anastopoulos, 1998; Barkley, 1998; Cunningham, Bremner, & Secord-Gilbert, 1998; Forehand & Long, 2002; Robin, 1998; Webster-Stratton, 1992; see Table 9.3 for downloadable materials for parents, including how to construct a home-based daily report card).

Related to behavioral parent training, parental psychopathology may co-occur with the presentation of child ADHD/ODD in primary care. Parental psychological problems, such as depression, substance abuse, or ADHD are overrepresented in families of children with ADHD and ADHD plus ODD/CD (Chronis et al., 2003); therefore, these problems often require concurrent treatment focused on these difficulties, particularly since these problems may interfere with effective parenting (i.e., Pelham, Lang et al., 1998; Sonuga-Barke, Daley, & Thompson, 2002). Physicians should refer parents to mental health professionals for psychosocial (e.g., a course designed to help parents cope with depression; Chronis, Gamble, Roberts, & Pelham, 2000) or psychiatric (e.g., stimulant medication for treating adult ADHD; Evans, Vallano, & Pelham, 1994) treatment when parental psychopathology is identified.

Classroom-Based Behavior Modification

Mental health professionals should adopt a consultative role in interacting with teachers about possible classroom interventions. Behavior modification strategies in schools have been shown to be effective across all three DBDs (Walker, Colvin, & Ramsey, 1995). Teachers can be trained to implement a continuum of behavioral strategies within their classrooms (see Table 9.3), ranging from school-wide discipline programs, through class-wide programs, to individualized programs for a targeted child. An effective tool that should be part of all school interventions is a daily report card (DRC; see Table 9.4). DRCs target individualized problems for children by setting behavioral goals, establishing procedures for the teacher to monitor and give feedback to the children for those problems, and providing feedback on a daily basis to parents on the children's school performance and behavior, for which parents provide a positive consequence at home (Kelley & McCain, 1995; O'Leary, Pelham, Rosenbaum, & Price, 1976). DRCs cost little, take little teacher time, and can be highly motivating for the child. In combination with appropriate praise, commands, and classroom/assignment structure, a DRC constitutes a level of school-based intervention that can easily be coordinated by primary care staff or collaborators. A downloadable packet that a teacher can use to establish a DRC with a parent is available (see Table 9.3). When this level of intervention is insufficient, more intensive work with the classroom teacher (e.g., teaching him or her to implement a point system) or placement in special education, if appropriate, typically yields improvement. Materials are available that can facilitate the instruction of these behavioral techniques to teachers (DuPaul & Stoner, 1994; Pfiffner, 1996; Walker et al., 1995; Walker & Eaton-Walker, 1991; see Table 9.3 for downloadable materials for teachers, including instructions for creating a school-based DRC).

Child Intervention

A typical child with ADHD, ODD, or CD will have areas of impairment and deficient competencies in important areas (e.g., social skills, academic achievement) that cannot be addressed in an office setting. The primary care provider must refer these patients to receive effective services that might include academic tutoring or evidence-based peer interventions such as intensive summer treatment programs (Pelham & Hoza, 1996; Pelham et al., in press). Such interventions are essential components of comprehensive care to target domains that are important predictors of long-term outcome, such as academic achievement or social relationships. Table 9.3 lists the components of such child-focused interventions.

TABLE 9.4 Sample School Daily Report Card

Child's Name: _____ Date: _____

	Special	Language Arts	Math	Reading	SS/Science
Follows class rules (no more than 3 rule violations per period).	Y N	Y N	Y N	Y N	Y N
Completes assignments within the designated time.	Y N	Y N	Y N	Y N	Y N
Completes assignments at 80% accuracy.	Y N	Y N	Y N	Y N	Y N
Complies with teacher requests (no more than 3 instances of noncompliance per period).	Y N	Y N	Y N	Y N	Y N
Gets along with peers (no more than 3 instances of teasing per period).	Y N	Y N	Y N	Y N	Y N
OTHER					
Follows lunch rules (2 or fewer violations).	Y N				
Follows recess rules (2 or fewer violations).	Y N				
Total Number of Yeses.					

_____.

Teacher's Initials: _____

Comments:

Combined Behavioral and Pharmacological Treatment

For ADHD, when behavioral interventions have produced improvement but it is insufficient, parents have a choice between more intensive behavioral treatment (e.g., special education placement) and adjunctive medication. If a parent opts for medication, then a structured assessment can be conducted by the primary care professional working with school staff or a mental health professional. This assessment will yield a good *starting* dose for a long-term medication regimen.

Over the past 20 years, a methodology for assessing individual medication response has been developed within the context of a summer treatment program (Pelham, 1993; Pelham, Bender, Caddell, Booth, & Moorer, 1985; Pelham, Aronoff et al., 1999, Pelham, Gnagy et al., 1999) and extended to other analogue settings (Pelham, Gnagy et al., 2001) and natural settings (MTA Cooperative Group, 1999a; Pelham, Hoza et al., 2002). This methodology is a short-term, double-blind, placebo-controlled medication assessment in which different medication doses (e.g., 0.3 mg/kg methylphenidate and 0.6 mg/kg methylphenidate) or different stimulants and placebo are randomized on a *daily* basis for a period of 4–5 weeks. We outline the procedures for an outpatient medication assessment in Table 9.5. A medication assessment in which medication is randomized by *day* and not by *week* reduces the confounding error variance associated with fluctuations in daily routines or other potential confounds (e.g., having a substitute teacher for a week) that may occur during an assessment. Error variance is distributed across all medication conditions rather than confounded with one condition, allowing for readily interpretable results.

It is well known that response to stimulant medication varies within and across children, depending on a number of factors, including the child's referring problems, the setting, the presence of a concurrent behavioral treatment, the time of day, and the nature of task demands

TABLE 9.5 Medication Treatment Guidelines for Practitioners Working in Primary Care for the Management of a Child With ADHD, ODD, or CD

1. Implement only following the development and implementation of an ongoing behavioral treatment program.

2. Conduct an initial controlled assessment of various doses/types of stimulant medication to select starting dose (instructions and instruments listed below are available, see "Conducting an Outpatient Medication Assessment and Ratings" at http://wings.buffalo.edu/adhd).

3. Decide on the type of medication to be included in the assessment. Start with either methylphenidate or amphetamine-based compounds. If the initial medication is ineffective, try the other stimulant molecule before other drug classes.

4. Determine need for t.i.d. dosing or long-acting medication (e.g., Concerta, Adderall XR) based on child's impairment across settings. Only use t.i.d. dosing or long-acting medication if there is documented impairment in the after-school setting. Likewise, prescribe medication for weekends only if there is documented impairment during weekend activities.

5. Explain the medication assessment procedures to child, parents, and teachers.

6. Emphasize to parents and teachers (if dosing at school) the necessity of standardized medication administration times.

7. Use the school-based DRC or other feasible indicators of impairment to objectively quantify the effectiveness of medication.

8. Have nurse or mental health professional randomly assign medication conditions to days of the week, and place capsules in daily pill minder to be used at home or school.

9. Have parents and teachers complete the Pittsburgh Side Effects Rating Scale daily.

10. Be alert for low base-rate but serious side effects, such as tachycardia and motor tics.

11. Inspect data of percentage of daily report card targets met on each condition, along with side effects ratings.

12. Determine if clinically significant gains were obtained on medication days versus placebo days.

13. Select the effective minimal dose to complement the behavioral intervention, leaving room for improvement (e.g., the child's daily report card remains challenging) and minimize side effects.

14. Monitor monthly using DRC or CIRS as indicator of functioning to adjust dosages both up and down and justify continued need; monitor height and weight.

15. Withdraw medication annually to document continued need; continue until no deterioration occurs when withdrawn.

(Pelham & Smith, 2000). Therefore, deciding whether stimulant medication confers beneficial effects for a given child is a complex undertaking, and in order to answer the question of whether medication benefits an individual child, a physician must systematically investigate the effectiveness of medication in the setting and on the measures in which the child is impaired. Because medication is typically being prescribed for school problems, obtaining objective, detailed information on medication response from the child's teacher is paramount. Research has shown the DRC (already established for the child as part of his or her behavioral treatment) to be a sensitive measure of medication effects, surpassing the utility of more expensive, time-consuming measures of medication effectiveness such as daily teacher ratings or classroom observations (Pelham, Hoza et al., 2002; Pelham, Gnagy et al., 2001).

For children who need medication, combined treatment has an incremental benefit over and above a pharmacological or behavioral treatment alone (e.g., Conners et al., 2001; Pelham & Waschbusch, 1999). For example, there are several reasons to speculate that long-term maintenance of treatment effects might be improved with a combined intervention. Children with ADHD exhibit impaired academic and social adjustment. To the extent that these skills are necessary for successful long-term outcome, treatment that includes a behavioral intervention focusing in part on building competencies in academic and social domains should improve the long-term outcome, which would not be achieved with medication alone. Similarly, to facilitate maintenance of behavioral treatment effects, the intervention should be such that it can be continued by the child's parents or teachers for a protracted time. Because the addition of a low dose of stimulant medication enables relatively greater effects to be achieved with less restrictive and more natural behavioral programs (e.g., Abramowitz, Eckstrand, O'Leary, & Dulcan, 1992), a combined treatment may be more likely to be maintained by parents and teachers over time.

In addition to the above-mentioned benefits of combined treatment, parents and teachers overwhelmingly prefer combined behavioral and stimulant medication interventions to medication alone. Adding behavioral treatment to medication dramatically reduces dissatisfaction with medication and doubles strong satisfaction among parents (Pelham et al., 2000). Furthermore, combined treatments typically result in the greatest normalization of functioning (e.g., Conners et al., 2001; Klein & Abikoff, 1997; Swanson et al., 2001). Finally, and importantly, combined treatments enable dramatic reductions in the dose of medication that is needed to yield optimal benefit—with reductions from 25–75% across a number of studies (Carlson, Pelham, Milich, & Dixon, 1992; Pelham et al., 1980; Vitiello et al., 2001). Given possible long-term side effects associated with high doses of medication, reduction in dose is a desired outcome.

Prevention Protocols

Along with facilitating treatment (e.g., tertiary prevention), primary care providers are in the perfect position to implement primary and secondary preventative measures, given their regular contact with families and established clinical relationships. Researchers have highlighted the importance of early intervention for children with ADHD and ODD/CD, to prevent and redirect negative developmental trajectories that might result in more serious psychosocial problems (Conduct Problems Prevention Group, 1999; Tremblay, LeMarquand, & Vitaro, 1999). Primary prevention for DBDs can begin as soon as parents sit down in the physician's waiting room. Handouts, informational packets, books, and videos on evidence-based assessment and treatment can be made available to waiting parents. In addition, primary care physicians should be aware of upcoming developmental transitions for all children (e.g., increased tantruming for 2 to 3 year olds; beginning of middle school) and use these opportunities to prepare and educate all parents for potential difficulties (e.g., instruct parents of toddlers on the proper use of time out, encourage parents to teach their beginner–middle school children how to use a daily assignment notebook). Secondary prevention may be handled in a similar fashion.

Costs of Effective Services for ADHD and ODD/CD

Clearly, families of children with ADHD use medical services at a greater rate and therefore have greater medical expenditures than families of children without ADHD. For example, in a birth cohort in Rochester, MN, the median costs of health-care expenditures for children with ADHD were twice that of children without ADHD (the median cost for children with ADHD was $4,306 versus $1,944 for those without ADHD), and contributing to this increased cost, children with ADHD were more likely to have visited emergency rooms and receive other inpatient and outpatient health services (Leibson, Katusic, Barbaressi, Ransom, & O'Brien, 2001). Kelleher (1998) has presented information from a Medicaid database showing that children with ADHD in western Pennsylvania were being provided mental health treatments with an average annual cost of $1,800 in

1994, comparable to the annual medical treatment of another chronic childhood problem—asthma. Given the low rate of utilization of evidence-based behavioral treatments in practice, it is unlikely that this $1,800 went to *appropriate* treatments other than medication, which is considerably less expensive than this cost.

Exacerbating the cost of these expenditures is the observation from surveys of doctors that only half the children in primary care settings are reported to receive care compatible with practice guidelines for ADHD treatment (Hoagwood et al., 2000), and those children are *only* receiving medication, not behavioral treatment, arguably an ineffective treatment for ADHD in the long run. For children with only ODD or CD, for whom medication is not indicated, the likelihood is that they receive no treatment in primary care.

The behavioral intervention (or the combined intervention) that we have outlined above—all of the components, including the intensive 8-week summer treatment program—is provided in our clinic (in 2003 dollars) for $4,000 per child per year. Without the summer program, the cost is on the order of $1,500 per year. If effective, evidence-based treatments can reduce health-care utilization, it is arguable that at least the low intensity behavioral intervention (parent training, school consultation, and medication) could be provided in a very cost-effective manner. For a managed care organization that spends $100/child/month for a primary care visit and the cost of Concerta, one of the newly approved medications for ADHD and the current market leader, the cost savings from having 75% of the ADHD children *unmedicated* could be put toward effective psychosocial treatments.

Consider the cost of special education and out-of-district placements for a school district. Special education typically costs two to three times what regular education costs. In addition, out-of-district placements (for the most disturbed children—almost always diagnosed as ADHD/ODD/CD) cost $20,000 to $30,000 per child per year. A school district that can prevent a high proportion of ADHD/ODD/CD children from being placed in special education or out-of-district placements by providing appropriate behavioral interventions (accompanied by low dosages of medication when necessary) in the regular classroom setting will achieve dramatic cost savings. The *combined* savings to the *community* across agencies and systems (e.g., health, education, justice) from effective treatments for ADHD and ODD/CD should be considerable even if more intensive evidence-based interventions are implemented for a substantial portion of the indicated children.

Finally, to the extent that providing effective interventions can prevent the development of later problems (e.g., substance abuse, criminal behavior) that are more costly to society and to the individual and family, effective intervention in primary care has the potential to not only be cost effective but also save an enormous amount of resources for society. Such an evaluation has not yet been conducted but is needed to justify the services that are called for in current guidelines.

Monitoring Functioning and Quality Assurance

In Tables 9.2 and 9.3, we have addressed guidelines for ongoing monitoring of treatment response. An example of a simple and idiographic mechanism for monitoring and tracking functioning in school was described above, the DRC. The utility of the DRC for monitoring and evaluating the effectiveness of medication in the short term has already been described. Indeed, the DRC is also useful for monitoring functioning in the individual child's most important domains of dysfunction (that is, the targeted behaviors on the DRC) over the long term. In contrast to the typical lack of communication among the school, parents, and the primary care provider, the DRC prompts daily contact and parental monitoring of the child's school functioning. This daily information affords parents the opportunity to reward and praise a child for daily successes and meeting successive approximations toward behavioral goals, and permits rapid response if behavior deteriorates (e.g., three days in a row of no behavior targets met might prompt a teacher meeting to determine an aspect of the intervention that needs to be modified). The DRC percentage of goals met is also easily graphed, and it provides parents with an ongoing assessment of their child's functioning that can be shared at appointments with the mental health professional and primary care physician, who can evaluate the child's progress at a glance. In addition, simple rating scales such as the CIRS described above can be repeated monthly, with parents bringing them in at appointment times. Although other monitoring systems focus on the *DSM* symptoms of ADHD and ODD/CD (e.g., AAP & NICHQ toolkit), the simple idiographic approach of the DRC is more efficient and arguably more valid (Pelham, Gnagy et al., 2001; Pelham, Hoza et al., 2002).

An Illustration of Comprehensive Treatment in Primary Care

To provide an idea of how these clinical procedures might be applied in a primary care setting, consider a prototypical child with ADHD/ODD. Prior to an office visit, the child's mother and teacher complete a standardized rating scale of ADHD/ODD symptoms and an impairment rating scale. These ratings are mailed in ahead of the visit, and an office staff member may then review the forms and begin to formulate appropriate treatment recommendations. After a diagnosis and evidence of significant psychosocial impairment are established, a nurse or mental health professional works with the child's teacher to develop and implement a DRC like the one in Table 9.4. The parents would be referred to a standard, manualized parenting program run by a nurse (perhaps in the office waiting room in the evening or on the weekend) or a local mental health professional. Finally, to address the child's peer relationships, the child would be enrolled in a program to address academic achievement and peer relationships, such as a Saturday or summer treatment program (Pelham & Hoza, 1996). At the next visit, the child's parent would be asked to bring back the school-based DRC and complete the same rating scales completed before the initial visit. If the child is still exhibiting psychosocial impairment based on parent and teacher reports on these measures, the behavioral interventions should be modified. Should the problems persist past the initial modification of the programs, the programs could be modified again (i.e., to make them more intensive), or a school-based medication assessment might be initiated (coordinated by a member of the office staff or local mental health professional). After a stable course of treatment is established, physicians then schedule frequent checkups to prevent relapse and maintain treatment gains.

Summary

ADHD and the other disruptive behavior disorders are prevalent; chronic mental health problems account for more than half of the referrals for pediatric psychosocial services, special education services, and mental health services. All contemporaneous guidelines and informed opinions indicate that ADHD, ODD, and CD need to be conceptualized as chronic mental health disorders. This necessitates a reformulation of treatment approaches for these disorders to be in line with other serious, chronic disorders such as autism and schizophrenia. Treatment for these three disruptive behavior disorders must be intensive, must be planned for the long term, and must include frequent check-ups and programs for relapse prevention, as we have outlined in Tables 9.2 and 9.3. It has been argued, for years, that the treatment of ADHD should take place in primary care settings (Christopherson, 1982). Sanders and Ralph (2001) noted that

> practitioners are frequently asked by parents for advice regarding their children's behavior. Family doctors are the most likely source of professional assistance sought by parents of children with behavioral and emotional problems and are seen by parents as credible sources of advice (p. 26).

Given that doctors are de facto care providers for these children, they must be educated and well versed in the ways to effectively evaluate and treat children with behavior disorders (Costello, 1986; Higgins, 1994). Because it would afford early identification and early intervention, an emphasis on identifying and treating these disorders in the primary care setting would be consistent with many of the recommendations made in the recent *Report of the Surgeon General's Conference on Children's Mental Health* (U.S. Public Health Service, 2000).

Conducting a functional assessment of the child's impairment in daily life functioning should be the thrust of assessment. Standardized rating scales, obtained from parents and teachers, along with interviewing the parents, will identify areas of impairment and targeted behaviors for treatment. Behavioral treatments should be employed as the first-line treatment for ADHD, ODD, and CD, with combined pharmacological and behavioral treatments for ADHD and co-morbid children being an effective and recommended adjunctive alternative if a child fails to show acceptable levels of improvement with only behavioral strategies in place. It is important that, as in any chronic disease model, treatment be ongoing. Primary care practitioners should stress the maintenance of treatment and provide systematic follow-up, involving the evaluation of treatment responsiveness and assessment of emerging problems that may lead to treatment nonadherence or failure. In following the evidence-based guidelines to assessment and treatment of ADHD and ODD/CD, primary care practitioners can effectively reduce current impairment, build competencies in important functional domains, and prevent the progression of behavior problems into more serious disorders and dysfunction.

References

Abramowitz, A. J., Eckstrand, D., O'Leary, S. G., & Dulcan, M. K. (1992). ADHD children's responses to stimulant medication and two intensities of a behavioral intervention. *Behavior Modification, 16,* 193–203.

Achenbach, T. M. (1991). *Manual for the Child Behavior Checklist/4–18 and 1991 profile.* Burlington, VT: University of Vermont, Department of Psychiatry.

American Academy of Child and Adolescent Psychiatry (AACAP). (1997a). Practice parameters for the assessment and treatment of children, adolescents, and adults with attention-deficit/hyperactivity disorder. *Journal of the American Academy of Child and Adolescent Psychiatry, 36*(suppl. 10), 85–121.

American Academy of Child and Adolescent Psychiatry (AACAP). (1997b). Practice parameters for the assessment and treatment of children and adolescents with conduct disorder. *Journal of the American Academy of Child and Adolescent Psychiatry, 36*(suppl. 10), 122–139.

American Academy of Child and Adolescent Psychiatry (AACAP). (2002). Clinical practice guideline: Treatment of the school-aged child with attention-deficit/hyperactivity disorder. *Journal of the American Academy of Child and Adolescent Psychiatry, 41,* 537.

American Academy of Pediatrics (AAP). (1996). The classification of child and adolescent mental diagnoses in primary care. In M. L. Wolraich, M. E. Felice, & D. Drotar (Eds.), *Diagnostic and statistical manual for primary care (DSM-PC) child and adolescent version.* Elk Grove Village, IL: Author.

American Academy of Pediatrics (AAP). (2000). Clinical practice guideline: Diagnosis and evaluation of the child with attention-deficit/hyperactivity disorder. *Pediatrics, 105,* 1158–1170.

American Academy of Pediatrics (AAP). (2001). Clinical practice guideline: Treatment of the school-aged child with attention-deficit/hyperactivity disorder. *Pediatrics, 108,* 1033–1044.

American Academy of Pediatrics and National Initiative for Children's Healthcare Quality (AAP & NICHQ). (2002). *Caring for children with ADHD: A resource toolkit for clinicians.*

American Psychiatric Association (APA). (1994). *Diagnostic and statistical manual of mental disorders* (4th ed.). Washington, DC: Author.

Anastopoulos, A. D. (1998). A training program for parents of children with attention-deficit/hyperactivity disorder. In J. M. Briesmeister & C. E. Schaefer (Eds.), *Handbook of parent training: Parents as co-therapists for children's behavior problems* (2nd ed., pp. 27–60). New York: Wiley.

Angold, A., Costello, E. J., Farmer, E. M., Burns, B. J., & Erkanli, A. (1999). Impaired but undiagnosed. *Journal of the American Academy of Child and Adolescent Psychiatry, 38,* 129–137.

Atkins, M. S., Pelham, W. E., & Licht, M. (1985). A comparison of objective classroom measures and teacher ratings of attention deficit disorder. *Journal of Abnormal Child Psychology, 13,* 155–167.

Barkley, R. A. (1998). *Attention-deficit hyperactivity disorder: A handbook for diagnosis and treatment.* New York: Guilford.

Biederman, J., Heiligenstein, J. H., Faries, D. E., Galil, N., Dittman, R., Emslie, G. J. et al. (2002). Efficacy of Atomoxetine versus placebo in school-aged girls with attention-deficit/hyperactivity disorder [Online]. *Pediatrics, 110.* Retrieved April 18, 2003, from http://www.pediatrics.org/cgi/content/full/110/6/e75.

Biederman, J., Lopez, F. A., Boellner, S. W., & Chandler, M. C. (2002). A randomized, double-blind, placebo-controlled, parallel-group study of SLI381 (Adderall XR) in children with attention-deficit/hyperactivity disorder. *Pediatrics, 110*, 258–266.

Brestan, E. V., & Eyberg, S. M. (1998). Effective psychosocial treatments of conduct-disordered children and adolescents: 29 years, 82 studies, and 5,272 kids. *Journal of Clinical Child Psychology, 27*, 180–189.

Campbell, S. B., Szumowski, E. K., Ewing, L. J., Gluck, D. S., & Breaux, A. M. (1982). A multidimensional assessment of parent-identified behavior problem toddlers. *Journal of Abnormal Child Psychology, 10*, 569–591.

Carlson, C. L., Pelham, W. E., Milich, R., & Dixon, J. (1992). Single and combined effects of methylphenidate and behavior therapy on the classroom performance of children with attention deficit hyperactivity disorder. *Journal of Abnormal Child Psychology, 20*, 213–232.

Castellanos, F. X. (1999). The psychobiology of attention-deficit/hyperactivity disorder. In H. C. Quay & A. E. Hogan (Eds.), *Handbook of disruptive behavior disorders* (pp. 179–198). New York: Kluwer Academic/Plenum Publishers.

Castellanos, F. X., Lee, P. P., Sharp, W., Jeffries, N. O., Greenstein, D. K., Clasen, L. S. et al. (2002). Developmental trajectories of brain volume abnormalities in children and adolescents with attention-deficit/hyperactivity disorder. *JAMA, 288*, 1740–1748.

Chamberlain, P., & Patterson, G. R. (1995). Discipline and child compliance in parenting. In M. Bornstein (Ed.), *Handbook of parenting: Vol. 4. Applied and practical parenting* (pp. 205–225). Mahwah, NJ: Erlbaum.

Christopherson, E. R. (1982). Incorporating behavioral pediatrics into primary care. *Pediatric Clinics of North America, 29*, 261–295.

Chronis, A. M., Gamble, S. A., Roberts, J. E., & Pelham, W. E. (2000, November). *Cognitive-behavioral therapy for mothers of children with ADHD: Changing distorted maternal cognitions about child behavior.* Paper presented at the annual meeting of the Association for the Advancement of Behavior Therapy, New Orleans.

Chronis, A. M., Lahey, B. B., Pelham, W. E., Kipp, H. L., Baumann, B. L., & Lee, S. S. (2003). Psychopathology and substance use in young children with attention-deficit/hyperactivity disorder. *Journal of the American Academy of Child and Adolescent Psychiatry, 42*, 1424–1432.

Coie, J. D., & Dodge, K. A. (1998). Aggression and antisocial behavior. In W. Damon (Series Ed.) & N. Eisenberg (Vol. Ed.), *Handbook of child psychology: Vol. 3. Social, emotional, and personality development* (5th ed., pp. 779–862). New York: Wiley.

Conduct Problems Prevention Research Group. (1999). Initial impact of the FAST Track prevention trial for conduct problems: II. Classroom effects. *Journal of Consulting and Clinical Psychology, 67*, 648–657.

Conners, C. K., Epstein, J. N., March, J. S., Angold, A., Wells, K. C., Klaric, J. et al. (2001). Multimodal treatment of ADHD in the MTA: An alternative outcome analysis. *Journal of the American Academy of Child and Adolescent Psychiatry, 40*, 159–167.

Conners, C. K., Sitarenios, G., Parker, J. D. A., & Epstein, J. N. (1998). Revision and restandardization of the Conners Teacher Rating Scale (CTRS-R): Factor structure, reliability, and criterion validity. *Journal of Abnormal Child Psychology, 26*, 279–291.

Costello, E. J. (1986). Primary care pediatrics and child psychopathology: A review of diagnostic, treatment, and referral practices. *Pediatrics, 78*(6), 1044–1051.

Costello, E. J. (1989). Child psychiatric disorders and their correlates: A primary care pediatric sample. *Journal of the American Academy of Child and Adolescent Psychiatry, 28*(6), 851–855.

Cunningham, C. E., Bremner, R., & Secord-Gilbert, M. (1998). *The community parent education (COPE) program: A school based family systems oriented course for parents of children with disruptive behavior disorders.* Unpublished manual.

DuPaul, G. J., & Eckert, T. L. (1997). The effects of school-based interventions for attention deficit hyperactivity disorder: A meta-analysis. *School Psychology Review, 26*, 5–27.

DuPaul, G. J., Power, T. J., McGoey, K. E., Ikeda, M. J., & Anastopoulos, A. D. (1998). Reliability and validity of parent and teacher ratings of attention-deficit/hyperactivity disorder symptoms. *Journal of Psychoeducational Assessment, 16*, 55–68.

DuPaul, G. J., & Stoner, G. (1994). *ADHD in the schools: Assessment and intervention strategies.* New York: Guilford.

Epstein, J. N., Conners, C. K., Erhardt, D., Arnold, L. E., Hechtman, L., Hinshaw, S. P. et al. (2000). Familial aggregation of ADHD characteristics. *Journal of Abnormal Child Psychiatry, 28*, 505–594.

Evans, S. W., Pelham, W. E., Smith, B. H., Bukstein, O., Gnagy, E. M., Greiner, A. R. et al. (2001). Dose-response effects of methylphenidate on ecologically-valid measures of academic performance and classroom behavior in ADHD adolescents. *Experimental and Clinical Psychopharmacology, 9*(2), 163–175.

Evans, S. W., Vallano, G., & Pelham, W. (1994). Treatment of parenting behavior with a psychostimulant: A case study of an adult with attention-deficit hyperactivity disorder. *Journal of Child and Adolescent Psychopharmacology, 4*, 63–69.

Fabiano, G. A., Pelham, W. E., Gnagy, E. M., Kipp, H., Lahey, B. B., Burrows-MacLean, L. et al. (1999, November). *The reliability and validity of the children's impairment rating scale: A practical measure of impairment in children with ADHD.* Poster presented at the annual meeting of the Association for the Advancement of Behavior Therapy, Toronto, ON.

Forehand, R., & Long, N. (2002). *Parenting the strong-willed child.* New York: McGraw-Hill.

Frick, P. J., & Loney, B. R. (1999). Outcomes of children and adolescents with oppositional defiant disorder and conduct disorder. In H. C. Quay & A. E. Hogan (Eds.), *Handbook of disruptive behavior disorders* (pp. 507–524). New York: Kluwer Academic/Plenum Publishers.

Goldman, L. S., Genel, M., Bezman, R. J., & Slanetz, P. J. (1998). Diagnosis and treatment of attention-deficit/hyperactivity disorder in children and adolescents. *Journal of the American Medical Association, 279*, 1100–1107.

Guevara, J., Lozano, P., Wickizer, T., Mell, M., & Gephart, H. (2002). Psychotropic medication use in a population of children who have attention-deficit/hyperactivity disorder. *Pediatrics, 109*, 733–739.

Higgins, E. S. (1994). A review of unrecognized mental illness in primary care. *Archives of Family Medicine, 3*, 908–917.

Hinshaw, S. P. (1992). Externalizing behavior problems and academic underachievement in childhood and adolescence: Causal relationships and underlying mechanisms. *Psychological Bulletin, 111*, 127–155.

Hoagwood, K., Kelleher, K. J., Feil, M., & Comer, D. (2000). Treatment services for children with ADHD: A national perspective. *American Academy of Child and Adolescent Psychiatry, 39*, 198–206.

Hoza, B., Pelham, W. E., Dobbs, J., & Owens, J. (2002). Do boys with attention-deficit/hyperactivity disorder have positive illusory self-concepts? *Journal of Abnormal Psychology, 111*, 268–278.

Jacob, R., & Pelham, W. E. (1999). Behavior therapy. In H. Kaplan & B. Sadock (Eds.), *Comprehensive textbook of psychiatry* (7th ed., pp. 2080–2127). New York: Williams & Wilkins.

Jensen, P. S., Bhatara, V. S., Vitiello, B., Hoagwood, K., Feil, M., & Burke, L. B. (1999). Psychoactive medication prescribing practices for U.S. children: Gaps between research and clinical practice. *Journal of the American Academy of Child and Adolescent Psychiatry, 38*, 557–565.

Kelleher, K. J. (1998). Use of services and costs for youth with attention deficit hyperactivity disorder and related conditions. *NIH Consensus Development Conference: Diagnosis and Treatment of Attention Deficit Disorder Programs and Abstracts*, 229–235.

Kelley, M. L., & McCain, A. P. (1995). Promoting academic performance in inattentive children. *Behavior Modification, 19*, 357–375.

Klein R. G., & Abikoff, H. (1997). Behavior therapy and methylphenidate in the treatment of children with ADHD. *Journal of Attention Disorders, 2*, 89–114.

Kolko, D. J., Bukstein, O. G., & Barron, J. (1999). Methylphenidate and behavior modification in children with ADHD and comorbid ODD and CD: Main and incremental effects across settings. *Journal of the American Academy of Child and Adolescent Psychiatry, 38*, 578–586.

Kramer, J. R., Loney, J., Ponto, L. B., Roberts, M. A., & Grossman, S. (2000). Predictors of adult height and weight in boys treated with methylphenidate for childhood behavior problems. *Journal of the American Academy of Child and Adolescent Psychiatry, 39*, 517–524.

Kurlan, R., Goetz, C. G., McDermott, M. P., Plumb, S., Singer, H., Dure, L. et al. (2002). Treatment of ADHD in children with tics: A randomized controlled trial. *Neurology, 58*, 527–536.

Kwasman, A. Tinsley, B. J., & Lepper, H. S. (1995). Pediatricians' knowledge and attitudes concerning diagnosis and treatment of attention deficit and hyperactivity disorders: A national survey approach. *Archives of Pediatric and Adolescent Medicine, 149*, 1211–1216.

Lahey, B. B., Miller, T. L., Gordon, R. A., & Riley, A. W. (1999). Developmental epidemiology of the disruptive behavior disorders. In H. C. Quay & A. E. Hogan (Eds.), *Handbook of disruptive behavior disorders* (pp. 23–48). New York: Kluwer Academic/Plenum Publishers.

Leibson, C. L., Katusic, S. K., Barbaressi, W. J., Ransom, J., & O'Brien, P.C. (2001). Use and costs of medical care for children and adolescents with and without attention-deficit/hyperactivity disorder. *Journal of the American Medical Association, 285*, 60–66.

Liu, C., Robin, A. L., Brenner, S., & Eastman, J. (1991). Social acceptability of methylphenidate and behavior modification for treating attention deficit hyperactivity disorder. *Pediatrics, 88*, 560–565.

Lynam, D. R. (1996). Early identification of chronic offenders: Who is the fledgling psychopath? *Psychological Bulletin, 120*, 209–234.

Mannuzza, S., & Klein, R. G. (1999). Adolescent and adult outcomes in attention-deficit/hyperactivity disorder. In H. C. Quay & A. E. Hogan (Eds.), *Handbook of disruptive behavior disorders* (pp. 279–294). New York: Kluwer Academic/Plenum Publishers.

Mash, E. J., & Johnston, C. (1990). Determinants of parenting stress: Illustrations from families of hyperactive children and families of physically abused children. *Journal of Clinical Child Psychology, 19*, 313–328.

Mash, E. J., & Terdal, L. G. (1997). Assessment of child and family disturbance: A behavioral-systems approach. In E. J. Mash and L. G. Terdal (Eds.), *Assessment of childhood disorders* (3rd ed., pp. 3–68). New York: Guilford.

McGee, R., & Williams, S. (1999). Environmental risk factors in oppositional-defiant disorder and conduct disorder. In H. C. Quay & A. E. Hogan (Eds.), *Handbook of disruptive behavior disorders* (pp. 419–440). New York: Kluwer Academic/Plenum Publishers.

McMahon, R. J., & Wells, K. C. (1998). Conduct problems. In E. J. Mash & R. A. Barkley (Eds.), *Treatment of childhood disorders* (2nd ed., pp. 111–207). New York: Guilford.

Meichenbaum, D. L., Gnagy, E. M., Flammer, L., Molina, B., & Pelham, W. E. (2001, April). *Why stop success? Exploration of long-term use of medication in a clinical ADHD sample from childhood through young adulthood.* Paper presented at the meeting of the eighth Florida Conference on Child Health Psychology, Gainesville, FL.

Moser, S. E., & Kallail, K. J. (1995). Attention-deficit hyperactivity disorder: Management by family physicians. *Archives of Family Medicine, 4*, 241–244.

MTA Cooperative Group. (1999a). 14-month randomized clinical trial of treatment strategies for attention deficit hyperactivity disorder. *Archives of General Psychiatry, 56*, 1073–1086.

MTA Cooperative Group. (1999b). Moderators and mediators of treatment response for children with attention-deficit/hyperactivity disorder: The multimodal treatment study of children with attention-deficit/hyperactivity disorder. *Archives of General Psychiatry, 56*, 1088–1096.

MTA Cooperative Group. (2004). National Institute of Mental Health multimodal treatment study of ADHD follow-up: Changes in effectiveness and growth after the end of treatment. *Pediatrics, 113*, 762–769.

National Institutes of Health (NIH). (2000). National Institutes of Health Consensus Development Conference statement: Diagnosis and treatment of attention-deficit/hyperactivity disorder (ADHD). *Journal of the American Academy of Child and Adolescent Psychiatry, 39*(2), 182–193.

O'Leary, K. D., Pelham, W. E., Rosenbaum, A., & Price, G. H. (1976). Behavioral treatment of hyperkinetic children. *Clinical Pediatrics, 15,* 510–515.

Pelham, W. E. (1993). Pharmacotherapy for children with attention-deficit hyperactivity disorder. *School Psychology Review, 22,* 199–227.

Pelham, W. E. (1999). The NIMH multimodal treatment study for attention-deficit hyperactivity disorder: Just say yes to drugs alone? *Canadian Journal of Psychiatry, 44,* 981–990.

Pelham, W. E., & Waschbusch, D. A. (2003). Assessment and treatment of attention deficit hyperactivity disorder (ADHD) in schools. In R. Brown (Ed.) *Handbook of pediatric psychology in school settings* (pp. 405–430). New York: Guilford.

Pelham, W. E., Aronoff, H. R., Midlam, J. K., Shapiro, C. J., Gnagy, E. M., Chronis, A.M. et al. (1999). A comparison of Ritalin and Adderall: Efficacy and time-course in children with attention-deficit/hyperactivity disorder [Online]. *Pediatrics, 103(4).* Retrieved May 1, 2002, from http://pediatrics.aappublications.org/cgi/content/full/103/4/e43

Pelham, W. E., Bender, M. E., Caddell, J., Booth, S. & Moorer, S. (1985). The dose-response effects of methylphenidate on classroom academic and social behavior in children with attention deficit disorder. *Archives of General Psychiatry, 42,* 948–952.

Pelham, W. E., Carlson, C., Sams, S. E., Vallano, G., Dixon, M. J., & Hoza, B. (1993). Separate and combined effects of methylphenidate and behavior modification on the classroom behavior and academic performance of ADHD boys: Group effects and individual differences. *Journal of Consulting and Clinical Psychology, 61,* 506–515.

Pelham, W. E., & Fabiano, G. A. (2000). Behavior modification. *Child and Adolescent Psychiatric Clinics of North America, 9,* 671–688.

Pelham, W. E., Fabiano, G. A., Gnagy, E. M., Greiner, A. R., & Hoza, B. (in press). The role of summer treatment programs in the context of comprehensive treatment for ADHD. In E. Hibbs & P. Jensen (Eds.) *Psychological treatments for child and adolescent disorders: Empirically based strategies for clinical practice.* New York: APA Press.

Pelham, W. E., Gnagy, E. M., Burrows-Maclean, L., Williams, A., Fabiano, G. A., Morrissey, S. M. et al. (2001). Once-a-day Concerta methylphenidate versus t.i.d. methylphenidate in laboratory and natural settings [Online]. *Pediatrics, 107.* Retrieved May 8, 2002, from http://www.pediatrics.org/cgi/content/full/107/6/e105.

Pelham, W. E., Gnagy, E. M., Chronis, A. M., Burrows-MacLean, L., Fabiano, G. A., Onyango, A. N. et al. (1999). A comparison of morning, midday, and late-afternoon methylphenidate with morning and late-afternoon Adderall in children with attention-deficit/hyperactivity disorder. *Pediatrics, 104,* 1300–1311.

Pelham, W. E., Gnagy, E. M., Greenslade, K. E., & Milich, R. (1992). Teacher ratings of *DSM-III-R* symptoms for the disruptive behavior disorders. *Journal of the American Academy of Child and Adolescent Psychiatry, 31,* 210–218.

Pelham, W. E., Gnagy, E. M., Greiner, A. R., Hoza, B., Hinshaw, S. P., Swanson, J. M. et al. (2000). Behavioral vs. behavioral and pharmacological treatment in ADHD children attending a summer treatment program. *Journal of Abnormal Child Psychology, 28,* 507–526.

Pelham, W. E., Gnagy, E. M., Greiner, A. R., & the MTA Cooperative Group. (in press). Parents and teacher evaluation of treatment in the MTA: Consumer satisfaction and perceived effectiveness. *Journal of Consulting and Clinical Psychology.*

Pelham, W. E., & Hoza, B. (1996). Intensive treatment: A summer treatment program for children with ADHD. In E. Hibbs & P. Jensen (Eds.), *Psychosocial treatments for child and adolescent disorders: Empirically based strategies for clinical practice* (pp. 311–340). New York: APA Press.

Pelham, W. E., Hoza, B., Kipp, H. L., Gnagy, E. M., & Trane, S. T. (1997). Effects of methylphenidate and expectancy on ADHD children's performance, self evaluations, persistence, and attributions on a cognitive task. *Experimental and Clinical Psychopharmacology, 5,* 3–13.

Pelham, W. E., Hoza, B., Pillow, D. R., Gnagy, E. M., Kipp, H. L., Greiner, A. R. et al. (2002). Effects of methylphenidate and expectancy on children with ADHD: Behavior, academic performance, and attributions in a summer treatment program and regular classroom settings. *Journal of Consulting and Clinical Psychology, 70,* 320–335.

Pelham, W. E., & Lang, A. R. (1999). Can your children drive you to drink? Stress and parenting in adults interacting with children with ADHD. *Alcohol Research and Health, 23,* 292–298.

Pelham, W. E., Lang, A. R., Atkeson, B., Murphy, D. A., Gnagy, E. M., Greiner, A. R. et al. (1998). Effects of deviant child behavior and parental alcohol consumption: Stress induced drinking in parents of ADHD children. *American Journal on Addictions, 7,* 103–114.

Pelham, W. E., & Murphy, H. A. (1986). Attention deficit and conduct disorder. In M. Hersen (Ed.), *Pharmacological and behavioral treatment: An integrative approach* (pp. 108–148). New York: Wiley.

Pelham, W. E., Schnedler, R., Bologna, N., & Contreras, A. (1980). Behavioral and stimulant treatment of hyperactive children: A therapy study with methylphenidate probes in a within-subject design. *Journal of Applied Behavior Analysis, 13,* 221–236.

Pelham, W. E., & Smith, B. H. (2000). Prediction and measurement of individual responses to Ritalin by children and adolescents with attention deficit hyperactivity disorder. In L. L. Greenhill and B. B. Osman (Eds.), *Ritalin: Theory and practice* (2nd ed., pp. 193–218). Larchmont, NY: Mary Ann Liebert.

Pelham, W. E., & Waschbusch, D. A. (1999). Behavioral intervention in attention-deficit/hyperactivity disorder. In H. C. Quay & A. E. Hogan (Eds.), *Handbook of disruptive behavior disorders* (pp. 255–278). New York: Kluwer Academic Publishers.

Pelham, W. E., Waschbusch, D. A., Hoza, B., Pillow, D. R., & Gnagy, E. M. (2001). Effects of methylphenidate and expectancy on ADHD boys' performance, self-evaluations, persistence, and attributions on a social task in boys with ADHD. *Experimental and Clinical Psychopharmacology, 9,* 425–437.

Pelham, W. E., Wheeler, T., & Chronis, A. (1998). Empirically supported psychosocial treatments for ADHD. *Journal of Clinical Child Psychology, 27,* 190–205.

Pfiffner, L. J. (1996). *All about ADHD: The complete practical guide for classroom teachers*. New York: Scholastic Professional Books.

Pierce, E. W., Ewing, L. J., & Campbell, S. B. (1999). Diagnostic status and symptomatic behavior of hard-to-manage preschool children in middle childhood and early adolescence. *Journal of Clinical Child Psychology, 28*, 44–57.

Pliszka, S. R. (1999). The psychobiology of oppositional defiant disorder and conduct disorder. In H. C. Quay & A. E. Hogan (Eds.), *Handbook of disruptive behavior disorders* (pp. 371–395). New York: Kluwer Academic/Plenum Publishers.

Robin, A. L. (1998). *ADHD in adolescents: Diagnosis and treatment*. New York: Guilford.

Rushton, J., Bruckman, D., & Kelleher, K. (2002). Primary care referral of children with psychosocial problems. *Archives of Pediatric Adolescent Medicine, 156*, 592–598.

Sanders, M. R., Markie-Dadds, C., Tully, L. A., & Bor, W. (2000). The triple p-positive parenting program: A comparison of enhanced, standard, and self-directed behavioral family intervention for parents of children with early onset conduct problems. *Journal of Consulting and Clinical Psychology, 68*, 624–640.

Sanders, M. R., & Ralph, A. (2001). *Practitioners manual for primary care: TEEN Triple P*. Milton, Queensland: Family International Publishing.

Sanson, A., & Prior, M. (1999). Temperament and behavioral precursors to oppositional defiant disorder and conduct disorder. In H. C. Quay & A. E. Hogan (Eds.), *Handbook of disruptive behavior disorders* (pp. 397–417). New York: Kluwer Academic/Plenum Publishers.

Schuhman, E. M., Foote, R. C., Eyberg, S. M., Boggs, S. R., & Algina, J. (1998). Efficacy of parent-child interaction therapy: Interim report of a randomized trial with short-term maintenance. *Journal of Clinical Child Psychology, 27*, 34–45.

Scotti, J. R., Morris, T. L., McNeil, C. B., & Hawkins, R. P. (1996). DSM-IV and disorders of childhood and adolescence: Can structural criteria be functional? *Journal of Consulting and Clinical psychology, 64*, 1177–1191.

Sleator, E., Ullmann, R., & von Neumann, A. (1982). How do hyperactive children feel about taking stimulants and will they tell the doctor? *Clinical Pediatrics, 21*, 474–479.

Smith, B. H, Pelham, W. E., Evans, S. W., Gnagy, E. M., Molina, B., Bukstein, O. et al. (1998). Dosage effects of methylphenidate on the social behavior of adolescents diagnosed with attention deficit hyperactivity disorder. *Experimental and Clinical Psychopharmacology, 6*, 187–204.

Sonuga-Barke, E. J. S., Daley, D., & Thompson, M. (2002). Does maternal ADHD reduce the effectiveness of parent training for preschool children's ADHD? *Journal of the American Academy of Child and Adolescent Psychiatry, 41*, 696–702.

Spencer, T., Biederman, J., Wilens, T., Harding, M., O'Donnell, D., & Griffin, S. (1996). Pharmacotherapy of attention-deficit hyperactivity disorder across the life cycle. *Journal of the American Academy of Child and Adolescent Psychiatry, 35*, 409–432.

Swanson, J. M., Kraemer, H. C., Hinshaw, S. P., Arnold, L. E., Conners, C. K., Abikoff, H. B. et al. (2001). Clinical relevance of the primary findings of the MTA: Success rates based on severity of ADHD and ODD symptoms at the end of treatment. *Journal of the American Academy of Child and Adolescent Psychiatry, 40*, 168–179.

Swanson, J. M., McBurnett, K., Christian, D. L., & Wigal, T. (1995). Stimulant medications and the treatment of children with ADHD. In T. H. Ollendick & R. J. Prinz (Eds.), *Advances in Clinical Child Psychology, 17*, 265–322.

Tremblay, R. E., LeMarquand, D., & Vitaro, F. (1999). The prevention of oppositional defiant disorder and conduct disorder. In H. C. Quay & A. E. Hogan (Eds.), *Handbook of disruptive behavior disorders* (pp. 525–555). New York: Kluwer Academic/Plenum Publishers.

U.S. Public Health Service. (2000). *Report of the surgeon general's conference on children's mental health: A national action agenda*. Washington, DC: Author.

Vitello, B., Severe, J. B., Greenhill, L. L., Arnold, L. E., Abikoff, H. B., Bukstein, O. G. et al. (2001). Methylphenidate dosage for children with ADHD over time under controlled conditions: Lessons from the MTA. *Journal of the American Academy of Child and Adolescent Psychiatry, 40*, 188–196.

Walker, H. M., Colvin, G., & Ramsey, E. (1995). *Antisocial behavior in school: Strategies and best practices*. Pacific Grove, CA: Brooks/Cole.

Walker, H. M., & Eaton-Walker, J. E. (1991). *Coping with noncompliance in the classroom: A positive approach for teachers*. Austin, TX: Pro-Ed.

Wasserman, R. C., Kelleher, K., Bocian, A., Baker, A., Childs, G. E., Indacocea, F. et al. (1999). Identification of attentional and hyperactivity problems in primary care: A report from pediatric research in office settings and the Ambulatory Sentinel Practice Network. *Pediatrics, 103*, E38.

Webster-Stratton, C. (1992). *The incredible years: A trouble-shooting guide for parents of children aged 3–8*. Toronto: Umbrella Press.

Wolraich, M. L., Lindgren, S., Stromquist, A. Milich, R., Davis, C., & Watson, D. (1990). Stimulant medication use by primary care physicians in the treatment of attention deficit hyperactivity disorder. *Pediatrics, 86*, 95–101.S

Zito, J. M., Safer, D. J., dos Reis, S., Gardner, J. F., Magder, L., Soeken, K. et al. (2003). Psychotropic practice patterns for youth: A 10-year perspective. *Archives of Pediatric Adolescent Medicine, 57*, 17–25.

Chapter 10
Providing Integrated Care for Smoking Cessation

ELIZABETH V. GIFFORD, KATHLEEN M. PALM, AND ANDREA DILORETO

Cigarette smoking presents a costly challenge for smokers, health-care professionals, and policymakers. Of the 17 million smokers who yearly make a serious attempt to quit, only 1.3 million are successful (Fiore, 1992; Hatziandreu et al., 1990). Even if no one were to begin smoking from this time forward, tobacco would still cause 10 million deaths worldwide within the next 20 years (see Warner, 1998). In the United States smoking remains the leading cause of preventable illness and death (U.S. Department of Health and Human Services, 2004). Tobacco-related diseases have reached "epidemic" proportions (Cinciripini, Hecht, Henningfield, Manley, & Kramer, 1997). Furthermore, treatment for smoking-related illnesses costs over $50 billion annually, and indirect costs from lost time at work and disability cost an additional $47 billion–50 billion (AHRQ, 1996; USPHS, 2000).

According to the Agency for Health Care Policy and Research 1996 *Smoking Cessation* Guideline:

> Smoking cessation interventions offer clinicians and health care providers *their greatest opportunity to improve the current and future health of all Americans* (U.S. Department of Health and Human Services [DHHS], 1989).

As described by Orleans (1993) and others, the majority of current smokers will never enroll in smoking treatment but will see a primary care physician each year. The primary care setting is thus the obvious vehicle for dissemination of smoking cessation interventions. For this reason, the U.S. Department of Health and Human Services (USDHHS) states that it is crucial that physicians and health-care delivery systems consistently identify, document, and treat every tobacco user seen in a health-care setting (Fiore, 2000).

The tobacco control field has led the way toward integrating behavioral health issues in medical settings (Davis, 1988). Efforts to encourage integrated care for smoking have been undertaken at the federal and state policy levels, and among nonprofit and for-profit health-care organizations. These efforts have begun to bear fruit. For example, based on its surveys, the National Committee for Quality Assurance (NCQA), in its 2000 report on the "State of Managed Care Quality," states that the average percentage of adult smokers who received advice to quit smoking from a medical professional increased from 1996 to 1999 by 4.3% (from 61% to 65.3%). This 4.3% improvement (on average) means more than 1,000 additional smokers were advised to quit, and 33 smokers quit smoking per their health plan. These numbers represent a financial savings of $68,000 per plan.

In 1999, approximately 6 million current or recent American smokers received advice from their physicians to quit. Although this figure represents an improvement over previous years, there is still a long way to go. According to NCQA, the lowest performing managed care organizations (MCOs) reported physician advice rates of 56%; the top performers reported rates of 73%. If all Americans were enrolled in top-quality plans with 73% rates, "28 million smokers would receive such advice, 715,000 more smokers would quit, and the health care system would save over 1.5 billion per year" (NCQA, 2000, pp. 10–11).

In this chapter we present state-of-the-art smoking cessation treatments, methods for delivering smoking treatment in primary care settings, and guidelines for integration at the organizational level. Tobacco cessation benefits from a relatively long history of integration efforts. Perhaps the most important of these lessons is the fundamental value of integration: systematic methods for integrating medical and behavioral concerns can result in profoundly meaningful health-related behavior change—change for the individual smoker, for the health-care delivery organization, and for the larger community.

Smoking-Related Health Risks

In a report recently released by the Centers for Disease Control (CDC) and Prevention (2000), chronic diseases emerged as the leading cause of death in the United States. In 1996 alone, an estimated 2.3 million people died from various forms of cardiovascular disease, cancer, and respiratory/pulmonary disorders. Cumulatively, these chronic diseases account for almost 70% of all deaths.

Smoking has been identified as a primary or secondary risk factor in virtually all the aforementioned diseases, and has, as a result, become *the* leading preventable cause of death and disability in the nation. The CDC reports that approximately 430,000 deaths each year can be directly attributed to cigarette smoking, a number that exceeds the combined number of deaths attributable to AIDS, alcohol, drug abuse, car crashes, murders, suicides, and fires. Half of all regular tobacco users will die from smoking-related complications (CDC, 2000).

Cigarette smoking and its link to emphysema and lung disease are well known, yet the harmful effects of smoking are widespread and extend beyond the respiratory system. Cardiovascular diseases have been identified as the number one cause of death, a category including coronary heart disease, cerebrovascular disease, atherosclerotic disease, and hypertension, and the risk of developing one of these disorders increases with the number of cigarettes smoked and the duration of smoking (McBride, 1992). Smoking has also been implicated in the development of a number of types of cancer, and according to the National Institute on Drug Abuse, rates of death from cancer are twice as high among smokers as nonsmokers, with rates increasing to four times as high with heavy smokers (NIDA, 2001). Smoking has been established as a major cause of lung, laryngeal, oral, and esophageal cancers; 80–90% of deaths from these cancers are attributable to smoking. Lower, yet significant percentages of deaths due to bladder, kidney, pancreatic, and stomach cancers (20–50%) are likewise attributable to smoking. In all cases, a smoker's risk of cancer is increased anywhere from 2 to 10 times that of a nonsmoker (Newcomb & Carbone, 1992). In addition to contributing to the development of cardiovascular diseases and cancer, cigarette smoking is the primary cause of pulmonary illnesses including chronic obstructive pulmonary disorder (COPD), chronic bronchitis, and emphysema. Smokers also experience an increased incidence of respiratory infections (Sherman, 1992).

Female smokers are particularly vulnerable to a number of health problems. In addition to the aforementioned diseases affecting all smokers, women who smoke have an increased risk of developing cervical cancer, and for women taking oral contraceptives, the risk of coronary heart disease increases. Pregnant women who smoke not only increase their own risk for disease, but also adversely affect the health of their infant or unborn fetus. Secondhand cigarette smoke is considered to be a risk factor for conduct disorders in childhood and causes SIDS and low birth weight. Women who smoke while pregnant also increase their risks of spontaneous abortion and ectopic pregnancy (USDHHS, 2004).

Despite the long-term damage caused by smoking, quitting and staying quit can markedly improve a smoker's health. If a smoker quits smoking before the age of 50, he or she doubles the chance of living for the next 15 years (CDC, 2000). The risk of cardiovascular disease is dramatically reduced within 6 months to 2 years of abstinence. A pregnant woman who stops smoking early in pregnancy reduces her risk of complications to the same level as a woman who has never smoked (USDHHS, 1990).

According to the American Lung Association (1991), within 20 minutes of smoking the last cigarette, blood pressure, pulse rate, and temperature of hands and feet return to normal levels. Nine months after quitting, carbon monoxide and oxygen levels in the blood become normal, lung capacity increases up to 30%, and the body's overall energy level increases. Furthermore, 5 years after quitting, the risk of lung cancer for the average smoker (one pack per day) decreases from 137 per 100,000 to 72 per 100,000. The message is clear: quitting smoking significantly reduces health risks.

Empirically Supported Smoking Treatments

Several different pharmacological and behavioral treatments for smoking cessation have been found effective. Choosing the appropriate treatment or treatments for a particular smoker may depend on the smoker's preference and the person's readiness to change. In this section, we describe effective pharmacological smoking cessation treatments and psychosocial interventions.

Nicotine Replacement Therapy

Nicotine replacement therapy (NRT) has been well documented as an efficacious and safe treatment for smoking cessation. The nicotine transdermal patch, polacrilex gum, nasal spray, and vapor inhaler have been shown to attenuate withdrawal symptoms experienced by smokers by slowly reducing the overall levels of nicotine in the body (Hatsukami & Mooney, 1999). In addition to offering relief from withdrawal, some forms of NRT, specifically the nasal spray, gum, and vapor inhaler, may also produce effects that are perceived by some smokers as benefits of smoking, including arousal or relaxation (Benowitz & Peng, 2000).

Although the patch, gum, nasal spray, and vapor inhaler show comparable overall outcomes, they differ in their availability, administration, immediacy of effect, and side effects, factors that should be taken into consideration when choosing an NRT (see Fiore, 2000). Both the nicotine patch and gum are available over the counter (OTC) in a variety of dosages. Sold as Nicoderm or Nicotrol, the patch is available in 21/14/7 mg, 15 mg, and 22/11 mg doses, and is administered once a day for either 16 or 24 hours, providing a steady level of nicotine throughout the day. The nicotine gum, under the brand name Nicorette, is available in 2 and 4 mg pieces and is administered either according to craving or at a fixed interval. The gum should be chewed slowly at first and then held between the lip and gum so that optimum nicotine absorption can occur (AHCPR, 1996).

The nasal spray and vapor inhaler are available only through prescription under the trade name Nicotrol. Among the various forms of NRT, nicotine delivery via the nasal spray more closely approximates that of smoking, with continine levels reaching roughly 30% of smoking levels (Schneider et al., 1995). The nasal spray delivers 1 mg of nicotine in each dose (0.5 mg per nostril) and is administered ad libitum. The nicotine inhaler, a plastic tube with a perforated plug containing

4 mg of nicotine, delivers nicotine via a puff or inhalation, with each cartridge containing enough nicotine for approximately 80 puffs (AHCPR, 1996).

Because each delivery system is unique, it is possible that combining two forms of NRT may further improve success rates. It has been shown that the combined use of the patch and the gum can significantly increase abstinence rates when compared with either treatment alone. One study reported a 50% higher abstinence rate at the end of the treatment period when those using a 16-hour active patch along with active gum were compared with those receiving only the active patch. Although there was no significant difference between the two groups at the 6-month follow-up, the investigators did find that the amount of time before relapse was significantly longer for those receiving both active treatments (Kornitzer, Bousten, Dramaix, Thijs, & Gustavsson, 1995).

It is important to note that while there is a great deal of evidence supporting the clinical utility of NRT in the treatment of smoking, the ability of each of these treatments to work alone varies and each treatment appears to more effective with the addition of some form of behavioral intervention. Virtually all the studies considered included psychosocial interventions in addition to the medication, and many authors acknowledge and advocate group and individual support, both brief and intensive, as an adjunct to NRT (AHCPR, 1996; Cinciripini & McClure, 1998; Hjalmarson, Franzon, Westin, & Wiklund, 1994; Silagy, Mant, Fowler, & Lodge, 1994).

Nonnicotine Therapies

Although NRT has continued to be the most frequently used pharmacological treatment for smoking cessation, many studies on nonnicotine medications are ongoing. Currently, only bupropion, clonidine, and nortriptyline have sufficient empirical support for inclusion in the AHCPR guideline. Nonnicotine medications are thought to aid in smoking cessation by lessening withdrawal symptoms, mimicking the beneficial physiological effects of smoking, or creating an aversion to smoking (Cinciripini & McClure, 1998). Antidepressants have begun to emerge as the most promising nonnicotine medications for smoking cessation.

Bupropion SR. Presently, sustained release bupropion (bupropion SR) is the only nonnicotine medication recommended as a first-line treatment by the AHCPR and approved by FDA for the treatment of smoking. Although the precise mechanism of action for this antidepressant has not been identified, it is thought that bupropion SR (a dopamine reuptake inhibitor) may mimic some neurochemical effects of nicotine, including the release of dopamine, noradrenaline, and serotonin (Benowitz & Peng, 2000).

Empirical support for this medication is derived from two large-scale controlled trials (Hurt et al., 1997; Jorenby et al., 1999). In both studies, patients reported a number of side effects, the most prominent being dry mouth and insomnia. In the Jorenby study, dropout rates were 12% and 11% for the bupropion group and combined treatment group, respectively, while attrition was only 7% in the patch group and 4% in the placebo group. The Hurt study reported three serious adverse events linked to the higher dosage of bupropion SR. It should be noted that, as with the majority of studies on NRT, these trials examining the efficacy of bupropion also included some form of behavioral intervention. (Benowitz, & Peng, 2000; Jorenby et al., 1999)

Clonidine. The antihypertensive medication clonidine is recommended by the AHCPR only as second-line pharmacotherapy to be used in the event that first-line medications, including NRT and bupropion SR, are insufficient or ineffective for a patient. Clonidine can be administered either transdermally or orally and should be taken before the quit date. Empirical support for clonidine remains contradictory, but in a meta-analysis of nine studies, clonidine was reported to have outperformed placebo, particularly when the patient was female (Covey & Glassman, 1991).

Because the FDA has not yet approved the use of clonidine as an aid for smoking cessation and the adverse effects are frequent, it should be dispensed cautiously on a case-by-case basis under a physician's direction (AHCPR, 1996). In a review of studies of clonidine, adverse experiences were reported by 23–92% of patients taking clonidine, the most common side effects being dry mouth, sedation, and dizziness. Given the frequency of these adverse effects, it has been suggested that this treatment be reserved for patients who experience intense agitation and anxiety when attempting to quit smoking (Gourlay & Benowitz, 1995).

Nortriptyline. The tricyclic, antidepressant medication nortriptyline, like clonidine, is recommended only as second-line pharmacotherapy for smoking cessation because of its lack of approval from the FDA for this purpose and its potential adverse effects. In its review of treatments for smoking cessation, the AHCPR found only two studies offering evidence in support of nortriptyline. Both clinical trials reported that significantly higher abstinence rates were obtained with nortriptyline when compared with placebo: 24% versus 12% and 14% versus 3%, respectively. Nortriptyline did not effectively reduce withdrawal symptoms. Reported adverse effects included dry mouth, lightheadedness, shaky hands, blurred vision, altered taste, drowsiness, and gastrointestinal distress (Hall et al., 1998; Prochazka et al., 1998). According to Benowitz and Peng (2000), nortriptyline blocks noradrenaline uptake in a manner similar to bupropion, thereby increasing the overall level of noradrenaline; nortriptyline does not block dopamine reuptake but does block serotonin reuptake. Due to the risk of serious adverse events, including myocardial infarction, arrhythmia, and stroke, nortriptyline requires intensive patient screening and monitoring.

Psychosocial Treatments/Behavioral Interventions

The effectiveness of these pharmacological treatments increases significantly when they are combined with behavioral interventions. Indeed, certain pharmacological interventions have been tested primarily in combination with counseling. For example, it is an often-overlooked fact that the two major studies that established bupropion SR as an empirically supported frontline intervention included a behavioral counseling component (Hurt et al., 1997; Jorenby et al., 1999), and that bupropion SR has not been studied as a stand-alone treatment. There is also a substantial body of literature describing the efficacy of behavioral and counseling interventions alone (Antonuccio, Boutilier, Ward, Morrill, & Graybar, 1992). It is important for medical personnel to familiarize themselves with the behavioral options described below, as well as local resources for obtaining these services if they do not already exist in-house.

Self-Help Interventions

Self-help materials such as pamphlets, manuals, and videos, are designed to increase smokers' motivation to quit and to communicate cessation skills. These types of materials are appealing for a number of reasons: high-quality intervention expertise can be widely distributed at a fairly low cost, materials can be customized according to stage of readiness or demographic characteristic, and smokers can adapt the program to their individual needs (Curry, 1993).

According to the AHCPR guideline, these materials, irrespective of media presentation, do not appear to be particularly effective and are not recommended as stand-alone treatments for smoking (AHCPR, 1996). Despite the lack of empirical support for self-help as a primary method of treatment, these materials do appear to be somewhat beneficial for smokers who are less dependent on nicotine and who are highly motivated to quit. The efficacy of self-help strategies can likewise be augmented by tailoring materials to individual users and by the addition of telephone support or counseling. In a study of over 3,000 smokers, Zhu and colleagues (1996) examined the extent to which self-help interventions and telephone counseling facilitate smoking cessation. They found significantly higher abstinence rates among those groups receiving single and multiple telephone counseling sessions.

Behavioral Interventions

Smoking is a behavior that is, in large part, developed and maintained through learning processes. Interventions and techniques addressing the behavioral determinants of smoking have long been empirically supported (Shiffman, 1993). Specific behavioral techniques are directed toward helping smokers identify and change behaviors that lead to smoking, reinforce nonsmoking, and teach avoidance and relapse prevention skills (APA, 2001). Among the behavioral techniques, aversive techniques, scheduled smoking, contingency management, cognitive behavioral therapy, and practical counseling and supportive care have gained the most empirical support.

Aversive smoking techniques create a conditioned aversive response by diminishing the pleasurable effects of smoking and inducing nausea or dizziness. Rapid smoking, rapid puffing, smoke holding, and focused smoking all involve using cigarettes and smoking as aversive agents. In rapid puffing and rapid smoking, clients puff on a cigarette every few seconds; in rapid smoking, the client will actually inhale the smoke until the cigarette is finished or the client is unable to continue. In smoke holding, the client inhales and holds the smoke in the mouth while continuing to breathe through the nose. Focused smoking requires the client to smoke at a slow and regulated rate (APA, 2001; Lando, 1993; Schwartz, 1992). These aversive techniques are effective, and they can be used with clients for whom other interventions have not worked. In a meta-analysis of 62 studies estimating the efficacy of counseling and behavior therapies, rapid smoking and other aversive techniques produced abstinence rates of up to 19.9% (AHCPR, 1996).

Scheduled smoking places smokers on fixed interval schedules linked to preexisting smoking levels. This technique gradually and systematically reduces the amount of nicotine in the smoker's system, weaning the smoker from nicotine without the use of nicotine replacement therapy. In addition, fixed schedules may reduce stimulus control over smoking, as smokers learn to perform behaviors other than smoking during times they previously smoked. The amount of time between cigarettes is also gradually and systematically increased. In one particular study, scheduled smoking produced higher abstinence rates when compared with abrupt cessation and uncontrolled reduction, and also reduced tension, fatigue, withdrawal, and urges to smoke (Cinciripini et al., 1995; Cinciripini & McClure, 1998).

The implementation of rewards and punishment in a system commonly referred to as contingency contracting or contingency management has likewise been supported empirically. In this intervention, smokers typically gain or lose money based on their current smoking status. During the course of treatment, abstinence earns rewards, while relapse earns punishment. Contingency management appears to be most effective during the treatment period, and long-term efficacy has yet to be empirically supported (APA, 2001). It has been shown that different schedules of reinforcement can produce differential abstinence effects. Incorporating relapse contingencies appears to improve effects. A progressive increase in magnitude of reward with a reset contingency for relapse appears to be more effective than a fixed magnitude or progressive increase without a reset contingency (Roll & Higgins, 2000).

Cognitive behavioral treatment is defined by efforts to help clients identify and anticipate situations that predispose them to smoke. Clinicians problem-solve with patients by helping them recognize internal and external states that threaten their abstinence and help them learn how to cope effectively with these states by imparting skills. Specifically, clients learn how to avoid or cope with these triggers through behavioral or cognitive techniques. Methods of behavioral coping include replacing the behavior with another, escaping the situation, or using skills to manage the triggers to smoke. Cognitively, clients can identify and challenge maladaptive beliefs or habitual patterns of thinking. Clients who engage in problem-solving and relapse-prevention training have achieved significant sustained abstinence rates; therefore, these methods are recommended as a core component of any behavioral intervention (AHCPR, 1996; Lando, 1993).

Strong social support from friends and family is often predictive of abstinence from smoking, yet attempts to implement social support in empirical settings have proven elusive (APA, 2001; Lando, 1993 Lichtenstein, Glasgow, & Abrams, 1986). Supportive care from a clinician, however, can significantly enhance quit rates. By expressing feelings of concern about the patient's smoking status, providing information about smoking and quitting, and encouraging the patient to talk about his or her feelings, a clinician can have a positive influence on a patient's smoking status. With supportive care and practical counseling, abstinence rates of approximately 15% can be achieved (AHCPR, 1996).

Using several techniques in concert appears to increase efficacy, outperforming no-contact controls and yielding 6-month abstinence rates of 20–25% (AHCPR, 1996; APA, 2001; Baillie, Mattick, Hall, & Webster, 1994; Glasgow & Lichtenstien, 1987; Lando, 1993; Law & Tang, 1995; Schwartz, 1992). The most effective multimodal, or multicomponent, therapies appear to incorporate skills training for both quitting and maintaining abstinence. It has also been suggested that multimodal treatments may enhance cessation rates by allowing clients to tailor the treatment to their own particular situation (Lando, 1993).

Although the aforementioned psychosocial interventions are frequently considered inconvenient or time consuming, their importance for the treatment of smoking cannot be underestimated. The AHCPR concluded that person-to-person contact can have a significant impact on cessation rates, and as treatment intensity increases, so does treatment effectiveness. This dose-response relationship is evident in as many as 43 studies, and for this reason, behavioral interventions have been identified as a necessary and effective component of any smoking cessation treatment program (AHCPR, 1996).

Assessment and Treatment in the Primary Care Setting

The literature is very clear: simple smoking cessation interventions performed by physicians in primary care settings have profound effects. Providing a short message and advice to quit results in 1-year quit rates of 6% (Anderson & Wetter, 1997). More frequent physician contacts or combining physician messages with self-help or pharmacologic agents increases this number to 22% (Houston Miller & Barr Taylor, 2000). According to Robinson, Laurent, and Little (1995), physicians are more likely to provide smoking cessation information to patients when physicians consistently inquire about smoking status. The very process of identifying smokers can serve not only as an integral part of a medical assessment, but also as an intervention (Fiore, et al., 2000). In practice, according to the National Ambulatory Medical Care Survey ($n = 1,558$) (Jaén, Stange, Tumiel & Nutting, 1997), physicians tend to conduct smoking assessments only with patients who are at risk because of other chronic illnesses (e.g., cardiovascular disease). Unfortunately, this selection criteria means the vast majority of smokers are not advised by their physicians to quit smoking.

Smoking Status

One concern about implementing an effective screening system is the practicality of adding another assessment to the limited time constraints with which physicians' offices have to work. Identifying patient smoking status, however, can be easily integrated into standard procedures. Including smoking status as a vital sign increases the rate of identifying smokers and assisting patients with smoking cessation (Fiore et al., 1995; Robinson et al., 1995). The AHCPR clinical guidelines for smoking cessation provide an example of how to incorporate the assessment of smoking status into standard practice by treating it as a vital sign (see Table 10.1). They suggest that clinicians assess every patient to determine whether the patient currently uses, never used, or used to use tobacco.

Nicotine Dependence

Assessment of nicotine dependence can be important in determining an appropriate treatment program for smokers. Research has found that highly nicotine-dependent smokers are likely to need more intensive therapy (Orleans, 1993). The CAGE questionnaire, the "Four Cs" test, and the Fagerstrom Tolerance Questionnaire are all efficient self-report tools commonly used to assess addiction (Etter, Vu Duc, & Perneger, 1999; Prokhorov et al., 2000; Rustin, 2000). These assessments inquire about patients' feelings of control over their own behavior, withdrawal symptoms, impact of smoking on their thoughts and feelings, and acknowledgment of consequences related to the addictive behavior. In particular, the Fagerstrom scale assessments have been found to predict success at smoking cessation and which smokers will benefit from nicotine gum or nasal spray (Fagerstrom & Schneider, 1989; Pomerleau, Majchrzak, & Pomerleau, 1989). Simply asking whether the first cigarette of the day is smoked within 30 minutes of awakening is a simple but reliable index of nicotine dependency (Fagerstrom, 1978; Pomerleau et al., 1989).

Smoking History

This assessment should include smoking rate, years smoked, desire to quit, stage of quitting (Prochaska & DiClemente, 1983), and past quit attempts. The majority of smokers have made at least one attempt to stop smoking (Fiore, 2000). Although most smokers who try to quit are no longer abstinent 1 year after quitting, each attempt increases their chance of quitting completely (Fiore, 2000). With each effort to quit, the smoker learns which skills are effective or ineffective. In order for the physician to help identify an effective cessation intervention for the client, it is important to assess circumstances related to past quit attempts; for example, past reasons for quitting, cause of relapse, length of time patient remained abstinent, and prior cessation strategies.

Environmental and Psychosocial Variables

Identifying rewarding aspects of smoking can be very useful in tailoring treatment for patients. Although it is important to ask the patient about past smoking behavior and quit attempts, it is useful and often informative for clinicians to inquire about current smoking behaviors and the functions smoking currently serves, for example, "Where do you smoke?" "When do you smoke?" and "Why do you smoke?" These questions should be used to identify external triggers (e.g., "When I'm with friends and we're out drinking") and internal triggers (e.g., "I smoke because I'm stressed").

There are several smoking functions commonly endorsed by patients (Rustin, 2000):

1. The act of smoking often provides the patient with physical stimulation (i.e., warmth, taste, feel in fingers, puffing, smoke, moving hand to mouth, etc.).

TABLE 10.1 Vital Signs

Blood Pressure: _____		
Pulse: _____	Weight: _____	
Temperature: _____		
Respiratory Rate: _____		
Tobacco Use: (circle one) Current	Former	Never

2. Many patients perform rituals that become habits that are difficult to change.
3. Patients often identify who they are by their smoking behavior. For example, they have learned to identify themselves as "rebellious" or by the brand of cigarette they smoke.
4. Many smokers report smoking cigarettes in an effort to achieve emotional relief.

The function of smoking may also vary depending on the patient's social context. Social support has been shown to be a major predictor of smoking cessation (Lichtenstein et al., 1986; Orleans, 1993). Smokers who have friends and family who are supportive of their quit attempt are more likely to remain abstinent. Therefore, identifying the smoking status of people in the patient's environment and their willingness to support the client in current and past quit attempts should be assessed. Reducing contact with smokers, enlisting the support of smokers (i.e., asking them to smoke outdoors, not to offer cigarettes, etc.), or encouraging significant others to join them in quit attempts are all helpful when smokers are part of the individual's social network.

Assessment of additional psychosocial factors may be useful in making a prognosis of whether patients will achieve and sustain cigarette abstinence (Orleans, 1993). Patients with greater self-esteem, effective coping skills, more confidence about their ability to quit, positive health habits, manageable life stress, and good self-management skills have a better prognosis. Furthermore, smokers who abuse alcohol or drugs have a more difficult time quitting smoking. Thus, clinicians should also assess whether patients use alcohol or other substances.

Readiness to Change

A great deal of smoking cessation literature has focused on the predictive utility of assessing patients' readiness to change (Dijkstra, De Vries, & Roijackers, 1999; Pine, Sullivan, Sauser, & David, 1997; Prochaska & DiClemente, 1983; Rohren, et al., 1994). Prochaska and DiClemente (1983) have described a model that outlines stages of willingness to change among smokers. These stages include precontemplation, contemplation, preparation, action, and maintenance. Based on the patient's stage of change, health-care providers can implement appropriate interventions that are likely to move patients into the next stage (Pine et al., 1997; Velicer, Prochaska, Rossi, & Snow, 1992). Research suggests that patients who are not considering quitting may benefit from different treatment strategies than those who identify with other stages of willingness to change (Pine et al., 1997). For example, when confronted with a precontemplator, the role of the physician becomes motivational, and the goal is to get the patient to consider quitting. Patients in the preparation stage may benefit from more specific advice regarding treatment, and patients in the action or maintenance stage will benefit from discussion of relapse potential and problem-solving aimed at relapse prevention.

Despite the fact that some patients are motivated and ready to change their behaviors, there are common barriers that make it difficult to quit, including for example, fears of weight gain and withdrawal symptoms. Identifying reasons and barriers for smoking cessation can be useful when motivating the client to quit (AHRQ, 2003). In addition to assessing for reasons and barriers, motivation can be enhanced by inquiring about patients' treatment preferences.

Biochemical Markers

Patients' self-reports of smoking are often adequate; however, some patients provide inaccurate reports of their smoking. Inaccurate reports could be due to reasons ranging from memory problems to shame about smoking. If the physician desires accurate monitoring of the patient's smoking, then there are devices that can be used to obtain objective readings that reflect smoking behavior. Some of these biological indices include carbon monoxide level readings and serum level testing. In addition to providing objective records of smoking, showing patients changing carbon monoxide levels can provide motivational enhancement. For example, carbon monoxide levels can be measured quickly and easily by expelling breath into a device that reflects smoking over the past several hours (Secker-Walker, Vacek, Flynn, & Mead, 1997; Velicer et al., 1992). Nicotine and cotinine levels can be measured in blood, saliva, and urine (Jarvis, Tunstall-Pedoe, Feyerabend, Vesey, & Saloojee, 1987). CO readings assess tobacco use over the past 24 hours, nicotine level assesses tobacco use over the past few hours. Cotinine, a metabolite of nicotine, is sensitive to smoking in the past week and provides a better assessment of total daily nicotine exposure (Secker-Walker et al., 1997).

Integrated Treatment Models

The success of smoking cessation and prevention programs depends on the integration of assessment and treatment strategies into systems that are acceptable and effective for staff and patients. Effective systems can vary in form but most share certain essential components: repeated assessment of smoking status and motivation to quit, identification of barriers, and multiple follow-up contacts.

The AHRQ Clinical Practice Guidelines suggest treatment strategies that health-care providers should be prepared to use with patients who are willing to quit smoking (Fiore et al., 2000). The first strategy, commonly referred to as the "5 As," involves the following:

- Ask the patient about his or her smoking status.
- Advise the smoker to quit.
- Assess willingness to quit.
- Assist those who are willing to quit.
- Arrange follow-up appointments to help prevent relapse.

Research suggests that practicing these guidelines will help identify and treat smokers more effectively. Research also shows that using more "As" improves outcomes. Health Plan Employee Data Information Set (HEDIS), released by the National Committee for Quality Assurance (NCQA), is a set of guidelines for performance measurement in health care delivery. HEDIS 3.0, the third version of HEDIS, was released in 1998. Asking and advising smokers to quit, as emphasized by HEDIS 3.0, has been called the "2A model" (Hollis et al., 2000). Although this is certainly better than nothing, and may serve as a motivational enhancement for some precontemplative smokers, the full 4A model generates exponential improvement in cessation rates. Hollis says:

Delivering brief advice to 60% of the smokers who see a clinician each year across the country might generate about 126,000 additional quitters over and above the spontaneous rate. If we increase the simple advice rate to 90%, we would produce something like 189,000 additional clinician generated quitters, which would be a substantial achievement. But suppose, once each year, clinicians advised 90% of smokers and that, for the half of these smokers who are at least considering quitting at any given time ("contemplators" in Prochaska's model), clinicians or their staff also provided 10 minutes of actual cessation counseling and assistance. The AHCPR meta-analyses estimate that 10 minutes of cessation assistance yields a much higher 2:4 odds ratio. This would yield about 756,000 additional quitters per year or a six-fold increase in the number of clinician generated quitters over current practice. My point here is that the third and fourth As in the 4A model really do matter, and we need to overcome the very real barriers that are preventing the delivery of systematic and comprehensive tobacco intervention in most primary care settings today (pp. 18–19).

Many smokers report that they are not ready or willing to quit smoking at this time. There are crucial steps health-care providers can take in order to increase patients' motivation to stop smoking. The AHCPR panel (Fiore, 2000) suggested a treatment strategy referred to as the "5 Rs": relevance, risks, rewards, roadblocks, and repetition. The health-care provider should encourage the patient to identify *reasons* why smoking cessation is relevant to him or her. In addition, the clinician can assist the client in clarifying the potential *risks* of not quitting and the *rewards* he or she might experience from quitting. Further, it is often useful to predict *roadblocks*, or barriers, that the patient might encounter when trying to stop smoking. Identification of barriers can assist the patient and the clinician in including treatment strategies into the cessation program that are helpful when encountering those roadblocks. Finally, these strategies should be *repeated* whenever these patients visit the clinic.

Orleans (1993) describes a stepped-care model for the treatment of nicotine dependence in medical settings. This model is based on Prochaska and DiClemente's (1983) multistage model, described above, with the addition of a "relapse and recycling" stage "with those who slip or relapse after achieving abstinence returning to any earlier stage" (Orleans, 1993, p. 150). Because accomplishing sustained abstinence often requires multiple quit attempts, health-care environments should provide multiple intervention opportunities, and every health-care visit should be viewed as an opportunity to help the smoker take "the next step."

Orleans's (1993) model starts with establishing a facilitative environment. This includes preparing the organizational environment and systems, including establishing a "smoking cessation coordinator," and identifying and resolving barriers to implementation (e.g., lack of time among primary care physicians and dentists means that much of the assessment and treatment must be delegated once the smoker is identified). Once the environment is established, all patients' smoking status is assessed, including a brief smoking and quitting history. In addition, assessment should occur repeatedly. Failures to quit should be treated as "practice" and used to provide more information regarding the individual's smoking assessment needs. This information should be summarized in the progress notes.

The next stage in the model involves enhancing motivation, that is, moving smokers to the next stage. Personal health risks and benefits should be addressed, and if possible, linked to existing medical conditions and delivered by the primary care provider. Barriers and fears regarding quitting should be explored if patients fall into the majority category of "contemplators" who are considering quitting. Importantly, this educational intervention should include strong advice to quit. Orleans suggests the following statement: "As your physician (dentist) I strongly advise that you stop smoking. If we can give you some help, are you willing to give it a try?" (1993, p. 154).

If smokers are willing to make a commitment, they should be directed to treatment. Patient preference regarding treatment should be included, and pharmacological and counseling preferences and options should be discussed. Minimal self-help interventions in combination with a follow-up phone call provide a starting point, and there are a number of self-help materials oriented to particular populations, including women, African-American and Hispanic smokers, older smokers, and teen smokers. Patients who feel over 70% sure they will be successful at quitting on their own likely will benefit from simple self-help materials (Houston Miller & Barr Taylor, 2000). For many smokers, quitting on their own is most preferred, and repeated minimal contact interventions involving primary care providers are the most efficient method. The best method for the individual patient will depend on his or her history of success or failure and the particular triggers he or she describes. Make sure that you or your office staff has information on community resources, including program costs, methods used, and a contact person.

Indicators for more intensive treatment include patient preference, a history of many prior treatments or self-help failures, higher levels of nicotine dependency, and a lack of support, skills, or motivation. Formal treatment programs, involving either counseling or medication, or, preferably, both (Fiore et al., 2000), should be provided. Such treatment should be offered again if treatment failure occurs. Frequently, relapsed patients may become, for a time, "precontemplators," unwilling to make the commitment to try again. Patients should not be reintroduced to formal treatment options, including medication, until they are willing to initiate a quit attempt or program. Finally, at the same time that quit dates are established, follow-up contacts should be discussed and planned with all those in the contemplation stage of change or above. Such discussions alone improve quit attempts and quit successes. Follow-up should consist of a phone contact or a return office visit, along with personalized self-help mailings (e.g., notes accompanying motivational or advice pamphlets).

Organizational Systems/Systems Changes

More than half the U.S. population, and up to 85% of privately insured individuals, are enrolled in managed care plans. For example, in 1996, 100 million Americans were enrolled in employer-sponsored HMOs and PPOs (CFAH, 2000). The *Surgeon General's Report on Treating Tobacco Use and Dependence* states: "research shows clearly that systems-level changes can reduce smoking prevalence among enrollees of managed health care plans" (PHS, 2000, p. 1). The U.S. Public Health Service (PHS) guideline recommends the following strategies:

- Every clinic should implement a tobacco-user identification system.
- All health care systems should provide education, resources, and feedback to promote provider interventions.
- Clinical sites should dedicate staff to provide tobacco dependence treatment and assess the delivery of this treatment in staff performance evaluations.
- Hospitals should promote policies that support and provide tobacco dependence services.
- Insurers and managed care organizations (MCOs) should include tobacco dependence treatments (both counseling and pharmacotherapy) as paid or covered services for all subscribers or members of health insurance packages.
- Insurers and MCOs should reimburse clinicians and specialists for delivery of effective tobacco dependence treatments and include these interventions among the defined duties of clinicians (p. 2).

Many exemplary, integrated, smoking cessation treatment programs exist, including Blue Cross-Blue Shield of Maine, Benefits Health Plan, Network Health Plan, HealthPartners, and others (e.g., see PHS, 2000). One of the best examples of a comprehensive approach to smoking prevention and cessation is Seattle Group Health Cooperative (GHC). Through the development of an integrated system, with the goal of decreasing smoking prevalence within its enrolled population, GHC increased participation in its smoking cessation programs tenfold, from 180 per year in 1991 to 1,500–2,000 per year since 1993 (McAfee & Thompson, 1998). They also increased identification of smoking status from 30% to over 85% in their primary care clinics, and doubled physician's documentation of advice to quit among physicians. Seventy-one percent of GHC patients who smoke in postvisit surveys reported that their physicians talked to them about smoking during their office visit. Their legislative lobbyist worked to support passage of a state law banning cigarette vending machines and other community-based interventions including media campaigns. As a result of these changes, over the past decade smoking prevalence among GHC members has decreased from 25% to 15% (a 10% drop), versus statewide decreases from 25% to 23% (only a 2% drop).

Managed Care Organizations and Smoking Cessation Interventions

What interventions produced these commendable results? There are several key strategies, all of which begin with a single factor: put smoking cessation efforts in the organizational mission. It has been argued that health maintenance organizations (HMOs) or managed care organizations (MCOs) have a financial interest in targeting smoking prevention (e.g., McAfee & Thompson, 1998; Yox, 1995). Given the extraordinarily deleterious health effects of tobacco consumption, such interests seem obvious. For example, numerous studies have shown that quitting smoking results in decreased use of inpatient and outpatient health-care services, as well as reducing risk for cardio-vascular and cardiopulmonary disease, low birth-weight infants, and work-related absenteeism (USDHHS, 2004). Smoking cessation programs pay for themselves in 3 or 4 years by reducing hospitalization utilization alone (Wagner, Curry, Grothaus, Saunders, & McBride, 1995).

However, it is important to acknowledge that in for-profit MCOs, there are factors working against integration of the prevention agenda, particularly the rapid cycling of members through some MCOs, and a focus on short-term cost decreases by some MCO managers (McAfee & Thompson, 1998). McAfee and Thompson (1998) recommend that the organization develop a division for prevention that is entrusted with certain functions: (a) emphasizing the marketing value of prevention services and the public-relations benefits of adopting these strategies; and (b) emphasizing the "higher" goals of the organization, namely, improving and saving lives, not just reducing costs. Just as necessary therapeutic interventions such as appendectomies are unquestioningly provided, critical prevention interventions such as smoking cessation should be automatically administered.

Influencing organizational leaders requires knowledge about the cost effectiveness of programs, knowledge about program implementation, and knowledge about the particular integration opportunities available within the health plan system (Krejci, 2000). Dacey (2000) states:

> Support at all the different levels of the organization, from the top leadership down, is critical. A successful program involves laying this groundwork. Endorsement from the chief executive officer, the quality structure leadership, the clinic manager, and the medical chief, as well as individual providers and their teams, must be gained. Gaining this support starts with creating a sound evidence based argument as to why the program is central to the health of the patient (p. 2).

Fortunately, the smoking cessation literature provides well-articulated evidence on smoking and health care, and well-developed, easily accessible guidelines for evidence-based practice. For example, the American Association of Health Plans' *Addressing Tobacco in Managed Care: A Resource Guide for Health Plans* (2001), and the U.S. Department of Health and Human Services' *Treating Tobacco Use and Dependence* (2000c).

With leadership support for a prevention effort, the next step is to set goals. These goals can include numbers of enrollees in smoking treatment programs, membership smoking rate reduction, reduction of cardiac or other disease events, numbers of smokers receiving advice to quit, and so forth. Once organizational goals are defined, it is necessary to develop systems to monitor progress and implementation; for example, systems to identify and document smoking status, to provide treatment, and to evaluate outcomes. There are several simple ways of monitoring or flagging client files to prompt providers to assess for smoking status. First, once a patient's smoking status has been identified, a sticker corresponding with the appropriate status should be placed on the folder. For example, Etter, Rielle, and Perneger (2000) found that placing "Smoker" stickers on patients' charts increased the likelihood that physicians would advise smokers to quit smoking. Second, a stamp with spaces to track smoking status and other useful smoking information can be printed on the patient file or, similarly, a tracking note inserted into the file. Fiore and colleagues (1995) found that tracking smoking as a vital sign on progress notes significantly increased the rate of identifying smokers, advising them to quit, and assisting with smoking cessation. These data systems must be in place before programs are implemented. Building on existing organizational data systems should occur wherever possible.

Managers, clinicians, and researchers who have been involved in dissemination continue to report their real-world experiences in the literature. Several general principles guiding successful smoking cessation systems implementation are as follows:

1. *Keep it simple.* For example, use tobacco chart stickers and vital sign stamps. It is imperative to consider the time demands of busy practice environments (Dacey, 2000, p. 30). Every step, including documentation of smoking status and interventions and referrals to smoking counselors, should be easy and should fit efficiently into office flow (Hollis et al., 2000).

2. *Delegate time-intensive tasks.* Provide systems so busy physicians can refer patients to specialists within the organization, such as trained RNs, or specialist programs within the organization that provide individualized treatment (Dacey, 2000, p. 31).

3. *Provide centralized support/staffing and dedicated funding for this staff* (Dacey, 2000; see also Krejci, 2000, p. 34). Orleans (1993) suggests each primary care practice or practice setting select a tobacco cessation coordinator who is responsible for integration of nicotine dependence treatment into the clinic or organization. Where members can access the services directly, it is important to notify the primary care provider (and members must be informed that such notification will occur). In network model health plans, a centralized and integrated delivery system is recommended because it increases efficiency with office requirements (e.g., a common toll-free number for participants in different markets), staff training (i.e., telephone counseling staff are in the same place), and staff supervision and support.

4. *Design programs that use follow-up and permit consistent contact with staff responsible for delivering services or maintaining systems.* According to Krejci (2000), "consistent 'one-on-one' coaching by a trained cessation specialist is paramount to the members' success, and we believe this is the reason we have maintained quit rates above 40% at one year" (p. 34). Counselors can be health education specialists (i.e., those with undergraduate or graduate degrees in health education or public health), registered nurses, social workers, crisis counselors, substance abuse counselors, or others.

5. *"Measure outcomes, evaluate the processes, and provide feedback"* (Dacey, 2000, p. 31). Three key areas to evaluate are utilization, member/provider satisfaction, and quit rates (Krejci, 2000). It is important to establish automated systems that permit audits and develop or utilize existing quality feedback reports, such as patient outcomes, electronic chart reviews, numbers of smokers identified, patient satisfaction.

6. *"Identify individuals at all levels accountable for measurable outcomes"* (Dacey, 2000, p. 31). Program evaluation should assess "implementation, data collection, staff, and operational integrity and effectiveness" (Krejci, 2000, p. 35). For example, medical assistants responsible for chart stickers, providers responsible to intervene and document intervention in chart, quality implementation team responsible to oversee clinic performance should be monitored (Dacey, 2000, p. 31). Accountability should be built into programs from the beginning.

7. *Provide incentives for change.* For example, certain health plans offer financial incentives to member clinics based on targeted goals such as smoking status identification and documented cessation counseling (Solberg, 2000, p. 37–38). Clinics can pass along these

"bonuses" to staff delivering services to encourage compliance with 5A protocols. Performance reviews are another important means of creating incentives (Hollis et al., 2000). Incentive measures and recognition should also be kept simple and meaningful (Isham, 2000).

8. *Execute "ongoing, multiple promotion" to the membership in order to increase utilization* (Krejci, 2000, p. 35). Krejci states, "We have learned that it is necessary to apply multiple promotion strategies—repeat your efforts and often. Consider multiple methods of promotion such as targeted mailings, newsletters, brochures, and publications, open enrollments, health fairs, 'on hold' phone messages, and public presentations. Send a brochure to a smoker identified through a health questionnaire. Target high risk populations such as members with diabetes, cardiovascular disease, or pregnancy through hospitalizations, pharmacy, or claims data" (p. 35).

9. *Cover the cost of cessation programs to reduce patient barriers to treatment* (Dacey, 2000; Krejci, 2000). Complete versus partial coverage has been proven to increase treatment utilization rates among patients (PHS, 2000). Small co-pays such as $20 may not function as barriers, but noncoverage of nicotine replacement will significantly reduce the number of enrollees. Coverage may also function as a "carrot" (Krejci, 2000, p. 33–34), and eligibility can then be contingent on compliance with in-person or telephone counseling, for example, nicotine replacement only provided to those who also fulfill their counseling.

Choosing the System for Your Office

Although many smoking prevention and cessation programs have proven to be effective in decreasing rates of smoking, the cost-effectiveness of implementing such programs is a concern for most health-care providers today. Two outcomes that are of particular interest to providers are total financial cost and cost of the treatment per life-year saved. The financial cost of treatment includes the cost of the resources consumed by smoking cessation treatments; for example, personnel, facilities, equipment, supplies, and medications (Yates, 1996). Cost of treatment per life-year saved is a cost-effectiveness ratio of the cost to the desirable outcome, which is improved health status and quality of life.

Cromwell and colleagues (1997) assessed the cost-effectiveness of the 15 smoking interventions recommended by the AHCPR clinical guidelines. Analyses were based on recommended resources inputs found in the AHCPR report. Researchers combined three counseling interventions for primary care clinicians (minimal, brief, and full) and two counseling interventions for smoking cessation specialists (individual intensive and group intensive) with or without transdermal nicotine and nicotine gum. The researchers found that, in general, greater spending on interventions yielded more net benefit. Specifically, more intensive interventions were related to lower costs per life-year saved. Furthermore, full or intensive counseling plus the nicotine patch resulted in greater quit rates and more life-years saved (Cromwell et al., 1997). Other studies have found that using the patch as an adjunctive treatment to brief counseling resulted in better health and lower costs per life-year saved when compared with brief counseling alone (Stapleton, Lowin, & Russell, 1999).

Nielson and Fiore (2000) analyzed the cost-effectiveness of the nicotine patch versus sustained-release bupropion, minimal counseling plus placebo, and the combination of the patch plus bupropion SR. These researchers assessed costs from an employer's perspective and accounted for absenteeism, medical care and workers' compensation costs, and lost productivity in their analyses. Results indicated that bupropion SR was more cost-beneficial than the patch, minimal counseling plus placebo, and the patch plus bupropion. In this study, minimal counseling plus placebo cost less than bupropion but also had a significantly lower quit rate than the bupropion alone.

Buck, Richmond, and Mendelsohn (2000) assessed the cost-effectiveness of integrating assessments of readiness to change with behavioral interventions and NRT. The researchers provided informational booklets to smokers who were assessed as precontemplative or contemplative. The booklet for precontemplative smokers included information about smoking and an invitation to return to the health-care provider to discuss quitting. The contemplative booklet also included information about smoking but also presented a brief motivation interview. Finally, prepared smokers received information on quitting, three visits for behavioral consultation, and advice on using the nicotine chewing gum. Buck and colleagues found that the integration of assessing readiness to change, behavioral interventions, and nicotine chewing gum was more cost-effective than self-help manuals and behavioral interventions alone.

In sum, implementing any smoking cessation intervention seems to provide at least some small net benefit (Nielson & Fiore, 2000). Studies suggest, however, that a combination of counseling and pharmacological interventions results in more impressive quit rates and greater cost-effectiveness.

Smoking and Public Policy

Integrative efforts in the smoking cessation field are not limited to jointly delivered medical and mental health care. Tobacco control efforts demonstrate integration in the broadest sense, uniting regulatory, educational, clinical, and community health efforts. Since 1964, when the first connection between smoking and lung cancer was made, the changes in social norms and public policy have dramatically decreased the nation's rate of smokers, from over 42% to the current rate of approximately 23% (MMWR, 2004). The national peak occurred in the early 1960s. Since then, the surgeon general's reports, the World Conferences on Smoking and Health, broadcast advertising bans, the nonsmokers' rights movement, increases in federal cigarette taxes, and other national factors have contributed to the dramatic reduction in adult per-capita cigarette consumption (USDHHS, 1999).

The Federal Drug Administration (FDA), as described by Koop, Warner, and others (see Henningfield, 2000, p. 4), has tried to combat the fact that "it is easy to get the disease, hard to get the treatment" (Henningfield, 2001, p. 4). The FDA's tobacco rule addressed the susceptibility of nicotine addiction by (a) establishing that nicotine is a drug, and cigarettes and smokeless tobacco products are drugs and drug delivery systems (FDA, 1995), and (b) designing a program to reduce nicotine access to young people (e.g., by preventing sales to youth, by refusing to permit advertising in youth-oriented publications, etc.; FDA, 1996). However, on March 21, 2000, the U.S. Supreme Court ruled that nicotine regulation does not fall under the FDA's jurisdiction, preventing the implementation of the FDA's efforts to reduce youth exposure to nicotine (American Medical Association, 2001). This ruling effectively passes the burden of prevention to the states.

According to the 1992 Synar amendment, states are required to establish and enforce laws prohibiting the sale of tobacco to anyone under 18. In addition, the Substance Abuse Mental Health Services Administration (SAMHSA) issued the Synar Regulation, which requires states to conduct unannounced, random inspections of state tobacco vendors, and establish annual target rates moving toward a goal of an inspection failure rate of less than 20% by the year 2003. Current ongoing funding for substance abuse prevention and treatment through SAMHSA may be denied to those states failing to achieve their annual targets.

One of the most effective means of reducing smoking among smokers of all ages is increasing excise tax rates. For example, Oregon passed a voter-approved measure to increase cigarette excise taxes by 30 cents (to 68 cents per pack), and to implement new prevention programs (CDC, 2000). These measures reversed a 4-year trend of increased smoking rates and lowered rates by 11.3%. According to the CDC's Morbidity and Mortality Weekly Report (USDHHS, 1999) "a 10% increase in the price of cigarettes can lead to a 4% reduction in the demand for cigarettes" (CDC, 1999, p. 989). California, Massachusetts, and Arizona have also passed voter initiatives (these initiatives, perhaps not coincidentally, bypass heavily lobbied state legislatures) to increase state tobacco taxes and develop tobacco prevention programs. As a result, "tobacco use rates in adults and youth have declined in these states, relative to use rates in the nation as a whole" (Henningfield, 2000, p. 5).

Summary

Integrating smoking treatment into the primary care setting is an essential step in reducing smoking and its human and economic costs. Integration efforts in the smoking field provide important lessons in integrated behavioral health care and the evolution of organized behavioral health-care practices. Summarized, these lessons include the following. First, good intentions are not enough. Busy primary care providers will put out visible fires and will not focus on behavioral correction or prevention. Second, systems need to be put in place that "make visible" the importance of these interventions and trigger their provision. Third, implementing these systems requires thought and effort. Provision of feedback (for all personnel involved in delivery) is essential, particularly as the effects of these interventions are often cumulative and delayed, and health-care providers can become discouraged by what they perceive as a lack of efficacy. In addition, change requires effort, and feedback provides extra incentives. Fourth, the MCO, the community, and the state and federal governments can be vital partners in the integration mission. Promoting health through behavior change improves the lives of all members of a community or organization, and leaders need contact with this data. Last but not least, the most important lesson for smoking cessation and the larger behavioral health-care community is that *integration works*. Assessing for and intervening in smoking behavior is an extremely productive use of time and resources in primary care settings. We have the knowledge and the means to make a difference.

References

Agency for Healthcare Research and Quality (AHRQ). (1996). *Overview: Smoking cessation recommendations for clinicians.* Retrieved January 2001, from http://www.ahcpr.gov/news/press/smoview.htm.

Agency for Healthcare Research and Quality (AHRQ). (1996). Smoking cessation and clinical practice guideline. Clinical Practice Guideline, No.18. AHCPR, Publication no. 96-0692, April 1996.

Agency for Healthcare Research and Quality (AHRQ). (2003). *Treating tobacco use and dependence—clinician's packet. A how-to guide for implementing the public health service clinical practice guideline,* March 2003. U.S. Public Health Service, Agency for Healthcare Research and Quality. Rockville, MD: http://www.ahrq.gov/clinic/tobacco.

American Association of Health Plans. (2001). *Addressing tobacco in managed care: A resource guide for health plans.* Washington, DC: American Association of Health Plans.

American Lung Association. (1991). *Benefits of quitting smoking.* Mimeographed handout.

American Medical Association (2001). *Annual tobacco report 2001* (Report 14 of the Board of Trustees, A-01). Washington, DC: D. Ted Lewers.

American Psychiatric Association (APA). (2001). Smoking cessation [Online]. Clinical resources. Retrieved January 2001, from www.psych.org/clin_res/pg_nicotine_3.cfm.

Anderson, C. B., & Wetter, D. W. (1997) Behavioral and pharmacologic approaches to smoking cessation. *Cancer and Metastasis Reviews, 16:* 393–404.

Antonuccio, D. O., Boutilier, L. R., Ward, C.H., Morrill, G. B., & Graybar, S. R. (1992). The behavioral treatment of cigarette smoking. *Progress in behavior modification, 28,* 119–181.

Baillie, A. J., Mattick, R. P., Hall, W., & Webster, P. (1994). Meta-analytic review of the efficacy of smoking cessation intervention. *Drug and Alcohol Review, 13,* 157–170.

Benowitz, N. L., & Peng, M. W. (2000). Non-nicotine pharmacotherapy for smoking cessation. *CNS Drugs, 13,* 265–285.

Buck, D. J., Richmond, R. L., & Mendelsohn, C. P. (2000). Cost-effectiveness analysis of a family physician delivered smoking cessation program. *Preventive Medicine, 31,* 641–648.

Centers for Disease Control and Prevention (CDC). (1999). Achievements in public health, 1900–1999: Tobacco use—United States, 1900–1999. *Morbidity and Mortality Weekly Report, 48,* 986–993.

Centers for Disease Control and Prevention (CDC). (2000). Cigarette smoking among adults—United States, 1998. *Morbidity Mortality Weekly Report, 48*(43), 993–996.

Center for the Advancement of Health (CFAH). (2000). *Health behavior change in managed care: A status report.* HMO Medical Director's Report. Retrieved from http://www.cfah.org/pdfs/health_HMOdirectors.pdf.

Cepeda-Benito, A. (1993). Meta-analytical review of the efficacy of nicotine chewing gum in smoking treatment programs. *Journal of Consulting and Clinical Psychology, 61,* 822–830.

Cinciripini, P. M., Hecht, S. S., Henningfield, J. E., Manley, M. W., & Kramer, B. S. (1997). Tobacco addiction: Implications for treatment and cancer prevention. *Journal of the National Cancer Institute, 89,* 1852–1867.

Cinciripini, P. M., Lapitsky, L. G., Seay, S., Wallfisch, A., Kitchens, L., & Vunakis, H. V. (1995). The effects of smoking schedules on cessation outcome: Can we improve on common methods of gradual and abrupt withdrawal? *Journal of Consulting and Clinical Psychology, 63,* 388–399.

Cinciripini, P. M., & McClure, J. B. (1998). Smoking cessation: Recent developments in behavioral and pharmacological interventions. *Oncology, 12,* 249–259.

Covey, L. S., & Glassman, A. H. (1991). A meta-analysis of double-blind placebo-controlled trials of clonidine for smoking cessation. *British Journal of Addiction, 86,* 991–998.

Cromwell, J., Bartosch, W. J., Fiore, M. C., Hasselblad, V., & Baker, T. (1997). Cost-effectiveness of the clinical practice recommendations in the AHCPR guideline for smoking cessation. *JAMA, 278,* 1759–1766.

Curry, S. J. (1993). Self-help interventions for smoking cessation. *Journal of Consulting and Clinical Psychology, 61,* 790–803.

Dacey, S. (2000). Tobacco cessation program implementation-from plans to reality: Skill building workshop-group model. *Tobacco Control, 9*(suppl. 1), 30–32.

Davis, R. M. (1988). Uniting physicians against smoking: The need for a coordinated national strategy. *Journal of the American Medical Association, 259,* 2900–2901.

Dijkstra, A., De Vries, H., & Roijackers, J. (1999). Targeting smokers with low readiness to change with tailored and nontailored self-help materials. *Preventive Medicine, 28,* 203–211.

Etter, J. F., Rielle, J. C., Perneger, T.V. (2000). Labeling smoker's charts with a "smoker" sticker: Results of a randomized controlled trial among private practitioners. *Journal of General Internal Medicine 15*(6), 421–424.

Etter, J. F., Vu Duc, T., & Perneger, T. V. (1999). Validity of the Fagerstrom test for nicotine dependence and of the Heaviness of Smoking Index among relatively light smokers. *Addiction, 94,* 269–281.

Fagerstrom, K. O. (1978). Measuring degree of physical dependence to tobacco smoking with reference to individualization of treatment. *Addictive Bahaviors 3*(3–4): 235–241.

Fagerstrom, K., & Schneider, N. G. (1989). Measuring nicotine dependence: A review of the Fagerstrom Tolerance Questionnaire. *Journal of Behavioral Medicine, 12,* 159–182.

Fiore, M. C. (1992). Trends in cigarette smoking in the United States: The epidemiology of tobacco use. *Medical Clinics of North America, 76,* 289–303.

Fiore, M. C. (2000). A clinical practice guideline for treating tobacco use and dependence: A US Public Health Service report. *JAMA, 283,* 3244–3254.

Fiore, M. C., Jorenby, D. E., Schensky, A. E., Smith, S. S., Bauer, R. R., & Baker, T. B. (1995). Smoking status as the new vital sign: Effect on assessment and intervention in patients who smoke. *Mayo Clinic Proceedings, 70,* 209–213.

Fiore, M., Thompson, S., & Lawrence, D. (2000). Helping Wisconsin women quit smoking: A successful collaboration. *Wisconsin Medical Journal, 99*(2) (April): 68–72.

Food and Drug Administration (1996). Regulations restricting the sale and distribution of cigarettes and smokeless tobacco to protect children and adolescents; final rule. *Federal Register, 61,* 4395–5318.

Food and Drug Administration (1995). Regulations restricting the sale and distribution of cigarettes and smokeless tobacco to protect children and adolescents; final rule. *Federal Register, 60,* 41314–787.

Glasgow, R. E., & Lichtenstein, E. (1987). Long-term effects of behavioral smoking cessation interventions. *Behavior Therapy, 18*(4), 297–324.

Gourlay, S. G., & Benowitz, N. L. (1995). Is Clonidine an effective smoking cessation therapy? *Drugs, 50*(2): 197–207.

Hall, S. M., Reus, V. I., Munoz, R. F., Sees, K. L., Humfleet, G., Hartz, D. T. et al. (1998). Nortriptyline and cognitive-behavioral therapy in the treatment of cigarette smoking. *Archives of General Psychiatry, 55,* 683–690.

Hatsukami, D. K., & Mooney, M. E. (1999). Pharmacological and behavioral strategies for smoking cessation. *Journal of Clinical Psychology in Medical Settings, 6,* 11–38.

Hatziandreu, E. J., Pierce, J. P., Lefkopoulou, M., Fiore, M. C., Mills, S. L., Novotny, T. E. (1990). Quitting smoking in the United States in 1986. *Journal of the National Cancer Institute, 82,* 402–406.

Henningfield, J. E. (2000). Tobacco dependence treatment: Scientific challenges; public health opportunities. *Tobacco Control, 9,* 3–10.

Hjalmarson, A., Franzon, M., Westin, A., & Wiklund, O. (1994). Effect of a nicotine nasal spray on smoking cessation: A randomized, placebo-controlled, double-blind study. *Archives of Internal Medicine, 154,* 2567–2572.

Hollis, J. F., Bills, R., Whitlock, E., Stevens, J. J., Mullooly, J., & Lichtenstein, E. (2000). Implementing tobacco interventions in the real world of managed care. *Tobacco Control, 9*(suppl. 1), 18–24.

Houston Miller, N., & Barr Taylor, C. (2000). *Smoking cessation and relapse prevention manual for health care professionals.* Stanford University Cardiac Rehabilitation Program. Unpublished manuscript.

Hurt, R. D., Sachs, D. P. L., Glover, E. D., Offord, K. P., Johnston, J. A., Dale, L. C. et al. (1997). A comparison of sustained-release bupropion and placebo for smoking cessation. *New England Journal of Medicine, 337,* 1195–1202.

Isham, G. J. (2000). A proactive health plan: Taking action on tobacco control. *Tobacco Control, 9*(suppl.), 1–5. Retrieved January 2001, from http://tc.bmjjournals.com/cgi/content/full/9/suppl_1/i15.

Jaén, C. R., Stange, K. C., Tumiel, L. M., & Nutting, P. (1997). Missed opportunities for prevention: Smoking cessation counseling and the competing demands of practice. *Journal of Family Practice, 45,* 348–354.

Jarvis, M. J., Tunstall-Pedoe, H., Feyerabend, C., Vesey, C., & Saloojee, Y. (1987). Comparison of tests used to distinguish smokers from nonsmokers. *American Journal of Public Health, 77,* 1435–1438.

Jorenby, D. E., Leischow, S. J., Nides, M. A., Rennard, S. I., Johnston, J. A., Hughes, A. R. et al. (1999). A controlled trial of sustained-release bupropion, a nicotine patch, or both for smoking cessation. *New England Journal of Medicine, 340,* 685–691.

Kornitzer, M., Bousten, M., Dramaix, M., Thijs, J., & Gustavsson, G. (1995). Combined use of nicotine patch and gum in smoking cessation: A placebo-controlled clinical trial. *Preventive Medicine, 24,* 41–47.

Krejci, R. (2000). Tobacco cessation program implementation—from plans to reality: Skill building workshop-network model. *Tobacco Control, 9*(suppl. 1), 33–36.

Lando, H. A. (1993). Formal quit smoking treatments. In C. Orleans (Ed.), *Nicotine addiction: Principles and management* (pp. 221–244). New York: Oxford University Press.

Law, M., & Tang, J. L. (1995). An analysis of the effectiveness of interventions intended to help people stop smoking. *Archives of Internal Medicine, 155,* 1933–1941.

Lichtenstein, E., Glasgow, R. E., & Abrams, D. B. (1986). Social support in smoking cessation: In search of effective interventions. *Behavior Therapy, 17,* 607–619.

McAfee, T., & Thompson, R. S. (1998). Improving community-based prevention by transforming managed care organizations into health improvement organizations. *Journal of Public Health Management Practice, 4,* 55–65.

McBride, P. E. (1992). The health consequences of smoking: Cardiovascular disease. *Medical Clinics of North America, 76,* 333–353.

National Committee for Quality Assurance (NCQA). (2000). State of managed care quality report. Washington, DC: Author.

National Institute on Drug Abuse (NIDA). (2001). Nicotine addiction. Research Report Series. Retrieved from October 2002, www.nida.nih.gov/researchreports/nicotine.

Newcomb, P. A., & Carbone, P. P. (1992). The health consequences of smoking: Cancer. *Medical Clinics of North America, 76,* 305–331.

Niaura, R., Abrams, D. B., Shadel, W. G., Rohsenow, D. J., Monti, P. M., & Sirota, A. D. (1999). Cue exposure treatment for smoking relapse prevention: A controlled clinical trial. *Addiction, 94,* 685–695.

Nielsen, K., & Fiore, M. C. (2000). Cost-benefit analysis of sustained-release bupropion, nicotine patch, or both for smoking cessation. *Preventive Medicine, 30,* 209–216.

Orleans, C. T. (1993). Treating nicotine dependence in medical settings: A stepped-care model. In C. T. Orleans & J. D. Slade (Eds.), *Nicotine addiction: Principles and management* (pp. 145–161). New York: Oxford University Press.

Pine, D., Sullivan, S., Sauser, M., & David, C. (1997). Effects of a systematic approach to tobacco cessation in a community-based practice. *Archives of Family Medicine, 6,* 363–367.

Pomerleau, C. S., Majchrzak, M. J., & Pomerleau, O. F. (1989). Nicotine dependence and the Fagerstrom Tolerance Questionnaire: A brief review. *Journal of Substance Abuse, 1,* 471–477.

Prochaska, J. O., & DiClemente, C. C. (1983). Stages and processes of self-change of smoking: Toward an integrative model of change. *Journal of Consulting and Clinical Psychology, 51,* 390–395.

Prochazka, A. V., Weaver, M. J., Keller, R. T., Fryer, G. E., Licari, P. A., & Lofaso, D. (1998). A randomized trial of nortriptyline for smoking cessation. *Archives of Internal Medicine, 158,* 2035–2039.

Prokhorov, A. V., De Moor, C., Pallonen, U. E., Hudmon, K. S., Koehly, L., & Hu, S. (2000). Validation of the modified Fagerstrom Tolerance Questionnaire with salivary cotinine among adolescents. *Addictive Behaviors, 25,* 429–433.

Robinson, M. D., Laurent, S. L., & Little, J. M. (1995). Including smoking status as a new vital sign: It works! *Journal of Family Practice, 40,* 556–561.

Rohren, C. L., Croghan, I. T., Hurt, R. D., Offord, K. P., Marusic, Z., & McClain, F. L. (1994). Predicting smoking cessation outcome in a medical center from stage of readiness: Contemplation versus action. *Preventive Medicine, 23,* 335–344.

Roll, J. M., & Higgins, S. T. (2000). A within-subject comparison of three different schedules of reinforcement of drug abstinence using cigarette smoking as an exemplar. *Drug and Alcohol Dependence, 58,* 103–109.

Rustin, T. A. (2000). Assessing nicotine dependence. *American Family Physician, 62,* 579–584.

Schneider, N. G., Olmstead, R., Mody, F. V., Doan, K., Franzon, M., Jarvik, M. E. et al. (1995). Efficacy of a nicotine nasal spray in smoking cessation: A placebo-controlled, double-blind, trial. *Addiction, 90,* 1671–1682.

Schwartz, J. L. (1992). Methods of smoking cessation. *Medical Clinics of North America, 76,* 451–476.

Secker-Walker, R. H., Vacek, P. M., Flynn, B. S., & Mead, P. H. (1997). Exhaled carbon monoxide and urinary cotinine as measures of smoking in pregnancy. *Addictive Behaviors, 22,* 671–684.

Sherman, C. B. (1992). The health consequences of cigarette smoking: Pulmonary diseases. *Medical Clinics of North America, 76,* 335–375.

Shiffman, S. (1993). Smoking cessation treatment: Any progress? *Journal of Consulting and Clinical Psychology, 61,* 718–722.

Silagy, C., Mant, D., Fowler, G., & Lodge, M. (1994). Meta-analysis on efficacy of nicotine replacement therapies in smoking cessation. *Lancet, 343,* 139–142.

Solberg, L.I. (2000). Incentivising, facilitating, and implementing an office tobacco cessation system. *Tobacco Control, 9*(suppl. 1), 37–41. Retrieved January 2001, from http://tc.bmjjournals.com/cgi/content/full/9/suppl_1/i37.

Stapleton, J. A., Lowin, A., & Russell, M. A. H. (1999). Prescription of transdermal nicotine patches for smoking cessation in general practice: Evaluation of cost-effectiveness. *Lancet, 354,* 208–213.

U.S. Department of Health and Human Services (USDHHS). (1999). *Best practices for comprehensive tobacco control programs.* U.S. Department of Health and Human Services, Centers for Disease Control and Prevention, National Center for Chronic Disease Prevention and Health Promotion, Office of Smoking and Health. Retrieved from http://www.cdc.gov/tobacco/research_date/stat_nat_data/byfactsheet.htm.

U.S. Department of Health and Human Services (USDHHS). (2001). *HHS fact sheet: Preventing disease and death from tobacco use.* Washington, DC: Author. Retrieved from January 2001, http://sss.hhs.gov/news/press/2001pres/01fstbco.html.

U.S. Department of Health and Human Services (USDHHS) (2004). *January 11, 2004, marks the 40th anniversary of the inaugural surgeon general's report on smoking and health.* United States Department of Health and Human Services, Centers for Disease Control and Prevention, National Center for Chronic Disease and Health Promotion, Office on Smoking and Health.

U.S. Department of Health and Human Services (USDHHS). (2000a). *Oregon—Reducing cigarette consumption through a comprehensive tobacco control program.* Tobacco information and prevention source (TIPS). Centers for Disease Control and Prevention; National Center for Chronic Disease Prevention and Health Promotion. Washington, DC: Author. http://www.cdc.gov/tobacco/research_data/intervetnions/mm299fs.htm

U.S. Department of Health and Human Services (USDHHS). (2000b). *Reducing tobacco use: A report of the surgeon general.* Atlanta: U.S. Department of Health and Human Services, Centers for Disease Control and Prevention, National Center for Chronic Disease and Health Promotion, Office of Smoking and Health.

U.S. Departmetn of Health and Human Services (USDHHS). (1990). *The health benefits of smoking cessation: A report of the Surgeon General.* Atlanta, GA: U.S. Department of Health and Human Services, Centers for Disease Control and Prevention, National Center for Chronic Disease Prevention and Health Promotion, Office of Smoking and Health.

U.S. Department of Health and Human Services (USDHHS) (2004). *The health consequences of smoking: A report of the Surgeon General.* Atlanta, GA: U.S. Department of Health and Human Services, Centers for Disease Control and Prevention, National Center for Chronic Disease Prevention and Health Promotion, Office on Smoking and Health.

U.S. Department of Health and Human Services (USDHHS). (2000c, November). *Treating tobacco use and dependence. A guide for health care administrators, insurers, managed care organizations, and purchasers.* Retrieved January 2001, from http://www.surgeongeneral.gov/tobacco/systems.htm.

U.S. Public Health Service (PHS). (June 2000). Achievements in tobacco cessation: Case studies. http://www.surgeongeneral.gob/tobacco/smcasest.htm.

U.S. Public Health Service (PHS). (2000). Treating tobacco use and dependence—a systems approach. A guide for health care administrators, insurers, managed care organizations, and purchasers. Retrieved from http://www.surgeongeneral.gov/tobacco/systems.htm.

Velicer, W. F., Prochaska, J. O., Rossi, J. S., & Snow, M. G. (1992). Assessing outcome in smoking cessation studies. *Psychological Bulletin, 111,* 23–41.

Wagner, E. H., Curry, S. J., Grothaus, L., Saunders, K. W., & McBride, C. M. (1995). The impact of smoking and quitting on health care use. *Archives of Internal Medicine, 155,* 1789–1795.

Warner, K. E. (1998). *Report from the 10th world conference on tobacco and health. Effective strategies for smoking cessation in primary care practice.* Darien, CT: SCP/Cliggott Communications.

Yates, B. T. (1996). *Analyzing costs, procedures, processes, and outcomes in human services.* Newbury Park, CA: Sage.

Yox, S. B. (1995). The HMO Group Conference: Tobacco use prevention and reduction. *HMO Practice, 9,* 123–127.

Zhu, S., Stretch, V., Balabanis, M., Rosbrook, B., Sadler, G., & Pierce, J. P. (1996). Telephone counseling for smoking cessation: Effects of single-session and multiple-session interventions. *Journal of Consulting and Clinical Psychology, 64,* 202–211.

Chapter 11
Infertility

NEGAR NICOLE JACOBS

Most individuals grow up with romantic illusions of getting married and starting a family at a time of their choosing (Galst, 1986). For many, becoming a parent is a developmental milestone that signals adult social status, as well as normality and sexual adequacy. On the societal and biological levels, there may be an expectation that productive members of society will propagate in order to ensure continuity and survival of the species. So strong is this cultural expectation that most family members ask newly married couples *when* they plan to have children and *how many* children they plan to have as opposed to *whether* they plan to have children. Given this individual and cultural context, few men or women are prepared for the shock of infertility. Dreams of having children playing within a house surrounded by a white-picket fence may be devastatingly shattered when the diagnosis of infertility is made (Galst, 1986). Infertile individuals commonly report reactions of anger, sadness, grief, guilt, and a sense of failure. In addition, there may be a sense of existential crisis when previously held expectations about the future and meaning of parenthood are challenged by infertility.

The standard definition of infertility is the inability to conceive a pregnancy after 1 year of engaging in sexual intercourse without the use of contraception (Leiblum, 1988). The time period of one year was chosen because of the observation that approximately 25% of couples will conceive within the first month of sexual intercourse without the use of contraception, roughly 60% will conceive within the first 6 months, and around 80% will achieve pregnancy within the first 12 months (Olsen, 1990). A distinction is made between primary and secondary infertility: A couple who has never been able to conceive a pregnancy is defined as having primary infertility (30% of infertile couples), whereas a couple who already has previously conceived but is currently unable to conceive is diagnosed as having secondary infertility (70% of infertile couples).

Reported rates of infertility vary between studies, but lie in a range of 8–16% of couples in the United States (American Society for Reproductive Medicine, 1998; Menning, 1980; Mosher & Pratt, 1990). One population-based study found that at least one in six couples were infertile (Hull et al., 1985). A number of factors have been hypothesized (Leiblum, 1988; Page, 1988; Stanton & Dunel-Schetter, 1991) to be responsible for this high incidence of infertility: (a) declining age of onset of sexual activity, (b) liberalization of sexual attitudes and behaviors; (c) rising numbers of sexually transmitted diseases, which can damage reproductive organs; (d) increased exposure to toxic environmental agents; (e) greater use of contraceptive devices, which can damage the reproductive tract; (f) increased average age at first attempt to conceive; and (g) rising divorce rate and subsequent remarriage.

Biopsychosocial Theory of Infertility

Williams, Bischoff, and Ludes (1992) provide a biopsychosocial framework for understanding the issues surrounding infertility. The authors posit that clinicians working with infertile couples must be able to understand the medical, psychological, and social origins of the couple's problems. They maintain that these factors transact to produce the common sequelae associated with infertility, including feelings of stress, depression, grief, marital difficulties, and social isolation.

Biological and Medical Aspects of Infertility

A basic understanding of the biological and medical aspects of infertility is essential in the development and implementation of any treatment for infertile couples. Clinicians who are knowledgeable about the medical aspects of infertility will be better able to understand the multiple stresses to which infertile couples are subjected (Williams et al., 1992). Men and women are equally affected by the biological causes of infertility (Menning, 1988). In 35% of cases the female partner receives the diagnosis of infertility, while in 35% of cases the male partner is infertile. Infertility is a combined problem between the male and female partners in 20% of the cases. The cause of infertility is unknown in the remaining 10% of cases.

There are three primary medical causes of infertility in women. First, if a woman has hormone problems or ovarian cysts, she may not produce or release mature eggs. Second, any scars or adhesions of the fallopian tubes may obstruct delivery of the egg to the uterus. Finally, the fertilized egg may not be able to properly implant itself into the uterine wall if the woman has structural abnormalities or hormone problems (Moghissi, 1978; Williams et al., 1992).

Male fertility relies upon the production and delivery of a sufficient quantity of sperm that are normal, motile, and mobile (Leiblum, 1988). Therefore, causes of infertility in the male include inadequate sperm production, structural abnormalities in the reproductive organs, and sexual disorders, including erectile dysfunction (Keye, 1999; Leiblum, 1988; Williams et al., 1992).

Psychological Aspects of Infertility: The Experience of Infertility

The experience of infertility can be devastating for any couple who desires a child (Leiblum, 1988). Most couples assume that they will be able to have children with a minimum of effort. When attempts at conception are unsuccessful, couples are often faced, for the first time in their lives, with failure and an inability to achieve a highly desired goal. Firmly held beliefs of being able to achieve a desired goal if they work hard enough are challenged. If the couple believes that parenting is a sign of adulthood, they may have to redefine their worldviews. Couples who have planned a future around desired children may have to grieve the loss of the potential to raise their own children. They must either adapt to the "transition to nonparenthood," begin the difficult and often painful process of medically assisted reproduction, or consider alternatives such as adoption.

The experience of infertility can take a significant emotional toll on both partners. In one study (Freeman, Boxer, Rickels, Tureck & Mastroianni, 1985) of 200 couples undergoing in vitro fertilization (IVF) treatment, researchers found that 49% of the women and 15% of the men considered infertility as the most upsetting experience of their lives. Mahlstedt, McDuff, and Bernstein (1987) found that 80% of their sample of infertile clients reported that their experience with infertility was either "stressful" or "extremely stressful." Other researchers have estimated that as many as 40% of infertile individuals have significant emotional distress that carries the possibility of long-term implications (e.g., Mahlstedt, 1985). In fact, infertility has been labeled a "biopsychosocial crisis" by some researchers (Cook, 1987; Taymor, 1979).

Common reactions to the diagnosis of infertility include feelings of failure, guilt, shock, anger, grief, depression, and a search for meaning. The failure to conceive may generalize to sexual insecurity or even to feelings of failure as a human being. Individuals may wonder "Why me?" (McDaniel, Hepworth, & Doherty, 1992). One infertility specialist reported that a high proportion of her patients believed that their infertility was a punishment from God for a past sexual transgression or other sin (Menning, 1988). Individuals may feel anger or resentment toward women who have abortions. They may also feel jealous or envious of other women's pregnancies.

Although the relationship between stress and infertility has been well documented, it remains less clear whether high levels of stress are the cause or the consequence of infertility (Brkovich & Fisher, 1998; Wright, Allard, Lecours, & Sabourin, 1989). A number of studies have investigated the relationship between stress and physiological patterns in infertile patients. However, owing to methodological shortcomings (e.g., correlational data only, lack of longitudinal designs, lack of control groups) in these studies relating psychological distress to physiological patterns in individuals with infertility, no conclusions about causality can be made (Brkovich & Fisher, 1998; Wright et al., 1989). Although there seems to be an association between extreme levels of environmental stress and infertility, the relationship is tenuous in the majority of infertility cases (Leiblum, 1988). It remains unclear whether stress resulting from infertility causes the above physiological changes, or if existing physiological differences in certain individuals cause infertility. However, although the specific links between psychological stress and physiological aspects of infertility are not yet delineated, it is clear that the experience of infertility takes an emotional toll and taxes the psychological resources of many couples (Stanton & Burns, 1999).

Infertile individuals may also feel a loss of control (McDaniel, Hepworth, & Doherty, 1992). Not only have they lost the ability to conceive on their own, but they now have to expose intimate details of their private lives as well as their private parts to doctors (Kraft, Palombo, Mitchell, Dean, Meyers et al., 1980). Medical treatment for infertility can be invasive, painful, embarrassing, and stressful. Many treatments for infertility involve close monitoring by vaginal ultrasound and blood work, which are often assessed early every morning for up to 2 weeks per menstrual cycle (Domar, 1997). Thus, the impact of infertility on job or career plans can be profound (Domar, 1997). Early morning monitoring can make women late to work, and women may have to switch to a job that offers them the flexibility to pursue treatment. For women who have to travel as part of their jobs, their travel plans may also have to be altered around times of ovulation, so as to ensure access to insemination by their husbands. Women taking infertility medications may experience such side effects as fatigue, nausea, bloating, headaches, hot flashes, irritability, depression, or anxiety (Domar, 1997), which can have detrimental effects on daily functioning. The financial aspect of infertility treatment may also be stressful for couples who cannot afford it. Neumann, Gharib, and Weinstein (1994) concluded that the typical cost for a successful delivery with IVF ranges from $44,000 to $211,940.

The experience of infertility has been likened to an "emotional roller-coaster" (Stanton & Dunkel-Schetter, 1991). Couples may experience feelings of anxiety before ovulation, hopefulness around the time of ovulation, and depression upon learning of a failure to conceive or a miscarriage. Hunt (1992) maintains that women are left in a state of "psychological pregnancy" for up to 2 weeks after embryo replacement from in vitro fertilization and may experience each lost embryo as a miscarriage.

Feelings of depression can often accompany the psychological distress experienced by many infertile individuals. However, studies investigating the level of depression experienced by infertile individuals have found contradictory results. In a critical review of this literature, Greil (1997) concluded that studies using standardized measures of depression were split almost evenly between those finding moderately higher levels of depression among infertile individuals (e.g., Domar Zuttermeister, Seibel, & Benson, 1992a) and those finding normative levels (e.g., Downey et al., 1989). Greil (1997) further concluded that there was little evidence of clinically significant elevations among those studies describing elevated levels of depression.

The experience of depression may be associated with feelings of loss and grief (Lukse & Vacc, 1999). Menning (1980) argued that the most common, appropriate, and necessary reaction to a conclusive diagnosis of infertility is grief. Losses due to infertility may include the loss of potential children, the loss of a dream, the loss of genetic continuity, the loss of miscarriages, the loss of self-esteem, the loss of security, the loss of control over one's body, the loss of pregnancy experiences, and loss of a sense that life is fair and predictable (cf. Cook, 1987; Mahlstedt et al., 1987; Menning, 1988; Williams et al., 1992).

Social Factors of Infertility

Impact on Couple. Medically assisted reproduction may also affect the couple's relationship. Couples may argue over the financial aspects of treatment or the course of treatment. They may have differing reactions to infertility, and their coping mechanisms may clash (Mahlstedt, 1985). Infertility treatment may also affect the couple's sexual relationship. The prescription for scheduled intercourse at specified points in the cycle may destroy spontaneous sexual contact or otherwise diminish sexual pleasure. In addition, males may feel a demand to perform if they know there will be a post-coital test immediately following intercourse.

Like any crisis, infertility has the potential to either cause problems in the relationship or unite the couple. As such, researchers investigating the relationship between infertility and marital functioning have produced mixed results. Some researchers have reported that infertility-related conflict is common and can result in decreased marital functioning (e.g., Andrews, Abbey, & Halman, 1991), possibly through such negative reactions as anger, guilt, estrangement, blaming or feeling blamed, lack of feeling supported, feeling misunderstood, and fearing a possible breakup of the relationship (Epstein & Rosenberg, 1997; Mahlstedt, 1985). Other researchers have reported that infertility does not adversely affect marital functioning (e.g., Daniluk, 1988; Downey et al., 1989). However, Leiblum (1993) reported that couples undergoing in vitro fertilization rated their relationships as better than average throughout the course of their treatment.

Although sexual dysfunctions have been implicated in infertility, Leiblum (1993) concluded that only 2.6–5.0% of infertile individuals actually have any evidence of a sexual dysfunction. Moreover, whereas sexual problems have been correlated with infertility in some studies (e.g., Andrews et al., 1991), a critical review of the literature (Greil, 1997) concluded that the majority of studies of sexual satisfaction have found few, if any, differences between infertile and fertile couples. However, Tuschen-Caffier, Florin, Krause, and Pook (1999) noted that 50% of infertile women in their sample did not have intercourse during the fertile period of their menstrual cycle, and that 14% of couples did not know how to mark the fertile period correctly. These researchers found that rates of live births could be increased by targeting *adherence* to a treatment regimen of timed intercourse during the most fertile period of the menstrual cycle. Researchers found that helping couples to differentiate between task-oriented sex during fertile days of the menstrual cycle and pleasure-oriented sex during the rest of the cycle helped couples practice timed intercourse more reliably and without decrements to sexual pleasure and satisfaction.

Social Stigma and Isolation. Greil (1991) describes the experience of infertile individuals living in a fertile world. Couples with infertility are often asked private questions about when they plan to have children or why they have not had children yet. Infertile couples often feel that these questions are an invasion of their privacy, and make them feel like they are outsiders or failures (Greil, 1991). When the pain of infertile couples is recognized, fertile individuals often treat it as trivial or inconsequential. They might give such advice as "just relax," or "just take a trip and you'll get pregnant," or they may minimize the complexity of treatment by saying such things as, "just do in vitro fertilization." Thus, infertile individuals have reported feelings of abnormality, rejection, abandonment, and being outcast and unlovable (Domar, Seibel, & Benson, 1990). There have also been reports of feelings of otherness, shame, guilt, failure, inadequacy, incompleteness, being devalued, and not being whole (Whiteford & Gonzales, 1995). Furthermore, infertile women often report that they feel they have deviated from societal norms and have broken gender roles by not having children (Whiteford & Gonzales, 1995).

The feelings and experiences of infertile individuals may cause them to self-isolate in order to minimize the possibility of being hurt. Individuals with infertility problems often avoid social gatherings, especially those related to fertility, such as baby showers, birthdays, communions, Bar Mitzvahs, graduations, family reunions, and company picnics (Epstein & Rosenberg, 1997). In addition, Epstein and Rosenberg (1997) have described a milestone-induced agoraphobia, in which infertile individuals avoid any events that involve fertility or mark the passage of time.

Assessment

Given the variety of psychological sequelae of infertility, a thorough assessment is essential in order to fully understand the presenting problem and select treatment targets. However, it must also be remembered that many infertility patients feel the medical community is already intruding upon their personal lives, and they may be reluctant to complete lengthy psychological assessment batteries in addition. Thus, it is suggested that assessment of the psychological sequelae of infertility be as brief as it is thorough. Brief assessment also lends itself well to repeated use in order to assess change in psychological functioning over time. Patients will be much more likely to repeatedly complete, and will be much less fatigued by, brief assessment batteries as opposed to lengthy batteries.

As noted above, common psychological sequelae of infertility include stress/anxiety, depression, and marital difficulties. Standardized tools for the assessment of these sequelae exist in brief versions. For example, the State-Trait Anxiety Inventory (STAI; Spielberger, Gorsuch, Luschene, Vagg, & Jacobs, 1983) is a psychometrically sound (Spielberger, Gursuch, & Luschene, 1970) and widely used measure of subjective anxiety that comprises two sets of 20 statements describing feelings of tension, worry, and apprehension. The state anxiety scale asks how the respondent feels *right now*, and the trait anxiety scale asks how the respondent *generally* feels. All items are rated on a 4- point Likert scale. The shortened form of the STAI is a 6-item scale that produces scores similar to those obtained using the full form, is sensitive to fluctuations in state anxiety, and has acceptable reliability and validity (Marteau & Bekker, 1992). The standard self-report measure of depression in the field is the Beck Depression Inventory (BDI; Beck & Steer, 1987, revised 1993). Although there is no shortened form of the BDI, the full-length questionnaire consists of only 21 self-report items. The BDI assesses the severity of depression in both normal and psychiatric populations. Questions about the symptoms of depression are rated on a 4-point scale ranging from 0 to 3, with higher scores indicating greater depressive symptomatology. The BDI has established reliability and validity (Beck, Steer, & Garvin, 1998). Meta-analysis of several studies has yielded a mean coefficient alpha of 0.81 for nonpsychiatric subjects (Beck et al., 1998). The most commonly used measure of marital adjustment/distress in the research literature is the Dyadic Adjustment Scale (DAS; Spanier, 1976). The DAS-7 (Hunsley, Pinsent, Lefebvre, James-Tanner, & Vito, 1995; Sharpley & Rogers, 1984) is a 7-item, abbreviated form of the original DAS, and has been found to have excellent psychometric properties, including good internal consistency, criterion validity, and construct validity (Hunsley et al., 1995; Sharpley & Cross, 1982; Sharpley & Rogers, 1984). The DAS-7 has also been found to conserve, without loss of variance, the pattern of relations found between the DAS and related constructs (Hunsley et al., 1995).

Despite the standardization and widespread use of the above measures, there are a number of drawbacks and limitations in using such instruments in the population of infertility patients. First, the above measures were not standardized for the infertility population. Thus, it is difficult to interpret scores in the absence of norms specific to patients with fertility problems. Second, many commonly used instruments in the field were developed for and tested with psychiatric patients, not medical patients. Accordingly, medical patients may interpret and respond differently to items than psychiatric patients, especially with items assessing somatic symptoms. Third, studies assessing psychiatric symptomatology in the infertile population have found mixed results, with most studies concluding that patients with infertility do not meet criteria for anxiety or mood disorders. However, patients clearly report that the psychological sequelae of their fertility problems are disrupting their lives. Thus, it may be that standardized questionnaires lack sensitivity to infertility-related issues. Therefore, clinicians working with infertility patients should also consider infertility-specific assessment tools.

The Fertility Problem Inventory (FPI; Newton, Sherrard, & Glavac, 1999) is a 46-item, self-report measure of infertility-related stress. Subjects are asked to indicate their degree of agreement with each item on a 6-point Likert scale. The FPI is a multidomain measure, producing scores on the following scales: social concern, sexual concern, relationship concern, need for parenthood, and rejection of child-free lifestyle. The FPI also produces a score on global stress. Newton et al. (1999) found the scale to have acceptable reliability (internal consistency alpha ranged from 0.77 to 0.93 for all scales; test-retest reliability for the global stress scale was 0.83 for women and 0.84 for men). In cross-validation with the BDI, STAI, and DAS, the FPI was found to have acceptable convergent validity. Newton et al. (1999) also found that the FPI was more sensitive to the effects of infertility on marital issues than was the DAS.

The Fertility Adjustment Scale (FAS; Glover, Hunter, Richards, Katz, & Abel, 1999) is a measure of psychological adjustment to infertility. Adjustment is operationally defined as "the way in which individuals acknowledge and process information about the course of their fertility problem and its investigation, treatment, and possible outcomes" (Glover et al., 1999, p. 624). The scale is designed to assess the extent to which subjects with infertility have come to terms with the possibilities of having or not having a biological child of their own. Subjects indicate their level of agreement with 12 items on a 6-point Likert scale. The FAS was found to be normally distributed in the sample of 100 infertility patients and was found to have acceptable reliability and validity (Glover et al., 1999, p. 624).

The Infertility Questionnaire (IFQ; Bernstein, Potts, & Mattox, 1985) was developed to assess the impact of infertility on the domains of self-esteem, blame/guilt, and sexuality. The IFQ is a 21-item self-report measure in which subjects are asked to indicate their level of agreement on a 5-point Likert scale. The test was found to have adequate reliability and validity (Bernstein et al., 1985). Developers of the scale suggest its use, in conjunction with a standard measure of psychological distress, by nurse specialists in order to assess the need for counseling.

In summary, a standard battery for infertility patients should include a brief measure of anxiety (such as the shortened form of the STAI), a measure of depression (such as the BDI), a brief measure of relationship satisfaction (such as the DAS-7), and at least one measure of infertility-specific distress (such as the FAS). Because of the ease of administering and interpreting these measures, the battery could be administered by nurses and office clerks as well as by mental health professionals MHPs. The battery should be given to all incoming infertility patients upon intake in order to assess the psychological status of each patient, to begin prevention protocols, and to develop treatment targets. The battery should be readministered at monthly intervals to monitor changes in patient status on these common psychological sequelae of infertility. Any changes in patient status should be shared with both the physician and the MHP. Finally, the battery should be administered on termination of treatment to assess the effectiveness of any psychosocial treatment administered and to make referrals for additional treatment if necessary.

When special situations or populations are involved, such as in third-party reproduction, care should be taken to tailor the assessment. For example, in the case of donor insemination (DI), Zoldbrod and Covington (1999) suggest that practitioners assess the couple's feelings about male-factor infertility and the meanings that each partner assigns to it, the couple's readiness for DI, and the indications and contraindications for DI. Greenfeld (1999) outlines issues to consider in the assessment of patients considering the use of oocyte donation (OD), including grieving the loss of a potential child that shares a genetic relationship with both parents. Clinicians working with potential gamete donors should refer to Applegarth and Kingsberg (1999), who outline issues to include in a structured clinical interview for potential donors. If clinicians wish to screen out major psychopathology, they should employ standardized measures of psychopathology, such as the Minnesota Multiphasic Personality Inventory (MMPI) in addition to clinical interviews.

Existing Treatments for Infertility

Medical Options

It is crucial that mental health professionals working in the field of infertility have a thorough understanding of the medical procedures involved in infertility treatment. Knowledge of such medical treatments for infertility will not only increase the credibility of psychological involvement in the treatment of infertility, but will also facilitate communication with both clients and medical personnel involved in treatment. Descriptions of medical options for infertility treatment can be found in existing literature (Keye, 1999; McDaniel, Hepworth, & Doherty, 1992; Meyers et al., 1995; Williams et al., 1992).

Adjunct Psychological Interventions

Given the psychological problems that can be co-morbid with infertility, such as stress, depression, and marital difficulties, a number of psychological interventions have been developed and implemented with infertile individuals who are distressed. Despite the use of these interventions, there is a paucity of research examining their effectiveness (Domar, Seibel, & Benson, 1990; Domar, Zuttermeister, Seibel, & Benson, 1992b). Typical goals of existing interventions include conducting a thorough assessment, treating any psychological problems uncovered during the assessment, providing psychoeducation as to the workings of the reproductive system and assisted reproduction, giving the couple an estimate of their fertility potential, providing emotional support, and counseling the couple as to the various options available to have children (Klock, 1999).

Psychoeducation. Most clinicians agree that any form of psychological intervention should include a component of psychoeducation, where couples are taught about the reproductive system, assisted reproduction techniques, and the psychological problems that can be concomitant with infertility (e.g., Daniluk, 1991). Clinicians and researchers also agree that it is important to help individuals by normalizing their strong reactions to infertility (Mahlstedt et al., 1987), especially so that they feel they are not "crazy" for feeling the way they do (McNaughton-Cassill et al., 2000).

Support Groups. Many infertile couples turn to support groups during times of infertility-related distress. These support groups can serve a normalizing function for couples, where they learn that they are not the only ones experiencing the psychological sequelae of infertility (McNaughton-Cassill et al., 2000). RESOLVE is a national support and informational network for individuals with infertility. Developed by Barbara Eck Menning, the organization has chapters that offer support groups in many major cities. Support groups may primarily function to provide solace and comfort, but are often also used as a venue to teach cognitive behavioral techniques such as relaxation skills, stress management skills, and other coping skills.

Cognitive Behavior Therapies. The majority of therapies conducted with infertility clients utilize a group format and employ some form of cognitive behavior therapy (CBT) as the intervention. Thus, CBT is commonly applied to problems with stress management, relaxation, depression, coping skills, and grief counseling. Myers and Wark (1996) argue that a cognitive behavioral approach is the most appropriate intervention to use with infertile couples for a variety of reasons. First, they argue that the cognitive behavioral approach has established empirical support for a vast array of couples issues (e.g., Baucom & Hoffman, 1986; Gurman, Kniskern, & Pinsof, 1986; Jacobson, Schmaling, & Holtzworth-Munroe, 1987). Second, the cognitive behavioral approach has instituted techniques for awareness and modification of automatic thoughts (Beck, Rush, Shaw, & Emery, 1979) and could address such dysfunctional thoughts in infertile couples. Third, the cognitive behavioral approach also makes use of behavior modification strategies that can be used with infertile couples to overcome avoidance behavior and to alleviate stress and depression. Fourth, the cognitive behavioral approach has been established as an effective way to help couples improve their communication skills, and could help infertile couples express their emotions and needs. Finally, the sexual difficulties experienced by infertile couples could be addressed through validated cognitive behavioral techniques to treat sexual dysfunctions (Masters & Johnson, 1966, 1970). As such, cognitive behavioral therapies applied to the infertile population have received empirical support (Tuschen-Caffier et al., 1999).

McNaughton-Cassill et al. (2000) have developed and investigated the effectiveness of a brief stress management support group for couples in IVF treatment. The group employed a cognitive behavioral format, in which cognitions about fertility were identified and challenged, links between irrational thoughts and expectations and emotional distress were explored, and couples were taught techniques for reframing attributions and generating alternative thoughts and solutions for their problems. Data indicated that overall, couples valued the social support offered in the group and felt the group helped them deal with the stress of IVF treatment.

Domar and colleagues (Domar et al., 1990; 1992b; Domar, Friedman, & Zuttermeister, 1999) have developed and tested the Mind/Body Program for the treatment of stress in infertile couples. These researchers reasoned that it might be useful to apply the relaxation response to the infertile population since it has been established that regular use of the relaxation response leads to decreased tension and stress, and there are data to indicate a relationship between stress and fertility. Researchers tested the hypotheses that infertile women using the relaxation response would have decreased levels of stress and increased rates of conception after completing their 10-week course by collecting pre- and posttreatment measures of stress, anxiety, mood, and anger. The Mind/Body Program for Infertility consists of teaching patients how to elicit the relaxation response, practicing relaxation exercises in a group, and a weekly lecture on a variety of cognitive behavioral topics (e.g., psychoeducation about the relationship between stress and the reproductive system, explanation of the physiology of stress, diaphragmatic breathing, cognitive restructuring and affirmations, nutrition, mindfulness, and emotions). Results indicated dramatic changes from pre- to postintervention. There were significant decreases in measures of depression, tension, and anxiety. Significant increases occurred in measures of mood and activity, and there was a trend to increase the healthy expression of anger. There were also dramatic improvements in subjective reports of feelings of control, security, well-being, and self-esteem. Furthermore, 34% of the participants conceived within 6 months of completing the program. Researchers concluded that regular elicitation of the relaxation response could increase the potential for conception in couples with infertility (Domar et al., 1990). Similar results were found on replication (Domar et al., 1992b; 1999).

Given the effectiveness of the above cognitive behavioral techniques applied to the infertile population, clinicians should also consider using other standard and empirically supported cognitive behavioral therapies, such as those recommended by the Division 12 Task Force on Psychological Interventions (Task Force on Promotion and Dissemination of Psychological Procedures, 1995; Woody & Sanderson, 1998), with clients struggling with stress, depression, and marital difficulties associated with infertility. Empirically supported treatments for relaxation training include Progressive Relaxation Training by Bernstein and Borkovec (1973; see also Carlson & Bernstein, 1995). Linehan's (1993a, 1993b) Dialectical Behavior Therapy has also received empirical support for teaching coping skills to reduce distress.

Cognitive behavioral therapy can also be applied to alleviate the symptoms of depression commonly associated with infertility. Empirically supported cognitive behavioral therapies for depression (Beck, 1995; Beck et al., 1979; Burns, 1980; Lewinsohn, Antonuccio, Breckenridge, & Teri, 1984; Lewinsohn, Munoz, Youngren, & Zeiss, 1992) can help infertility clients through identification of dysfunctional thoughts, relearning/reframing/reattribution and modification of these faulty cognitions, and teaching effective behavioral skills, such as activity schedules, exposure, and behavioral rehearsal of skills aimed at improving mood.

Hunt and Monach (1997) have adapted principles of CBT to the cognitive distortions commonly held by infertility clients. They define and identify the following examples of such thinking with respect to male-factor infertility. First, overgeneralization is defined as taking one event or aspect of an event and drawing a general conclusion from it, such as thinking, "If I cannot father a child, I am not a man at all" (p. 192). Second, selective abstraction is taking one aspect of a situation and defining the entire situation based on that detail, as in thinking, "I cannot have a proper sexual relationship if my spermatozoa are infertile" (p. 192). Third, magnification and minimization are defined as exaggerating the importance of negative aspects of a situation or inappropriately shrinking the positive aspects of the situation, respectively. Examples of magnification and minimization are, "My wife cannot enjoy sex with me if I am not fertile," and "My wife only says she loves me still because she pities me," respectively (pp. 192–193). Fourth, personalization involves seeing oneself as the cause of some negative external event whereas there was actually no personal responsibility. An example of personalization with respect to infertility is thinking, "Now the doctor says that she is not ovulating, maybe this is because of my sperm problems" (p. 193). Finally, Hunt and Monach (1997) define arbitrary inference as jumping to a conclusion without adequate evidence, such as in thinking, "If I had had fewer sexual partners I would still be fertile" (p. 193). In the CBT tradition, clients should be taught how to maintain records of automatic thoughts, which include recording the situation, the feelings experienced, the automatic thought, a challenge to the automatic thought, and the subsequent outcome (Hunt & Monach, 1997). They should also be taught the importance of engaging in pleasant activities, especially those that include sources of satisfaction alternative to fertility (Myers & Wark, 1996).

Given that infertility is commonly associated with relationship difficulties, infertile couples suffering from marital dissatisfaction should be offered an empirically supported cognitive behavioral therapy for couples (e.g., Gottman & Rushe, 1995; Jacobson & Margolin, 1979). In the context of such therapies, couples should learn how to identify and challenge cognitive distortions about infertility and marriage, learn the relationship between behavior exchange and relationship satisfaction, be encouraged to engage in mutually pleasurable activities, be encouraged to seek out sources of satisfaction other than childrearing (Callan & Hennessey, 1989), learn communication skills in order to express and understand each other's feelings about infertility, learn problem-solving skills aimed at helping the couple decide on treatment issues and deal with insensitive social comments, be warned about dangerous interaction patterns of communication such as demand-withdraw (e.g., Christensen & Heavey, 1990), and learn the importance of having sexual intercourse during the most fertile times of the cycle.

Adapting Empirically Supported Treatments to the Medical Setting. Robinson (chapter 2, this volume) has made a number of suggestions for successfully adapting evidence-based treatments into the medical setting. Consistent with her suggestion to reduce treatment length and intensity of treatment, it is suggested that mental health professionals working with infertility patients distil the essence of the above empirically supported treatments into a number of condensed treatment modules. For example, a module on stress reduction and relaxation could be drawn from the empirically supported work of McNaughton-Cassill et al. (2000), Domar and colleagues (Domar et al., 1990, 1992b, 1999), Bernstein and Borkovec (1973), and Linehan (1993a, 1993b). This module could target how to apply cognitive behavioral relaxation and stress reduction techniques to the stress associated with infertility. Similarly, another module for combating the depression commonly associated with infertility could be developed based on the empirically supported work of Beck and colleagues (Beck, 1995; Beck et al., 1979), Burns (1980), Lewinsohn and colleagues (1984, 1992), and Hunt and Monach (1997). This module could target how cognitive distortions associated with infertility affect mood, and how patients can modify their cognitions and use effective behavioral skills in order to enhance their mood. The empirically supported cognitive behavioral work of Gottman and Rushe (1995) and Jacobson et al. (1979) in relationship satisfaction could be used to develop a third module on the relationship problems commonly associated with infertility. This module could target combating cognitive distortions associated with infertility and marriage as well as relationship skills needed to solve marital difficulties resulting from infertility. A fourth module could address assertiveness skills based on the empirically supported work of Gambril (1995). In this module, infertility patients could learn cognitive behavioral skills to deal with intrusive friends and family members and with the social stigmas associated with being infertile in a fertile world. Consistent with Robinson's (chapter 2, this volume) suggestion that mental health professionals working in medicine adopt a "patient education, self-management model," a psychoeducational module aimed at explaining and normalizing the psychological sequelae of infertility, as well as a brief introduction to self-management skills, should be included in the series of modules offered to patients with infertility. The module should outline the causes, diagnoses, and various treatments for infertility. It should also cover options for family building, including the psychosocial issues associated with each. This psychoeducational module, along with referrals to appropriate self-help books and infertility support groups such as RESOLVE, should be part of a standard prevention protocol instituted for each patient in the practice.

All modules should be 2–12 weeks in duration and should meet for 30 to 60 minutes weekly in a group format. Groups should be open, allowing in new patients at any time. Consistent with the Primary Behavioral Health Care Model (Robinson, chapter 2, this volume) group sessions should be conducted in an office nested in the infertility clinic. This approach has the likelihood of further integrating medical and psychosocial care, including the potential benefits of an integrated care program (e.g., Katon et al., 1992; Robinson & Strosahl, 2000). In the context of a stepped-care model, patients should first be referred to these groups then further referred to individual therapy if their symptoms persist or worsen.

Ideally, patients entering medical treatment for infertility would be given a brief battery of psychological measures aimed at assessing the level of distress associated with their fertility problems. Consistent with the population care model used in medicine, all infertility patients, regardless of their scores on the measures, would be offered the psychoeducational and self-management skills module described above. This model of service delivery aims to improve the health of the entire community of infertile patients by preventing psychosocial distress associated with infertility, identifying and treating distress early on, and supporting healthy lifestyles in order to maximize chances of pregnancy and live birth (Robinson, chapter 2, this volume). However, patients with elevated scores on measures of psychosocial distress would be referred to modules appropriate to their type of distress. All patients should be given a brief battery of psychosocial questionnaires on a monthly basis to monitor their progress on the psychological sequelae of infertility. Patients with improved scores can then titrate their treatment by decreasing the number of sessions they attend and eventually terminating sessions. These patients should schedule follow-up and booster sessions as needed. Patients with scores indicating increased distress should either attend group sessions more often or more consistently, or should be offered individual sessions in the context of a stepped-care model. Of course, any change in the patient's psychosocial status should be communicated with physicians immediately.

Treatment Compliance. Little empirical data exist with respect to the treatment compliance of patients seeking medical treatment for infertility. Given the highly desirable outcome of having their own biological child, the tremendous financial investment in the treatment, and patient's willingness to undergo painful and invasive fertility procedures for years, it can be assumed that infertility patients are highly motivated for treatment and tend to be compliant with treatment. One study investigating the reasons for termination of fertility treatment did not cite problems with compliance as a common reason to discontinue treatment (Hofmann, Jeschke, & Jeschke, 1985). In a study analyzing the motivation and compliance of andrology patients, researchers concluded that patients who desired a child demonstrated higher levels of cooperation and compliance (Pusch, 1985).

Compliance with psychosocial treatments for the psychological sequelae of infertility has also received little empirical analysis. Most treatment-outcome studies in this field did not cite attrition rates or explicitly make any references to problems with treatment compliance. However, Domar et al. (1992b) reported that only 5–10% of self-referred patients evaluated for group therapy did not join the group, and many did not join for practical reasons (e.g., scheduling conflicts, geographical relocation, conception before treatment). Although it is likely that infertility patients will be generally compliant with psychosocial treatments for the psychological sequelae of infertility, it is important to monitor and address compliance, especially upon initial referral and if patients are concerned with the stigmas of infertility or psychotherapy. In order to maximize compliance with psychosocial treatment, it is essential to integrate it with medical treatment for infertility. All patients who enter treatment should be given a full psychosocial assessment and attend a psychoeducational treatment module on the psychological sequelae of infertility. Patients who demonstrate elevated scores on specific psychological symptoms should be referred to other appropriate treatment modules. Physicians and MHPs should be in close communication regarding any changes in patient status, and the relationships between mental health, physical health, and fertility should be explained to all patients.

Long-Term Management. Because successful medical treatment for infertility can take many years and because some couples are never able to achieve live birth through medically assisted reproduction despite years of trying, it is important to consider long-term management of infertility. Within the context of a stepped-care model, patients demonstrating psychological sequelae of infertility should be initially treated in a group-therapy format. If their symptoms persist or worsen, these patients should be referred to individual therapists for treatment of their psychological problems associated with infertility. However, if their symptoms improve, patients seeking continued psychosocial treatment could be referred to community support groups for infertility, such as those provided by RESOLVE.

Patients with prolonged medical treatment failures should be advised to consider the option of stopping medical treatment for infertility. Many patients are so hopeful to have a biologically related child that they have not even considered alternatives, even in the face of continued treatment failures (Stephenson, 1987). MHPs can gently help such infertility patients to gradually consider and get used to the idea that they may not have biological children of their own. However, MHPs should emphasize to patients that they still have choices, even though those choices may not include biologically related children. MHPs can help infertility patients to explore alternatives such as adoption, artificial insemination by donor, surrogate motherhood, and child-free living. The pros and cons of each alternative, as well as couple's reactions to these alternatives, should be processed. Issues of couple disagreement over alternatives should be addressed. In addition, it is important to help patients grieve the loss of the potential for having biologically related children.

Collaboration Between Mental Health Professionals and Infertility Physicians. It is important to note that the above therapies received empirical support when they were delivered by competent master's- or doctoral-level psychotherapists. Thus, treatment for the psychological sequelae of infertility should be delivered by licensed psychologists or psychiatrists, or by therapists being supervised by such licensed professionals. These MHPs should collaborate with the physicians whose clients they share in order to ensure the most integrated and continuous care. Collaboration between MHPs and physicians can be maximized in the following ways. First, the MHP should emphasize to the physicians the potential benefits of collaboration. The pressures faced by infertility specialists are similar to those faced by primary care doctors with respect to heavy patient loads, being confronted with the psychosocial problems of their patients, having limited time with their patients, and dealing with treatment compliance issues. MHPs should describe how they could reduce the physician's treatment load by splitting the responsibilities such that MHPs address the patient's psychosocial issues and the physicians address the medical issues. Consistent with the Primary Behavioral Health Model, MHPs would not take charge of the patient's care but would manage the patient within the structure of the integrated health-care team (Robinson, chapter 2, this volume). Given the possible connection between stress and infertility, it should also be emphasized that improved psychological well-being may also increase the physician's conception rates. MHPs should also explain how they can use psychological principles (such as motivational interviewing) to improve patient compliance with medical regimens. Second, on a broader level, MHPs can maximize collaboration with physicians by publishing in medically oriented infertility journals. Such publications could educate physicians about the psychological sequelae associated with infertility, the relationship between stress and infertility, psychosocial treatments for the emotional sequelae of infertility, and the importance of collaboration with MHPs. Third, these topics could also be addressed in workshop format. Such workshops could be presented by MHPs at national conferences for reproductive endocrinologists and obstetricians/gynecologists. Fourth, MHPs could benefit by forming a professional alliance with national organizations for reproductive endocrinologists and obstetricians/gynecologists (e.g., American Fertility Society, American College of OB/GYN). Finally, on an individual and local basis, MHPs can maximize collaboration with physicians by keeping open the lines of communication regarding their shared patients. The more physicians are given updates regarding the patients they refer to MHPs, the more likely they will be to reciprocate with vital medical information that may affect psychological functioning, act as a team with MHPs in providing the most seamless patient care and maximizing treatment outcomes, and continue referring patients with mental health concerns. Ideally, all members of the integrated health care team, including MHPs, nurses, and physicians, would meet weekly to discuss the status of each patient and to provide the most seamless and integrated patient care.

Prior to starting psychotherapy, all patients should have a clear understanding of the collaborative nature of the relationship between their MHP and their fertility specialist. Patients should know that their therapist and their physician will be discussing their case in order to provide the most integrated care and to maximize the chances of live births for the patients. However, this open sharing of information between therapists and physicians may impede some patients from seeking mental health services or from being forthcoming with psychological difficulties if patients fear the doctors will deem then "bad patients" or "bad parents" and discontinue treatment for infertility. Because patients must rely on their infertility specialist to help them achieve their dream of having a baby, they may conceal their true feelings of fear, anxiety, sadness, anger, disappointment, and grief. They may also conceal marital difficulties for fear that their doctor may see them as potentially poor parents. If patients know that their therapist will share information with their physician, they may also avoid disclosing their emotional difficulties to their mental health specialist. Validating and normalizing their reactions to infertility and medical treatment can assuage patient's fears. It is also crucial for therapists to share with patients the parameters around confidentiality and the types of information that can be shared with physicians.

It is suggested that physicians not have access to patient's weekly session notes, but that a monthly progress checklist noting patient attendance in sessions, changes in scores on psychological measures of distress, and a listing of general patient issues being addressed be used. For example, therapists can share with physicians that their patients attended three group sessions this month in which the following topics were addressed: relaxation techniques, increasing pleasant events, and communication skills. Scores on psychological measures could be relayed in graph format, charting changes in scores across time. MHPs should be sure to include brief remarks on the clinical meanings and significance of the scores. Therapists should also be sure to convey information about techniques used to increase patient compliance with medical regimens. As noted above, although motivation for treatment and patient compliance tend to be very high in this population, one area of difficulty in compliance is getting couples to abstain from sexual intercourse during certain nonfertile parts of the menstrual cycle and to engage in intercourse during the fertile times of the cycle. Therapists should note to physicians that they are addressing this problem using behavioral techniques.

Potential Medical Cost Offset

If there is indeed a connection between stress and fertility, and if a reduction of stress does contribute to increased fertility rates, as has been suggested in the literature (e.g., Harrison, O'Moore, & O'Moore, 1986a; 1986b; McGrady, 1984; Moghissi & Wallach, 1983; O'Moore, O'Moore, Harrison, Murphy, & Carruthers, 1983; Pook, Rohrle, & Krause, 1999), then it may be hypothesized that a reduction of stress and other psychological problems co-morbid with infertility has the potential to enhance the effectiveness of medical infertility treatment. Couples who are less distressed, using effective coping skills, and communicating well may be more likely to adhere to infertility treatment; cope well with the stress of treatment; stay in treatment long enough to conceive (Domar, 1997); have regular sexual intercourse, especially during times of greatest possible fertility; and therefore maximize their chances of conceiving.

Although there is a logically compelling argument for the addition of behavioral health care to the standard medical treatment of infertility, there are as yet no data regarding the potential medical cost offset of such an addition. Empirical analysis is needed in order to assess the effects of adding psychosocial treatments for patients suffering from the psychological sequelae of infertility. Such analysis should consider the direct costs, such as therapist fees (approximately $120–150 per hour of group sessions led by a Ph.D.-level therapist and $50–75 for a master's-level therapist or social worker). It is also crucial to consider potential indirect costs for infertility patients, such as reduced productivity and days off work due to psychosocial symptoms related to infertility, and the threat to the reproduction and continuity of the patient's family. If stress does diminish fertility, then additional potential indirect costs include decreased effectiveness (rate of successful pregnancies) and efficiency (number of cycles required to achieve successful pregnancy) of medical fertility treatments, which may then lead to increased medical costs and cyclical deterioration of psychological functioning.

References

American Society for Reproductive Medicine (1998). *Fact sheet: in vitro fertilization (IVF)*. Birmingham, AL: Author.

Andrews, F. M., Abbey, A., & Halman, L J. (1991). Stress from infertility, marriage factors, and subjective well-being of wives and husbands. *Journal of Health and Social Behavior, 32*(3), 238–253.

Applegarth, L. D., & Kingsberg, S. A. (1999). The donor as patient: Assessment and support. In L. H. Burns & S. N. Covington (Eds.), *Infertility counseling: A comprehensive handbook for clinicians* (pp. 357–374). New York: Parthenon.

Baucom, D. H., & Hoffman, J. A. (1986). The effectiveness of marital therapy: Current status and application to the clinical setting. In N. S. Jacobson & A. S. Gurman (Eds.), *Clinical handbook of marital therapy* (pp. 597–620). New York: Guilford.

Beck, A. T., Rush, A. J., Shaw, B. F., & Emery, G. (1979). *Cognitive therapy of depression*. New York: Guilford.

Beck, A. T., & Steer, R. A. (1987) (revised 1993). *Beck depression inventory manual*. New York: Psychological Corporation/Harcourt Brace Jovanovich.

Beck, A. T., Steer, R. A., & Garbin, M. (1998). Psychometric properties of the Beck Depression Inventory: Twenty-five years of evaluation. *Clinical Psychology Review, 8*, 77–100.

Beck, J. S. (1995). *Cognitive therapy: Basics and beyond*. New York: Guilford.

Bernstein, D. A., & Borkovec, T. D. (1973). *Progressive relaxation training: A manual for the helping professions*. Champaign, IL: Research Press.

Bernstein, J., Potts, N., & Mattox, J. H. (1985). Assessment of psychological dysfunction associated with infertility. *Journal of Obstetrics, Gynecology, and Neonatal Nursing, 14*(6 suppl.), 63s–66s.

Brkovich, A. M., & Fisher, W. A. (1998). Psychological distress and infertility: Forty years of research. *Journal of Psychosomatic Obstetrics and Gynaecology, 19*(4), 218–228.

Burns, D. D. (1980). *Feeling good: The new mood therapy*. New York: Avon Books.

Callan, V. J., & Hennessey, J. F. (1989). Strategies for coping with infertility. *British Journal of Medical Psychology, 62*, 343–354.

Carlson, C. R., & Bernstein, D. A. (1995). Relaxation skills training: Abbreviated progressive relaxation. In W. T. O'Donohue & L. Krasner (Eds.), *Handbook of psychological skills training: Clinical techniques and applications*. Boston: Allyn & Bacon.

Christensen, A., & Heavey, C. L. (1990). Gender and social structure in the demand-withdraw pattern of marital conflict. *Journal of Personality and Social Psychology, 59*, 73–81.

Cook, E. P. (1987). Characteristics of the biopsychosocial crisis of infertility. *Journal of Counseling & Development, 65*(9), 465–470.

Daniluk, J. C. (1988). Infertility: Intrapersonal and interpersonal impact. *Fertility and Sterility, 49*(6), 982–990.

Daniluk, J. C. (1991). Strategies for counseling infertile couples. *Journal of Counseling and Development, 69*, 317–320.

Domar, A. D. (1997). Stress and infertility in women. In S. R. Leiblum (Ed.), *Infertility: Psychological issues and counseling strategies* (pp. 67–82). New York: Wiley.

Domar, A. D., Broome, A., Zuttermeister, P. C., Seibel, M., & Friedman, R. (1992). The prevalence and predictability of depression in infertile women. *Fertility and Sterility, 58*(6), 1158–1163.

Domar, A. D., Friedman, R., & Zuttermeister, P. C. (1999). Distress and conception in infertile women: A complementary approach. *Journal of the American Women's Association, 54*(4), 196–198.

Domar, A. D., & Seibel, M. (1990). Emotional aspects of infertility. In M. M. Seibel (Ed.), *Infertility: A comprehensive text* (pp. 23–35). Norwalk, CT: Appleton & Lange.

Domar, A. D., Seibel, M., & Benson, H. (1990). The mind/body program for infertility: A new behavioral treatment approach for women with infertility. *Fertility and Sterility, 53*(2), 246–249.

Domar, A. D., Zuttermeister, P. C., Seibel, M., & Benson, H. (1992a). The prevalence and predictability of depression in infertile women. *Fertility and Sterility, 58*(6), 1158–1163.

Domar, A. D., Zuttermeister, P. C., Seibel, M., & Benson, H. (1992b). Psychological improvement in infertile women after behavioral treatment: A replication. *Fertility and Sterility, 58*(1), 144–147.

Downey, J., Yingling, S., McKinney, M., Husami, N., Jewelewicz, R. & Maidman, J. (1989). Mood disorders, psychiatric symptoms, and distress in women presenting for infertility evaluation. *Fertility and Sterility, 52*(3), 425–432.

Epstein, Y. M., & Rosenberg, H. S. (1997). He does, she doesn't; she does, he doesn't: Couple conflicts about infertility. In S. R. Leiblum (Ed.), *Infertility: Psychological issues and counseling strategies* (pp. 129–148). New York: Wiley.

Freeman, E. W., Boxer, A. S., Rickels, K., Tureck, R., & Mastroianni, L. (1985). Psychological evaluation and support in a program of *in vitro* fertilization and embryo transfer. *Fertility and Sterility, 43*(1), 48–53.

Galst, J. P. (1986). Stress and stress management for the infertile couple: A cognitive-behavioral approach to the psychological sequelae of infertility. *Infertility, 9*, 171–179.

Gambril, E. (1995). Assertion skills training. In W. T. O'Donohue & L. Krasner (Eds), *Handbook of psychological skills training: Clinical techniques and applications* (pp. 81–118). Needham Heights, MA: Allyn & Bacon.

Glover, L., Hunter, M., Richards, J., Katz, M., & Abel, P. D. (1999). Development of the Fertility Adjustment Scale. *Fertility and Sterility, 72*(4), 623–628.

Gottman, J., & Rushe, R. (1995). Communication skills and social skills approaches to treating ailing marriages: A recommendation for a new marital therapy called "Minimal Marital Therapy." In W. T. O'Donohue & L. Krasner (Eds.), *Handbook of psychological skills training: Clinical techniques and applications* (pp. 287–305). Boston: Allyn & Bacon.

Greenfeld, D. A. (1999). Recipient counseling for oocyte donation. In L. H. Burns & S. N. Covington (Eds.), *Infertility counseling: A comprehensive handbook for clinicians* (pp. 345–356). New York: Parthenon.

Greil, A. L. (1991). *Not yet pregnant: Infertile couples in contemporary America.* New Brunswick: Rutgers University Press.

Greil, A. L. (1997). Infertility and psychological distress: A critical review of the literature. *Social Science and Medicine, 45*(11), 1679–1704.

Gurman, A. S., Kniskern, D. P., & Pinsof, W. M. (1986). Research on the process and outcome of marital and family therapy. In S. L. Garfield & A. E. Bergen (Eds.), *Handbook of psychotherapy and behavior change* (3rd ed., pp. 565–624). New York: Wiley.

Harrison, R. F, O'Moore, R. R., & O'Moore, A. M. (1986a). Stress and fertility: Some modalities of investigation and treatment in couples with unexplained infertility in Dublin. *International Journal of Infertility, 31*, 153–155.

Harrison, R. F, O'Moore, R. R., & O'Moore, A. M. (1986b). Stress and fertility: Some modalities of investigation and treatment in couples with unexplained infertility in Dublin. *International Journal of Infertility, 31*, 156.

Hofmann, R., Jeschke, A., & Jeschke, B. (1985). Problems in the discontinuation of sterility treatment. *Zentralbl Gynakol., 107*(5), 294–299.

Hull, M. G. R., Glazener, C. M. A., Kelly, N. J., Conway, D. I., Foster, P. A., Hinton, R. A. et al. (1985). Population study of causes, treatment, and outcome of infertility. *British Medical Journal, 291*, 1693–1697.

Hunsley, J., Pinsent, C., Lefebvre, M., James-Tanner, S., & Vito, D. (1995). Construct validity of the short forms of the Dyadic Adjustment Scale. *Family Relations, 44*, 231–237.

Hunt, J. (1992). Issues in infertility and adoption. In A. Burnell, D. Reich, & P. Sawbridge (Eds.), *Infertility and adoption* (pp.). London: Post Adoption Centre.

Hunt, J., & Monach, J. H. (1997). Beyond the bereavement model: The significance of depression for infertility counselling. *Human Reproduction, 12*(11 suppl.), 188–194.

Jacobson, N. S., & Margolin, G. (1979). *Marital therapy: Strategies based on social learning and behavior exchange principles.* New York: Brunner/Mazel.

Jacobson, N. S., Schmaling, K. B., & Holtzworth-Munroe, A. (1987). Component analysis of behavioral marital therapy: Two-year follow-up and prediction of relapse. *Journal of Marital and Family Therapy, 13*, 187–195.

Katon, W., Von Korff, M., Lin, E., Bush, T., Lipscomb, P., & Russo, J. (1992). A randomized trial of psychiatric consultation with distressed high utilizers. *General Hospital Psychiatry, 14*, 86–98.

Keye, W. R., Jr. (1999). Medical aspects of infertility for the counselor. In L. H. Burns & S. N. Covington (Eds.), *Infertility counseling: A comprehensive text for clinicians* (pp. 27–46). New York: Parthenon.

Klock, S. C. (1999). Psychosocial evaluation of the infertile patient. In L. H. Burns & S. N. Covington (Eds.), *Infertility counseling: A comprehensive text for clinicians.* New York: Parthenon.

Kraft, A. D., Palombo, J., Mitchell, D., Dean, C., Meyers, S., & Schmidt, A. W. (1980). The psychological dimension of infertility. *American Journal of Orthopsychiatry, 50*(4), 618–628.

Leiblum, S. R. (1988). Infertility. In E. A. Blechman & K. D. Brownell (Eds.), *Handbook of behavioral medicine for women* (pp. 116–125). New York: Pergamon.

Leiblum, S. R. (1993). The impact of infertility on sexual and marital satisfaction. *Annual Review of Sex Research, 4*, 99–120.

Lewinsohn, P. M., Antonuccio, D. O., Breckenridge, J. S., & Teri, L. (1984). *The coping with depression course.* Eugene, OR: Castalia.

Lewinshohn, P. M., Munoz, R. F., Youngren, M. A., & Zeiss, A. M. (1992). *Control your depression.* New York: Simon & Schuster.

Linehan, M. M. (1993a). *Cognitive-behavioral treatment of borderline personality disorder.* New York: Guilford.

Linehan, M. M. (1993b). *Skills training manual for treating borderline personality disorder.* New York: Guilford.

Lukse, M. P., & Vacc, N. A. (1999). Grief, depression, and coping in women undergoing infertility treatment. *Obstetrics and Gynecology, 93*(2), 245–251.

Mahlstedt, P. P. (1985). The psychological component of infertility. *Fertility and Sterility, 43*, 335–346.

Mahlstedt, P. P., McDuff, S., & Bernstein, J. (1987). Emotional factors and the in vitro fertilization and embryo transfer process. *Journal of In Vitro Fertilization and Embryo Transfer, 4*, 232–236.

Marteau, T. M., & Bekker, H. (1992). The development of a six-item short-form of the Speilberger State-Trait Anxiety Inventory (STAI). *British Journal of Clinical Psychology, 31*(3), 301–306.

Masters, W. H., & Johnson, V. E. (1966). *Human sexual response.* Boston: Little, Brown.

Masters, W. H., & Johnson, V. E. (1970). *Human sexual inadequacy.* Boston: Little, Brown.

McDaniel, S. H., Hepworth, J., & Doherty, W. (1992). Medical family therapy with couples facing infertility. *The American Journal of Family Therapy, 20*(2), 101–122.

McGrady, A. V. (1984). Effects of psychological stress on male reproduction: A review. *Archives of Andrology, 13*, 1.

McNaughton-Cassill, M. E., Bostwick, M., Vanscoy, S. E., Arthur, N. J., Hichman, T. N., Robinson, R. D. et al. (2000). Development of brief stress management support groups for couples undergoing *in vitro* fertilization treatment. *Fertility and Sterility, 74*(1), 87–93.

Menning, B. E. (1980). The emotional needs of infertile couples. *Fertility and Sterility, 34*(4), 313–319.

Menning, B. E. (1988). *Infertility: A guide for the childless couple* (2nd ed.). New York: Prentice Hall.

Meyers, M., Diamond, R., Kezur, D., Scharf, C., Weinshel, M., & Rait, D. S. (1995). An infertility primer for family therapists: I. Medical, social, and psychological dimensions. *Family Process, 34*(2), 219–229.

Moghissi, K. S. (1978). Maternal nutrition in pregnancy. *Clinical Obstetrics and Gynecology, 21*(2), 297–310.

Moghissi, K. S., & Wallach, E. E. (1983). Unexplained infertility. *Fertility and Sterility, 39*(1), 5–31.

Mosher, W. D., & Pratt, W. F. (1990). Fecundity and infertility in the United States, 1965–1988. *Advance Data, 192*, 1–9.

Myers, L B., & Wark, L. (1996). Psychotherapy for infertility: A cognitive-behavioral approach for couples. *American Journal of Family Therapy, 24*(1), 9–20.

Neumann, P. J., Gharib, S. D., & Weinstein, M. C. (1994). The cost of a successful delivery with in vitro fertilization. *New England Journal of Medicine, 331*(4), 239–243.

Newton, C. R., Sherrard, M. A., & Glavac, I. (1999). The Fertility Problem Inventory: Measuring perceived infertility-related stress. *Fertility and Sterility, 72*(1), 54–62.

Olsen, J. (1990). Subfecundity according to age of the mother and father. *Danish Medical Bulletin, 37*, 281–282.

O'Moore, A. M., O'Moore, R. R., Harrison, R. F., Murphy, G., & Carruthers, M. E. (1983). Psychosomatic aspects in idiopathic infertility: Effects of treatment with autogenic training. *Journal of Psychosomatic Research, 27*(2), 145–151.

Page, H. (1988). The increasing demand for infertility treatment. *Health Trends, 20*(4), 115–118.

Pook, M., Rohrle, B., & Krause, W. (1999). Individual prognosis for changes in sperm quality on the basis of perceived distress. *Psychotherapy and Psychosomatics, 68*(2), 95–101.

Pusch, H. H. (1985). Motivation and compliance of andrology patients. *Andrologia, 17*(2), 194–199.

Robinson, P., & Strosahl, K. (2000). Improving care for a primary care population: Depression as an example. In M. E.Marnish (Ed.), *Handbook of psychological assessment in primary care settings* (pp. 687–711). Mahwah, NJ: Lawrence Erlbaum.

Sharpley, C. F., & Cross, D. G. (1982). A psychometric evaluation of the Spanier Dyadic Adjustment Scale. *Journal of Marriage and the Family, 44*, 739–741.

Sharpley, C. F., & Rogers, H. J. (1984). Preliminary validation of the Abbreviated Spanier Dyadic Adjustment Scale: Some psychometric data regarding a screening test of marital adjustment. *Educational and Psychological Measurement, 44*, 1045–1049.

Spanier, G. B. (1976). Measuring dyadic adjustment: New scales for assessing the quality of marriage and similar dyads. *Journal of Marriage and the Family, 38*, 15–28.

Spielberger, C. D., Gorsuch, R. L., & Luschene, R. (1970). *The State-Trait Anxiety Inventory manual.* Palo Alto: Consulting Psychologists Press.

Spielberger, C. D., Gorsuch, R. L., Luschene, R., Vagg, P. R., & Jacobs, G. A. (1983). *Manual for the State-Trait Anxiety Inventory (Form Y) (Self-evaluation questionnaire).* Palo Alto, CA: Consulting Psychologists Press.

Stanton, A. L., & Burns, L. H. (1999). Behavioral medicine approaches to infertility counseling. In L. H. Burns & S. N. Covington (Eds.), *Infertility counseling: A comprehensive text for clinicians* (pp. 129–147). New York: Parthenon.

Stanton, A. L., & Dunkel-Schetter, C. (1991). *Infertility: Perspectives from stress and coping research.* New York: Plenum.

Stephenson, L. R. (1987). *Give us a child: Coping with the personal crisis of infertility.* New York: Harper & Row.

Taymor, M. L. (1979). Emotional stress and infertility. *Infertility, 2*(1), 39–47.

Task Force on Promotion and Dissemination of Psychological Procedures. (1995). Training in and dissemination of empirically-validated psychological treatments: Report and recommendations. *Clinical Psychologist, 48*(1), 3–23.

Tuschen-Caffier, B., Florin, I., Krause, W., & Pook, M. (1999). Cognitive-behavioral therapy for idiopathic infertile couples. *Psychotherapy and Psychosomatics, 68*(1), 15–21.

Whiteford, L. M., & Gonzales, L. (1995). Stigma: The hidden burden of infertility. *Social Science and Medicine, 40*(1), 27–36.

Williams, L., Bischoff, R., & Ludes, J. (1992). A biopsychosocial model for treating infertility. *Contemporary Family Therapy: An International Journal, 14*(4), 309–322.

Woody, S. R., & Sanderson, W. C. (1998). Manuals for empirically supported treatments: 1998 update. *Clinical Psychologist, 51*(1), 17–21.

Wright, J., Allard, M., Lecours, A., & Sabourin, S. (1989). Psychosocial distress and infertility: A review of controlled research. *International Journal of Fertility, 34*(2), 126–142.

Zolbrod, A. P., & Covington, S. N. (1999). Recipient counseling for donor insemination. In L. H. Burns & S. N. Covington (Eds.), *Infertility counseling: A comprehensive handbook for clinicians* (pp. 325–344). New York: Parthenon.

Chapter 12
The Integration of Psychosocial Interventions Into the Oncology Practice

ADRIENNE H. KOVACS AND ARTHUR C. HOUTS

More than one third of North Americans will be diagnosed with cancer during their lifetimes (Greenlee, Hill-Harmon, Murray, & Thun, 2001; National Cancer Institute of Canada, 2001). Cancer is the second-leading cause of death in the United States (Greenlee et al., 2001). Cancer is not a single disease; rather, it is a group of related diseases that involve the uncontrolled growth and spread of abnormal cells. Tumors that are formed from this atypical cell division may be benign or malignant, and it is the malignant tumors that are diagnosed as cancer. Not all cancers result in the formation of tumors, however. Cancer cells may also exist in the blood and blood-forming organs (bone marrow, lymphatic system, and spleen). Among men, the most common diagnoses are prostate, lung and bronchus, and colorectal cancers, whereas among women, breast, colorectal, and lung and bronchus cancers are most frequently diagnosed (Greenlee et al., 2001). In a process known as metastasis, cells from malignant tumors may invade other tissues and organs by breaking away from the original tumor site and entering the bloodstream or lymphatic system. As cancer in this new location still consists of abnormal cells from the original site, it retains the original name. For example, if breast cancer spreads to the brain, this is referred to as metastatic breast cancer (i.e., not brain cancer). In addition to description referring to the original site of the abnormal cell activity, cancers are "staged" according to the extent of the disease, with higher stages indicative of disease that is more advanced and has spread from the original site. Within the tumor node metastasis (TNM) staging system, tumors are assigned a stage of I, II, III, or IV; within the summary staging system, cancers are labeled as in situ, local, regional, or distant.

Treatment options include surgery, radiation, chemotherapy, hormonal therapy, and immunotherapy. In addition to the surgical removal of the cancerous tumor, surrounding tissue and lymph nodes may also be removed. Surgery is often accompanied by radiotherapy, the use of high-energy particles or waves to destroy cancer cells at a specific site. Radiation therapy may be used before surgery for the purpose of shrinking the tumor (neoadjuvant surgery) or afterward in order to destroy any remaining cancer cells (adjuvant therapy). Radiotherapy can also be used without surgery, particularly if surgery is not possible, and it may also be recommended for pain relief. In contrast to the localized effects of surgery and radiation therapy, chemotherapy, hormone therapy, and immunotherapy are referred to as systemic treatments because they do not target one specific location. Chemotherapy, the administration of drugs to kill cancer cells, may be the only treatment, may be used in conjunction with radiotherapy, and may precede or follow surgery in a neoadjuvant or adjuvant fashion. Chemotherapy drugs, which can be administered orally or injected, travel through the bloodstream and reach all cells, both cancerous and healthy. Side effects often occur as a result of the drugs' impact on healthy cells, including cells that fight infection, carry oxygen throughout the body, or line the digestive tract. The side effects associated with these five treatments may be short term (e.g., fatigue, hair loss, nausea, and vomiting) or long term and even permanent (e.g., loss of fertility). Hormone therapy refers to the administration of drugs that interfere with hormone activity or the surgical removal of hormone-producing glands. This treatment targets cancers that involve hormones in the proliferation of abnormal cells (e.g., ovarian and testicular cancer). Immunotherapy, also known as biological therapy, enhances the body's own immune system to fight against treatment side effects or the cancer itself. For example, patients may undergo bone marrow transplantation or stem cell transplantation in order to replace those cells damaged by chemotherapy or radiotherapy with healthy cells. Each of these five treatment options may be used alone or in combination with other treatments. The overall treatment approach is determined by several factors including the location and stage of cancer and whether the disease has spread throughout the body. Cancer is a physical disease, but as with many other diseases, cancer affects the broader overall functioning of patients.

Biopsychosocial Aspects of Cancer

This chapter presents a biopsychosocial conceptualization of the cancer experience. In addition to changes at the cellular level, cancer typically has broader effects on an individual's physical, psychological, and interpersonal functioning.

The impact of cancer on one's body is not limited to specific cancerous cells. The disease and its treatment can affect physical well-being in a variety of ways. Fatigue is one of the most commonly reported symptoms. Estimates of Canadian and American cancer patients who experience fatigue range from 70–78% (Ashbury, Findlay, Reynolds, & McKerracher, 1998; Smets, Garssen, Schuster-Uitterhoeve, & de Haes, 1993). Patients undergoing chemotherapy or radiation therapy typically report greater levels of fatigue than cancer-free individuals (Irvine, Vincent, Graydon, Bubela, & Thompson, 1994; Jacobsen et al., 1999). In addition to increased reports of fatigue, almost half of all cancer patients experience sleep disturbance (Beszterczey & Lipowski, 1977). Regular sleep patterns are particularly susceptible to disruption during hospitalization or when a patient is experiencing pain attributed to treatment or the disease itself. Individuals with cancer may experience pain at any stage of the disease process, and this pain may be persistent (Greenwald, Bonica, & Bergner, 1987). Daut and Cleeland (1982) observed that, depending on the location and stage of cancer, the prevalence of patient-reported pain ranged from 0% to 75%. It was highest among cancer patients with metastatic disease. Unfortunately, research suggests that unmet analgesic needs and situations in which doctors' estimates of patient pain are less than patient reports are rather common (Peteet, Tay, Cohen, & MacIntyre, 1986; Zhukovsky, Gorowski, Hausdorff, Napolitano, & Lesser, 1995). Among individuals with cancer, it is clear that the majority will experience at least some degree of pain, fatigue, and/or sleep disturbance.

With regard to the psychological changes that may accompany cancer diagnoses and treatments, the experiences are likely to vary among individuals. The impact of cancer on mood and symptoms of depression and anxiety is addressed in the next section. There are, however, other ways in which cancer can affect an individual's emotional or cognitive functioning. Individuals with cancer may strive to make meaning of this event or to reprioritize aspects of their lives (Curbow, Somerfield,

Baker, Wingard, & Legro, 1993; Taylor, 1983). They may experience a change in self-identity when faced with changes in appearance, such as the loss of a breast, postsurgical scarring, or hair loss due to chemotherapy. Depending on the size and location of the tumor, individuals with cancer of the brain may undergo changes in personality or memory. At the behavioral level, whether by necessity or choice, cancer patients commonly experience at least a temporary change in their daily activities. For example, daily radiotherapy appointments may replace morning routines for several weeks. Individuals may also decide to change their diet, exercise patterns, or tobacco and alcohol consumption after receiving a cancer diagnosis. In summary, cancer patients typically experience psychological changes across affective, cognitive, and behavioral domains.

The various physical and psychological changes associated with cancer diagnoses and treatments do not affect only the patient. They may also affect family members, friends, and coworkers as well as patients' relationships with these individuals. Within marriages, communication difficulties and role shifts may occur (Lichtman, Taylor, & Wood, 1988). It has also been estimated that 20–90% of cancer patients experience sexual dysfunction or dissatisfaction, with higher rates of sexual difficulties reported among gynecologic patients (Andersen, 1985). Such changes in communication and sexual functioning affect both patients and their partners. In addition, cancer patients may experience rather significant changes in their social environments. For example, they may begin spending increased time interacting with members of their health-care team and other cancer patients, and spend less time with coworkers or casual friends. Friends and family members, who may themselves be attempting to find meaning in their loved one's cancer, may alter the way in which they interact with the patient. They may withdraw due to personal discomfort or fear regarding the situation. Alternatively, they may begin spending increased amounts of quality time with the cancer patient. There are also situations in which social interactions may be extremely affected due to the cancer experience. In order to avoid infections, individuals who have recently undergone bone marrow transplantation, for example, have extremely limited social contact, even with close family members.

Although cancer diagnoses and treatments are often associated with biological, psychological, or social changes, these three domains are not easily separated. For example, it is rarely possible to separate physical effects from the psychological or social changes that accompany cancer. Fatigue, one of the most commonly reported symptoms among cancer patients, is associated with greater levels of anxiety and depression and poorer physical and mental health (Hann, Jacobsen, Martin, Azzarello, & Greenberg, 1998). Spiegel, Sands, and Koopman (1994) have found that cancer patients who reported higher levels of pain were more likely to be given a clinical diagnosis of depression. This was observed despite a history of more frequent episodes of major depression among individuals who reported lower pain. In addition, Daut and Cleeland (1982) have reported that cancer patients with the highest reports of physical pain were more likely to report that this pain interfered with their usual activity level and enjoyment of life. As a general strategy, it is inappropriate to explore any single change associated with the cancer experience in isolation of other changes.

Assessment Strategies

Within this biopsychosocial framework, it is evident that the majority of individuals will experience at least some degree of change when coping with a cancer diagnosis and its subsequent treatment. Mental health professionals have moved from the traditional mental health field into oncology settings and offered interventions in order to improve patients' cancer experiences. It would be very appealing if there were an accurate method of identifying a select group of cancer patients who are in most need of intervention, are most likely to participate in interventions, and would realize the most benefits from participation. In addition to the attempt to identify the need for treatment, there are two other reasons why mental health professionals should be aware of methods used in the assessment of cancer patients. First, consistent with the scientist-practitioner model, even individuals who do not plan to publish their results should assess the impact of their interventions. Second, issues of quality assurance demand the systematic evaluation of treatment effectiveness. In order to survive in the oncology setting, mental health professionals must be prepared to "prove" their worthiness to physicians and managed-care organizations. The clear interpretation of results obtained from standardized assessment instruments should aid in this process. Two approaches for the systematic assessment of cancer patients for the purposes of recruitment into psycho-oncology interventions and the systematic evaluation of these interventions are presented. Finally, a third approach that could be applied to all cancer patients is considered.

Traditional Mental Health Assessment

Many researchers have offered support for the psychological screening of cancer patients (Greer, 1989; McDaniel, Musselman, & Nemeroff, 1997; Payne, Hoffman, Theodoulou, Dosik, & Massie, 1999; Zabora, Smith-Wilson, Fetting, & Enterline, 1990). This approach is based upon the notion that such screening will be an efficient way of determining who is in most need of psychological intervention. Some researchers limit participation in psychosocial interventions to individuals who report high levels of psychological distress (Ford et al., 1990; Greer et al., 1992; Telch & Telch, 1986; Worden & Weisman, 1984).

Others advocate the position that, due to difficulties associated with the accurate identification of depressed medical patients through current screening processes and the paucity of evidence linking screening with improved outcomes, there is little evidence in favor of psychological screening (Campbell, 1987; Coyne, Thompson, Palmer, Kagee, & Maunsell, 2000; U.S. Preventive Services Task Force, 1996). In addition to a lack of evidence in support of blanket screening, possible risks associated with this practice have been proposed. The domain of somatic symptoms included in many standardized mental health instruments may lead to confusion. Health-care team members might neglect either the physical causes or psychological causes of high-scorers' somatic complaints (Tope, Ahles, & Silberfarb, 1993). Other potential risks include the inaccurate labeling of screened patients with mental health diagnoses, the withdrawal of attention from disorders with effective screening methods, and damage to the patient-doctor relationship (Campbell, 1987).

As the debate regarding psychological screening is not likely to soon dissipate, it is helpful to review the research literature on the psychological functioning of cancer patients. After administering self-report measures of depression or anxiety, many research teams have concluded that individuals with cancer, as opposed to the general population, are more likely to report symptomatology in the clinical range (Epping-Jordan et al., 1999; Glinder & Compas, 1999; Pinder et al., 1993; Watson et al., 1991). There is significant variation in terms of the published rates of psychological symptomatology among cancer patients; the prevalence rates of depression and anxiety have ranged from 0–50% and from 0.9–49%, respectively (McDaniel, Musselman, Porter, Reed, & Nemeroff, 1995; Van't Spijker, Trijsburg, & Duivenvoorden, 1997).

The majority of research investigating the psychological status of cancer patients has relied on self-report measures. There are many readily available measures of mood and symptoms of depression and anxiety that have often been used for this purpose. This list includes the Beck Depression Inventory (BDI; Beck & Beck, 1972), the Hospital Anxiety and Depression Scale (HADS; Zigmond & Snaith, 1983), and the Profile of Mood States (POMS; McNair, Lorr, & Droppleman, 1971). However, after conducting clinical interviews with 215 cancer patients undergoing medical treatment, Derogatis et al. (1983) assigned a *DSM-III* (*Diagnostic and Statistical Manual of Mental Disorders*) major affective disorder diagnosis to only 6% of the sample. In similar fashion, Lansky and colleagues (1985) administered clinical interviews to women with a history of cancer and found that 5.3% of the women were experiencing clinical levels of depression. Among this group of 505 women, in which the time since diagnosis ranged from 2 weeks to 23 years, time since diagnosis did not differentiate between the depressed and nondepressed women. Within the cancer population, research suggests that only one third to one half of cancer patients who report significant distress on self-report measures will receive a clinical diagnosis after an interview has been conducted (Kathol, Mutgi, Williams, Clamon, & Noyes, 1990; Payne et al., 1999). Therefore, there is quite a contrast between the self-report of depressive symptoms and diagnoses obtained through formal clinical interviews.

There is other research to suggest that cancer patients are quite similar to physically healthy individuals in terms of their psychological status. In one study, cancer patients were found to report less mood disturbance than both college students and outpatient psychotherapy clients (Cella et al., 1989). In another study, the mental health of medical patients, including those with cancer, was observed to be similar to the mental health of the general population and better than individuals undergoing treatment for depression (Cassileth et al., 1984). In their meta-analysis, Van't Spijker et al. (1997) found that cancer patients did not report more symptoms of anxiety or distress than nonpatients. When the analysis was limited to studies published after 1987, cancer patients did not report more symptoms of depression than their healthier counterparts. Due to equivocal research findings using self-report measures, it would appear to be inaccurate and inappropriate to presume that cancer patients commonly experience significant levels of psychological distress.

Therefore, the administration of self-report measures of psychosocial distress does not appear to be a particularly effective solution for those wishing to identify cancer patients for whom an intervention would be most appropriate. Mental health professionals working in the oncology setting must also not forget that they are working with cancer patients rather than typical mental health patients. Cancer patients may not welcome the routine assessment of their psychological status during visits with their oncologists. This is not to suggest, however, that psychological disturbance is absent in the cancer population. It is likely that a continuum of psychological health exists; some cancer patients will meet diagnostic criteria for a psychological disorder, others will experience increased distress without reaching clinical levels, and still others will experience minimal change in their psychosocial functioning.

Global Assessments of Functioning and Quality of Life

Rather than focus on traditional mental health concerns and screen cancer patients with standard psychological assessment tools, an alternate strategy is to assess the varied and unique concerns of individuals with cancer. Consistent with the biopsychosocial approach, the strength of these instruments lies in their ability to assess the impact of cancer on global functioning or overall quality of life rather than focus on specific psychological symptoms. Quality of life is a multidimensional construct that includes physical, psychological, social, and spiritual factors (Aaronson et al., 1991; Tope et al., 1993). Instruments that have been developed for such use with medical patients include the Sickness Impact Profile (Gilson et al., 1975), the Psychosocial Adjustment to Illness Scale (PAIS; Derogatis & Derogatis, 1990), and the Medical Outcomes Study 36-Item Short Form Health Survey (MOS SF-36; Ware, Snow, Kosinski, & Gandek, 1993). In contrast to these generic measures, other instruments have been developed specifically for use with individuals with cancer. Table 12.1 presents a summary of six of these assessment tools.

In a comparison of women with and without a history of bone marrow transplantation for the treatment of breast cancer, cancer patients received lower scores on six of the subscales of the SF-36 (physical functioning, physical role functioning, general health, vitality, social functioning, and

TABLE 12.1 Global Assessments of Cancer Functioning, Adjustment, and/or Quality of Life

Name of Instrument	Authors and Year	Description
Cancer Care Monitor	Fortner (2003)	38-item, notebook computer–administered clinical screening and quality-of-life measure consisting of six normalized screening measures (physical symptoms, treatment side effects, acute distress, despair, impaired ambulation, and impaired performance)
Cancer Rehabilitation Evaluation System (CARES)	Schag & Heinrich (1990)	139-item, self-report measure of cancer-related problems and quality of life with five summary scores (physical, psychosocial, marital, sexual functioning, and medical interaction). Short-form version is also available
European Organization for Research and Treatment of Cancer–Quality of Life Questionnaire (EORTC QLC-C30)	Aaronson et al. (1993)	30-item questionnaire with five functional scales (physical, role, emotional, social, and cognitive functioning), three symptom scales (fatigue, pain, nausea/vomiting), one global health/quality of life scale, and several single items
Functional Assessment of Cancer Therapy–General (FACT-G)	Cella et al. (1993)	28-item questionnaire with four subscales (physical, functional, social, and emotional well-being)
Functional Living Index–Cancer (FLIC)	Schipper, Clinch, McMurray, & Levitt (1984)	22-item, self-report measure of quality of life in which items address physical, psychological, family, and social functioning
M.D. Anderson Symptom Inventory (MDASI)	Cleeland et al. (2000)	13 core symptoms plus additional disease-specific items evaluating the degree to which symptoms interfere with life. It can be administered by questionnaire or interview, and there is current research into the administration via interactive voice response (IVR) system in which patients respond to items using telephone keypad

emotional role functioning), but did not report lower levels of mental health (Hann et al. 1997). As stated earlier in this chapter, the separation of psychological functioning from physical and social changes that are likely to occur during the experience of cancer is a limiting conceptualization. As a result, a broader focus on the varied changes that may be associated with the cancer experience is appropriate.

A Third Option: Providing Interventions to All Interested Participants

Despite the appeal of an assessment tool that is able to accurately identify cancer patients most suitable for intervention, we currently lack such an instrument. Although the assessment of more global aspects of functioning and quality of life is an improvement over an exclusive focus on traditional mental health issues, there is another approach to consider, namely, the provision of psychosocial oncology interventions to all interested participants. The benefits of psychosocial oncology interventions do not appear to be limited to cancer patients with higher reports of psychological distress. Meyer and Mark (1995) conducted a meta-analysis of psychosocial interventions with cancer patients and found no differences associated with participants' risk for psychological distress or the use of psychological screening. Sheard and Maguire (1999) meta-analyzed intervention studies in which participation was not determined by psychological screening and found moderate and weak effect sizes for anxiety and depression outcomes, respectively. An examination of 402 cancer patients who participated in a brief group coping-skills program suggests that enhancements of mood and quality of life did not differ by gender, marital status, religion, education, or prior experience with mental self-help techniques, although improvements in quality of life were lower in patients with recurrent disease (Cunningham, Lockwood, & Edmonds, 1993). It should be noted that the benefits of group participation were not immediate in the older patients, although this group showed equal improvement with their younger counterparts 3 months later.

Taylor, Falke, Shoptaw, and Lichtman (1986) have compared cancer patients who had and had not participated in cancer support groups. The two groups were similar in terms of cancer site, age, marital status, and perceived health. Those who had not participated in such groups had more recent diagnoses, and those who had attended support groups were more likely to be of a higher social class and to report a negative interaction with members of the medical community, prior use of social support resources, and concerns that were both related and unrelated to the cancer experience. It is interesting to note that scores on the POMS subscales indicated no differences between attenders and nonattenders, with the exception that those who participated in support groups were actually less likely to report depressive symptoms.

In addition to evidence suggesting that the benefits of participation are not limited to a preselected group of patients, the possibility of improved medical outcomes is a second reason why it might be appropriate to offer interventions to all interested cancer patients. Not without methodological limitations, studies have linked a number of psychosocial factors with lower cancer survival rates. This list includes lower patient-reported quality of life, higher levels of emotional distress, greater use of depressive coping, higher levels of helplessness/hopelessness, higher pessimism (among patients between the ages of 30 and 59), lower emotional expression, and less perceived emotional support (Faller, Bülzebruck, Drings, & Lang, 1999; Ganz, Lee, & Siau, 1991; Reynolds et al. 2000; Schulz, Bookwala, Knapp, Scheier, & Williamson, 1996; Watson, Haviland, Greer, Davidson, & Bliss, 1999). However, we are regularly reminded that the evidence is contradictory regarding the relationship between psychosocial factors and cancer progression (Garssen & Goodkin, 1999; Kidman & Edelman, 1997). For example, Dean and Surtees (1989) found that women who met the criteria for a psychiatric illness before breast cancer surgery and those who engaged in denial after surgery had less chance of cancer recurrence. Similarly, Fawzy and colleagues (1993) found that higher levels of baseline mood disturbance were associated with better medical outcomes 5 to 6 years later. The causal relationship between the various psychosocial correlates of cancer and medical outcomes for cancer patients is by no means clear.

Preliminary evidence suggests that participation in psychosocial oncology interventions may be associated with improved survival rates (Fawzy et al., 1993; Shrock, Palmer, & Taylor, 1999; Spiegel, Bloom, Kraemer, & Gottheil, 1989). These research teams have offered various hypotheses for the health benefits of their interventions, including greater compliance with medical treatment, enhanced social support, improved coping and stress management, and due to a self-selection bias or placebo effect in participation in the intervention, an increased will to live. Researchers in the field of psychoneuroimmunology have begun exploring specific mechanisms that may be involved (Folkman, 1999; van der Pompe, Antoni, Visser, & Garssen, 1996; Walker, Heys, & Eremin, 1999). Research investigating a possible link between interventions and increased survival is not unequivocal, and other research teams have failed to observe this relationship (Cunningham et al., 1998;

Edelman, Lemon, Bell, & Kidman, 1999; Ilnyckyj, Farber, Cheang, & Weinerman, 1994). However, based on the results of three studies in which psychosocial oncology interventions were associated with enhanced survival, Dreher (1997) argued that we have both scientific and moral imperatives for the broad-based institution of interventions with this population. If we restrict participation to cancer patients who report high psychological distress, we miss the opportunity to enhance the quality and, possibly, the quantity of life for greater numbers of cancer patients.

Interventions for Cancer Patients

Psychosocial Interventions in the Oncology Setting

Qualitative reviewers of psychosocial oncology interventions have concluded that these interventions have positive effects for individuals who participate (Andersen, 1992; Fawzy, Fawzy, Arndt, & Pasnau, 1995; Trijsburg, van Knippenberg, & Rijpma, 1992). The results of three published meta-analyses also indicate that participation in these interventions is associated with positive outcomes (Devine & Westlake, 1995; Meyer & Mark, 1995; Sheard & Maguire, 1999). The interventions included in these reviews compose a very heterogeneous group and include education, behavior training, supportive-expressive approaches, and more structured interventions. Educational interventions are designed to increase knowledge regarding the prevention and treatment of cancer and the medical environment (e.g., Rainey, 1985). Mental health professionals who provide behavioral interventions use relaxation training and systematic desensitization to reduce anticipatory nausea and vomiting associated with chemotherapy and radiotherapy (e.g., Burish & Jenkins, 1992; Morrow et al., 1992). Compas, Haaga, Keefe, Leitenberg, and Williams (1998) concluded that the use of progressive muscle relaxation to address these treatment-related symptoms met the criteria for an efficacious treatment. Within the less-structured approach of those who offer supportive-expressive interventions, there is a pronounced emphasis on open sharing, self-disclosure, and fostering high levels of cohesion (e.g., Ilnyckyj et al., 1994; Spiegel et al., 1989; Spiegel, Bloom, & Yalom, 1981). An often-cited study is that of Spiegel and colleagues (1981, 1989) who studied the effects of participation in a year of supportive group meetings on women with metastatic breast cancer. Group participation was associated with significantly less mood disturbance, maladaptive coping responses, and phobias, as well as improved length of survival.

We have chosen to focus on the final category of interventions, namely, those with a structured cognitive behavioral approach. In these interventions, similar material is covered with each participant. Although some investigators have not detected a difference between outcomes associated with structured versus unstructured approaches (Meyer & Mark, 1995; Worden & Weisman, 1984), the results of other research teams point to the relative superiority of structured interventions (Cunningham & Tocco, 1989; Helgeson & Cohen, 1996; Telch & Telch, 1986). Because mental health professionals working in the oncology setting must consider convenience as a major factor when offering interventions to cancer patients, we have emphasized brief structured interventions. Regarding the duration of the interventions, unlike traditional mental health patients, medical patients typically do not expect to remain in therapy indefinitely. Psycho-oncology researchers have called for increased acceptability and accessibility of psychosocial interventions (Meyer & Mark, 1995; Moynihan, Bliss, Davidson, Burchell, & Horwich, 1998). One needs only to look at the reasons cited for nonparticipation to understand the need for brief onsite interventions: travel constraints, commitment to regular group attendance, and competing schedule demands (Alter et al., 1996; Cunningham, Jenkins, Edmonds, & Lockwood, 1995; Cunningham et al., 1998). As approximately 70% of cancer patients report feeling tired and fatigued during radiation treatment and chemotherapy (Smets et al., 1993), it is inappropriate to expect these patients to commit to a long-term intervention at an offsite location. In fact, positive outcomes have been associated with brief one- or two-session interventions (Burish, Snyder, & Jenkins, 1991; Larson, Duberstein, Talbot, Caldwell, & Moynihan, 2000). As further indication of recent awareness of the importance of convenience, psychosocial support is now being offered via telephone (Alter et al., 1996; Marcus et al., 1998; Mermelstein & Holland, 1991) and Internet (Sharf, 1997). In addition to patient convenience, briefer interventions, by their very nature, are also less expensive to provide.

Brief Structured Interventions

We have reviewed 17 published psychosocial oncology interventions that followed a structured format (Kovacs & Houts, 2004). In recognition of the need for brief interventions, our review was limited to interventions with a maximum duration of six sessions. The total length of the interventions ranged from 90 minutes to 12 hours, with an average of 6.8 hours calculated from the studies that presented specific information regarding the duration of the intervention. Nine interventions were administered in a group format, seven were administered on an individual basis, and one study varied in terms of the administration. The number of participants in each study ranged from 20 to 205. Among the various studies, a wide range of cancer experiences was represented. The average reported age of participants ranged from 40 to 65 years, and the majority of interventions were provided to both male and female cancer patients. Thirteen of the interventions targeted adults with newly diagnosed cancer; seven were limited to recently diagnosed cancer of specific sites (Bridge, Benson, Pietroni, & Priest, 1988; Christensen, 1983; Fawzy, 1995; Fawzy et al., 1990a, 1990b; Larson et al., 2000; Moynihan et al., 1998; Shrock et al., 1999), and six did not have specific inclusion criteria regarding the location of the cancer (Burish et al., 1991; Decker, Cline-Elsen, & Gallagher, 1992; Edgar, Rosberger, & Nowlis, 1992; Ferlic, Goldman, & Kennedy, 1979; Greer et al., 1992; Worden & Weisman, 1984). In the remaining four studies, each sample was heterogeneous in terms of cancer site and time since diagnosis (Cunningham et al., 1995; Cunningham & Tocco, 1989; Heinrich & Schag, 1985; Telch & Telch, 1986).

In our review, we classified the treatment components of each structured intervention into a 10-category system. Rather that looking for unique contributions of the individual interventions, the goal was to discern common features. However, it was not a simple process to categorize the treatment components, as there was extreme variation in the attention that researchers devoted to explaining the specific content of their interventions (an observation also made by Andersen, 1992). Table 12.2 presents a brief description of each of the categories along with their frequency among the 17 reviewed brief structured interventions.

As is evident from Table 12.2, the majority of the interventions included relaxation training, and progressive muscle relaxation (PMR) was the most common technique. In standard PMR, an individual alternates between tensing and relaxing specific muscle groups in order to produce an increased sense of physical relaxation. There are many published PMR scripts (e.g., Davis, Eshelman, & McKay, 1995), the majority of which are variations of Jacobson's (1929) original program. Some of the interventions added visual imagery, and it has been observed that this addition may be useful for cancer patients with physical limitations that make muscle contraction difficult (Edgar et al., 1992). When participants in one study were asked what they perceived to be the most helpful components of the interventions, relaxation training was the most common response (Heinrich & Schag, 1985). However, although the participants may have appreciated relaxation training, this does not imply that they actually increased their overall sense of relaxation. No studies included an assessment of subjective physical relaxation, and blood pressure and heart rate were assessed in only one study (Burish et al., 1991).

TABLE 12.2 Common Components of Brief Structured Interventions (N = 17)

Component	Description	Recommended References	Number of Studies
Relaxation training	Training in specific techniques to increase sense of relaxation (e.g., progressive muscle relaxation, visual imagery, deep breathing)	Davis, Eshelman, & McKay (1995); Horowitz & Breitbart (1993)	15 (88%)
Problem solving	Training in specific problem-solving approaches and the application to personal situations, or the identification of areas of desired change followed by discussion or behavioral practice in order to enact change	Fawzy & Fawzy (1994)	10 (59%)
Supportive discussion	Specific allotment of time for informal discussion, specific reference to within-group support, or specific stated objective of provision of psychological support or supportive discussion	Classen et al. (1997); Spiegel, Bloom, & Yalom (1981)	10 (59%)
Education	Provision of information (e.g., cancer and its treatment, health-care system, impact of stress) without skills training or application of this knowledge	Burish, Snyder, & Jenkins (1991); Ferlic, Goldman, & Kennedy (1979)	9 (41%)
Cognitive therapy	Identification of maladaptive thought patterns and the promotion of more effective ways of thinking	Beck (1995); Edgar, Rosberger, & Nowlis (1992)	7 (41%)
Stress management	Assessment of individual's stress, stress monitoring, or the provision of strategies to improve coping with stress	Davis, Eshelman, & McKay (1995); Fawzy & Fawzy (1994)	7 (41%)
Activity/lifestyle management	Completion of lifestyle checklist and discussion of health lifestyles, increased engagement in pleasant events, or exercise	Davis, Eshelman, & McKay (1995)	7 (41%)
Communication skills	Promotion of effective communication (e.g., between patient and spouse), which may include the open expression of feelings during sessions	Christensen (1983)	4 (24%)
Goal setting	Instruction in principles of effective goal-setting in order to organize priorities or provide sense of accomplishment/control	Davis, Eshelman, & McKay (1995); Cunningham et al. (1991)	3 (18%)

TABLE 12.2 (continued)

Healing imagery	Visualization of effective functioning of immune system or patient's body overcoming cancer	Cunningham et al. (1991)	3 (18%)

Note. Adapted from Kovacs and Houts, in press.

In addition to relaxation training, the intervention components that were administered with greatest frequency were problem solving, supportive discussion, and education. It is worth noting that not all the interventions that offered problem-solving training assessed problems faced by cancer patients or participants' abilities to cope with or adjust to problems, and not all the interventions that provided education assessed whether there was any improvement in the knowledge of the participants. Therefore, it appears that there has not been adequate assessment of whether these interventions produce the changes that the developers targeted.

In addition to often neglecting to provide adequate information on the specific content of the interventions, researchers did not always provide a clear theoretical rationale for the development of their intervention. Although replication is important to determine the efficacy of an intervention (Compas et al., 1998), the current practice results in a lack of development of more novel approaches. As an example, participants in 15 of the 17 interventions received at least one form of relaxation training. Mental health professionals working in the cancer setting may therefore assume that relaxation training is an essential component of an intervention. This is a premature assumption, however, as there is a paucity of research comparing interventions that offer relaxation training with those that do not. In fact, in one study that compared the impact of a 90-minute multicomponent preparatory intervention, multiple relaxation training sessions, and a combined intervention consisting of the preparatory intervention and relaxation training, it was observed that the single session was the most effective at increasing knowledge and reducing nausea, hostility, depression, and interference in daily and work lives (Burish et al., 1991). Although it is inappropriate to eliminate relaxation training in psychosocial oncology interventions based on the results of a single study, this does suggest that further investigation is necessary in order to determine whether the seemingly automatic inclusion of relaxation training is warranted.

This commentary was not offered to suggest that the commonly used treatment components are not useful. In fact, in 16 of the 17 brief interventions that were reviewed, research teams observed positive outcomes associated with participation. In addition to reductions in reported psychosocial distress, various research teams also found that individuals who participated in the interventions experienced less interference in daily and work lives, fewer and less severe problem situations, enhanced problem solving, adjustment to cancer, and quality of life, and improved survival rates. A list of common intervention components was included in order to provide a starting base for mental health practitioners and provide an impetus for researchers in this area.

Summary

This chapter was primarily directed toward mental health professionals who wish to integrate interventions in the oncology setting. For individuals who plan to establish a full psycho-oncology unit within a cancer setting, however, the process will be more involved. Jimmie Holland (1998), founder of the Memorial Sloan-Kettering psycho-oncology program in New York, has offered guidelines for individuals who wish to undertake this project. Holland provided information for the development of a unit proposal and mission statement, staff recruitment, development of ties with community organizations, working within the traditional oncology setting, establishing educational and research programs, and advocacy and ethical issues. As the provision of a psycho-oncology unit is likely beyond the scope of the majority of readers, we have focused on the more general concerns of individuals interested in offering a psychosocial intervention to cancer patients.

When considering assessment strategies, it is important to maintain a biopsychosocial approach and recognize the varied impacts of cancer. There are physical and social changes associated with cancer diagnoses and treatment, and there likely exists a continuum of psychological well-being among cancer patients. Although this chapter reviewed evidence to suggest that the majority of cancer patients do not experience significant psychological disturbance, the aim was not to suggest that we neglect true psychological disturbance among the minority of cancer patients who experience it. Mental health professionals working in the oncology setting must be prepared to deal with cancer patients who experience serious emotional problems. The practice of traditional psychological screening, however, is not likely to serve as an effective way to identify these individuals. In addition, although clinically depressed and anxious cancer patients require increased attention, this does not mean that we should neglect other patients who may be experiencing significant changes in other areas of functioning.

As to the actual intervention, it is important to select treatment components that reflect the goal of the intervention. As stated earlier, some mental health researchers have limited participation to cancer patients who reported high levels of emotional distress. Therefore, these studies explicitly targeted the presumed psychological distress of cancer patients. However, with a primary focus on the emotional impact of cancer, mental health professionals run the risk of minimizing other aspects of cancer, such as fatigue, sleep disturbance, pain, and changes in interpersonal functioning. Although psychological interventions that address the stresses associated with cancer, teach relaxation training, or reduce sleep-related anxiety have been recommended (Berlin, 1984; Horowitz & Breitbart, 1993), none of the brief interventions in this review included assessments of their ability to improve sleep in cancer patients. Thomas and Weiss (2000) encouraged the use of psychoeducation, supportive psychotherapy, and cognitive behavioral therapy, in addition to traditional pharmacotherapy, to target cancer pain. Mental health professionals who are planning to introduce psychosocial interventions in an oncology setting may find it useful to consider the options included in Table 12.2. The focus need not be limited to this list. The inclusion of novel treatment components with a strong theoretical rationale is also encouraged. For example, optimism is one factor that has been associated with fewer reported symptoms of mood disturbance, anxiety, and depression as well as more effective coping and higher self-esteem (Bjorck, Hopp, & Jones, 1999; Carver et al., 1993; Epping-Jordan et al., 1999). Mental health professionals may wish to offer interventions with the intention of enhancing the optimism of cancer patients. Of the 17 studies in our review, four research teams expanded their focus beyond psychosocial variables and investigated the effects of psychosocial oncology interventions on physiological or health outcomes (Burish et al., 1991; Fawzy et al., 1990b, 1993; Larson et al., 2000; Shrock et al., 1999). Among these studies, outcome measures included immunological functioning, blood pressure, heart rate, self-reported health, self-reported ratings of nausea and vomiting, and survival or recurrence rates several years later. This type of unique combination of both physical health outcome measures and psychosocial functioning outcome measures needs to be promoted in future investigations.

In summary, the adoption of a biopsychosocial perspective to cancer is crucial in order to understand the impact of cancer diagnoses and treatment. The negative impact of cancer on an individual's overall quality of life and the possible role of psychology in minimizing this disruption are receiving increasing attention. For this reason, this is an exciting time for both clinicians and researchers interested in the expanding role of psychology within the oncology setting.

References

Aaronson, N. K., Ahmedzai, S., Bergman, B., Bullinger, M., Cull, A., Duez, H. J. et al. (1993). The European Organization for Research and Treatment of Cancer QLC-C30: A quality of life instrument for use in international clinical trials in oncology. *Journal of the National Cancer Institute, 85*, 365–376.

Aaronson, N. K., Meyerowitz, B. E., Bard, M., Bloom, J. R., Fawzy, F. I., Feldstein, M. et al. (1991). Quality of life research in oncology: Past achievements and future priorities. *Cancer, 67*(3), 839–843.

Alter, C. L., Fleishman, S. B., Kornblith, A. B., Holland, J. C., Biano, D., Levenson, R. et al. (1996). Supportive telephone intervention for patients receiving chemotherapy: A pilot study. *Psychosomatics, 37*(5), 425–431.

Andersen, B. L. (1985). Sexual functioning morbidity among cancer survivors: Current status and future research directions. *Cancer, 55*, 1835–1842.

Andersen, B. L. (1992). Psychological interventions for cancer patients to enhance the quality of life. *Journal of Consulting and Clinical Psychology, 60*(4), 552–568.

Ashbury, F. D., Findlay, H., Reynolds, B., & McKerracher, K. (1998). A Canadian survey of cancer patients' experiences: Are their needs being met? *Journal of Pain and Symptom Management, 16*(5), 298–306.

Beck, A. T., & Beck, R. W. (1972). Screening depressed patients in family practice: A rapid technique. *Postgraduate Medicine, 52*, 81–85.

Beck, J. S. (1995). *Cognitive therapy: Basics and beyond.* New York: Guilford.

Berlin, R. M. (1984). Management of insomnia in hospitalized patients. *Annals of Internal Medicine, 100*(3), 398–404.

Beszterczey, A., & Lipowski, Z. J. (1977). Insomnia in cancer patients (letter). *Canadian Medical Association Journal, 116*(4), 355.

Bjorck, J. P., Hopp, D. P., & Jones, L. W. (1999). Prostate cancer and emotional functioning: Effects of mental adjustment, optimism, and appraisal. *Journal of Psychosocial Oncology, 17*(1), 71–85.

Bridge, L. R., Benson, P., Pietroni, P. C., & Priest, R. G. (1988). Relaxation and imagery in the treatment of breast cancer. *British Medical Journal, 297*, 1169–1172.

Burish, T. G., & Jenkins, R. A. (1992). Effectiveness of biofeedback and relaxation training in reducing the side effects of cancer chemotherapy. *Health Psychology, 11*(1), 17–23.

Burish, T. G., Snyder, S. L., & Jenkins, R. A. (1991). Preparing patients for cancer chemotherapy: Effect of coping preparation and relaxation interventions. *Journal of Consulting and Clinical Psychology, 59*(4), 518–525.

Campbell, T. L. (1987). An opposing view. *Journal of Family Practice, 25*(2), 184–187.

Carver, C. S., Pozo, C., Harris, S. D., Noriega, V., Scheier, M. F., Robinson, D. S. et al. (1993). How coping mediates the effect of optimism on distress: A study of women with early stage breast cancer. *Journal of Personality and Social Psychology, 65*(2), 375–390.

Cassileth, B. R., Lusk, E. J., Strouse, T. B., Miller, D. S., Brown, L. L., Cross, P. A. et al. (1984). Psychosocial status in chronic illness: A comparative analysis of six diagnostic groups. *New England Journal of Medicine, 311*(8), 506–511.

Cella, D. F., Tross, S., Orav, E. J., Holland, J. C., Silberfarb, P. M., & Rafla, S. (1989). Mood states of patients after the diagnosis of cancer. *Journal of Psychosocial Oncology, 7*(1/2), 45–54.

Cella, D. F., Tulsky, D. S., Gray, G., Sarafian, B., Linn, E., Bonomi, A. et al. (1993). The Functional Assessment of Cancer Therapy Scale: Development and validation of the general measure. *Journal of Clinical Oncology, 11*, 570–579.

Christensen, D. N. (1983). Postmastectomy couple counseling: An outcome study of a structured treatment protocol. *Journal of Sex and Marital Therapy, 9*(4), 266–275.

Classen, C., Abramson, S., Angell, K., Atkinson, A., Desch, C., Vinciguerra, V. P. et al. (1997). Effectiveness of a training program for enhancing therapists' understanding of the supportive-expressive treatment model for breast cancer groups. *Journal of Psychotherapy Practice and Research, 6*, 211–218.

Cleeland, C. S., Mendoza, T. R., Wang, X. S., Chou, C., Harle, M. T., Morrissey, M. et al. (2000). Assessing symptom distress in cancer patients: The M.D. Anderson Symptom Inventory. *Cancer, 89*(7), 1634–1646.

Compas, B. E., Haaga, D. A. F., Keefe, F. J., Leitenberg, H., & Williams, D. A. (1998). Sampling of empirically supported psychological treatments from health psychology: Smoking, chronic pain, cancer, and bulimia nervosa. *Journal of Consulting and Clinical Psychology, 66*(1), 89–112.

Coyne, J. C., Thompson, R., Palmer, S. C., Kagee, A., & Maunsell, E. (2000). Should we screen for depression? Caveats and potential pitfalls. *Applied and Preventive Psychology, 9*(2), 101–121.

Cunningham, A. J., Edmonds, C. V. I., Hampson, A. W., Hanson, H., Hovanec, M., Jenkins, G. et al. (1991). A group psychoeducational program to help cancer patients cope with and combat their disease. *Advances, 7*(3), 41–56.

Cunningham, A. J., Edmonds, C. V. I., Jenkins, G. P., Pollack, H., Lockwood, G. A., & Warr, D. (1998). A randomized controlled trial of the effects of group psychological therapy on survival in women with metastatic breast cancer. *Psycho-oncology, 7*, 508–517.

Cunningham, A. J., Jenkins, G., Edmonds, C. V. I., & Lockwood, G. A. (1995). A randomised comparison of two forms of a brief, group, psychoeducational program for cancer patients: Weekly sessions versus a "weekend intensive." *International Journal of Psychiatry in Medicine, 25*(2), 173–189.

Cunningham, A. J., Lockwood, G. A., & Edmonds, C. V. I. (1993). Which cancer patients benefit most from a brief, group, coping skills program? *International Journal of Psychiatry in Medicine, 23*(4), 283–398.

Cunningham, A. J., & Tocco, E. K. (1989). A randomized trial of group psychoeducational therapy for cancer patients. *Patient Education and Counseling, 14*, 101–114.

Curbow, B., Somerfield, M. R., Baker, F., Wingard, J. R., & Legro, M. W. (1993). Personal changes, dispositional optimism, and psychological adjustment to bone marrow transplantation. *Journal of Behavioral Medicine, 16*(5), 423–443.

Daut, R. L., & Cleeland, C. S. (1982). The prevalence and severity of pain in cancer. *Cancer, 50*, 1913–1918.

Davis, M., Eshelman, E. R., & McKay, M. (1995). *The relaxation and stress reduction workbook* (4th ed.). Oakland, CA: New Harbinger Publications.

Dean, C., & Surtees, P. G. (1989). Do psychological factors predict survival in breast cancer? *Journal of Psychosomatic Research, 33*(5), 561–569.

Decker, T. W., Cline-Elsen, J., & Gallagher, M. (1992). Relaxation therapy as an adjunct in radiation oncology. *Journal of Clinical Psychology, 48*(3), 388–393.

Derogatis, L. R., & Derogatis, M. F. (1990). *Psychosocial adjustment to illness scale: Administration, scoring, and procedures manual—II.* Baltimore: Clinical Psychometric Research.

Derogatis, L. R., Morrow, G. R., Fetting, J., Penman, D., Piasetsky, S., Schmale, A. M. et al. (1983). The prevalence of psychiatric disorders among cancer patients. *Journal of the American Medical Association, 249*(6), 751–757.

Devine, E. C., & Westlake, S. K. (1995). The effects of psychoeducational care provided to adults with cancer: Meta-analysis of 116 studies. *Oncology Nursing Forum, 22*(9), 1369–1381.

Dreher, H. (1997). The scientific and moral imperative for broad-based psychosocial interventions for cancer. *Advances, 13*(3), 38–48.

Edelman, S., Lemon, J., Bell, D. R., & Kidman, A. D. (1999). Effects of group CBT on the survival time of patients with metastatic breast cancer. *Psycho-oncology, 8,* 474–481.

Edgar, L., Rosberger, Z., & Nowlis, D. (1992). Coping with cancer during the first year after diagnosis: Assessment and intervention. *Cancer, 69,* 817–828.

Epping-Jordan, J. E., Compas, B. E., Osowiecki, D. M., Oppedisano, G., Gerhardt, C., Primo, K. et al. (1999). Psychological adjustment in breast cancer: Processes of emotional distress. *Health Psychology, 18*(4), 315–326.

Faller, H., Bülzebruck, H., Drings, P., & Lang, H. (1999). Coping, distress, and survival among patients with lung cancer. *Archives of General Psychiatry, 56,* 756–762.

Fawzy, F. I., Cousins, N., Fawzy, N. W., Kemeny, M. E., Elashoff, R., & Morton, D. (1990a). A structured psychiatric intervention for cancer patients: I. Changes over time in methods of coping and affective disturbance. *Archives of General Psychiatry, 47,* 720–725.

Fawzy, F. I., & Fawzy, N. W. (1994). A structured psychoeducational intervention for cancer patients. *General Hospital Psychiatry, 16,* 149–192.

Fawzy, F. I., Fawzy, N. W., Arndt, L. A., & Pasnau, R. O. (1995). Critical review of psychosocial interventions in cancer care. *Archives of General Psychiatry, 52,* 100–113.

Fawzy, F. I., Fawzy, N. W., Hyun, C. S., Elashoff, R., Guthrie, D., Fahey, J. L. et al. (1993). Malignant melanoma: Effects of an early structured psychiatric intervention, coping, and affective state on recurrence and survival 6 years later. *Archives of General Psychiatry, 50,* 681–689.

Fawzy, F. I., Kemeny, M. E., Fawzy, N. W., Elashoff, R., Morton, D., Cousins, N. et al. (1990b). A structured psychiatric intervention for cancer patients: II. Changes over time in immunological measures. *Archives of General Psychiatry, 47,* 729–735.

Fawzy, N. W. (1995). A psychoeducational nursing intervention to enhance coping and affective state in newly diagnosed malignant melanoma patients. *Cancer Nursing, 18,* 427–438.

Ferlic, M., Goldman, A., & Kennedy, B. J. (1979). Group counseling in adult patients with advanced cancer. *Cancer, 43,* 760–766.

Folkman, S. (1999). Thoughts about psychological factors, PNI, and cancer. *Advances in Mind-Body Medicine, 15,* 255–259.

Ford, M. F., Jones, M., Scannell, T., Powell, A., Coombes, R. C., & Evans, C. (1990). Is group psychotherapy feasible for oncology outpatient attenders selected on the basis of psychological morbidity? *British Journal of Cancer, 62,* 624–626.

Fortner, V. B. (2003). The cancer care monitor: Preliminary examination of a computer administered system for symptom screening and quality of life in adult cancer patients. *Journal of Pain and Symptom Management, 26*(6), 1077–1092.

Ganz, P. A., Lee, J. J., & Siau, J. (1991). Quality of life assessment: An independent prognostic variable for survival in lung cancer. *Cancer, 67*(12), 3131–3135.

Garssen, B., & Goodkin, K. (1999). On the role of immunological factors as mediators between psychosocial factors and cancer progression. *Psychiatry Research, 85,* 51–61.

Gilson, B. S., Gilson, J. S., Bergner, M., Bobbitt, R. H., Kressell, J., Pollard, W. E. et al. (1975). The Sickness Impact Profile: Development of an outcome measure of health care. *American Journal of Public Health, 65,* 1304–1310.

Glinder, J. G., & Compas, B. E. (1999). Self-blame attributions in women with newly diagnosed breast cancer: A prospective study of psychological adjustment. *Health Psychology, 18*(5), 475–481.

Greenlee, R. T., Hill-Harmon, M. B., Murray, T., & Thun, M. (2001). Cancer statistics, 2001. *CA—A Cancer Journal for Clinicians, 51,* 15–36.

Greenwald, H. P., Bonica, J. J., & Bergner, M. (1987). The prevalence of pain in four cancers. *Cancer, 60,* 2563–2567.

Greer, S. (1989). Can psychological therapy improve the quality of life of patients with cancer? *British Journal of Cancer, 59,* 149–151.

Greer, S., Moorey, S., Baruch, J. D. R., Watson, M., Robertson, B. M., Mason, A. et al. (1992). Adjuvant psychological therapy for patients with cancer: A prospective randomized trial. *British Medical Journal, 304,* 675–680.

Hann, D. M., Jacobsen, P., Martin, S., Azzarello, L., & Greenberg, H. (1998). Fatigue and quality of life following radiotherapy for breast cancer: A comparative study. *Journal of Clinical Psychology in Medical Settings, 5*(1), 19–33.

Hann, D. M., Jacobsen, P. B., Martin, S. C., Kronish, L. E., Azzarello, L. M., & Fields, K. K. (1997). Quality of life following bone marrow transplantation for breast cancer: A comparative study. *Bone Marrow Transplantation, 19,* 257–264.

Heinrich, R. L., & Schag, C. C. (1985). Stress and activity management: Group treatment for cancer patients and spouses. *Journal of Consulting and Clinical Psychology, 53*(4), 439–446.

Helgeson, V. S., & Cohen, S. (1996). Social support and adjustment to breast cancer: Reconciling descriptive, correlational, and intervention research. *Health Psychology, 15*(2), 135–148.

Holland, J. C. (1998). Establishing a psycho-oncology unit in a cancer center. In J. C. Holland (Ed.), *Psycho-oncology* (pp. 1049–1054). New York: Oxford University Press.

Horowitz, S. A., & Breitbart, W. (1993). Relaxation and imagery for symptom control in cancer patients. In W. Breitbart & J. C. Holland (Eds.), *Psychiatric aspects of symptom management in cancer patients* (pp. 147–171). Washington, DC: American Psychiatric Press.

Ilnyckyj, A., Farber, J., Cheang, M. C., & Weinerman, B. H. (1994). A randomized controlled trial of psychotherapeutic intervention in cancer patients. *Annals of the Royal College of Physicians and Surgeons of Canada, 27*, 93–96.

Irvine, D., Vincent, L., Graydon, J. E., Bubela, N., & Thompson, L. (1994). The prevalence and correlates of fatigue in patients receiving treatment with chemotherapy and radiotherapy: A comparison with the fatigue experienced by healthy individuals. *Cancer Nursing, 17*(5), 367–378.

Jacobsen, P. B., Hann, D. M., Azzarello, L. M., Horton, J., Balducci, L., & Lyman, G. H. (1999). Fatigue in women receiving adjuvant chemotherapy for breast cancer: Characteristics, course, and correlates. *Journal of Pain and Symptom Management, 18*(4), 233–242.

Jacobson, E. (1929). *Progressive relaxation: A physiological and clinical investigation of muscular states and their significance in psychology and medical practice.* Chicago: University of Chicago Press.

Kathol, R. G., Mutgi, A., Williams, J., Clamon, G., & Noyes, R. (1990). Diagnosis of major depression in cancer patients according to four sets of criteria. *American Journal of Psychiatry, 147*(8), 1021–1024.

Kidman, A. D., & Edelman, S. (1997). Developments in psycho-oncology and cognitive behavior therapy in cancer. *Journal of Cognitive Psychotherapy: An International Quarterly, 11*(1), 45–62.

Kovacs, A. H., & Houts, A. C. (in press). *A review of brief psychosocial oncology interventions: Suggestions for an expanded focus.*.

Lanksy, S. B., List, M. A., Herrmann, C. A., Ets-Hokin, E. G., DasGupta, T. K., Wilbanks, G. D. et al. (1985). Absence of major depressive disorder in female cancer patients. *Journal of Clinical Oncology, 3*(11), 1553–1559.

Larson, M. R., Duberstein, P. R., Talbot, N. L., Caldwell, C., & Moynihan, J. A. (2000). A presurgical psychosocial intervention for breast cancer patients: Psychological distress and the immune response. *Journal of Psychosomatic Research, 48*, 187–194.

Lichtman, R. R., Taylor, S. E., & Wood, J. V. (1988). Social support and marital adjustment after breast cancer. *Journal of Psychosocial Oncology, 5*(3), 47–74.

Marcus, A. C., Garrett, K. M., Cella, D., Wenzel, L. B., Brady, M. J., Crane, L. A. et al. (1998). Telephone counseling of breast cancer patients after treatment: A description of a randomized clinical trial. *Psycho-oncology, 7*, 470–482.

McDaniel, J. S., Musselman, D. L., & Nemeroff, C. B. (1997). Cancer and depression: Theory and treatment. *Psychiatric Annals, 27*(5), 360–364.

McDaniel, J. S., Musselman, D. L., Porter, M. R., Reed, D. A., & Nemeroff, C. B. (1995). Depression in patients with cancer: Diagnosis, biology, and treatment. *Archives of General Psychiatry, 52*, 89–99.

McNair, P. M., Lorr, M., & Droppleman, L. (1971). *Profile of mood states manual.* Sand Diego, CA: Educational and Industrial Testing Services.

Mermelstein, H. T., & Holland, J. C. (1991). Psychotherapy by telephone: A therapeutic tool for cancer patients. *Psychosomatics, 32*(4), 407–412.

Meyer, T. J., & Mark, M. M. (1995). Effects of psychosocial interventions with adult cancer patients: A meta-analysis of randomized experiments. *Health Psychology, 14*(2), 101–108.

Morrow, G. R., Asbury, R., Hammon, S., Dobkin, P., Caruso, L., Pandya, K. et al. (1992). Comparing the effectiveness of behavioral treatment for chemotherapy-induced nausea and vomiting when administered by oncologists, oncology nurses, and clinical psychologists. *Health Psychology, 11*(4), 250–256.

Moynihan, C., Bliss, J. M., Davidson, J., Burchell, L., & Horwich, A. (1998). Evaluation of adjuvant psychological therapy in patients with testicular cancer: Randomised controlled trial. *British Medical Journal, 316*, 429–435.

National Cancer Institute of Canada. (2001). *Canadian cancer statistics 2001.* Toronto, Canada: Author.

Payne, D. K., Hoffman, R. G., Theodoulou, M., Dosik, M., & Massie, M. J. (1999). Screening for anxiety and depression in women with breast cancer: Psychiatry and medical oncology gear up for managed care. *Psychosomatics, 40*(1), 64–69.

Peteet, J., Tay, V., Cohen, G., & MacIntyre, J. (1986). Pain characteristics and treatment in an outpatient cancer population. *Cancer, 57*, 1259–1265.

Pinder, K. L., Ramirez, A. J., Black, M. E., Richards, M. A., Gregory, W. M., & Rubens, R. D. (1993). Psychiatric disorder in patients with advanced breast cancer: Prevalence and associated factors. *European Journal of Cancer, 29A*(4), 524–527.

Rainey, L. C. (1985). Effects of preparatory patient education for radiation oncology patients. *Cancer, 56*, 1056–1061.

Reynolds, P., Hurley, S., Torres, M., Jackson, J., Boyd, P., Chen, V. W. et al. (2000). Use of coping strategies and breast cancer survival: Results from the Black/White Cancer Survival Study. *American Journal of Epidemiology, 152*(10), 940–949.

Schag, C. A. C., & Heinrich, R. L. (1990). Development of a comprehensive quality of life measurement tool: CARES. *Oncology, 4*, 135–138.

Schipper, H., Clinch, J., McMurray, A., & Levitt, M. (1984). Measuring the quality of life of cancer patients: The Functional Living Index–Cancer: Development and validation. *Journal of Clinical Oncology, 2*, 472–483.

Schulz, R., Bookwala, J., Knapp, J. E., Scheier, M., & Williamson, G. M. (1996). Pessimism, age, and cancer mortality. *Psychology and Aging, 11*(2), 304–309.

Sharf, B. F. (1997). Communicating breast cancer on-line: Support and empowerment on the Internet. *Women and Health, 26*(1), 65–85.

Sheard, T., & Maguire, P. (1999). The effect of psychological interventions on anxiety and depression in cancer patients: Results of two meta-analyses. *British Journal of Cancer, 80*(11), 1770–1780.

Shrock, D., Palmer, R. F., & Taylor, B. (1999). Effects of a psychosocial intervention on survival among patients with stage I breast and prostate cancer: A matched case-control study. *Alternative Therapies, 5*(3), 49–55.

Smets, E. M. A., Garssen, G., Schuster-Uitterhoeve, A. L. J., & de Haes, J. C. J. M. (1993). Fatigue in cancer patients. *British Journal of Cancer, 68*, 220–224.

Spiegel, D., Bloom, J. R., Kraemer, H. C., & Gottheil, E. (1989). Effect of psychosocial treatment on survival of patients with metastatic breast cancer. *Lancet, 2*, 888–891.

Spiegel, D., Bloom, J. R., & Yalom, I. (1981). Group support for patients with metastatic cancer: A randomized prospective outcome study. *Archives of General Psychiatry, 38*, 527–533.

Spiegel, D., Sands, S., & Koopman, C. (1994). Pain and depression in patients with cancer. *Cancer, 74*, 2570–2578.

Taylor, S. E. (1983). Adjustment to threatening events: A theory of cognitive adaptation. *American Psychologist, 38*, 1161–1173.

Taylor, S. E., Falke, R. L., Shoptaw, S. J., & Lichtman, R. R. (1986). Social support, support groups, and the cancer patient. *Journal of Consulting and Clinical Psychology, 54*(5), 608–615.

Telch, C. F., & Telch, M. J. (1986). Group coping skills instruction and supportive group therapy for cancer patients: A comparison of strategies. *Journal of Consulting and Clinical Psychology, 54*(6), 802–808.

Thomas, E. M., & Weiss, S. M. (2000). Nonpharmacological interventions with chronic cancer pain in adults. *Cancer Control, 7*(2), 157–164.

Tope, D. M., Ahles, T., & Silberfarb, P. M. (1993). Psycho-oncology: Psychological well-being as one component of quality of life. *Psychotherapy and Psychosomatics, 60*, 129–147.

Trijsburg, R. W., van Knippenberg, F. C. E., & Rijpma, S. E. (1992). Effects of psychological treatment on cancer patients: A critical review. *Psychosomatic Medicine, 54*, 489–517.

U.S. Preventive Services Task Force. (1996). *Guide to clinical preventive services: Report of the U.S. Preventive Services Task Force* (2nd ed.). Baltimore: Williams & Wilkins.

van der Pompe, G., Antoni, M., Visser, A., & Garssen, B. (1996). Adjustment to breast cancer: The psychobiological effects of psychosocial interventions. *Patient Education and Counseling, 28*, 209–219.

Van't Spijker, A., Trijsburg, R. W., & Duivenvoorden, H. J. (1997). Psychological sequelae of cancer diagnosis: A meta-analytic review of 58 studies after 1980. *Psychosomatic Medicine, 59*, 280–293.

Walker, L. G., Heys, S. D., & Eremin, O. (1999). Surviving cancer: Do psychosocial factors count? *Journal of Psychosomatic Research, 47*(6), 497–503.

Ware, J. E., Snow, K. K., Kosinski, M., & Gandek, B. (1993). *SF-36 health survey: Manual and interpretation guide.* Boston: Health Institute, New England Medical Center.

Watson, M., Greer, S., Rowden, L., Gorman, C., Robertson, B., Bliss, J. M. et al. (1991). Relationships between emotional control, adjustment to cancer and depression and anxiety in breast cancer patients. *Psychological Medicine, 21*, 51–57.

Watson, M., Haviland, J. S., Greer, S., Davidson, J., & Bliss, J. M. (1999). Influence of psychological response on survival in breast cancer: A population-based cohort study. *Lancet, 354*, 1331–1336.

Worden, J. W., & Weisman, A. D. (1984). Preventive psychosocial intervention with newly diagnosed cancer patients. *General Hospital Psychiatry, 6*, 243–249.

Zabora, J. R., Smith-Wilson, R., Fetting, J. H., & Enterline, J. P. (1990). An efficient method for psychosocial screening of cancer patients. *Psychosomatics, 31*(2), 192–196.

Zhukovsky, D. S., Gorowski, E., Hausdorff, J., Napolitano, B., & Lesser, M. (1995). Unmet analgesic needs in cancer patients. *Journal of Pain and Symptom Management, 10*(2), 113–119.

Zigmond, A. S., & Snaith, R. P. (1983). The hospital anxiety and depression scale. *Acta Psychiatr Scand, 67*, 361–370.

Chapter 13
Managing Obesity in Primary Care

MARK W. CONARD, WALKER S. CARLOS POSTON, AND JOHN P. FOREYT

Obesity is a major health problem in the United States and other industrialized nations (Mokdad et al., 2004; NHLBI, 1998). Obesity has been traditionally defined as an excess of body fat (i.e., 25% body fat in men and 33% in women; Bray, 1998). This increased body fat is associated with greater risk for a number of health problems including cardiovascular disease, diabetes, and some cancers (Anderson & Wadden, 1999). The prevalence of obesity in primary care appears to be high due its increasing rates in the general population as well as in individuals with obesity-associated medical conditions (e.g., type 2 diabetes, dyslipidemia, and hypertension) seeking treatment (Gray, 1999), with many obese patients (from 50% to 75%) reporting not receiving advice from their health-care providers regarding weight management strategies (Galuska et al., 1999; Potter, Vu, & Croughan-Minihane, 2001; Stafford, Farhat, Misra, & Schoenfeld, 2000). A recent study of family practice offices found that 64% of the patients were obese (Gray, 1999), With such large-scale prevalence, obesity management and treatment should be seen as a problem requiring the involvement of primary care providers as well as specialists in the field.

Obesity Prevalence in the United States

At the present time, 61% of the adult population in the United States is either overweight (i.e., body mass index [BMI] of 25 to 29.9) or obese (a BMI of 30 or more) (CDC, 2000). Approximately 34% are overweight and 27% are obese. These data indicate a 14-percentage-point increase since 1980. The highest prevalence is within the minority population, with 36.5% of African American women and 33.3% of Mexican American women obese. In contrast, the lowest prevalence is in Caucasian men (20.0%) and African American men (20.6%) (Foreyt & Pendleton, 2000). Although obesity prevalence typically increases through age 59 and then declines, the rate of obesity in children is increasing rapidly, with estimates ranging from 20–30% (Gortmaker, Dietz, Sobol, & Wehler, 1987; Troiano & Flegal, 1998). Various studies have noted significant increases in the prevalence of obesity in children over the past several decades. The Bogalusa heart study found that among 6-to-11-year-olds, there has been a 50% increase in the rates of obesity since 1973 (Freedman, Srinivasan, Valdez, Williamson, & Berenson, 1997). Another study reported that there has been an 80% increase in the incidence of obese children becoming obese adults (Schonfeld-Warden & Warden, 1997). Adults with childhood onset of obesity have more severe obesity and earlier onset of co-morbidities. The likelihood of an obese child becoming an obese adult increases as children age and remain obese (Foreyt & Pendleton, 2000).

Costs of Obesity

In the United States, the costs of obesity were estimated to be $99.2 billion in 1995 with approximately $51.6 billion being direct medical costs associated with the treatment of obesity-related diseases (NHLBI, 1998). These direct costs represented about 5.7% of the national health expenditure within the United States (Wolf & Colditz, 1998). The indirect costs, which represent the value of lost output caused by morbidity and mortality, the effects of other medical conditions, and the personal and societal level impacts of obesity, were $47.6 billion (Wolf & Colditz, 1998). For example, cardiovascular disease and type 2 diabetes accounted for 48% and 17.5%, respectively, of the indirect costs (Colditz, 1999).

In a study of the relationship between BMI and future health-care costs, individuals with BMIs of 20 to 24.9 had averaged total costs of outpatient services of $7,673, inpatient care of $5,460, pharmacy services of $2,450, and of all medical care of $15,583 over the 8-year period of the investigation (Thompson, Brown, Nichols, Elmer, & Oster, 2001). In contrast, for those with BMIs of 30 or greater, the averaged total costs of outpatient services was $8,826, for inpatient care was $7,885, use of pharmacy services was $5,000, and total medical costs were $21,711.

Other researchers reported that average annual total costs were 25% higher among individuals with BMIs of 30 to 34.9 (mild obesity) and 44% higher among those with BMIs of 35 or greater (moderate to severe obesity) compared with normal-weight individuals (Quesenberry, Caan, & Jacobson, 1998). Similar results were obtained by Pronk, Tan, and O'Connor (1999), who found that the expected mean annualized costs were approximately 12% higher for those individuals with BMIs of 30 to 34 and approximately 19% higher for those with BMIs of 35 to 39 compared with normal-weight individuals.

In contrast, the cost offsets of intervention programs to lower obesity have had positive economic effects (Pronk et al., 1999). Shephard (1992) investigated the economic impact of a physical activity intervention and found that after 12 years of operation, the intervention yielded a $6.85 return for every $1.00 invested. In addition, the intervention saved $679 in medical costs per year for each participant. Pronk et al. (1999) found similar results for the effects of physical fitness on lowering obesity costs.

Etiology of Obesity

Obesity is a complex, multifaceted chronic disease that involves metabolic, physiological, biochemical, genetic, behavioral, social, and cultural factors (Foreyt & Pendleton, 2000). It is a result of an imbalance between the energy individuals expend and the amount of calories they consume. However, public opinion has tended to view obesity as the result of gluttony and sloth, a behavioral disorder of overeating and laziness (i.e., obese individuals would lose weight if they would just eat less and exercise). There is some basis for this belief. For example, Americans have become more sedentary in both work and leisure (USDHHS, 1996). In addition, Americans consume about 150 more calories per day than they did 10 years ago (Poston & Foreyt, 1999). However, these are not the only reasons behind the epidemic of obesity.

Research has suggested that there is a substantial genetic component to obesity. Genetic influences have been found to contribute to differences among resting metabolic rate (Rice, Tremblay, Deriaz, Perusse, Rao, & Bouchard, 1996), body fat distribution (Bouchard, Perusse, Rice, Rice, & Rao, 1998), and weight gain in response to overfeeding (Bouchard et al., 1990). Some individuals appear to be more predisposed to obesity than others. Thus, environmental factors that interact with obesity-promoting genes have become more available and salient in today's society (Poston & Foreyt, 1999).

Health Risks of Obesity

Increasing body mass is associated with greater mortality risk (NHLBI, 1998; Solomon & Manson, 1997; Mokdad et al., 2004; Pi-Sunyer, 2002). Figure 13.1 provides a graphical representation of the relationship between increased BMIs and mortality rates.

Obesity increases the risk of cardiovascular disease–related mortality one- to twofold (NHLBI, 1998; Singh & Linstead, 1998). A study of coronary patients found that a BMI greater than 35 was associated with an increase in mortality risk (Ellis, Elliott, Horrigan, Raymond, & Howell, 1996).

Obesity has been found to contribute to an increased risk of multiple co-morbid medical conditions including hypertension, dyslipidemia, coronary heart disease, type 2 diabetes, gallbladder disease, sleep apnea, osteoarthritis, various forms of cancer, pulmonary problems, and complications with pregnancy (Ellis et al., 1996; Gray, 1999; Mokdad et al., 2003; NHLBI, 2002; Pi-Sunyer, 2002). Individuals with BMIs of 30 or more are substantially more likely to have some co-morbid condition compared with individuals with BMIs of 19.0 to 24.9 (Quesenberry et al., 1998). Obese patients are 1.7 times more likely to have heart disease, 2 times more likely to have hypertension, and 3 times more likely to have type 2 diabetes compared with normal-weight individuals (Quesenberry et al., 1998).

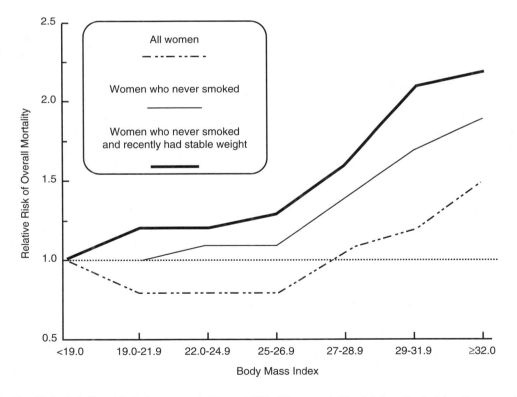

Fig. 13.1 Relationship between mortality and BMI. When mortality risk is adjusted for disease-related health status and smoking, the leanest women (BMI < 20) have the lowest mortality and that mortality risk increases with increasing BMI (adapted from WHO, 1998).

With the increase in obesity, it is not surprising that primary care physicians are seeing more co-morbidities. What we do not know is how frequently primary care physicians are treating the obesity or focusing only on the co-morbid conditions.

Assessment of Obesity

Before prescribing weight loss intervention, primary care providers should assess the patient's level of obesity, need for treatment, and readiness for change. Assessment will help determine the type of treatment to prescribe and how to best tailor interventions to each patient's needs. Areas of assessment involve determining the degree of obesity, level of health risk involved, current diet and eating patterns, level of physical activity, emotional state, and readiness to change. These assessments are warranted when the physician believes the patient is presenting with early signs and symptoms of obesity or associated co-morbid medical conditions that require attention.

Assessing the degree of obesity provides the practitioner a useful starting point for selecting the most appropriate treatment modality (Foreyt & Pendleton, 2000). For example, cognitive behavioral techniques have been used most often with patients who are overweight to moderately obese (BMIs from 25–40), while other approaches, such as gastric bypass surgery, have been indicated for patients with severe obesity (BMI greater than 40) (NHLBI, 1998).

Assessment Tools

There are numerous assessment tools for determining the degree of obesity or body fatness of a patient. These tools include hydrodensitometry (underwater weighing), air displacement plethysmography, dual x-ray absorptiometry (DEXA), isotope dilution, total body potassium, skin-fold measurements, bioelectrical impedance, ultrasound, total body conductivity (TOBEC), computed tomography (CT), magnetic resonance imaging (MRI), neutron activation, waist circumference, and BMI (Foreyt & Pendleton, 2000; NHLBI, 2000).

Hydrodensitometry. In hydrodensitometry, the patient is weighed on a special scale while completely submerged underwater. The technique is based on the principle that fat floats and nonfat components sink. This method was the "gold standard" until the advent of dual x-ray absorptiometry (DEXA).

Dual X-Ray Absorptiometry. The DEXA method requires patients to lie on a table while low-energy x-rays are beamed through their bodies. Estimates of lean body mass, body fat, and bone content are possible. The cost of the DEXA equipment ranges from $40,000–100,000. Patients weighing in excess of 300 pounds may not be testable because of the structural limitations of the equipment (Foreyt & Pendleton, 2000).

Skin-Fold Measurements. The skin-fold method entails the measurement of subcutaneous fat at predefined points on the body utilizing a special pincher-like device known as a skin caliper (Foreyt & Pendleton, 2000). Skin-fold measurements are one of the more common, inexpensive methods of estimating body fat because of the ease of administration. However, there are concerns regarding the skin-fold method's accuracy as compared with hydrodensitometry and DEXA because of variation in measurement instrumentation and difficulties with interrater reliability. Another limitation of the method is related to the inability of the jaws of the calipers to open wide enough to measure extremely large deposits of fat.

Bioelectrical Impedance. Bioelectrical impedance uses a weak electric current to determine the level of body fat in the patient (Foreyt & Pendleton, 2000). This weak electric current is passed through the body with the current flow being aided by hydrated, fat-free tissue and impeded by dense adipose tissue. Thus, the more body fat, the more inhibited and slower the current. Although this technique is advanced in its use of technology, it appears to be less accurate than DEXA because it is sensitive to the patient's level of hydration.

Imaging Techniques. Several imaging techniques have been found to be useful in assessing body fat (Foreyt & Pendleton, 2000). One technique is a portable ultrasound meter. It measures subcutaneous fat using sound reflectance. Ultrasound has good reliability and is not limited by the size of the patient being assessed. Another technique is TOBEC, which relies on the change in electromagnetic characteristics as a function of fat and water. Other imaging methods that are accurate in measuring body fat are CT and MRI. However, similar to DEXA, CT, MRI, and TOBEC, the imaging equipment is expensive and in clinical settings these costs might be restrictive. Less-expensive methods such as skin-fold measurements and ultrasound can produce results with 95–97% accuracy when performed according to recognized protocols (McArdle, Katch, & Katch, 1991).

Waist Circumference. Waist circumference is positively correlated with abdominal fat content (NHLBI, 1998). This method provides a clinically acceptable measurement for determining a patient's abdominal fat content. Sex-specific cutoffs have been determined to identify the increased relative risk for the development of obesity-related risk factors in most adults with BMIs of 25 to 34.9. High-risk cutoffs for men and women are a waist circumference greater than 102 cm (greater than 40 in.) and 88 cm (greater than 35 in.), respectively.

Body Mass Index (BMI). A quick method to determine the level of obesity is to assess BMI, which is determined by taking weight in kilograms and dividing it by height in meters squared (NHLBI, 1998). BMI also can be calculated by dividing weight in pounds by height in inches squared and multiplying the product by 704.5 (as shown in the Nonmetric Formula for Calculating BMI, Equation 13.1). Table 13.1 provides a BMI chart commonly used to assess obesity.

$$BMI = \frac{Weight(pounds)}{Height(inches)^2} \times 704.5$$

BMI has been divided into classes to define underweight (BMI less than 18.5), normal weight (BMI 18.5–24.9), and overweight (BMI 25–29.9) individuals (see Table 13.2). For obesity (BMI 30 or greater), there are three further classifications divided in terms of severity: Class I—mild obesity (BMI of 30.0 to 34.9), Class II—moderate obesity (BMI of 35.0 to 39.9), and Class III—severe obesity (BMI of 40 or greater) (NHLBI, 1998). The advantages of using the BMI in primary care include its ease of use, its accuracy in measuring both weight and height, and its use of similar criteria independent of gender (Foreyt & Pendleton, 2000). However, BMI does not work well with well-muscled athletes who have unusually high levels of lean muscle mass. In addition, the BMI categories are restricted to individuals who are past puberty. Classifying children using BMI could result in incorrect estimations of their body composition (McArdle et al., 1991).

Health Risk Assessment

Figure 13.1 indicates the relationship between BMI and increased mortality. As illustrated by the figure, higher BMIs tend to be associated with higher rates of mortality. With the increased prevalence of other medical conditions that are related to obesity, it is important to assess the level of health risk of the patient. Some obese patients with multiple health risks need to lose weight more than patients who are otherwise relatively healthy. Likewise, heavier patients usually have more co-morbid medical conditions than those who are not as heavy.

TABLE 13.1 Example of Body Mass Index (BMI) Chart

BMI	19	20	21	22	23	24	25	26	27	28	29	30	31	32	33	34	35
Height								*Weight (in pounds)*									
4'10" (58")	91	96	100	105	110	115	119	124	129	134	138	143	148	153	158	162	167
4'11" (59")	94	99	104	109	114	119	124	128	133	138	143	148	153	158	163	168	173
5' (60")	97	102	107	112	118	123	128	133	138	143	148	153	158	163	168	174	179
5'1" (61")	100	106	111	116	122	127	132	137	143	148	153	158	164	169	174	180	185
5'2" (62")	104	109	115	120	126	131	136	142	147	153	158	164	169	175	180	186	191
5'3" (63")	107	113	118	124	130	135	141	146	152	158	163	169	175	180	186	191	197
5'4" (64")	110	116	122	128	134	140	145	151	157	163	169	174	180	186	192	197	204
5'5" (65")	114	120	126	132	138	144	150	156	162	168	174	180	186	192	198	204	210
5'6" (66")	118	124	130	136	142	148	155	161	167	173	179	186	192	198	204	210	216
5'7" (67")	121	127	134	140	146	153	159	166	172	178	185	191	198	204	211	217	223
5'8" (68")	125	131	138	144	151	158	164	171	177	184	190	197	203	210	216	223	230
5'9" (69")	128	135	142	149	155	162	169	176	182	189	196	203	209	216	223	230	236
5'10" (70")	132	139	146	153	160	167	174	181	188	195	202	209	216	222	229	236	243
5'11" (71")	136	143	150	157	165	172	179	186	193	200	208	215	222	229	236	243	250
6' (72")	140	147	154	162	169	177	184	191	199	206	213	221	228	235	242	250	258
6'1" (73")	144	151	159	166	174	182	189	197	204	212	219	227	235	242	250	257	265
6'2" (74")	148	155	163	171	179	186	194	202	210	218	225	233	241	249	256	264	272
6'3" (75")	152	160	168	176	184	192	200	208	216	224	232	240	248	256	264	272	279

Note. Evidence Report of Clinical Guidelines on the Identification, Evaluation, and Treatment of Overweight and Obesity in Adults, 1998. NIH/National Heart, Lung, and Blood Institute (NHLBI).

TABLE 13.2 Classification of Obesity Using BMI

	BMI
Underweight	< 18.5
Normal weight	18.5–24.9
Overweight	25–29.9
Mild obesity	30–34.9
Moderate obesity	35–39.9
Severe obesity	> 40

Diet/Eating Patterns Assessment

Because diet plays a major role in the development of obesity, an assessment of dietary patterns is an essential component for devising a treatment plan (Foreyt & Pendleton, 2000). However, the labor-intensive nature of traditional assessment techniques (i.e., 24-hour recall and food-frequency questionnaires) challenges the primary care provider's ability to deliver quality service in a time-efficient manner. In response, brief dietary assessment questionnaires have been developed. These questionnaires include the MEDFICTS Dietary Assessment Questionnaire (National Cholesterol Education Program, 1993), the Rate Your Plate dietary assessment questionnaire (which aims at the management of cholesterol) (SCORE, 1988), and the Eating Pattern Assessment Tool (which is directed at patients interested in maintaining a heart-healthy diet) (Physician Based Nutrition Program, 1990).

These tools assess the frequency at which certain food groups are eaten per week along with typical serving sizes (Foreyt & Pendleton, 2000). Although these tools are specific to particular medical conditions, they can be generalized easily to obesity management because they provide a description of the patient's daily eating patterns. An advantage of these brief tools is that the primary care provider can capture reliable and general data concerning the patient's eating patterns in a relatively short time. In addition, patients gain self-awareness of their eating behaviors. If more detailed dietary patterns are required, primary care physicians can refer the patient to a registered dietitian.

Physical Activity Assessment

Similar to assessing dietary patterns, examining the patterns and levels of physical activity can augment treatment planning. However, like traditional dietary assessments, these techniques tend to consume large amounts of time (Foreyt & Pendleton, 2000). To shorten the assessment, more cost-effective methods to examine a patient's physical activity have been developed. For example, general patterns of physical activity can be efficiently assessed by the Self-Administered 7-Day Physical Activity Recall Questionnaire (Blair, 1984). The instrument provides a means of capturing general information concerning the patient's level of moderate-to-vigorous physical activity over the most recent 7-day period.

Emotional Assessment

The assessment of a patient's emotional state is important in determining the proper treatment for obesity. About 25–30% of obese patients who seek some form of weight reduction therapy reportedly suffer from marked depression or other psychological disturbances (Fitzgibbon, Stolley, & Kirschenbaum, 1993). There also is a high prevalence of depression among obese patients who binge (Marcus, 1993), along with increased emotional distress (Yanovski, 1993). Patients suffering from depression tend to have more difficulty in adhering to weight management programs and may achieve greater success if the depression is treated effectively before a weight loss program is implemented (Foreyt & Pendleton, 2000). Obese patients with marked depression, anxiety, or binge eating may require some form of psychotherapy or pharmacotherapy before beginning any form of weight loss treatment (Anderson & Wadden, 1999).

There are several well-documented instruments that can aid in assessing depression, including the Beck Depression Inventory for Primary Care (BDI-PC; Steer, Cavalieri, Leonard, & Beck, 1999) and the Center for Epidemiologic Studies Depression Scale (CES-D; Miller & Harrington, 1997a). The BDI-PC is a self-administered, 7-item questionnaire that reliably identifies depression in a primary care setting (Steer et al., 1999). The CES-D also is self-administered. It contains 20 items with good psychometric properties and is simple to use (Miller & Harrington, 1997a).

In addition to assessment instruments for depression, there also are brief and valid measures of general distress, anxiety, and binge eating available. For example, the General Well-Being Schedule is an 18-item questionnaire that was developed to measure well-being and distress as part of the U.S. Health and Nutrition Examination Survey (McDowell & Newell, 1987). It has established cut points, and its reliability and validity have been evaluated in a variety of populations (Miller & Harrington, 1997b; Poston et al., 1998; Taylor et al., 2003). For assessment of anxiety, a well-known and brief measure is the State-Trait Anxiety Inventory (Spielberger, Syderman, Owen, & Marsh, 1999). This brief measure assesses both state (situation specific) and trait (general) anxiety symptom ratings and has been studied in a number of relevant patient samples (Spielberger et al., 1999). Finally, the Binge Eating Scale is a 16-item questionnaire designed to assess distress associated with binge eating and severity of bingeing. Although it is not equivalent to a diagnosis of binge-eating disorder, it has been found to be a useful outcome measure in obesity and binge-eating intervention studies and has established norms and validity data (Gormally, Black, Daston, & Rardin, 1982; Pike, Loeb, & Walsh, 1995; Stellefson & O'Neil, 1997).

Stages of Change Assessment

A final area that should be assessed by the primary care provider before developing a treatment plan is to examine the patient's readiness for change (Foreyt & Pendleton, 2000). For any type of therapy or treatment to be effective, the patient needs to be motivated to make the appropriate changes. Obese patients will present at differing levels of readiness to change. It is likely that some severely obese patients with multiple medical conditions will not be ready to change their habits to reduce their weight. The primary care provider needs to recognize this fact and work with these patients to educate them about the issues involved.

The Transtheoretical Model (or Stages of Change Model) categorizes individuals into five stages: precontemplation, contemplation, preparation, action, and maintenance (Prochaska, Norcross, & DiClemente, 1994). *Precontemplators* are individuals who are not at all concerned about their obesity. *Contemplators* express some concerns about their weight but are not yet certain about taking some type of action. For example, if obese patients are not ready to begin reducing their caloric intake and increasing their exercise, such suggestions will fall on deaf ears and may even increase their resistance. In this instance, discussion between the primary care physician and the obese patient focused on education and personalization of the risks involved might be more beneficial. Individuals in the *preparation stage* have decided to make some change but have not yet done so. These individuals need encouragement to take action as well as to make a commitment to change their behaviors. Individuals in the *action stage* recently have started to make changes in their habits and tend to benefit most from behavioral interventions such as goal setting and self-monitoring (Foreyt & Pendleton, 2000). Obese patients in the *maintenance stage* are working on continuing the changes they have made and tend to benefit from moral support and recognition.

To assess the level of readiness of an obese patient, primary care physicians can use the questions developed by Prochaska and colleagues (1994). Table 13.3 illustrates some diagnostic questions that could be used to assess a patient's current stage of change with respect to dieting behaviors.

Similar questions can be used to assess various target behaviors. Recently, a study was conducted using this method to assess stages of change of six weight-related behaviors among a group of obese patients at a family practice clinic (Logue, Sutton, Jarjoura, & Smucker, 2000). The researchers found that patients in a particular stage were distributed across all five stages for other behaviors. The stage of change was associated significantly with BMI or waist girth.

A shortened form of the University of Rhode Island Change Assessment Scale (URICA) relates the stages of change to weight management (Prochaska & DiClemente, 1992). It consists of four dichotomous items that relate precisely to weight management behavior. One study using this assessment tool found that obese individuals in the precontemplation and contemplation stages were more likely to have negative feelings toward weight management strategies, while those in the action stage were more likely to have positive, directed coping approaches (Cowan, Britton, Logue, Smucker, & Milo, 1995).

Treatment Strategies for Obesity

Psychosocial Treatments

In working with obese patients, a central component of management and treatment is the modification of the patient's lifestyle. The focus is on increasing physical activity, normalizing caloric

TABLE 13.3 Examples of Stages of Change Questions for Dieting Behaviors

Which statement most accurately describes you?

Precontemplation—I do not diet and have no plans to start.

Contemplation—I plan to begin dieting in the next 6 months.

Preparation—I plan to begin dieting in the next month.

Action—I have begun dieting on a regular basis for more than 6 months.

Maintenance—I have been dieting on a regular basis for more than 6 months.

consumption, and creating realistic expectations for success. There are seven basic lifestyle modification approaches used to decrease caloric consumption and to increase physical activity: setting realistic goals, self-monitoring, stimulus control, cognitive restructuring, stress management, relapse prevention training, and social support (Foreyt & Pendleton, 2000).

Setting Realistic Goals. A patient will, on average, lose 8–10% of baseline weight in an intervention program, but most obese patients want to lose more. Therefore, an important early treatment strategy is to assist patients in setting more realistic weight-loss goals. For example, a physician might encourage a patient to make small behavioral changes in eating and physical activity and to concentrate on the health benefits associated with these changes (Foreyt & Pendleton, 2000). This type of approach provides the patient with dual benefits, including feelings of success for meeting the short-term goals as well as moving toward the long-term goal of weight loss that can be maintained (Foreyt & Pendleton, 2000).

Self-Monitoring. One of the most of important lifestyle modification strategies is self-monitoring (Foreyt & Pendleton, 2000). Self-monitoring involves the systematic observation and recording of specific target behaviors, related feelings, and environmental cues (Baker & Kirschenbaum, 1993). This technique is particularly useful for someone attempting weight loss because it raises the awareness of the patient's eating behaviors and levels of physical activity as well as what affects these behaviors. Self-monitoring tools include food diaries to record total caloric intake, total fat grams consumed, food groups used, and situations when overeating is common; physical activity logs to record frequency, duration, and intensity of exercise; electronic devices that count the number of steps taken; and weight scales or body composition measures to record changes in weight, body fat, or lean body mass (Poston & Foreyt, 1999).

Accuracy in self-reporting of behaviors is desirable but does not usually occur, and absolute accuracy is not necessary (Foreyt & Pendleton, 2000). This strategy is beneficial even with some inaccuracy (i.e., patients tend to underestimate caloric consumption by about one-third and overestimate physical activity by about one-half) because it provides an increased awareness of eating and physical activity behaviors possibly leading to some type of improvement (Foreyt & Goodrick, 1991; Foreyt & Poston, 1996). Self-monitoring strategies have been found to be consistently effective in improving treatment outcomes, with patients reporting that they are one of the most helpful tools in obesity management (Baker & Kirschenbaum, 1993; Boutelle & Kirschenbaum, 1998; Kayman, Bruvold, & Stern, 1990). However, physicians tend not to ask their patients to keep food diaries, and patients do not like to fill them out even though diaries are the single most helpful tool for raising patients' awareness of their eating and physical activity behaviors (Foreyt & Pendleton, 2000).

Stimulus Control. Stimulus control involves the identification and modification of the environmental cues that contribute to overeating and inactivity (Baker & Kirschenbaum, 1993). Once the environmental cues have been identified, patients can devise strategies to control them, which can be useful in maintaining long-term weight loss (Foreyt & Goodrick, 1993). Various techniques to help control common environmental cues include eating only at the kitchen table without watching television, keeping no snack foods in the house, and placing exercise clothes out the night before as a reminder to jog in the morning.

Cognitive Restructuring. Cognitive restructuring refers to encouraging patients to examine their inner thoughts, feelings, and beliefs about themselves and their weight and challenging them to change those beliefs that are inaccurate or counterproductive (Foreyt & Goodrick, 1993). This method is particularly useful with obese patients because many of them have poor self-esteem and distorted body images. Some are unrealistic about how much weight they can lose as well as the benefits of weight loss (Poston & Foreyt, 2000). The goal of cognitive restructuring is to identify these self-defeating cognitions and to assist the patient in replacing them with more productive and affirming ones (Foreyt & Pendleton, 2000).

Stress Management. Stress management training is useful in the management of weight loss because stress has been found to be a strong predictor of overeating and relapse (Kayman et al., 1990; Pendleton et al., 2001). There are a number of techniques to manage stress and reduce associated sympathetic nervous system arousal. These techniques include diaphragmatic breathing, stress innoculation training, progressive muscle relaxation, and meditation (Poston & Foreyt, 2000). They have been found to be highly effective in helping manage a number of health-related problems including obesity (Everly, 1989).

Relapse Prevention. Relapse prevention training attempts to normalize lapses as an acceptable part of weight-loss management (Foreyt & Goodrick, 1991, 1994). The method teaches patients to accept lapses as inevitable and prepares them to manage lapses by minimizing the damage and getting patients back on the road to weight loss as quickly as possible. This technique lessens the chance that a full relapse will occur.

Social Support. Research consistently has shown that patients with high levels of social support tend to have greater success in achieving and maintaining weight losses than those lacking in support (Kayman et al., 1990). High levels of social support also improve adherence to obesity management programs (Foreyt & Goodrick, 1991; Klem, Wing, Simkin-Silverman, & Kuller, 1997). Improving social support involves including family members and friends in the weight loss intervention, participation in community-based programs, involvement in outside social activities (e.g., university or community education courses, health clubs, and church-related activities), or referrals to groups of individuals with similar goals (Foreyt & Pendleton, 2000; Poston & Foreyt, 2000). Social support helps patients become more self-accepting, develop new norms for interpersonal relationships, and manage stressful work- or family-related situations (Foreyt & Goodrick, 1993; Kayman et al., 1990).

Results of Behavioral Interventions

Incorporating lifestyle modification strategies into obesity management programs produces average weight losses of about 10 kg (22 lb) over 6 months (Poston & Foreyt, 2000). Intervention programs last about 20–24 weeks and usually including multiple treatment strategies. Patients tend to maintain, on average, about two thirds of their initial weight loss 9 to 10 months after the termination of their treatment. Although 5–10% losses of initial bodyweight can confer health benefits, it is not known how long these health benefits last or how quickly the gradual weight gain after treatment termination mitigates these benefits (NHLBI, 1998). Attrition rates are generally low (less than 18%). There is greater weight loss when multiple lifestyle modification strategies are used (NHLBI, 1998; Wing, 1998).

Physical Activity

Physical activity is associated with reductions in a number of co-morbid, obesity-related medical conditions. It is an important predictor of weight maintenance (NHLBI, 1998; USDHHS, 1996). The type, frequency, intensity, and duration should be considered when adding physical activity to a weight loss program (Foreyt & Pendleton, 2000; Miller & Wadden, 2004). The types selected should be matched to the individual's physical and psychological limitations to ensure consistency and enhance adherence.

The American College of Sports Medicine has recommended specific guidelines for exercise-induced weight loss (Jakicic et al., 2003). These guidelines recommend that overweight and obese individuals lower their current level of energy intake by 500–1,000 kcal per day combined with a reduction in dietary fat intake to < 30% of total energy intake. Furthermore, these individuals are recommended to progressively increase their level of physical activity to a minimum of 150 minutes (30 minutes, 5 times per week) of moderate-intensity exercise. For long-term weight loss, the guidelines suggest an eventual increase to higher amounts of exercise (e.g., 200–300 minutes per week or approximately 2,000 kcal per week of leisure-time physical activity). However, this goal might not be realistic for obese patients just beginning a weight loss program. Obese patients should begin a program slowly, building to moderate levels of activity (e.g., brisk walking) for 30 to 40 minutes, 3 to 5 times a week (an expenditure of 150 to 225 kcal per session) (NHLBI, 1998). The focus of physical activity should be weight loss where maximum physical exertion is not required. Moderate-intensity lifestyle activity can be as effective as higher intensity exertion in burning calories (Andersen et al., 1999; Dunn et al., 1999; Foreyt & Pendleton, 2000). Talking with patients about the benefits of moderate-intensity exercise and encouraging even some modest increases in physical activity might lead them to value even modest efforts and contribute to overall treatment adherence.

Diet

The USDA guidelines recommend a reduction of 500–1,000 calories per day, which will lead to a weight loss of 0.45–0.9 kg (1–2 lb) per week (NHLBI, 1998). According to these guidelines, women should follow a diet of 1,000 to 1,200 kcal per day, and men 1,200 to 1,500 kcal per day (NHLBI, 1998). A reduction of 500 calories per day will result in a loss of one pound per week (Foreyt & Pendleton, 2000). Determining an appropriate caloric intake, along with self-monitoring, will enable patients to attain better control over their diet. However, knowing the amount of calories in a given meal is not easy. When in doubt, patients should focus on portion sizes, especially with those foods known to be high in fat content (Foreyt & Pendleton, 2000).

In addition to reducing calories, patients should be encouraged to lower the amount of fat and empty calories they ingest. The Food Guide Pyramid (USDA, 1992) and the Exchange Lists for Meal Planning (American Dietetic Association and American Diabetes Association, 1989) can be helpful in determining what foods to eat and the number of servings that promote healthy eating. By following a balanced, reduced-calorie diet, with choices made according to USDA recommendations, patients will have more long-term success with weight loss and subsequent management.

Components of Obesity Treatment Strategies

The above treatment strategies can be delivered either individually or in group formats, depending on the needs of the patient and the facility's ability to provide the needed services. Currently, most behavioral programs are delivered in weekly, small-group programs consisting of 10–20 patients over 20 or more weeks (Wing, 2004). The duration of obesity treatment programs has steadily increased over the past 30 years from an average of 8.4 weeks in 1974 to an average of 27 weeks by the mid-1990s (Wing, 2004). This shift has occurred as researchers began to realize that obesity treatment is a lifelong disease-management process. In addition to traditional individual and group delivery of obesity treatment, long-term approaches include the use of support groups and promoting intermittent individual treatments. Several current examples of obesity treatment programs that follow a lifelong maintenance approach to obesity treatment include the LEARN Program (Brownell, 2000), Structure House, and the Duke Diet and Fitness Centers programs. It is important to note that not all these strategies need to be used by a patient, nor is there a particular order in delivering these approaches. The use of these strategies should be determined on an individual basis by the physician or in consultation with the rest of the health-care team.

Pharmacotherapy Treatments

Although lifestyle modifications appear to be helpful for most obese patients, they do not ensure long-term, weight-loss maintenance (Poston & Foreyt, 2000). Without recurrent contact, most or all of the weight patients lose will be regained within 3 to 5 years (Wing, 2004; Perri & Foreyt, 2004). Many patients need additional intervention. Current National Institutes of Health clinical guidelines view pharmacotherapy as an adjunct to lifestyle modification programs (NHLBI, 1998). Pharmacotherapy is appropriate for patients with a BMI of 30 or greater or with a BMI of 27 or greater with other co-morbidities (e.g., hypertension, dyslipidemia, or type 2 diabetes) (NHLBI, 1998).

Researchers comparing the effectiveness of drug treatment alone, behavior therapy alone, and combined drug treatment and behavior therapy found that behavior therapy alone and the combined behavior therapy with drug treatment resulted in greater weight loss than a wait-list control group or the drug alone group (Craighead, Stunkard, & O'Brien, 1981; Stunkard, Craighead, & O'Brien, 1980). Obesity drugs in conjunction with dietary programs typically result in modest weight losses compared with placebo groups (NHLBI, 1998). The effects of drug treatments maximize within the first 6 months of initiation, with weight loss being generally maintained for the duration of the treatment (Poston & Foreyt, 2000). Table 13.4 lists examples of available obesity medications.

Noradrenergic Drugs. Noradrenergic drugs affect weight by suppressing a patient's appetite. Noradrenergic drugs include phentermine resin (Ionanmin), mazindol (Sanorex), phenylpropanolamine (Dexatrim), phendimetrazine (Plegine), and diethylpropion (Tenuate). When combined with dietary programs, these medications produce modest, short-term weight losses compared with placebo. The U.S. Food and Drug Administration (FDA) has not approved any of these drugs for the long-term treatment (i.e., 1 year) of obesity (Poston & Foreyt, 2000). Side effects of these drugs can include increased heart rate and blood pressure, insomnia, constipation, and dry mouth (Yanovski & Yanovski, 2002).

Serotonin and Noradrenaline Reuptake Inhibition. Sibutramine (Meridia) is a serotonin and noradrenaline reuptake inhibitor. It is approved by the FDA for the long-term treatment of obesity. Sibutramine was developed initially as an antidepressant (Luque & Rey, 1999). However, weight loss was seen in depressed patients who were not actively attempting to lose weight (Foreyt & Pendleton, 2000). Clinical studies have shown that sibutramine produces weight losses of 4.7 to 7.6 kg (10.3 to 16.7 lb) in patients receiving the drug compared with placebo. The weight losses are dose-dependent and level off at 6 months (Lean, 1997; Seagle, Bessesen, & Hill, 1998; Bray & Ryan,

TABLE 13.4 List of Obesity Drugs

Agent	DEA Schedule	Action
Diethylpropion (Tenuate)	IV	Noradrenergic
Mazindol (Sanorex)	IV	Noradrenergic
Orlistat* (Xenical)	None	Lipase Inhibitor
Phendimetrazine (Plegine)	III	Noradrenergic
Phentermine (Fastin)	IV	Noradrenergic
Phentermine resin (Ionamin)	IV	Noradrenergic
Phenylpropanolamine (Dexatrim)	Over-the-counter	Noradrenergic
Sibutramine* (Meridia)	IV	SNRI

DEA = Drug Enforcement Agency; SNRI = serotonergic noradrenergic reuptake inhibitor.
*Orlistat and sibutramine are the only drugs labeled by the Food and Drug Administration for long-term treatment of obesity.

2004). In more than 20 trials weight losses were significantly greater in sibutramine-treated patients (who lost about 6–10% of body weight over 6–12 months) than in those given the placebo (Foreyt & Pendleton, 2000). Sibutramine also has been studied in a number of unique populations including obese controlled hypotencives, diabetics, and ethnic minorities further establishing its effectiveness (Poston & Foreyt, 2004).

Side effects of sibutramine include a mean increase in blood pressure of 1–3 mm Hg as well as a mean increase in heart rate of about 4 bpm (Lean, 1997). A few patients experience a significant increase in blood pressure, so blood pressure needs to be monitored (Lean, 1997). These potentially clinically significant increases have been documented with an incidence of 2% relative to placebo in patients with uncomplicated obesity (Foreyt & Pendleton, 2000). Care should be used when prescribing sibutramine in patients with a history of hypertension, and it should not be given to those with uncontrolled or poorly controlled blood pressure. There have been no reported cases of ischemic coronary problems, arrhythmias, cerebrovascular difficulties, neurotoxicity, primary pulmonary hypertension, or valvular heart disease with patients taking sibutramine compared with placebo (Bray & Ryan, 2004; Foreyt & Pendleton, 2000; Lean, 1997). There are drug interactions with monoamine oxidase inhibitors (MAOIs), selective serotonin reuptake inhibitors (SSRIs), erythromycin, and ketoconazole (Foreyt & Pendleton, 2000).

Lipase Inhibition. Orlistat (Xenical) is a lipase inhibitor that works by reducing the body's absorption of dietary fat. It is a nonsystemic drug that blocks about 30% of dietary fat (Hvizdos & Markham, 1999; Van Gaal & Bray, 2004). Orlistat has been approved by the FDA for long-term use. One clinical study reported weight losses of about 5 kg (11 lb) after 12 weeks of treatment with orlistat (360 mg per day) compared with 2-to-3-kg losses (4.4 to 6.6 lb) in the placebo group (Drent et al., 1995). The weight losses appeared to be dose-dependent, with lower doses producing smaller weight losses. Another study found that patients given orlistat over a 2-year period experienced substantial improvements in weight and other health parameters (e.g., improvements in low-density lipoprotein [LDL] cholesterol and insulin) compared with the placebo group (Davidson et al., 1999). A number of 2-year, randomized, double-blind prospective studies have found that patients lose significantly more weight with orlistat than placebo and improve their health profiles (Foreyt & Pendleton, 2000). Recent findings suggest that adding Orlistat to lifestyle-change programs provides an added benefit of lowering the incidence of type 2 diabetes in obese patients with a risk reduction of 37.3% over a four year period (Torgerson & Boldrin, Hamptman, & Sjostrom, 2004).

The contraindications for the use of orlistat include chronic malabsorption syndrome or cholestasis (Foreyt & Pendleton, 2000). Side effects include changes in bowel habits, such as oily or loose stools, the need to have a bowel movement quickly, bloating, or oily spotting. These side effects tend to occur when individuals consume more than 30% of calories from fat. They can be minimized once patients lower the fat in their diet to less than 30%. Orlistat reduces the absorption of fat-soluble vitamins A, D, E, and K as well as beta-carotene. Patients taking orlistat should take a multivitamin supplement containing fat-soluble vitamins (Foreyt & Pendleton, 2000).

Surgery

Past surgical treatments for obesity have included wiring the patient's jaw to lower caloric intake and jejunoileal bypass to induce malabsorption. However, both these treatments were abandoned because of lack of long-term efficacy (jaw wiring) or unacceptable side effects (jejunoileal bypass) (Gray, 1999). Currently, gastric partitioning is used to decrease the intake of food by increasing satiety through decreasing the size of the patient's stomach. The current NIH guidelines for surgical interventions indicate that this option is only acceptable for carefully selected patients with clinically severe obesity (BMIs of 40 or greater or BMIs of 35 or greater with co-morbid conditions) when less-intensive techniques have not worked and the patients are at high risk for obesity-related morbidity and mortality (NHLBI, 1998).

Severely obese patients have traditionally not been helped by the more conservative interventions such as lifestyle modification (Foreyt & Pendleton, 2000). The surgical option is seen as a reasonable approach for severely obese patients who are at increased risk for premature death and whose potential benefits from the procedure outweigh the involved risks (National Institute of Health Consensus Development Conference Statement, 1992; Sjostrom, 2004). The effectiveness of surgical interventions has been well documented, with weight losses of 100 lb or more after 12 months following surgery (Foreyt & Pendleton, 2000; Sjostrom, 2004).

Treatment Guidelines

Traditionally, the choice of obesity treatment has been based primarily on the amount of excess body weight (Hill, 1998), with the more aggressive therapies targeted toward patients who are more obese or who have more health complications (Anderson & Wadden, 1999). Interventions for overweight patients (BMIs of 25 to 29.9) have typically focused on lifestyle modification strategies. Treatments for obese patients (BMIs of 30 to 39.9) usually require more aggressive options such as pharmacological treatments, very low-calorie diets, or residential programs. Those who are severely obese (BMIs of 40 or greater) may need gastric bypass surgery (Anderson & Wadden, 1999; Hill, 1998; NHLBI, 1998). The NIH has created a treatment algorithm for the evaluation of overweight or obese individuals (see Figure 13.2) (NHLBI, 1998).

The initial decision is based on BMI. Additional steps consist of evaluations of related factors, including individual history, physical examination, laboratory tests, and motivation to lose weight. These steps help determine the type, frequency, and level of weight loss strategies the patient should attempt (NHLBI, 1998).

In addition to the NIH clinical guidelines, Hill (1998) has proposed three general models of obesity management based on the extent to which primary care providers are willing and able to be involved in the chronic management of their obese patients. The minimal model involves the assessment of risk followed by referral of those with high risk to more comprehensive obesity programs. The intermediate model consists of the primary care providers evaluating risk; establishing treatment goals; providing information concerning lifestyle modification strategies, pharmacotherapy, and reduced calorie diets; and evaluating treatment outcomes. The third model includes all

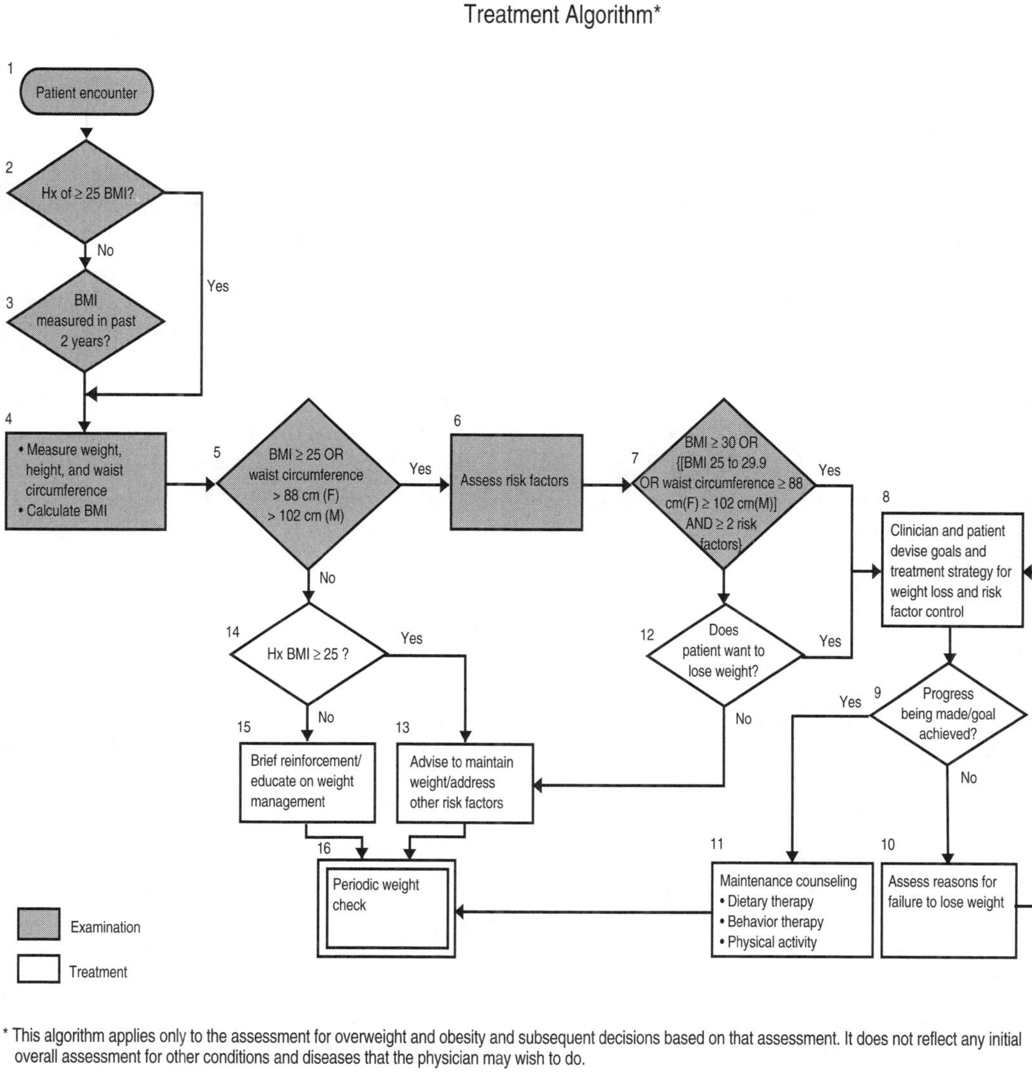

Treatment Algorithm*

Fig. 13.2 NIH obesity treatment algorithm (from NHLBI, 1998).

* This algorithm applies only to the assessment for overweight and obesity and subsequent decisions based on that assessment. It does not reflect any initial overall assessment for other conditions and diseases that the physician may wish to do.

aspects of the intermediate model but additionally emphasizes long-term maintenance of reduced body weight (Hill, 1998).

Role of the Behavioral Health-Care Specialist in Obesity Treatment

In some instances, physicians consult with behavioral health-care specialists (BHS) to aid them in obesity treatment. The BHS functions as an integral part of the patient's multidisciplinary team by providing additional support and training in how to most effectively implement lifestyle modifications and maintain them over time (Foreyt & Poston, 1998). The BHS can aid the physician, the multidisciplinary health-care team, and the patient with strategies for implementing and maintaining the obesity treatment strategies. Additionally, the BHS can act as a research consultant in determining more effective and efficacious treatments for obesity. Discussions between the physician and BHS can occur at multidisciplinary meetings, case conferences, individual rounds, and through medical charts. Information pertaining to treatment progress and recommendations are typically shared during these various discussions.

Review of Obesity Prevention

Prevention includes the primary prevention of obesity itself, secondary prevention or avoidance of weight regain following weight loss, and prevention of further weight increases in obese patients unable to lose weight (Jeffery, 1998; National Task Force on Prevention and Treatment of Obesity, 1994). Most strategies for the prevention of obesity have focused on modifying the obese patient's behaviors (predominantly diet and physical activity). However, they have provided little in the way of actual procedures or guidelines for prevention (Nestle & Jacobson, 2000) and have not been very effective.

Primary prevention of obesity should include strategies that focus on the environmental influences that affect obesity. These influences include food marketing practices, media and advertising, transportation patterns, community organization, and lack of opportunities for physical activity during the workday (French, Story, & Jeffery, 2001; James, 1995; Jeffery, 1991; Poston & Foreyt, 1999). Creating policies and procedures that promote healthy eating and increased physical activity will enhance the promotion of weight loss and reduction in the prevalence of obesity. Obesity prevention needs to be recognized by both the government and health-care payers (HMOs and PPOs).

Primary care providers can play an important role in obesity prevention because of the high proportion of overweight and obese patients who come for treatment in the primary care setting. Primary care providers have a significant role in preventing obesity and its related medical disorders through control of dyslipidemia, high blood pressure, and type 2 diabetes (NHLBI, 1998). Because children and adolescents visit primary care settings frequently as they grow, primary care providers can play an integral part in the prevention of childhood obesity by educating and treating the early signs of overweight.

Summary

Obesity is a complex chronic disease that requires long-term management similar to other chronic medical disorders (e.g., hypertension or type 2 diabetes). Current treatment guidelines suggest that lifestyle interventions utilizing behavior modification principles (e.g., goal-setting, self-monitoring, etc.) are helpful for many patients, particularly those with BMI less than 30. Patients with severe obesity or with obesity-related, co-morbid conditions (e.g., hypertension, heart disease, type 2 diabetes) may benefit from adjunctive pharmacotherapies or obesity surgery in extreme cases. Mental health professionals can assist in the interdisciplinary treatment of obesity by providing primary care physicians with training in the use of behavior modification strategies and by assisting in the assessment and triaging of patients into appropriate treatments.

Acknowledgment

This work was partially supported by a grant from the National Institutes of Health (NIDDK DK58299).

References

American Dietetic Association and American Diabetes Association. (1989). *Exchange lists for weight management.* Chicago: Author.

Andersen, R. E., Wadden T. A., Bartlett, S.J., Zemel, B., Verde, T. J., & Franckowiak, S. C. (1999). Effects of lifestyle activity vs. structured aerobic exercise in obese women: A randomized trial. *Journal of the American Medical Association, 281*, 335–340.

Anderson, D. A., & Wadden, T. A. (1999). Treating the obese patient: Suggestions for primary care practice. *Archives of Family Medicine, 8,* 156–167.

Baker, R. C., & Kirschenbaum, D. S. (1993). Self-monitoring may be necessary for successful weight control. *Behavior Therapy, 24,* 377–394.

Blair, S. N. (1984). How to assess exercise habits and physical fitness. In J. D. Matazrazzo, S. M. Weiss, J. A. Herd, & N. E. Miller (Eds.), *Behavioral health* (pp. 424–447). New York: Wiley.

Bouchard, C., Perusse, L., Rice, T., & Rao, D. C. (1998). The genetics of human obesity. In G. A. Bray, C. Bouchard, & W. P. T. James (Eds.), *Handbook of obesity* (pp. 157–190). New York: Marcel Dekker.

Bouchard, C., Tremblay, A., Despres, J. P., Nadeau, A., Lupien, P. J., Theriault, G. et al. (1990). The response to long-term overfeeding in identical twins. *New England Journal of Medicine, 322,* 1477–1482.

Boutelle, K. N., & Kirschenbaum, D. S. (1998). Further support for consistent self-monitoring as a vital component of successful weight control. *Obesity Research, 6,* 219–224.

Bray, G. A. (1998). *Contemporary diagnosis and management of obesity.* Newton, PA.: Handbooks in Health Care.

Bray, G. A., & Ryan, D. H. (2004). Sympathomimetic and serotonergic drugs used to treat obesity. In G. A. Bray & C. Bouchard (Eds.), *Handbook of obesity: Clinical applications.* 2nd ed. (pp. 201–252). New York: Marcel Dekker.

Brownell, K. (2000). *The LEARN program for weight management 2000.* Dallas: American Health.

Centers for Disease Control and Prevention (CDC). (2000). Prevalence of overweight and obesity among adults: United States, 1999. Retrieved May 24, 2003, from www.cdc.gov/nchs/products/pubs/pubd/hestats/obese/obese99.htm.

Colditz, G. (1999). Economic costs of obesity and inactivity. *Medicine and Science in Sports and Medicine, 31,* S663–S667.

Cowan, R., Britton, P. J., Logue, E., Smucker, W., & Milo, L. (1995). The relationship among the transtheoretical model of behavior change, psychological distress, and diet attitudes in obesity: Implications for primary care intervention. *Journal of Clinical Psychology in Medical Settings, 2,* 249–267.

Craighead, L. W., Stunkard, A. J., & O'Brien, R. M. (1981). Behavior therapy and pharmacotherapy for obesity. *Archives of General Psychiatry, 38,* 763–768.

Davidson, M. H., Hauptman, J., DiGirolamo, M., Foreyt, J. P., Halsted, C. H., Heber, D. et al. (1999). Weight control and risk factor reduction in obese subjects treated for 2 years with orlistat: A randomized controlled trial. *Journal of the American Medical Association, 281,* 235–242.

Drent, M. L., Larsson, I., William-Olsson, T., Quaade, F., Czubayko, F., von Bergmann, K. et al. (1995). Orlistat (RO 18-0647), a lipase inhibitor, in the treatment of human obesity: A multiple dose study. *International Journal of Obesity and Related Metabolic Disorders, 19,* 221–226.

Dunn, A. L., Marcus, B. H., Kampert, J. B., Garcia, M. E., Kohl, H. W., III, & Blair, S. N. (1999). Comparison of lifestyle and structured interventions to increase physical activity and cardiorespiratory fitness: A randomized trial. *Journal of the American Medical Association, 281,* 327–334.

Ellis, S. G., Elliott, J., Horrigan, M., Raymond, R. E., & Howell, G. (1996). Low-normal or excessive body mass index: Newly identified and powerful risk factors for death and other complications with percutaneous coronary intervention. *American Journal of Cardiology, 78,* 641–646.

Everly, G. S. (1989). *A clinical guide to the treatment of the human stress response.* New York: Plenum.

Fitzgibbon, M. L., Stolley, M. R., & Kirschenbaum, D. S. (1993). Obese people who seek treatment have different characteristics than those who do not seek treatment. *Health Psychology, 12,* 342–345.

Foreyt, J. P., & Goodrick, G. K. (1991). Factors common in successful therapy for the obese patient. *Medicine and Science in Sports and Exercise, 23,* 292–297.

Foreyt, J. P., & Goodrick, G. K. (1993). Evidence for success of behavior modification in weight loss and control. *Annals of Internal Medicine, 119,* 698–701.

Foreyt, J. P., & Goodrick, G. K. (1994). Attributes of successful approaches to weight loss and control. *Applied Preventative Psychiatry, 3,* 209–215.

Foreyt, J. P., & Pendleton, V. R. (2000). Management of obesity. *Primary Care Reports, 6,* 19–30.

Foreyt, J. P., & Poston, W. S. C. (1996). Building better compliance: Factors and methods common to achieving a healthy lifestyle. In A. M. Gotto, R. Paoletti, L. C. Smith, A. L. Catapano, & A. S. Jackson. (Eds.), *Drugs affecting lipid metabolism: Risk factors and future direction* (pp. 489–496). Dordrecht, The Netherlands: Kluwer.

Foreyt, J. P., & Poston, W. S. C. (1998). The role of the behavioral counselor in obesity treatment. *Journal of the American Dietetic Association, 98,* S27–31.

Freedman, D. S., Srinivasan, S. R., Valdez, R. A., Williamson, D. F., & Berenson, G. S. (1997). Secular increases in relative weight and adiposity among children over two decades: The Bogalusa Heart Study. *Pediatrics, 99,* 420–426.

French, S. A., Story, M., & Jeffery, R. W. (2001). Environmental influences on eating and physical activity. *Annual Review of Public Health, 22,* 309–335.

Galuska, D. A., Will, J. C., Serdula, M. K., & Ford, E. S. (1999). Are health care professionals advising obese patients to lose weight? *Journal of American Medical Association, 282,* 1576–1578.

Gormally, J., Black, S., Daston, S., & Rardin, D. (1982). The assessment of binge eating severity among obese persons. *Addictive Behaviors, 7,* 47–55.

Gortmaker, S. L., Dietz, W. H., Jr., Sobol, A. M., & Wehler, C. A. (1987). Increasing pediatric obesity in the United States. *American Journal of Diseases of Children, 141,* 535–540.

Gray, D. S. (1999). Obesity. In B. D. Wiess (Ed.), *Twenty common problems in primary care* (pp. 27–50). New York: McGraw-Hill.

Hill, J. O. (1998). Dealing with obesity as a chronic disease. *Obesity Research, 6*(suppl. 1), 34S–38S.

Hvizdos, K. M., & Markham, A. (1999). Orlistat: A review of its use in the management of obesity. *Drugs, 58,* 743–760.

Jakicic, J. M., Clark, K., Coleman, E., Donnelly, J. E., Foreyt, J., Melanson, E., Volek, J., Volpe, S. L., & American College of Sports Medicine (2003). American College of Sports Medicine position stand. Appropriate intervention strategies for weight loss and prevention of weight regain for adults. *Medicine and Science in Sports and Exercise, 33,* 2145–2156.

James, W. P. (1995). A public health approach to the problem of obesity. *International Journal of Obesity and Related Metabolic Disorders, 19*(suppl. 3), S37–S45.

Jeffery, R. W. (1991). Population perspectives on the prevention and treatment of obesity in minority populations. *American Journal of Clinical Nutrition, 53*(suppl. 6), 1621S–1624S.

Jeffery, R. W. (1998). Prevention of obesity. In G. A. Bray, C. Bouchard, & W. P. T. James (Eds.), *Handbook of obesity* (pp. 819–830). New York: Marcel Dekker.

Kayman, S., Bruvold, W., & Stern, J. S. (1990). Maintenance and relapse after weight loss in women: Behavioral aspects. *American Journal of Clinical Nutrition, 52,* 800–807.

Klem, M. L., Wing, R. R., Simkin-Silverman, L., & Kuller, L. H. (1997). The psychological consequences of weight gain prevention in healthy, premenopausal women. *International Journal of Eating Disorders, 21,* 167–174.

Lean, M. E. (1997). Sibutramine—a review of clinical efficacy. *International Journal of Obesity and Related Metabolic Disorders, 21*(suppl. 1), S30–S36.

Logue, E., Sutton, K., Jarjoura, D., & Smucker, W. (2000). Obesity management in primary care: Assessment of readiness to change among 284 family practice patients. *Journal of the American Board of Family Practice, 13,* 164–171.

Luque, C. A., & Rey, J. A. (1999). Sibutramine: A serotonin-norepinephrine reuptake-inhibitor for the treatment of obesity. *Annals of Pharmacotherapy, 31,* 968–978.

Marcus, M. D. (1993). Binge eating in obesity. In C. Fairburn & G. T. Wilson (Eds), *Binge eating: Nature, assessment, and treatment* (pp. 77–96). New York: Guilford.

McArdle, W. D., Katch, F. I., & Katch, V. L. (1991). *Exercise physiology: Energy, nutrition, and human performance* (3rd ed.). Philadelphia: Lea & Febiger.

McDowell, I., & Newell, C. (1987). *Measuring health: A guide to rating scales and questionnaires.* New York: Oxford University Press.

Miller, G. D., & Harrington, M. E. (1997a). Center for epidemiologic studies depression scale. In S. T. St. Jeor (Ed.), *Obesity assessment: Tools, methods, interpretations* (pp. 457–464). New York: Chapman & Hall.

Miller, G. D., & Harrington, M. E. (1997b). General well-being schedule. In S. T. St. Jeor (Ed.), *Obesity assessment: Tools, methods, interpretations* (pp. 457–464). New York: Chapman & Hall.

Miller, W. C., & Wadden, T. A. (2004). Exercise as a treatment for obesity. In G. A. Bray & C. Bouchard (Eds.), *Handbook of obesity: Clinical applications.* 2nd ed. (pp. 169–184). New York: Marcel Dekker.

Mokdad, A. H., Ford, E. S., Bowman, B. A., Dietz, W. H., Vinicor, F., Bales, V. S., & Marks, J. S. (2003). Prevalence of obesity, diabetes, and obesity-related health risk factors, 2001. *JAMA, 289,* 76–79.

Mokdad, A. H., Marks, J. S., Stroup, D. F., & Gerberding, J. L. (2004). Actual causes of death in the United States, 2000. *JAMA, 291,* 1238–1245.

National Cholesterol Education Program. (1993). Short dietary questionnaire to assess adherence to step I and step II diet. In National Institutes of Health, National Heart, Lung, and Blood Institute, *Second report of the expert panel on detection, evaluation, and treatment of high blood cholesterol in adults* . Bethesda, MD: IIA-I.

National Heart Lung and Blood Institute (NHLBI). (1998). Clinical guidelines on the identification, evaluation, and treatment of overweight and obesity: The evidence report. *Obesity Research, 6*(suppl. 2), 51S–210S.

National Heart Lung and Blood Institute (NHLBI). (2002). The practical guide: Identification, evaluation, and treatment of overweight and obesity in adults. NIH Publication II: 02-4084. Available at: http://www.nhlbi.nih.gov/guidelines/obesity/practgde.htm.

National Institutes of Health (NIH): National Heart, Lung, and Blood Institute (NHLBI). (2000). Clinical guidelines on the identification, evaluation, and treatment of overweight and obesity in adults. Publication no. 98-4083. Bethesda, MD: National Institute of Health.

National Institutes of Health Consensus Development Conference Statement. (1992) Gastrointestinal surgery for severe obesity. *American Journal of Clinical Nutrition, 55,* 615S–619S.

National Task Force on the Prevention and Treatment of Obesity. (1996). Long-term pharmacotherapy in the management of obesity. *Journal of American Medical Association, 276,* 1907–1915.

Nestle, M., & Jacobson, M. F. (2000). Halting the obesity epidemic: A public health policy approach. *Public Health Reports, 115,* 12–24.

Pendleton, V. R., Willems, E., Swank, P., Poston, W. S. C., Goodrick, G. K., Reeves, R. S. et al. (2001). Stress and the outcome of treatment for binge eating. *International Journal of Eating Disorders.*

Perri, M. G., & Foreyt, J. P. (2004). Preventing weight regain after weight loss. In G. A. Bray & C. Bouchard (Eds.), *Handbook of obesity: Clinical applications.* 2nd ed. (pp. 185–200). New York: Marcel Dekker.

Physician Based Nutrition Program and Department of Medicine and Division of Epidemiology. (1990). *Eating assessment tool.* Minneapolis: University of Minnesota Press.

Pike, K. M., Loeb, K., & Walsh, B. T. (1995). Binge eating and purging. In D. B. Allison (Ed.), *Handbook of assessment methods for eating behaviors and weight-related problems* (pp. 303–346). Thousand Oaks, CA: Sage.

Pi-Sunyer, F. X. (2002). The medical risks of obesity. *Obesity Surgery, 12,* 6S–11S.

Poston, W. S. C., & Foreyt, J. P. (1999). Obesity is an environmental issue. *Atherosclerosis, 146,* 201–209.

Poston, W. S. C., & Foreyt, J. P. (2000). Successful management of the obese patient. *American Family Physician, 61,* 3615–3622.

Poston, W. S. C., Olvera-Ezell, N. E., Yanez, C., Haddock, C. K., Dunn, J. K., Hanis, C. L. et al. (1998). Evaluation of the factor structure and psychometric properties of the General Well-Being Schedule (GWB) with Mexican American women. *Women and Health, 27*, 49-62.

Potter, M. B., Vu, J. D., & Croughan-Minihane, M. (2001). Weight management: What patients want from their primary care physicians. *Journal of Family Practice, 50*, 513–518.

Prochaska, J. O, & DiClemente, C. C. (1992). The transtheoretical approach. In J. C. Norcross & M. R. Goldfried (Eds.), *Handbook of psychotherapy integration* (pp. 300–334). New York: Basic Books.

Prochaska, J. O., Norcross, J. C., & DiClemente, C. C. (1994). *Changing for good*. New York: Avon Books.

Pronk, N. P., Tan, A. W. H., & O'Connor, P. (1999). Obesity, fitness, willingness to communicate and health care costs. *Medicine and Science in Sports and Exercise, 31*, 1535–1543.

Quesenberry, C. P., Caan, B., & Jacobson, A. (1998). Obesity, health services use, and health care costs among members of a health maintenance organization. *Archives of Internal Medicine, 158*, 466–472.

Rice, T., Tremblay, A., Deriaz, O., Perusse, L., Rao, D. C., & Bouchard, C. (1996). A major gene for resting metabolic rate unassociated with body composition: Results from the Quebec Family Study. *Obesity Research, 4*, 441–449.

Schonfeld-Warden, N., & Warden, C. H. (1997). Pediatric obesity. An overview of etiology and treatment. *Pediatric Clinics of North America, 44*, 339–361.

SCORE. (1988). *Rate your plate*. Pawtucket, RI: Memorial Hospital.

Seagle, H. M., Bessesen, D. H., & Hill, J. O. (1998). Effects of sibutramine on resting metabolic rate and weight loss in overweight women. *Obesity Research, 6*, 115–121.

Shephard, R. J. (1992). Twelve years experience of a fitness program for the salaried employees of a Toronto life insurance company. *American Journal of Health Promotion, 6*, 292–301.

Singh, P. N., & Linstead, K. D. (1998). Body mass and 26-year risk of mortality from specific disease among women who never smoked. *Epidemiology, 9*, 246–254.

Sjostrom, L. (2004). Surgical treatment of obesity: An overview and results from the SOS study. In G. A. Bray & C. Bouchard (Eds.), *Handbook of obesity: Clinical applications*. 2nd ed. (pp. 359–390). New York: Marcel Dekker.

Solomon, C. G., & Manson, J. E. (1997). Obesity and mortality: A review of the epidemiologic data. *American Journal of Clinical Nutrition, 66*(4 suppl.), 1044S–1050S.

Spielberger, C. D., Syderman, S. J., Owen, A. E., & Marsh, B. J. (1999). Measuring anxiety and anger with the State-Trait Anxiety Inventory (STAI) and State-Trait Anger Expression Inventory (STAXI). In M. E. Maruish (Ed.), *The use of psychological testing for treatment planning and outcome assessment* (pp. 993–1021). Hillsdale, NJ: Erlbaum.

Stafford, R. S., Farhat, J. H., Misra, B., & Schoenfeld, D. A. (2000). National patterns of physician activities related to obesity management. *Archives of Family Medicine, 9*, 631–638.

Steer, R. A., Cavalieri, T. A., Leonard, D. M., & Beck, A. T. (1999). Use of the Beck depression inventory for primary care to screen for major depression disorders. *General Hospital Psychiatry, 21*, 106–111.

Stellefson, E., & O'Neil, P. M. (1997). Binge eating scale. In S. T. St. Jeor (Ed.), *Obesity assessment: Tools, methods, interpretations* (pp. 337–351). New York: Chapman & Hall.

Stunkard, A. J., Craighead, L. W., & O'Brien, R. (1980). Controlled trial of behaviour therapy, pharmacotherapy, and their combination in the treatment of obesity. *Lancet, 2*, 1045–1047.

Taylor, J. E., Poston, W. D. 2nd, Haddock, C. K., Blackburn, G. L., Heber, D., Heymsfeld, S. B., & Foreyt, J. P. (2003). Psychometric characteristics of the general well-being schedule (GWB) with African-American women. *Quality of Life Research, 12*, 31–39.

Thompson, D., Brown, J. B., Nichols, G. A., Elmer, P. J., & Oster, G. (2001). Body mass index and future healthcare costs: a retrospective cohort study. *Obesity Research, 9*, 210–218.

Torgerson, J. S., Boldrin, M. N., Hamptman, J., & Sjostrom, L. S. (2004). Xenical in the prevention of diabetes in obese subjects (XENDOS) study: A randomized study of orlistat as an adjunct to lifestyle changes for the prevention of type 2 diabetes in obese patients. *Diabetes Care, 27*, 155–161.

Troiano, R. P., & Flegal, F. M. (1998). Overweight children and adolescents: Description, epidemiology, and demographics. *Pediatrics, 101*(suppl.), 497–504.

U.S. Department of Agriculture (USDA). (1992). *The food guide pyramid*. Home and Garden Bulletin #252. Washington, DC: U.S. Government Printing Office.

U.S. Department of Health and Human Services, Office of the Surgeon General (USDHHS). (1996). *Physical activity and health: A report of the surgeon general*. Atlanta: U.S. Dept. of Health and Human Services, Centers for Disease Control and Prevention, National Center for Chronic Disease Prevention and Health Promotion.

Van Gaal, L. F. & Bray, G. A. (2004). Drugs that modify fat absorption and alter metabolism. In G. A. Bray & C. Bouchard (Eds.), *Handbook of obesity: Clinical applications*. 2nd ed. (pp. 253–274). New York: Marcel Dekker.

Wing, R. R. (1998). Behavioral approaches to the treatment of obesity. In G. A. Bray, C. Bouchard (Eds.), *Handbook of obesity: Clinical applications*. 2nd ed. (pp. 147–169). New York: Marcel Dekker.

Wolf, A. M., & Colditz, G. A. (1998). Current estimates of the economic costs of obesity in the United States. *Obesity Research, 6*, 97–106.

World Health Organization (WHO). (1998). *Obesity: Preventing and managing the global epidemic. Report of a WHO consultation on obesity*. Geneva: Author.

Yanovski, S. Z. (1993). A practical approach to treatment of the obese patient. *Archives of Family Medicine, 2*, 309–316.

Yanovski, S. Z., & Yanovski, J. A. (2002). Drug therapy: Obesity. *New England Journal of Medicine, 346*, 591–602.

Chapter 14

As Precise as the Scalpel's Cut ... Sort of: Psychological and Self-Regulation Treatments in Preparation for Surgery and Invasive Medical Procedures

RODGER S. KESSLER

There is a compelling argument in support of psychological preparation for surgery, supported by 40 years of clinical and research literature. Such efforts have been demonstrated as effective in improving medical outcomes as well as saving health-care resources. Despite this, psychological preparation for surgery is not widely used. In addition to the observation that most psychological interventions in medicine are underused, there are particular dilemmas, having to do with lack of financial incentives, the difficulty of adding another process to the tight time frame in the surgical suite, and the fact that surgery, as a complex psychological and emotional experience, frequently needs to be psychologically responded to, but currently is not a part of the theme of surgery.

In addition to a surgery problem, psychological attention to upcoming surgery is clearly a primary care problem. Primary care is the place where high utilizers of medical services will present pre- and postsurgical problems. Also, patients who have had a poor history with surgical experiences or who are specifically stressed by an upcoming procedure will present these issues in primary care.

After reviewing these issues, this chapter will present an intervention model based on the research of the past 40 years. Hallmarks of the intervention include self-efficacy, face-to-face contact, assessment of individual differences, psychoeducation, and tailored intervention. The steps of the procedure, including strategies for selecting treatment options, are then elaborated.

More than 40 years ago, Janis (1958) first theorized that patients receiving preoperative information about their upcoming surgery would generate "the work of worry," reduce anxiety, and facilitate recovery. Egbert, Battit, and Turndorf (1963) demonstrated that providing a presurgical visit the night before surgery would reduce anxiety and improve recovery. Both of these observations continue to inform contemporary practice. However, strategies that enhance patients' beliefs in their ability to successfully cope with the demands of surgery appear to have the most robust support (Kessler & Dane, 1996; Van Dalfsen & Syrjala, 1990) and have influenced most contemporary applications. Evidence suggests that contemporary surgical preparation can be defined as a face-to-face assessment of individual differences, followed by a brief, tailored intervention delivered in vivo using some combination of procedural and sensory information and training in coping strategies, combined with surgery-specific suggestions for enhanced function and recovery (Kessler & Dane, 1996).

Increasingly, providing the best clinical care to surgery patients in the least amount of time is a key requisite of surgical care. In some areas of surgery and technology the level of surgical skill has improved outcomes to the extent that minimal improvement in postoperative return to function is expected (e.g., laparoscopic cholecystectomy). In other aspects of return to function, recovery is greatly affected by the patient's response to the surgical intervention (Kessler & Whalen, 1999).

The above observations are not surprising if one is familiar with the clinical and research literature in the area of surgical preparation. Psychology, nursing, and anesthesiology have researched preparation for surgery for over 40 years (Kessler & Dane, 1996). There have been numerous findings concluding that preparation for surgery has demonstrated effectiveness in assisting patient functioning pre-, intra-, and postsurgically, improved rates of return to function, and saved health-care resources (Arthur, Daniels, McKelvie, Hirsch, & Rush 2000; Blankenfield, 1991; Johnston & Vogele, 1993; Mumford, Schlessinger, & Glass, 1982; Rogers & Reich, 1986). Strategies used in these preparations have ranged from procedural and sensory information provision, coping skills training, brief cognitive and behavioral treatments for anxiety, relaxation training, imagery, suggestion, and hypnosis. Most contemporary research in the area has used some combination of these interventions.

Preparation as an Empirically Supported Treatment

Chambless and Hollon (1998) have developed what appears to be the most widely used criterion for empirical support applied to psychological treatments. They suggest that empirically supported therapies (ESTs) can be used to describe treatments that have been shown to be efficacious in controlled research with specific populations. The literature on surgery preparation demonstrates that surgical preparation meets the designation as an EST.

There have been at least four meta-analyses of the surgical preparation literature that support designation as an empirically supported treatment. In the initial review Mumford, Schlessinger, and Glass (1982) concluded that of 34 controlled outcome studies, covering approximately 2,000 patients, patients receiving preparation for surgery physically recovered more quickly, felt better psychologically, and had a 2.4-day shorter hospital stay than those who did not. Rogers and Reich (1986) noted that the evidence was compelling that both for surgery and obstetrics preparation had a significant effect clinically and economically. Blankenfield (1991) reviewed 18 studies that used hypnotic suggestion or relaxation to prepare patients for surgery. He found that 16 of the 18 studies supported the effectiveness of the intervention in accelerating postoperative function. He also observed that among the dimensions affected by surgical preparation, seven studies demonstrated shortened hospital stay, seven studies demonstrated less postoperative narcotic use, five studies demonstrated lower postoperative pain, six studies demonstrated lower postoperative anxiety, two studies demonstrated less blood loss, and three studies demonstrated earlier return of gastrointestinal function. Johnston and Vogele (1993) reviewed 38 studies and concluded that there is substantial agreement that psychological preparation for surgery offers substantial clinical and cost benefit. The meta-analysis conducted by Chiles, Lambert, and Hatch (1999) of the effect of psychological interventions on medical cost offset concluded that the most dramatic treatment effects were for the behavioral medicine treatments of surgical inpatients, resulting in significant decrease in length of stay and an increase in psychological well-being. They further concluded that the greatest demonstration of effect was in the area of providing psychoeducational intervention to assist hospitalized surgical patients.

The number of studies quantifying cost savings is limited, but compelling. In the Mumford et al. (1982) analysis of approximately 2,000 intervention and control patients, it was found that for the intervention group, there was a 2.4-day reduction in hospitalization compared with patients who did not receive intervention. In 1991, Rapkin, Straubing, and Holroyd compared hypnotic preparation with the usual preparation in head and neck surgery. In addition to significant clinical outcomes, the hypnotic preparation group had a 5-day shorter postoperative stay and an average reduction in hospitalization costs of $6,725 per hospitalization. In 1993, Disbrow, Bennett, and Owings reported on their study of return of gastrointestinal ileus. A post hoc analysis of the data showed a 1.5-day reduction in hospitalization in favor of the preparation group, with a per surgery savings of $1,200, in addition to the clinical outcomes. Bennett remarked that when one of his colleagues approached him with a request to analyze the cost data post hoc, he initially questioned the idea. His reasoning was that in the period of time since the Mumford et al. analysis, much had changed in hospitals, people were discharged earlier, and the Mumford findings would not stand up to contemporary hospital economics. He eventually consented to the analysis that produced these findings (H. Bennett, personal communication, 1995). Recently Lang and Rosen (2002) demonstrated that hypnosis in combination with sedation reduces the cost of interventional radiologic procedures by more than half compared with the cost of the procedure with standard sedation. Taken together, the data have been sufficiently compelling to lead Johnson and Vogele (1993) to observe that a large number of nonsignificant findings would have to exist to challenge the significance of findings of benefit.

In reviewing the surgical preparation literature, the majority studied surgeries that require hospitalization for one or more nights. Recently, Lang, Benotsch, and Fick (2000) reported on a study of patients receiving interventional radiology procedures, some of whom were ambulatory. The study randomized 241 patients to standard medical treatment, structured attention, or self-hypnotic relaxation with structured attention. Results demonstrated that in the relaxation preparation condition there was less analgesia used, procedural duration was shorter, there was no increase in pain scores, and there were fewer patients with hemodynamic instability.

Preparation Is Not Widely Used

Despite such a lengthy history, clinical and research literature, publications in the most widely read medical journals, demonstrated health-care savings, and specificity of procedures that define this area of psychological intervention in medicine, use of such preparatory strategies is limited outside of experimental situations. This appears particularly accurate in nontertiary medical care. There are a number of reasons that might explain this.

At this point of development, psychological interventions are not well known within medicine. Psychological professionals and their services are still establishing a foothold and validity in medical settings. Efforts to integrate psychology and medicine are encouraging, but their acceptance and integration in general medicine is still far off. Also, psychological aspects of medicine are still lumped within the generic mental health system, which is seen as difficult to access and a black hole into which patients may or may not flow, and the content and results of which are essentially unknown (Gray, Brody, & Hart, 2000).

This is an era where the field of medicine is struggling with pressure to be evidence based and is often overwhelmed with the amount of available evidence. Clinical pathways and evidence-based treatments may be well developed, but in many areas the sheer overwhelmingness of contemporary medical practice is a barrier or a limitation to their implementation. The result is treatments that often have limited evidence to support their use or motivation to change practice. This leaves psychological treatments—and most certainly psychological treatments in surgery—with no easy platform from which to offer or implement its evidence.

As has been observed elsewhere in this volume, in fee-for-service environments there are no financial incentives to consider the utility of integrated treatment strategies. Even in capitated models I am not aware of any system that has regularly used psychological interventions in surgery to enhance clinical outcomes and cost efficiencies. In the carve-out models, which have become the norm for managing psychological treatments, there is a disincentive to consider the psychological issues in medicine, even though primary care has been dubbed the de facto mental health system (Regier et al., 1993). Since penetration rates and the strategies employed by managed care to limit access to mental health services are based on their estimates of community utilization, they are certainly not motivated to pursue strategies that increase penetration and thus utilization.

It should be clear that attending to psychological issues in surgery does not currently fit either the theoretical or practical dimensions of surgery practice. Primary care views surgery as something to refer out to specialty care (surgeons) to evaluate, manage, and (hopefully) resolve. Surgery is seen as a primarily technical problem where a part of the body (e.g., leg, back, etc.) or organ (heart, lung, etc.) has a problem, is isolated, worked on, and the issue resolved as best it can be. That surgery is a complex psychological and emotional experience requiring specific attention as part of the surgical process has not been historically viewed as a primary focus of care. Even the most minimalist additional psychological intervention is experienced as a perturbation to a system that has not discerned that a problem exists and as such is neither aware of nor interested in resolving that which is not perceived as a problem. Also the referral from primary care to surgical evaluation and through surgery is a well-orchestrated flow, with few easy opportunities for significant changes in that flow.

Why Does Surgical Preparation Work?

When we practice psychological medicine, we are constantly reminded to practice as medicine does. Medical interventions are mostly brief and specific. Surgical preparations are brief and specific. In my clinical practice, the most frequent number of patient contacts for a preparation is one. In less than 20% of cases there are two, and rarely more than that. In an often-cited study of reducing the postsurgical time until return of bowel function, Disbrow et al. (1993) used an instructional intervention that was less than 20 minutes in length. Lang and Rosen's (2002) intra-procedural hypnotic intervention occurred once, during the procedure, and yet increased the rate of hemodynamic stability in invasive radiology procedures. In the Chiles et al. (1999) meta-analysis there was support for the idea that specificity of the type of intervention affects outcome. They found that psychoeducational interventions have significantly higher effect sizes than psychotherapeutic interventions. Similar findings characterize the surgical preparation literature. It has been observed that activating cognitive coping strategies is a core component in successful preparation (Kessler, 1997; Salmon, 1994). Additionally, surgical preparation appears to be effective because it can be equated to capturing the Holy Grail—demonstrating that psychological interventions can affect physiological and biochemical processes.

It is well established that the stress response to an upcoming surgical event is a complex neuroendocrine affector-effector response elicited by a large number of exogenous and endogenous stimuli (Kessler & Whalen, 1999), including fear, anxiety, and pain response in addition to surgical trauma, infection, and exogenous drugs. There have been consistent reports of preparation being associated with lowered anxiety, lowered pain, and less use of analgesic drugs (Evans & Richardson, 1991; Evans & Stanley, 1991; Syrjala, Cummings, & Donaldson, 1992). In addition, there have been findings that support the role of psychological preparation in decreased serum cortisol levels and more rapid wound healing (Holden-Lund, 1988), diminished blood loss at the surgical site (Bennett, Benson, & Kuiken, 1986; Enqvist, von Konow, & Bystedt, 1995), rapid return of gastrointestinal motility (Disbrow et al., 1993), and increased vital capacity and pulmonary functioning (Hathaway, 1986). Montgomery, Weltz, and Bovbjerg (2002) have recently broadened the scope of these findings to excisional breast biopsy patients, with their finding that a 10-minute hypnotic procedure administered on the day of surgery reduced both postsurgical pain and distress.

The Suggestibility of Critical Moments

Psychologically, patients accurately view surgery as a critical event, independent of the severity of the procedure (Kessler & Whalen, 1999). Early on, Egbert et al. (1963) demonstrated that establishing a helping relationship with a patient before surgery contributed to patient readiness, tolerance of, and recovery from surgery. Dabney Ewing (1986), a surgeon who works with severe industrial burn patients, has observed that during acute, serious medical conditions patients are universally advanced in their ability to be receptive to instruction and suggestion. Such openness to instruction and suggestion has been observed to be a function of hypnotic susceptibility in some settings (Kirsch, 1997), the response to reasonably presented realistic instructions (Barber, 1984), or the logical consequence of the interaction of characteristic coping style with a caregiver response that is tailored to that coping style (Kessler, Dane, & Galper, 2002).

Patients often have heightened autonomic arousal and distorted and catastrophic cognitive styles prior to surgery. The focus of information and cognitive coping-based preparation strategies assists in the creation of a focused sense of order. It reframes the amorphous set of surgical experiences into a set of discreet steps that enable focus and attention on activities designed to enhance successful participation in and recovery from the surgical process. In this way, surgical preparation resembles the kind of self-efficacy training offered by Bandura (1986), who found self-efficacy to be learning successful strategies and engaging in them, with those successes generalizing to an overall view of confidence and success. In surgery preparation, training for self-efficacy prior to the event and the actual occurrence of the event are closely tied in time, allowing the recency of the cognitive, behavioral, and physiological self-regulation of the preparation to generalize the surgical event.

A patient came to see me who was preparing to have both knees surgically replaced. She came fearful about the procedure and because she did not understand what was going to happen to her. When asked to describe what she really wanted to happen she replied "I wish that the first one was already done so I could know everything that happened. You know, the first thing then the second thing and so on. Then I would feel better because I would know what was to happen." We used a rehearsal strategy as preparation, going through as many steps as possible for her to be able to anchor her experience.

Surgery as a Primary Care Problem

For the purposes of this discussion, primary care is defined as (1) the office within which primary care physicians practice and (2) the local specialty care medical/hospital services the primary care physician accesses in the routine care of patients. Therefore, psychosocial concerns generated by medical events that occur outside of the primary care office, such as surgery, are still primary care issues. Increased psychosocial reactivity is certainly frequently part of patient reaction to surgery, particularly those for whom stress reactivity due to life occurrences activates medical utilization. Three subsets of patients are likely to look to primary care for guidance and support as they prepare for upcoming surgeries: high utilizers of medical services, patients with previous negative medical and surgical experiences, and patients for whom an upcoming surgery is a particularly stressful or threatening experience.

The top 10% of utilizers of medical services account for more activity than the lowest 50% of utilizers of a practice (Katon et al., 1990). It also has been demonstrated that about 50% of high utilizers have psychiatric co-morbidities (Katon et al., 1990). I am not aware of data specifying differences in surgery rates for high medical utilizers. It stands to follow, however, that patients who are psychiatrically co-morbid and who use medical services to support psychosocial distress are likely both to be consumers of surgeries and to have increased difficulty both preparing for and recovering from surgery, with increased service demand from primary care.

A primary care physician and her surgeon referred a woman to me. The surgeon refused to operate until I felt the patient could successfully undergo a colostomy closure. She had a lengthy history of invasive procedures, accompanied by lengthy hospitals stays in excess of what was predicted, difficulty discontinuing postsurgery narcotics, which became a management problem for the primary care physician, and the patient was labeled as being difficult to deal with. I saw the patient three times, supported her to discharge affect, helped her problem solve about her children and how to heat her house in Vermont winter while she was in the hospital, and used very good imaginative skills to teach her dissociative imagery with imaginal review of a successful experience. The previous sequalae never occurred during the hospitalization or upon follow-up by the primary care physician.

It seems equally clear that among the primary care patient population there are those who have had previous negative medical surgical experiences. As will be discussed shortly, patients with these experiences have a greater likelihood of repeated difficulties with current surgeries (Kessler & Dane, 1996), have greater rates of complications, and have longer postoperative stays (Kessler & Whalen, 1999). Also, patients with early pain histories or who have grown up in families with medically related pain histories are likely to experience greater adult pain and to cope more poorly with medical and surgical events (Bachiocco, Scesi, Morselli, & Carli 1993; Lester, Lefebre, & Keefe, 1994).

An obstetrician referred a woman for assistance prior to her first delivery. She had poor tolerance of any medical care and had a needle phobia. The needle phobia was easily desensitized, and during the interview, a number of poor experiences with pediatric medicine were revealed, including her mother's observation about the pain that was suffered during the patient's childbirth. The guilt and embarrassment of these two early experiences had never been revealed, and after that discussion and related emotion, the patient quickly learned imagery-base relaxation for needle insertion and had a successful childbirth.

It is equally important to identify any patients with unremarkable psychological histories who view and respond to upcoming surgery as a major and significant psychological event that they are not sure how to cope with. Lack of clarity about seriousness of the surgery or its consequences, confronting real or catastrophic potential mortality, logistics, and expenses may each or in combination be sufficient to generate levels of reactivity that may become the focus of a primary care visit. Such visits may be regular, scheduled visits for a presurgical history and physical, or for some other surgery-related concern that masks the psychosocial distress. So, it is clear that primary care is often involved in assisting psychosocial adaptation to surgery, particularly for certain at-risk subpopulations of patients.

A man was referred for orthopedic arm surgery. Intellectually he had no problems with the upcoming procedure, but was left with a sense of anticipatory dread. In our single contact he was able to identify fear of having a heart attack on the table. He explained that his father had gone to the hospital for a routine procedure and had had a heart attack and died while in the hospital some 3 years prior. He realized that his own fear related to the fear that the same thing would happen to him, despite his overall good health. After that realization the dread diminished and there were no further complications.

Poor presurgical adaptation or postsurgical hospital adaptation is often associated with problematic consequences posthospitalization (Rogers, Liang, Poss, & Cullen, 1982). Although the surgeon attends to some of these consequences, it is often the primary care physician who is called upon by the postsurgical patient for further management. Patient expectations of postsurgical recovery and functioning vary, and may or may not match the expected medical course. Energy, strength, pain, concentration, attention, or medication issues may prompt primary care physician consultation, and psychological issues surrounding adaptation and recovery often need to be addressed, particularly if these issues were not satisfactorily responded to presurgically. So patient psychological functioning before and after surgery is a primary care issue, whether or not it is specifically the focus of primary medical care.

A man had a hip replaced, which resulted in a prolonged, difficult rehabilitation. He began the use of antianxiety medication prescribed by his primary care physician and continued its use for a number of years postrecovery. His physician asked him to see me because of concerns about ongoing use of the medication. He was seen for almost 5 months. The patient was able to identify that the hip replacement gave him a message about his aging and eventual mortality, which he feared. He was not one who could talk of such things with his physician, nor did he discuss the matter with his family. He understood that the medication was not helping him and agreed to talk to me because he wanted to eliminate the medication. The ensuing months were spent helping him confront his aging as well as adapting strategies that would allow him to focus on successful living.

So we are left with empirically supported interventions to specific patients with specified clinical presentations who can benefit from the service, and a setting that is in the best position to identify patient need for the service. The next task is to identify the components of the intervention and the steps necessary to reengineer current primary care practice to accommodate it.

Developing the Intervention: The Steps of the Process

The research literature has not generated sufficient data to allow us to comparatively evaluate different intervention models. We are therefore left to construct models based on different empirical findings that, taken together, can be viewed as empirically formulated models, but not yet comparatively evaluated. The intervention model proposed here is based on the following set of empirical findings concerning the best outcomes for surgical preparation:

1. Self-efficacy promotion via active coping strategies enhances the outcomes of surgical preparation (Salmon, 1994).
2. A face-to-face intervention delivered preoperatively is probably more effective than either a taped intervention or an intervention delivered intraoperatively (Enqvist, von Konow, & Bystedt, 1995).
3. An assessment of specified individual differences optimizes the ability to select the most effective intervention strategy (Kessler & Dane, 1996).
4. Greatest effects are associated with a psychoeducational focus to intervention, including procedural and sensory information (Chiles et al., 2000, Salmon, 1994).
5. A brief and tailored intervention based on variation in individual differences promoting effective and successful coping appears to be more effective than a standardized intervention (Syrjala et al., 1992; H. Bennett, personal communication, 1995).

Rapid Self-Efficacy Promotion Is the Key

Patients distressed by upcoming surgeries have been characterized as having high levels of distorted cognitions and beliefs that exceed probable expectations (Blacher, 1987a). The product of this is limited effectiveness in coping with the demands of the upcoming procedure. Therefore, no matter the strategy employed, it may be said that the goal of preparation for surgery is to train, practice, and implement effective management of the time before, during, and after hospitalization to effectively manage the issues that are distressing during those times. Such a goal not only defines the tasks of the preparation but also helps physicians identify patients who can benefit most from a preparation procedure. The research literature does not adequately inform us how to identify patients who will benefit as opposed to those who will not. Preoperative psychological state has not been found to be a useful predictor of surgical outcome or preparation effectiveness (Salmon, 1994), so we are left with clinical observation to determine selection strategy. Certainly patients whose ability to tolerate surgery is negatively affected because of psychological functioning should be candidates. This can range from anxiety about survival, phobias of insertion of IVs, or emotional volatility that does not appear to have a clear antecedent. Patients who have had previously compromised or negative surgical or anesthesiology experiences are also particularly deserving of attention. Also, as with other aspects of medical psychology, patients with limited coping capacities or support systems might be considered. It is left to further research to give us clearer parameters to assist in patient selection.

Depending on the method employed, the task is to promote adaptive health behavior based on the demands of the situation (Auerbach, 1989). Such adaptive coping is a patient-initiated process of attaching strategies that the patient feels have a good probability of being helpful to desirable cognitive, physiological, and emotional states. With the ability to accomplish this, patients feel empowered to use an effective coping strategy in an identified situation, which relates to *successful* coping with the upcoming procedure. Such a procedure is solution-focused rather than problem-focused, with attention focused on successful future outcomes rather than present or past problems (Kessler & Miller, 1995). The desired treatment outcome is a presurgery focus on the future success of the surgery and recovery, and a patient's belief in and active use of efficacious strategies to create that success. The next sections discuss the steps of that process.

Getting Them There

Surgical preparation is a very portable procedure. It typically requires only one or two visits, each lasting as short as 30 minutes (Bennett, 1993) to 1 hour (Kessler & Dane, 1996). I have done preparations in an office within the hospital, in my clinical office, in the emergency room, and in the preoperative cubicle in the OR suite. Timing of intervention tends to be determined by when a physician determines a need and the length of time until surgery. I have seen patients a week before surgery or just the day of surgery. Complexity of the psychological presentation is a determinant of what appears to be optimal timing. In a complex presentation, 5–7 days prior to surgery seems to be optimal, because it allows for the scheduling of a follow-up before the surgery. If acuity appears more manageable, then seeing a patient around 3 days prior to the surgery appears to be optimal.

Promoting a Rapid Story: Framing What Is to Be Resolved

Often, patients present generalized anxieties or concerns about surgery. This is an example of the state of anxiety (Spielberger, Gorsuch, & Lushene, 1970) that has often been found to accompany surgery (Salmon, 1994). But this is a trap. A treatment focused on the generalized picture defocuses both patient and treatment from the story of the surgery. Given the rapid time frame for preparation, it is critical to quickly identify the specific history, incidents, or perceptions about the surgery that are stimulating the generalized arousal. Examples might be family pain history, a difficult pediatric hospitalization, or a bad experience with anesthesia. In my clinical experience of over 10 years in this area, virtually every patient seen for surgical preparation has been able to identify specific antecedents to his or her anxiety. The framing of the telling of the story about the antecedent is always asking the patient to "Tell me about your surgery/procedure." This enables a patient to identify the issues that have become the focus for the brief intervention. It is told within the context of the clinicians needing specific assessment data from which to tailor an intervention. This information focuses on assessing previous medical history, primary coping focus, and suggestibility.

Assessing Previous Medical History, Coping Focus, and Suggestibility

Although it is important to support the telling of the story, this task establishes the nature of the disruption and elicits information the literature suggests is keenly important in constructing the intervention. Previous medical history is a predictor of functioning before, during, and after the surgery or procedure (Kessler & Dane, 1996). There have been multiple reports that negative surgical experience impacts subsequent functioning and healing (Blacher, 1987b; Rogers & Reich, 1986). Further, individual pain history has been demonstrated to predict intensity, duration, and onset of postsurgical pain (Bachiocco et al., 1993).

The patient's characteristic coping style and how it interacts with the coping demands of the surgery will also influence how a patient will cope with a surgical experience. Coping "repressors," those who cope by denying and avoiding, experience more pain and anxiety if given more information presurgically, while coping "sensitizers," patients who deal best with information and taking action, improve their rate of surgical recovery when given information (Cohen & Lazarus, 1973). Paradoxically, if sensitizers' need for attention and information is not addressed, it has been found they have the poorest postsurgical recovery (Cohen & Lazarus, 1973). The data reviewed strongly suggest that preexisting medical and surgical history and predominant coping style must be assessed. Fortunately, doing so is quite simple. Table 14.1 contains the Medical Surgical Experiences Rating Scale (Kessler, 1992). The scale helps patients rate to what degree an upcoming surgery is being influenced by a previous hospitalization, surgery, anesthesia, injection, or other similar experience. It should be completed as part of the initial intake, and it takes less than a minute.

Although there are many measures of coping style, for the purposes of the brief assessment preparation, simply asking a patient often works really well. Asking the question, "Some people like to know as much as they can about the upcoming procedure so they can actively participate, and some people don't want to know very much at all. Which best describes you?" is often sufficient to elicit this information. In some situations a surgery may have multiple coping demands that require

TABLE 14.1 The Medical Surgical Experience Rating Scale

To what degree are any of the following affecting your upcoming surgery? (Please circle appropriate number)

	not at all	a little	somewhat	very much	a lot
a hospitalization	1	2	3	4	5
a surgery	1	2	3	4	5
anesthesia	1	2	3	4	5
getting a needle or injection	1	2	3	4	5
pain during any other medical experience	1	2	3	4	5
another family member's medical experience	1	2	3	4	5

© Rodger Kessler, Ph.D., 1993.

different coping responses. For a discussion of this infrequent but important issue the reader is referred to Kessler and Dane (1996) for further elaboration.

Suggestibility may seem an odd construct to be part of this discussion. It is included for two reasons. The first is that there have been a number of studies observing that higher suggestibility influences recovery from surgery and the efficacy of presurgical interventions (Disbrow et al. 1993; Rapkin et al., 1991; Rondi et al., 1993). Although these findings are interesting, by themselves they are not clinically instructive. However, the second reason for including suggestibility in this discussion relates to selection of clinical strategies for preparation. A patient's suggestibility has been demonstrated to be a factor that influences clinical ability to modify the components of a patient's experience, or at least the type of strategies that optimize or limit such change (Kessler, Dane, & Galper, 2002). It has been further observed that treatment responsiveness is an interaction between this suggestibility factor and the contextually and experientially shaped level of participation in the experience, which is so crucial to its success (Kessler et al., 2002). Therefore, as part of the assessment we conduct to develop an optimal clinical strategy, some information about relative suggestibility is instructive in shaping treatment selection.

From Assessment to Treatment Options: The Logical Consequences Position

As a starting point for selecting treatment options, one should consider the logical consequences that follow from the assessment data just collected. If one respects the story, assesses previous medical experiences and predominant coping strategies, and further generates an assessment of gross level of suggestibility, then much of the treatment progression is laid out (Kessler, 1997). Such information tells you:

- The overall focus of the intervention.
- Whether the intervention needs to include the distinction between historic medical surgical experiences and the current upcoming procedure.
- Whether more or less information provision is indicated as part of the intervention.
- Whether an imaginal or dissociative strategy is indicated, or whether a more here-and-now set of coping strategies is probably going to be helpful.

This matrix is summarized in Table 14.2. Once the general framework is laid out, the next step is deciding the specifics of the intervention by making key decisions about specific treatment options.

Selecting Treatment Options

Earlier it was identified that a preparation will probably include some combination of information and self-regulation with the product being usable coping strategies that a patient perceives as assisting his or her self-efficacy. Because of the resource utilization and scheduling issues inherent in surgical preparation, there have been multiple efforts to utilize procedures that consume less resources and time. Unfortunately, these efforts have been at best equivocal and have resulted in the most frequently reported procedures needing to be face to face and individual, with some possible utility to an adjunctive tape of the preparation for later review and practice. Since it appears that tailoring to patient need optimizes interventions, previously prepared tapes or written material appear of limited utility.

Following from that observation, the issues discussed earlier about coping style outline an intervention strategy suggesting that the role of information provision be tailored to a patient's characteristic coping style. This certainly influences clinician selection of a point on the self-regulation continuum from which to intervene. A key dimension distinguishing self-regulation therapies and

TABLE 14.2 The Logical Consequences of Differences in Previous Medical History, Coping Style, and Suggestibility in Selecting a Preparation Strategy

	Differences	Logical Consequences	Strategies
Coping Style	Avoidant	Does not want information; does not want to actively participate; disempowered; passive	Distraction; dissociative strategies; empower medical professionals; passive strategies; absorbing comfortable imagery
	Confronting	Wants information; wants to participate; active involvement	Information; future rehearsal; active strategies; active self-regulation; participation
Suggestibility	More	Rapid; dissociative; rapid relationship development; easily absorbed; high imaginal abilities	Rapid use of hypnotic strategies; dissociative strategies; use of relationship; imagery
	Less	Less absorption; internal locus of control; stepwise learned involvement; less dissociative ability	Promote internal locus of control; use of self-control; stepwise learned strategies; less reliance on power of immediate relationship; rehearsal; less dissociative and imaginative strategies
Previous Negative Medical Experiences	Significant	Distorted cognitions; negative affect; lack of historic/present boundaries in time and emotion; physiologic hyperarousal	Cognitive restructuring; affective release; dissociative distinguishing history from present; mind/body self-regulation

selecting one for the focus of treatment is the degree of active self-involvement that a strategy requires, as compared with interventions that rely on more imaginal and perhaps dissociative strategies. This continuum is illustrated in Table 14.3.

This clinical decision about selecting self-regulation strategy draws on at least two dimensions of patient characteristics generated during the assessment phase. When evaluating patient interest in active participation in treatment, coping sensitizers will probably be more interested in active involvement, and selection of an active self-regulation strategy is indicated. Conversely, coping avoiders may well just want the whole thing done, and would be just as happy to have little if any active involvement, therefore suggesting a more distracting and perhaps dissociative strategy. The second patient characteristic that will certainly influence selection of a point on the self-regulation continuum is clinician assessment of suggestibility. If there appears to be a substantial degree of imaginative ability and a preference to use it, then a point closer to the hypnotic end of the continuum may be indicated. Wickramsekera (1988) has noted that suggestibility is an important consideration in selecting the most useful psychophysiological treatment strategies. He notes that patients with lower suggestibility will do better with the structure and cognitive attentional focus of biofeedback. Patients with substantial suggestibility will do worse with biofeedback and better with the open-endedness and cognitive freedom of hypnosis. Once the clinician has selected a self-regulation focus, he or she is ready to proceed with the tailoring of a preparation strategy.

TABLE 14.3 The Voluntary Self-Regulation Continuum

Relaxation	Progressive Muscle Relaxation	Autogenics	Imagery	Hypnosis

Tailoring Treatment as Outcome of Standard Assessment

The above assessment and treatment selection strategies suggest that the research literature prescribes a set of assessment procedures that generally forms a useful framework for most surgical preparation activity. However, that does not imply that the treatment delivered to our patients follows a standardized procedure. There is emerging data that suggest the contrary, that the best effects are generated from tailoring the intervention to the needs of the patient. Although it has been insufficiently researched, there appears to be support that tailored, individualized interventions generate superior outcomes to standardized interventions (Enqvist et al., 1995; Syrjala et al., 1992). Therefore, the product of this effort is usually a brief, somewhat standardized assessment of specified dimensions, which generates data allowing for a tailored intervention that respects coping style and medical history and takes advantage of levels of suggestibility that might enhance the treatment. The goal is for the patient to finish the formal preparation; having told his or her story, with a different future-focused orientation toward successfully employing identified coping strategies the patient believes to be efficacious.

How to Prepare Medical Offices

Preparing medical offices is a very difficult area with little mapping to rely on. To review briefly, historically surgical preparation has primarily occurred experimentally, and it is generally not integrated as usual clinical care anywhere I am aware of, with the exception of a small number of anesthesiologists' individual practices around the country. Examples of psychologists being active in surgical preparation as a regular part of medical practice are even more rare. The steps to involve physicians and their offices parallel the steps necessary to be successful in any aspect of medical or hospital practice, with some additions. First, generate credibility. In medical settings credibility starts with being credentialed as part of the medical staff of the hospital. Currently, in most hospitals that means becoming part of some variation of the allied health professional staff. That may even mean finding a physician member of the active staff and having him or her sponsor you and perhaps serve as your supervising physician. It is probably accurate that more hospitals than not require psychologists to be supervised if they are on staff. If that is what it takes to start, then it must be done. However, that is only a necessary but not sufficient step to generating credibility. Within the scope of your privileges, attend medical staff meetings and get on medical staff committees, even if it means 7 A.M. meetings, as it does in my institution. Be present on site and attend continuing education seminars. Get known. If you get referrals from physicians make sure they are pleased. Communicate regularly and *develop strong and positive relationships*. Next, know both the psychological and medical literature and be ready to share it. Being involved in surgical preparation means dealing with a variety of medical and nursing professionals, including primary care physicians, anesthesiology surgeons, and cardiologists. It is important to know the key literature in each of those areas.

Where Does One Start? The Current Condition

The literature and experience suggest that primary care has the most advantageous view of patient adaptation and coping and is currently the least involved in the process after referring to a surgeon, once a decision to do surgery is made. In the primary care practice in which I work, of the 82 referrals that were made to me between January 1, 2000, and December 31, 2000, only one was made specifically for preparation for surgery. In terms of best ability to assess patient need and willingness, primary care practice offers the greatest opportunity. In terms of current organization of medicine, primary care physicians have been rarely involved.

Anesthesiology is responsible for much of the research literature on surgical preparation. There are advantages and disadvantages to approaching these professionals to consider efforts in this area. The advantages include concern with patient psychological functioning as surgery approaches and usual contact with a patient before surgery. The disadvantages include the tendency to conduct brief, snapshot assessments of patient psychosocial need, using no formal assessment system, having an often inflexible schedule, and lacking the ability to predict that the anesthesiologist who sees a patient preoperatively will be in the operating room during the procedure. In terms of recognizing need and utility of surgical preparation, anesthesiology may be the most open. Unfortunately, because of the volume and pace of operating rooms and patient flow to and from surgery, it is not easy to accommodate significant change in routine.

Interestingly, it is surgeons who provide my practice with the greatest number of referrals after years of involvement in this work. However, when a surgeon does not refer a patient for preparation it means that physicians who probably know the patient better, and who have been involved in earlier stages of acuity, have not seen a need to involve a patient in surgical preparation. One explanation is that it is the acuity of the visit with the surgeon or the closeness in time with the procedure that generates the patient reactivity and prompts a surgeon to take action. The dilemma is that by the time that surgeon is that closely involved, acuity is often higher and time to surgery is usually quite brief. In addition, surgery training is procedural training, and surgeons probably have the most limited biopsychosocial view of the process. These factors suggest that there is a greater advantage to earlier detection and intervention. On the other hand, when a surgeon does refer there is usually an acute, compelling reason that, unresolved, might affect the occurrence or outcome of the upcoming procedure.

How to Communicate

The single largest complaint I have heard about behavioral health professionals is that they are unavailable when needed, and that they do not know how to communicate! To be effective in any aspect of medicine is to be available and to provide rapid, focused feedback. This advice is particularly relevant when working in surgery, where acuity of need, rapidity of intervention, and feedback are integral to everyday life. A practice model of someone leaving a message on a telephone answering machine or voice mail is probably an impediment. My pager number is printed on the staff roster, and I encourage medical offices to use it. In most cases, I can be interrupted while with patients by crisis or acute-need pages or calls. Even if my schedule for a day is full, I will make time to see a patient who a physician feels needs to be seen acutely, and I always find the time to see a patient prior to surgery. This is not outstanding behavior; rather it is emulating the model in which I want to participate. After a number of years of this, I have begun to become credible.

Similarly, equal consistency in how one reports back to medical colleagues is critical. Getting consent from a patient to communicate with a referring physician is a basic tenet of practice. I have not once encountered a patient who was unwilling to grant a release for that communication. I have developed a standard preparation feedback document, which takes only a couple of minutes to complete, and which is delivered back to the referring physician after my intervention is completed. It is brief, summarizes key presenting issues, what was done as intervention, and includes recommendations about what the physician might consider doing with the patient, either before the surgery or as follow-up. That document usually becomes part of the medical record or the physician file. An example is included in Table 14.4. Most of the time that document is sufficient communication. On occasion, there is a request for a face-to-face or phone conversation.

TABLE 14.4 Presurgical Preparation Form

Type of surgery:
Surgeon:
Scheduled date of surgery:
Date of preparation:
Summary:
Patient's primary concerns:
Relevant history:
Description of preparation:
Patient's response:
Recommended procedure:

Who Comes, Who Doesn't Come, and Who Should Come

Part of the dilemma in discussing surgical preparation clinically, while commenting from the research perspective, is that there are certainly obvious differences in the populations included. For example, to be able to have representative groups in a research sample, certain parameters for inclusion in that sample need to be established. This might mean age or gender parameters, prior history of psychopathology, or cutoff scores on a psychological measure. However, this also implies that research samples may be made up of a more restricted set of patients than a clinical sample in a primary hospital setting.

One group that appears in the clinical setting but is often not included in research samples is the psychologically distressed high utilizers of medical services described earlier. Such patients not only use more primary care and more specialist consultation time, but also have a higher volume of surgeries than other medical patients. They are often particularly challenging, because their histories with primary care physicians are often difficult and they will often pose a challenge for consultant surgeons and anesthesiologists. Such patients may need extra time and attention, make more requests for presurgical and postsurgical medication, have greater pain complaints, and may need extended hospital stays and higher frequency of ancillary supports. As in other parts of the medical system this population appears to be small, but consumes greater resources. Referrals for psychological assistance with these patients almost always come from the surgeon or anesthesiologist. The primary focus of intervention is actively managing the crises and demands that may be more frequent.

Clinically, the population that appears most frequently in both the clinical and research literatures are patients with acute co-morbid psychological issues that interfere with the progression leading up to surgery and the surgery itself. When the surgeon or anesthesiologist sees such a patient, the co-morbidity makes medical management more difficult. Adherence with preoperative instruction, need for sedation, greater expression of negative effect, higher levels of acute anxiety, and concerns about surviving the surgery are among the problems with such patients. Often, there is negative prior medical surgical history, either personally or with family members, and active coping is compromised. Focus needs to be on rapid assessment of dimensions identified earlier, and brief psychological intervention targeted on remediation of distortions generated from previous medical surgical experience, attention to resolving presenting symptoms, and successful coping using the primary historic coping strategy as focus.

Another small but interesting clinical population that will sometimes either self-refer to a psychologist for preparation or make that request through a primary care physician or surgery are patients whose model of medicine is a mind-body experience. Their self-preparation for the upcoming surgical experience is quite reasonable, but they nevertheless feel that surgery is a mind-body experience and see preparation as a way to enhance this experience. Often such a patient is quite sophisticated psychologically, has previous positive experience with self-regulation techniques, and has a predisposition to active coping. Intervention with such patients usually consists of supporting their use of self-regulation and assisting the focus on specific healing outcomes, such as comfort, rapid healing, and rapid return to function using active coping strategies including active self-participation.

By and large, the primary criterion for referral for surgical preparation has been some version of psychological pathology, interfering with medical functioning or the normal functioning of the institutional surgical process. This could be getting the normal set of injections or insertion of the IV; demonstrating reasonable effect that does not translate into extra time in the surgeon's office or the anesthesia preoperative visit. Implicitly, it is as if there were a trait of psychological distress about surgery. However, despite many efforts to observe such relationships, measures of *pathology* have not consistently correlated with *poorer surgical outcome* (Salmon, 1993). Patients may have greater anxiety before surgery or even have greater amounts of trait anxiety. However, such presentations have not been demonstrated to consistently correspond to any specific negative outcome dimension (Kessler & Whalen, 1999). In fact, it has been observed that there have been functional or physiological improvements even when controlling for psychological pathology (Salmon, 1994). Therefore, using observable pathology as the activator of surgical preparation, while of value, is not the sole criterion to be considered. Other dimensions of functioning have been demonstrated to compromise surgical outcomes, yet they are infrequently considered as initiators of use of psychological surgical preparation.

As already mentioned, poor coping and compromised medical surgical history are related to poorer outcomes of surgery and recovery. In addition, patients who have had multiple surgeries or surgeries with compromised outcomes are likely to cope poorly with additional surgeries and therefore have greater need to be considered for active psychological preparation. Certain surgeries, such as organ or body part loss, gastric bypass, or having a colostomy, require significant coping and adaptation in preparation for the surgery and significant lifestyle changes afterward. Such procedures have clear psychological dimensions that need to be, yet are infrequently formally, addressed.

Again, even in some of the studies that have only allowed patients without identifiable psychological co-morbidity to participate, clinical and cost benefits of preparation have been demonstrated. This last point should be underscored. In an era where the cost of procedures and patient care is under scrutiny, probably the largest group of patients who could benefit from preparatory strategies do not receive them. This both increases patients' personal distress and suffering, and costs the health-care system large amounts of money based on the cost data that have been generated in this field in the past 20 years.

Obstacles

It is assumed that most of the readership of this book have a more diverse knowledge base concerning psychological interventions in medicine than the majority of the medical and psychological community. It is further assumed that even for this readership this chapter has discussed somewhat unfamiliar techniques and outcomes, compared with other aspects of medical psychology. The observation is probably more focused if the readership includes surgeons and primary care physicians. I have not read a family practice textbook, or a general surgery text, that provides more than a cursory review of the psychological issues of patients undergoing surgery and no substantive discussion of the psychological preparation of the surgery patient. This subject has been sufficiently obscure that it has not appeared even as mainstream as other areas of behavioral medicine, despite the length and substance of its research, its ease of use and transportability, and its savings to the health-care system. Additionally, what is known is often limited and inaccurate, which has resulted in the association between referral for surgical preparation and significant presentation of psychopathology, or disbelief that such a brief psychological intervention could have such profound clinical and cost consequences. Changing the current status is a complicated task. First, it involves substantial education. Second, education is generally insufficient to change medical behavior. It is well documented in the medical education literature that information is a necessary but not sufficient intervention, and that giving physicians experience with the change, in their site, and assisting them in learning and experiencing its value is an important component that influences physician behavior change (Davis, Thompson, Oxman, & Haynes, 1992; Kroenke, Taylor-Vaisey, Dietrich, & Oxman, 2000). Third, such a shift cuts across multiple disciplines, and both outpatient and hospital practice. The strategies that need to be employed must address the interests, needs, and concerns of each of the disciplines, respecting and addressing the different organizations, medical staff departments, hospital departments, and employing organizations. Each has a relationship and interest in patient care, organization of care, and administrative issues that are involved in different aspects of the clinical and administrative care that is part of surgery.

Another dimension that must be considered and resolved if psychologists are to be involved in surgery preparation is the payment for psychological services. When a colleague and I first began a surgical preparation service in our rural medical center, it received a front-page headline in the largest newspaper in Vermont. This was followed shortly by a letter from the medical director of the largest insurer in Vermont, wondering if we expected that they would pay for the service. After we wrote them a letter outlining many of the points made in this chapter, and after they reviewed the literature cited in this chapter, the matter was resolved to everyone's satisfaction. However, despite this, the financing of psychology in medicine is the same obstacle in this area of medicine as it is in other areas of health psychology. In general, carve-out models of behavioral health do not assist resolution because intervening with medical patients does not fit their model, which has relied on limiting, not increasing, access to behavioral health care of any type. For them there is no incentive to reasonably support medically and psychologically integrated care, since it would just increase their expense target and reduce profit, and if a patient does not receive needed psychological preparation, the increased medical expense does not come out of their budget.

The Limitations of the Data and Need for Further Research

Despite the large and lengthy supporting literature that has been identified, there is still work to be done. The models of organizing surgical preparation and the specificity of our interventions are not quite as precise as a scalpel's cut. Because this area of research has not been near the top of the national research funding agenda, most of the treatment effectiveness studies have been conducted at single sites with smaller samples than would be optimal. Large multiple-site trials with consistent methodology and the same specified outcomes are needed. These trials need to assess both intra- and postsurgical outcomes, but also longer-term follow-up of posthospitalization function, such as return to work and ongoing medical utilization.

Given the auspicious data from studies reviewing the cost consequences of these interventions and meta-analyses including cost, greater consideration needs to be given to evaluating the cost consequences of both preparation before compared with during surgery and nonpreparation. Also, there are different preparation models. In two of their published studies, Bennett and colleagues (Bennett, Benson, & Kuiken, 1986; Disbrow, Bennett, & Owings, 1993) used a brief semistandardized intervention that took less than 15 minutes while generating significant important outcomes, the first demonstrating lowered blood loss during the surgery and the other rapid return of bowel motility. This is contrasted with other models, such as my own work, which average around 1 hour and include a standardized assessment and tailored intervention, as well as other variations of intervention strategy.

Assessing Effectiveness

Once more there is the opportunity for research to inform practice. The variables that have been used to demonstrate surgical preparation's effectiveness in the research literature are available for use in clinical practice. The variables used to assess the effectiveness of this medical intervention are the variables that medicine notices. Analogue pain ratings are often regularly kept in patient's charts and are now more likely to be present due to attention on pain from the Joint Commission. Also, data concerning premedication prior to surgery is available, as are amounts of postoperative pain medications. Nursing notes, usually containing observational data about patients' overall and psychological function and length of hospital stay, are easily available. However, the best measure in terms of changing physician perception and behavior is seeing the changes in individual functioning of their patients. As powerful as the measurable outcomes have been to my success, one surgeon's report to his colleagues of a remarkably labile and difficult patient was probably just as important. The surgeon had labeled the patient the most emotionally difficult patient he had ever worked with during her first surgery, but after a preparation the patient had an easy, rapid surgery and recovery and early discharge.

Summary

This chapter started with the proposition that there has been successful development of clinical technologies to demonstrate that over a lengthy period of time, psychological preparation for surgery and invasive medical procedures is an effective intervention that has demonstrated clinical, administrative, and financial benefits to patients and the medical system. It is not quite as precise as a scalpel's cut, however, because greater specificity and commonalties of outcomes to be measured need to be defined. More work needs to be done concerning the contribution and implications of individual differences, and greater clarity in matching procedures to patient subtypes needs to be demonstrated. But even with these constraints it should be clear that this is a technology that should be endorsed to patients, physicians (especially in primary care), nurses, administrators, and insurers. It is disappointing to say that presently such endorsement has fallen on mostly deaf ears; therein lies the task.

In some areas of health psychology there is openness to the provision of adequately developed technical solutions. I would say that smoking cessation fits that bill, where despite great efforts and some promise, there is a clear limitation in the effectiveness of the technology. Preparation for surgery suffers from the converse. There is a demonstrated effective technology waiting for the opportunity to be used. The primary tasks in this clinical area are no longer developing a treatment technology. Rather the task is reengineering primary care medicine to regularly include screening for patients who are at risk for compromised psychological and physiological surgical outcomes because of psychological distress. If this can be accomplished we need to move on to integrated systems of referral and cotreatment to lessen or eliminate these risks and to provide improved patient care. Surgery does not begin with the scalpel's cut. It begins with a system of care that respects both the mind's and the body's contribution to functioning, to healing, to living. That is our contribution, and our patients deserve nothing less.

References

Arthur, H., Daniels, C., McKelvie, R., Hirsch J., & Rush, B. (2000). Effect of a preoperative intervention on preoperative outcomes in low-risk patients awaiting elective coronary artery bypass surgery. *Annals of Internal Medicine, 133,* 253–262.

Auerbach, S. (1989). Stress management and coping research in the health care setting: An overview and methodological commentary. *Journal of Consulting and Clinical Psychology, 57,* 388–395.

Bachiocco,V., Scesi, M., Morselli, A., & Carli, G. (1993). Individual pain history and familial pain tolerance models: Relationships to post-surgical pain. *Clinical Journal of Pain, 9,* 266–271.

Bandura, A. (1986). *Social foundations of thought and action: A social psychological theory.* Englewood Cliffs, NJ: Prentice Hall.

Barber, T. X. (1984). Changing "unchangeable" bodily processes by suggestions: A new look at hypnosis, cognitions, imagining, and the mind body problem. In A. Sheikh (Ed.), *Imagination and healing* (pp. 69–128). Farmingdale, NY: Baywood.

Blacher, R., (1987). Brief psychotherapeutic intervention for the surgical patient. In R. Blacher (Ed.), *The psychological experience of surgery.* New York: Wiley.

Blacher, R. (1987). General surgery and anesthesia: The emotional experience. In R. Blacher (Ed.), *The psychological experience of surgery* (pp. 202–220). New York: Wiley.

Blankenfield, R. (1991). Suggestion, relaxation and hypnosis as adjuncts in the care of surgery patients: A review of the literature. *American Journal of Clinical Hypnosis, 33,* 172–187.

Bennett, H. (1993). Personal communication.

Bennett, H., Benson, D., & Kuiken, D. (1986). Preoperative instructions for decreased bleeding during spine surgery. *Anesthesiology, 65,* A245.

Chambless, D., & Hollon, S. (1998). Defining empirically supported therapies. *Journal of Consulting and Clinical Psychology, 66*(1), 7–18.

Chiles, J., Lambert, M., & Hatch, A. (1999). The impact of psychological interventions on medical cost offset: A meta-analytic review. *Clinical Psychology Science and Practice, 6,* 204–220.

Cohen, F., & Lazarus, R. (1973). Active coping processes, coping disposition, and recovery from surgery. *Psychosomatic Medicine, 35,* 375–389.

Davis, D., Thompson, M., Oxman, A., & Haynes, R. (1992). Evidence for the effectiveness of CME: A review of 50 randomized trials. *Journal of the American Medical Association, 268*(9), 1111–1117.

Disbrow, E., Bennett, H., & Owings, J. (1993). Effect of preoperative suggestion on postoperative motility. *Western Journal of Medicine, 158,* 488–492.

Egbert, L., Battit, G., & Turndorf, H. (1963). The value of the preoperative visit by the anesthetist: A study of doctor-patient rapport. *Journal of the American Medical Association, 185,* 553–555.

Enqvist, B., von Konow, L., & Bystedt, H. (1995). Pre and perioperative suggestion in maxillofacial surgery: Effects on blood loss and recovery. *International Journal of Clinical and Experimental Hypnosis, 43,* 284–294.

Evans, B., & Richardson, R. (1991). Improved recovery and increased postoperative stay after therapeutic suggestions during general anesthesia. *Lancet, 2,* 491–493.

Ewing, D. (1986). Emergency room hypnosis for the burned patient. *American Journal of Clinical Hypnosis, 29*(1), 7–12.

Gray, G., Brody, D., & Hart, M. (2000, March) Primary care and the *de facto* mental health care system: Improving care where it counts. *Managed Care Interface,* 62–65.

Hathaway, D. (1986). Effect of preoperative instruction on postoperative outcomes: A meta-analysis. *Nursing Research, 35,* 269–275.

Holden-Lund, C. (1988). Effects of relaxation and guided imagery on surgical stress and wound healing. *Research in Nursing and Health, 11,* 235–244.

Janis, I. (1958). *Psychological stress.* New York: Wiley.

Johnson, M., & Vogele, C. (1993). Benefits of psychological preparation for surgery: A meta-analysis. *Annals of Behavioral Medicine, 15,* 245–256.

Katon, W., VonKorff, M., Lin, E., Lipscomb, P., Russo, J., Wagner, E. et al. (1990). Distressed high utilizers of medical care: DSM III diagnosis and treatment needs. *General Hospital Psychiatry, 12,* 355–362.

Kessler R. (1992). Hypnotizability and hypnotic responsiveness: Modifying responsiveness in clinical practice. In M. Hunter (Ed.), *Frontiers of hypnosis* (vol. 2). Vancouver: SeaWalk Press.

Kessler, R., & Dane, J. (1996). Psychological preparation for anesthesia and surgery: An individual differences perspective. *International Journal of Clinical and Experimental Hypnosis, 74*(3), 189–207.

Kessler, R., Dane, J., & Galper, D. (2002). Assessing and accessing hypnotic responsiveness to enhance hypnotic experience in clinical practice. *American Journal of Clinical Hypnosis, 44*(3), 273–282.

Kessler, R., & Miller, S. (1995). The use of future time frame in psychotherapy. *American Journal of Clinical Hypnosis, 38*(1), 39–46.

Kessler, R., & Whalen, T. (1999). Hypnotic preparation in anesthesia and surgery. In R. Temes (Ed.), *Medical hypnosis: An introduction and clinical guide* (pp. 43–64). New York: Churchill Livingstone.

Kirsch, I. (1997). Hypnotic suggestion: A musical metaphor. *American Journal of Clinical Hypnosis, 39*, 271–277.

Kroenke, K., Taylor-Vaisey, A., Dietrich, A., & Oxman, T. (2000). Interventions to improve provider diagnosis and treatment of mental disorders in primary care. *Psychosomatics, 41*(1), 271–277.

Lang, E., Benotsch, E., & Fick, L. (2000). Adjunctive non-pharmacological analgesia for invasive medical procedures: A randomized trial. *Lancet, 355*, 1486–1490.

Lang, E. V., & Rosen, M. P. (2002). Cost analysis of adjunct hypnosis with sedation during outpatient interventional radiologic procedures. *Radiology, 222*(2), 375–382.

Lester. N., Lefebre, J., & Keefe, F. (1994). Pain in young adults: Relationship to gender and family pain history. *Clinical Journal of Pain, 10*, 282–289.

Montgomery, G., Weltz, C. R., & Bovbjerg, D. H. (2002). Brief presurgery hypnosis reduces distress and pain in excisional breast biopsy patients. *International Journal of Clinical and Experimental Hypnosis, 50*(1), 17–32.

Mumford, E., Schlesinger, H., & Glass, G. (1982). The effects of psychological intervention on recovery from surgery and heart attacks: An analysis of the literature. *American Journal of Public Health, 72*, 141–151.

Rapkin, D., Straubing, M., & Holroyd, J. (1991). Guided imagery hypnosis and recovery from head and neck cancer surgery: An exploratory study. *International Journal of Clinical and Experimental Hypnosis, 39*, 215–226.

Regier, D., Narrow, W., Rae, D., Manderscheid, R., Locke, B., & Goodwin, F. (1993). The de facto U.S. mental and addictive services system: Epedimiologic catchment area prospective 1-year prevalence rates of disorders and services. *Archives of General Psychiatry, 50*, 85–94.

Rogers, M., Liang, M., Poss, R., & Cullen, K. (1982). Adverse psychological sequalae associated with joint replacement surgery. *General Hospital Psychiatry, 34*, 155–158.

Rogers, M., & Reich, P. (1986). Psychological intervention with surgery patients: Evaluation outcome. *Advances in Psychosomatic Medicine, 15*, 25–50.

Rondi, G., Bowers, K., Buckley, D., Merikle, P., Dunn,G., & Rondi, P. (1993). Postoperative awareness of information presented under general anesthesia. In P. Sobel, B. Bonke, & E. Winograd (Eds.), *Memory and awareness in anesthesia* (pp. 187–195). Englewood Cliffs, NJ: Prentice Hall.

Salmon, P. (1994). Psychological factors in surgical recovery. In H. Gibson (Ed.), *Pain and anesthesia* (pp. 229–258). London: Chapman & Hall.

Spielberger, C., Gorsuch, R., & Lushene, R. (1970). *Manual for the State Trait Anxiety Inventory.* Palo Alto, CA: Consulting Psychologist Press.

Syrjala, K., Cummings, C., & Donaldson, G. (1992). Hypnosis and cognitive behavioral training for the reduction of pain and nausea during cancer treatment: A controlled clinical trial. *Pain, 48*, 137–148.

Van Dalfsen, P., & Syrjala, K. (1990). Psychological strategies in acute pain management. *Critical Care Clinics, 6*, 421–432.

Wickramsekera, I. (1988). *Clinical behavioral medicine.* New York: Plenum.

Suggested Reading

Chiles,J., Lambert, M., Hatch, A. (1999) The impact of psychological interventions on medical cost offset: A meta-analytic review. *Clinical Psychology Science and Practice* 6: 204-220.

Kessler R., Dane J., (1996) Psychological preparation for anesthesia and surgery: An individual differences perspective. *International Journal of Clinical and Experimental Hypnosis* 74,3. 189-207

Kessler R., Whalen T., (1999) Hypnotic preparation in anesthesia and surgery. In R. Temes (ed.), *Medical hypnosis: An introduction and clinical guide.* New York: Churchill Livingstone, 43-64.

Chapter 15
Assessment and Treatment of Chronic Benign Headache in the Primary Care Setting

JOHN G. ARENA AND EDWARD B. BLANCHARD

Chronic pain (that is, pain that lasts for at least 6 months), with the exception of influenza and the common cold, is the most frequent cause of visits to primary health-care settings (Sobel, 1993), and presents an extremely frustrating challenge for most traditional medically oriented health-care providers. Headache is one of the most common pain complaints, and research has shown that over a 10-year period from 1987 to 1996, primary care providers have seen an increasing number of individuals with pain-related diagnoses primarily due to an increase in headache patients (Andersson, Ejlertsson, Leden, & Schersten, 1999). Khan, Khan, Harezlak, Tu, and Kroenke (2003) have noted that headache is a particularly refractory diagnosis for primary care providers. The direct health-care costs of headaches are significant (Mannix, 2001), and the cost of headaches to employers is exceedingly high. In a study that examined lost workdays and decreased work effectiveness associated with headache in the workplace, Schwartz, Stewart, and Lipton (1997) found that headache sufferers lost the equivalent (they accounted for both actual lost workdays and reduced effectiveness at work) of 4.2 workdays per year because of headache.

A large body of literature on both the pharmacotherapy and psychological treatment of headache has emerged during the past three decades. Reviews of the behavioral literature have generally shown two techniques, biofeedback and relaxation therapy, to be effective in significantly reducing headache activity in 40–60% of both tension and vascular (migraine and combined migraine-tension) headache patients (Arena & Blanchard, 2000; Blanchard & Arena, 1999; Costa & Vandenbos, 1990; Craig & Weiss, 1990; Gatchel & Blanchard, 1993; Holroyd, 1993; Shumaker, Schron, & Ockene, 1990). In this chapter, we will review the basics of nonpharmacological treatments for migraine and tension-type headaches (the two major types of headache categories), placing special emphasis on the frontline mental health professional in a primary care setting. Whenever possible, we will include clinical guidelines that are based on both the available research literature and our clinical experience.

Characteristics of Migraine and Tension-Type Headache

Clinicians who work with headache patients should use a standardized set of inclusion and exclusion criteria for diagnosis, such as those of the Ad Hoc Committee on the Classification of Headache (1962) or the newer Headache Classification Committee of the International Headache Society (1988).

Migraine headache is episodic and characterized by a throbbing/pulsating/pounding type of pain that generally starts on one side of the head, although as the headache progresses, it often encompasses both sides. It typically starts over an eye or in the temple region and can last anywhere from 2 hours to 3 days. Frequently it is accompanied by nausea and, sometimes, vomiting, as well as sensitivity to noise (termed phonophobia) and, especially, light (termed photophobia). A migraine can occur on a frequency of two a week to only one or two a year; the average migraineur has one to two headaches a month. Approximately 10% of migraine headache patients have a prodrome—that is, preheadache symptoms that can occur up to 30 minutes before a headache, such as seeing flashing lights or squiggly lines, experiencing a disturbance in speech, or a tingling feeling in the arms or hands. Those migraine headache sufferers with a prodrome are described as classic migraineurs; those without a prodrome are termed common migraineurs.

Tension headache is generally less episodic and is characterized by a steady, dull ache or pressure that is generally on both sides of the head. It is sometimes described as a tight band or cap around the head, a soreness, a nagging, or a vice-like pain. It typically begins in the forehead, temple, back of the head and neck, or shoulder regions, and encompasses the entire head. A tension headache can last from 30 minutes to 7 days. If headache occurs less than 15 days a month, it is termed episodic tension-type headache; if the headache is experienced 15 or more days a month, it is termed chronic tension-type headache. The pain associated with tension headache is considered to be of generally lesser intensity than that of migraine headache.

Up to half of patients with migraine headache also meet the criteria for tension headache. These individuals have been labeled as having "Mixed Migraine and Tension-Type Headache" or "Combined Migraine and Tension-Type Headache." Most clinicians and researchers have typically lumped both pure migraine and mixed migraine and tension headaches together under the label of "Vascular Headache" and treated them similarly.

Headaches are a true biopsychosocial phenomenon, affecting psychological and social factors of an individual's life as well as the more obvious physiological concerns. Depression, anxiety, and anger are common sequelae of headache, as are dysfunctions in occupational areas, such as lowered job productivity and increased days off from work, and interpersonal relations, such as being unable to participate in family outings and social functions (e.g., parties, picnics, etc.). Of course, the reverse is also true, that psychological and social factors affect headache intensity, frequency, and duration. For example, psychological stress has been shown to exacerbate and bring on head pain.

Epidemiology of Migraine and Tension-Type Headache

Tension-type headache is believed to be the most prevalent form of headache. It is more common in females than males, with a male-to-female ratio of approximately 1:1.5 (Rasmussen, 1999). Age of onset is generally in the second decade, and it peaks between the ages of 30 and 39. Rasmussen, Jensen, Schroll, and Olesen (1991), using the diagnostic criteria of the International Headache Society, found that lifetime prevalence of episodic or chronic, tension-type headache was 78% for men and women combined, 69% for men, and 88% for women. In that study, the prevalence of tension headache in the previous month was 48% overall. Interestingly, among subjects with migraine in the previous month, 62% had coexisting tension headache. This study is extremely important because it is the first investigation to include a representative random population, to use operational diagnostic criteria, and to include a clinical interview as well as a general physical and neurological examination of all participants. It suggests that the incidence and prevalence of chronic tension headache is much higher than previously believed. Silberstein and Lipton (2000) estimated that 4–5% of the U.S. population suffer from primary chronic daily headache, of which the majority are tension-like.

Migraine headache is predominantly a disorder of women during the childbearing years. In prepubertal children, migraine is approximately equally distributed across the sexes. With the onset of menarche, females having migraines begin to outnumber males by about 2 or 3 to 1. An outstanding epidemiological survey (Stewart, Lipton, Celentano, & Reed, 1992) involving over 20,000 participants across the United States found 17.6% of females and 5.7% of males have one or more migraine headaches per year, with almost 4.5 million adults suffering from one or more migraine headaches *per month*. (In our experience, women outnumber men by 4 or 5 to 1 in terms of seeking psychosocial treatment for migraine headaches.)

Establishing a Relationship With a Primary Care Provider: The Clinician's Initial Task

While not always essential for high-quality treatment per se of the headache patient, if at all possible, the psychologist should try to establish a relationship with primary care providers who have sent, or will likely provide, referrals. Optimally, one should establish this relationship prior to receiving any referrals from the primary care provider. This is easily done if the behavioral healthcare provider operates in the same setting as the primary care provider and is located in the primary care clinic or office. Daily interactions with providers are therefore easy and expected. Often, the mental health professional has lunch or coffee with the primary care providers, meets them in the hall and informally discusses cases, and so forth. Unfortunately, it is often the case that the mental health professional is not integrated into the primary care setting, and this makes it quite difficult to establish such relationships. Sometimes establishing such relationships before receiving referrals is not feasible, especially in medical schools or a teaching hospital where large numbers of students, residents, and staff rotate frequently through the primary care setting. Establishing an alliance with the primary care provider will likely pay dividends, not only with headache sufferers currently being treated, but with subsequent headache patients. Taken as an aggregate, we have found that primary care providers are more receptive to psychological approaches to chronic pain than are other medical specialists, such as those in orthopedics, neurology, or neurosurgery, although there is great variability among providers.

As noted above, being integrated into the primary care clinic or offices is preferable, and it makes it easy to establish a relationship with the primary care providers. However, this often is not the case. If you are located in a hospital or clinic and are operating in the same setting as the primary care providers, we suggest the preferred method is to walk to the primary care provider's office and introduce yourself. It is important to keep in mind that primary care providers are usually extremely busy, so limit your initial visit to a brief greeting. Then set up a longer stretch of time (no more than 20 minutes, however) to explain in outline form what services you can offer. Keep it very pragmatic and avoid the use of jargon. If you are a psychologist in private practice and your office is located some distance away from the primary care provider's office, getting acquainted by phone will do the trick.

In your interactions with primary care providers, in addition to letting them know what you can do and what you are about, we would urge you to briefly discuss your strengths and weaknesses. (This, of course, necessitates that you are aware of your strengths and weaknesses. If you are not, simply ask your spouse, children, or friends!) If you do not work well with certain populations—such as the mentally retarded or individuals who are extremely angry or ruminative—let them know that and if possible furnish them with the names of individuals who do work well with such populations. Above all, *do not promise more than you can deliver.* That is by far the biggest mistake psychologists and other mental health professionals who work in primary care settings or with primary care providers make. We have found that when you are dealing with health-care professionals, a little humility goes a long way. Discuss in a realistic way the clinical outcome data (detailed below) on the nonpharmacological treatment of headache and always remember that the stringent inclusion and exclusion criteria employed in most research protocols (i.e., they generally exclude individuals with major depression or who have serious medical illnesses, etc.) probably influence that data in a positive direction. This initial interaction will pave the way for subsequent meetings and "prime the pump" for the beginning of a two-way learning process between the primary care provider and the mental health professional.

Two final notes here: First, the adage about not promising more than you can deliver applies to both primary care patients and providers. Second, for those mental health professionals located in primary care clinics, we have found that the optimal place for an office is in the quietest part of the clinic, as far away as possible from the examination and procedure rooms. The examination and procedure rooms are generally very active, noisy places that are usually not conducive to nonpharmacological interventions. In this way, the primary care provider or his or her staff can walk the headache patient over to your office, and you can briefly introduce yourself and schedule an appointment. This significantly reduces initial no-show rates.

Understanding the Primary Care Provider's Practice Style and Preferences and Beginning a Collaborative Process: The Clinician's Next Task

The collaborative process that a mental health professional has with the primary care provider can, depending on circumstances, be either extremely rewarding or punitive. A great deal depends on the mental health clinician's obtaining an understanding of the practice style and personal preferences of the primary care provider. The process that underlies this is a subtle one that begins with the initial introduction and continues along the life of the relationship. There are some things, however, that we feel are nearly always useful for the mental health provider to discover about the primary care provider.

One of the most important things to ascertain about primary care providers is how they prefer obtaining information about the status of their patients. Some providers want you to keep them updated constantly, with a copy of the initial report faxed to them, coupled with an e-mail, phone call, or fax after each treatment session, as well as a copy of the termination report. Others simply want a copy of the initial report and termination report, yet others feel that once they send you the patient he or she is "owned" by you (a terrible phrase that is unfortunately used by too many health-care providers) unless they hear otherwise. Deciding what is the referral source's preferred style of communication regarding status of patients is essential for the psychologist or other mental health professional working in a primary care setting. It is easy to irritate providers by sending them too much or too little information. In our experience, the vast majority of primary care providers wish to be updated periodically about patients' status, usually at the beginning of treatment with your clinical impressions and at the end of treatment with a global percentage of improvement and, if the patient did not achieve sufficient relief, suggestions for further treatment or referrals. But do not assume this—ask. Furthermore, do not always assume that primary care providers accurately provided their true desires concerning how often they wish to be updated regarding a patient's status—sometimes they give the response they believe they should give or the response they assume you would want to hear. As you treat a few of their patients and get to know your referral sources, you will discover whether the information they gave you initially was accurate, and you can modify your information delivery style as necessary. For example, a provider may have initially told you that he or she wanted information on a patient only after treatment is completed. However, if that provider repeatedly calls you about the patient's progress, you can infer that he or she really wants periodic updates. You should then change your frequency of reporting on that provider's patients.

We also find it helpful to tell the primary care provider that if certain things change regarding the headache (for example, the headache characterization changes, switches location, or suddenly becomes constant and unremitting, or the patient suddenly loses coordination, or gets drowsy or confused when she has a headache), you will immediately let him or her know about these changes. This lets the primary care provider know that you are aware of the medical aspects of headache, and that you respect his or her discipline.

Another rather delicate issue to touch upon is the personality, reasoning, and desires (conscious or unconscious) underlying the referral from a provider. An overall feeling about this generally comes after receiving a couple of referrals from the provider. If at all possible, try to find out what the provider really wants from the referral and why the provider is truly referring the patient to you. The documented referral question does not always contain the only reason for a referral. It is important to keep in mind that a primary care provider will not generally refer a headache sufferer to a mental health professional unless the patient has proved refractory to a number of pharmacological and medical interventions.

Does the primary care provider want the mental health provider to give him/her absolution, to say that it was not his/her fault that this patient did not improve, that no primary care provider could help this patient? If this is the case, it is important to include phrases such as, "this very difficult pain management case" or "this complex pain problem" in your report. As you develop a relationship with that particular provider, you may wish to do some brief psychotherapeutic interventions concerning this attitude. For example, in your conversations with the primary care provider, you can delicately discuss how difficult you find some of these patients to work with, how having patients that prove refractory to treatment can be frustrating, and here is how you and others have dealt with such types of patients, etc.

Does the provider want you to identify whether the patient has significant psychological problems that interfere with medical treatment response, but really does not want you to treat the patient? Some primary care providers do not want a mental health professional to be involved in the headache treatment process, but they want to understand better the psychological makeup of their headache patients. In this instance, education and time are your best assets, because as the provider gets more information concerning the psychological aspects of headache, the provider will quickly see the benefits of nonpharmacological treatment (as well as the fact that it takes specialized skills to help their patients).

Is the primary care provider referring the headache patient because this a very difficult patient that the provider wants to dump on the mental health professional? If this is the case, and the mental health professional will quickly realize this—generally after four or five completely inappropriate consults who have failed to respond to nonpharmacological treatment (if they make the mistake of treating them)—psychoeducation will typically in our experience fail. Generally the best approach is to discourage that particular provider from sending referrals.

Is the provider at his or her wits' end and going on a "fishing expedition" in the hopes of finding something that might work? This is the most common nonstraightforward referral pattern, and it is actually easy to deal with. Education about when to send a patient to a mental health professional—hopefully well before a primary care provider gets to the "end of his/her rope"— usually also does the trick here.

Finally, does the provider want some excuse not to treat this patient, and is hoping that a psychologist's report will give him or her the justification? Here, education of the provider about when to transfer a patient to another primary care provider, and discussion of transference and countertransference (if appropriate to the primary care provider's level of sophistication about psychological factors) is appropriate. One way to do this is to discuss difficult patients you have had and how you have had to transfer patients to other mental health providers because you just could not work with someone. Usually, this will begin a dialogue that most medically oriented professionals have never had and they are often grateful for the chance to discuss such a sensitive topic.

One way some mental health professionals try to help both themselves and the referring provider is to have either a separate checklist that providers can then attach to consults, or a list of usual reasons for referrals to the mental health professional that they can refer to when formulating referrals for difficult patients. The referral slip (e.g., sort of a "check the box" slip), that does not go in the actual chart, delineates reasons for referral (e.g., patient is refractory to numerous treatments, I believe there may be mental health problems; I think that this patient is depressed; etc.) that the medical care provider would fill out and give to the mental health care provider. This is often a useful tool for the mental health professional in the primary care setting.

Another personal preference that is useful for the mental health provider to ascertain concerning a respective primary care provider is his or her interest in the headache and psychological clinical research literature. Some primary care providers enjoy reading research articles, and others do not. Some prefer review articles, chapters, or books to research articles. Some enjoy reading about pharmacological or medical approaches to headache, but wish no information about nonpharmacological approaches. (Here one needs to be careful, as the mental health provider does not wish to be seen as stepping into the primary care provider's turf. If we do provide such information, we usually provide an article that compares a nonpharmacological approach with a pharmacological one.) Some primary care providers enjoy getting articles about headache epidemiology, others about pathophysiology. Still others do not want any educational materials—at least not those given to them by a mental health professional. Determining the provider's style concerning educational aspects of the relationship comes with experience and time, generally after the mental health professional has established a personal relationship with the primary care provider.

The Clinical Interview, Headache Diagnosis, and Nonpharmacological Treatment Prognosis: The Initial Step With Every Headache Patient

The first formal step in any assessment procedure involves conducting an extensive headache history, which is necessary in determining a diagnosis. The clinical interview for a headache patient is the clinician's most valuable tool, not only for diagnosis but also for prognosis. The interview we currently use is a slightly modified version of one used in previous research and requires about 60 minutes to complete. We have published (Blanchard & Andrasik, 1985) this version of our clinical interview. For readers wishing a revised version, please contact the authors.

The clinical interview for a headache patient is very similar to the clinical interview for a psychiatric patient, with one major exception: it is important that the mental health provider avoids talking about psychological issues for at least the first half of the interview. This way one avoids having the patient attempt to characterize the mental health professional as a "shrink" who is not really interested in his or her pain. If patients tell you that they feel like harming themselves when their pain is severe, or that they use alcohol to attenuate their pain, or that stress makes their pain worse, do not deviate from your initial goal of obtaining information about their headache, do not start asking questions concerning suicide, alcohol abuse, or stress. If the patient persists in wanting to talk about psychological problems before the headache aspects of the interview are completed, we say: "I really want to find out all about your pain now. I promise you we'll discuss these other issues later."

The headache interview should, of course, cover the history of the patient's headaches. Intensity, duration, and frequency should be reviewed, as well as where the headache starts, how it progresses over time, associated symptoms, what exacerbates the head pain, is there a menstrual relationship, what attenuates the head pain, family history of headache, and so forth. One of the most important questions to ask is whether patients have more than one kind of headache. If they answer yes to this question, we would urge you to take a separate headache history for each type of headache, to ascertain whether they do, indeed, suffer from combined migraine-tension headache. Sometimes patients state they have more than one kind of headache but, upon examination, they are making a differentiation based on intensity or location alone. This does not meet the criteria for combined migraine-tension headache.

Another important question to ask is, "How would you describe the pain? Is it a dull ache, throbbing, burning, piercing, cramping, sharp, or an electric pain?" Here you are looking not only at the descriptors, but the manner in which they describe the pain. Generally, the clinician is looking for extremes. Individuals who matter-of-factly state, "It's a bad pain" or who floridly state, "It's like a spider web of pain, a labyrinth of agony. It feels like my brain is too big for my skull—like someone is taking a skinny pair of pliers and twisting and pulling my brain out through my eyeball," are both, in our clinical experience, poor treatment responders.

Another thing to explore in the clinical interview is possible secondary gains, that is, overt reasons why it may be beneficial for a person to create or maintain his or her headaches. The usual sources are: spouse (attention, acceptable reason for decreased sexual activity, decreased nagging, etc.), children and grandchildren (attention, quiet, reason for them to stay at home and not date, etc.), work (socially acceptable reason to not work), financial remuneration (paid sick leave, litigation, disability), and that pain is often a socially acceptable reason to not participate in activities such as church, parties, picnics, dancing, sports, and so forth. Clinically, we have found that the presence of significant secondary gains is a good predictor of poor treatment outcome.

In addition to obtaining a complete headache history, it is important to ask about what is going on in the headache patient's life. Issues such as marriage, work, how they get along with parents, etc., are vitally important. If they ask why you are inquiring, we tell them: "We know that most pain is made worse by stress, so we're looking for possible areas of stress in your life." Another significant area of inquiry is to ascertain what they do on a typical day. This will give you important information about their activity level, as well as insight as to why they may be depressed. For example, many individuals with chronic daily tension or combined migraine-tension headache have days that consist mainly of staying at home and watching television. This, of course, leads to elevated levels of depression, as well as poor muscle tone. High levels of depression and anxiety have both been found to be good predictors of poor treatment outcome for nonpharmacological interventions.

Above all, *do not skip the mental status examination*. Many clinicians feel that since they are dealing with a headache patient, they do not need to do a formal mental status examination. However, we feel that such questions are vitally important. For example, we know that headache patients who are significantly depressed have much worse outcomes than those who are not, and some headache patients are schizophrenics with somatic delusions. Every clinician has stories of individuals who seem to be functioning within normal limits until the very end of the interview when, responding to a question such as, "Do you have any special powers?," report that, "I cause the sun to rise every morning and set every evening." If you overlook the mental status examination, you overlook vitally important clinical information.

It is important to reflect on the interview process upon completion of the interview. Questions the mental health provider should ask him/herself are: Were there antisocial personality traits present? Were there histrionic personality traits present? Was there hostility or inappropriate anger present? Was the patient trying to present him/herself in an unusually good light (e.g., "everything would be perfect in my life if it were not for this darn pain")? In our clinical practice, we have found that these characteristics retard the treatment process.

Other prognostic indicators of poor treatment outcome are: pain that is constant, pain that remains at the same level throughout the day regardless of activity level (i.e., it is always an 8 on a scale of 1 to 10), a diffuse pain ("It's all over") as opposed to a specific pain ("It's right over my eye"), pain that is in multiple areas of the body, individuals who are involved in litigation or have quit their jobs as a result of the headaches, headache sufferers who have no or a large number of associated symptoms, patients who have previously proved refractory to nonpharmacological intervention, and individuals with preexisting psychiatric conditions. Unfortunately, in the non-pharmacological treatment of headache, the prognostic indicator of good treatment outcome is generally the absence or low number of prognostic indicators of poor treatment outcome. Tables 15.1 and 15.2 present brief checklists of prognostic indicators of poor and good treatment outcome.

All information obtained in the clinical interview should be included in the body of the consultation report. Very often patients will tell the mental health professional things that they have not told their primary care provider. Often, patients believe that they have told their primary care provider information that they have not. Therefore, as a rule, we include all information in the consultation report. Major points are covered in a section that we term, "Summary and Recommendations." Less important points are placed in a section that we term, "History and Interview Data."

There is certain information that the mental health professional may obtain during the clinical interview that requires immediate consultation with the primary care provider, rather than simply noting it in the consultation report. Many of these are obvious, such as a patient who admits he or she is a substance abuser or is suicidal. Other less-apparent instances are when patients decide to discontinue medication on their own, use more than the prescribed dosage, or enhance the effects with alcohol. It is also prudent to alert the primary care provider when patients complain of new sensory or motor deficits that occur before or during the headache that are not typically associated with migraine prodromes, such as weakness or numbness in an extremity, or twitching of the hands or feet, as the patient may have had a stroke. Aphasia or slurred speech may be caused by a vascular malformation. Twitching—especially on one side of the face or in only one hand—could indicate focal seizures due to a tumor or other structural lesions. If the patient has had some trauma to the head since being seen by the primary care provider, especially if unconsciousness occurred even momentarily, immediately alert the primary care provider. This matter is even more urgent if the topography of the headache has changed since the trauma. If the patient's headaches have gone from being intermittent and variable in intensity to constant and unremitting, alert the primary care provider. If the patient has tension headaches and the intensity has been steadily increasing over a period of weeks to months with no relief, alert the primary care provider because the headache may be due to uncontrolled hypertension or a tumor causing increased intracranial pressure. If the patient's family tells you that there has been a noticeable change in behavior, personality, memory, or intellectual functioning recently, alert the primary care provider as this may be indicative of a frontal lobe tumor. If the patient complains of sudden onset of headache during exertion (lifting/weight training, sexual intercourse, heated arguments, etc.) alert the primary care provider as this may be due to a leaking cerebral aneurysm. Finally, if the patient tells you of any family history of vascular abnormalities, polycystic kidneys, or cerebral aneurysm, immediately notify the referring primary care provider, as the patient may not have informed the provider about this family history.

The Headache Diary: The Clinician's Next Step With Every Headache Patient

At the first visit, you should have the patient begin to record a daily headache diary. In this diary, the patient notes degree of headache activity using a 6 (0–5) point scale, an 11 (0–10) point scale, or a visual-analogue scale, generally four times a day (awakening, lunch, dinner, bedtime). We have

TABLE 15.1 Prognostic Indicators of Poor Response to Nonpharmacological Treatment

_____ Antisocial personality traits present to a significant degree (i.e., married numerous times, long history of substance abuse, long arrest record, history of fighting, etc.)

_____ Atypical headache

_____ Cognitive functioning at low levels

_____ Constantly present headache

_____ Depression that is at a moderate/severe/marked level

_____ Diffuse pain (i.e., "It's all over my body")

_____ Extremely dramatic pain presentation

_____ Extremely matter-of-fact pain presentation with no affect (only when discussing pain)

_____ Few associated symptoms (e.g., dizziness, difficulty walking, crying, concentration problems, anger, stomach problems)

_____ More than seven associated symptoms (e.g., fatigue, loss of bladder control, blurred vision, irritability, depression, profuse sweating)

_____ Headache that is always at the same intensity level (i.e., pain level unchanged regardless of activities)

_____ Histrionic personality traits present to a significant degree (i.e., dramatic presentation throughout the interview, flirtatiousness, etc.)

_____ Hostility or inappropriate anger present to a significant degree

_____ Litigation pending or ongoing

_____ Low motivation level

_____ Significant MMPI-2 findings: (a) invalid profile (especially if they attempted to "fake bad"); (b) scale 1 > 70T; (c) scale 3 > 70T; (d) scale 4 > 65T (check Harris and Lingoes subscales to make sure not due to family problems) (e) scale 6 > 70T; (f) scale 8 > 75T (not due to bizarre sensory experiences—check Harris and Lingoes subscales); (g) presence of conversion V—scales 1 and 3 > 65T and scale 2 at least 10 T points lower than 1 and 3.

_____ Multiple types of pain or multiple pain sites

_____ Patient trying to present in an unusually good light (e.g., "Everything would be perfect in my life if it were not for this darn pain")

_____ Patient very skeptical about the effectiveness of nonpharmacological treatments ("That stuff just doesn't work")

_____ Poor work history (particularly prior to onset of headaches)

_____ Preexisting psychiatric conditions

_____ Previously failed nonpharmacological interventions

_____ Secondary gains:

    _____ Children and grandchildren (attention, quiet, reason for them to stay at home and not date, etc.)

    _____ Financial remuneration (paid sick leave, litigation, disability)

    _____ Socially acceptable reason to not participate in activities (such as church, parties, picnics, dancing, sports, etc.)

    _____ Spouse (attention, acceptable reason for decreased sexual activity, decreased nagging, etc.)

    _____ Work (socially acceptable reason to not work)

    _____ Typical day consists of few activities and pleasant events

    _____ Quit job as a result of headaches

TABLE 15.2 Prognostic Indicators of Good Response to Nonpharmacological Treatment

_____	Antisocial personality traits *not* present to a significant degree (i.e., married only once or twice, no history of substance abuse, no arrest record, no history of fighting, etc.)
_____	Appropriate number (between 3 and 6) of associated symptoms (e.g., dizziness, difficulty walking, crying, concentration problems, anger, stomach problems)
_____	Cognitive functioning at normal or above levels
_____	Good work history (particularly prior to onset of headaches)
_____	Headache follows typical pattern
_____	Headache intensity changes
_____	Headache is intermittent, not constant
_____	Histrionic personality traits (i.e., dramatic presentation throughout the interview, flirtatiousness, etc.) *not* present to a significant degree
_____	Hostility or inappropriate anger *not* present to a significant degree
_____	Litigation *not* pending or ongoing
_____	Moderate or greater motivation level
_____	No depression present or present at low levels
_____	No easily observable secondary gains
_____	No history of poor response to nonpharmacological interventions
_____	No preexisting psychiatric conditions
_____	No significant MMPI-2 findings
_____	Normal pain presentation (i.e., not dramatic or matter-of-fact)
_____	Pain localized to headache only
_____	Patient *not* trying to present in an unusually good light
_____	Patient expresses strong belief in the efficacy of nonpharmacological interventions
_____	Patient referred by someone who was a nonpharmacological treatment success (or patient knows someone who was a success)
_____	Typical day consists of many activities and pleasant events

generally used the 6-point scale, but there is no evidence suggesting any one scale is more advantageous than another. Medication usage can also be recorded.

Measures generally derived from the headache diary are (1) The average daily headache activity score per week, termed the *headache index*. This is the most sensitive and frequently used measure since it combines intensity and duration. (2) Number of headache-free days per week. (3) The highest, or peak, single headache rating for each week. This measures whether the more debilitating headaches are being relieved. At the end of one week, we usually have the patient return to have the diary checked. If the records are not being adequately kept, the procedures should be explained again. Although ideally the headache diary should be kept for at least 28 days before treatment starts for vascular headache sufferers, and for 7 to 14 days for tension headache patients, one needs at least 2 weeks of diary for vascular headache and 1 week for tension headache.

The headache diary is essential for documenting treatment results. It can also give the provider an indication of how well patients will adhere to the treatment regimen. Obviously, if the patient cannot correctly fill out the diary or refuses to fill out the diary, that is likely a harbinger of poor treatment results. It is certainly "grist for the therapy mill"—that is, inquiry about why the patient is having problems with the diary will likely lead to discussion of areas of possible stress in his or her life or salient personality characteristics that would need to be addressed by the mental health professional. If a patient adamantly refuses to fill out a headache diary, however, we generally will continue to treat him or her, although many clinicians would not. Appendix A includes a sample of a headache diary.

Psychological Testing

Readers interested in an in-depth discussion of the personality factors associated with headache and the nuts and bolts of psychological testing with headache and pain patients should avail themselves of the excellent reviews that are already available (e.g., Block, 1996; Cao, Zhang, Wang, Wan, & Wang, 2002; Holroyd, Stensland, Lipchik, Hill, O'Donnell, & Cordingley, 2000; London, Shulman, & Diamond, 2001; Turk and Melzack, 1992). We believe that psychological testing is not always necessary or cost-effective with headache patients, especially given the generally high rates of success of nonpharmacological treatments (see below). Clinically, unless we can identify certain markers during the headache interview, we do not administer psychological tests with headache patients. Indications that psychological testing may be helpful include significant depression, anxiety, or anger; and a history of physical, sexual, or substance abuse.

There are many instruments that the mental health professional can use to assess their pain patients personality characteristics (e.g., Beck Depression Inventory, MMPI, Million Clinical Multiaxial Inventory, Million Behavioral Health Inventory, SCL-90, Spielberger State-Trait Anxiety Inventory, Spielberger Anger Expression Inventory, etc.), and cognitive factors such as pain beliefs and coping styles (e.g., Coping Strategies Questionnaire, McGill Pain Questionnaire, Vanderbilt Pain Management Inventory, Ways of Coping Checklist, etc.). From the primary care perspective, we would advance that, for personality assessment, the MMPI-2 should be strongly considered for use with headache patients. Our reasoning is threefold. First, the MMPI-2 is the most widely employed psychological test, generating more research literature than any other instrument (Green, 2000). Second, most primary care providers know of and respect this test. Frequently those mental health professionals working in a teaching hospital will get consults requesting "MMPI" when new residents and fellows come onboard. (They are quickly educated about appropriate psychological testing consults, of course.) Third, and most important, from our clinical experience, it has seemed to answer our needs better than most other instruments. As the reader will see below, high levels of anxiety and depression are predictors of poor treatment response.

Descriptions of the Three Major Psychological Treatment Modalities

Biofeedback Training

Biofeedback, as it is generally employed at the present time, is a procedure in which a therapist monitors a patient's bodily responses (such as muscle tension, surface skin temperature, or heart rate) through the use of a machine and then relays this information back to the patient. The physiological feedback is usually supplied to the patient either through an auditory modality (e.g., a tone that goes higher or lower as muscle tension goes higher or lower) or a visual modality (e.g., a computer screen where surface skin temperature is graphed on a second-by-second basis during each minute or, more simply, the actual skin temperature in degrees Fahrenheit is presented). Through this physiological feedback, it is assumed that over time a patient will learn how to control his or her bodily responses. A more formal definition of biofeedback is

> a process in which a person learns to reliably influence psychophysiological responses of two kinds: either responses which are not ordinarily under voluntary control or ordinarily are

easily regulated but for which regulation has broken down due to trauma or disease (Blanchard & Epstein, 1978, p. 2).

There are two major modalities of biofeedback for chronic headache: EMG or electromyographic activity biofeedback, and thermal or surface skin temperature biofeedback. In EMG biofeedback, sensors are placed on the forehead, neck, or shoulders and tension headache patients are taught to decrease their muscle tension, as it has traditionally been assumed that tension headaches are caused by elevated levels of muscle tension in these muscle regions. It is also believed that learning to decrease EMG levels enhances an individual's ability to deal with stressful situations.

In temperature biofeedback, a small temperature-sensitive device is attached to the skin, usually the fingertips, and vascular headache patients (migraineurs and mixed migraine-tension headache sufferers) are taught to increase their hand temperature. It is believed that increasing one's hand temperature decreases overall stress levels, decreases sympathetic nervous system arousal, and increases peripheral vasodilation.

Relaxation Therapy

Relaxation therapy is a systematic approach to teaching people to gain awareness of their physiological responses and achieve both a cognitive and physiological sense of tranquility without the use of the machinery employed in biofeedback. There are various forms of relaxation techniques (see Lichstein, 1988, or Smith, 1990, for excellent reviews of the various types of relaxation therapy). The major relaxation therapies employed today, however, are progressive muscle relaxation therapy (Bernstein & Borkovec, 1973; Jacobson, 1929), meditation (Lichstein, 1988), autogenic training (Luthe, 1969-1973), and guided imagery (Bellack, 1973). By far, the most widely used relaxation procedures in headache are variants of Jacobsonian progressive muscle relaxation therapy and guided imagery, and when we discuss treatment outcome we will be mostly emphasizing those procedures. We have elsewhere described in detail a nine-session abbreviated Jacobsonian progressive muscle relaxation therapy regimen that we have used with our headache patients (Arena & Blanchard, 1996).

Because relaxation therapy and biofeedback are believed to directly influence both an individual's physiology and psyche, they are commonly referred to as psychophysiological interventions, and we shall refer to them this way throughout the remainder of this chapter.

Cognitive Behavioral Therapy

Cognitive behavioral therapies for headache are based on the assumption that an individual's thoughts, emotions, and behaviors influence his or her physiology. Therefore, cognitive behavioral treatments generally involve identifying thoughts, emotions, and behaviors that routinely precede or exacerbate headache activity, with the therapist subsequently teaching patients in a systematic manner to modify these thoughts, feelings, and behaviors. Cognitive behavioral therapies are generally combined with relaxation or biofeedback procedures. We have elsewhere described in detail our cognitive behavioral procedures (Arena, 2002; Blanchard & Andrasik, 1985).

Treatment of Headache in the Primary Care Setting

The actual treatment of headache in the primary care setting is much the same as treatment of headache outside the primary care setting. For a much more detailed how-to description of the EMG and thermal biofeedback procedures, interested readers are referred to Arena and Devineni (in press); Arena and Blanchard (1996, 2000, 2002); for details on relaxation therapy, please refer to Arena, Bruno, Hannah, and Meador (1995), or Arena and Blanchard (1996); for additional information concerning cognitive behavior therapy, please refer to Blanchard and Arena (1999) or Blanchard and Andrasik (1985).

It is essential for the nonphysician mental health provider working in the primary care setting or with primary care providers to familiarize him- or herself with the essentials of the physical and neurological examination of the patient with headache, as well as the neurodiagnostic imaging procedures used in the investigation of headache. Learning to at least understand what the terms and procedures used by medical providers are may save you embarrassment later on. Understanding the basic pharmacological treatment approaches to both migraine and vascular headache is also useful. We would urge the nonphysician mental health provider to get a copy of what most headache experts consider the "bible" of headache—*Diamond's and Dalessio's The Practicing Physicians Approach to Headache* (Diamond & Solomon, 1999a)—and read the relevant chapters carefully. We would also urge that nonphysician mental health providers purchase a medical dictionary and keep it on their desk or at their computer for quick reference.

The psychophysiological interventions—biofeedback and relaxation therapy—can be and are administered by many health care professionals, such as nurses, psychologists, physicians assistants, individuals with master's degrees in psychology, social workers, physical therapists, chiropractors, and physicians. Generally, however, physicians assistants and physicians in a busy primary care setting do not conduct such interventions, generally leaving it up to a nurse, physical therapist, or mental health professional. Cognitive behavior therapy should be conducted only by a trained mental health professional.

Nonpharmacological Outcome Results

Tension Headache

A beneficial manner of reporting outcome is the average proportion or fraction of a sample of headache patients who achieve a clinically significant reduction in headache activity, as documented by the daily headache diary. In chronic pain, a 50% or greater reduction in pain activity is generally considered a treatment success. With tension headache, the biofeedback approach used is EMG (muscle tension) feedback from the forehead, neck, or shoulders. For relaxation therapy alone, this value ranges from 40–55%, for EMG biofeedback alone, from 50–60%, and for cognitive therapy, from 60–80%; when EMG biofeedback and relaxation are combined, the average improves from about 50% to 75%; when relaxation and cognitive therapy are combined, success increases from 40–65%.

Migraine Headache

For patients with pure migraine headache, hand surface temperature (or thermal) is the biofeedback modality of choice, and it leads to clinically significant improvement in 40–60% of patients. Cognitive therapy by itself has about 50% success. A systematic course of relaxation training seems to help when added to thermal biofeedback (increasing success from about 40–55%), but cognitive therapy added to the thermal biofeedback and relaxation does not improve outcome on a group basis. Relaxation training alone gets success in from 30–50% of patients, and adding thermal biofeedback boosts that success (from about 30–55%).

Combined Migraine-Tension Headache

For patients with both kinds of the primary benign headache disorders (migraine and tension-type), the results with thermal biofeedback alone are a bit lower, averaging 30–45% success; relaxation training alone leads to 20–25% success. The best results come when thermal biofeedback and relaxation training are combined. With this combination treatment, results show 50–55% success rates (adding thermal biofeedback to relaxation raises success from 20–55%; adding relaxation therapy to thermal biofeedback increases success from 25–55%). We strongly recommend a combination of the two treatments for these headache sufferers.

Special Headache Populations

There are a number of special headache populations for which nonpharmacological interventions are beneficial, and two where the research has demonstrated that they are relatively ineffective. There is now a sizable body of research attesting to the efficacy of thermal biofeedback with pediatric migraine (see Arena & Blanchard, 2002). In addition, headaches in the elderly can also be effectively treated with biofeedback and relaxation techniques (Arena, Hightower, & Chang, 1988; Arena, Hannah, Bruno, & Meador, 1991; Kabela, Blanchard, Appelbaum, & Nicholson, 1989; Nicholson & Blanchard, 1993), as can those individuals who consume excessive levels of medication (Blanchard, Taylor & Dentinger, 1992; Michultka, Blanchard, Appelbaum, Jaccard & Dentinger, 1989). Hickling, Silverman, and Loss (1990), as well as Turk and his colleagues (Marcus, Scharff & Turk, 1995; Scharff, Marcus & Turk, 1996), have demonstrated that a combination treatment including relaxation therapy and biofeedback is efficacious for treating headaches during pregnancy. Because pregnant women are not able to use most pain medications, we feel that techniques such as the psychophysiological interventions and psychotherapy should be the first-line intervention for headache during pregnancy (Marcus, 2002).

Cluster headache, which is a very rare type of headache and tends to be found predominantly in males, is generally diagnosed by its very distinctive temporal pattern. In episodic cluster headache, the patient is headache-free for months to years and then enters a so-called cluster bout. During the cluster bout, the one-sided headaches appear fairly regularly, once or twice per day to every other day. The headaches are described as intense, excruciating pain that often makes it impossible for the patient to lie still; they last from 15–30 minutes to 2–3 hours. Many patients are so debilitated by this type of headache that it can take hours for them to return to a normal level of functioning. The cluster bout lasts several weeks to several months and then disappears. Some unfortunates have continuous cluster headache. Nonpharmacological interventions have been found to be relatively ineffective for cluster headache (Blanchard, Andrasik, Jurish & Teders, 1982) and, given these poor results and our clinical experience, we no longer see such patients in our practice.

Blanchard and colleagues (Barton & Blanchard, 2001; Blanchard, Appelbaum, Radnitz, Jaccard, & Dentinger, 1989) have identified a relatively refractory headache type they have labeled "chronic, daily high-intensity headache." Individuals with this type of headache describe their headache as present essentially all the time (at least 27 out of 28 days) at a moderately severe to severe level of pain and distress. Thus, although these patients usually meet the nominal criteria for tension-type headache, their severity ratings are like those of migraine patients and show little variability. In a retrospective case-control analysis, Blanchard et al. (1989) found that only 13% of patients with chronic, daily high-intensity headache responded favorably to combinations of biofeedback, relaxation, and cognitive therapy. Barton and Blanchard (2001), in a prospective study using a 20-session intensive combination treatment, had only 17% respond favorably.

Cost Effectiveness

Treatment of chronic headache through the techniques described in this chapter by experienced practitioners can result in considerable savings in health-care dollars over the patient's lifetime. The reason for this, of course, is that successful treatment of the headache problem results in a marked decrease in physician office visits, diagnostic procedures, and prescriptions for pain medication. One study that addressed this issue (Blanchard, Jaccard, Andrasik, Guarnieri, & Jurrish, 1985) found that, when one compared the total medical expenses a set of chronic headache patients had incurred in the 2 years prior to receiving nondrug therapy to the expenses for the 2 years following nondrug therapy, the average reduction was almost 90%. In 1985 dollars, the reduction was from an average of $200 per patient for all headache-related medical care in the 2 years prior to treatment to approximately $25 in the 2 years following treatment. To the best of our knowledge, formal cost-effectiveness studies have not been performed; however, these data from Blanchard and colleagues certainly indicate a marked reduction in expenses following psychosocial treatment of the headache.

Prevention of Chronic Benign Headache

Unfortunately, research on the prevention of chronic benign headache is in the fetal stage of development. To our knowledge, there have been no prospective or retrospective primary, secondary, or even tertiary prevention studies conducted. We do, however, have a research literature base from which the careful clinician or researcher can make logical inferences that may enable a mental health professional to assist in educating the primary care provider to identify individuals who may be at elevated risk for headache. The primary care provider may be able to either prevent headache from occurring or stop headaches in the early stages, averting them from becoming a significant health problem.

The strongest evidence suggesting that prevention may be possible comes from the epidemiological literature, which has repeatedly demonstrated that migraine, as opposed to tension or cluster headache, is a familial and possibly hereditary illness:

> If both parents have experienced migraine, there is a 70% chance that the children will also have migraine; if only one parent has had migraine, the children's chances are reduced to about 45%. If neither parent has had migraine but there is a history of migraine in other family members, it will occur in about 25% of the children (Diamond & Solomon, 1999b, pp. 20–21).

Given this strong familial pattern, we advance that it would be prudent to inform all migraine patients that their children ought to be carefully observed and brought in to the primary care clinic at first signs of a headache problem. Parents should also be instructed to be particularly sensitive in detecting certain psychological characteristics that may be harbingers of future headache problems, especially depression (see below), and to seek early intervention should they occur. In very young children (preschool), the presence of nausea may be a precursor of migraine headache. The mental health professional may wish in his or her communications with primary care providers to suggest that they routinely pursue a similar course of education and prevention with their migraine patients.

It has long been known that there is a relationship between headache and depression and that both are significant primary care problems. In a recent large-scale study (Wu, Parkerson, & Doraiswamy, 2002) it was found that primary care patients with high levels of anxiety or depression had nearly double the amount of headaches of those with lower levels (4.4 versus 2.3). In an important study, Breslau et al. (2000) examined the relationship between headache and major depression by eliminating the risk for the onset of major depression in persons with prior migraine and the risk for onset of migraine in persons with prior major depression. Unfortunately, this study was confounded by including tension headache subjects in a nonmigraine group, which they termed "severe headache" (59% of the severe headache group was composed of tension-headache subjects); however, their findings certainly hold for migraine headache. Results indicated a lifetime prevalence of major depression of 49% for those migraineurs with auras, and 37% for migraineurs without auras; the severe headache group (composed mostly of tension headache) had a 36% lifetime prevalence for major depression, and the nonheadache controls had a 16% lifetime prevalence. The authors found a bidirectional relationship between migraine and depression:

> Migraine signaled an increased risk for the first onset of major depression, and major depression signaled an increased risk for the first time occurrence of migraine. ... In contrast, severe headache signaled an increased risk for major depression, but there was no evidence of a significant influence in the reverse direction, from major depression to severe headache (Breslau et al., 2000, p. 311).

Given this relationship between headaches and depression, there are a number of strategies the mental health professional can take to assist the primary care provider in preventing headaches and in preventing depression in headache patients (see chapter 17 by Callaghan, Ortega, and Berlin, this volume) for prevention of depression in primary care. We have focused in this chapter on strategies especially relevant to headaches and depression.

All patients who have headaches should be carefully assessed for depression and treated accordingly. Often, headache patients—especially migraineurs and chronic, daily high-intensity headache sufferers—stay around the house mostly and engage in few pleasurable events in their lives. As a result, they become significantly depressed, which increases their pain levels and starts a vicious pain-depression cycle. If no or very low levels of depression are present, we have found that the primary care provider cautioning pain patients not to isolate themselves, to maintain normal interactions with family and friends, and continue engaging in pleasurable events is generally much more effective in preventing depression than a mental health professional stating the same concerns.

If moderate to severe depression is found, cognitive behavioral therapy and/or pharmacological intervention is warranted. Given the fact that high levels of depression have been shown to lead to poorer psychophysiological treatment outcome (Andrasik et al., 1982; Arena & Blanchard, 2000; Blanchard, Andrasik & Arena, 1984; Blanchard, Andrasik, Neff et al., 1982), we would suggest that, if possible, the depression should be treated prior to the onset of such treatments. Finally, although exercise can bring on some types of headache, and there is even a rare form of headache termed *benign exertional headache* (Kunkel, 1999), anecdotally we have found that exercise is often extremely helpful in treating depression in headache patients, as it has in the general depressed population (Blumenthal, Babyak, Moore, Craighead, & Herman, 1999). After obtaining medical approval, we routinely suggest that our headache patients engage in a regular exercise regimen. Often this is as simple as walking briskly (3–4 miles per hour) for 30 minutes three to four times a week.

Given the fact that both depression and migraine are familial illnesses, the mental health professional may wish to communicate to their migraine patients that their children should be carefully observed and brought in to the clinic if they evidence early signs of depression. Other emotions have been implicated in headache, such as anxiety and obsession (Arena, Blanchard, Andrasik, & Applebaum, 1986; Arena, Andrasik, & Blanchard, 1985; Arena, Blanchard, & Andrasik, 1984; Blanchard et al., 1984) and anger (Arena, Bruno, Rozantine, & Meador, 1997; Ham, Andrasik, Packard, & Bundrick, 1994), although the relationship is not as clearly demonstrated as that of depression, and clinicians may wish to communicate this information to their headache patients, as well as to primary care providers.

Dietary Factors in Prevention

It is reasonably well recognized (for a detailed account see Diamond and Dalessio, 1999) that in some individuals with migraine headache, the headaches are triggered by certain foods. Some of the common food triggers are chocolate and tyramine-containing substances, such as red wine, aged cheese, and alcohol. It thus becomes possible to prevent these food-triggered migraine headaches by eliminating those foods from the patient's diet. As a first step, the primary care physician might inquire if the patient has ever noticed any association between eating certain kinds of food or drinking certain kinds of beverages and developing a migraine headache in the next day or two. A list of potential food triggers can be found in Diamond and Dalessio (1999). This list could also be given to the patient. The patient will have to perform the experiments on him- or herself to see whether he or she has a food sensitivity that triggers migraine headache. However, in our experience, just mentioning this idea causes an awakening of potential associations in certain patients. More details on an empirical approach to the use of elimination diets and food testing can be found in articles by Radniz, Blanchard, and Bylina (1990) and Radnitz and Blanchard (1991). In the first paper, individuals who proved refractory to intensive psychosocial treatments were led through elimination diets and food challenges to identify which foods caused their headaches. Elimination of those foods from the diet then had a profoundly positive effect on their headache intensity, frequency, and duration.

There is data to suggest that migraines may be highly correlated to a high-fat diet. Bic, Blix, Hopp, Leslie, and Schell (1999) had 54 migraine subjects monitor their food intake for 28 days and then restricted their fat intake to no more than 20 grams a day. "Subjects significantly decreased their ingestion of dietary fat in grams between baseline (mean 65.9 g/day, $p < 0.0001$) and the postintervention period (mean 27.8 g/day). The decreased dietary fat intervention was associated with statistically significant decreases in headache frequency, intensity, duration, and medication intake (all $p < 0.0001$). There was a significant positive correlation between baseline dietary fat intake and headache frequency ($r = .44$, $p = 0.02$)" (p. 623). Thus, a low-fat diet can reduce headache frequency, intensity, and duration, and medication intake.

Changing an individual's eating habits and asking him or her to eliminate certain foods can be a very difficult task for the patient to carry forward. Consultation with a registered dietician may be needed to help the patient in this area.

Summary

In this chapter we have reviewed the basics of nonpharmacological treatments for migraine and tension-type headache, placing special emphasis on the frontline mental health professional in a primary care setting. We hope we have demonstrated that the application of psychological constructs to chronic pain disorders is simple and straightforward, that effective nonpharmacological treatments are now well established for headache and do not require a great deal of specialized training, and that the mental health professional can easily apply such skills to traditional medical domains such as pain. Collaborative efforts between the mental health professional and primary care provider will likely lead to more positive outcomes in headache treatment.

Acknowledgment

This chapter was supported by a Department of Veterans Affairs Merit Review awarded to John G. Arena, and by National Institute of Mental Health Grant No. MH-41341 awarded to Edward B. Blanchard.

Appendix A Headache Diary

Date Diary Started: _____/_____/_____

Last 4 digits of social security: _____ **Phone #** _____

Please record:
       (1) **Headache Pain** (0–10 scale; see Pain Rating Scale for details)
       (2) **Stress Level** (0–10 scale: 0 = no stress 10 = most stress I have ever had)
       (3) **Pain Medication** (A–J; see Pain Medication List)

Time of Day	Day of the week	SU	M	TU	W	TH	F	S
B R E A K F A S T	Headache Pain Level (0–10)							
	Stress Level (0–10)							
	Medication Code (A–J)							
L U N C H	Headache Pain Level (0–10)							
	Stress Level (0–10)							
	Medication Code (A–J)							
D I N N E R	Headache Pain Level (0–10)							
	Stress Level (0–10)							
	Medication Code (A–J)							
B E D T I M E	Headache Pain Level (0–10)							
	Stress Level (0–10)							
	Medication Code (A–J)							
Best estimate of total # of hours of pain								

APPENDIX A (continued)

Pain Rating Scale:

0 = No Pain
2 = Mild Pain: aware of it only when paying attention to it
4 = Mild Pain: can be ignored at times
6 = Moderate Pain: pain is noticeably present
8 = Severe Pain: difficult to concentrate, but can do undemanding tasks
10 = Intense Pain: excruciating, intolerable, or incapacitating pain

---

Pain Medication List

Please record pain medication information and transfer the letter A–J to the Headache Diary.

Examples:			
A	Tylenol	2 tablets	500 mg acetaminophen
B	Percocet	1 tablet	325 mg acetaminophen, 5 mg oxycodone
C	Imitrex	1 injection	6 mg sumatriptan succinate

Medicine Code	Brand Name Of Medication	Quantity	Dose (mg) and Type of drug in each tablet (or injection)
A			
B			
C			
D			
E			
F			
G			
H			
I			
J			

References

Ad Hoc Committee on the Classification of Headache. (1962). Classification of headache. *Journal of the American Medical Association, 179,* 127–128.

Andersson, H. I., Ejlertsson, G., Leden, I., & Schersten, B. (1999). Musculoskeletal chronic pain in general practice: Studies of health care utilization in comparison with pain prevalence. *Scandinavian Journal of Primary Health Care, 17,* 87–92.

Andrasik, F., Blanchard, E. B., Arena, J. G., Teders, S. J., Teevan, R. C., & O'Keefe, D. M. (1982). Psychological functioning in headache sufferers. *Psychosomatic Medicine, 44,* 171–182.

Arena. J. G. (2002). Chronic pain: Psychological approaches for the front-line clinician. *In-Session/Journal of Clinical Psychology.*

Arena, J. G., Andrasik, F., & Blanchard, E. B. (1985). The role of personality in the etiology of chronic headache. *Headache, 25*, 296–301.

Arena, J. G., & Blanchard, E. B. (1996). Biofeedback and relaxation therapy for chronic pain disorders. In R. J. Gatchel & D.C. Turk (Eds.), *Chronic pain: Psychological perspectives on treatment* (pp. 179–230). New York: Guilford.

Arena, J. G., & Blanchard, E. B. (2000). Biofeedback therapy for chronic pain disorders. In J. D. Loeser, D. Turk, R. C. Chapman, & S. Butler (Eds.), *Bonica's management of pain* (3rd ed., pp. 1755–1763). Baltimore: Williams & Wilkins.

Arena, J. G., & Blanchard, E. B. (2002). Biofeedback for chronic pain disorders: A primer. In R. J. Gatchel & D. C. Turk (Eds.), *Chronic pain: Psychological perspectives on treatment* (2nd ed., pp. 159–186). New York: Guilford.

Arena, J. G., Blanchard, E. B., & Andrasik, F. (1984). The role of affect in the etiology of chronic headache. *Journal of Psychosomatic Research, 28*, 79–86.

Arena, J. G., Blanchard, E. B., Andrasik, F., & Applebaum, K.A. (1986). Obsessions and compulsions in three kinds of headache sufferers: Analysis of the Maudsley Questionnaire. *Behaviour Research and Therapy, 24*, 127–132.

Arena, J. G., Bruno, G. M., Hannah, S. L., & Meador, K. J. (1995). A comparison of frontal electromyographic biofeedback training, trapezius electromyographic biofeedback training, and progressive muscle relaxation therapy in the treatment of tension headache. *Headache, 35*, 411–419.

Arena, J. G., Bruno, G. M., Rozantine, G. S., & Meador, K. J. (1997). A comparison of tension headache sufferers and non-pain controls on the State-Trait Anger Expression Inventory: An exploratory study with implications for applied psychophysiologists. *Applied Psychophysiology and Biofeedback, 22*, 209–214.

Arena, J. G., & Devineni, T. (in press). Module 1: Introduction to biofeedback. To appear in A. Crider & D. Montgomery (Eds.), *Association for Applied Psychophysiology and Biofeedback home study biofeedback course*. Wheat Ridge, CO: Association for Applied Psychophysiology and Biofeedback.

Arena, J. G., Hannah, S. L., Bruno, G. M., & Meador, K. J. (1991). Electromyographic biofeedback training for tension headache in the elderly: A prospective study. *Biofeedback and Self-Regulation, 16*, 379–390.

Arena, J. G., Hightower, N. E., & Chang, G. C. (1988). Relaxation therapy for tension headache in the elderly: A prospective study. *Psychology and Aging, 3*, 96–98.

Arena, J. G., & Schwartz, M. S. (2003). Psychophysiological assessment and biofeedback baselines for the front-line clinician: A primer. In M. S. Schwartz (Ed.), *Biofeedback: A practitioner's guide* (3rd ed.). (pp. 128–148) New York: Guilford.

Barton, K. A., & Blanchard, E. B. (2001). The failure of intensive self-regulatory treatment with chronic daily headache: A prospective study. *Applied Psychophysiology and Biofeedback, 26*, 311–318.

Bellack, A. (1973). Reciprocal inhibition of a laboratory conditioned fear. *Behaviour Research and Therapy, 11*, 11–18.

Bernstein, D. A., & Borkovec, T. D. (1973). *Progressive relaxation training*. Champaign, IL: Research Press.

Blanchard, E. B., & Andrasik, F. (1985). *Management of chronic headache: A psychological approach*. New York: Pergamon.

Blanchard, E. B., Andrasik, F., & Arena, J. G. (1984). Personality and chronic headache. In B. A. Maher & W. B. Maher (Eds.), *Progress in experimental personality research* (vol. 13, pp. 303–364). New York: Academic Press.

Blanchard, E. B., Andrasik, F., Jurish, S. E., & Teders, S. J. (1982). The treatment of cluster headache with relaxation and thermal biofeedback. *Biofeedback and Self-Regulation, 7*, 185–191.

Blanchard, E. B., Andrasik, F., Neff, D. F., Arena, J. G., Ahles, T. A., Jurish, S. E. et al. (1982). Biofeedback and relaxation training with three kinds of headache: Treatment effects and their prediction. *Journal of Consulting and Clinical Psychology, 50*, 562–575.

Blanchard, E. B., Appelbaum, K. A., Radnitz, C. L., Jaccard, J., & Dentinger, M. P. (1989). The refractory headache patient: I Chronic, daily, high intensity headache. *Behaviour Research and Therapy, 27*, 403–410.

Blanchard, E. B., & Arena, J. G. (1999). Biofeedback, relaxation training and other psychological treatments for chronic benign headache. In M. L. Diamond & G. D. Solomon (Eds.), *Diamond's and Dalessio's The practicing physician's approach to headache* (6th ed., pp. 209–224). New York: Saunders.

Blanchard, E. B., & Epstein, L. H. (1978). *A biofeedback primer*. Reading, MA: Addison-Wesley.

Blanchard, E. B., Jaccard, J., Andrasik, F., Guarnieri, P., & Jurish, S. E. (1985). Reduction in headache patients' medical expenses associated with biofeedback and relaxation treatments. *Biofeedback and Self-Regulation, 10*, 63–68.

Blanchard, E. B., Taylor, A. E., & Dentinger, M. P. (1992). Preliminary results from the self-regulatory treatment of high medication consumption headache. *Biofeedback and Self-Regulation, 17*, 179–202.

Block, A. R. (1996). *Presurgical psychological screening in chronic pain syndromes: A guide for the behavioral practitioner*. Mahwah, NJ: Erlbaum.

Blumenthal, J., Babyak, M. A., Moore, K. A., Craighead, W. E., & Herman, S. (1999). Effects of exercise training on older patients with major depression. *Archives of Internal Medicine, 159*, 2349–2356.

Breslau, N., Schultz, L. R., Stewart, W. F., Lipton, R. B., Lucia, V. C., & Welch, K. M. A. (2000). Headache and major depression: Is the association specific to migraine? *Neurology, 54*, 308–313.

Cao, M., Zhang, S., Wang, K., Wang, Y., & Wang, W. (2002). Personality traits in migraine and tension-type headaches: A five-factor model study. *Psychopathology, 35*(4): 254–258.

Costa, P. T., & Vandenbos, G. R. (Eds.). (1990). *Psychological aspects of serious illness: Chronic conditions, fatal diseases, and clinical care*. Washington, DC: American Psychological Association.

Craig, K. D., & Weiss, S. M. (Eds.). (1990). *Health enhancement, disease prevention and early intervention: Biobehavioral strategies*. New York: Springer.

Diamond, M. L., & Solomon, G. D. (Eds.). (1999a). *Diamond's and Dalessio's The practicing physician's approach to headache* (6th ed.). New York: Saunders.

Diamond, M. L., & Solomon, G. D. (1999b).Taking a headache history. In M. L. Diamond & G. D. Solomon (Eds.), *Diamond's and Dalessio's The practicing physician's approach to headache* (6th ed., pp. 16–25). New York: Saunders.

Flor, H., Miltner, W., & Birbaumer, N. (1992). Psychophysiological recording methods. In D. C. Turk & R. Melzack (Eds.), *Handbook of pain assessment* (pp. 169–192). New York: Guilford.

Gatchel, R. J., & Blanchard, E. B. (Eds.). (1993). *Psychophysiological disorders: Research and clinical applications.* Washington, DC: American Psychological Association.

Green, R. (2000). *The MMPI-2: An interpretive manual* (2nd ed.). Boston: Allyn & Bacon.

Ham, L. P., Andrasik, F., Packard, R. C., & Bundrick, C. M. (1994). Psychopathology in individuals with post-traumatic headaches and other pain types. *Cephalgia, 14,* 118–126.

Headache Classification Committee of the International Headache Society. (1988). Classification and diagnostic criteria for headache disorders: Cranial neuralgias and facial pain. *Cephalgia, 8*(suppl. 7), 29–34.

Hickling, E. J., Silverman, D. J., & Loos, W. (1990). A non-pharmacological treatment of vascular headache during pregnancy. *Headache, 30,* 407–410.

Holroyd, K. A. (1993). Behavioral treatment strategies. In J. Olesen & J. Schoenen (Eds.), *Tension-type headache: Classification, mechanisms and treatment* (pp. 245–254). New York: Raven.

Holroyd, K., Stensland, M., Lipchik, G., Hill, K., O'Donnell, F., & Cordingley, G. (2000). Psychosocial correlates and impact of chronic tension-type headaches. *Headache, 40*(1): 3–16.

Jacobson, E. (1929). *Progressive relaxation.* Chicago: University of Chicago Press.

Kabela, E., Blanchard, E. B., Appelbaum, K. A., & Nicholson, N. (1989). Self-regulatory treatment of headache in the elderly. *Biofeedback and Self-Regulation, 14,* 219–228.

Khan, A., Khan, A., Harezlak, J., Tu, W., & Kroenke, K. (2003). Somatic symptoms in primary care: Etiology and outcome. *Psychosomatics: Journal of Consultation Liaison Psychiatry, 44*(6): 471–478.

Kunkel, R. S. (1999). Complicated and rare forms of migraine. In M. L. Diamond & G. D. Solomon (Eds.), *Diamond's and Dalessio's The practicing physician's approach to headache* (6th ed., pp. 95–105). New York: Saunders.

Lichstein, K. L. (1988). *Clinical relaxation strategies.* New York: Wiley.

London, L., Shulman B., & Diamond S. (2001). The role of psychometric testing and psychological treatment in tension-type headache. *Current Pain and Headache Reports, 5*(5): 467–71.

Luthe, W. (Ed.) (1969–1973). *Autogenic therapy* (6 vols.) New York: Grune & Stratton.

Mannix, L. K. (2001). Epidemiology and impact of primary headache disorders. *Medical Clinics of North America, 85,* 887–895.

Marcus D. (2002). Managing chronic pain in the primary care setting. *American Family Physician, 66*(1): 36, 38, 41.

Marcus, D. A., Scharff, L., & Turk, D. C. (1995). Nonpharmacological management of headaches during pregnancy. *Psychosomatic Medicine, 57,* 527–535.

Michultka, D. M., Blanchard, E. B., Appelbaum, K. A., Jaccard, J., & Dentinger, M. P. (1989). The refractory headache patient: II. High medication consumption (analgesic rebound) headache. *Behaviour Research and Therapy, 27,* 411–420.

Nicholson, N. L., & Blanchard, E. B. (1993). A controlled evaluation of behavioral treatment of chronic headache in the elderly. *Behavior Therapy, 25,* 395–408.

Radnitz, C. L., & Blanchard, E. B. (1991). Assessment and treatment of dietary factors in refractory vascular headache. *Headache Quarterly, 2,* 214–220.

Radnitz, C. L., Blanchard, E. B., & Bylina, J. (1990). A preliminary report of dietary therapy as a treatment for refractory migraine headache. *Headache Quarterly, 1,* 239–243.

Rasmussen, B. K. (1999) Epidemiology and socio-economic impact of headache. *Cephalalgia, 25*(suppl.), 20–23.

Rasmussen, B. K., Jensen, R., Schroll, M., & Olesen, J. (1991). Epidemiology of headache in a general population—A prevalence study. *Journal of Clinical Epidemiology, 44,* 1147–1157.

Scharff, L., Marcus, D. A., & Turk, D. C. (1996). Maintenance of effects in the nonmedical treatment of headaches during pregnancy. *Headache, 36,* 285–290.

Schwartz, B. S., Stewart, W. F., & Lipton, R. B. (1997). Lost workdays and decreased work effectiveness associated with headache in the workplace. *Journal of Occupational and Environmental Medicine, 39,* 320–327.

Shumaker, S. A., Schron, E. B., & Ockene, J. K. (Eds.). (1990). *The handbook of health behavior change.* New York: Springer.

Silberstein, S. D., & Lipton, R. B. (2000). Chronic daily headache. *Current Opinions in Neurology, 13,* 277–283.

Smith, J. C. (1990). *Cognitive-behavioral relaxation training: A new system of strategies for treatment and assessment.* New York: Springer.

Sobel, D. S. (1993). Mind matters, money matters: The cost-effectiveness of clinical behavioral medicine. *Mental Medicine Update, 2,* 1–8.

Stewart, W. F., Lipton, R. B., Celentano, D. D., & Reed, M. L. (1992). Prevalence of migraine headache in the United States. *Journal of the American Medical Association, 267,* 64–69.

Sturgis, E. T., & Arena, J. G. (1984). Psychophysiological assessment. In M. Hersen, R. Eisler, & P. M. Miller (Eds.), *Progress in behavior modification* (vol. 17, pp. 1–30). New York: Academic Press.

Turk, D. C., & Melzack, R. (1992). *Handbook of pain assessment.* New York: Guilford.

Wu, L., Parkerson, G., & Doraiswamy P. (2002). Health perception, pain, and disability as correlates of anxiety and depression symptoms in primary care patients. *The Journal of the American Board of Family Practice, 15*(3): 183–190.

Chapter 16
Addressing Chronic Pain in Primary Care Settings

RICHARD C. ROBINSON, MARGARET GARDEA, ANN MATT
MADDREY, AND ROBERT J. GATCHEL

Chronic pain is a devastating condition that impacts virtually all areas of a person's life. Despite the distinct symptoms of different chronic pain disorders (e.g., fibromyalgia, postherpetic neuralgia, musculoskeletal pain, etc.), all share the central symptom of pain, which often leads to emotional suffering. Our knowledge of these different disorders continues to grow; however, chronic low back pain (CLBP) remains the condition about which we know the most and provides us with a starting point to discuss chronic pain conditions in general. An estimated 70–80% of adults will suffer from a spinal disorder at some point during their lives, but the majority of these spinal disorders (90%) will resolve within 6 months of onset (Deyo, Cherkin, Conrad, & Volinn, 1991; Lanes et al. 1995). In addition, 15% of the U.S. population is totally and permanently disabled by chronic spinal disorders (Gatchel, Polatin, & Mayer, 1995). In a more recent study, Linton, Hellsing, and Hallden (1998) reported a 1-year prevalence of 66% for musculoskeletal pain in persons 35–45 years of age. More alarming, 25% of those individuals reported significant pain and disability.

The costs of chronic pain are staggering. An estimated 80% of physician visits are related to pain disorders (Gatchel & Epker, 1999). With regard to spinal pain patients, approximately $16 billion is spent annually on treatment (Holbrook, Grazier, Kelsey, & Stauffer, 1984), and with regard to all musculoskeletal pain patients, $27 billion is spent annually (Gatchel et al., 1995). When other costs associated with disability (e.g., social security, lost productivity, etc.), are included with the treatment costs, $20–60 billion is lost annually to musculoskeletal disorders (Mayer & Gatchel, 1988).

Psychosocial factors play an important role in the perception and reporting of pain. Engel in 1959 postulated that certain personality characteristics might predispose an individual to chronic pain. He believed that factors, such as a history of defeat in one's personal life, significant guilt, and unsatisfied aggressive impulses might place a person at greater risk. Melzack and Wall's (1965) Gate Control Theory of pain provided a conceptual framework for the role of higher cognitive processes in the perception of pain. These researchers proposed that a neurophsyiological "gate" was located in the dorsal horn of the spinal column and that both ascending and descending nerve fibers influenced the gate. At the dorsal horn, afferent peripheral signals could be modified by signals originating in the higher cortical regions, increasing or decreasing the final peripheral signals that reached the brain.

With the advent of the Gate Control Theory of pain, our conceptualization of pain moved from the biomedical model to the biopsychosocial model. Chronic pain has defied traditional biomedical explanations, because the amount of tissue damage frequently failed to coincide with the amount of reported pain. Although Engel first suggested the biopsychosocial model, Turk and Rudy (1987) elaborated upon it so that it could be applied to chronic pain. Their model considered the cognitive, affective, psychosocial, behavioral, and physiological components of pain so that the entire person could be understood. In addition, according to their model, the role that psychosocial factors play increases as suffering increases, which, in turn, increases pain behavior and causes additional suffering.

At this point it may be helpful to note the qualitative distinction between acute and chronic pain. According to Grzesiak (1991), acute pain serves as a biological signal. The clinician determines the somatic cause and is assisted with the appropriate interventions based on the location, pattern, and description of the pain. In contrast, according to the biopsychosocial model, chronic pain serves a different function altogether. Rather than assisting by pinpointing a causal somatic problem, chronic pain serves as a signal to the health-care professional that something is wrong somewhere in the patient's life. The origin of these problems may be biological, psychological, or social in nature.

Psychosocial Factors

Several excellent review articles and chapters have been written concerning psychosocial factors associated with chronic pain that place individuals at risk for developing chronic pain (Gatchel & Epker, 1999; Mayer & Gatchel, 1988). However, at this time, no one variable or set of variables can accurately predict who will go on to develop a chronic pain condition. Several of the most important and well-researched psychosocial variables will be briefly touched upon in this chapter.

Psychopathology

Although we have come to understand that a host of psychosocial variables place a patient at risk for developing chronic pain, the presence of psychopathology, and specifically depression, has received thorough investigation. Numerous studies have found rates of major depression in chronic pain patients that exceed those found in the normal population. In CLBP patients, current rates of 45% and lifetime rates of 65% have been found. In upper-extremity patients, even higher rates have been reported (i.e., 80% for current and lifetime; Kinney, Gatchel, Polatin, Fogarty, & Mayer, 1993; Polatin, Kinney, Gatchel, Lillo, & Mayer, 1993). These figures stand in stark contrast to the occurrence of depression in the normal population, which is 5% current and 17% lifetime (American Psychiatric Association, 1987).

Fishbain, Cutler, Rosomoff, and Rosomoff (1997) explored the relationship between pain and depression through a meta-analysis of 23 studies. They found that 21 studies reported an association between the intensity of pain and the degree of depression. Further, other studies reviewed found associations between pain duration and the development of depression, between pain frequency and depression, and between the number of pain sites and depression. The relationship between pain and depression exists, but the nature of the interaction has only begun to be understood.

The relationship between pain and depression is far from simple. Several studies have looked at interactions among pain, depression, and other demographic and work variables. Averill, Novy, Nelson, and Berry (1996) studied 254 chronic pain patients and found a significant negative relationship between work status and depression in chronic pain patients. Further, Magni, Moreschi,

Rigatti-Luchini, and Mersky (1994) also found that unemployment was associated with depression. Complicating matters further, these investigators reported a relationship among depression, age, and gender in chronic pain patients. Younger women appear more depressed than younger men, and older men appear more depressed than older women (Magni et al., 1994). Further, other investigators reported that working chronic pain patients who planned litigation had higher levels of depression than working patients who were not planning litigation (Tait, Chibnall, & Richardson, 1990).

The recognition and treatment of depression is an important goal in and of itself. However, addressing depression in chronic pain patients is a clear necessity for appropriate treatment of their pain. Weickgenant et al. (1993) demonstrated that CLBP patients who are depressed avoid activities and social support and engage in more self-blame than those patients who are not depressed. Dworkin, Handlin, Richlin, Brand, and Vanucci (1986) demonstrated that depressed chronic pain patients were less likely to benefit from treatment. Haley, Turner, and Romano (1985) found that antidepressant medication given to pain patients resulted in lowered self-reports of pain, and other researchers have found that patients who are depressed have lowered pain tolerances and a propensity to magnify symptoms (Averill et al., 1996). Obviously, patients who are depressed are going to be less likely to engage in a number of activities that would help them with their pain, such as actively engaging in physical therapy, resolving workers' compensation issues, and practicing relaxation management techniques.

Depression is not the only form of psychopathology that has been associated with chronic pain. Polatin et al. (1993) used the Structured Clinical Interview for the *Diagnostic and Statistical Manual of Mental Disorders-III-Revised* and reported that 77% of CLBP patients met lifetime diagnostic criteria for a psychiatric disorder. These researchers found the highest rates for depression, substance abuse, and anxiety disorders. Further, 51% of the patients they examined met diagnostic criteria for a personality disorder.

When discussing pain and depression, or pain and psychological distress, the question often arises, Which came first, the pain or the psychopathology? Unfortunately, there is no simple answer, but this question continues to receive a great deal of attention. Several studies have attempted to examine this question by looking at the difference between acute and chronic pain patients, as well as looking at patients before and after successful treatment. Sternbach, Wolf, Murphy, and Akeson (1973) examined the Minnesota Multiphasic Personality Inventory (MMPI) profiles of acute and chronic pain patients and reported that chronic pain individuals were more distressed as measured by the first three clinical scales of the MMPI (Scale 1 Hypochondriasis; Scale 2 Depression; and Scale 3 Hysteria; also known as the "neurotic triad"). Barnes, Gatchel, Mayer, and Barnett (1990) reported that MMPI profiles in chronic pain patients reporting distress returned to normal levels 6 months after successfully competing an intensive 3-week functional restoration treatment program.

Gatchel (1991) attempted to clarify this complex relationship between pain, psychopathology, and personality by theorizing about the progression from of acute to chronic pain. He refers to the psychological changes that occur as a person progresses from acute to chronic pain as a "layering of behavioral/psychological problems over the original nociception of the pain experience itself" (p. 34). His model is based on a three-stage progression from acute to subacute to chronic disability following the experience of pain as a result of an identifiable injury. Stage 1 encompasses the resulting emotional reactions (e.g., fear, anxiety, and worry) that arise as a consequence of perceived pain. Stage 2 begins when the pain persists past a reasonable, acute time period. It is at this stage that the development or exacerbation of psychological and behavioral problems occurs. Gatchel (1991) notes that the form these difficulties take depends primarily on the premorbid personality and psychological characteristics of the individual (i.e., a diathesis), as well as current socioeconomic and environmental stressors. For instance, an individual with a tendency to become depressed may develop a depressive disorder in response to the economic and social stress of being unable to work as a result of pain (Gatchel & Turk, 1996). Weisberg, Vittengle, Clark, Gatchel, and Garen (2000) have also recently amplified such a "diathesis-stress" model.

This complex interaction of physical and psychosocioeconomic factors leads to Stage 3 of the model. As the patient's life begins to totally and completely revolve around the pain as a result of the chronic nature of the problem, the patient begins to accept the sick role. By doing so, the patient is excused from normal responsibilities and social obligations, which may serve to reinforce the maintenance of the sick role (Gatchel, 1991).

Further adding to the "layers" of behavioral and psychosocial difficulties is the addition of physical deconditioning, which generally accompanies patients during their progression toward chronic disability. The physical deconditioning syndrome generally leads to the progressive lack of use of the body, as when an individual is physically and emotionally distressed. Research has shown that this physical deconditioning can produce a circular effect, leading to increased mental deconditioning. The combined interaction of the symptoms as they reinforce one another negatively impacts the emotional well-being and self-esteem of an individual. Conversely, these same negative emotional reactions can reinforce the physical deconditioning through decreased motivation to participate in work and recreational activities. Further complicating the process, when patients engage in an activity that produces acute pain, they are likely to associate the pain with the initial hurt. This causes patients to fear and avoid pain and possible pain-producing situations (Gatchel & Turk, 1996). Unfortunately, pain often accompanies physical reconditioning and the additional steps needed in order to resume normal responsibilities and social obligations. Therefore, patients must be taught that hurt and harm are not the same (Fordyce, 1988).

Coping

An increasing area of interest concerns how a person copes with the stress often associated with chronic pain. The Multidimensional Pain Inventory (MPI), formerly the West-Haven Yale Multidimensional Pain Inventory, developed by Kerns, Turk, and Rudy (1985) is a widely used measure in the pain area that examines a person's perception of his or her pain and coping ability. Turk and Rudy (1988) found three types of coping styles on the MPI in chronic pain patients: dysfunctional (43%), interpersonally distressed (28%), and adaptive copers (29.5%). The dysfunctional group members reported extreme pain and interference from their pain in their lives. Patients in the interpersonally distressed group indicated that they perceived a lack of support and understanding from important individuals in their lives. Adapative copers reported high levels of activity and lower levels of pain, interference in their lives from pain, and affective distress.

Epker, Gatchel, and Ellis (1999) used the MPI in temporomandibular patients and found that either dysfunctional or interpersonally distressed profiles on the MPI had more biopsychosocial difficulties than patients with adaptive coper profiles. In addition, Brown and Nicassio (1987) found an association between decreased pain and coping strategies that were more active, rather than passive, in nature, such as staying busy and using distraction techniques.

A specific maladaptive coping strategy or response to stress that has received increasing empirical scrutiny is *catastrophizing*. Catastrophizing is said to occur when a person has exaggerated, negative cognitions about events and stimuli. For instance, a patient who has pain that has lasted 9 months may catastrophize by thinking to him- or herself, "This is the worse thing that has ever happened and I will never get better." Butler, Damarin, Beaulieu, Schwebel, and Thorn (1989) found that catastrophizing was associated with higher levels of pain in patients who had undergone surgery. Jacobsen and Butler (1996) studied 59 females who underwent surgery for breast cancer and found a positive relationship between catastrophizing and pain as well as between catastrophizing and analgesic use. Sullivan, Stanish, Waite, Sullivan, and Tripp (1998) found that catastrophizing was positively related to disability, pain, and unemployment. Interestingly, they found that catastrophizing was related to disability independent of the level of anxiety or depression.

Occupational Functioning

Job satisfaction is an especially important variable associated with pain and disability. Both retrospective (Bigos et al., 1986) and prospective (Bigos et al., 1991; Cats-Baril & Frymoyer, 1991; Croft et al., 1995) studies have found an association between pain and job satisfaction. That is, low job satisfaction appears related to increased pain and disability. Williams and colleagues (1998) found that job satisfaction may help prevent patients from progressing from acute to chronic pain, and that job dissatisfaction may increase the chances of long-term disability. As with many risk factors, there are important interactions with other demographic variables. For instance, Vingard and colleagues (2000) found that job dissatisfaction increased the risk of low back pain in males, but not in females.

Often related to the area of work and job satisfaction is the notorious topic of secondary gain. Secondary gain includes factors such as potential monetary gain, avoidance of work duties, or avoidance of social and familial responsibilities. Primary care physicians should be aware that secondary gain issues might inadvertently reinforce the patient's pain. Research suggests secondary gain may serve as a powerful disincentive and barrier to recovery.

Perhaps one of the most powerful secondary gain factors is monetary compensation. Many studies have found that patients with compensation cases have poorer outcomes than patients without any such issues. The presence of active compensation has shown a significant impact on the continuance of disability (Beals, 1984). Rohling, Binder, and Langhinrichsen-Rohling (1995) found a relationship between compensation and increased pain and decreased treatment efficacy. Another study found that the most robust predictor of poor postoperative outcome was the presence of pending litigation associated with a workers' compensation disability claim (Vaccaro, Ring, Scuderi, Cohen, & Garfin, 1997). A study of a large U.S. worker sample was undertaken by Gatchel et al. (1995). The researchers followed 421 acute low back pain patients for 1 year. Logistic regression analyses discriminated between employed subjects versus those not working due to their original back injury. Workers' compensation and personal injury insurance status were one of the four psychosocial variables found to play a role in the development of a chronic pain condition and to contribute to unemployment status. Rainville, Sobel, Hartigan, and Wright (1997) found subjects in the compensation group reported a greater amount of pain, depression, and disability than the individuals without compensation involvement. Overall, these findings suggest that given the same physical symptoms, patients with compensation issues may not interpret their improved physical capacity as impacting their daily functioning compared with to noncompensation patients. It is possible that the reinforcing nature of the secondary gains received from their compensation involvement may result in the reluctance of patients to report significant improvement.

On the other hand, further research has found that compensation in itself may not be a barrier to outcome. Rainville et al. (1997) recognized that in their study, compensation patients had more severe chronic back pain syndromes and, therefore, depict a more complex challenge for the treating physician. Sanderson, Todd, Holt, and Getty (1995) suggest that employment status may influence disability more than compensation. In general, the investigators found that the presence of compensation and unemployment resulted in higher disability scores. However, when patients receiving compensation were analyzed according to employment status, notable differences were found. Patients who were still working had significantly less disability when compared with those who remained unemployed. The authors conclude that while both unemployment and compensation status impact disability, the most important factor appears to be employment status.

Finally, Ambrosius, Kremer, Herkner, DeKraker, and Bartz (1995) evaluated 60 back pain patients enrolled in a functional restoration program. Subjects were divided into two groups according to their compensation-seeking status. A high return-to-work frequency was achieved for both groups. Overall, 91% of the compensation-seeking subjects and 100% of the noncompensation group returned to employment.

Although the research on secondary gains is mixed, the variables underlying this relationship are only beginning to be understood. The majority of the evidence demonstrates a powerful impact on outcome. Preliminary research has established a relationship between compensation and decreased treatment efficacy and productivity, in addition to increased reported pain levels, depression, and disability. Primary care physicians working with chronic pain patients must identify secondary gain issues that may impede treatment. Once recognized, the physician should work together with the psychologist to address the matter with the patient.

Assessment

To properly assess a chronic pain patient, one must understand the biopsychosocial aspects of the patient. Several instruments have been developed that serve to answer these questions. A list of these instruments is provided here so the primary care physician can become familiar with the most common ones in use. However, administration and interpretation of these instruments should be limited to those individuals who have been trained to integrate data from various sources.

Minnesota Multiphasic Personality Inventory (MMPI-2). The MMPI-2 is a 567-item, self-report questionnaire that provides information on psychiatric symptoms and personality organization. Internal consistency typically ranges from .60 to .90, depending on the specific scale and population being tested (Graham, 1993). This instrument provides a wealth of information, but often takes pain patients several hours to complete and must be interpreted by an individual who has received specialized training.

Structured Clinical Interview for DSM-IV–Nonpatient Version (SCID-NP). The SCID-NP is a highly structured interview that yields diagnoses corresponding to the criteria within the *DSM-IV.* It has been shown to have moderately high reliability for both current and lifetime Axis I diagnoses, with kappa coefficients of .61 for current diagnoses and .69 for lifetime diagnoses (Spitzer & Williams, 1986). The SCID represents the gold standard for psychiatric diagnosis, but requires training in administration and can be fairly time consuming.

Hamilton Rating Scale of Depression (HRSD). The HRSD is a clinician-administered rating scale that consists of 17 items, with total scores ranging from 0 to 50. In a previous study, the interrater reliability has been found to be adequate (Rush, Beck, Kovacs, & Hollon, 1977). This is a fairly easy instrument to learn to administer, and it takes only a few minutes to complete.

Beck Depression Inventory (BDI). The BDI is a self-report measure containing 21 items related to physical and emotional symptoms of depression and is currently one of the most widely used measures of depression in both medical and psychological research. It was developed by Beck, Ward, Mendelson, Mock, and Erbaugh (1961) in order to offer a reliable and valid measure of the presence and severity of depression. This is a frequently used self-report measure of depression that takes a patient only a few minutes to complete.

The Dallas Back Pain Questionnaire (DBPQ). This analogue scale is a 15-item, self-report questionnaire containing items related to pain and disability. Subjects indicate their response to each question by picking a point on a 10-cm line representing a range of possible answers from 0 to 10. For instance, endpoints of the scale may signify: "No Problems" and

"Totally Cannot Work" for questions related to disability. Million, Haavik-Nilson, Jayson, and Baker (1981) developed the scale and validated it through correlation with clinicians' findings. The total score is the sum of all responses. Scores of 0 to 39 indicate "mildly disabling" pain, 40 to 84 indicate "moderately disabling pain," and 85 and above indicate "severely disabling pain." The Dallas Pain Questionnaire has particular utility when the self-report of pain exceeds what would be expected given physical findings. This finding might suggest the existence of a psychosocial component in the patient's disability (Capra, Mayer, & Gatchel, 1985).

The Multidimensional Pain Inventory (MPI). The MPI is a brief, self-report pain inventory theoretically based on the cognitive behavioral perspective of evaluating and managing pain. It was normed on chronic pain patients. Eight scales are provided to determine patient perception of pain, and three clusters can be determined according to patient coping style (adaptive, interpersonally distressed, and dysfunctional). Internal consistency reliability estimates range from .70 to .90 for the different scales. Stability estimates range from .62 to .91. Adequate validity was determined through correlation with a variety of measures related to the different MPI scales (Kerns et al., 1985). Again, this is a quick and easy test to administer.

One question frequently asked by practitioners is "What is the best assessment test to use with my pain patients?" There is no single answer to this question, because the question itself needs to be prefaced by various more specific questions, such as: For what purpose is the assessment being performed (e.g., comprehensive patient management/treatment planning; surgical prescreening determination; palliative care, etc.)? Is the assessment purely for clinical purposes or for treatment outcome documentation purposes? Is there a health-care specialist available to help with integrating the assessment test results? The first of these more specific questions is the most-often asked. In answering the question, What is the best battery of assessment tests to use for comprehensive patient management/treatment planning? Gatchel (2000) has recommended a stepwise approach where one chooses the most time- and cost-effective biopsychosocial assessment of patients. Of course, one must not make the assumption that there is a single instrument that can serve as the best assessment method. For most patients, several assessment methods will be needed. Rather than asking what method should be used, a better question is, What sequence of testing should I consider to develop the best understanding of potential biopsychosocial problems that might be encountered with the patient? With a stepwise approach, briefer instruments are administered initially and more thorough assessment instruments are used only with patients who appear to be experiencing more complex psychosocial problems as assessed by briefer measures or interview data. In addition, collecting psychosocial data requires staff who are appropriately trained to interpret and make appropriate referrals when needed, such as a psychologist or other mental health-care professional.

In addition to the above measures, approaching chronic pain patients from a biopsychosocial perspective will allow one to intuitively understand which questions to ask. For instance, in addition to questions related to physical symptoms, questions about their mood and the impact pain has had on their lives would provide excellent information. Many primary care physicians will often ask these questions when time permits. However, an often-overlooked area is patients' occupational functioning and their feelings about their jobs. Questions about their workers' compensation status as well as any ongoing litigation may also be of great benefit.

At this time, no widely used or accepted screening instruments exist to assess the potential for opioid abuse in chronic, nonmalignant pain patients. Fortunately, investigators such as Chabal, Erjavec, Jacobson, Mariano, and Chaney (1997) have attempted to remedy this situation by developing a "prescription abuse checklist" that consists of five criteria:

1. A focus on opiate issues during clinic visits impeding progress with other treatment issues and persisting beyond the third appointment.
2. A pattern of early refills or escalating drug use in the absence of any clinical change.
3. Multiple phone calls or visits about opiate prescriptions.
4. A pattern of prescription "problems" (lost, spilled, stolen, etc.).
5. Supplemental sources of opiates.

Further, Compton, Darakjian, and Miotto (1998) developed a 42-item questionnaire based on the criteria developed by the American Society of Addiction Medicine. These researchers found that nonaddicted patients did not use multiple prescription providers, use illegal sources for medication, or use others' medication. Three items correctly classified 92% of the cases: (a) a tendency to increase opioid dose and use, (b) having a preference for route of administration, and (c) considering oneself addicted.

Treatment

Traditionally, primary care treatment for chronic pain patients has focused on eliminating the physical pathology. The rational being that once the pain is taken care of, the other common complaints such as lack of sleep, nervousness, and work-related difficulties will no longer exist. However, as we have discussed earlier in this chapter, solely addressing the physical pathology is insufficient and will likely result in poor outcome. Consequently, many chronic pain patients go from doctor to doctor in an effort to find a "cure" for their pain (Turk & Gatchel, 1999). Moreover, both physician and patient often experience increased frustration over the patient's lack of improvement, given the repeated efforts.

Chronic pain is best conceptualized as an ongoing, long-term, dynamic condition with reciprocal interplay between the patient's biological, cognitive, affective, behavioral, and social factors (Dworkin, Von Korff, & LeResche, 1990). As mentioned earlier, chronic illness is a debilitating, demoralizing, and often overwhelming condition that drastically impacts all aspects of the patient's life. Effective treatment, therefore, must address all components—biological, psychological, and social aspects—of the illness.

Ideally, an interdisciplinary approach is the best paradigm to properly assess, conceptualize, and treat individuals suffering from ongoing pain conditions. The International Association for the Study of Pain (IASP) identifies an interdisciplinary clinic as a facility with a diverse group of health-care professionals comprising of physicians, psychologists, nurses, physical therapists, occupational therapists, case managers, and other specialists. In this setting, the health-care providers work as a team and offer various therapeutic assessments and interventions (Loeser, 1991). Table 16.1 presents a list of standard interdisciplinary-treatment team members. The primary care physician is capable of serving as the team leader and, therefore, is responsible for all related medical issues associated with the patient's pain. Given the extensive nature of this list, one will have to decide which health-care professionals are essential in attaining the treatment goals for each patient.

In assembling a group of health-care workers, one must consider several factors. First, it is extremely important that the primary care physician find team members who share the same rehabilitative philosophy. For instance, many times a physician will order physical therapy for a patient, intending him or her to receive a specialized active-oriented intervention such as functional restoration therapy. However, the physical therapist may practice a passive mode of treatment or provide a standard "shake-and-bake" intervention that is not necessarily suited to the patient's specific needs. Thus, the execution of the treatment plan is inconsistent, and the health-care professionals are striving for conflicting goals. As a result, the treatment outcome will likely be poor.

TABLE 16.1 Interdisciplinary Treatment Team Members

Physician/Medical director. Team leader; responsible for all medical matters related to complaints of pain including diagnoses and management of physiological, anatomical, and pathological processes.

Nurse. Plays a crucial role in obtaining patient histories, assessing patients' lifestyle, and identifying issues that may impact response to treatment, monitor medications.

Psychologist. Aids in treatment planning with psychosocial evaluations including personality, psychopathology, social support, level of motivation, and coping resources. In treatment, addresses and monitors these issues.

Physical Therapist. Performs a comprehensive musculoskeletal assessment of reflexes, sensation, neurological indices, range of motion, gait, and postural abnormalities. Once completed, tailors a program specifically for the patient's needs.

Occupational Therapist. Serves as a link between injured workers and their employer to help ensure needed job modifications. Makes pre- and posttreatment evaluations focusing on the patient's daily activities, including work and recreational activities and the patient's body mechanics and energy conservation. Oversees the incremental increase of functional activity to facilitate the utmost normal level of activity for the patient.

Medical Disability Case Manager. Typically a vocational rehabilitation professional or an occupational therapist serves in this capacity. Monitors the patients overall progress including adherence, performance, and posttreatment development. Also promotes vocational and social reactivation throughout treatment, and addresses occupational planning, sequencing, and socioeconomic issues.

Second, it is imperative for all team members to recognize the importance of properly addressing each treatment area. This includes tackling the psychological and social issues as well as the physical pathology. One common error is to neglect the importance of psychosocial variables, especially when there is a clear pathology such as a ruptured disk. On the other hand, physicians are quick to remember the psychological aspects of pain whenever functional disability exceeds what is to be expected given the physical pathology. Turk (1996) notes it is crucial to address all the facets of the biopsychosocial model. Specifically, he states that as an illness progresses, each model component may be weighted differently. For example, in the early stage of illness, biological aspects may dominate; however, as the syndrome progresses, the psychological and social factors may come to the forefront. Still, when a clear-cut physical pathology is present, it is tempting to treat the chronic pain patient with a single modality such as medications, surgery, or physical therapy. Nevertheless, it is crucial to address all the issues and not choose one single treatment over another, be it medication, psychological intervention, or physical therapy. "No single factor in isolation—pathophysiological, psychological or social—will adequately explain chronic pain status" (Gatchel & Turk, 1996, p. 7). Consequently, owing to the encompassing nature of ongoing illness, all chronic pain patients will benefit from a comprehensive multidisciplinary intervention, not just a few. In order to properly address these psychosocial issues, the primary care physician will want to work carefully with a health psychologist or rehabilitation counselor properly trained in psychological assessments, behavioral interventions, and stress management.

Third, one must work carefully with the patient to explain the importance of all aspects of multidisciplinary treatment. Because the treating physician often has increased power to influence patients, he or she is in a unique position to organize and highlight the importance of adhering to the complete program, not just certain aspects. For example, patients are often hesitant to see a psychologist. If the patient refuses, the primary care physician must be emphatic and must adequately explain to the patient that all components are integral to his or her well-being. Making the next doctor's appointment contingent on completing the behavioral medicine assessment may solve this compliance problem. (Additionally, assuring patients that you know their pain is real and not in their head, and that you don't think they are crazy may also help.) In doing this, the physician conveys the importance of each treatment component to the patient.

Finally, and perhaps most important, frequent communication among health-care providers is essential. The constant communication helps ensure consistent treatment interventions and philosophies as well as improved patient adherence. Moreover, any conflicting information reported by the patient, or attempts to "split" the staff, can be handled in a straightforward manner. Many chronic pain patients are skillful at splitting clinicians. A typical example of this is when the patient provides team members with inconsistent information ("Doc, physical therapy was really hard on me today; my pain is excruciating and the physical therapist thinks I need more medicine"). Pitfalls such as this can be avoided with an interactive team approach.

Gatchel and Turk (1999) have outlined the essential ingredients of interdisciplinary pain management. One of the most important components is a regularly scheduled staff meeting consisting of all team members. The information presented affords staff members essential data allowing each team member to work more effectively with the patient. Moreover, patient care conferences, with all treatment team members present, facilitate the most valid perception of the patient and help unite the team with regard to the direction and progress of treatment. The result of this free flow of information and team interaction is an alignment regarding treatment goals, and it helps ensure that a consistent message and clear expectations are presented to the patient, another crucial factor in properly treating pain patients.

Finally, the unified approach limits the opportunity of staff splitting. Table 16.2 summarizes the essential factors that can significantly promote success of the interdisciplinary pain management program.

Once essential team members have been selected, the team leader must set treatment goals. Determining successful treatment for chronic pain patients can be a difficult task. According to Katz (1998), the goal of pain management "often cannot be complete relief of all pain" (p. 2S). Keeping this in mind, ascertainable treatment goals should focus on a *functional rehabilitative model* versus an *investigative curative approach*. As such, the goals are usually specific, definable, operationalizable, and realistic. This includes identifying and managing any unresolved medical problems, reducing and improving symptoms, eliminating any unnecessary medications, and curtailing inappropriate use of the health-care system. Another important aim is increasing patient independence and restoring physical, social, and occupational functioning in the patient's life. In order to achieve these goals, the treatment team must form a strong alliance with patients and instill in them the need to self-manage their pain and take responsibility for their well-being (Bendix et al., 1996). Turk and Gatchel (1999) note that implicit in interdisciplinary treatment is a transfer of responsibility from the health-care provider to the patient.

TABLE 16.2 Essential Elements of Interdisciplinary Pain Management Programs

Schedule regular meetings to (1) ensure proper communication between team clinicians and (2) strengthen established mutual goals for each patient.
Communication value and respect for each treatment team member's skills and mutual reinforcement with regard to each member's role and efforts with the patient.
Systematic monitoring of the patient's progress and outcome is essential to optimize quality assurance.
All staff members must understand and accept the treatment philosophy and interventions of the treatment team.

Tertiary prevention has been described in the above paragraphs. However, primary prevention of chronic pain is an intense area of study at this time. Unfortunately, few prevention measures have undergone rigorous empirical evaluation and those that have do not currently appear promising (Linton, 1999). Most attempts at interventions have focused on instructing workers at risk in physically demanding jobs on safer ways to perform their duties, such as lifting, or making the job safer for the worker (Frank et al., 1996). Educational measures, such as instructing the patient how to properly lift, appear mediocre at best. Exercise appears to offer some benefit as an early intervention (Linton, Bradley, Jensen, Spangfort, & Sundell, 1989).

Summary and Conclusion

Our conceptualization of chronic pain has changed with the adoption of the biopsychosocial approach. It recognizes the various forces that impact a person's perception of his or her pain and disability. It guides us in both our approach to assessment as well as to treatment. When patients undergo care that focuses on these important aspects, their chances for success are greater than if only one aspect is examined.

It should also be noted that several important organizations in the United States have recently developed new standards for the evaluation of pain. The Joint Commission on Accreditation of Health Care Organizations requires that physicians now consider pain as a fifth vital sign (added to the other vital signs of pulse, blood pressure, core temperature, and respiration). It requires that pain severity be documented using a pain scale, in addition to the patient's own words to describe his or her pain (such as location, duration, etc.). This information, along with the present pain management regimen and effectiveness, the patient's pain goal, and the physical examination, should be documented on initial assessment. These new standards are now being scored for compliance in accredited health-care organizations (JCAHO, 1999). Moreover, the nonprofit American Pain Foundation has created a "Pain Care Bill of Rights" informing patients of this requirement. Such initiatives have created a new mandate for primary care physicians to successfully assess and manage all types of pain, malignant as well as nonmalignant.

Acknowledgment

The writing of this article was supported in part by grants 2 KO2 MH01107, RO1 DE10713 and RO1 MH 46452, awarded to the second author, from the National Institutes of Health.

References

Ambrosius, F. M., Kremer, A. M., Herkner, P. B., DeKraker, M., & Bartz, S. (1995). Outcome comparison of workers' compensation and noncompensation low back pain in a highly structured functional restoration program. *Journal of Orthopaedic and Sports Physical Therapy, 21*(1), 7–12.

American Psychiatric Association (Ed.). (1987). *Diagnostic and statistical manual of mental disorders* (3rd ed., revised). Washington, DC: Author.

Averill, P. M., Novy, D. M., Nelson, D. V., & Berry, L. A. (1996). Correlates of depression in chronic pain patients: A comprehensive evaluation. *Pain, 65*, 93–100.

Barnes, D., Gatchel, R. J., Mayer, T. G., & Barnett, J. (1990). Changes in MMPI profiles of chronic low back pain patients following successful treatment. *Journal of Spinal Disorders, 3*, 353–355.

Beals, R. (1984). Compensation and recovery from injury. *Western Journal of Medicine, 140*, 233–237.

Beck, A. T., Ward, C. H., Mendelson, M., Mock, J., & Erbaugh, J. (1961). An inventory for measuring depression. *Archives of General Psychiatry, 4*, 561–569.

Bendix, A. E., Bendix, T., Vaegter, K., Lund, C., Frolund, L., & Holm, L. (1996). Multidisciplinary intensive treatment for chronic low back pain: A randomized, prospective study. *Cleveland Clinic Journal of Medicine, 63*, 62–69.

Bigos, S. J., Battie, M. C., Spengler, D. M., Fisher, L. D., Fordyce, W. E., Hansson, T. H. et al. (1991). A prospective study of work perceptions and psychosocial factors affecting the report of back injury. *Spine, 16*(1), 1–6.

Bigos, S. J., Spengler, D. M., Martin, N. A., Zeh, J., Fisher, L., Nachemson, A. et al. (1986). Back injuries in industry: A retrospective study. *Spine, 11*, 241–256.

Brown, G. K., & Nicassio, P. M. (1987). Development of questionnaire for the assessment of active and passive coping strategies in chronic pain patients. *Pain, 31*, 53–64.

Butler, R. W., Damarin, F. L., Beaulieu, C., Schwebel, A. L., & Thorn, B. E. (1989). Assessing cognitive coping strategies for acute postsurgical pain. *Journal of Consulting and Clinical Psychology: Psychological Assessmnet, 1:* 41–45.

Capra, P., Mayer, T. G., & Gatchel, R. J. (1985). Adding psychological scales to your back pain assessment. *Journal of Musculoskeletal Medicine, 2,* 41–52.

Cats-Baril, W. L., & Frymoyer, J. W. (1991). Identifying patients at risk of becoming disabled because of low-back pain. The Vermont Rehabilitation Engineering Center predictive model. *Spine, 16,* 605–607.

Chabal, C., Erjavec, M. K., Jacobson, L., Mariano, A., & Chaney, E. (1997). Prescription opiate abuse in chronic pain patients: Clinical criteria, incidence, and predictors. *Clinical Journal of Pain, 13*(2), 150–155.

Compton, P., Darakjian, J., & Miotto, K. (1998). Screening for addiction in patients with chronic pain and "problematic" substance use: Evaluation of a pilot assessment tool. *Journal of Pain and Symptom Management, 16,* 355–363.

Croft, P. R., Papageorgiou, A. C., Ferry, S., Thomas, E., Jayson, M. I. V., & Silman, A. J. (1995). Psychological distress and low back pain. Evidence from a prospective study in the general population. *Spine, 20,* 2731–2737.

Deyo, R. A., Cherkin, D., Conrad, D., & Volinn, E. (1991). Cost, controversy, crisis: Low back pain and the health of the public. *Annual Review of Public Health, 12,* 141–156.

Dworkin, R. H., Handlin, D. S., Richlin, D. M., Brand, L., & Vanucci, C. (1986). Unraveling the effects of compensation, litigation, and employment on treatment response in chronic pain. *Pain, 23,* 46–59.

Dworkin, S. F., Von Korff, M. R., & LeResche, L. (1990). Multiple pains and psychiatric disturbance: An epidemiologic investigation. *Archives of General Psychiatry, 47,* 239–244.

Engel, G. L. (1959). "Psychogenic" pain and the pain-prone patient. *American Journal of Medicine, 26,* 899–918.

Epker, J. T., Gatchel, R. J., & Ellis, E. (1999). A model for predicting chronic TMD: Practical applications in clinical settings. *Journal of the American Dental Association, 130,* 1470–1475.

Fishbain, D. A., Cutler, R., Rosomoff, H. L., & Rosomoff, R. S. (1997). Chronic pain-associated depression: Antecedent or consequence of chronic pain? A review. *Clinical Journal of Pain, 13,* 116–137.

Fordyce, W. E. (1988). Pain and suffering: A reappraisal. *American Psychologist, 43,* 276–283.

Frank, J. W., Brooker, A. S., DeMaio, S. E., Kerr, M. S., Maetzel, A., Shannon, H. S. et al. (1996). Disability resulting from occupational low back pain. Part II: What do we know about secondary prevention? A review of the scientific evidence on prevention after disability begins. *Spine, 21*(24), 2918–2929.

Gatchel, R. J. (1991). Early development of physical and mental deconditioning in painful spinal disorders. In T. G. Mayer, V. Mooney, & R. J. Gatchel (Eds.), *Contemporary conservative care for painful spinal disorders* (pp. 278–289). Philadelphia: Lea & Febiger.

Gatchel, R. J. (2000). How practitioners should evaluate personality to help manage chronic pain patients. In R. J. Gatchel & J. N. Weisberg (Eds.), *Personality characteristics of patients with pain* (pp. 241–258). Washington, DC: American Psychological Association.

Gatchel, R. J., & Epker, J. T. (1999). Psychosocial predictors of chronic pain and response to treatment. In R. J. Gatchel & D. C. Turk (Eds.), *Psychosocial factors in pain: Critical perspectives* (pp. 412–434). New York: Guilford.

Gatchel, R. J., Polatin, P. B., & Mayer, T. G. (1995). The dominant role of psychosocial risk factors in the development of chronic low back pain disability. *Spine, 20*(24), 2702–2709.

Gatchel, R. J., & Turk, D. C. (Eds.). (1996). *Psychological approaches to pain management: A practitioner's handbook.* New York: Guilford.

Gatchel, R. J., & Turk, D. C. (1999). Interdisciplinary treatment of chronic pain patients. In R. J. Gatchel & D. C. Turk (Eds.), *Psychosocial factors in pain: Critical perspectives* (pp. 435–444). New York: Guilford.

Graham, J. R. (1993). *MMPI-2. Assessing personality and psychopathology* (2nd ed.). New York: Oxford University Press.

Grzesiak, R. C. (1991). Psychologic considerations in temporomandibular dysfunction. A biopsychosocial view of symptom formation. *Dental Clinics of North America, 35*(1), 209–226.

Haley, W. E., Turner, J. A., & Romano, J. M. (1985). Depression in chronic pain patients: Relation to pain, activity, and sex differences. *Pain, 23,* 337–343.

Holbrook, T., Grazier, K., Kelsey, J., & Stauffer, R. (1984). *The frequency of occurrence impact and cost of selected musculoskeletal conditions in the United States.* Rosemont, IL: American Academy of Orthopedic Surgeons.

Jacobsen, P. B., & Butler, R. W. (1996). Relation of cognitive coping and catastrophizing to acute pain and analgesic use follwoing breast cancer surgery. *Journal of Behavioral Medicine, 19,* 17–23.

Joint Commission on Accreditation of Health Care Organizations (JCOAOH). (1999). *Comprehensive accreditation manual for hospital: Pain management standards.* Chicago: Author.

Katz, W. A. (1998). The needs of a patient in pain. *American Journal of Medicine, 105*(1B), 2S–7S.

Kerns, R., Turk, D., & Rudy, T. (1985). The West Haven-Yale Multidimensional Pain Inventory. *Pain, 23,* 345–356.

Kinney, R. K., Gatchel, R. J., Polatin, P. B., Fogarty, W. J., & Mayer, T. G. (1993). Prevalence of psychopathology in acute and chronic low back pain patients. *Journal of Occupational Rehabilitation, 1993,* 95–103.

Lanes, T. C., Gauron, E. F., Spratt, K. F., Wernimott, T. J., Found, E. M., & Weinstein, J. N. (1995). Long-term follow-up of patients with chronic back pain treated in a multidisciplinary rehabilitation program. *Spine, 18,* 1103–1112.

Linton, S. J. (1999). Prevention and special reference to chronic musculoskeletal disorders. In R. J. Gatchel & D. C. Turk (Eds.), *Psychosocial factors in pain: Critical perspectives* (pp. 374–389). New York: Guilford.

Linton, S. J., Bradley, L. A., Jensen, I., Spangfort, E., & Sundell, L. (1989). The secondary prevention of low back pain: a controlled study with follow-up. *Pain, 36*(2), 197–207.

Linton, S. J., Hellsing, A. L., & Hallden, K. (1998). A population-based study of spinal pain among 35-45-year-old individuals. Prevalence, sick leave, and health care use. *Spine, 23*(13), 1457–1463.

Loeser, J. D. (1991). The role of pain clinics in managing chronic back pain. In J. Frymoyer (Ed.), *The adult spine: Principles and practice*. New York: Raven.

Magni, G., Moreschi, C., Rigatti-Luchini, S., & Mersky, H. (1994). Prospective study on the relationship between depressive symptoms and chronic musculoskeletal pain. *Pain, 56*, 289–298.

Mayer, T. G., & Gatchel, R. J. (1988). *Functional restoration for spinal disorders: The sports medicine approach*. Philadelphia: Lea & Febiger.

Melzack, R., & Wall, P. D. (1965). Pain mechanisms: A new theory. *Science, 150*, 971–979.

Million, R., Haavik-Nilsen, J., Jayson, M. I. V., & Baker, R. D. (1981). Evaluation of low back pain and assessment of lumbar corsets with and without back supports. *Annals of the Rheumatic Diseases, 40*, 449–454.

Polatin, P. B., Kinney, R. K., Gatchel, R. J., Lillo, E., & Mayer, T. G. (1993). Psychiatric illness and chronic low-back pain. The mind and the spine—Which goes first? *Spine, 18*(1), 66–71.

Rainville, J., Sobel, J., Hartigan, C., & Wright, A. (1997). The effect of compensation involvement of the reporting of pain and disability by patients referred for rehabilitation of chronic low back pain. *Spine, 22*(17), 2016–2024.

Rohling, M. L., Binder, L. M., & Langhinrichsen-Rohling, J. (1995). Money matters: A meta-analytic review of the association between financial compensation and the experience and treatment of chronic pain. *Health Psychology, 14*(6), 537–547.

Rush, A. J., Beck, A. T., Kovacs, M., & Hollon, S. (1977). Comparative efficacy of cognitive therapy and pharmacotherapy in the treatment of depressed outpatients. *Cognitive Therapy and Research, 1*, 17–37.

Sanderson, P. L., Todd, B. D., Holt, G. R., & Getty, C. J. (1995). Compensation, work status, and disability in low back pain patients. *Spine, 20*(5), 554–556.

Spitzer, R. L., & Williams, J. B. W. (1986). *Structured clinical interview for DSM-III—Nonpatient version* (modified for Vietnam Veterans Readjustment Study 4/1/87 ed.). New York: Biometrics Research Department, New York State Psychiatric Institute.

Sternbach, R. A., Wolf, S. R., Murphy, R. W., & Akeson, W. H. (1973). Aspects of chronic low back pain. *Psychosomatics, 14*, 52–56.

Sullivan, M. J., Stanish, W., Waite, H., Sullivan, M., & Tripp, D. A. (1998). Catastophizing, pain and disability in patients with soft-tissue injury. *Pain, 77*, 253–260.

Tait, R. C., Chibnall, J. T., & Richardson, W. D. (1990). Litigation and employment status: Effects on patients with chronic pain. *Pain, 43*, 37–48.

Turk, D. C. (1996). Biopsychosocial perspective on chronic pain. In R. J. Gatchel & D. C. Turk (Eds.), *Psychological approaches to pain management: A practitioner's handbook* (pp. 3–32). New York: Guilford.

Turk, D. C., & Gatchel, R. J. (1999). Multidisciplinary programs for rehabilitation of chronic low back pain patients. In W. H. Kirkaldy-Willis & J. T. N. Bernard (Eds.), *Managing low back pain* (4th ed., pp. 214–239). New York: Churchill Livingstone.

Turk, D. C., & Rudy, T. E. (1987). Towards a comprehensive assessment of chronic pain patients. *Behavioral Research and Therapy, 25*, 237–249.

Turk, D., & Rudy, T. (1988). Toward an empirically derived taxonomy of chronic pain patients: Integration of psychological assessment data. *Journal of Consulting and Clinical Psychology, 56*, 233–238.

Vaccaro, A. R., Ring, D., Scuderi, G., Cohen, D. S., & Garfin, S. R. (1997). Predictors of outcome in patients with chronic back pain and low-grade spondylolisthesis. *Spine, 22*(17), 2030–2034; discussion on p. 2035.

Vingard, E., Alfredsson, L., Hagberg, M., Kilvom, A., Theorell, T., Waldenstrom, M. et al. (2000). To what extent do current and past physical and psychological occupational factors explain care-seeking for low back pain in a working population? *Spine, 25*, 493–500.

Weickgenant, A. L., Slater, M. A., Patterson, T. L., Atkinson, J. H., Grant, I., & Garfin, S. R. (1993). Coping activities in chronic low back pain: Relationship to pain and disability. *Pain, 53*, 95–103.

Weisberg, J. N., Vittengle, J. R., Clark, L. A., Gatchel, R. J., & Garen, A. A. (2000). Personality and pain: Summary and future directions. In R. J. Gatchel & J. N. Weisberg (Eds.), *Personality characteristics of patients with pain*. Washington, DC: American Psychological Association.

Williams, R. A., Pruitt, S. D., Doctor, J. N., Epping-Jordan, J. E., Wahlgren, D. R., Grant, I. et al. (1998). The contribution of job satisfaction to the transition from acute to chronic low back pain. *Archives of Physical Medicine and Rehabilitation, 79*, 366–374.

Chapter 17
Psychosocial Interventions With Type 1 and 2 Diabetes Patients

GLENN M. CALLAGHAN, JENNIFER A. GREGG, ENRIQUE ORTEGA, AND
KRISTOFFER S. BERLIN

Diabetes mellitus is a chronic disease that is very costly, both in terms of medical care expenditures and disability, for the nearly 17 million Americans who live with it. In the past decade, researchers have demonstrated that intensive pharmacological and self-management treatment can prevent or postpone complications of diabetes, such as blindness, amputations, renal failure, and death. However, given the high level of self-management required, many patients do not adhere to recommendations. In this chapter, we describe a biopsychosocial approach to diabetes, which utilizes key psychosocial factors and diabetes management, for the treatment of diabetes in a primary health-care setting.

Diabetes as a Biopsychosocial Phenomenon

Diabetes mellitus is a chronic, costly, and potentially fatal disease that requires a large amount of self-management by patients. The extensive behavior and lifestyle change required places a large amount of treatment responsibility on the patient, rather than the clinician, and makes successful adherence to medical recommendations for diabetes very difficult for many patients. Thus, the psychosocial and behavioral aspects of treatment for this chronic condition play an important role in successful treatment.

Definition

Diabetes mellitus is a metabolic disorder affecting the body's capacity to produce or respond to insulin, a hormone that allows blood glucose to be used for energy. Diabetes falls into two main categories, types 1 and 2. Type 1 is characterized by problems with the body's production of insulin and typically has an onset during childhood or adolescence. Type 2, the more common form of the disease, is characterized by a failure to produce sufficient levels of insulin or to sufficiently utilize the insulin that is produced by the body. Historically, type 2 diabetes has had an onset usually occurring after age 45, though it is becoming more common to see onset of type 2 diabetes at an earlier age.

Type 1 diabetes requires continual maintenance of proper insulin levels. To date there are no strategies for the prevention of type 1 diabetes. Type 2 diabetes is associated with obesity and a family history of the disease (CDC, 2002). Type 2 diabetes has potential prevention strategies to avoid its onset, aimed at lifestyle choices (such as diet and exercise) associated with the disease. Physical inactivity as well as race or ethnicity (e.g., African American, Hispanic, American Indian, some Asian American and Pacific Island groups) also contribute as risk factors for the disease. Type 2 diabetes accounts for 90–95% of all cases of diabetes (CDC, 2002). The prevalence of both types of diabetes comprises an estimated 17 million people in the United States, or approximately 6.2% of the population. Nearly 450,000 deaths are attributed to diabetes per year, and diabetes remains the sixth-leading cause of death in the United States (CDC, 2002).

Heart disease is the leading cause of death among individuals with diabetes, with an incidence two to four times greater than that of the nondiabetic population. In addition to death, physical complications of diabetes include cardiopulmonary diseases, stroke, blindness, kidney disease, nervous system diseases including diabetic neuropathies, retinopathy, lower extremity amputations, dental disease, and pregnancy complications (CDC, 2002). Sixty to sixty-five percent of individuals with diabetes have chronic hypertension, contributing to the higher incidence of stroke with diabetes patients (e.g., Simonson, 1988).

Diabetes Self-Management

More than 10 years ago, the Diabetes Control and Complications Trial Research Group (DCCT, 1993) drastically changed the way diabetes is treated by reporting that in this controlled, prospective trial of more than 1,400 individuals with type 1 diabetes, intensive management of blood glucose levels led to tighter glucose control, which led to reduced diabetes-related complications. Five years later, similar results were demonstrated with more than 5,000 individuals with type 2 diabetes in the United Kingdom Prospective Diabetes Study (UKPDS, 1998).

Given these and other results, the contemporary medical management of diabetes attempts to keep blood glucose levels near nondiabetic levels. This treatment varies depending on the type of diabetes and can include a carefully calculated diet, planned physical activity, blood glucose testing multiple times per day, use of medications to improve natural insulin production and response, and the administration of exogenous insulin (ADA, 2000). The medical interventions for type 1 diabetes include instructions about dietary restrictions and information about physical exercise and insulin administration in the form of two or more injections per day or the use of an insulin pump. Medical interventions for type 2 diabetes can include instruction about diet and increased exercise, the use of oral prescription medication for the regulation of glucose levels (e.g., metformin) and increasing effective responses to insulin (e.g., pioglitazone), as well as daily insulin injections for some patients (ADA, 2000). Self-management, or the patient's control and regulation of the disorder, is integral to the treatment of diabetes (ADA, 1998). Recent American Diabetes Association (2000) treatment recommendations and guidelines suggest that treatment should be tailored to the individual and should address medical, psychosocial, and lifestyle issues.

Although the medical management of diabetes is important, the need for psychoeducation interventions is apparent, given the high level of self-management required in diabetes. Despite the repeated recommendations by the American Diabetes Association (2000) and the clear need for a more comprehensive, integrated-care model, Clement (1995) reports that fewer than 50% of individuals with diabetes ever receive more than limited self-management education. Of individuals with type 2 diabetes who do not use insulin, 76% report never having attended any educational program for their diabetes (Coonrod, Betschart, & Harris, 1994).

Despite the importance of diabetes education, however, education alone may not be sufficient to bring about desired behavior change. In a review of diabetes self-management interventions, Clement (1995) reported that none of the seven studies using only didactic education methods demonstrated improvement in glucose control. In contrast, he reported that interventions that utilized behavior change strategies, in addition to education, produced improvements.

Another issue related to diabetes self-management education is the setting in which treatment is delivered. Janes (1995) reported that individuals with diabetes are more likely to receive medical care for their diabetes in a primary care setting, while another study found that individuals with diabetes receive better care from diabetes-focused treatments than general medical clinics (Ho, Marger, Beart, Yip, & Shekelle, 1997). Regardless of where treatment is delivered, a multidisciplinary health-care team is continually advocated in the area of diabetes intervention (e.g., Boland, Ahern, & Grey, 1998; Funnell, 1996; Harris & Lustman, 1998). This multidisciplinary team provides education about and treatment of psychological problems, as they are related to diabetes, together with the necessary medical treatment. This coordinated-care approach results in a better standard of living for the patient and has been demonstrated to be more cost-effective than conventional (i.e., medical only) treatments (Jacobson, 1996; Neff, 1999; Tucker, 1999).

Psychological Complications

Psychological complications contribute significantly to the health of the individual with diabetes. The initial distress of being diagnosed with such a disease is only the beginning of a difficult psychological path for these patients. According to a recent study, as many as 25% of individuals with diabetes experience recurring emotional problems such as depression, anxiety, and eating disorders (Harris & Lustman, 1998). Psychological problems suffered by diabetes patients have been related to the risk of elevated glucose and difficulties in controlling these levels (Jacobson, 1996).

Depression has been found to be much more prevalent among patients with diabetes than those without diabetes (18.5% versus 11.4%, respectively; Neff, 1999). Approximately 15–25% of adults with either type 1 or type 2 diabetes have major depression (Tucker, 1999). This is more than twice the level of depression found in the general population. Depression has also been associated with an increased risk for diabetic complications, poor control of glycemic levels, and a reduced quality of life, although the mechanisms of this relationship are not yet fully understood (Lustman et al., 2000; Tucker, 1999).

Economic Cost

Complications created by psychological problems and nonadherence lead to a very high economic burden for the individual patient and managed-care systems (Selby, Ray, Zhang, & Colby, 1997). Of the $44.1 billion estimated direct medical expenditures for diabetes in 1997, $11.8 billion was attributed to the treatment of chronic complications (ADA, 1998). Indirect costs of diabetes (including work absenteeism, disability, and premature death) have more recently been estimated at $132 billion yearly (ADA, 2000). Although the literature has not yet investigated a direct relationship between psychological problems and the direct cost of chronic diabetes complications, the two may have an important relationship. For example, depression is associated with poor glycemic control, which increases the risk of complications, and, thus, the costs associated with treating diabetes (Lustman et al., 2000). Total annual health-care costs are significantly higher for individuals with diabetes and depression ($6,800 average per person) than for individuals with diabetes without depression ($4,300 average per person; Neff, 1999). This relationship between depression, adherence, and its associated costs indicates the necessity of addressing psychological disorders when treating diabetes from a coordinated-care perspective. Further, these findings support the importance of a behavioral health-care provider's being involved in the treatment of the individual with diabetes. The treatment of depression for individuals with diabetes would likely improve their glycemic control indirectly by facilitating better adherence to the treatment program.

One efficient way to address both psychological and self-management issues for individuals with diabetes is through the delivery of diabetes self-management education in a psychoeducational group. Efficiency is increased because at one group session a behavioral health-care provider can see as many as 10 to 15 patients, and in this area group education has been shown to be as effective as individual education (Norris, Engelgau, & Narayah, 2001). Given the potential benefits in efficiency and social support of delivering care in a group format, the recommendations in this chapter for psychoeducational interventions for patients with diabetes are made with group treatment in mind. However, if patients require additional psychological services or have difficulty participating in a group format, individual sessions may be used as well.

Diabetes serves as a model disease for the integration of psychosocial or psychoeducational treatments into standard medical management. Psychoeducational treatment components directly address the prevention and treatment of both medical and psychological complications and promote the adherence necessary for the successful management of diabetes.

The Integrated Care Treatment Model of Diabetes

Targeted Areas of Intervention

Recommendations based on research for psychoeducational treatments for diabetes can be categorized into five main areas: (1) educational information, (2) coping skills and stress management, (3) social support, (4) diet, and (5) exercise. We suggest a comprehensive psychoeducational approach to the treatment of diabetes that combines elements of each of these areas. This comprehensive treatment better serves patients with diabetes than treatments focusing on only one or two areas (see, e.g., Howorka et al., 2000). Although type 1 and type 2 diabetes remain different in important ways with respect to onset and medical management, the principles of psychosocial interventions apply to both, and an intervention can be conducted that serves both types of patients simultaneously. For this reason, this discussion will group both types of diabetes patients together. Specific considerations for each type of diabetes are highlighted for behavioral interventions for diet and exercise, but the other components address psychosocial issues common to both types.

Each of the five main areas listed above have been investigated as separate interventions and have gained empirical support as being necessary but not sufficient interventions for the successful management of the disease. Only recently have researchers advocated the integration of psychological interventions with more traditional areas of focus such as education, diet, and exercise (e.g., Harris & Lustman, 1998; Howorka et al., 2000). To date, there are no standard, empirically supported treatments that have integrated all five areas of intervention.

The Take Charge! Treatment Protocol

Three of the authors of this chapter (GC, EO, & KB) have created a new treatment manual based on recommendations from the empirical literature that combines each of these five areas into one 5-week protocol called *Take Charge!* (Callaghan & Ortega, 2001; Callaghan, Ortega, Uribe, & Berlin, 2001). All five of these areas were integrated as an attempt to help patients successfully manage the disease in combination with taking their prescribed medications. In this treatment, each of the five areas is addressed as its own module in a group treatment. There is a strong emphasis on gaining social support for successful management of the disease throughout the treatment. To this end, patients are encouraged to bring one "support person" to each session. This person may be a partner, family member, or friend. Ideally, it is someone who is invested in the patient's health and well-being.

The group is structured so that it meets once per week, and meetings last for 90 minutes. Doctoral-level psychologists and psychology trainees conduct the groups. Each module presents information didactically and requires each patient to complete specific in-and-out-of-session activities. Because the treatment is conducted in a group format, as many as 10 patients can be seen at a time. The protocol is designed so that only one health-care professional is needed to conduct the group.

This *Take Charge!* treatment protocol was recently evaluated in a small treatment outcome study. Although the results of the study are preliminary and based on a small, uncontrolled sample, they suggest that this treatment may be effective in increasing adherence to medical treatment, decreasing blood glucose levels (as measured by HbA_{1C}), increasing psychological functioning, and increasing quality of life in a community primary health-care clinic (Dhanjal, Callaghan, Rosito, Wang, & Waddel, 2002). These changes were related to social support and psychological health, dietary changes, amount of exercise, as well as increases in the frequency of glucose self-monitoring. At a 3-month follow-up, several patients reported lasting decreases in HbA_{1C} blood glucose values, indicating sustained behavioral improvements relating to diabetic management.

The following presents a discussion of each of the five areas of intervention in the contemporary management of diabetes. The modules are numbered in sequence to correspond to the order in which they appear in our treatment protocol. We have ordered them this way because it makes conceptual sense to build upon the information related to education about the disease; however, there is no evidence to suggest that they cannot be conducted in a different order than provided here.

Education. Education about diabetes has evolved considerably in the past 20 years. The American Diabetes Association (ADA) recognizes diabetes education programs that train individuals in programs that meet ADA standards. Education areas typically focus on information about how diabetes affects the body, nutrition, and self-monitoring of glucose levels. Meta-analyses of research on education interventions repeatedly show that education is important in the management of diabetes (Brown, 1988, 1992; Padgett, Mumford, Hynes, & Carter, 1988), but, as noted above, it may not be sufficient for effective self-management interventions (Clement, 1995).

Areas of education that are important to address in psychoeducational interventions include the following:

- Information about what diabetes is as a disease.
- An understanding of the role of insulin in the body and how insulin relates to diabetes.
- Information about causes for both types 1 and 2 diabetes.
- Understanding the difference between type 1 and type 2 diabetes and knowing which type a patient has.
- Information on the importance of maintaining healthy glucose levels, what those levels are, and how to conduct the self-monitoring tests.
- Understanding hypo- and hyperglycemic events.
- Information and instruction about the importance of foot and eye care including self-monitoring for problems.

Education about diabetes, particularly more comprehensive programs that include the areas emphasized above, remains an integral part of any psychologically based intervention because it may help to promote patient compliance through an understanding of diabetes and the disease process. For example, a basic understanding of how changes in blood sugar levels affect the patient's feeling of having energy may provide better prompts for maintaining appropriate glucose levels. Similarly, patients who understand the relationship between circulation problems and nerve damage (peripheral neuropathy) may be motivated to better take care of their feet.

Although these interventions may be important, the disconnection between diabetes and education and behavior change suggests that there may be additional barriers that prevent patients from acting on this education material. These barriers can be addressed in the following components, focusing on coping skills and stress management strategies.

Coping Skills and Stress Management. As described earlier, depressive disorders in individuals with diabetes have been linked to poor glycemic control (Lustman et al., 2000) and a corresponding increased risk of complications (Anderson, Lustman, Clouse, De Groot, & Freedland, 2001). The fact that the prevalence of depression among individuals with diabetes is nearly twice as high as that of the general population in the United States indicates the necessity to include the screening and appropriate treatment for depression and other psychological problems among diabetes patients.

Stress, difficulties coping with diabetes, and difficulties making necessary behavioral changes have also been associated with poor glycemic control and increased risk of complications (Kramer, Ledolter, Manos, & Bayless, 2000). Research investigating the inclusion of coping skills training in the treatment of diabetes indicates that these skills help patients lower glucose levels, assist with their medical management of the disease, and decrease the negative impact of diabetes on their quality of life (Grey, Boland, Davidson, Li, & Tamborlane, 2000). The coping-skills training to be implemented by the behavioral health-care provider includes social problem solving, cognitive and behavior modification, and conflict resolution.

Suggestions for psychoeducational treatment components in this area include:

• Screening for depression and appropriate treatment if mood disorder is present.
• Coping-skills training using cognitive behavioral strategies.
• Focusing on such topics as family adjustment, stress management, eating disorders.
• Focusing on parenting and marital issues as they are related to diabetes and an adjustment to a new lifestyle.

More general and long-term suggestions for treatment approaches in this area include the use of support group meetings that facilitate sharing of information, treatment plans, effective coping skills, anecdotal experiences, and resources by the patients. These groups can be conducted in tandem with the psychoeducational intervention, or they could be offered as less structured, after-care support groups. The overarching suggestion for this aspect of diabetes treatment is that the mental health professional be competent to facilitate behavioral changes that assist patients' adherence to treatment, develop patients' coping and adjustment to new lifestyles, as well as address eating disorders if present. This may entail using a psychotherapist such as a licensed marriage family therapist or licensed clinical social worker who has had experience delivering psychosocial or psychological interventions.

In our *Take Charge!* treatment protocol we propose specific tasks for developing effective coping skills and stress management strategies. These include (1) teaching patients how to decrease the general levels of stress in their lives; (2) the use of relaxation strategies and meditation, the use of exercise; (3) taking a time-out from stressful situations; and (4) using social supports to help deal with stress. We suggest that it is also useful to address the specific stress that diabetes can add to a patient's life. We advocate helping patients to adjust to the changes in their lives slowly and in small steps in areas where this is possible. Helping patients prioritize which areas need to be addressed and changed first (e.g., with diet or exercise due to obesity or pulmonary problems) is also a key task.

One of the difficulties patients encounter with managing their diabetes occurs as a result of avoiding the thoughts or feelings associated with being diagnosed and living with a chronic disease. Acceptance of the fact that patients have the disease, and that they wish they did not, may also be an important coping strategy to teach. We further discuss the role of acceptance later in the chapter.

Social Support. Social support has been recognized as an important element in the treatment and management of diabetes. Family and friends play an important role in this process through their assistance with selecting and preparing meals, providing care, and helping the patient cope with stress. Social support and encouragement greatly influence the patient's coping, management, and attitude toward their condition (Wallhagen, 1999).

Considerations for treatment interventions regarding social support include

- Orienting patients to the importance of social support and involving friends and family to assist them with the management of their disease.
- Helping patients understand that they are not alone in having diabetes, that they do not have to struggle in isolation.
- Informing patients of other social support outlets.
- Providing group sessions with other individuals with diabetes to promote the development of support networks and learning new coping strategies from others.
- Providing an "awareness" session with the patient's friends and family about the importance that they have in the treatment and management of their loved one's condition.
- Assisting the patient and their friends or family with the adjustment process of having and managing diabetes.

Providing the above components in a social support intervention can be very beneficial to the individual with diabetes. As discussed earlier, we recommend directly involving at least one primary support member for a patient. This person can come to each of the psychoeducational group sessions to better understand how to help the patient manage his or her disease. Both the patient and family member need to understand that diabetes is a lifelong management issue. Together, the patient with diabetes and his or her family member or friend can work as a team. With effective management the patient can live a long, happy, and healthy life.

We also propose that it is useful to teach patients some basic social skill strategies including using active listening strategies and assertion skills. One important area in which to implement these socially based strategies is with the patients' physician, and the behavioral health-care specialist can address patients' concerns about how to talk with their doctor and instruct them in making clear, specific requests about their medical needs. In the service of helping the patient become more effective and to manage costs associated with unnecessary health-care visits, it is also useful to teach the patient to discriminate when a diabetic emergency occurs, when to contact the physician, and when to rely on other sources of support.

Diet. Nutrition, diet, and obesity continue to be among the most problematic areas for intervention, for both patients with diabetes and for health-care service providers. Despite the consistent need for a balanced diet and the empirical documentation of the role that nutrition and obesity play in chronic health problems, particularly with diabetes, there are no consistent research findings to suggest the best intervention with respect to dietary change strategies for individuals with diabetes. Historically, dietary recommendations for both type 1 and 2 diabetes have focused on

(1) providing an extensive list of prohibited foods to prevent glycemic events and increased levels of hemoglobin A_{1c} values (ADA, 1994), and (2) giving explicit recommendations to individuals with type 2 diabetes to lose weight. These two traditional approaches have met with limited success. More recently, there has been much attention paid to low carbohydrate diets for individuals with diabetes, but, given the numerous health problems experienced by these patients, such recommendations have not been applied broadly by most physicians. Ultimately, dietary change is complicated, and in diabetes there is no specific diet or meal plan that will work for everybody, so encouraging individuals with diabetes to lose weight through a plan that takes into account their specific circumstances is often most effective.

Although there is no magic diet, there are some general suggestions and guidelines for addressing behavioral change in diet and nutrition (ADA, 1994). These suggestions state that health service providers consider important contextual variables such as race or ethnicity and previous dietary habits when planning any individualized diet plan. According to the American Diabetes Association, for medical nutrition therapy to be effective, an individualized meal plan should be developed that considers the individual's normal eating habits, being sensitive to cultural and ethnic food values, as well as what the individual is willing and not willing to do (ADA, 2000). Meal plans should be developed keeping in mind specific goals, such as improved metabolic control, maintaining healthy body weight, and preventing short- and long-term complications. Because many dietary factors may be complex to the untrained person, it is recommended that a dietitian or nutritionist knowledgeable about diabetes be involved in meal planning as well as any type of nutrition assessment.

General suggestions for a diabetes diet-intervention protocol include the following considerations:

- A nutrition assessment should be conducted to determine the patient's individualized meal plan as well as treatment goals.
- Group meetings can be held in which specific information is presented on the relationship of nutrients to blood glucose levels, serum lipid levels, as well as the optimum levels of calories, carbohydrates, fat, protein, and cholesterol that meals and diets should include.
- Instruction in counting carbohydrates and grams of fat should be provided to help the patient keep track of nutritional intake.
- A dietician or other health-care provider should give information and assistance on the use of insulin, insulin regimens, as well as insulin and food adjustment procedures.
- Information should be provided in group meetings on short- and long-term complication risks and how certain foods and diets prevent these.
- A periodic assessment of goals and adherence to dietary plans should occur throughout treatment.

Specific recommendations for dietary changes for better health must to be tailored to the individual. However, some recommendations apply to many individuals with diabetes, including these:

- Recommend that the patient try choosing food products low in sodium, sugar, and fat when grocery shopping.
- Advise the patient to prepare meals that are baked, broiled, or grilled and not fried.
- Recommend that the patient try flavoring foods with herbs or lemon juices instead of using salt and to try to minimize or reduce foods with creamy sauces, butter, and rich desserts.
- Suggest that patients eat lean meats and plenty of vegetables.
- Suggest that patients consult with their doctor about how much fruit is acceptable to eat, given the risk of glycemic events associated with natural sugars.

In an ideal treatment setting, patients with diabetes would be referred to a nutritionist who would help the patient develop a tailored diet plan based on his or her precise needs. This is often not the case, but the role of the nutritionist should not be overlooked in any setting. If the patient has been diagnosed as having nutrition-related health deficiencies, evidences or reports of food allergies, specific food requirements or restrictions based on an ideology or belief system, or other needs that go beyond the general recommendations made in a psychoeducational intervention, a nutritionist should be consulted.

Another area of focus with dietary considerations concerns the use of tobacco and alcohol. It is in most patients' best interest to reduce or eliminate smoking. For individuals with diabetes, circulatory and cardiovascular problems are especially prominent, and smoking tobacco is known to be related to heart and lung disease. Given the prominence of heart disease with this population, specific counseling on the effects of smoking is highly recommended.

Alcohol consumption is a difficult issue for individuals with diabetes. It may be necessary to treat a co-morbid alcohol dependence problem for some patients. However, for those patients who drink in moderation, it is important to assess the quantity of alcohol consumed and provide some basic education on the relationship between alcohol and diabetes. Metabolizing alcohol can be difficult for some individuals with diabetes. The symptoms of hypoglycemia and intoxication are similar (e.g., thick-tongued speech, shaking, staggering walk, mental confusion, etc.), and people may confuse these symptoms and ignore or delay treatment of diabetic insulin reactions.

Some individuals with diabetes can drink alcohol in moderation with few adverse health effects, but only if their diabetes is in good control. It is recommended that individuals with diabetes not drink more than one serving a day, where one serving is 4 ounces of wine, 12 ounces of beer, or 1.5 ounces of hard liquor. Additionally, individuals with diabetes should drink only when eating a meal and they should be advised to avoid sweet liqueurs or mixes because of their high sugar content.

Exercise. Nutritional recommendations are most effective as dietary and weight loss strategies when coupled with an exercise program. As with planning a diet, diabetes patients should consult with their physicians to determine the best exercise regimen for them. Exercise helps control blood sugar levels, reduces the risk of complications such as nerve and eye damage, and protects against heart disease (Stanten, 2000). However, many individuals with diabetes receive minimal information about exercising, perhaps owing to complexities involved in maintaining normal blood sugar levels during such activities (Colberg, 2000).

Type 1 diabetes patients need a basic education of physiology to understand how varying blood sugar levels produce negative effects such as an increased risk of cardiovascular, foot, and hypoglycemic problems. For this reason, individuals trained in exercise physiology with knowledge in the area of diabetes are recommended to assist the patient develop an exercise program. The healthcare provider should understand and have the necessary training to analyze the risks and benefits of exercise to the patient (ADA, 2000).

For individuals with type 1 diabetes, research indicates that exercise does not help improve diabetes management with respect to glycemic control. However, exercise helps boost cardiovascular fitness. For individuals with type 2 diabetes, exercise programs, when combined with appropriate medical treatment, increase glycemic control and reduce risk factors for heart and circulatory problems (ADA, 1996).

General recommendations for planning exercise-based interventions for individuals with diabetes include the following:

• A detailed medical evaluation, a thorough screening for cardiovascular conditions, and an individualized risk evaluation should be conducted for each patient. This evaluation should include specific assessments for hypertension, neuropathy, retinopathy, and ischemic heart disease. An exercise EEG may be indicated for patients over 35 (ADA, 1996).

- Education should be provided about basic physiology as related to body and exercise (energy use, bodily responses, body fuels).
- Patients should continue to self-monitor glycemic levels and immediately adjust their exercise regimen accordingly.
- Patients should have a personalized training regime based on individualized evaluations.

Specific recommendations for an exercise plan, as with the dietary intervention, should be tailored to the individual and be done in coordination with the patient's physician. Some additional recommendations also include the following:

- The patient should always wear something that identifies him- or herself as a person with diabetes.
- The patient should have a card with his or her name and the phone number of contact persons in case of an emergency. This is especially important when exercising outside.
- The patient should set aside a special time during the day, and days of the week, to exercise.
- It is important to remind the patient to eat at least 1 to 2 hours before exercising and to be aware of how exercise affects the body.
- If the patient feels weak or faint, he or she should immediately discontinue exercising and make sure to tell the doctor.
- Patients should always carry a fast-acting sugar such as glucose tablets, honey, or a hard candy in the event a hypoglycemic event occurs.
- Patients should continue to monitor their blood-sugar levels frequently to notice any changes. If blood-sugar levels become too high or low, the patient should discontinue any activity immediately so that he or she can normalize glucose levels with certain foods with fast-acting sugars or extra insulin as appropriate.

Issues Associated With Successful Treatment Delivery

The following sections address some of the specific issues associated with delivering a psychoeducational treatment protocol effectively in a health-care setting. These issues include the motivation of patients with respect to treatment adherence, problems associated with emotional avoidance, and the type of practitioner needed to deliver psychoeducational treatments.

Addressing Motivation and Patient Adherence

Patient adherence to treatment recommendations can be difficult to achieve. The research literature on promoting adherence is scant and has centered largely on educating patients about the disease. Recently, psychological behavior change models, such as Prochaska and DiClemente's (1982, 1986) stages of change model, have been applied theoretically to diabetes (e.g., Ruggiero & Prochaska, 1993). Increased attention is being paid to the utilization of psychological principles to tackle motivation with this population.

In our approach, we have attempted to address this by having patients explicitly state their goals and values for healthy living. We then tailor the intervention to each patient in the group based on his or her own goals. This assumes, however, that patients hold the goals of healthy living. It is unclear how to motivate or increase a desire to live a healthy life if it is not held as a value.

Alternatively, another factor thought to be a motivator in diabetes is information on the costs of not taking care of one's diabetes—specifically information about complications such as blindness, amputation, and death. It remains unclear, however, whether this knowledge will motivate behavior change (e.g., Clement, 1995).

Avoidance, Acceptance, and Diabetes

Acceptance as a strategy for coping with a chronic disease has recently emerged as an area of potential focus for interventions. Acceptance theorists suggest that it is the avoidance of psychological discomfort, such as thoughts and feelings about having to deal with diabetes for the rest of one's life, that may contribute to nonadherence to treatment recommendations (e.g., Hayes, Strosahl, & Wilson, 1999). For example, a patient with diabetes may be distressed about the possibility of blindness, amputation, or even death, and may therefore avoid thoughts about having diabetes in order to not have to feel this distress. This avoidance may then lead to a decrease in diabetes self-management behaviors.

Acceptance theorists advocate treatments that develop skills that reduce avoidance strategies and increase patients' abilities to experience aversive emotions related to their disease, such as acceptance and commitment therapy. This area is new to disease management and is only just now being investigated in diabetes; we include it here because it may be an important area of assessment and intervention. Recently, a measure has been developed (Acceptance/Avoidance Diabetes Questionnaire, AADQ; Callaghan & Gregg, 2001) that assesses the extent to which individuals with diabetes actively avoid their thoughts and feelings associated with the disease. Each patient's response to the AADQ helps identify areas of avoidance that may inhibit the patient's ability to fully engage self-management behaviors. For example, if a patient indicates that he or she is working very hard not think about his or her diabetes and will avoid the stimuli or materials associated with diabetes, that patient may be less likely to test his or her blood glucose. In this case, we would focus on helping the patient learn to experience those feelings of fear of the disease, to accept those as natural feelings, *and* to engage in the behaviors necessary to prevent an early death and have a healthier life.

Health-Care Providers for Diabetes Interventions

In an integrated health-care model, the medical management of diabetes remains under the direction of the physician. However, any behavioral health-care provider with proper training (except of course, where a specialist is required) can provide all the components of the psychoeducational interventions described above. In addition, certified health-care specialists such as physicians' assistants, nurse practitioners, certified diabetes educators, or registered nurses can provide these interventions in coordination with the primary care physician. Regardless of who conducts the intervention, any health-care provider working with patients with diabetes must know the limits of their knowledge. Due to some of the specified knowledge required for physiology and nutritional aspects of a comprehensive approach to diabetic care, health-care providers should continue to consult with a physician, and when possible, involve specialists such as dieticians, nutritionists, and others.

Assessment of Variables Important to Diabetes

There are many domains to assess with diabetes interventions. These fall into five main categories: knowledge, medical, diet, psychosocial, and economic costs. There are numerous devices available in each of these domains, and they can provide important information about the effectiveness of the psychoeducational intervention and provide an assessment of accountability to the patient and service provider. The specific devices described below can be given pre- and posttreatment to help determine the effectiveness of the intervention. These devices are applicable to all individuals with diabetes, though they require the patient to be able to read. Literacy and vision impairments (e.g., retinopathy) should be determined before using these assessments.

A good general comprehensive assessment device is the Diabetes Care Profile (Fitzgerald et al., 1996), which assesses multiple domains pertaining to diabetes including dietary strategies, amount of education received, impact of diabetes on lifestyle, and level of psychological distress. Another general assessment device is the Diabetes Self-Management Profile (Harris et al., 2000), which assesses various components of the regimen including exercise, management of hypoglycemia, diet, blood glucose testing, and insulin administrations and dose adjustment. However, a broadband multimethod assessment approach is advocated with interventions for individuals with diabetes. Improvements shown on one assessment device for one domain should correlate with improvements shown in other domains, but this is not necessarily the case. It is important to determine the nature of discrepancies in divergent or inconsistent data from assessments of the different domains.

Knowledge

Knowledge assessments such as the Diabetes Knowledge Scale (Hess & Davis, 1983) or Brief Diabetes Knowledge Scale (Fitzgerald et al., 1998) attempt to determine what the patient knows about the facts of the disease. This is a good assessment device to use to determine the effectiveness of an educational intervention.

Medical

The primary variable assessed for diabetes is the effective maintenance of healthy glucose levels. Typically a test called glycosylated hemoglobin or hemoglobin A1c (GHb or HbA_{1c} is used. The HbA_{1c} is a measure of average blood glucose for the preceding 3 months and is considered the gold standard for indexing metabolic control (Goldstein, Little, Wiedmeyer, England, & McKenzie, 1986). Two variables that patients with diabetes report to physicians and health-care specialists are the frequency of self-monitoring or testing of glucose levels and the value of the glucose level at each test. Assessing glucose levels is useful to determine whether behavioral interventions lead to an increased frequency of testing and impact glucose levels (e.g., Clement, 1995). Assessments of blood pressure, medication compliance, foot and eye problems, and emergency room visits should also be considered obligatory in this domain.

Diet

Variables related to dietary practices and changes can be readily assessed using measures of weight loss, body mass indices, and self-monitored, weekly diet or meal record.

Psychosocial

Psychological or behavioral variables are numerous. The choice of an assessment device in this domain should be tailored to the individual's particular problems such as anxiety or mood problems. A general assessment of social support may be useful to track changes in utilization of support networks (e.g., the Social Support Questionnaire by Sarason, Sarason, Shearin, and Pierce, 1987).

Because depression is so prominent among patients with diabetes, a good basic depression self-report inventory is the Beck Depression Inventory (BDI or BDI-II; Beck, Steer, & Brown, 1996; Beck, Steer, & Garbin, 1988; Beck, Ward, Mendelson, Mock, & Erbaugh, 1961). The BDI is an instrument that rapidly assesses depression symptoms and provides an index for severity of distress. Although the BDI is not a diagnostic tool, it is very helpful in determining the severity of a patient's affective disturbance and can be useful for determining the appropriateness of a referral to another subspecialty clinic.

Assessing anxiety can be accomplished using the Beck Anxiety Inventory (Beck & Steer, 1997). This brief self-report device has been reported to be both psychometrically sound and useful in primary care settings for a variety of problems (e.g., Ferguson, 2000). General levels of stress can be effectively assessed using the Symptom Checklist-90 (SCL-90-R; DeRogatis, 1977). The SCL-90-R can yield a general index of psychological distress (Cyr, McKenna-Foley, & Peacock, 1985) that can be used as in pre-to-posttreatment assessment.

Assessing treatment satisfaction can also be considered an important psychological variable, particularly as it relates to the motivation of a patient to continue with the treatment. The Diabetes Treatment Satisfaction Questionnaire (Bradley, 1994) is one example of many devices that address patients' satisfaction with the intervention.

Economic Costs

Assessment of economic costs can be conducted for both patients and service providers or health-care agencies. For individuals with diabetes, assessments can include tracking the amount of money patients spend on self-care supplies (e.g., testing strips, insulin, medication, syringes, and other prescriptions), number and cost of doctor visits, emergency room visits, and specialty foods. Per capita medical expenditures for individuals with diabetes have been estimated at $10,071 per year, compared with $2,669 for people without diabetes (CDC, 1998). The economic costs of diabetes come largely from treating complications due to poor management of the disease.

Economic Analysis of Treating Diabetes and Cost Offset Opportunities

The most obvious way to reduce costs associated with diabetes lies in prevention of chronic complications. The costs for managing diabetes are high; however, the costs associated with complications such as amputations, emergency room visits, retinopathy, and nephropathy are staggering. The single largest cost offset for a diabetes intervention would be to reduce the $11.8 billion spent annually on treatment of complications.

A recent economic analysis of diabetes interventions yielded mixed empirical support for the different types of treatment strategies (Klonoff & Schwartz, 2000). This report categorized interventions according to their economic impact, from clearly cost-saving to unclear impact, based on the available data for the intervention. Cost-saving interventions include those focused on eye care (prevention of retinopathy) and preconception care, nephropathy prevention in type 1 diabetes, and improved glycemic control. These interventions produced clear savings medically and economically and ranged from cost savings between $1,000 to over $21,000 per patient per year depending on the intervention (with higher savings for prevention of nephropathy).

Interventions that indicate equivocal findings with respect to demonstrated cost savings include nephropathy prevention in type 2 diabetes and self-management training, case management, nutrition therapy, self-monitoring of blood glucose, foot care instruction, blood pressure, smoking cessation, exercise interventions, and weight loss (Klonoff & Schwartz, 2000). These equivocal findings should not necessarily preclude the health-care provider from utilizing interventions focused on these variables. For example, while the larger summary analysis by Klonoff and Schwartz indicated questionable findings for the cost effectiveness of foot care interventions, Litzelman and colleagues (1993) found a dramatic reduction in costs of health care using a basic intervention for foot care. Other studies have shown similarly large cost savings, particularly in the reduction of foot amputations, using similar approaches (Malone et al., 1989). In addition, reductions in direct costs for amputations do not necessarily reflect the potentially massive savings in indirect costs associated with the prevention of becoming physically disabled.

Enlisting and Maintaining Physician Collaboration

There is no empirical literature on enlisting and maintaining physician collaboration in the treatment of diabetes. Clearly, a multidisciplinary team is not only advocated but required to accomplish the multiple demands of a successful intervention. The following suggestions are based on a conceptualization of how to effectively create a psychosocial intervention in the context of primary care. First, the behavioral health-care specialist should determine that there is a need to provide additional care for patients with diabetes in a primary care setting. This can be done by explaining that the path to having physicians provide the best care for their patients with diabetes is to address the psychosocial variables in addition to the medical side of disease management. One way to approach this is to ask the director of a health-care agency of a primary care physician what he or she needs to *supplement* the care for their patients with diabetes.

Second, the behavioral health-care specialist can then describe the services that he or she can provide to the patient that would accomplish the goals for the agency in treating the patient. The health-care provider should develop clear and simple channels of communication with each key team member in the primary care setting. This communication is essential for providing follow-through and follow-up information to (a) inform the physician about progress and (b) determine the medical impact of the psychoeducational intervention on the patient. This information is essential to reevaluate the intervention for opportunities to improve the treatment for the patient and for the physician.

The overall key to involving physicians and other primary care management staff is to demonstrate the effectiveness of a psychoeducational intervention in the collaborative management of diabetes. This can be done by (1) conveying the effectiveness of the intervention as demonstrated in the empirical literature, and (2) by gathering specific data for the patients treated by the behavioral health-care specialist. Providing feedback about patients' successes medically, psychologically, and behaviorally is essential to demonstrating the important role that the behavioral health-care specialist serves on this type of treatment team.

Prevention of Diabetes

Prevention of diabetes depends largely on perspective and the point of intervention. Secondary and tertiary prevention efforts are geared toward the avoidance of complications as described above. Primary prevention efforts are currently being intensely investigated (e.g., Julius, Schatz, & Silverstein, 1999), including examining the possibility of administering insulin to people at risk for type 1 diabetes to prevent or delay onset of the disease. Other prevention efforts for type 1 diabetes are geared at screening and counseling at-risk individuals. Risk factors for the development of type 1 diabetes includes first-degree relatives of patients with type 1 diabetes and ethnicity.

Prevention efforts for type 2 diabetes are aimed at preventing obesity and reduction in weight for those who are obese. The risk of developing type 2 diabetes increases with age, obesity, and lack of physical activity. Other risk factors for developing type 2 diabetes include those individuals with a family history of diabetes and membership in certain racial or ethnic groups. The screen used to detect the development of diabetes is the fasting plasma glucose test.

The role of the behavioral health-care specialist rests with preventing type 2 diabetes. Efforts aimed at weight reduction, developing proper dietary habits, and increasing physical activity may all work to help prevent the onset of the disease. The health-care specialist may also choose to provide interventions aimed at the children of individuals with diabetes about the importance of maintaining a good diet and engaging in exercise either through parenting instruction or directly to children.

Summary

We have attempted in this chapter to outline the critical areas for a psychosocial intervention with patients with type 1 or 2 diabetes. As a biopsychosocial phenomenon, diabetes affects patients in numerous areas of their physical and psychological functioning. As such, health-care interventions must address these multiple domains. A multidisciplinary intervention is warranted in treating diabetes to develop better self-management skills. This intervention should address the areas of education about the disease, the development of coping skills and stress management, use and facilitation of social support, development of better dietary habits, and engagement in an effective and healthy exercise plan. With this multifaceted intervention, a systematic attempt is made to delay, prevent, or ameliorate many of the medical and psychological complications associated with type 1 and type 2 diabetes so that patients with this disease can live healthier and happier lives.

References

American Diabetes Association (ADA). (1994). Nutrition recommendations and principles for people with diabetes mellitus. *Diabetes Care, 17*, 519–522.

American Diabetes Association (ADA). (1996). Diabetes mellitus and exercise. *Diabetes Care, 19*(suppl. 31), S30–S36.

American Diabetes Association (ADA). (1998). Economic consequences of diabetes mellitus in the U.S. in 1997. *Diabetes Care, 21*, 296–336.

American Diabetes Association (ADA). (2000). Standard of medical care for patients with diabetes mellitus, clinical practice recommendations. *Diabetes Care, 23*(suppl.), 32–42. Retrieved February 1, 2001, from http://www.diabetes.org/clinicalrecommendations/CareSup1Jan01.htm.

Anderson, R. J., Lustman, P. J., Clouse, R. E., De Groot, M., & Freedland, K. E. (2001). The prevalence of comorbid depression in adults with diabetes: A meta-analysis. *Diabetes Care, 24*, 1069–1078.

Beck, A. T., & Steer, R. A. (1997). Beck Anxiety Inventory. In C. P. Zalaquett & R. J. Wood (Eds.), *Evaluating stress: A book of resources* (pp. 23–40). Lanham, MD: Scarecrow.

Beck, A. T., Steer, R. A., & Brown, G. K. (1996). The Beck Depression Inventory-2. San Antonio, CA: Harcourt-Brace.

Beck, A. T., Steer, R. A., & Garbin, M. G. (1988). Psychometric properties of the Beck Depression Inventory: Twenty-five years of evaluation. *Clinical Psychology Review, 8*, 77–100.

Beck, A. T., Ward, C. H., Mendelson, M., Mock, J., & Erbaugh, J. (1961). An inventory for measuring depression. *Archives of General Psychiatry, 4*, 53–63.

Boland, E. A., Ahern, J., & Grey, M. (1998). A primer on the use of insulin pumps in adolescents. *Diabetes Educator, 24*(1), 78–86.

Bradley, C. (1994). Diabetes Treatment Satisfaction Questionnaire (DTSQ). In C. Bradley (Ed.), *Handbook of psychology and diabetes: A guide to psychological measurement in diabetes research and practice* (pp. 111–132). Philadelphia: Harwood Academic Publishers/Gordon & Breach Science Publishers.

Brown, S. A. (1988). Effects of educational interventions in diabetes care: A meta-analysis of findings. *Nursing Research, 37*, 223–230.

Brown, S. A. (1992). A meta-analysis of diabetes patient education research: Variations in intervention effects across studies. *Research in Nursing and Health, 15*, 409–419.

Callaghan, G. M., & Gregg, J. A. (2001). *Acceptance/avoidance diabetes questionnaire.* San Jose, CA: San Jose State University.

Callaghan, G. M., & Ortega, E. (2001). *Take Charge! Diabetes treatment workbook: Psychosocial education for type 1 & type 2 diabetes.* San Jose, CA: San Jose State University.

Callaghan, G. M., Ortega, E., Uribe, E., & Berlin, K. (2001, May). *Integration of psychosocial interventions with type 1 and 2 diabetic patients.* Paper presented at the 81st annual meeting of the Western Psychological Association, Maui, HI.

Centers for Disease Control and Prevention (CDC). (1998). *National diabetes fact sheet: National estimates and general information on diabetes in the United States (rev. ed.).* Atlanta: U.S. Department of Health and Human Services, Centers for Disease Control and Prevention.

Centers for Disease Control and Prevention (CDC). (2002). *National diabetes fact sheet: General information and national estimates on diabetes in the United States, 2000.* Atlanta: U.S. Department of Health and Human Services, Centers for Disease Control and Prevention.

Clement, S. (1995). Diabetes self-management education. *Diabetes Care, 18*, 1204–1214.

Colberg, S. R. (2000). Practical management of type 1 diabetes during exercise. *Journal of Physical Education, Recreation and Dance, 71*, 24.

Coonrod, B. A., Betschart, J., & Harris, M. I. (1994). Frequency and determinants of diabetes patient education among adults in the U.S. population. *Diabetes Care, 17*, 852–858.

Cyr, J. J., McKenna-Foley, J. M., & Peacock, E. (1985). Factor structure of the SCL-90-R: Is there one? *Journal of Personality Assessment, 49*, 571–578.

DeRogatis, L. R. (1977). *SCL-90-R: Administration, scoring and procedures manual-II.* Towson, MD: Clinical Psychometric Research.

Dhanjal B., Callaghan, G. M., Rosito, O., Wang, T.-C., & Waddel, M. (2002, April). *Psychosocial interventions for type 2 diabetes in primary care.* Paper submitted at the 82nd annual meeting of the Western Psychological Association, Irvine, CA.

Diabetes Control and Complications Trial Research Group (DCCT). (1993). The effect of intensive treatment of diabetes and the development and progression of long-term complications in insulin-dependent diabetes mellitus. *New England Journal of Medicine, 397*, 977–986.

Ferguson, R. J. (2000). Using the Beck Anxiety Inventory in primary care. In M. E. Maruish (Ed.), *Handbook of psychological assessment in primary care settings* (pp. 509–535). Mahwah, NJ: Erlbaum.

Fitzgerald, J. T, Davis, W. K., Connell, C. M., Hess, G. E., Funnell, M. M., & Hiss, R. G. (1996). Development and validation of the diabetes care profile. *Evaluation Health Profession, 19*, 208–230.

Fitzgerald, J. T., Funnell, M. M., Hess, G. E., Barr, P. A., Anderson, R. M., Hiss, R. G. et al. (1998). The reliability and validity of a brief diabetes knowledge test. *Diabetes Care, 21*, 706–710.

Funnell, M. M. (1996). Integrated approaches to the management of NIDDM patients. *Diabetes Spectrum From Research to Practice, 9*, 55–59.

Goldstein, D. E., Little, R. R., Wiedmeyer, H. M., England, J. D., & McKenzie, E. M. (1986). Glycosylated hemoglobin: Methodologies and clinical applications. *Clinical Chemistry, 32*(suppl.), B64–B70.

Grey, M., Boland, E. A., Davidson, M., Li, J., & Tamborlane, W. V. (2000). Coping skills training for youth with diabetes mellitus has long-lasting effects on metabolic control and quality of life. *Journal of Pediatrics, 137*, 107–113.

Harris, M. A., & Lustman, P. J. (1998). The psychologist in diabetes care. *Clinical Diabetes, 26*(2), 91–93.

Harris, M. A., Wysocki, T., Sadler, M., Wilkinson, K., Harvey, L. M., Buckloh, L. M. et al. (2000). Validation of a structured interview for the assessment of diabetes self-management. *Diabetes Care, 23*, 1301–1304.

Hayes, S. C., Strosahl, K. D., & Wilson, K. G. (1999). *Acceptance and commitment therapy: An experiential approach to behavior change.* New York: Guilford.

Hess, G. E., & Davis, W. K. (1983). The validation of a diabetes patient knowledge test. *Diabetes Care, 6*, 591–596.

Ho, M., Marger, M., Beart, J., Yip, I., & Shekelle, P. (1997). Is the quality of diabetes care better in a diabetes clinic or in a general medicine clinic? *Diabetes Care, 20*, 472–475.

Howorka, K., Pumprla, J., Wagner-Nosiska, D., Grillmayr, H., Schlusche, C., & Schabmann, A. (2000). Empowering diabetes out-patients with structured education: Short-term and long-term effects of functional insulin treatment on perceived control over diabetes. *Journal of Psychosomatic Research, 48*, 37–44.

Jacobson, A. M. (1996). The psychological care of patients with insulin-dependent diabetes mellitus. *New England Journal of Medicine, 334*, 1249–1254.

Janes, G. (1995). Ambulatory medical care for diabetics. In M. Harris, C. Cowie, G. Reiber, E. Boyko, M. Stern, & P. Bennett (Eds.), *Diabetes in America* (NIH Publication # 95-1468; 2nd ed., pp. 541–552). Washington, DC: U.S. Government Printing Office.

Julius, M. C., Schatz, D. A., & Silverstein, J. H. (1999). The prevention of type I diabetes mellitus. *Pediatric Annals, 28*, 585–588.

Klonoff, D. C., & Schwartz, D. M. (2000). An economic analysis of interventions for diabetes. *Diabetes Care, 23*, 390–404.

Kramer, J. R., Ledolter, J., Manos, G. N., & Bayless, M. L. (2000). Stress and metabolic control in diabetes mellitus: Methodological issues and an illustrative analysis. *Annals of Behavioral Medicine, 22*, 17–28.

Litzelman, D. K., Slemenda, C. W., Langefeld, C. D., Hays, L. M., Welch, M. A., Bild, D. E. et al. (1993). Reduction of lower extremity clinical abnormalities in patients with non-insulin-dependent diabetes mellitus. A randomized, controlled trial. *Annals of Internal Medicine, 119*, 36–41.

Lustman, P. J., Anderson, R. J., Freedland, K. E., De Groot, M., Carney, R. M., & Clouse, R. E. (2000). Depression and poor glycemic control: A meta-analytic review of the literature. *Diabetes Care, 23*, 934–942.

Malone, J. M., Snyder, M., Anderson, G., Bernhard, V. M., Holloway, G. A., Jr., & Bunt, T. J. (1989). Prevention of amputation by diabetic education. *American Journal of Surgery, 158*, 520–524.

Neff, M. (1999). Depression increases health costs in patients who have diabetes. *American Family Physician, 60*, 2359.

Norris, S. L., Engelgau, M. M., & Narayan, K. M. (2001). Effectiveness of self management training in type 2 diabetes: A systematic review of randomized controlled trials. *Diabetes Care, 24*, 561–587.

Padgett, D., Mumford, E., Hynes, M., & Carter, R. (1988). Meta-analysis of the effects of educational and psychosocial interventions on management of diabetes mellitus. *Journal of Clinical Epidemiology, 41*, 1007–1030.

Prochaska, J. O., & DiClemente, C. C. (1982). Transtheoretical therapy: Toward a more integrative model of change. *Psychotherapy: Theory, Research, and Practice, 19*, 276–288.

Prochaska, J. O., & DiClemente, C. C. (1986). Toward a comprehensive model of change. In W. R. Miller & N. Heather (Eds.), *Treating addictive behaviors: Processes of change* (pp. 3–27). New York: Plenum.

Ruggiero, L., & Prochaska, J. O. (1993). Application of the transtheoretical model to diabetes management. *Diabetes Spectrum: From Research to Practice, 6*, 58–59.

Sarason, I. G., Sarason, B. R, & Shearin, E. N. (1986). Social support as an individual difference variable: Its stability, origins, and relational aspects. *Journal of Personality and Social Psychology, 50*, 845–855.

Sarason, I. G., Sarason, B. R., Shearin, E. N., & Pierce, G. R. (1987). A brief measure of social support: Practical and theoretical implications. *Journal of Social and Personal Relationships, 4*, 497–510.

Selby, J. V., Ray, T. R., Zhang, D., & Colby, C. J. (1997). Excess costs of medical care for patients with diabetes in a managed care population. *Diabetes Care, 20*, 1396–1406.

Simonson, D. C. (1988). Etiology and prevalence of hypertension in diabetic patients. *Diabetes Care, 11*, 821–827.

Stanten, M. (2000). Exercising with diabetes. *Prevention, 52,* 78.

Tucker, M. E. (1999). Screen all diabetics for depression. *Family Practice News, 29*, 11.

UK Prospective Diabetes Study Group (UKPDS 33). (1998). Intensive blood-glucose control with sulphonylureas or insulin compared with conventional treatment and risk of complications in patients with type 2 diabetes. *Lancet, 352,* 837–853.

Wallhagen, M. I. (1999). Social support in diabetes. *Diabetes Spectrum, 12,* 254.

Suggested Reading/Websites for Diabetes Patients

Suggested Reading

Becker, B. (2001). The first year: Type 2 diabetes: An essential guide for the newly diagnosed. Marlowe.

Bernstein, R. K. (2003). Dr. Bernstein's diabetes solution: The complete guide to achieving normal blood sugars (revised & updated). Little Brown.

Rubin, A. L. (1999). Diabetes for dummies. For Dummies Publishers.

Websites

American Diabetes Association: www.ada.org

World Diabetes Foundation: http://www.worlddiabetesfoundation.org/

CDC Diabetes home page: http://www.cdc.gov/diabetes/

National Institute of Diabetes and Digestive and Kidney Disease: http://www.niddk.nih.gov/health/diabetes/diabetes.htm

Chapter 18
Increasing Medication Adherence in Chronic Illnesses: Guidelines for Behavioral Health-Care Clinicians Working in Primary Care Settings

ERIC R. LEVENSKY

Across patient populations and medical settings, inadequate adherence to prescribed medications is a significant barrier to effective health-care delivery (Rogers & Bullman, 1995). Although advancements in medicine have yielded effective medications for many illnesses, the beneficial effects of these medications are often not realized because an estimated 50% of patients fail to sufficiently follow the prescribed regimens (Sackett & Snow, 1979). This lack of adherence to medications not only reduces the impact of potentially effective treatments, but also can incur substantial and unnecessary health and social costs (Cleemput, Kesteloot, & DeGeest, 2002). Adherence is a particular concern for patients with chronic illnesses because patients on long-term medication regimens generally have poorer adherence than those on shorter regimens, and medication adherence tends to worsen over time (Cramer, Scheyer, & Mattson, 1990; Haynes, Taylor, & Sackett, 1979).

Behavioral health-care clinicians are increasingly being integrated into primary care settings in an effort to better address psychosocial issues affecting patients' physical and mental health (see chapter 1 of this volume). The purpose of this chapter is to provide these clinicians with information and strategies they can use to facilitate patients' adherence to medication regimens. A large body of research on adherence to medical treatment regimens has shown that inadequate adherence to medications is often mediated by psychosocial factors and can be impacted by psychosocial interventions (see below). Therefore, the task of increasing medication adherence is well suited to the training and skills of behavioral health-care clinicians.

Specifically, this chapter will (a) discuss the nature and consequences of inadequate adherence to prescribed medications, (b) briefly review the current state of the literature on factors related to inadequate adherence, as well as strategies for increasing adherence, (c) discuss methods of assessing patient adherence to medications, and (d) propose and describe guidelines for a medication adherence intervention that can be integrated into primary care settings. Although the focus of this chapter is on working with patients who have been prescribed long-term medication regimens, much of this information has been found to apply to facilitating adherence to short-term and nonpharmaceutical regimens such as dietary and exercise regimens as well (see Dunbar-Jacob, Burke, & Puczynski, 1995; Meichenbaum & Turk, 1987; Shumaker, Schron, Ockene, & McBee, 1998).

The Nature of Adherence and Nonadherence

Although there is much variability in the definition of the term *adherence*, it generally refers to the extent to which patients follow the instructions they are given for prescribed treatments (Haynes, McDonald, Garg, & Montague, 2002, p. 2). In recent years, the term adherence has begun to be used in place of the more traditionally used term *compliance*. This shift in terminology has occurred because many researchers and clinicians believe that compliance suggests passivity and obedience on the part of patients, whereas adherence implies patient-provider collaboration and an active role of patients in their treatment (Rogers & Bullman, 1995).

Nonadherence to medications can take a number of forms. These can include the following:

- Not filling the medication prescription or not initiating the treatment.
- Taking too many or too few pills at each dose.
- Taking too many or too few doses.
- Taking medications at the incorrect times (e.g., taking doses too close together or too far apart).
- Not following special dosing instructions (e.g., food/beverage requirements).
- Terminating the treatment prematurely.

To the complexity of nonadherence, whether or not a patient is considered nonadherent to a specific medication can depend on how closely the regimen for that medication must be followed for the treatment to be effective. For example, researchers have found that, in order for highly active antiretroviral therapy (HAART) mediations to be effective in the treatment of HIV infection, patients are required to take at least 95% of the doses, and the medication is also quite sensitive to variations in the timing of doses (Andrews & Friedland, 2000; Barlett, 2002; Low-Beer, Yip, O'Shaughnessy, Hogg, & Montaner, 2000; Paterson et al., 2002). Therefore, the definition of adherence to HAART is often based on these criteria.

Health and Financial Consequences of Nonadherence

Poor adherence to medication treatments has been found to have a number of substantial health and financial consequences (Rogers & Bullman, 1995). Health consequences can include (a) no change in the illness or a worsening of the illness, (b) the development of collateral illnesses or problems (e.g., opportunistic infections, resistance to the treatment), (c) the provider's being unable to evaluate the effectiveness of the treatment and erroneously increasing the medication or discontinuing a potentially effective medication, and (d) death of the patient.

Financial consequences can include the cost of additional services and treatments needed to address consequences of poor adherence (e.g., additional doctor visits, medications, and tests; emergency room visits, hospitalizations, etc.), as well as decreases in the productivity of the patient. Poor adherence to prescribed medications is estimated to cost over $100 billion each year in the United States through increasing health-care utilization and decreasing patient productivity (Grahl, 1994; National Pharmaceutical Counsel, 1994).

Factors Related to Adherence and Nonadherence

Over the past several decades, a wide range of factors have been found to be associated with adherence and nonadherence to mediations. However, most of these factors account for a relatively small proportion of the variance in adherence and are not consistently related to adherence across studies (see Fincham, 1995; Meichenbaum & Turk, 1987; Morris & Schulz, 1992; for reviews). Table 18.1

TABLE 18.1 Factors Related to Poor Adherence to Medication in Chronic Illness Populations

Factors related to the patient:

- Lack of knowledge of regimen requirements (e.g., what to take, how much to take, when to take it, etc.)
- Cognitive deficits (e.g., forgetfulness)
- Lack of adherence-related skills (e.g., problem-solving, organizational, memory aid skills, etc.)
- Lack of resources (e.g., financial, housing, transportation, time, etc.)
- Substance abuse (i.e., alcohol abuse and illicit drug use)
- Language deficits/poor literacy
- Stressful life events (e.g., death of loved one, loss of job, ending of important relationship)
- Emotional health problems (especially depression and anxiety disorders)
- Problematic beliefs about:
  - Need for treatment/seriousness of the disease
  - Efficacy of the treatment
  - Importance of adherence
  - Relative costs and benefits of adhering to the treatment
  - Ability to adhere (i.e., self-efficacy)
- Inadequate social support (emotional, practical/instrumental support; help with medication taking; encouragement of adherence, etc.)
- Apathy about health/future
- Problematic past experiences with adherence (e.g., ability to adhere, costs and benefits, etc.)
- Lack of intent to adhere
- Fear of stigma of taking medication/having illness
- Problematic responses to slips in adherence
- Taking medication is an unwelcome reminder of illness

Factors related to the medication regimen:

- High complexity/demands of the regimen (e.g., number of pills, frequency/timing of dosing, food/water requirements, size of pills, storage requirements, etc.)
- Poor fit between regimen requirements and patient's lifestyle/daily activities (e.g., eating and sleeping patterns, work schedule, social life, other daily activities, etc.)
- Long duration of the treatment
- Frequent/severe side effects
- High cost of medication
- Poor portability of medication
- Inconvenient packaging of medication

Factors related to the patient-provider relationship:

- Poor communication between patient and provider
- Provider does not adequately assess problems with treatment/adherence
- Patient has difficulty bringing up problems with treatment/adherence
- Patient uncertain about provider's ability to help
- Patient lacks trust/comfort with provider
- Patient dissatisfied with provider

TABLE 18.1 (continued)

Factors related to the clinical setting:

- Poor accessibility of services (e.g., availability of staff, hours of operation, wait/lines for services, etc.)
- Lack of continuity/cohesiveness of care
- Concerns about confidentiality
- Lack of child care
- Unfriendly/unhelpful staff
- Poor reputation of clinic

Features of the disease:

- Disease not serious or threatening to health
- Long-term duration of disease
- Lack of symptoms experienced by patient
- Symptoms of disease interfere with adherence (e.g., cognitive deficits, lack of mobility, problems with vision, etc.)

Note. Factors taken from the following reviews of the literature on treatment adherence: Dunbar-Jacob & Mortimer-Stephens, 2001; Fincham, 1995; Ickovics & Meisler, 1997; Meichenbaum & Turk, 1987; Morris & Schulz, 1992; Myers & Midence, 1998; Shumaker, Schron, Ockene, & McBee, 1998; Vermeire, Hearnshaw, & Van Royen, 2001. Organization of these factors is based on model of adherence developed by Ickovics & Meisler, 1997.

summarizes factors that have at least some empirical support for their association to poor adherence to medications. Several themes appear to emerge from this literature. First, medication adherence appears to be complex and multidetermined. That is, many different types of factors can impact patients' adherence to medications, including factors related to the patient, disease, treatment, provider, and clinical setting. Second, patients appear to be quite heterogeneous in terms of if and how any of these factors will impact their adherence. For example, depression is a factor that has been found to have a strong association with rates of medical treatment adherence (DiMatteo, Lepper, & Croghan, 2000). However, this does not mean that every patient who is depressed will have poor adherence. Additionally, for patients experiencing depression that is affecting their adherence, this effect could be occurring for a number of reasons related to depression (e.g., sleeping through doses, apathy about life, fatigue, problems with memory, social isolation, etc.). Third, these factors do not provide a reliable means for predicting whether any one patient will adhere adequately to a regimen.

Putting these themes together suggests that conducting a thorough assessment of potential barriers and developing an individualized adherence plan with each patient is warranted. Despite the limitations of the barriers-to-adherence literature, it can serve to facilitate this process by orienting clinicians to potential barriers to patients' adherence, as well as to potentially effective interventions. The Prescriptive Adherence Counseling and Education (PACE; Levensky & O'Donohue, 2002) intervention described later in this chapter provides an example of how these factors can be used in this way.

Interventions for Increasing Medication Adherence

The effectiveness of interventions to increase medication adherence is also somewhat unclear. This is because a relatively small number of studies have been conducted examining these interventions (see Haynes et al., 2002 for a review of this literature). Additionally, interpreting the results of these studies is difficult because of methodological problems in many of the studies, including inaccurate measures of adherence, lack of control groups, confounding variables, small sample sizes, short follow-up periods, lack of detailed descriptions of the interventions, and differing definitions of adherence across studies (Haynes et al., 2002). Another problem that has made it difficult to draw conclusions from this literature is that methodologically sound studies of similar interventions have produced different outcomes (e.g., Haynes, Wang, & Da Mota Gomes, 1987).

Despite these limitations, however, the results of these studies have generally suggested that (a)no single strategy is clearly most effective, (b) multicomponent interventions are generally more effective than single-strategy interventions, (c) interventions that involve multiple sessions or follow-ups are more effective in sustaining adherence over time than one-time interventions, and (d) the impact of these interventions is generally modest, with effect sizes rarely exceeding 0.34 (Haynes et al., 1987, 2002; Haynes, McKibbon, & Kanani, 1996; Morris & Schulz, 1992; Roter et al., 1998). These findings are consistent with the notion that adherence involves a complex and multidetermined set of behaviors that are not easily changed.

Interventions found to be effective generally include educational, cognitive, and behavioral components. The primary strategies used in these effective interventions are summarized in Table 18.2. It should be noted that many of these strategies have been evaluated as part of multicomponent interventions and have not been examined as stand-alone interventions.

Measuring Adherence to Medications

An important component in facilitating mediation adherence is identifying when a patient is having trouble with adherence. There are a number of methods for accomplishing this. Each method has its relative strengths and weaknesses in terms of reliability, validity, utility, and practicality, and there is no gold standard for measuring adherence. Andrews and Friedland (2000), Dunbar (1984), Miller and Hays (2000), Rand and Weeks (1998), and Vitolins, Rand, Rapp, Ribisl, and Sevick (2000) provide useful reviews of the literature on methods of assessing medication adherence. The descriptions below are taken primarily from these reviews.

Self-Report

Self-report is the most commonly used method of assessing adherence in clinical practice because this method is relatively quick, easy, and inexpensive. Common methods of obtaining self-report data include questionnaires, medication diaries, and interviews. Although self-report is the most practical method of adherence assessment, the accuracy of this method is often reduced by patients' hesitancy to report missed doses and by limitations in patients' ability to recall missed doses (Rand & Weeks, 1998). Specifically, self-report tends to overestimate rates of adherence. When compared with more accurate methods of measuring adherence (e.g., Medication Events Monitoring System Caps, see below), self-report has generally been found to be a 20% overestimate of adherence (Andrews & Friedland, 2000).

Despite these limitations, however, self-report can be a valuable clinical tool, and it has been found to be a predictor of adherence and clinical outcomes (Rand & Weeks, 1998; Stone, 2001). In addition, an important advantage of the self-report method over some of the other methods (e.g., pill counts) is that it can provide information about the patterns and timing of pill taking as well as information about barriers to adherence. This can be particularly the case when patients keep daily medication diaries. Additionally, although self-report tends to produce overestimates of adherence, the method does tend to have good specificity for nonadherence. That is, if patients indicate they are nonadherent, this is likely to be the case (Vitolins et al., 2000). Methods that have been shown to increase the accuracy of patient self-report of adherence include (a) using brief, structured questionnaires, (b) asking patients to report on levels of nonadherence rather than on levels of adherence, (c) specifying a time frame, (d) assessing a recent time frame (e.g., no more than the

TABLE 18.2 Strategies for Increasing Adherence to Medication in Chronic Illness Populations

Assessing to readiness to begin treatment

- Assessing past adherence patterns and current health beliefs/concerns about the treatment
- Discussing pros and cons of initiating treatment
- Using a "practice trial" with jelly beans or other nonactive medication analogue
- Assessing for potential barriers to treatment and intervening on these
- Waiting to initiate treatment until the patient is ready

Increasing treatment-related knowledge:

- Educating patient on the:
  - nature of disease
  - action of the treatment
  - requirements of the treatment regimen
  - importance of adherence
  - nature and management of side effects
- Using simple, understandable language
- Using visual aids
- Assessing comprehension
- Providing all information in written form
- Having patient demonstrate proficiency

Increasing adherence skills:

- Providing regimen-related organizational and memory-aid tools/skills including:
  - special packaging (e.g., blister packaging)
  - pillboxes/medication organizers
  - alarms
  - cues for dosing (e.g., notes and stickers)
  - linking medication taking to daily activities such as morning/bedtime routines, meals, television shows, etc.
  - teaching self-monitoring (e.g., use of pill diary or calendar)
  - helping patient adjust daily routine to better fit regimen
- Teaching skills on how to respond to slips in adherence
- Teaching problem-solving skills
- Improving patient's communication with provider, including:
  - asking questions
  - reporting problems with treatment such as side effects, adherence, etc.
- Planning for medication-taking on a typical day, as well as nontypical days, such as weekends, vacations, nights out, etc.
- Role playing

Increasing resources and support:

- Referring to social services/social worker for assistance with accessing resources (e.g., financial, housing, transportation, childcare, etc.)
- Increasing social support, including:
  - support group/individual counseling
  - medication "buddy"
  - telephone "check-ins" from staff
  - help with medication taking from friends or family

TABLE 18.2 (continued)

Increasing motivation:

- Simplifying regimen as much as possible (few pills/dosing times, long acting medication, few food restrictions, convenient dosing times, etc.)
- Tailoring regimen to fit patient's lifestyle
- Working with patient to fit regimen into daily routine (e.g., setting up dosing schedule, food requirements to match routines)
- Having patient take an active role the treatment planning and decisions
- Reframing problematic health beliefs and beliefs about the treatment
- Getting firm commitment from patient regarding specific adherence behaviors
- Establishing reinforcement system for adherence (e.g., social, financial, other tangible reinforcements)
- Orienting patient to benefits of adherence and costs of nonadherence (e.g., on health, future goals, etc.)
- Providing feedback to patient regarding the impact of his or her adherence and nonadherence on clinical outcomes
- Enhancing patient's self-efficacy
- Treating mental health problems (e.g., depression, substance abuse)
- Treating side effects
- Minimizing barriers at clinic (long waits, scheduling problems, limited appointment times, etc.)
- Using Motivational Interviewing techniques with patient (Miller & Rollnick, 1996)

Follow-up:

- Implementing telephone reminders, check-ins regarding problems with treatment/adherence
- Scheduling regular follow-up visits with patient
- Directly assessing for barriers to adherence and problem solving methods of overcoming identified barriers on regular basis

---

Note. Strategies were taken from the following reviews of the literature on treatment adherence: Dunbar-Jacob & Mortimer-Stephens, 2001; Fincham, 1995; Haynes, McDonald, Garg, & Montague, 2002; Ickovics & Meisler, 1997; Meichenbaum & Turk, 1987; Mullen, Green, & Persinger, 1985; Myers & Midence, 1998; Roter et al., 1998; Shumaker, Schron, Ockene, & McBee, 1998; Vermeire, Hearnshaw, & Royen, 2001.

past 7 days of medication taking), (e) using cues to facilitate recall, (f) having patients keep a medication diary in which they record their daily medication taking, and (g) reassuring patients that problems with adherence are normal, they will not be punished for nonadherence, and that accurate reporting of adherence problems is crucial for effective treatment (Andrews & Friedland, 2000; Dunbar-Jacob et al., 1995; Rabkin & Chesney, 1999; Stone, 2001; Vitolins et al., 2000). Four brief yes-or-no questions that have been found to be good predictors of clinical outcomes are: (1) Do you ever forget to take your medicine?, (2) Are you careless at times about taking your medicine?, (3) When you feel better do you sometimes stop taking your medicine?, and (4) Sometimes if you feel worse when you take the medicine, do you stop taking it? A "yes" to any of these questions indicates a problem with adherence (Morisky, Green, & Lavine, 1986).

Pill Counts

Another fairly common method for assessing patient adherence to medications is pill counts. Doing pill counts involves determining how many pills a patient should have left, (given the number of days since the prescription was filled and the number of pills to be taken each day), counting all the patient's medications to determine how many pills the patient currently has, and then calculating the difference between how many pills the patient should have and the number of pills the patient actually has. A strength of this method is that it can be more objective than report in that it does not rely on a patient's memory of missed doses. For clinical use, this method is limited by the requirements of patients bringing in all of their medications and of clinical staff taking the time to count the pills. The accuracy of this method is limited by patients failing to bring in all of their pills (e.g., forgetting to bring in pills not kept in bottles, or intentionally leaving pills at home to appear adherent). Additionally, this method does not provide information about the patterns of adherence and nonadherence (e.g., timing of doses, when doses were missed, etc).

Assessing patients' pharmacy records (i.e., determining if refills were obtained on time) has also been used in research and clinical settings as an objective measure of adherence. This method has many of the same drawbacks as pill counts; however, it tends to be a less sensitive measure and can be difficult to use with patients who go to more than one pharmacy to fill prescriptions.

Medication Event Monitoring System (MEMS) Caps

MEMS caps are rarely used in clinical practice owing to their expense, but are frequently used in research because of the relatively high accuracy of the method (e.g., Liu et al., 2001). MEMS caps are electronic devices that serve as caps to patients' medication bottles. These caps log the date and time of every opening and closing of the medication bottles. This information can then be downloaded and examined by the clinician to assess rates and patterns of adherence and nonadherence. Strengths of this method are that it does not rely on patient report, and that it is more convenient for both the patient and the clinical staff than is the pill count method. Additionally, it provides information about the timing of medication taking. Disadvantages of the method are that the caps are rather expensive (between $80 and $100 per cap), and that it cannot be determined whether a patient actually took pills out of the bottle when it was opened, how much was taken out, or if the patient actually consumed the medication if it was taken out. An additional disadvantage of MEMS caps is that they are not compatible with patients using pillboxes or otherwise storing medications outside the capped bottles.

Biological Indicators

Biological markers are used in both clinical and research settings to assess patient adherence to medications. Typically, this involves taking blood or urine samples and assessing these for correlates of the presence of the medication, or for traces of the medication itself. Although this method is an objective measure of adherence, its accuracy can be affected by a number of factors such as recency of ingestion, individual differences in absorption, and the presence of biological elements other than the medication that can influence readings (Miller & Hays, 2000). Additionally, this method can be expensive and impractical, and such measures are not available for many medications.

Many researchers and clinicians advocate using a combination of these methods, although it is not yet clear how this can be done most effectively (Rand & Weeks, 1998). The use of self-report in combination with a more objective measure, such as pill counts or assessing pharmacy records, would likely be useful and feasible in many clinical settings.

Prescriptive Adherence Counseling and Education (PACE) Intervention

Levensky and O'Donohue (2002) have developed the Prescriptive Adherence Counseling and Education (PACE) intervention, an individualized assessment-based HIV medication adherence enhancement intervention. The PACE intervention has been found to produce modest, yet significant, improvement in rates of self-reported adherence to HIV medications at 2- and 12-week follow-ups as compared with treatment as usual, and was also found to have high patient satisfaction and follow-though with the adherence plans (Levensky et al., 2002).

The PACE intervention is described in detail here to serve as a set of guidelines that behavioral health-care clinicians working in primary care settings can use to facilitate patients' adherence to long-term medication regimens. Although this intervention was developed for and evaluated with HIV patients, it is hypothesized that the principles and strategies described here can be implemented successfully with other chronic illness populations. The PACE intervention has been evaluated using only a clinical pharmacist to deliver it; however, the intervention was designed to be effectively delivered by most health-care providers, including nurses, pharmacists, health-care educators, and behavioral health-care clinicians. Additionally, the intervention was designed to be delivered in a one-on-one counseling session, but could, at least theoretically, be delivered in a group format.

The PACE intervention is designed to (a) aid clinicians in identifying important, causal, and changeable barriers to individual HIV patient's medication adherence, (b) guide clinicians in developing and implementing effective tailored interventions for these identified barriers, (c) be trainable and usable for a broad range of HIV clinicians (e.g., doctors, pharmacists, nurses, social workers, health advocates, etc.), and (d) be acceptable, efficient, cost effective, and practical in a wide range of HIV and primary care treatment settings (e.g., specialty clinics, hospitals, community health centers, pharmacies, private offices, etc.). A primary assumption of the PACE intervention is that the ability to adhere is not a patient "trait," but rather adherence is a set of behaviors that can be facilitated by increasing information, skills, tools, and resources and by decreasing environmental barriers.

The content of the PACE intervention is based on a guiding model of adherence. This guiding model organizes the determinants of HIV medication adherence into four theoretical factors:

1. Adherence-related knowledge and skills (e.g., knowledge of specific requirements of the regimen and importance of adherence, organizational and memory-aid skills, assertiveness skills with treatment provider).
2. Resources and lifestyle (e.g., stability of housing, transportation, and finances; social support; match between medication regimen and daily routine; health status; depression; substance abuse).
3. Direct rewards and punishers of adherence (e.g., responses of social network and medical staff to adherence and nonadherence, side effects, reminder of illness, stigma, barriers at the clinic).
4. Beliefs about HIV and the treatment (e.g., one's beliefs about the need for treatment, effectiveness of treatment/provider, relative costs and benefits of adherence, one's ability to adhere).

The PACE intervention consists of four components: (1) the Barriers to HAART Adherence Questionnaire (BHAQ), (2) the intervention guidelines, (3) the adherence planning sheets, and (4) a manual for using these components. The intervention is relatively brief, taking about 40–50 minutes to complete (once the patient has completed the BHAQ). Each of the intervention components is described below.

Barriers to HARRT Adherence Questionnaire (BHAQ)

The BHAQ is a self-report questionnaire (using both written and Likert scale responses) that is designed to assess for current and potential barriers to individual HIV patient's adherence to HIV medications. The BHAQ consists of 46 items, which assess for 14 adherence "domains" related to the model of adherence described above. These barrier domains are:

1. Knowledge of prescribed HIV medication regimen.
2. Appropriateness and complexity of the prescribed medication regimen.
3. Adherence-related lifestyle, skills, and resources.
4. Responses to slips in adherence.
5. Social support.
6. Recreational drug use.
7. Alcohol abuse.
8. Depression.
9. Health and functional problems.
10. Missing doses to avoid adverse consequences.
11. Side effects from HIV medication.
12. Adherence barriers at the clinic.
13. Relationship with or beliefs about provider at clinic.
14. Beliefs about HIV and HIV medications.

Three additional items on the BHAQ assess current adherence to the medication, and ask patients to identify additional barriers to their adherence as well as facilitators of their adherence.

Patients complete this questionnaire before meeting with the adherence counselor. If a patient is not able to read, the clinician reads the questions and response choices to the patient and records his or her answers. The adherence counselor then examines the completed BHAQ for potential adherence barriers, which are easily identified by a quick scan of the patient's responses on the questionnaire's Likert scales. The BHAQ has not been psychometrically evaluated because it consists of a set of face-valid items intended to alert the clinician to potential adherence barriers, which he or she is then guided in further assessing.

Intervention Guidelines

The intervention guidelines are designed to guide adherence counselors in designing individualized plans for addressing the adherence barriers that have been identified on the BHAQ. The content of these guidelines is guided by the model of adherence described above, and they incorporate strategies and techniques shown to be effective in producing health behavior change or are components of effective health behavior change interventions (e.g., Meichenbaum & Turk, 1987; Safren et al., 2001; Shumaker et al., 1998). These include

1. Providing information regarding the nature of HIV/AIDS, HAART, the requirements of the regimen, and the importance of adherence.
2. Increasing adherence-related skills such as stimulus control strategies (i.e., use of cues for medication taking), self-monitoring, organization, fitting the regimen into the daily routine, communicating with providers, and anticipating, preventing, and dealing with slips in adherence. Also included is providing medication organizers, diaries, and reminder alarms as needed.

3. Increasing resources and support, such as practical and emotional social support (e.g., obtaining help with medication taking, going to support groups, increasing contact with exiting social network), and financial, housing, transportation, and food resources (through referrals to social services).

4. Increasing motivation (i.e., increasing reinforcement and reducing punishment), such as orienting patient to benefits of adherence and costs of nonadherence, providing feedback on the impact of the patient's adherence on his or her health status, increasing the patient's sense of adherence self-efficacy, increasing social reinforcement for adherence, treating medication side effects and other health problems, providing treatment for depression and substance abuse, addressing fears about the medication, and simplifying and tailoring the regimen to fit one's lifestyle.

The manual for delivering the intervention includes instructions for the clinician in the use of general counseling methods found to be effective in producing health behavior change. These counseling methods are used throughout the intervention: skills training (O'Donohue & Krasner, 1995), behavior modification (Epstein & Cluss, 1982), problem solving (D'Zurilla, 1986), Motivational Interviewing (Miller & Rollnick, 2002), increasing self-efficacy (Bandura, 1986), commitment strategies (Linehan, 1994), and behavioral contracting (Kirschenbaum & Flanery, 1983). Some of these same counseling techniques were employed in another HAART adherence intervention recently found to produce some promising results (Safren et al., 2001).

Additional important aspects of the manual are that it instructs the counselor in (a) assessing *if* and *how* an identified barrier actually functions to interfere with a patient's adherence to the medications, (b) developing plans both to reduce identified barriers to adherence and to improve adherence despite persistent barriers, and (c) working collaboratively with the patient in developing the adherence plans.

The intervention guidelines consist of 14 separate, one-to-three-page guidelines, each of which is specific to one of the adherence barrier domains assessed for in the BHAQ (i.e., knowledge of prescribed HIV medication regimen, adherence-related lifestyle, skills, resources, etc.). An intervention guideline for a specific barrier domain is followed when at least one of the items representing that domain has been sufficiently endorsed on the BHAQ. For each barrier domain, there are both "general guidelines" and "specific guidelines." The general guidelines are followed when any of the BHAQ items representing that domain have been endorsed. The specific guidelines are followed in addition to the general guidelines and are followed only when specific BHAQ items representing that domain have been endorsed.

Adherence Planning Sheets

The adherence planning sheets are intended as a record of the adherence plans that have been developed. There is one adherence planning sheet for each intervention guideline. After the adherence counselor and patient have agreed upon an adherence plan for a particular barrier domain, the patient is asked to record the plan on the appropriate adherence planning sheet. A completed adherence planning sheet describes all the important details of each adherence plan (e.g., how, what, were, when, why, etc.). Once all of the necessary BHAQ intervention guidelines have been followed, and all the necessary adherence planning sheets have been completed by the patient, the adherence counselor staples the adherence planning sheets into a booklet and gives this booklet to the patient to take home.

Specific PACE Assessment and Intervention Strategies

The following is a brief summary of the PACE assessment and interventions strategies for each of the adherence domains. The general counseling principles mentioned above are followed when implementing these strategies.

Knowledge of the Regimen

Assessment. Patients are asked to list the name of each medication they are prescribed and to indicate for each medication (a) the color and shape of the pills, (b) the number of pills taken at each dose, (c) the number of doses take each day, (d) the times of day does are to be taken, and (e) any special dosing instructions (e.g., with food or on an empty stomach). These questions were based on the AIDS Clinical Trials Group's (ACTG) medication adherence measure (Chesney et al., 2000). The patients' reports of their regimens are then compared with the prescribed regimen as indicated in the patient's chart.

Interventions. If there is a discrepancy between a patient's report of his or her regimen and the regimen documented in the chart, this discrepancy is pointed out to the patient, and the adherence counselor determines if the patient has made an error in documenting the regimen or is mistaken about the actual regimen requirements. If necessary, the adherence counselor consults with the patient's prescribing provider to get the patient back on the correct regimen. The patient is given written instructions for the correct regimen, including: (a) the names of the medications, (b) the color and shape of the pills, (c) the number of pills taken at each dose, (d) the number of doses taken each day, (e) the times of day doses are to be taken, and (f) any special dosing instructions (e.g., food and fluid restrictions).

Adherence to the Regimen

Assessment. Patients indicate how many doses of each prescribed medication they have missed on each day of the last week, and also rate on a 5-point Likert scale how frequently they have taken doses at the correct times and followed the special dosing instructions. The taking of partial doses is counted as missing a dose. Patients also make a more general rating of the frequency of missed doses in the past month. These questions were also based on the ACTG medication adherence measure (Chesney et al., 2000). The adherence counselor further assesses for patterns of nonadherence, including the times of day, particular days of the week, and specific types of situations, places, or people that precipitate problems with adherence. In this assessment, patients are asked to identify all the possible reasons they can think of for their missed doses. Patients are also often asked to identify a recent incident of a missed dose and to identify factors that contributed to this lapse in adherence. Commonly reported reasons for missed doses reported by patients include (a) simply forgetting, (b) sleeping through doses, (c) being away form home and not having the medication with them, (d) having a change in the daily routine, (e) being busy with other things, (f) feeling too sick or experiencing side effects, (g) feeling depressed, and (h) feeling good (Levensky et al., 2002). The extent to which nonadherence is intentional is also assessed.

Interventions. Adherence barriers identified by the patient here are noted and addressed by following one or more of the appropriate assessment and intervention guidelines described below.

Appropriateness of the Regimen

Assessment. The extent to which the prescribed medication regimen is the most appropriate possible for the patient is assessed. Specifically, the prescribed regimen is reviewed with three primary questions in mind.

- Is the prescribed medication the most effective treatment available for the patient?
- Is there an alternative, but equally effective, medication option that involves fewer pills at each dose, few doses, easier administration (e.g., easier to swallow), fewer food restrictions, or fewer (or less severe) side effects?
- Would it be possible to modify the dosing schedule of the currently prescribed medication to reduce its complexity and demands?

Interventions. If it appears that the medication regimen should be changed, simplified, or otherwise made less demanding, the clinician works with the patient and the prescriber to make these adjustments. The prescribing provider is consulted before a medication change is discussed with the patient.

Social Support

Assessment. The nature and quality of the patient's social support system is assessed, including the extent to which (a) important people in the patient's life know about his or her diagnosis and are supportive of the patient in taking the medication, (b) the patient has help with taking the medication (e.g., reminders, reinforcement, etc.), (c) the patient has people he or she can go to for general emotional and practical support, and (d) the patient is satisfied with these supports.

Interventions. The importance of social support in facilitating adherence to a long-term medication regimen is discussed with the patient. Depending on the identified needs of the patient, and the patient's willingness, interventions to increase social support include (a) encouraging and problem-solving with the patient to solicit support (e.g., emotional/practical support, help with taking medications, etc.) from existing friends and family members, and (b) increasing the patient's support network, including referring the patient to a support group or treatment advocate (an individual who regularly checks in with and supports the patient regarding adherence). An effort is made to identify at least one person (e.g., spouse, partner, friend, roommate, etc.) who can help with adherence. The patient may also be encouraged to tell appropriate individuals about his or her diagnosis so that the patient can get support around this issue.

Beliefs About the Disease and Treatment

Assessment. The patient's beliefs about his or her disease and about the prescribed medication are assessed in several domains based on the Health Beliefs Model (Janz & Becker, 1984). The belief domains assessed are (a) the likelihood of the disease worsening if left untreated, (b) the seriousness and threat of the disease to the patient's health, (c) the patient's ability to adhere to the medications, (d) the effectiveness of medication in treating the disease, (e) the relative costs and benefits of taking the medications, and (f) the necessity of taking the medication as prescribed for the treatment to be effective. If the patient indicates problematic beliefs in any of these domains, the specific nature of these beliefs is further assessed.

Interventions. Interventions for problematic beliefs include providing information about the progression of the disease if untreated and the importance of adherence to the medication. Additional interventions include orienting the patient to the benefits of adhering by helping the patient identify his or her long-term goals and values and relating these to adherence. If other adherence barriers are identified during the assessment of the patient's beliefs (e.g., lack of skill, depression, inadequate social support, side effects, etc.) the intervention guidelines for these other barriers are followed. The patient may also be referred to an HIV support group or medication "buddy" so that adherence-promoting beliefs can be reinforced.

Adherence-Related Lifestyle, Resources, and Skills/Tools

Assessment. Three domains are assessed to determine the extent to which they interfere with adherence: (1) the fit between the patient's lifestyle (e.g., eating and sleeping patterns, work schedule, activities, etc.) and the requirements of the regimen, (2) the patient's practical resources for day-to-day living, and obtaining and adhering to the medication (e.g., money, food, housing, transportation, medication storage, etc.), and (3) the effectiveness of the patient's medication organizational or memory-aid system (e.g., patient's ability to remember to take doses on time both on typical days and on nontypical days such as weekends, nights out, and vacations). The extent to which these factors impact adherence is often assessed by having the patient describe a typical day of adherence and a typical day of nonadherence and by discussing the specific types of circumstances in which doses have been missed. Additionally, the effectiveness of the patient's medication organizational or memory-aid system is evaluated by assessing the extent that doses are missed because of forgetting to take the dose, forgetting whether doses have been taken, being away from home and not having the medication available, running out of medication, sleeping through doses, being too busy, and having changes in daily routines. Also, the extent to which these factors affect the patient's taking medications at the correct times and following the food and liquid requirements is assessed.

Interventions. If a poor fit between the patient's daily routines and the requirements of the regimen appear to be affecting adherence, several interventions are considered. These include (a) discussing the usefulness and feasibility of maintaining regular bedtimes, wake-up times, and meal times so that these activities can serve to cue dosing and aid the patient in following dietary requirements for dosing, (b) problem solving with the patient on steps he or she can take to make these activities more regular, (c) problem solving with the patient on how to best adhere within the context of a variable schedule of activities, and (d) considering making modifications in the medication regimen or switching regimens to better fit the patient's lifestyle (e.g., switch to a different type of medication or to a longer-acting version of the same medication to reduce number of doses). Making medication changes is always discussed with the patient's prescribing provider. It is worth noting that in some cases, it may be more effective to have the patient take a less optimal medication that he or she will be more likely to actually take correctly than a more optimal medication to which the patient will not adhere.

If the patient indicates that a lack of specific practical recourses is impeding adherence, interventions include problem solving on how the patient can obtain these recourses or can adhere without them. The patient may be referred to a social worker for assistance in obtaining needed resources. Additionally, making a change in the medication regimen may be considered (e.g., medications that are less expensive, do not have food requirements, and do not need to be refrigerated).

If a lack of memory or organizational skills or tools is identified, these tools and skills are provided to the patient, including pillboxes, alarms, stickers and notes, self-monitoring sheets or diaries, and strategies for linking doses to daily activities. The provision of these skill and tools is frequently included in the PACE intervention and is, therefore, described in some detail here.

A pillbox can be a very useful tool to enhance patient adherence, and pharmaceutical companies usually will provide them for no charge. These medication organizers are typically designed to hold doses for an entire week, with separate compartments for morning, afternoon, and evening doses, and allow patients to remove each daily compartment so that it can be carried with them. These organizers not only facilitate patients' taking the correct medications at each dose, but also can remind patients whether or not doses have been taken. If a pillbox organizer is provided to a patient, the patient is instructed in how to fill and use it, and is asked to demonstrate this to the clinician. Additionally, a plan is made to fill the pillbox on a specific day each week. For medications that need to be refrigerated or kept in their original containers, small items such as candies serve as placeholders in the pillbox. Some long-term medications have begun to be available in blister packs, which preorganize doses for each day, and can serve similar functions as a pillbox.

Also commonly available at no cost from pharmaceutical companies are alarms that can be programmed to prompt patients to take medication doses at the appropriate times throughout the day. These alarms come in wristwatch and pocket formats and can serve to both remind patients to take doses and confirm whether or not doses have been taken. Not all patients are willing to use these alarms, or for that matter would benefit from them; however, all patients are informed that they are available and oriented to the usefulness of these devises. Patients may also have digital watches that can be used for this purpose, and prefer to use those. As with pillbox organizers, patients who are provided dosing alarms are instructed in their use and are asked to demonstrate proficiency.

Other useful memory-aid tools are stickers (e.g., colored dots) and notes to cue dosing (e.g., Safran et al., 2001). These cues are placed in locations where they are most likely to be seen at dosing times, such as on the bathroom mirror, coffee machine, television, alarm clock, the refrigerator, or the desk or computer at work. Stickers or notes can also be placed next to the front door and in the car to remind patients not to forget to bring needed medications when leaving home. Keeping the medications in locations where they will be readily seen can also serve as a cue for dosing.

Another strategy that can be used to aid patients in reducing missed doses is self-monitoring (Southam & Dunbar, 1986). This procedure often involves having patients record the time doses have been taken each day, as well as the number of pills that were taken at each dose, whether or not special dosing instructions were followed, and reasons for missed doses. Common methods for self-monitoring include the patient's keeping a medication diary or recording medication doses on a calendar. This can be made relatively easy by teaching the patient to use basic symbols (e.g., a checkmark or an X) in the diary or calendar to indicate whether doses have been taken. In addition to the possible benefits of reminding patients if doses have been taken, this type of self-monitoring can have the additional benefit of providing information to the clinician on the patterns of the patient's medication taking, as well as times of day and situations in which adherence problems occur. This information can be used by the clinician to problem solve with the patient on ways to increase adherence.

It can also be useful to teach patients to link taking medication to regular daily activities. This involves identifying activities that the patient engages in at regular times each day that correspond to dosing times, and using these activities as cues to take medication doses. Common examples of such activities include getting out of bed in the morning or getting in bed at night, regular meals, television shows, and toothbrushing or other regular hygienic activities. Patients are often asked to take their medications before doing these activities so that they will be less likely to forget to take the medication and may be rewarded for taking it.

Once the above adherence tools and skills have been discussed and the patient has decided which ones he or she will use, a specific and detailed plan for taking medication on typical days is developed. This involves identifying the components of the patient's typical day (waking up, getting showered and dressed, eating breakfast, going to work, coming home, etc.), and putting together the agreed-upon adherence skills and tools into a comprehensive and concrete plan for taking the medications throughout the day. Potential barriers to adherence on these typical days are identified and solutions for overcoming them are developed. Adherence plans for nontypical days (e.g., weekends, vacations, trips, parties, etc.) are also developed (see Safren, Otto, and Worth, 1999, for examples of these strategies). Plans are also made for when and how medication refills will be obtained. Key elements of these plans focus on how the patient will be reminded to take doses at correct times and how the patient will have access to the correct medications at those times. As with other adherence plans, these plans are provided the patient in writing.

Communication With and Beliefs About Prescribing Provider

Assessment. Areas assessed to identify possible problems with the patient-provider relationship include the extent to which the patient (a) believes the provider has the ability to help him or her, (b) trusts the provider, (c) can communicate with the provider (e.g., bring up problems with side effects, adherence, etc.), (d) feels understood by the provider, (e) believes the provider cares about him or her, (f) feels that he or she gets enough time during a visit with the provider, and (g) is satisfied with the treatment he or she is receiving from the provider.

Interventions. If identified problems with the patient-provider relationship appear to be interfering with adherence (e.g., decreasing the patient's motivation to adhere, preventing the patient from asking questions or bringing up problems), the interventions carried out include (a) discussing with the patient the importance of the patient-provider relationship (e.g., trusting the provider, getting questions answered, bringing up problems, etc.), and (b) providing the patient with basic skills for communicating effectively with his or her prescribing provider. These latter skills include (a) bringing a list of questions to appointments and asking them directly, and (b) informing the provider about side effects, difficulties with adherence, or other problems with the treatment. Role-playing with the patient is often used to teach these skills. Some patients feel uncomfortable with being assertive with their provider. This discomfort is assessed for and addressed. One solution to this is to have the patient bring an advocate (spouse, friend, family member) to the medical appointment to offer support in giving information to, and obtaining information from, the provider. In cases where patients feel quite dissatisfied or uncomfortable with their provider, consultation with the provider or switching to a new provider is implemented.

Adherence Barriers at the Clinic

Assessment. Current and potential barriers to the patient's adherence existing at the clinic are assessed. These may include difficulty in getting appointments at convenient times or when they are needed, long waits, concerns about confidentiality, difficulty obtaining refills, poor reputation of the clinic, and unfriendly or unhelpful staff.

Interventions. Interventions include problem solving with the patient on how to be assertive with staff to get needs met (using role playing as appropriate) and getting needs met despite these barriers. Additionally, consultation with staff to reduce these barriers is done as appropriate.

Missing Doses to Avoid Unpleasant Consequences

Assessment. Several types of potentially aversive consequences for taking medications, as well as the extent to which these consequences are interfering with adherence, is assessed. The consequences assessed are both actual consequences for taking the medication, as well as those that are anticipated by the patient. These include: (a) side effects of the medications, (b) difficult administration (e.g., hard to swallow, bad taste of medication, etc.), (c) not wanting others to notice the patient taking the medication (i.e., wanting to avoid stigma, or others knowing about the patient's illness), (d) worries that the medication will be harmful to the patient, (e) not wanting the medication to interfere with activities (e.g., drinking alcohol, eating certain foods, etc.), and (f) not wanting to be reminded of the illness. Additionally, the extent to which symptoms of the patient's current health or physical problems (e.g., fatigue, decreased mobility, etc.) make it difficult to take the medications as prescribed is assessed, as well as whether patients miss doses because they are "feeling good."

Interventions. Interventions involve problem-solving with the patient to reduce the identified aversive consequences of adherence. Common solutions include (a) working with the patient's provider to treat side effects, (b) helping the patient think about untreatable side effects as "signs that the treatment is working," (c) reframing thoughts of medications as a reminder that the patient is ill to a reminder that the patient is treating the illness, (d) teaching the patient how to take his or her medications more discretely when in public, (e) helping the patient prepare answers to unwanted questions from others about the purpose of the medications, (f) educating the patient on the consequences of missing doses, and (g) considering a change of medication to make administration easier or to reduce side effects. The clinician also works on helping the patient orient to the value of taking the medication, despite the aversive consequences, by having the patient discuss and orient to his or her long-term goals and values (e.g., health, family, friends, etc.). These interventions typically involve both reducing the aversive consequence of adherence, as well as helping the patient adhere with the unpleasant consequence in place. For identified, anticipated, aversive consequences that have not actually occurred (e.g., side effects), information on the likelihood of these consequences as well as the management of them is provided.

Reponses to Slips in Adherence

Assessment. Even for the best-intentioned patients with the greatest resources and skills, at least occasional missed doses are inevitable with long-term medication regimens. When patients do miss a dose, they can sometimes have a reduction in self-efficacy, believe they have "blown it," and stop trying to adhere to the medication. This phenomenon has been referred to as the *abstinence violation effect* (AVE; Marlatt & George, 1998). Patients are asked about this directly.

Interventions. Intervention strategies include discussing with the patient that (a) slips in adherence are normal, (b) the important thing is to learn from the slip and return to following the regimen, and (c) if necessary, the patient should inform his or her provider about the slip so that the patient can receive help with getting back on the regimen.

Depression

Assessment. To assess for depression, a 5-item questionnaire developed by Burns (1997) is used. This measure is highly correlated with the longer Beck Depression Inventory (Beck, Ward, Mendelsohn, Mock, & Ergaugh, 1961). The five items assess for feeling "sad or blue," "discouraged or hopeless," a "low self-esteem," "worthless or inadequate," and a "loss of pleasure." If depression has been identified, specific symptoms of depression that are interfering with adherence are assessed (e.g., loss of appetite, fatigue, sleeping through doses, apathy about life, loss of motivation to take medications, etc.).

Interventions. As with other interventions, both reducing depression and increasing the patient's adherence while depressed are targeted. Interventions include (a) working with the patient to increase his or her social support and other pleasant activities (i.e., behavioral activation), and (b) referring the patient for pharmaceutical treatment, a support group, or individual or group counseling.

Substance Abuse

Assessment. The frequency and quantity of alcohol and recreational drug use are assessed. The use of recreational drugs is assessed by each drug type (marijuana, cocaine, opiates, and amphetamines). The extent to which substance abuse is implicated in missed doses is assessed (e.g., forgetting, apathy, concerns about adverse interactions, etc.).

Interventions. The issue of alcohol and recreational drug use can be sensitive. The patient is told that the goal of the discussion about substance use is only to provide the patient information about the possible effects of substance use on adherence and the effectiveness of the treatment (e.g., more likely to miss doses, drug interactions, etc.). The patient is provided this information in a nonconfrontational way, so that the patient feels free to make a choice based on the information provided. If the patient indicates that he or she would like help with reducing substance use, he or she is referred to individual or group therapy. If the patient indicates that he or she wishes to continue substance use, the clinician problem-solves with the patient about how he or she can adhere while using these substances (provided that it is safe to do so). These can include taking mediations before drug or alcohol use (to prevent forgetting), and eating and drinking fluids soon after drug or alcohol use.

Follow-Up and Maintenance

Although a follow-up component was not included in the preliminary evaluation of the PACE intervention, such a component has been developed and will be evaluated in a study soon to be under way. The follow-up component involves having the patient meet with the adherence counselor 1 to 2 weeks after the initial visit, and then again after that as needed. Elements of these follow-ups are (a) assessment of adherence, (b) assessment of effectiveness of adherence plan, (c) reassessment of barriers to adherence, (d) reinforcing, modifying, and augmenting adherence plan as needed, (e) reinforcement of adherence, and (f) linking adherence to health outcomes.

Integrating an Adherence Intervention Into Primary Care

The process of integrating behavioral health-care interventions into primary care settings is discussed in detail in chapter 1 of this volume. However, several recommendations to facilitate the integration of a medication-adherence intervention into this setting are listed below. It is recommended that the behavioral health-care clinician

- Become educated on disease processes, medication treatments, and medication side effects and their management.
- Keep primary care providers and other relevant staff informed about the intervention and how to refer patients to it. Specifically, these providers should be informed about the

nature of the intervention, how to identify appropriate patients, and how to present the intervention to patients. This can be done by presenting in-services, distributing flyers, and checking-in with providers.

- Encourage primary care physicians and other relevant staff (nurses, pharmacists, health advocates, etc.) to regularly assess patients' adherence to medication regimens.
- Encourage primary care providers to present the intervention to patients as a standard part of chronic illness management, rather than a service for "problem patients."
- Regularly check with primary care providers about any patients who may be appropriate for the intervention.
- Collect outcome data that primary care physicians can appreciate and provide it to them. These data include the impact of the intervention on adherence rates, clinical outcomes, service utilization, and patient satisfaction. Also assess primary care providers' satisfaction with the intervention. Use these data to improve the intervention.
- Keep the primary care physicians and other relevant staff informed about (a) the nature of the patient's adherence problems, (b) the specific barriers to adherence for the patient, and (c) the adherence plans developed with patients and the outcomes of these plans.

References

Andrews, L., & Friedland, G. (2000). Progress in HIV therapeutics and the challenges of adherence to antiretroviral therapy. *Infectious Disease Clinics of North America, 14*(4), 901–928.

Bandura, A. (1986). Social foundations of thoughts and action: A social cognitive theory. Englewood Cliffs, NJ: Prentice-Hall.

Beck, A. T., Ward, C. H., Mendelsohn, M., Mock, J., & Erbaugh, J. (1961). An inventory for measuring depression. *Archives of General Psychiatry, 4*, 561–571.

Burns, D. D. (1997). *Therapist's toolkit, 1997 upgrade.* Los Altos, CA: Author.

Chesney, M., Ickovics, J., Chambers, D., Gifford, A., Neidig, J., Zwickl, B. et al. (2000). Self-reported adherence to antiretroviral medications among participants in HIV clinical trials: The AACTG adherence instruments. *Aids Care, 12*(3), 255–266.

Cleemput, I., Kesteloot, K., & DeGeest, S. (2002). A review of the literature on the economics of noncompliance. Room for methodological improvement. *Health Policy, 59*, 65–94.

Cramer, M., Scheyer, R., & Mattson, R. (1990). Compliance declines between clinic visits. *Archives of Internal Medicine, 150*(7), 1509–1510.

DiMatteo, M. R., Lepper, H. S., & Croghan, T. W. (2000). Depression is a risk factor for noncompliance in medical treatment. *Archives of Internal Medicine, 14*, 2101–2107.

Dunbar, J. (1984). Adherence measures and their utility. *Controlled Clinical Trials, 5*, 515–521.

Dunbar-Jacob, J., Burke, L. E., & Puczynski, S. (1995). Clinical assessment and management of adherence to medical regimens. In P. M. Nicassio & T. W. Smith (Eds.), *Managing chronic illness: A biopsychosocial perspective* (pp. 313–349). Washington, DC: American Psychological Association.

Dunbar-Jacob, J., & Mortimer-Stephens, M. (2001). Treatment adherence in chronic disease. *Journal of Clinical Epidemiology, 54*, S57–S60.

D'Zurilla, T. (1986). *Problem solving therapy: A social competence approach to clinical interventions.* New York: Springer.

Epstein, L., & Cluss, P. (1982). A behavioral medicine perspective on adherence to long-term medical regimens. *Journal of Consulting and Clinical Psychology, 50*, 960–971.

Fincham, J. (Ed.) (1995). *Advancing prescription medicine compliance: New paradigms, new practices.* Binghamton, NY: Pharmaceutical Products Press.

Grahl, C. (1994). Improving compliance: Solving a $100 billion problem. *Managed Health Care*, S11–S13.

Haynes, B., McDonald, H., Garg, A. X., & Montague, P. (2002). Interventions for helping patients to follow prescriptions for medications (Chocrane Review). In *The Chocrane Library, Issue 4*. Oxford: Update Software.

Haynes, B., McKibbon, K., & Kanani, R. (1996). Systematic review of randomized trials of interventions to assist patients to follow prescriptions for medications. *Lancet, 348*, 383–386.

Haynes, B., Taylor, D., & Sackett, D. (1979). *Compliance in health care.* Baltimore: Johns Hopkins University Press.

Haynes, B., Wang, E., & Da Mota Gomes, M. (1987). A critical review of interventions to improve compliance with prescribed medications. *Patient Education and Counseling, 10*, 155–166.

Ickovics, J. R., & Meisler, A. (1997). Adherence in AIDS clinical trials: A framework clinical research and clinical care. *Journal of Clinical Epidemiology, 50*, 385–391.

Janz, N., & Becker, M. (1984). The health belief model: A decade later. *Health Education Quarterly, 11*, 1–47.

Kirschenbaum, D. S., & Flanery, R. C. (1983). Behavioral contracting: Outcomes and elements. In M. Hersen, R. M. Eisler, & P. M. Miller (Eds.), *Progress in behavior modification* (vol. 15). New York: Academic Press.

Levensky, E., & O'Donohue, W. (2002). *The Prescriptive Adherence Counseling and Education (PACE) intervention for increasing adherence to HIV medications.* Unpublished manuscript, University of Nevada, Reno.

Levensky, E., O'Donohue, W., Scott, J., Weisberg, M., Bolan, R., & Knox, L. (2002, December). *Increasing adherence to HAART with a brief assessment-based intervention: A preliminary evaluation.* Poster presented at Elements of Success, an International Conference on Adherence to Antiretroviaral Therapy, Dallas.

Linehan, M. (1994). *Cognitive behavioral therapy for borderline personality disorder.* New York: Guilford.

Liu, H., Golin, C. E., Miller, L. G., Hays, R. D., Beck, C. K., Sanandaji, S. et al. (2001). A comparison study of multiple measures of adherence to HIV protease inhibitors. *Annals of Internal Medicine, 134*, 968–977.

Low-Beer, S., Yip, B., O'Shaughnessy, M. V., Hogg, R. S., & Montaner, J. S. (2000). Adherence to triple therapy and viral load response. *Journal of Acquired Immune Deficiency Syndrome, 23*, 360–361.

Marlatt, G., & George, W. (1998). Relapse prevention and the maintenance of optimal health. In S. Shumaker, E. Schron, J. Ockene, & W. McBee (Eds.), *The handbook of health behavior change* (pp. 33–58). New York: Springer.

Meichenbaum, D., & Turk, D. (1987). *Facilitating treatment adherence: A practitioner's guidebook.* New York: Plenum.

Miller, W. R., & Rollnick, S. (2002). *Motivational interviewing: Preparing people for change.* (2nd ed.) (pp. xx, 428). New York: Guilford.

Miller, L. G., & Hays, R. D. (2000). Measuring adherence to antiretroviral medications in clinical trials. *HIV Clinical Trials, 1*(1), 36–46.

Morisky, D. E., Green, L. W., & Lavine, D. M. (1986). Concurrent and predictive validity of a self-report measure of medication adherence. *Medical Care, 24*, 67–74.

Morris, L., & Schulz, R. (1992). Patient compliance—An overview. *Journal of Clinical Pharmacy and Therapeutics, 17*, 283–295.

Mullen, P., Green, L., & Persinger, G. (1985). Clinical trials of patient education for chronic conditions: A comparative meta-analysis of intervention types. *Preventative Medicine, 14*, 753–781.

Myers, L., & Midence, K. (Eds.) (1998). *Adherence to treatment in medical conditions.* Amsterdam: Harwood Academic Publishers.

National Pharmaceutical Counsel. (1994). *Noncompliance with medications: An economic tragedy with important implication for health care reform.* Reston, VA: Author.

O'Donohue, W., & Krasner, L. (1995). *Handbook of psychological skills training: Clinical techniques and applications.* (pp. xvi, 432). Needham Heights, MA: Allyn & Bacon.

Paterson, D. L., Swindells, S., Mohr, J., Brester, M., Vergis, E. N., Sauier, C., Wagener, M. M., & Singh, N. (2002). Adherence to protease inhibitor therapy and outcomes in patients with HIV infection. *Annals of Internal Medicine, 133*(1), 21–30.

Rabkin, J. G., & Chesney, M. (1999). Treatment adherence to HIV medications, the Achilles heal of new therapeutics. In D. G., Ostrow & S. C. Kalichman (Eds,), *Psychosocial and public health impacts of new HIV therapies. AIDS prevention and mental health* (pp. 61–82). New York: Kluwer Academic/Plenum.

Rand, C. S., & Weeks, K. (1998). Measuring adherence with medication regimens in clinical care and research. In S. Shumaker, E. Schron, J., Ockene, & W. McBee (Eds.), *The handbook of health behavior change* (pp. 114–132). New York: Springer.

Rogers, H., & Bullman, W. (1995). Prescription medication compliance. A review of the baseline knowledge-A report of the National Council of Patient Information and Education. *Journal of Pharmacoepidemiology, 3*(2), 3–36.

Roter, D., Hall, J., Merisca, R., Nordstrom, B., Cretin, D., & Svarstad, B. (1998). Effectiveness of interventions to improve patient compliance: A meta-analysis. *Medial Care, 36*(8), 1138–1161.

Sackett, D., & Snow, J. (1979). The magnitude of compliance and non-compliance. In R. B. Haynes, D. W. Taylor, & D. L. Sackett (Eds.), *Compliance in healthcare* (pp. 11–22). Baltimore: Johns Hopkins University Press.

Safren, S., Otto, M., & Worth, J. (1999). Life-steps: Applying cognitive behavior therapy to HIV medication adherence. *Cognitive and Behavioral Practice, 6*, 332–341.

Safren, S., Otto, M., Worth, J., Salomon, E., Johnson, W., Mayer, K. et al. (2001). Two strategies to increase adherence to HIV medications: Life-Steps and medication monitoring. *Behavior Research and Therapy, 39*, 1151–1162.

Shumaker, S., Schron, E., Ockene, J., & McBee, W. (Eds.) (1998). *The handbook of health behavior change.* New York: Springer.

Southam, M., & Dunbar, J. (1986). Facilitating patient compliance with medical interventions. In K. Holroyd & T. Creer (Eds.), *Self-management of chronic disease* (pp.). New York: Academic Press.

Stone, V. E. (2001). Strategies for optimizing adherence for highly active antiretroviral therapy: Lessons from research and clinical practice. *Clinical Infectious Diseases, 33*, 865–872.

Vermerie, E., Hearnshaw, H., & Van Royen, P. (2001). Patient adherence to treatment: Three decades of research. A comprehensive review. *Journal of Clinical Pharmacy and Therapeutics, 26*, 331–342.

Vitolins, M. Z., Rand, C. S., Rapp, S. R., Ribisl, P. M., & Sevick, M. A. (2000). Measuring adherence to behavioral and medical interventions. *Controlled Clinical Trials, 21*, 188S–194S.

Chapter 19
The Integrated Management of Adult Asthma

MICHELLE R. BYRD, KYLE E. FERGUSON, DEBORAH A. HENDERSON, ERIN M. OKSOL, AND WILLIAM T. O'DONOHUE

Of the aspects of heath most often taken for granted, the ability to breathe is primary. However, for persons who suffer from chronic respiratory diseases, breathlessness is a terrifying and life-threatening reality. This chapter will address the most common respiratory ailment throughout one's lifespan—asthma.

Asthma can be conceptualized as a chronic inflammation of the bronchial tubes sometimes accompanied by respiratory distress. As yet, there is no clearly understood etiology of the disease. Individuals suffering from asthma intermittently experience such symptoms as wheezing, coughing, and difficulty catching their breath, with varying degrees of severity (NAEPP, 1997). Asthma is defined as a chronic disease, meaning that there is no cure, only long-term management of the disease. The primary target of asthma management is to avoid asthma exacerbations or attacks. Poorly managed asthma may have serious consequences, including permanent disability and death.

Asthma is one of the most prevalent chronic illnesses, affecting approximately 14–17 million people in the United States (CDC, 2004). Although science has made great advances in understanding and treating asthma, we are not yet able to prevent the onset or effectively control the course of the disease. In fact, the number of people affected by asthma is climbing; the national asthma prevalence rates have risen 75% since 1980 (CDC, 2004). Asthma is now diagnosed more often than any other illness in primary care visits, about 10 million times per year, and is the most frequently diagnosed illness upon hospital admission (CDC, 2004). Furthermore, in addition to rising prevalence rates, various markers of poorly managed asthma also appear to be rising, including hospitalization rate, morbidity, and mortality (Yoos & McCullen, 1996).

The personal and societal impact of asthma is staggering. Asthma attacks result in excess of 5,000 deaths, 468,000 hospital admissions (with an average length of stay of 5 days), and 3 million lost work days annually (CDC, 2004). Almost half of asthma sufferers report that the disease restricts their ability to participate in daily physical activities, such as walking up stairs or playing with their children (Collins, 1997).

A discussion of incidence and prevalence rates of asthma would not be complete without considering the cultural context in which the disease occurs and is managed. In approximately one decade, the overall death rate attributed to asthma rose 62%, with a greater increase among minority populations and low socioeconomic inner-city populations (CDC, 2004; Dinkevitch, Cunningham, & Crain, 1998). Specifically, African Americans have been found to have significantly higher rates of asthma diagnosis, more asthma-related hospitalizations, and asthma-linked morbidity when compared with nonminority samples (Blixen, Tilley, Haustad, & Zoratti, 1997). Gender must also be considered in the diagnosis and management of asthma. Males, regardless of ethnicity, were approximately 1.5 times more likely to die from asthma than females (CDC, 2004).

Not surprising, given the overall rates of utilization and disability, asthma costs more in health-care dollars than any other medical condition, including hypertension and cancer (Dyer, 1999). The direct cost of treating asthma is estimated to be $6.2 billion yearly, with the majority of that cost being attributed to emergency department visits, hospitalizations, and death (Weiss, Gergen, & Hodgson, 1992). Direct costs also include outpatient clinic visits and multiple medications per patients.

Indirect costs of asthma appear to be relatively equal to direct costs. In 1993, direct and indirect costs associated with asthma totaled $12.6 billion, with that figure having climbed to approximately $14.5 billion in 2000, the most recent year for which cost estimates are available. Because asthma affects approximately 5.2% of peak working-age people (18–44 years), losses of workdays, limitations in functioning, and subsequent lost wages are also significant (U.S. Department of Health and Human Services, 1996). The cost of lost workdays (outside the home) has been estimated to be about $284.7 million per year (Weiss, Gergen, & Hodgson, 1992). For those who work inside the home, the estimated economic value of lost housework is over $500 million (Weiss, Gergen, & Hodgson, 1992). In comparison, costs related to limitations in functioning, including hospitalizations, are approximately twice in patients with asthma compared with those rates reported in hypertensives (Collins, 1997).

Fortunately, treatments for asthma have been developed that, when properly implemented by both clinicians and patients, can effectively manage asthma, thereby limiting the number and severity of exacerbations and the associated increased risks of mortality, disability, and medical costs. Because the successful management of asthma requires both physical and behavioral interventions like many other chronic diseases, it is critical to take an integrated approach to asthma management. Although effective technologies exist, there is a wide gap between known best practices and the treatment of asthma as it is typically undertaken, resulting in a much lower than ideal rate of well-managed asthma patients.

The primary goal of this chapter is to orient the reader to the integrated treatment of asthma in the primary care setting. We will first provide a brief medical overview of the disease process and treatment of asthma. We will then describe how asthma is managed and the role mental health professionals might play in improving effective disease management. In particular, we will discuss barriers to successful asthma management and suggest ways of improving response to treatment.

Defining the Disease

Asthma is defined as a chronic inflammatory disorder of the airways characterized by symptoms including "recurrent episodes of wheezing, breathlessness, chest tightness, and cough, particularly at night and in the early morning" (NAEPP, 1997, p. 3). Asthma typically results in airflow obstruction and an increased sensitivity to a variety of bronchial irritants such as pollen, dust, and animal dander (NAEPP, 1997). Asthma is sometimes initially difficult to diagnose because symptoms may present as or occur in the context of less serious illnesses, such as a common cold or bronchitis.

Several techniques are commonly used to get a complete clinical picture to make a differential diagnosis, including obtaining a complete medical history (particularly history of asthmalike symptoms), conducting a physical examination, using spirometry to measure airflow (inhalation, exhalation, and speed of exhalation), taking chest x-rays, and conducting allergy tests.

For the clinical practitioner or epidemiologist, the gold standard for the definitive diagnosis of asthma is threefold: a history of recurrent symptoms (e.g., coughing, dyspnea, tightness of the chest, and wheezing), reversible airflow obstruction assessed using spirometry, and the exclusion of alternative diagnoses (e.g., pneumonia) (NAEPP, 1997, p. 3). In making the diagnosis, therefore, medical providers must consider the pattern of symptoms over time rather than solely the patient's clinical presentation at the time of evaluation. Reversible airflow obstruction may occur spontaneously or in response to medications. As such, asthma is partially defined by response to treatment. To meet the criterion for reversible airflow obstruction, the patient must have less than 65% of expected airflow prior to treatment with an asthma medication, such as a short-acting $beta_2$ agonist, and an improvement of at least 12% after treatment. Other physical findings that support the diagnosis of asthma but are not necessary for the diagnosis to be made are tachypnea, tachycardia, the use of accessory muscles in breathing, and pulsus paradoxus.

Asthma is classified by severity, which helps determine an individualized and appropriate level of care. The levels of classification are:

- *Mild asthma* (intermittent or persistent)—These patients experience either infrequent exacerbations or persistent but mild symptoms of cough, wheezing, and dyspnea or breathlessness. They are usually asymptomatic and have good tolerance for exercise between attacks. They do not require urgent or emergency care. Despite decreased airflow, their pulmonary functions are usually normal.
- *Moderate asthma*—These patients have symptoms intermediate between mild and severe.
- *Severe asthma*—These patients have daily symptoms and require urgent or emergency treatment several times per year. Due to the chronicity of inflammation, they also respond poorly to bronchidilators (described in more detail below).

Treating the Disease

Asthma is a well-researched problem, the focus of a huge body of literature and several journals. Based on this literature, practice guidelines have been developed to guide health professionals in efficiently and effectively treating patients with asthma. Before undertaking the integrated management of asthma, it is recommended that the clinician become familiar with the best practices.

Currently, the most recognized and accepted treatment guidelines for asthma are the National Asthma Education and Prevention Program's (NAEPP) *Expert Panel Report 2: Guidelines for the Diagnosis and Management of Asthma* (1997) (updated on selected topics in 2002), which were coordinated by the National Heart, Lung, and Blood Institute. The NAEPP guidelines specify both medical and psychological components for the effective management of asthma. These guidelines provide clear recommendations for the accurate medical diagnosis, treatment, and monitoring of asthma. In addition, the guidelines include patient education materials, treatment plan forms, and patient diary cards to assist clinicians in implementing the guidelines and to assist with patient education. Based on the guidelines, the *Practical Guide for the Diagnosis and Management of Asthma* (NAEPP, 1997) provides more specific suggestions for creating individualized programs. Another excellent resource is *Improving Asthma Care in Children and Adults*, which provides specific suggestions for creating the treatment "culture" in which the NAEPP guidelines can be most effectively implemented and tested.

The remainder of this chapter will summarize the current practice guidelines and make suggestions to extend the existing guidelines to include more recent research findings and adapt the recommended practices to the integrated-care environment. Although this chapter is aimed at behavioral health professionals who are committed to treating patients with asthma, in order to accomplish behavioral treatment goals the behavioral health provider must first have an elementary understanding of the medical management of asthma, particularly because behavioral health-care providers may play an integral role in increasing adherence to medical protocols.

Medical Management of Asthma

Asthma is best treated in a disease management model. This model was first developed at the Mayo Clinic in an attempt to provide a systematic process to identify at-risk patients, provide both preventive care and intervention, and monitor short- and long-term health outcomes. Consistent with a disease management approach, both prevention and treatment are key elements of asthma management according to the NAEPP guidelines.

The first target of successful asthma management is avoiding (preventing) medical crises by treating the chronic pulmonary inflammation associated with asthma. This is usually accomplished through the use of "maintenance" medications, which can be either taken orally or inhaled. Long-term control medications include inhaled steroids, oral steroids, and long-acting bronchodilators. Inhaled steroids are the most potent medication currently available and are usually well-tolerated and safe at recommended doses. Inhaled asthma medication is usually administered through a metered-dose inhaler (MDI), which provides a controlled amount of medication. There are also some new orally administered maintenance medications now being prescribed; however, these medications have not yet been integrated into the current practice guidelines.

In the use of MDI, the most common maintenance-medication method of administration, there are several important components to successful self-administration. Unlike the use of oral agents, patients must be taught not only when to use their inhaled medications, but also how. In particular, there are techniques patients should be taught to a level of mastery prior to being sent home to manage their disease, such as correctly measuring distance between their mouth and their inhaler. The form of administration should be periodically evaluated for adherence to prescribed protocol. It must be noted that these types of maintenance medications must be taken once to several times daily, even when the patient does not feel ill, presenting an inherent challenge to compliance.

The second component of asthma management is avoiding or limiting exposure to allergens or other asthma triggers. Asthma may be exacerbated by a variety of triggers such as molds, animals, smoke, exercise, respiratory infections or colds, and experiencing strong emotions (NAEPP, 1997). Obviously, many of these stimuli cannot or should not be avoided (e.g., exercise or laughing), however, patients must be instructed how to manage their disease when they do encounter triggers. Behavioral health-care providers in primary care settings may be able to help patients develop self-management plans so they are better able to prevent attacks from occurring by modifying their environment or their response to their environment when the triggers cannot be eliminated.

In addition, there are several co-morbid medical conditions that must be monitored by both patient and physician to predict and potentially prevent asthma exacerbations. These conditions include allergies, smoking, rhinitis, sinusitis, gastroesophageal reflux, sulfite sensitivity, medication interactions (for example, beta blockers and aspirin are potentially fatal in asthma patients), occupational exposures to harmful substances, and viral respiratory infections. Although these common medical problems may pose only minimal health risk to nonasthmatics, in this population the common cold, left untreated, may precipitate a fatal medical event.

It is critical that patients learn to monitor their symptoms, recognize when they are likely to have an exacerbation, and take appropriate steps to protect their airways. One of the primary components of self-monitoring is the use of a peak flow meter. Patients should be instructed by their health-care treatment team in the use of peak flow meters to assess respiratory function between office visits. Monitoring peak flow is akin to hypertensive patients learning to take their own blood pressure at home or diabetic patients learning to measure their blood glucose in order to titrate their insulin appropriately.

Peak flow is defined as the greatest velocity of forced exhalation from fully inflated lungs. One patient was noted to have conceptualized obtaining his peak flow as "giving it all he's got." Using peak flow monitoring at home may increase the probability of predicting and hence, preventing, impending asthma exacerbations (NIH, 1995). Importantly, consistently and validly measuring and recording peak flow provides a quantitative record of lung function, which may be useful in letting the patient know when to seek medical attention and letting the treatment team know the pattern of lung functioning over time, in addition to having an additional index of patient compliance.

When more acute symptoms emerge and or when mild-to-moderate symptoms do not abate, respiratory crises must be treated with quick relief or "rescue" medications (such as short-acting inhaled beta$_2$ agonists and oral steroids) and may require emergency medical intervention. Most often, these medications are delivered through a MDI. Under special circumstances, anticholinergics are prescribed for this purpose when the preferred medications are not well tolerated.

In order to facilitate adequate self-maintenance, per the NAEPP guidelines, patients should establish with their primary medical provider an asthma action plan, which serves as a written reminder of the patient's management plan. An asthma action plan is a flowchart for patients and their caregivers to determine what steps to take to best manage their asthma with particular symptom presentations. For example, if the patient is experiencing symptoms suggesting that his or her asthma is getting worse (e.g., activity restriction, waking at night due to coughing or wheezing), the asthma action plan would indicate what pharmacological changes to make, including what medication(s) to take, dosage, and when to take the medication. If the symptoms persist or worsen, the asthma action plan may indicate to take additional doses, add additional medications, or call the doctor after having waited for a specified period of time after having dosed. Always included in the asthma action plan are warning signs of an impending medical emergency to indicate to the patient when he or she should go to the emergency department or call an ambulance.

Clearly communicating the information contained in the asthma action plan directly by health-care providers to the patient helps obtain mutual agreement for the treatment plan. This, in turn, enhances the likelihood of compliance on the part of the patient, who then has the same perceived goals as the physician and understands the rationale for treatment, follow-up, and appropriate alterations in the therapeutic plan. In addition, the patient will have a better understanding of the need to recognize and avoid external and internal precipitants and the potential for medication-induced adverse effects.

Obviously, self-monitoring is a key component of successful outpatient management of asthma, yet it is often the missing link in the behavioral chain. It is recommended that persons with asthma have three or four "well" outpatient visits per year to monitor progress and adjust medication and behavior management plans. Between these visits, asthma patients must continually monitor and treat their disease and have the assessment abilities to determine when they need additional contact with medical professionals. Specifically, because of the intermittently emergent nature of asthma, patients with the disease and people in their support system must be knowledgeable about the signs and symptoms of an asthmatic emergency and what steps to take to terminate the episode quickly or lessen the severity of the episode to provide a window of time in which to obtain professional medical assistance. To establish this level of competence in their own care, asthma patients must learn about the disease from their doctors and honestly report their levels of symptomatology and compliance during regular visits.

Like patients with other chronic illnesses, asthma patients must take a greater-than-average responsibility for their health and well-being and, in doing so, develop a strong working relationship with their primary care treatment team. This type of relationship is necessary in the context of asthma to provide patient compliance. When patients fail to obtain regular care for their disease outside of acute exacerbations, the probability of relapse is greatly increased. Understandably then, the lack of an identified primary care physician and the inability or failure to obtain prescribed medications have been shown to be significantly related to short-term relapse (Emerman & Cydulka, 1998).

Finally, to understand the medical management of asthma, the emotional valence of coping with asthma must not be overlooked. Asthma, particularly when first diagnosed, is a frightening disease. Asthma is typically diagnosed after an acute episode of breathlessness, which is typically not only terrifying to the patient, but also to others who witnessed the asthma attack or other members of the patient's support system who learn of the event later. Patients commonly have the post hoc observation that they genuinely thought they were dying during their first moderate-to- severe asthma attack. Unfortunately, it is under these less-than-ideal learning circumstances that patients are given their first education about asthma, including being instructed on appropriate medication administration. Given the relative complexity of self-management required of asthma patients, at the very minimum patients should be provided upon diagnosis written instructions regarding the proper use and administration of medications, the clinical rationale for the various medications they will likely be prescribed, instructions on self-monitoring, signs and symptoms to monitor that would indicate a need for additional medical attention on both outpatient and emergency bases, and signs and symptoms that long-term therapies are decreasing in effectiveness (NAEPP, 1997). Having such information in writing will enable the patient to review and consult it, in addition to providing some education as to the patient's support system, who may not be present during the medical visit.

Behavioral Management of Asthma

As should be apparent to the reader at this point, successful asthma management cannot be defined by medical intervention alone, but requires a great deal of behavioral management as well. Psychological factors must be addressed in asthma management, even when these factors do not amount to a co-morbid, diagnosable, psychological disorder. Behavioral strategies may be employed both to reduce the occurrence of asthma exacerbations and to help patients better manage acute episodes when they occur. Many behavioral protocols have been developed to meet these targets, in accordance with the NIH guidelines. Common elements of these protocols include educating patients on their illness, improving compliance with maintenance and rescue medication regimens, compliance with environmental management strategies, and management of psychological symptoms that may contribute to the severity or duration of symptoms. Lehrer, Feldman, Giardino, Song, and Schmaling (2002) suggest several biopsychosocial markers of successful behavioral intervention: quality-of-life measures, reduction in medication usage, change in current status of asthma severity, and the ability to regain normal flow volumes during an acute asthma exacerbation.

Several studies have examined the effectiveness of behavioral protocols for improving patient knowledge and management of asthma (e.g., Hockemeyer & Smyth, 2002; Lucas et al., 2001). Both individual as well as group protocols have been utilized and studied. Although the quality of the data varies, generally speaking, these programs have been associated with improvements in a number of outcome variables including knowledge of asthma, use of self-management strategies, emergency department visits, asthma-related inpatient hospitalizations, physician visits, medication compliance and reduction where appropriate, and number of asthma attacks or exacerbations.

These findings suggest that the implementation of a behavioral intervention administered at the time of diagnosis with supplemental interventions provided on an as-needed basis could prevent unnecessary suffering and financial costs. In cases of poorly controlled asthma, management protocols that include control of environmental asthma precipitants, enhanced medication regimens, and smoking cessation have been shown to improve functioning (e.g., Irwin, Curley, & French, 1993). However, additional research is certainly warranted, as we do not yet have an empirically supported protocol for behavioral management and we have not yet measured all the potentially relevant outcome variables (such as medical cost offset).

There are two main roles that behavioral health-care providers can play in improving asthma patient care: improving adherence to prescribed protocols when asthma is poorly managed and treating co-morbid psychological and behavioral problems.

Improving Adherence and Compliance

Unfortunately, asthma treatment guidelines are not always implemented as suggested, and even when they are, patients are not always compliant with treatment. In fact, patient compliance with asthma treatment protocols is only around 50% (Center for the Advancement of Health, 2000). In one study of asthma patients recently treated for exacerbations in the emergency department, 34% had furry pets in their home, only 15% had mattress covers, hypoallergenic pillows, or covers, and only 50% vacuumed their carpets weekly, all recommended management strategies (Emerman & Cydulka, 1998). There are several possible reasons for lack of adherence and compliance at both the patient and physician levels.

Physicians may not be aware that there is an empirically validated treatment protocol for the diagnosis and treatment of asthma or may not know where to find the protocol materials. Alternatively, they may know of the treatment guidelines but may not be familiar enough with them to implement them effectively. They may not know (or may not be convinced) that adherence to the guidelines is important for increasing the probability of patient compliance. It should also be noted that physicians are typically operating under a number of different contingencies, including time pressures and huge patient case loads; they may not feel they have the resources to implement the guidelines as they ideally should.

Patients as well may fail to comply with their asthma treatment plan for a number of reasons. They may not understand the rationale for the treatment protocol and therefore take it less seriously than they should. They may not clearly understand what asthma is, what conditions may exacerbate their symptoms, or how and when to use their medications. They may not know how to identify asthma triggers or know what preventive steps they should take. They may be unmotivated to make important lifestyle changes or lack the support necessary to do so. They may see managing their asthma as a barrier to life satisfaction or unnecessary when they are not symptomatic. Patients may also be reluctant to seek additional help when needed, or may not know that they need additional help in managing their asthma. Effective asthma management includes several complex components and in order to increase the probability that the patient will comply with this kind of comprehensive treatment, a system of care must be developed to provide prophylactic guidance in asthma management as well as ongoing monitoring and intervention to collaborate with the patient in managing his or her condition.

There are several signs of poorly managed asthma that may serve as a cue in primary care settings to initiate a collaborative effort between a behavioral health-care provider, the patient, the patient's support system, and other members of the primary care team (NIH, 1995). Signs of poorly controlled asthma include: nighttime exacerbations more than twice per week, increased or overuse of "rescue" medications, underuse of maintenance medications, failure to achieve quick and sustained relief when medications are administered during an acute episode, activity-induced exacerbations, the use of over-the-counter respiratory medications, interference in activities of daily living (attending and participating in work or school, regular physical activities, etc.), emergency department visits, or hospitalizations related to an exacerbation (NIH, 1995).

If any of these symptoms should become apparent to any member of the health-care team, a thorough functional analysis should be conducted by a behavioral health provider to determine what antecedents interfere with the patient's ability to follow his or her treatment plan. Then, we can problem solve with patients about how to overcome barriers to adherence and develop contingency management plans to improve their adherence through contingent reinforcement of adherent behaviors.

Some strategies that may be applied at the antecedent level are obtaining verbal or written agreement from the patient and key members of his or her support system to actively participate in managing the disease. This may take the form of a self-contract. Another useful self-management strategy is to establish precommitment by building asthma management tasks into the patient's daily routine.

At the level of consequences, patients should be encouraged to structure contingent reinforcement for having complied with their treatment plan. Obviously, patients should receive praise at medical visits when there is evidence that they have improved management of their asthma; however, visits are too infrequent to provide a sufficient schedule of reinforcement to maintain compliance for most patients. Initially patients should be encouraged to develop a plan for reinforcement to be delivered each time they perform a management task that has previously not been complied with. For example, one patient who had been noncompliant with the medication planned to eat a small piece of candy after he used his maintenance medication each day. Another patient developed a token economy as a means of providing reinforcement for monitoring his symptoms, taking his medication, and avoiding asthma triggers (e.g., vacuuming and changing his pillowcase every day), a plan he found to be very successful. For some patients, involving their spouses or other significant support persons in their contingency management plan may increase the likelihood of compliance. Once compliance has reached acceptable levels, the schedule of reinforcement can be thinned to best maintain the desired management behavior.

Finally, cultural beliefs or practices may be interfering with a patient's ability to comply with his or her treatment plan, and this requires special consideration. As described at the start of this chapter, minority patients and particularly African American patients experience higher rates of asthma-related death and exacerbations requiring emergent medical intervention (Blixen, Tilley, Havstad, & Zoratti, 1997) than their Caucasian peers. Furthermore, one study suggests that African Americans have less access to asthma specialists and are less likely to fill prescriptions for inhaled or oral steroids (Zoratti et al., 1998). Unfortunately, the studies that examined the differential impact of asthma on populations of color have been correlational and have not shed light on causal factors. On an individual basis, however, behavioral health-care providers should attempt to understand what sociocultural factors are impacting a patient's ability to successfully manage his or her asthma.

Other Mental Health Services

In addition to improving adherence, behavioral health-care providers may offer a variety of other services to asthma patients in the primary care or specialty mental health-care settings. If emotional arousal triggers an attack, as is often the case, behavioral health-care providers could assist by providing brief relaxation training. Skill training in the areas of communication and assertiveness may also be helpful in assisting particular patients to learn how to communicate with health-care providers and other people in the their lives who may be involved in their disease management. Furthermore, more specialized treatments may be incorporated depending on patient need, including smoking cessation and treatment of diagnosed psychological disorders.

Smoking Cessation. The prevalence of smoking and the importance of smoking cessation among the asthmatic population must be given special consideration. Among different samples diagnosed with asthma, 24–50% report a history of smoking and 15–43% report that they are currently smoking (Bailey et al., 1990; Cline, Dodge, Lebowitz, & Burrows, 1994; Emerman & Cydulka, 1998). In addition, lifelong smoking has been associated with asthma mortality (Ulrik & Fredericksen, 1995). Given these factors, when an asthma patient is also a smoker, he or she must be immediately referred to a smoking cessation program for evaluation and treatment (see chapter 10 for more detailed information on smoking cessation).

Treating Co-Morbid Psychological Disorders

As with other chronic illnesses, a patient's psychological distress or disorders can jeopardize the successful management of asthma. Specifically, anxiety, depression, and generalized psychological distress have been demonstrated to have a significant impact on the course of the disease and, as such, must be treated concurrently with the medical treatment of asthma. Although we will provide an overview here, for a complete review of the relevant literature, Lehrer, Feldman, Giardino, Song, and Schmaling's (2002) "Psychological Aspects of Asthma" is recommended reading.

Anxiety and Asthma

There is a significant overlap between experiences of respiratory distress and anxiety. For example, at the diagnostic level, in the general population it is estimated that between 2–4% of people will, at some point in their lifetimes, develop panic disorder (Eaton, Kessler, Wittchen, & Magee, 1994). However, among asthma patients, 6–30% are estimated to meet diagnostic criteria for panic disorder (Carr, Lehrer, Rausch, & Hochron, 1994; Shavitt, Gentil, & Mandetta, 1992) and an additional estimated 13% are agoraphobic (Shavitt et al., 1992). At the symptom level, there are several physical symptoms common to both anxiety disorders and asthma that patients may experience, including dyspnea, or shortness of breath, accelerated heart rate, a sense of being smothered, feeling lightheaded, a fear of dying during the acute event, a feeling of choking, sweating, and chest pain (Smoller, Pollack, Otto, Rosenbaum, & Kradin, 1996). Because of the overlap in symptoms, differential diagnosis between asthma, anxiety (especially panic), or both is sometimes challenging and must be skillfully undertaken (Smoller et al., 1996).

The data on asthma and anxiety raise a classic chicken-egg question: Which comes first, anxiety or asthma? Simply, there is evidence supporting both sides. There is some evidence to suggest that symptoms of panic (perhaps particularly hyperventilation) may quickly evolve into asthma attacks (Lehrer, Isenberg, & Hochron, 1993). To the contrary, there is also evidence to suggest that patients with preexisting asthma appear to have greater "anxiety sensitivity," meaning that they may interpret bodily sensations related to asthma (described above) as being more serious or dangerous than they are in reality, although their pulmonary function may not be more compromised than other patients (Carr, Lehrer, Rausch, & Hochron, 1994). Indeed, the fear of being breathless has been shown to precipitate panic attacks in some asthma patients (Carr et al., 1992). The literature also posits that there may be a bidirectional pathway between anxiety and asthma (see Lehrer, Feldman, Giardino, Song, & Schmaling, 2002 for a review).

There have been several studies that suggest untreated anxiety in asthma patients may result in decreased quality of life and increased health-care utilization. Among asthma patients with anxiety-related symptoms or disorders, higher levels of use and sometimes overuse of asthma medications, increased frequency and duration of hospitalizations due to asthma exacerbations, and higher levels of mortality related to asthma have been observed (Mascia et al., 1989; Mawhinney et al., 1993; Van der Shoot & Kaptein, 1990). For asthma patients with concurrent anxiety, treatment of both disorders appears to be imperative, however, no empirical testing of concurrent treatment protocols have yet been published. In lieu of an empirically established treatment, we recommend that existing empirically validated treatments for anxiety be used (e.g., cognitive behavior therapy or CBT).

Depression and Asthma

Not only does anxiety figure significantly in the comprehensive treatment of asthma, but depression is also a prevalent co-morbid condition. In the case of depression, the research suggests that coping with the challenges of living with the disease may give rise to depressive symptomatology (Bell, Jasnoski, Kagan, & King, 1991). Some have hypothesized that when asthma patients choose to assume a "sick role" and engage in behaviors symptomatic of learned helplessness that they are more likely to subsequently become depressed (Chaney et al., 1999). In addition, the experience of fatigue is common to both disorders, making a differential diagnosis important (Lehrer, Feldman, Giardino, Song, & Schmaling, 2002).

Based on the limited available data on depression and asthma, it is recommended that integrated-care clinicians carefully assess for concurrent depression in asthma patients, with a special emphasis on evaluating the patient's sense of control over the disease. Based on clinician assessment, several treatment strategies may be appropriate, although none have been empirically validated. First, additional psychoeducation may be necessary to help patients learn active coping strategies for managing their asthma symptoms. Second, clinicians should carefully assess for the presence of secondary-gain issues. In particular, if the patient's observed limitations (activities, etc.) exceed his or her known level of disability, the clinician would be well advised to assess for a pattern of negative reinforcement, that is, is the patient experiencing a removal of aversive stimuli based on his or her behavior? For example, a patient may be unable to participate in carrying a full laundry basket to a downstairs laundry room because of the high probability of breathlessness on exertion. However, the patient may then assert that she is unable to load the laundry into the washing machine, a task she finds undesirable, due to her asthma, although appropriate accommodations in completing this task may be available. Thus, the patient is no longer responsible for laundering clothing, although she may be physically able to complete at least some of the tasks involved.

Stress and Asthma

Among asthma patients and their treatment providers, there appears to be a commonsense understanding that psychological stress may precede asthma exacerbations. Research has only begun to investigate and understand the potential relationship between asthma and stress; however, several studies have suggested a significant causal relationship (Busse et al., 1995). Several correlational studies have shown that asthma patients have heightened bronchoconstriction in response to stress than nonasthma patients (e.g., Ritz, Steptoe, DeWilde, & Costa, 2000). There is some additional evidence to suggest that this pattern of physiological responding may be related to a passive style of coping with stressful situations (cf. review by Isenberg, Lehrer, & Hochron, 1992).

Two primary questions remain to be answered by the research literature with regard to the relationship between stress and asthma. The first question relates the role of operant conditioning in the relationship between stress and asthma attacks. Second, the potential treatment benefits of teaching stress management strategies or assertiveness skills to persons who suffer from stress-related exacerbations are unknown.

Although the research is not yet developed sufficiently to answer these questions, it is our recommendation that integrated-care practitioners conduct a functional analysis of asthma exacerbations occurring in the context of a stressful situation. In addition, because there are no empirically based treatment recommendations for stress-related asthma, we recommend that the integrated-care clinician use theoretically sound treatment strategies for stress management and improving active coping.

How Much Can We Do?: A Stepped-Care Model of Asthma Management

Several researchers have suggested a stepped-care model for the management of chronic illness that details optimal roles and responsibilities for health-care professionals to improve patient adherence and outcomes that take into account the severity of illness (Glasgow, 1995; Katon, Von Korff, Lin, & Simon, 2001; Von Korff & Tiemens, 2000). Several studies have demonstrated that the use of "care extenders," meaning health professionals other than physicians such as nurses, nurse practitioners, social workers, and psychologists, to provide auxiliary services improves the process and outcome of health care related to asthma (Bailey, Kohler, & Richards, 1999; Winsor, Bailey, & Richards, 1990).

Applying a stepped-care model to the management of asthma, the following steps are recommended.

Level 1: Prevention, Diagnosis, Outcome Monitoring, Patient Education

- The patient is diagnosed with asthma, ideally by the primary care physician or, in cases of acute respiratory crisis, by emergency department physicians. The physician may initiate treatment at this time if the complexity of the case is within his or her scope of practice or immediately refer to a specialist if indicated.
- After the diagnosis is made, the patient is prescribed medications and is given some brief education from his or her primary care physician or a care extender during that initial visit. Condensed information should be provided regarding the disease itself, the importance of compliance, and modifications to make to the patient's environment to reduce exposure to allergens.
- Asthma action plans are developed for each patient to provide individualized instructions for short-term management of exacerbations and long-term management of the disease.
- All newly diagnosed asthma patients are invited to attend weekly, behaviorally based, informational series held in a group format on the management of their disease. Ideally, groups should be held in the familiar primary care setting and lead by a behavioral health-care provider or other care extender.
- Patients should be monitored by the primary care team for adherence to and compliance with medication and behavioral regimens.

The following handouts should be included as educational components of this group (NAEPP, 1997):

1. "What everyone should know about asthma control"
2. "How to use your metered-dose inhaler the right way"
3. "How to use your peak flow meter"
4. "How to control things that make your asthma worse"
5. "Patient self-assessment form for environmental and other factors that can make asthma worse"

Level 2: Active Treatment in Primary Care

- Patients may be identified as failing to comply with their prescribed treatment. The decision regarding when a patient is not complying with treatment can be made by a number of professionals including his or her primary care physician, care extenders such as nurses, pharmacist, ER staff, the patient him- or herself or a family member, or his or her managed care company if utilization does not correspond with illness severity.
- Behavioral health-care providers (with the support of the primary care team) conduct a functional analysis of noncompliance and actively problem solve with patients about how to improve self-management.
- Minimal supplemental education outside of Level 1 group may be provided within the context of primary care visits (e.g., patient does not adequately understand when to use crisis inhaler and requires more instruction).

Level 3: Specialty Care Within the Primary Care Setting

- If determined that additional behavioral factors may be interfering with management, such as co-morbid psychological diagnoses or smoking, involve colocated behavioral health-care providers in the primary care visit to provide supplemental education or treatment.

Level 4: Referral to Specialty Care Setting

- For patients who have poorer outcomes at lower levels of disease severity, are chronically noncompliant, or have more complex clinical presentations, refer to treatment providers in the community who specialize in the management of asthma and pulmonary disease, including specialty mental health-care providers such as psychologists and psychiatrists.
- At this level, the specialist and the primary care team must decide to establish a collaborative relationship to provide for the continued management of the patient's needs.

Figure 19.1 exemplifies a decision tree for the suggested stepped-care model.

Potential for Medical Cost Offset

At the time of this writing, we know of no studies directly measuring medical cost offset as an outcome of successful asthma management. However, managing patients with optimum effectiveness and efficiency has clearly been articulated as a main goal of disease management. Unfortunately, cost outcomes are rarely reported in the clinical outcome literature. In one published study, researchers developed a seven-session (90 minutes each), group self-management intervention that featured self-monitoring of peak flow rates and managing exacerbations (Kotses et al., 1995; Kotses, Stout, & McConnaughy, 1996). The program cost approximately $200 per patient to implement, but savings in direct and indirect asthma-related bills the following year per patient averaged $500. These savings were attributed primarily to a reduced number of absences from work and hospitalizations. If the medical cost offset observed in this program is generalizable, it may be hypothesized that more effectively managing asthma across settings could result in not only improved patient care, but economic benefit for health-care systems and third-party payers as well.

Summary

In this chapter we have provided a primer for behavioral health providers in caring for asthma patients both in primary (integrated) as well as specialty mental health-care settings. Although the

ASTHMA MANAGEMENT DECISION TREE

Patient diagnosed with asthma by MD

Medications prescribed/brief education provided by MD during same visit

More extensive education provided in group format

Adherence and compliance monitored

 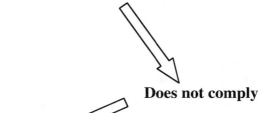

Complies   **Does not comply**

Specialty care within primary care setting

 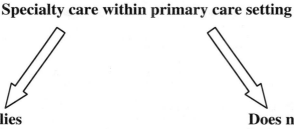

Complies   **Does not comply**

Specialty care provided outside of primary care setting

Fig. 19.1 Decision tree for stepped-care model.

complexities of and barriers to participating as a member of an asthma treatment team are numerous, it is our belief that, given the existing data, behavioral health-care providers could provide much-needed services to patients and their families, ultimately resulting in improved health and quality of life for our patients.

References

Bailey, W., Kohler, C., & Richards, J. (1999). Asthma self-management: Do patient education programs always have an impact? *Archives of Internal Medicine, 159*, 2422–2428.

Bailey, W. C. Richards, J. M., Jr., Manzella, B. A., Brooks, C. M., Winsor, R. A., & Soong, S. J. (1990). Characteristics and correlates of asthma in university clinic population. *Chest, 98*, 821–828.

Bell, I. R., Jasnoski, M. L., Kagan, J., & King, D. S. (1991). Depression and allergies: Survey of a nonclinical population. *Psychotherapy and Psychosomatics, 55*(1): 24–31.

Blixen C. E., Tilley B., Havstad S., & Zoratti E. (1997). Quality of life, medication use, and health care utilization of urban African Americans with asthma treated in emergency departments. *Nursing Research, 46*(6): 338–341.

Busse, W. W., Kiecolt-Glaser, J. K., Coe, C., Martin, R. J., Weiss, S. T., & Parker, S. R. (1995). NHLBI workshop summary. Stress and asthma. *American Journal of Respiratory and Critical Care Medicine, 151*, 249–252.

Carr, R. E., Lehrer, P. M., & Hochron, S. M. (1992). Panic symptoms in asthma and panic disorder: A preliminary test of the dyspnea-fear theory. *Behavioral and Respiratory Therapy, 30*, 251–261.

Carr, R. E., Lehrer, P. M., Rausch, L. L., & Hochron, S. M. (1994). Anxiety sensitivity and panic attacks in an asthmatic population. *Behavioral and Respiratory Therapy, 32*, 411–418.

Center for the Advancement of Health. (2000). *Selected evidence for behavioral approaches to chronic disease management in clinical settings: Asthma.* Washington, DC: Author.

Centers for Disease Control and Prevention (CDC). (1995). Asthma—United States, 1989–1992. *Morbidity and Mortality Weekly Report, 43*, 952–955.

Centers for Disease Control and Prevention (CDC). (1996a, May 3). Asthma mortality and hospitalization among children and young adults, 1980-1993. *Morbidity and Mortality Weekly Report, 45*(17), 350–353.

Centers for Disease Control and Prevention (CDC). (1996b). Asthma mortality and hospitalization among children and young adults—United States, 1990–1993. *Morbidity and Mortality Weekly Report, 45*, 350–353.

Centers for Disease Control and Prevention (CDC). (1998, April 24). CDC surveillance summaries. *Morbidity and Mortality Weekly Report, Ap24*(SS-1), 47.

Centers for Disease Control and Prevention (CDC). (2004). Summary health statistics for U.S. adults: National health interview survey, 2000. *Vital and Health Statistics*, Series 10, Number 222.

Chaney, J. M., Mullins, L. L., Uretsky, D. L., Pace, T. M., Werden, D., & Hartman, V. L. (1999). An experimental examination of learned helplessness in older adolescents and young adults with long-standing asthma. *Journal of Pediatric Psychology, Vol 24*(3): 259–270.

Cline, M. G., Dodge, R., Lebowitz, M. D., & Burrows, B. (1994). Determinants of percent predicted FEV in current asthmatic subjects. *Chest, 106*, 1089–1093.

Collins, J. G. (1997). *Vital and health statistics: Prevalence of selected chronic conditions: United States, 1990–1992.* Series 10, data from the National Health Survey, no. 194. Publication no. PHS 97-1522. Hyattsville, MD: DHHS.

Dinkevich, E. I., Cunningham, S. J., & Crain E. F. (1998). Parental perceptions of access to care and quality of care for inner-city children with asthma. *Journal of Asthma, Vol 35*(1) 63–71.

Dyer, R. (1999). *Behavioral technologies in disease management: A new service model for working with physicians.* Bellevue, WA: Criterion Health.

Eaton, W. W., Kessler, R. C., Wittchen, H. U., & Magee, W. J. (1994). Panic and panic disorder in the United States. *American Journal of Psychiatry, 151*, 413–420.

Emerman, C. L., & Cydulka, R. K. (1998). Behavioral and environmental factors associated with acute exacerbation of asthma. *Annals of Allergy, Asthma, and Immunology, 81*, 239–242.

Glasgow, R. (1995). A practical model of diabetes management and education. *Diabetes Care, 18*, 117–126.

Hockemeyer, J., & Smyth, J. (2002). Evaluating the feasibility and efficacy of a self-administered manual-based stress management intervention for individuals with asthma: Results from a controlled study. *Behavioral Medicine, Vol 27*(4): 161–172.

Irwin, R. S., Curley, F. J., & French, C. L. (1993). Difficult-to-control asthma. *Chest, 103*(6), 1662–1669.

Isenberg S. A., Lehrer P. M., & Hochron, S. (1992). The effects of suggestion and emotional arousal on pulmonary function in asthma: a review and a hypothesis regarding vagal mediation. *Psychosomatic Medicine, 54*(2): 192–216.

Katon, W., Von Korff, M., Lin, E., & Simon, G. (2001). Rethinking practitioner roles in chronic illness: the specialist, primary care physician, and the practice nurse. *General Hospital Psychiatry, 23*(3): 138–144.

Kotses, H., et al., (1995). A self-management program for adult asthma: Part 1: Development and evaluation. *Journal of Allergy and Clinical Immunology, 95*, 529–540.

Kotses, H., Stout, H., & McConnaughy, K. (1996). Evaluation of individualized asthma self-management programs. *Journal of Asthma, 33*, 113–116.

Lehrer, P., Feldman J., Giardino N., Song, H. S., & Schmaling, K. (2002). Psychological aspects of asthma. *Journal of consulting and clinical psychology, 70*(3): 691–711.

Lehrer, P. M., Isenberg, S., & Hochron, S. M. (1993). Asthma and emotion: A review. *Journal of Asthma, 30*, 5–21.

Lucas, D. O., Zimmer, L. O., Paul, J. E., Jones, D., Slatko, G., Liao, W., & Lashley, J. (2001). Two-year results from the asthma self-management program: Long-term impact on health care services, costs, functional status, and productivity. *Journal of Asthma, Vol 38*(4): 321–330.

Mascia, A., Frank, S., Berkman, A., Stern, L., Lampl, L., Davies, M. et al. (1989). Mortality versus improvement in severe chronic asthma: Physiologic and psychologic factors. *Annals of Allergy, 62*, 311–317.

Mawhinney, H., Spector, S. L., Heitjan, D., Kinsman, R. A., Dirks, J. F., & Pines, I. (1993). As-needed medication use in asthma: Usage patterns and patient characteristics. *Journal of Asthma, 30*, 61–71.

National Asthma Education and Prevention Program (NAEPP). (1996). *National asthma education and prevention program task force on the cost effectiveness, quality of care, and financing of asthma care.* Publication no. 55-807. Bethesda, MD: National Institutes of Health.

National Asthma Education and Prevention Program (NAEPP). (1997). *Expert panel report 2: Guidelines for the diagnosis and management of asthma.* Publication no. 97-4051. Bethesda, MD: National Institutes of Health.

National Asthma Education and Prevention Program (NAEPP). (1997). *Practical Guide for the Diagnosis and Management of Asthma.* Publication no. 96-3659A. Bethesda: MD: National Institutes of Health.

National Institutes of Health (NIH): National Heart, Lung, and Blood Institute. (1995, July). *The role of the pharmacist in improving asthma care.* Publication no. 95-3280. Bethesda, MD: National Institutes of Health.

Ritz, T., Steptoe, A., DeWilde, S., & Costa, M. (2000). Emotions and stress increase respiratory resistance in asthma. *Psychosomatic Medicine, 62*, 401–412.

Shavitt, R. G., Gentil, V., & Mandetta, R. (1992). The association of panic/agoraphobia and asthma: Contributing factors and clinical implications. *General Hospital Psychiatry, 14*, 420–423.

Smoller, J. W., Pollack, M. H., Otto, M. W., Rosenbaum, J. F., & Kradin, R. L. (1996). Panic anxiety, dyspnea, and respiratory disease. *American Journal of Respiratory and Critical Care Medicine, 154*, 6–17.

Ulrik, C. S., & Fredericksen, J. (1995). Mortality and markers of risk of asthma death among 1,075 outpatients with asthma. *Chest, 108*(1), 10–15.

U.S. Department of Health and Human Services. (1996). *Vital and health statistics: Current estimates from the National Health Interview Survey.* Series 10, data from the National Health Survey, no 193. Publication no. PHS 96-1521. Hyattsville, MD: DHHS.

Van der Shoot, T. A., & Kaptein, A. A. (1990). Pulmonary rehabilitation in an asthmatic clinic. *Lung, 168*, 495–501.

Von Korff, M., & Tiemens, B. (2000). Individualized stepped care of chronic illness. *Western Journal of Medicine, 172*, 133–137.

Weiss, K. B., Gergen, P. J., & Hodgson, T. A. (1992). An economic evaluation of asthma in the U.S. *New England Journal of Medicine, 362*, 862–866.

Winsor, R., Bailey, W., & Richards, J. (1990). Evaluation and efficacy and cost-effectiveness of health education methods to increase medication adherence among adults with asthma. *American Journal of Public Health, 80*, 1519–1521.

Yoos, H. L., & McMullen, A. (1996). Illness narratives of children with asthma. *Pediatric Nursing, 22*(4), 285–90.

Zoratti E. M., Havstad S., Rodriguez, J., Robens-Paradise Y., Lafata J. E., & McCarthy, B. (1998). Health service use by African Americans and Caucasians with asthma in a managed care setting. *American Journal of Respiratory and Critical Care Medicine, 158*(2): 371–377.

Index